Teaching Developmental Reading

Historical, Theoretical, and Practical Background Readings

Second Edition

EDITED BY

Sonya L. Armstrong

Northern Illinois University

Norman A. Stahl

Northern Illinois University

Hunter R. Boylan

Appalachian State University

Bedford/St. Martin's   Boston ◆ New York

For Bedford/St. Martin's

Executive Editor for Developmental Studies: Alexis Walker
Developmental Editor: Jill Gallagher
Publishing Services Manager: Andrea Cava
Production Supervisor: Victoria Anzalone
Editorial Assistant: Nicholas McCarthy
Project Management: DeMasi Design and Publishing Services
Text Design: Claire Seng-Niemoeller
Cover Design: Marine Miller
Composition: Jouve
Printing and Binding: RR Donnelley and Sons

President, Bedford/St. Martin's: Denise B. Wydra
Editorial Director, English and Music: Karen S. Henry
Director of Marketing: Karen R. Soeltz
Production Director: Susan W. Brown
Director of Rights and Permissions: Hilary Newman

Manufactured in the United States of America.

8 7 6 5 4 3
f e d c b a

For information, write: Bedford/St. Martin's, 75 Arlington Street, Boston, MA 02116
(617-399-4000)

ISBN 978-1-4576-5895-2

Acknowledgments

Preface

This is a book for and about professional development. Members of the field of developmental reading were fortunate that Bedford/St. Martin's saw the need for a professional development resource text in 2003 when the first edition of *Teaching Developmental Reading: Historical, Theoretical, and Practical Background Readings* was published. Over the past decade, many professionals have turned to this text to read seminal works that combine theory, research, and practice on developmental reading instruction.

Although the first edition contains a number of timeless articles, it is time to issue a new edition of *Teaching Developmental Reading: Historical, Theoretical, and Practical Background Readings* that reflects the theories, research, and practices from the past decade. As you explore this second edition, we hope you'll recognize the central, underlying argument that drives this book's structure and selected readings: professional development is critical to our field; not just for some, but for *all* of us.

As professionals, we never stop learning, regardless of our career stage. This is evidenced by various reform initiatives within the field of developmental education across the past decade. Thus, those who are truly committed to the field are always *becoming* professionals in developmental reading by understanding the heritage of the profession, the theoretical and research foundations of today's best practices, and the promises for the future. This book demonstrates our own commitment to the field and our own experiences as we are forever becoming professionals, but in very different ways.

We represent the transgenerational experience that builds a field and sustains a profession. This book is a product, in a sense, of our own interests, of the people who have influenced us while we have been in the profession, of those who acculturated us and brought us into the field, and of those who have influenced our mentors as well. This edition of *Teaching Developmental Reading* therefore represents our own professional development experiences, urges others toward such experiences, and paints a picture of the professionalization of a field. Given this triad of purposes, it is entirely appropriate that the book's introduction, written by Hunter R. Boylan, outlines some of the major policies, reform initiatives, and legislation currently shaping the conversations within the field.

This book also represents a philosophy that being knowledgeable about the history of the field is prerequisite to fully understanding the present state of developmental reading. Very often, what prevails is a myopic view that fails to acknowledge the previous work that has shaped current thinking. Rather, we argue that in order to navigate the current antidevelopmental education politics and stay on course for the future, college reading professionals need to recognize that our collective teaching efforts and our current research have all stemmed from a long-standing, rich history.

Indeed, it should become immediately apparent as early as the first chapter that this book honors the past in terms of the shaping of our field; however, it also acknowledges an emerging generation of scholars, theoreticians, and researchers in college reading. This book is a call to action for these new professionals. It is a call to know the past in order to inform a more productive and student-centered present and anticipate a future with an even stronger field of college reading.

As in the first edition of this book, we have selected texts that represent the most current thought in the field; for the most part, we have purposefully sought out articles published within the last five years. However, this edition also very deliberately honors the past. For instance, Chapter 1 begins by exploring some of the important people who have helped shape our field. We've framed this chapter in terms of "Heroes and Heroines," and included three interviews with professionals we believe exemplify heroism through their service and scholarship. This chapter then concludes with a list of selected references of historical importance to the field of college reading and learning.

Following that first chapter, each of the book's remaining chapters begins with a Historically Significant Work (HSW) with which all professionals in college reading should be familiar. Each chapter's HSW also provides the necessary foundation and background for a critical examination of the current issues and recommendations in the field that follow within that chapter.

We believe that the articles in the first edition of this book are valuable and certainly worth reading even today, but through updating this edition we present new models and acknowledge the value of the current programming all the while giving credit to the progenitors. Therefore, the remainder of the text focuses on new and evolving models and programs that push us forward as a field.

Chapter 2, "Cross-Level Conversations," examines conversations that are, or should be, occurring between high school and college professionals. Currently, there is much discussion of strengthening the educational pipeline; however, in order to do so, professionals at both levels must begin to discuss the literacy expectations that define the secondary-postsecondary transition. The selections included in this chapter aim to help initiate such discussions.

The third chapter, "Student Population and Diversity," explores some aspects related to the ever-changing demographics of beginning college students. This chapter is intended to serve as a reminder that knowing the students we serve is a key component of professional development.

The next three chapters provide selections dedicated to the practice of teaching developmental reading. To begin, Chapter 4 examines some innovative approaches to how postsecondary reading can be structured. Chapter 5 then explores "Disciplinary Literacy Instruction," currently a major focus of literacy instruction at all levels. Then, Chapter 6, "Instruction:

From Vocabulary to Comprehension" explores practice on a classroom level.

Chapter 7, "Placement and Assessment," tackles a sometimes unpleasant topic, but one that is no less important, especially in this current age of accountability and data-driven decisions.

Finally, we close with Chapter 8, on "Professional Development," which includes a detailed listing of the most notable developmental reading training options, professional organizations, and publications.

This book is designed to provide a unified, comprehensive model for professional development, both for novices and for seasoned veterans. The underlying perspective driving this book is that professional development is more than simply what one does in class on Monday morning. Rather, true development as a professional in one's field involves knowing its roots, understanding its value system, and being an active participant in the shaping of its future. We hope that this book will help you to see the importance of professional development and will spark your interest in continuing on your own journey to becoming a professional, regardless of your career stage.

Acknowledgments

To the professionals who reviewed a draft of this second edition of *Teaching Developmental Reading* and provided thoughtful feedback (Christine Harrington of Middlesex Community College, Sheila Nicholson and Russ Hodges of Texas State University San Marcos, Thomasa Henry of Tarrant County College, Ashley Horak of Kankakee Community College, and Mary Dubbe of Thomas Nelson Community College): your insights and suggestions were instrumental in getting to the final draft of this manuscript. Thank you for the time you invested in this project.

To the professionals at Bedford/St. Martin's: Our thanks to Denise B. Wydra, President; Karen S. Henry, Editorial Director for English and Music; Erica T. Appel, Director of Development; Edwin Hill, Publisher for College Success and Developmental Studies; and Andrea Cava, Publishing Services Manager, for their commitment to providing excellent and accessible professional development resources and opportunities for developmental education instructors across several disciplines. We are especially grateful to Alexis Walker, Executive Editor for Developmental Studies, and our editor, Jill Gallagher, for their patience and good cheer through multiple revisions. We also want to thank DeMasi Design and Publishing Service for their copy editing brilliance, and for catching each and every em-dash error in the entire book.

To our contributors: Thank you for your excellent work and commitment to the field of developmental reading. We are especially grateful for the opportunity to showcase this work for others in the field.

To our readers: We hope this book provides you with opportunities to extend your knowledge base related to developmental reading.

Contents

Hunter R. Boylan presents an overview of past and present developmental education reform movements, as well as initiatives that impact developmental reading.

Martha E. Casazza and Laura Bauer present an interview with Martha Maxwell, a trailblazer in the field of college reading and study strategy instruction, as well as postsecondary learning assistance.

Norman A. Stahl presents an interview with Michele L. Simpson and Sherrie L. Nist, two key scholars in the field whose work sought to inform practice with research and theory.

Gene Kerstiens presents an interview with Walter Pauk. Fifty years ago, few individuals knew of this new faculty member at Cornell University; however, as the years progressed it can be said that virtually every individual in the field of postsecondary reading and study strategy instruction, as well as the overall field of reading pedagogy, came to know and value Dr. Pauk's scholarship.

Norman A. Stahl
Selected References of Historical Importance to the Field of College Reading and Learning

Norman A. Stahl provides a bibliography of key sources published across the past century that serve as seminal works in the field for each era and can be considered required reading for every college reading professional who seeks a scholarly knowledge of the field.

Chapter 2: Cross-Level Conversations

Frances Oralind Triggs
From Remedial Reading: The Diagnosis and Correction of Reading Difficulties at the College Level

In this historically important selection, Frances Oralind Triggs argues that, in general, the American public, including college graduates, does not read widely, often, or critically. Students do not receive specialized training in reading after the early grades, despite the fact that reading expectations are more specialized in high school and college.

Patricia A. Alexander
The Path to Competence: A Lifespan Developmental Perspective on Reading

Patricia A. Alexander presents a model of literacy development that accounts for reading growth from "womb to tomb." This framework provides six characteristics of reading development, each one accounting for changes that occur as readers develop across a lifetime.

Lisa Schade Eckert
Bridging the Pedagogical Gap: Intersections between Literary and Reading Theories in Secondary and Postsecondary Literacy Instruction

Lisa Schade Eckert discusses the pedagogical divide between the instructional practices of literacy and literature professionals, acknowledging that this divide has contributed to some of the instructional gaps between secondary and postsecondary education.

Chapter 3: Student Population and Diversity 104

Chapter 4: Structuring Postsecondary Reading 160

Elaine DeLott Baker, Laura Hope, and Kelley Karandjeff

Elaine DeLott Baker, Laura Hope, and Kelley Karandjeff provide background on and examples of a promising model for structuring instruction at the postsecondary level—contextualized teaching and learning (CTL).

Chapter 5: Disciplinary Literacy Instruction   270

David W. Moore, John E. Readence, and Robert J. Rickelman

In this historically significant selection, David W. Moore, John E. Readence, and Robert J. Rickelman examine recommendations for content area reading instruction from a historical perspective.

Timothy Shanahan and Cynthia Shanahan

Timothy and Cynthia Shanahan provide a discussion on disciplinary literacy instruction, including a distinction from more traditional content-area literacy instructional models, an overview of the background and history on the move away from such traditional models, and a review of relevant research across several disciplines.

Cynthia Hynd, Jodi Patrick Holschuh, and Betty P. Hubbard

Cynthia Hynd, Jodi Patrick Holschuh, and Betty P. Hubbard report on a study that investigated students' history-specific disciplinary literacy practices, including their strategy usage and epistemological beliefs about history.

Josh W. Helms and Kimberly Turner Helms

Josh W. Helms and Kimberly Turner Helms present an active reading strategy—note launchers—that was developed specifically for reading in mathematics texts.

Chapter 6: Instruction: From Vocabulary to Comprehension   **361**

Steven A. Stahl
To Teach a Word Well: A Framework for Vocabulary Instruction (363)

1985

In his seminal work, the late Steven A. Stahl offers literacy educators a cognitive processing framework for vocabulary instruction that has stood the test of time.

Donna Willingham and Debra Price
Theory to Practice: Vocabulary Instruction in Community College Developmental Education Reading Classes: What the Research Tells Us   *375*

Donna Willingham and Debra Price explore key theoretical constructs as well as extant research on vocabulary instruction for college reading students.

Marty Frailey, Greta Buck-Rodriguez, and Patricia L. Anders
Literary Letters: Developmental Readers' Responses to Popular Fiction   (388)

2004

Marty Frailey, Greta Buck-Rodriguez, and Patricia L. Anders extend the work of Nancy Atwell, whose groundbreaking research demonstrated the academic promise of "literary letters" for building elaboration competencies with middle grade youngsters. Here, the authors extend that work with literary letters as written by college developmental readers.

Dolores Perin
Facilitating Student Learning through Contextualization: A Review of Evidence   *409*

Dolores Perin presents a discussion of two forms of contextualization (contextualization and integrated instruction) as well as a review of the extant research.

Eric J. Paulson
Self-Selected Reading for Enjoyment as a College Developmental Reading Approach   (438)

2006

Eric J. Paulson proposes that college reading programs should prepare students for a lifetime of reading and that the common developmental studies skills-based, direct-instruction methods found in so many college reading programs fall short of meeting the goal of preparing life-long readers.

Chapter 7: Placement and Assessment 445

Michele L. Simpson and Sherrie L. Nist
Toward Defining a Comprehensive Assessment Model for College Reading 448

Michele L. Simpson and Sherrie L. Nist draw on David Cross and Scott Paris's (1987) work to define "assessment." Using the Cross and Paris triad of assessment purposes—sorting, diagnosing, and evaluating—the authors present their argument in favor of comprehensive assessment models for developmental reading programs.

Edward H. Behrman and Chris Street
The Validity of Using a Content-Specific Reading Comprehension Test for College Placement 460

Edward H. Behrman and Chris Street describe a study of the validity of a content-specific reading test used for purposes of placing students in college-level coursework or developmental reading.

Kouider Mokhtari and Carla A. Reichard
Assessing Students' Metacognitive Awareness of Reading Strategies 474

Kouider Mokhtari and Carla A. Reichard present an overview of the development and validation of the Metacognitive Awareness of Reading Strategies Inventory (MARSI), an instrument designed to assess readers' metacognitive awareness and perceived strategy use.

Chapter 8: Professional Development, Training, and Credentialing 499

William G. Brozo and Norman A. Stahl
Focusing on Standards: A Checklist for Rating Competencies of College Reading Specialists 502

William G. Brozo and Norman A. Stahl present the College Reading Specialist Competency Checklist, an informal measure for evaluating the competencies and experiences of college reading professionals.

Developmental Reading: Where We Are and What We Do

Hunter R. Boylan

Whether it has been called "preparatory," "remedial," or "developmental," the teaching of reading to underprepared college students has been a fixture of American higher education since the early 1800s (White, Martirosayin, & Wanjohi, 2009). Although the percentage of students requiring developmental education may come as a surprise to some, those familiar with the history of higher education in the United States are aware that there has never been a period when all students entering colleges and universities were fully prepared to be there. Toward the close of the nineteenth century, 80 percent of the colleges and universities in the United States reported having some form of developmental education as of 1889 (Brier, 1984). In the twentieth century, the National Center for Education Statistics reported that about 80 percent of colleges and universities in the United States had some form of developmental education as of 2000 (NCES, 2004).

Although some may find this hard to understand, it is altogether necessary that this fixture has been with us for so long. Few would argue against the concept that reading is the most basic and essential skill necessary for success in college, but many would wonder why it is necessary to teach it in college. After all, by the time students get to college they are "supposed" to know how to read. Knowing how to read novels, newspapers, and instructions, however, is not the same as being able to perform the myriad reading comprehension and analysis skills required for academic work. Furthermore, a large number of high school graduates simply do not possess the requisite reading skills necessary for college success. According to ACT (2010), 48 percent of high school graduates taking college readiness tests are underprepared for college-level reading.

Some erroneously regard the number of students underprepared for college reading as a growing crisis. Stanley (2010) points out, however, that "The crisis, in fact, has shown itself to have such remarkable staying power that the word *crisis* hardly applies" (p. 1) and points out that efforts to respond to the so-called literacy crisis among college students dates back to the 1870s. She goes on to suggest that one of the reasons the problem of underpreparedness never goes away in U.S. postsecondary education is that everyone tends to regard it as a temporary issue that will soon disappear as a result of some legislation, school reform, or policy initiative.

In fact, we are again currently engaged in a period of major reform in postsecondary developmental education and developmental reading. In 2004, the Lumina Foundation launched the Achieving the Dream initiative designed to increase the number of minority and low-income students completing community college credentials, either with an associate degree or a meaningful work certificate. Since 2004, the foundation has awarded more than $112 million in grants to colleges participating in the project. The main strategy of the Achieving the Dream initiative was not only to encourage innovation but also to encourage innovations based on a "culture of evidence" (Rutschow, Richburg-Hayes, et al., 2011). Simply defined, the culture of evidence refers to the use of data to drive innovation and reform. This initiative has now become its own foundation, the Achieving the Dream Foundation, and continues to promote the goals and philosophy of the original project.

Meanwhile, the Bill and Melinda Gates Foundation has spent millions and pledged millions more dollars to fund its own Developmental Education Initiative (Bill and Melinda Gates Foundation, 2008). This initiative is designed to bring successful innovations to scale at community colleges so that all underprepared students can benefit from programs that now serve only a small number of students. In addition, the Gates Foundation has also funded projects to improve the use of technology in developmental courses, to redesign developmental courses, and to explore statewide policies that might contribute to community college student completion.

The Ford Foundation has funded the Bridges to Opportunity project which has supported a number of activities designed to increase community college access and success for low-income students. One of its major and most successful efforts has been the State of Washington's I-BEST program (Zeidenburg, Cho, & Jenkins, 2010). In this project adult education and workforce skills are combined with vocational and technical instruction in an effort to get those from low-income and low-educational levels into the workforce quickly.

Complete College America is a nonprofit organization funded by the Bill and Melinda Gates Foundation, the Lumina Foundation, the Ford Foundation, the Carnegie Foundation, and the W. K. Kellogg Foundation. It is an alliance of states designed to close the college completion gap among underrepresented groups of students. It does this by gathering, collecting, and analyzing state-level data on college completion; promoting innovation and change; and recommending state policies that contribute to college completion (Collins, 2009).

The National Governors Association has also established its own initiative to improve college graduate rates. Through its Center for Best Practices, the association identifies and promotes promising institutional and state practices contributing to the retention and graduation of all students, particularly those from low-income backgrounds (National Governors Association, 2011). It also analyzes and recommends state education policies consistent with the goal of improving graduation rates.

The Education Commission of the States has set up a project called "Getting Past Go" designed to promote developmental education as a major component of state efforts to increase college graduation rates (Vandal, 2010). As part of this project, research reviews have been conducted, state-level data have been collected, and continuous online discussions have been held among leaders in the field to identify promising practices and policies. These are then widely disseminated to education decision makers at the state level as well as to the higher education professional community.

As a result of these projects, developmental reading, a field which has often been on the back burner of discussions on U.S. higher education, is now at the forefront. The millions of dollars spent by philanthropic foundations and the press coverage this money has generated have made developmental education in general and developmental reading in particular a highlight of policy analysis and development. Legislators and policy makers in every state in the Union are considering or implementing efforts to improve college readiness and promote higher graduation rates through some form of developmental education.

These investments and the discussions, policies, and programs generated by them have been useful and informative. We have already learned much from the investment of foundation dollars in research and demonstration as well as the innovative efforts of colleges and universities. We have also learned much about state and institutional policies that contribute to student success.

We have discovered new ways and rediscovered old ways of accelerating student progress through developmental courses (Edgecombe, 2011). We have learned that pairing developmental reading courses with student success courses, developmental mathematics courses, or college credit courses can contribute to greater student success (Rutschow & Schneider, 2011). We have learned how to harness the power of technology to modularize our courses, accelerate our students' progress, and improve our outcomes (Twigg, 2003). We have learned that student progress toward meaningful work credentials can be enhanced through contextualized learning (Perin, 2011). We have learned that student success courses can make an important contribution to student retention (ACT, 2010).

Nevertheless, as valuable as this research, policy analysis, and the resulting discussions and innovations may be, they tend to miss one very important fact. The most important variable in student success is what goes on in the college or university classroom between individual instructors and the students they teach. And, furthermore, we already know a great deal about how to teach developmental reading. We probably know more about teaching developmental reading than we know about any other subject in the developmental education curriculum. It is possible that some institutions hire reading instructors who are not familiar with the research and literature in the field and make few efforts to enhance their knowledge through professional development. It is possible that what we know is used poorly or ignored. It is possible that college curriculum standardization policies prohibit some instructors from using our knowledge base to teach developmental reading well. It is possible that some college developmental reading programs are so underfunded that they simply cannot take advantage of what we know about teaching reading in order to implement effective programs. The bottom line, however, is that we know much about how to do what we do, but we do not always use what we know to create high-quality classroom experiences.

This book contributes to improving what happens in the college reading classroom. It assembles some of the key research and literature in the field of developmental reading in a single volume. The editors hope that, armed with this information, classroom teachers will use what we know to better do what they do. The purpose of this volume, therefore, is to improve the quality of what goes on in the developmental reading classroom between individual instructors and their students.

References

American College Testing. (2010). *What works in student retention: Fourth national survey, colleges and universities with 20 percent or more black students enrolled.* Iowa City, IA: ACT.

Bill and Melinda Gates Foundation. (2008). *All students ready for college, career, and life: Reflections on the foundation's education investments, 2000–2008.* Seattle, WA: Bill and Melinda Gates Foundation.

Brier, E. (1984). Bridging the academic preparation gap: An historical view. *Journal of Developmental and Remedial Education, 8*(1), 2–5.

Collins, M. (2009). *Setting up success in developmental education: How state policy can help community colleges improve student success outcomes*. Boston, MA: Jobs for the Future.

Edgecombe, N. (2011, May). *Accelerating the academic achievement of students referred to developmental education* (CCRC Brief # 55). New York, NY: Community College Research Center, Teachers College, Columbia University.

National Center for Education Statistics. (2004). *Remedial education at degree granting postsecondary institutions, 2000*. Washington, DC: U.S. Department of Education.

National Governors Association. (2011). *Making education dollars work: Issue briefs*. Washington, DC: James B. Hunt, Jr. Institute for Legislation and Policy/National Governors Association.

Perin, D. (2011, April). *Facilitating student learning through contextualization* (CCRC Research Brief # 53). New York, NY: Community College Research Center, Teachers College, Columbia University.

Rutschow, E., & Schneider, E. (2011). *Unlocking the gate: What we know about improving developmental education*. New York, NY: MDRC.

Rutschow, E., Richburg-Hayes, L., Brock, T., Orr, G., Cerna, O., Cullinan, D., Reid-Kerrigan, M., Jenkins, D., Gooden, S., Martin, C. (2011, February). *Turning the tide: Five years of Achieving the Dream in community colleges*. New York, NY: MDRC.

Stanley, J. (2010). *The rhetoric of remediation: Negotiating entitlement and access to higher education*. Pittsburgh, PA: University of Pittsburgh Press.

Twigg, C. (2003). Improving learning and reducing costs: New models for online learning. *Educause, 5*(38) 28–38.

Vandal, B. (2010, May). *Getting past go: Rebuilding the remedial education bridge to college success*. Denver, CO: Education Commission of the States.

White, W., Martirosayin, R., & Wanjohi, R. (2009). Preparatory programs in nineteenth-century Midwest land grant colleges, Part 1. *Research in Developmental Education, 23*(1), 1–4.

Zeidenberg, M., Cho, S-W, & Jenkins, D. (2010, September). *Washington State's Integrated Basic Education and Skills Training program (I-BEST): New evidence of effectiveness* (CCRC Working Paper # 29). New York, NY: Community College Research Center, Teachers College, Columbia University.

Heroes and Heroines

Introduction

The first edition of *Teaching Developmental Reading: Historical, Theoretical, and Practical Background Readings* (2003) provided the reader with a chapter of readings on historical contexts for college reading instruction and research. That chapter began with a quotation from Franklin D. Roosevelt that bears repeating. In 1939, as the nation was at last emerging from the Great Depression, President Roosevelt wisely stated, "a nation must believe in three things. It must believe in the past. It must believe in the future. It must, above all, believe in the capacity of its own people so to learn from the past that they can gain in judgment in creating their own future."

President Roosevelt spoke to a nation facing an unknown future with the clouds of war on the horizon, but we believe that his sage advice is of equal value to our nation today as well as to our field of study and practice. Furthermore, we firmly believe that the field of reading pedagogy and research with college reading as an established component will never become a true academic profession until both scholars and practitioners alike are cognizant of our roots and then embrace the rich and valuable history that must be foundational to our future.

In the first edition of this text, the chapter on historical contexts provided readings that focused on institutions, programs, curricula, and instruction. It is a resource you should read if you have not already done so. In this new edition of the text we choose to celebrate our roots through the lives, both professional and at times personal, of individuals deserving to be viewed as heroes and heroines of the college reading and learning strategies movement across the past half century.

James R. King's research (1990) with K–12 teachers demonstrated quite convincingly the important role that professional heroes and heroines can play in the preparation and later lives of literacy specialists. Hence, we believe that whether a person views oneself as a scholar or as a practitioner, it is imperative that every individual in the college reading and learning strategies field have heroes and heroines to emulate.

We focus on four individuals whose nationally, if not internationally, recognized scholarship, pedagogy, and service define the very concept of heroism. In presenting these lived tales of Martha Maxwell, Michele L. Simpson and Sherrie L. Nist, and Walter Pauk, we draw upon the methods of oral history and interview.

As you read these works we encourage you to celebrate and learn from the contributions of these professionals to our field, but also to ask yourself who might be your heroes and heroines whether they are widely known or simply of importance in your more immediate professional life. Then ask yourself how your heroes and heroines have enriched your professional life, and hence, impacted the lives of your students.

Additional Readings

Acee, T. W. (2009). Strategic learning and college readiness: An interview with Claire Ellen Weinstein. *Journal of Developmental Education, 33*(1), 20–28.

Armstrong, S. L. (2012). The impact of history on the future of college reading: An interview with Norman A. Stahl. *Journal of Developmental Education, 35*(3), 24–27.

Bauer, L., & Casazza, M. E. (2007). Oral history of postsecondary access: Mike Rose, a pioneer. *Journal of Developmental Education, 30*(3), 16–22.

Calderwood, B. J. (2009). Learning center issues, then and now: An interview with Frank Christ. *Journal of Developmental Education, 32*(3), 24–28.

Casazza, M. E., & Bauer, L. (2006). *Access, opportunity, and success: Keeping the promise of higher education*. Westport, CT: Praeger.

Clifford, G. J. (1971). Sidney Leavitt Pressey. In H. G. Richey & R. J. Havinghurst (Eds.), *Leaders in American education: Seventieth yearbook of the National Society for the Study of Education, part 2*. Chicago, IL: University of Chicago Press.

Flippo, R. F., Cranney, A. G., Wark, D., & Raygor, B. R. (1990). From the editor and invited guests: In dedication to Al Raygor: 1922–1989. *Forum for Reading, 21*(2), 4–10.

Hodges, R., & Sparks, J. (2008). Words from experience: An interview with Gladys Shaw. *Journal of Developmental Education, 32*(1), 16–20.

Johri, A., & Sturtevant, E. G. (2010). Walter Pauk: A brief biography. In W. M. Linek (Ed.), *The College Reading Association legacy: A celebration of fifty years of literacy leadership,* Vol. 1 (p. 171). St. Cloud, MN: Association for Literacy Educators and Researchers.

Johri, A., & Sturtevant, E. G. (2010). Martha Maxwell: A brief biography. In W. M. Linek (Ed.), *The College Reading Association legacy: A celebration of fifty years of literacy leadership, Vol. 1* (pp. 155–156). St. Cloud, MN: Association for Literacy Educators and Researchers.

King, J. R. (1990). Heroes in reading teachers' tales. *International Journal of Qualitative Studies in Education, 4*(1), 45–60.

Kingston, A. J. (2003). A brief history of college reading. In E. J. Paulson, M. E. Laine, S. A. Biggs, & T. L. Bullock (Eds.), *College reading research and practice: Articles from the Journal of College Literacy and Learning* (pp. 7–12). Newark, DE: International Reading Association.

Lapp, D., Guthrie, L. A., & Flood, J. (2007). Ruth May Strang (1895–1971): The legacy of a reading sage. In S. E. Israel & E. J. Monaghan (Eds.), *Shaping the reading field: The impact of early reading pioneers, scientific research, and progressive ideas* (pp. 347–373). Newark, DE: International Reading Association.

Massey, D. D., & Pytash, K. (2010). Martha Maxwell: CRA president 1963–1964. In W. M. Linek (Ed.), *The College Reading Association legacy: A celebration of fifty years of literacy leadership, Vol. 1* (pp. 397–400). St. Cloud, MN: Association for Literacy Educators and Researchers.

Maxwell, M. (2001). College reading fifty years later. In W. M. Linek, E. G. Sturtevant, J. A. R. Dugan, & P. Linder (Eds.), *Celebrating the voices of literacy* (pp. 8–13). Commerce, TX: College Reading Association.

Piper, J. (1998). An interview with Martha Maxwell. *The Learning Assistance Review, 3*(1), 32–39.

Robinson, R. D. (n.d.). *Oscar Causey and Albert Kingston—Two founders of the National Reading Conference: A retrospective.* Retrieved from http://nrconline.org/pdf/causey-kingston.pdf

Roosevelt, F. D. (1939). Remarks at the Dedication of the FDR Library. Retrieved from http://fdrlibrary.files.wordpress.com/2012/07/transcript-of-dedication.pdf

Oral History of Postsecondary Access: Martha Maxwell, a Pioneer[1]

Martha E. Casazza and Laura Bauer

Martha E. Casazza and Laura Bauer present an interview with Martha Maxwell, a trailblazer in the fields of college reading and study strategy instruction, as well as postsecondary learning assistance. She was also a leader in professional organizations such as the College Reading and Learning Association, the National Association for Developmental Education, and the College Reading Association. Maxwell was the profession's benevolent matriarch and a heroine to a generation.

[1]Conducted in 1999, this narrative is one component of an oral history research project developed to record the stories of individuals who have all played a role in what lies behind opening the doors to higher education. The presentation of the oral history in this publication includes historic background material from the literature to help the reader understand the context of the narrative. Due to the nature of the oral history, the original wording from conversations has been left unchanged.

Truly a pioneer in the field of learning assistance and developmental education, Martha Maxwell has mentored hundreds, if not thousands, of professionals and students as well as authored a variety of reference shelf publications. Her career spanned 50 years. In her classic, *Improving Student Learning Skills*, she says there are seven persons named Martha Maxwell: counselor, teacher, academic advisor, reading/learning disabilities specialist, researcher, administrator, and perennial student.

Martha Maxwell: I think there are a few others. Cheerleader ought to be included. I would say that perennial student and cheerleader are the most apt descriptions. In our profession. we are dealing with students who come from backgrounds where success has not been part of their repertoire. They have not been encouraged: in fact, many of them have been discouraged in academia. So they feel they can't do it. Once you get them working, then I think you have to be a cheerleader and help them along that way.

Educational Background

I worked very hard in school. I did well in elementary and high school. I attended school at a time when high school students who wanted to attend selective colleges either took an extra year of high school or went to college preparatory schools.

When I got to college, I began by majoring in music, then I shifted to English, then to half a dozen fields, and finally majored in psychology . . . left school for a couple of years, came back and graduated with a split major in economics and psychology.

I started college before World War II at the University of Maryland at a time when many freshmen dropped out of college; there were no academic support services. We did have one psychology professor who helped some students with vocational counseling, but there was no counseling either. After the war when ex-GIs came to college in great numbers, colleges started counseling centers, reading and study skills programs, and offered free tutoring services. At first, these were just for ex-GIs, but later they were opened to all students.

I remember not knowing what I wanted to do in college, so when I was a senior in college we had a unit in career planning. One of the things we read about was the role of the vocational counselor. I said, "Gee, that sounds like a great job. I don't know what I want to be. Maybe if I were a vocational counselor, I'd learn about a lot of fields and be able to make my mind up." I did eventually become a vocational counselor.

When I had been a freshman, I had gone in for vocational counseling myself. I only saw one person, and he tested me and said, "You are an overachiever." That kind of hurt. What he meant was that you were working harder than you should, and you are getting higher grades than you are capable of. I don't think people worry about that today, but in those days I felt sort of taken aback about it. For the next 8 years I refused to take any of the standardized tests. But I also took an interest test from him, and he said, "Your interests look like you should go into college teaching." So here is an overachiever going into college teaching.

Early Professional Life

My first job was in the counseling center at American University after I had trained to be a counselor at the University of Maryland's counseling center. It was right after WWII, so most of the people we counseled were returning ex-GIs starting college. Many of them needed help in reading and study skills and how to study, and I had had some experience in that field. When I started at American University I was told, "Oh by the way, Martha, we want you to teach a reading course." I was not about to say no because it was a job that paid $3,000 a year for 12 months, and I needed it. So I ended up teaching a speed reading course to adults. . . . I guess I got interested in how students learn because of the jobs I was thrust into; those were the jobs one got placed in those days. Both at American University and later on when I went back to Maryland, I worked in their developmental education program teaching classes . . . that got me more interested in problems that students who have difficulties bring to college.

One day I got called into the president of American University's office, and he said, "By the way, we need a reading program for our students; they are not reading well enough." And I asked, "If we set up a reading program, what are we going to use for material?" He said, "Don't worry." And he leaned over and pulled a stack of communist *Daily Workers* from his bookshelves and gave them to me. This was in the middle of the McCarthy era in Washington, DC, and faculty members were worried about having FBI agents in their classes to report them to Congress.

My thesis advisor who had been teaching the American University reading class said, "Don't worry, Martha," as he handed me some 3x5 slips of paper which were his class notes. "Just take these. You can teach the course from these." I don't remember the text I used, but it wasn't quite appropriate for my class, which ranged from a Navy captain down to two black students from the deep South who had not finished high school.

The government gave ex-GIs back-to-school benefits if they went to high school or college or took any kind of training after they got out of the service. I don't think they expected so many to take advantage of it, but it really altered our colleges. One of the things it did was to force the development of counseling centers in large universities. They were veterans' counseling centers at first. And then of course many of these returning GIs needed very basic help in reading and study skills. So Reading and Study Skills programs were developed in colleges, and these eventually became learning centers. Students got many of the same things we are providing to students today. They had tutoring, skills courses, and lots of counseling. Maybe they even got a little better treatment than some of our developmental students today who are merely put into a course. At any rate, it paved the way for many students, who had not really considered going to college, to achieve satisfactorily and to take part in the community in ways that they had probably never dreamed about doing before going into the service.

The Educational Climate of the Sixties

In the 1960s the diverse voices that had been challenging the traditionalist approach to higher education became louder and clearer. The concept of open admissions challenged many of the earlier assumptions that had gradually been losing status over the years, and the surge of "grassroots" colleges reflected the growing importance of educational diversity (Hall, 1974).

In 1968 I took a job at the University of California at Berkeley and set up a reading and study skills center in their counseling center. When I was at the University of Maryland, I had been a member of the "Women of the South" and was viewed as a conservative. At Berkeley, I was considered a faculty "yippie" because I got involved in protests. Anybody who really had anything to say out there got labeled a radical. It was an interesting environment with an extremely conservative faculty: yet, most of the teaching was done by graduate students. All the radicalism came through the graduate students not the faculty.

Tear gas was the method of choice for containing protests as violence escalated. One never knew when or where you'd find tear gas. One morning someone opened the window in the reading lab and tear gas filled the room; we were next door to the Placement Office where military service groups were recruiting. You could walk across campus and get gassed in low places where tear gas clung. One day at high noon, the guard chased a group across Sprout Plaza and helicopters tear gassed staff and faculty going to lunch. Rioters firebombed the reading lab at a nearby community college, but we escaped fire damage. One morning someone found a crudely made pipe bomb on the inside stairway of our old wooden building. Fortunately, it failed to ignite; had it gone off our building would have been totally burned out.

Some faculty members tried to support the students, and some became official observers to monitor the police and National Guard activities. Those who taught smaller classes met students in their homes. Faculty, too, got their share of attacks. Those with graying hair were considered pariahs, just a little better than folks in uniforms, and were treated with contempt. Anonymous letters and calls threatened dire consequences if you didn't comply with their wishes. The first time I got a threatening call, a gruff male voice said, "Quit your job or we'll kill you." I panicked and called the campus police. The cop who answered said, "Look, lady, you're the 12th one to complain this week."

At Berkeley we had three major movements. First, and probably the biggest, were the protests against the Vietnam War which was not at all popular among young people. There were also protests for the affirmative action movement and for the women's movement. Affirmative action and women sort of merged in that, when the affirmative action bill passed, they included women as well as minorities. None of these were greeted with much enthusiasm by the faculty, to say the least.

I was active in the women's movement because when I went to Berkeley as a visiting associate professor from Maryland, the dean promised, "We will review you for tenure when you get here." They kept saying that for 3 years and then reduced me to a lecturer. I helped organize the protest to Department of Health, Education & Welfare on sexism and later was on the class action suit we filed. The lawsuit was eventually dismissed with prejudice against those of us who had filed it. After 3 years, the dean finally broke down and reviewed two of the women in education for tenure, myself and another woman, and two men. We all submitted our portfolios in the fall. The two men were validated by their committees in February and went ahead and got approved and got tenure, but the women's committees delayed until April. (My youngest granddaughter recently finished her senior thesis on the legal actions of the League of Academic Women, of which I was a member, against the University of California at Berkeley. She found that most of the women teaching at Berkeley today are still lecturers. Although only two percent of the full professors were women in 1970, today they represent four percent of that rank, not a great increase in 30 years (Maxwell email message, 2003).

I gave up fighting for tenure and took a full time administrative job as Director of the Student Learning Center. The learning center at Berkeley started out as a reading and study skills unit under the counseling center. Its reason for being was their realization that the administration was planning to admit more minorities who would need more help. At that point they had money for the EOP (Equal Opportunity Program) that was matched ten to one by the Regents to support the minority program. Finally the Chancellor decided that was not the way to do it, and he said that each campus would finance the EOP program. By putting it under the campus, instead of getting all those matching funds, we were able to set up learning centers. That was not an easy thing to do because we had Chicano Studies and other ethnic studies departments who had their own ideas on tutors and tutoring. We applied for money and grants, and they would fight us. Then when we got the money, and grants would come in, they would say, "You owe us half the budget." So it was an ongoing struggle, but by and large many students were helped and it became a large center.

Providing Learning Assistance

In addition to the students already described, other populations started coming through the doors of higher education. Beginning with the Rehabilitation Act of 1973, students with disabilities were granted easier access to college and also given assurances of academic assistance (Hardin, 1988). Continuing to 1990, with the passage of the Americans with Disabilities Act, access for the disabled became a matter of course for all postsecondary institutions. Schools have been charged to provide "reasonable" accommodation, and the number of disabled students attending college has grown steadily from the 1970s, in part due to increased support provided by the elementary and secondary schools. By 1994, 75% of disabled adults had completed high school (U.S. Department of Education), and 14,994 seniors took special editions of the SAT designed for the disabled (Casazza & Silverman, 1996).

One group of students at Berkeley, although I had met them at other places as well, were LD (learning disabled) students, who had become juniors and seniors. What was fascinating about them was how they had managed to find interesting ways to compensate for their disabilities. Some of them would get their textbooks for fall courses at the beginning of the summer and read them before fall. Others would spend 20 hours on an assignment, and some of them would totally avoid writing anything. One man very ingeniously would scotch tape and paste his essays together, and he got caught because he was a graduate student in social work where he had to write up his own cases. Another one was a Forestry major, very bright kid, and he just had a terrible time with reading and spelling, but he hired the secretary in the Forestry Department to type his papers. (There were poor spellers on the Forestry faculty, so she was used to it.) This student had very good ideas; one of his ideas was on reforestation in Africa. The professor took it and actually applied it to a project in Africa. These students were not dumb at all, but they had difficulty expressing what they knew and could do in written papers. I have always admired LD students because they work so much harder than anybody else.

Berkeley didn't really have a "revolving door," but it accepted a lot of students who were not qualified, and retention became a problem. Actually Berkeley was doing a better job than many state universities in terms of training and graduating minorities. It put a lot of effort into it, and did what it could to help the students.

Berkeley had a strong learning center. It was a well coordinated program that involved everything from placement to financial aid. They identified those who would need help early and nurtured the students when they got admitted. In the 1960s, they would just bring them in and send them a letter saying, "You are a special admit." This didn't mean anything to the student, so when they were asked to come in and get help, they refused. But when the program began to organize and get the students who needed help in early, it was much more effective. I still personally believe that, if you tell students they need help or if you think they know they need help, they will volunteer. But that is not the way it works. Most likely, they will run to the other end of campus before they will seek help.

A lot of southern states mandated testing and remedial courses, but there are always problems with forcing students into a program. There is really no one way, one best way, to deal with underprepared students. From a faculty point of view, if you can assign them to a course and get them out of your office you are fine. That is cheap and quick, but it doesn't assure success.

Two current indicators of the gradual professionalization of college tutoring programs are the increasing number of tutor training programs and the appearance of manuals and materials for tutor training. Surveys suggest that more than half the college tutoring programs offer some form of training for their tutors (Roueche & Snow, 1977; Woolley, 1976). As of 2003, the level of professionalization has grown rapidly as there are at least two professional associations, the College Reading and Learning Association and the National Association for Developmental Education, that have developed standards for the training of tutors and also offer formal certification based on these standards.

The importance of mentoring is often overlooked. The successful minority programs are those in which the counselors are mentors, and they have peer mentors as well. They can tell the students to go to SI (Supplemental Instruction), explain what it will do for them, and make sure they get there. Without that, weaker students still feel that "I don't want to be bothered; I can make it on my own." Students can certainly make good mentors if they are trained; they need support. It is not something that comes naturally. I know of open admission colleges where they use everybody from the janitors to the faculty, anybody that really shows an interest, in mentoring students. I think that's a good idea because then at least you have people who are interested and motivated. It is very hard to get college faculty to volunteer for any program for any extended period of time. That is true of mentoring, it is true of training tutors or being in learning centers. They just sort of fizzle out. You need motivated people, and they need support and training.

The Link to High School Preparation

I think we are really in a state of flux now because, after all, we have dumped (to use the term advisedly) billions of dollars into helping disadvantaged students to pull up their educational achievement. They are not on a par yet, but they are getting closer to the traditional students. There is still room for improvement, but compared to what they were 20 years ago many of them can compete successfully in today's programs. And we also have better high school preparation for many students. So although we have pulled up a lot of students, we are also getting a lot more who need help. The proportion of high school graduates who want to come to college is larger than we have ever seen. In some areas today, it is hitting close to 75%; groups are predicting it will be 80% in 5 years. It is as if everybody will be going to college, and there are more opportunities because you have even the armed services giving college courses as a recruiting tool.

I would like to tell potential students, "Look, if you are going to college, take college prep." For the third of the freshmen who are required to take our courses, most have not had the regular college prep program. I don't think you can bring them up to par in 1 semester or with a course or two. They need the rigorous courses that train them to think and reason. We are kidding ourselves if we think we can help them quickly get up to par when they haven't had 3 or 4 years of this back when they could learn it more readily. Besides, you have the attitudinal problems when they are in college and have gotten by without having had these courses.

The students who need help today are students in the bottom 20%, a lot of students from ESL, backgrounds where English is not spoken at home, refugees, and others who need developmental education.

I think the thing that has changed the least is that there is still a big gap between high school and college for many students. The courses, the demands, and the expectations of college instructors are quite different from high school faculty. I don't think that students realize it, and I don't think the high school faculty realize it. And I'm afraid a lot of developmental reading teachers don't realize it. What the reading students need in college is more than a general high school reading course they took before. It is not general reading, it is specific reading that you need to succeed in college. You need to be able to handle difficult academic material in different fields. I think that it's costly and unnecessary to hire a specially trained teacher to work individually with college students. Much of what we need to do with developmental students is tutoring, mentoring, and demonstrating skills in the courses. It takes much better if a student is in a class in sociology and is learning how to read sociology than just reading whatever.

It is almost as if there is a great wall between high school and college people. The college people don't go down and talk to the high school folks unless they happen to get a grant or have a special program that lasts 6 months; these never endure. There is a bar in terms of high school people chatting with college instructors to really explore these ideas, getting them out on the table and talking about what to do about it. There are places where learning specialists at the college level go down to high schools and work with the students to get them ready. That's the kind of preparation we should have more of, but it's not on most people's list of tasks to do this week.

I would like to see prep schools develop that can help students improve academically. Somebody has to say sooner or later to high schools, "Look you have got to do a better job because these students, whether you like it or not, are going to go to college." In other countries, where they have greater problems with matriculation, they do have opportunities for adults or any students who haven't mastered their high school courses to go back for a college prep year. We do it for the service personnel, and those programs have been successful. It seems to me that it makes more sense than taking a reading course if you are weak in reading or a reading and a math course because you need to have some content to broaden your background; it could be incorporated at the high school level. Back in the old days, in the 30s when I went to high school, there were students who wanted to go to college and knew they would have trouble. So they stayed on in high school and took a postgraduate year. They managed to do well when they got to college, but they needed that extra year.

Looking at the Future

I think it (relegating developmental education to 2-year colleges) is inevitable as we get more students in college because, with very few exceptions, 4-year college budgets are not growing. They have increased every year since WWII, and the public is saying, no more. Since 2-year college budgets are easier to increase, that puts the 4-year college in a position where it has to be more selective about students: They can't take everybody. And I think that will exacerbate the problem of underprepared students going to a 4-year college and help them to begin to shift more to 2-year schools. I think it will hit the 2-year schools too; they will probably become more selective.

I am still working on the idea that students should not be segregated in developmental courses, that programs, like learning centers, ought to be open to any student. Despite the evidence, people still feel that they need to be put off in a cave someplace. I do see some change in that, though we still have a way to go. That is what I would like to see in the future. I think in general we are a little better at looking at realistic parts of what we are doing with the exception of the fact that a lot of people don't realize that developmental students have a hang up about being called "developmental" students. It's a pejorative term. It's not, particularly for the people that work with them. They should be happy that we are doing all these good things for them. But if they are rejecting the idea, it's going to be very hard to work with them. We need to get away from the negative feeling of being branded developmental.

Developmental has so many negative connotations. It's been adopted by lots of different fields, so it has become a synonym for "remedial." I wish we could get rid of those terms we have inherited, "learning assistance" still hasn't got contaminated.

I still think we have to learn to avoid compartmentalizing people and stay open to the fact that they can improve. Not only do we need to give them a chance and the support to improve, we need to help them really believe that they can. That must be conveyed, so they have some hope.

References

Casazza, M., & Silverman, S. (1996). *Learning assistance and developmental education*. San Francisco: Jossey-Bass.

Cross, K. P. (1983). The impact of changing student populations on community colleges. *Community College Review, 10*(4), 30–34.

Hall. J. C. (1974). A history of baccalaureate programs for adults, 1945–1970 (National Institute of Education Report). Washington, DC: National Institute of Education. (ERIC Reproduction Service No. ED 101607).

Hardin, C. J. (1988). Access to higher education: Who belongs? *Journal of Developmental Education, 12*(1), 2–6, 19.

Hoyt. J. E., & Sorensen, C. T. (2001). High school preparation, placement testing, and college remediation. *Journal of Developmental Education, 25*(2), 27–34.

Maxwell, M. (1979). *Improving student learning skills*. San Francisco: Jossey-Bass.

Roueche. J. F., & Snow, J. J. (1977). *Overcoming learning problems*. San Francisco: Jossey-Bass.

Sandham, J. E. (1998, March 4). Focus on teacher preparation, not numbers, panel hears. *Education Week*, 22.

U. S. Department of Education. (1994). Number of disabled students taking special SATs rises, *Education Daily, 27*(170), 5.

Woolley, J. (1976, October). A summary of tutorial services offered by California community colleges. *About Tutoring*, 1–7.

Strategic Reading and Learning, Theory to Practice: An Interview with Michele Simpson and Sherrie Nist

Norman A. Stahl

Norman A. Stahl presents an interview with Michele L. Simpson and Sherrie L. Nist, two key scholars in the field whose work sought to inform practice with research and theory. With the coming of the 1980s there emerged in the literacy field a generation of scholars who were part of a paradigm shift from the tenets of behavioralism to the theories and research on cognitive science with foci on schema theory and constructivism. At the same time, the state of Georgia implemented developmental education programs throughout its public postsecondary institutions including the University of Georgia, which had a historic research mission in the field of literacy theory and pedagogy.

It was in this academic community that Nist and Simpson, as two young assistant professors, began a partnership that has spanned three decades. During this time they have published numerous articles in high-impact journals, chapters in scholarly publications, and highly regarded textbooks. Their scholarly trilogy of "College Reading and Learning Academic Assistance Programs," "College Studying," and "Encouraging Active Reading at the College Level" served as the foundational sources for a generation of new professionals in the field. Through their scholarly contributions, their mentorship, and their strong professionalism, Nist and Simpson serve as models for all individuals in the college reading field.

Norman Stahl (N.S.): Along with individuals such as Claire Weinstein and Michael Pressley, the team of Sherrie Nist and Michele Simpson can be credited with focusing the field's attention on the theory and research on strategic reading and learning. Why did you decide to approach reading and study instruction from a strategic perspective?

Michele Simpson (M.S.): For me it came from my experiences. I taught secondary reading back in the '70s where I also helped the students do well in high school. This experience set the tone or at least provided the foundation for my practice. When I worked at Arizona State University and later when I took my first job at the University of Northern Iowa, I worked in a drop-in program where people came in with their situations, their problems, and their failings. You had to be strategic to help them. You had to determine what courses they were taking, what texts they were reading, what the professor expected of them, and how they were studying, so it seemed like a natural approach. When you read Rummelhart, Bransford, or Ann Brown, the strategic perspective that I practiced intuitively with the students, made a lot of sense because these researchers were suggesting that learning is an interactive process, and it depends on the text and the task.

Sherrie Nist (S.N.): I had a similar experience, although I essentially fell into working and thinking about reading and studying from a strategic perspective. It wasn't such a conscious sort of thing. Before I went back to graduate school for the doctorate I had a job at a small 4-year institution in Florida, and I was working at a reading lab while I was undertaking my master's degree. We used early technology like controlled readers and instructional approaches focusing on the skill and drill philosophy. At the time I was thinking, this just doesn't seem to be working and so I started investigating different graduate programs and entered a doctoral program in the early days of the cognitive revolution. I knew that there had to be something more I could do to help students with their critical reading skills, but this was the era of skill drill approaches; strategic reading wasn't on the horizon yet.

In my cognitive psychology class, I was exposed to Bransford and the idea that learning and studying is a complex issue, and it just made so much sense to me. And so it wasn't so much that I got into this field because I knew about strategic learning or studying as an interactive process but more because I thought that there had to be something else out there. I happened to start my graduate program at a time when the field of reading and studying was moving from behaviorism to a cognitive approach of strategic learning.

M.S.: I don't know if my students in the UGA Developmental Studies program influenced me directly as much as did the research that Sherrie and I did collaboratively. We kept pushing the envelope and going out into the classes that students were taking, which then would reaffirm what we believed already. For both of us the previous experiences and the texts we read gave us the courage to go out and see what experiences our students were having in classes.

S.N.: The Division of Developmental Studies at the University of Georgia was my first job after I graduated from the University of Florida. I thought that I could teach the students a few strategies, and they would use these strategies in content classes and it would be magic. They would make good grades and classes would be easy for them. We found out, of course, after a couple of years that it just didn't work that way.

M.S.: At UGA we never had students do tasks that weren't from real college-level books. Sherrie's text, *Developing Textbook Thinking*, brought college textbook content into the developmental reading classroom. We also gave them assignments where they had to go out and do something with a lecture from a content field class or they had to integrate something from their assigned textbooks.

S.N.: At the time when we first started out at UGA, we worked with some very weak students, yet we persisted in the strategic approach to reading and studying. That was a hard pill to swallow for many of our colleagues, both in and out of the state. They said, "You're at the University of Georgia. You have better students than we do. You can use that approach. We can't." Interestingly we oftentimes found it difficult to fit in somewhere with the kind of research we were doing and with our approach to teaching the kind of students that we taught. We truly didn't fit in the higher education mainstream, and our colleagues in developmental reading weren't sure that we fit there either.

N.S.: When the two of you entered the field, behaviorism was beginning to give way to the constructivist theories of the cognitive revolution. In addition, you witnessed the shift from a quantitative research orientation to the acceptance, if not dominance, of qualitative research methodology. As you look back across the past decade what theories or research findings have fundamentally changed your thinking about how students learn and what are the implications for instruction?

S.N.: Both Michele and I entered this field at the beginning of the cognitive revolution, so the early work of theorists such as Bransford and Jenkins certainly influenced me then, and it influenced the whole body of work that I've done. The research and theory on meta-cognition such as Baker and Brown's work was of great importance as well. The early work was of researchers such as Alexander, Schallert, and Hare; Pintrich and Garcia; Hofer; and Thomas and Rowher was really a very strong influence on how we thought about the theoretical approach we took to our research and also the practical approach we took to teaching. The work of Patricia Alexander has been of importance across the years as well.

M.S.: I still quote Paris, Lipson, and Wixson's theory on "the skill and the will" and then the important difference between declarative, procedural, and conditional knowledge. I would add Wittrock and his theory of generative processing. It made so much sense because he was talking about processing. I liked Doyle's work on task because that's part of that tetrahedral model, and whether you use Brandford's, Jenkin's, or Brown's model, it's all there. The way Doyle talks about task and peels it out and defines it so it's not just this single entity was eye opening.

S.N.: The Jenkins–Bradford tetrahedral model gave way in my mind to self-regulated learning. It was sort of a natural progression when Thomas and Rowher came up with their early model of self-regulated learning. Their work, basically, was the same information repackaged, and so that's why the early work had such a strong influence on me. I'd also like to mention Ruth Garner in terms of metacognition as well as the work of E. Chiseri-Strater with academic literacies.

N.S.: How did the field's move from quantitative to qualitative research influence you?

M.S.: The emergence of the qualitative revolution really freaked out Sherrie and me. We were doing empirical studies, which you have to do to be promoted and tenured, but that was also the way we were brought up. And so we tested everything, from annotation to PLAE to PORPE. As we learned about qualitative research methodology it allowed us to figure out how to conduct research in actual classrooms in a productive manner. This made sense to us. One of the things we did was to look at "difference." What was the difference between students who do well and students who don't do well in classes? Using qualitative methodology in collecting materials and analyzing them, and our being imbedded in the classroom like a journalist, freed us up to investigate real questions that we were trying to answer.

S.N.: The qualitative work enabled us to peel away another layer. This was sort of the breakthrough in our understanding that strategic learning was more than just a series of strategies. when we first got this glimpse that there was something going on with the task. The students had to understand the task or they couldn't select the right strategies. You can teach all the strategies you want, but if students don't know what the task is, they are not going to be able to select the right strategy. So, it enabled us to look at the students' beliefs a little bit more. Without that qualitative piece we would have probably been back doing straight quantitative studies and really wouldn't have been any further ahead.

That said, there's still a lot we need to know about learning and studying that you can find out through actual experimental studies. And yet most of our research, or experiments that we did, was based on observation. We saw something happening with our students in class and out in other classes, and we wanted to be able to explain what was happening.

M.S.: I agree with you, Sher, and I'm glad you pointed that out because the PLAE model came from our asking why weren't the students enrolled in our classes doing what we hoped they would be doing. We realized that there was a missing piece. So PLAE came from our observations. We tried it out and tested it with our students. We researched it twice by comparing PLAE to the traditional time management skills instruction. Then we wrote about it in the *National Reading Conference Yearbook* and in the *Journal of Reading*.

N.S.: In the global context you have been influenced by the works of researchers such as Entwistle and Gibbs in the United Kingdom, Marton and Saljo in Sweden, and Biggs in Australia. What are the theories, research, and best practices that reading/learning specialists in North America should learn from researchers around the world?

S.N.: I think that one of the contributions that these researchers gave to us was the understanding of the complexity of learning and studying. Furthermore, this complexity cuts across all college students, not just developmental students or students who are struggling. All college students need to engage in strategic learning to be successful. The other contributions that these folks gave us were instruments to use to look at our students as either deep structure or surface structure learners. Still, the primary message that they gave to us was strategic learning could benefit all college students.

M.S.: Yes, they were ahead of theorists such as Schommer, Pintrich, and Hofer. They gave labels for things that we had already noticed. For example, they talked about cue seekers and help seekers—there are students who fall into such categories—and you know, we watched them. There were people who sought out cues from their professors or others who were totally clueless about cues that are given implicitly or explicitly. And they gave us language for concepts like "deep level strategies" and "surface level strategies" that we could use when we talked to students.

Someone who is interested in various aspects of strategic learning needs to know that there are important scholars beyond the United States. They look at the world and strategic learning differently than we do here in this country.

S.N.: The way the higher education is organized in Europe and Australia and so forth is considerably different than it is in the United States, and I suspect that in other kinds of systems students are going to have to be self-regulated learners, active learners, and strategic learners in order to be successful in those systems. It seems like the whole idea of self-regulated learning is infused more into the curriculum before students get to college in those countries than it is in the U.S.A.

N.S.: Both of you have been part of a growing number of individuals who have authored seminal works on how students' evolving epistemologies influence the reading/learning act. What should developmental educators know about the role of students' epistemologies for developing curriculum and delivering instruction? What theorists on the topic should specialists be reading?

M.S.: Students not only have beliefs about learning, but they have beliefs about reading as well. I talk to students about their definitions (beliefs) of reading, thinking, and learning at the beginning of the semester and again at the end of the semester. I try to determine if they think learning is quick and easy, if learning is something someone else does to them, and if the ability to learn is something they inherited or something they don't have the potential to do. A particular belief is going to influence how each student looks at tasks and the strategies each one will select. Developmental educators need to talk to students about the impact of beliefs on learning help them to determine their beliefs, and then hopefully assist them to develop more mature beliefs. Our colleagues should read the works by both Hofer and Pintrich including their coauthored article that won the award from AERA several years ago.

S.N.: Developmental educators should also read the articles authored by Schommer on epistemological belief research. Weinberg is a good read too; he certainly influenced our thinking about epistemologies in history and the way we conducted our research in history. Holschuh is doing some more work in epistemologies right now. She and I just had an article in the *Journal of College Reading and Learning* on a practical approach to epistemologies in the classroom.

For me, a late-coming idea was that students' beliefs about reading, studying, and learning are at the root of the strategies that they are going to select. I don't know how many times I've sat in my office with a student where he or she will say, "Well, I tried these strategies and none of them work for me." And then you start talking to the student a little bit more and you realize that, well, his beliefs about learning are such you know the strategies aren't going to work for him. The student is not going to select deep structure strategies because he believes that learning is, for example, simply mastering facts. Unless you can modify those belief systems for the students who have very naïve beliefs about studying and reading and learning, you can't move them forward in terms of being self-regulated learners. All the strategic models now have this component, this filter.

M.S.: When I looked at that filter construct I had my own ideas about what the filter was in the Thomas and Rowher model, but when I started reading some of the ideas from individuals like Gibbs and Marton and then later Pintrich and Hofer, I went, "Aha! Task definition is part of the filter." All of this later research really helped put things together for me and really shaped how I taught my students my last few years.

N.S.: Together as a team or with other colleagues from the Georgia connection you have authored seminal research reviews on college reading and strategic learning. Yet even with all that you have demonstrated, our field is focused equally or more so on traditional techniques than on what research suggests we should be doing. What do you view as the biggest obstacles to the incorporation of research findings from the professional discourse into reading/learning and developmental education practice?

S.N.: A curiculum based on the research and theories of strategic learning has not fully arrived in developmental reading classrooms. I think there are numerous reasons why the situation exists. From my experiences I find that there are still a lot of programs that are using skill at a time materials, teaching main idea, teaching inferencing, and using new technological forms of controlled readers. This situation puzzles me because many of the textbooks that are published today have more of a strategic approach. These are not comprised of brief paragraphs followed by 10 questions. Maybe it relates more to a lack of specific training for developmental reading educators. There are not many good graduate programs focusing on strategic learning, studying, and developmental reading. Many of the people that end up in the field still arrive by a circuitous route. And once in a position, particularly in the community college, the teaching load is often very heavy. These faculty members don't have to read theory and research regularly let alone undertake action research or formal research as part of the job responsibilities. We are still fighting this battle of getting the research and theory that informs good practice into actual developmental classrooms.

M.S.: I would agree with Sherrie on these points. When we present at conferences, without failure people come up to us to get clarification on what is the *Journal of Adolescent and Adult Reading* or sometimes they don't even know of the *Journal of Developmental Education*. How could there be an awareness of the research when individuals are not even aware of the publication outlets? I'm afraid that far too much professional development occurs through reading new editions of worktexts, which is not necessarily bad, but you're not going to get cutting edge research or anything that's packaged in a different way.

Too many people are teaching part-time at multiple institutions, so they don't really have time to keep current. Even if such an individual reflected, "What I'm doing isn't necessarily working," she likely wouldn't have the time or the energy to do something in depth about it. Yet, when interacting with faculty, there's that enthusiasm, that caring. They all care about the students.

S.N.: When you teach a strategic approach you have to give students a great amount of both written and oral feedback. We were fortunate enough to have smaller classes, and the teaching load wasn't too heavy. When you're teaching five classes and so many students it's very difficult to teach an approach where you have to give lots of feedback. But it's the only way a strategic approach works.

M.S.: The same issues apply with vocabulary instruction as with strategic learning. Scholars have studied effective vocabulary instruction for 30 years and now it's making research resurgence. We know much about what should be best practice in teaching vocabulary, so why is it then that we have nonresearch driven books for vocabulary instruction? Why is it that students don't learn the words and cannot use the words in their writing and speaking? It's the way it's being taught and the way the research is translated or interpreted in the books that the people use in classes. Why not use an approach that's more research based? Because it takes a lot of time to monitor growth, to provide individualized instruction with language-based activities (e.g., writing sentences). So as long as the professionals in our field are overworked and not fully aware of the breadth of literature sources, we're not going to change teaching practices.

S.N.: I do think some of the materials have changed. When we first started using this approach, *Developing Textbook Thinking*—the book that William Diehl and I wrote—was actually the first book of its kind out there, and there have been so very many others since then. One would think that they've had to have some kind of an influence on the field, but there are still a lot of skills based texts out there. I truly believe that there is still this very strong attitude that students coming to college who are not good readers will only benefit from a skills-oriented approach.

N.S.: When the two of you began your careers the concept of developmental education was emerging as both the philosophical and the administrative replacement for postsecondary remedial or compensatory education. Thirty years later has the concept—not merely the term—"developmental" truly displaced the deficit model embodied in remedial reading instruction?

M.S.: In our field developmental education external forces are tinkering always with what it is we do based on what they think we should do. That's where the state instructional mandates and the required tests come into play. As long as Boards of Regents and legislators make up rules, research-based progress will be stymied.

S.N.: The only thing that's changed is the name, and I think we're still operating this sort of deficit model. We still pigeonhole students whether you want to call them developmental programs or remedial programs or special studies programs by still operating from this deficit model. We see that in what are we doing with developmental programs at the college level. They have pretty much been relegated to community colleges or oftentimes outsourced to firms like Kaplan based on a "you take care of it" mindset. So I think the name has changed, but I'm not sure the model has changed.

M.S.: When we are looking at a deficit model or a model that worries about students' grade levels and performance on tests, we miss an important factor and that's retention at the university. When universities get rid of assistance programs that serve the academic unwashed, there is the misconception that this action takes care of all our academic performance issues. We've forgotten the big issue of the individual learner and that learner is anyone who might need assistance at any point in one's academic life. Hopefully we want to retain each student and have each student do well in college.

S.N.: The retention at UGA is actually pretty good. Now, that said, we still have the bottom 10 to 15% of the students that should be able to do college work: They've been accepted; they have fairly decent SAT scores; they look pretty good on paper. Yet, they are not critical readers, and they have very, very weak study skills and strategies. They don't understand the complexity of learning. They were very successful in high school, but they are not successful here. So you end up with these students going on probation. A true developmental model takes those students into consideration, and I don't think that is going on in most places.

N.S.: At the time when you first began your careers at the University of Georgia, specialists taught study skills such as SQ3R and the Cornell Notetaking System. Later, as you came of age professionally, you developed and validated strategic approaches such as PORPE for test taking and PLAE for the management of the learning act. What research driven learning strategies and teaching techniques would you recommend that our colleagues integrate regularly into their own classes as offered in 2006?

S.N.: The annotation studies that we did were really pivotal. They helped us recognize one key thing. It's not the strategy that makes the difference. It's the underlying processes. Then the rest of our research was based on this one key epiphany. We realized that annotation worked so well not because you should write in your book, but because students have to isolate information, they must monitor their learning, they have to paraphrase, and they have to elaborate. You can examine any of the research-based strategies, and it's very easy to understand why they tend to work—there's something else going on. When you look at study skills such as the SQ3R, if you take it as an algorithm where you survey and you question and you read and you recite and you review, it's a very perfunctory thing. If you're just doing this in a lock-step manner, it's not going to work. So it's those two pieces that annotation studies helped us understand: the processes and the flexibility of the strategy that makes it work.

M.S.: In a sense this goes back to that article that I cited by Wittrock about generative processing. Weinstein talked about processing later on and so did Mayer. Elaboration, selection, and organization are types of processes that we really believe are important. For instruction you find an artifact or event in which to imbed the strategy instruction but you must constantly emphasize processes. We've both had students in our office, and we'll say, "How are you doing?" "Are you annotating?" We get a response, "Oh, no. I don't annotate at all." But then when we dig deeper, you find out what it is that they do when they're reading and thinking. They're doing the processes. They may not be doing the actual imitation of the way we taught annotation. But they're thinking the way we espoused. They're elaborating, they're organizing, they're making connections, and so forth. Randall's research showed that many times they're not using the strategies, but they're using the processes. We need to teach students strategies and underlying processes and have an artifact that would embody them.

S.N.: When we talk to students and ask them what strategies they're using, it's very interesting. They might not say that they're annotating, but they're being flexible and if they're writing in their text in some way, they're doing something with that text, and they're using the processes. But it's even more than that. It's that they're doing more than one thing.

One of the strategies that students continue to use is concept cards. And they will often continue to use concept cards the way we taught them and not just for memorization of information. For instance, students will say, "Oh, I use concept cards, and you know, I like to map with my concept cards," I still believe that teaching the processes is the key. Now we teach them a lot of strategies too but the emphasis is on process.

M.S.: One of the things that distinguishes an A and a B student from a D and F student is that the A and B students have more ways of interacting with the course content and texts both cognitively and metacognitively. Good students have more tools, whereas the ones who don't do well are the ones who just go about it in one way that's probably surface level or not task appropriate.

S.N.: Every strategy that a student learns needs to have some sort of self-testing element (process). The students need to be able to monitor their learning. In so much of our research we found out that students don't monitor their learning. They can be taught to do that. As an example, annotation has a monitoring piece built in. Concept cards have a monitoring, self-testing piece. Every strategy that we teach the students has some way that they self-test themselves.

On another point, at the beginning of all of our reading and studying classes, one of the things that we do is teach the students about the complexity of the processes of reading, of understanding, and of being able to remember and retrieve information. Students do not understand the complexities of these four pieces that have to come together in order for them to understand a piece of text.

It's the whole issue of studying and reading being a cyclical process. There's something that you do before, there's something that you do during, and there's something that you do after reading or studying. But it is the flexibility that's built into reading and learning strategies. It's the process that's built into the actions that makes it different from an algorithm like SQ3R.

M.S.: Sherrie alluded to the idea of understanding the nature of learning. For example, a very simple thing that I teach professors and students is how little we remember about what we read. Sharing with them research, in a very graphic way, that after 24 hours you're going to forget much of what you read unless you do some sort of active processing so as to code that information has impact on them.

The other information about learning that we cover at the beginning of a term and then reinforce regularly is the nature of the declarative, conditional, and procedural knowledge. I am constantly saying to the students, "Now you want to know why you're doing this activity. Can you tell me why you might be doing that action? What are the advantages? What are the disadvantages?" We talk about the selection and procedural processes and then we debrief. It's not a strategy. Perhaps it's not a teaching technique, but it is imperative. It's knowledge about the learning process.

Our research has also demonstrated that it's important that we teach students how to evaluate what they did in approaching learning tasks and whether it was a productive approach, which was a part of PLAE. It's that "E" (evaluation) step in PLAE. This point goes back to task knowledge and monitoring. If we don't teach students to evaluate their learning and the strategies they're using, then we've just got one little small piece to the puzzle. So you should teach them strategies of what to do with the textbooks and what to do with lectures. But do not forget the evaluation process.

S.N.: Besides introducing students to a little bit of learning or reading theory another thing that we certainly do in our classroom is that we talk to students about beliefs. We use Schommer's basic types of beliefs about learning as a jumping-off point. Students have really never thought about beliefs. And so when you say, "Do you believe that learning should be quick? How much time are you willing to spend on a task?" the responses are very interesting, very telling. If the student believes that learning is quick or if the student believes that learning is something that is done to him, then the student is going to choose very different strategies from a student who really believes that he or she is a partner in learning, that learning's an interactive process, and that he has something to contribute. It's so important to lay that groundwork in order to get students to buy into the strategies, You know, it goes back to the "skill and will" concept. You can teach students the strategies, but they have to buy into them in order for the transfer to take place.

M.S.: I would add to that we regularly teach students how to define tasks using Doyle's model, and not just the tasks that we have in our classroom but also the ones that they might be encountering in the other classes that they're taking. Students need to think about what it is that they're being asked to do in class so that they develop task-appropriate products. Oftentimes the students are not developing good products because they're drawing from their past academic histories and beliefs (often high school) to define what they think it is that they are supposed to do in a college class.

We both believe that it's important to teach students how to study for college level essay tests because they rarely had such tests in high school. It's important as well to teach them how to prepare for short-answer tests. Even here, the task definition comes in to play because some professors believe short-answer tests are mini-essays and others believe that they are identification questions. It's very important to teach students not only how to define an essay test and a short-answer [test] but then to compose what it is that they are supposed to be writing.

Another thing we recommend is teaching students how to integrate information from multiple sources. For example, if you've got a Web page, a section from the textbook, and the professor's lecture notes as well, how do you synthesize that material? You might put it together with a map. You might put it together with a chart. Students need to learn integrative strategies. Otherwise they focus on individual sets of information. They must learn intertextual organizational strategies, which goes back to that processing issue.

S.N.: All reading programs are going to have to deal with the changing ways that students receive instruction. There are so many more professors on our campus that put class notes on the Web for example. How do you teach students to deal with that approach? The less sophisticated student will tell you, "I just copy the notes. I download the notes, and I don't have to go to class." That's not true. So how do you teach students to deal with both the academic responsibilities and the learning approaches for such an instructional environment? Teaching students how you evaluate information on the web is an evolving instructional concern. So much of what we teach in our reading and studying courses is changing bit by bit to meet this new kind of influence from technology.

What we have attempted to do with our program at UGA over all the years is to match what we teach in our reading and our studying classes to the tasks that students have to do in the instructional environment. That's why it's been a dynamic type of program. It hasn't become stagnant because the academic tasks and the ways students have to complete these tasks have changed dramatically over the years. And so, our program has changed, and the only way we can accomplish on a regular basis is by getting out there on campus and in the classrooms to see what students are experiencing.

M.S.: Another way we've done the outreach is by using the survey process. From the returned questionnaires we learned that we'd better be teaching students how to answer short-answer questions, because many professors were using them on tests, and we realized that we weren't teaching the students how to write such answers. So questionnaires that ask professors teaching the general education and survey courses to explain the writing and reading tasks that they are asking of the students are enlightening.

S.N.: Another instructional approach where we see a big change now is the whole issue of collaborative learning. More and more professors are requiring students to work together in groups and do collaborative learning. So if that's something that students encounter in history classes or sociology classes, this suggests new content to be covered effectively in our courses. We lead the students to understand that you still have to read and learn the information, but we ask how you do that within a group dynamic, how do you use a study group to your advantage, and how do you learn from others?

M.S.: If you have an at-risk group, you'd better teach vocabulary, and you'd better be doing it in a research-based program because it makes a major difference with the students. Whether they are at-risk learners or whether they are advanced learners, students enjoy learning words when they know that they are going to master them and be able to use them. If you're teaching freshmen and you're not providing formal vocabulary instruction through research-based approaches then you are really doing them a disservice.

First of all students have to know words beyond a mere definition. They also have to understand the connotation and the denotation; they have to be able to know examples and characteristics of the word. Students think that every word is a one-to-one relationship, but the words are in context. In our approach they use the words orally in sentences first. Then the students play with them, and once they get to a comfortable level, we write the sentences. We look the word up in the dictionary and write a sentence so there's a lot of oral language going on that precedes the writing. We create a demand for the writing. Finally based on the research we hold them to the commitment of knowing those words over a long-term basis.

S.N.: The students are exposed to the words in lots of different ways and so it's not just a dictionary definition or it's not just context. They might see it in a multiple-choice format, they might see it in terms of a sentence completion, they might have to write a sentence — so it's in multiple ways that they have to show that they understand the meaning of the word. It is not only the first definition of the word they encounter but also its deeper definitions. At one time instructors felt that it should all be context based, but research shows it's a combination of different ways of approaching vocabulary mastery, just like different ways of studying. It's being more than a one-trick pony.

M.S.: Finally there is an issue of assessment, as the testing has to match the techniques of instruction. With vocabulary instruction, if you only give students multiple-choice activities like they do in most workbooks, why would a student ever learn the word at a deeper level? So, you know, we've come up with a lot of devious ways to make students get to a more elaborative level. For instance, having four words in the group and asking which one doesn't belong and what do the other three have in common? When students know they have to know the words at deeper levels, they step up to the plate and they put the effort into it. Then they are thrilled because they retain the word for the long term.

The bibliography is comprised of one or two seminal works by each of the scholars mentioned in the interview.

Bibliography

Alexander, P. A. (2004). The development of expertise: The journey from acclimation to proficiency. *Educational Researcher, 32*(8), 10–14.

Alexander, P. A., Schallert, D. L., & Hare, V. C. (1991). Coming to terms. How researchers in learning and literacy talk about knowledge. *Review of Educational Research, 61*, 315–343.

Baker, L., & Brown, A. L. (1984). Metacognitive skills and reading. In P. D. Pearson, R. Barr, M. Karnil, & P. Mosenthal (Eds.), *Handbook of reading research* (Vol. I, pp. 353–394). New York: Longman.

Biggs, J. B. (1984). Learning strategies, student motivation patterns, and subjectively perceived success. In R. Kirby (Ed.) *Cognitive strategies and educational performance* (pp. 111–134). Orlando, FL. Academic Press.

Bransford, J. D., Brown, A. L., & Cocking, R. R. (1999). *How people learn: Brain, mind, experience, and school.* Washington, DC: National Academy Press.

Brown, A. L. (1982). Learning to learn from reading. In J. A. Langer & M. T. Smith Burke (Eds.), *Reader meets author/Bridging the gap* (pp. 26–64). Newark, DE: International Reading Association.

Chiseri-Strater, E. (1991). *Academic literacies: The public and private discourse of university students.* Portsmouth, NH: Boyton/Cook.

Doyle, W. (1983). Academic work. *Review of Educational Research, 53,* 159–199.

Entwistle, N. J. (1994). *Experiences of understanding and strategic studying.* (ERIC. Document Reproduction Service No. ED. 374–704).

Garner, R. (1990). When children and students do not use learning strategies: Toward a theory of settings. *Review of Educational Research, 60*, 517–529.

Gibbs, G. (1990). *Improving student learning: Project briefing paper.* Oxford, England: Oxford Polytechnic University. Oxford Center for Staff Development.

Hofer, B. K. (2001). Personal epistemology research: Implications for learning and teaching. *Journal of Educational Psychology Review, 13*, 353–882.

Hofer, B. K., & Pintrich, P. R. (1997). The development of epistemological theories: Beliefs about knowledge and their relation to learning. *Review of Educational Research, 67*, 88–140.

Holschuh, J. P. (1998). *Epistemological beliefs in introductory biology: Addressing measurement concerns and exploring the relationship with strategy use.* Unpublished doctoral dissertation, University of Georgia, Athens.

Jenkins, J. J. (1978). Four points to remember: A tetrahedral model of memory experiments. In L.S. Cermak & F.I.M. Craik (Eds.), *Levels of processing and human memory* (pp. 425–445). Hillsdale, NJ: Lawrence Erlbaum Associates.

Marton, E., & Saljo, R. (1976a). On qualitative differences in learning 1: Outcomes and process. *British Journal of Educational Psychology, 46*, 4–11.

Marton, E., & Saljo, R. (1976b). On qualitative differences in learning 2: Outcomes as a function of the learner's conception of task. *British Journal of Educational Psychology, 46,* 115–127.

Nist, S. L., & Simpson, M. L. (2000). College studying. In M. Kamil, R. Barr, P. Mosenthal, & P. D. Pearson (Eds.), *Handbook of reading research* (Vol. III, pp. 645–666). Mahwah, NJ: Lawrence Erlbaum Associates.

Paris, S. G., Lipson, M. Y., & Wixson, K. (1983). Becoming a strategic reader. *Contemporary Educational Psychology, 8,* 293–316.

Pintrich, P., & Garcia, T. (1994). Self-regulated learning in college students: Knowledge, strategies, and motivation. In P. Pintrich, D. Brown, & C. Weinstein (Eds.), *Perspectives on student motivation, cognition, and learning: Essays in honor of W. J. McKeachie* (pp. 113–133). Hillsdale, NJ: Lawrence Erlbaum Associates.

Randall, S. (2002). *An evaluation of an elective academic assistance course.* Unpublished doctoral dissertation, University of Georgia, Athens, GA.

Rumelhart, D. E. (1980). Schemata: The building blocks of cognition. In R. Spiro, B. Bruce, & W. Brewer (Eds.), *Theoretical issues in reading comprehension* (pp. 33–58). Hillsdale, NJ: Lawrence Erlbaum Associates.

Schommer, M. (1994). Synthesizing epistemological belief research: Tentative understandings and provocative confusions. *Educational Psychology Review, 6,* 293–319.

Simpson, M. L., Hynd, C. A., Nist, S. L., & Burrell, K. I. (1997). College reading and learning in academic assistance programs. *Educational Psychology Review, 9,* 39–87.

Simpson, M. L., & Nist, S. L. (2002). Encouraging active reading at the college level. In M. Pressley & C. Collins Block (Eds.), *Comprehension instruction: Research-based best practices* (pp. 365–379). New York, NY: Guilford Press.

Thomas, J. W., & Rowher, W. D. (1986). Academic studying: The role of learning strategies. *Educational Psychologist, 21,* 19–41.

Weinstein, C. F., & Mayer, R. F. (1986). The teaching of learning strategies. In M. C. Wittrock (Eds.), *Handbook of research on teaching* (pp. 315–327). New York, NY: Macmillan.

Wineberg, S. S. (1991). On the reading of historical texts: Notes on the breach between school and academy. *American Educational Research Journal, 28,* 495–519.

Wittrock, M. C. (1990). Generative processes of comprehension. *Educational Psychologist, 24,* 345–376.

Studying in College, Then and Now: An Interview with Walter Pauk

Gene Kerstiens

Gene Kerstiens presents an interview with Walter Pauk. Fifty years ago, few individuals knew of this new faculty member at Cornell University; however, it can be said that as the years progressed, virtually every individual in the field of postsecondary reading and study strategy instruction, as well as the overall field of reading pedagogy, came to know and value Dr. Pauk's scholarship. As the director of the Reading Study Center at Cornell University, Pauk developed study strategies such as the Cornell System of note taking that to this day continue to be taught to students in college reading and study strategy courses. Throughout a professional career spanning five decades, Pauk was active in professional organizations such as the International Reading Association and the College Reading Association, and he authored well over 100 articles, columns, and texts. His How to Study in College, *first published in 1962 and now in its eleventh edition, is the text that introduced many college reading instructors to the field of study strategies, and it has been used by thousands upon thousands of students learning study strategies. In addition to his teaching at Cornell, Pauk has taught at the University of the West Indies, Jamaica, and at the University of Liberia, West Africa.*

The following interview between Gene Kersteins and Walter Pauk was published in 1998 when the sixth edition of How to Study in College *had recently been released to the market. Hence, the reader must approach the interview within its historical context.*

I n the old days, the amount a student read, and presumably assimilated, was the measure of his reading skill.

Historically and currently, Walter Pauk is recognized as a prominent influence upon the profession. While serving as director of the Reading Study Center at Cornell University, he developed teaching strategies and materials that continue to enjoy widespread employment. Through more than 4 decades he has actively participated in professional organizations, is well represented in more than 125 of their publications, and has authored enduring college-level texts and other materials in reading study skills. His *How to Study in College . . .* is widely regarded as the benchmark to which similar texts are compared. In addition to his teaching at Cornell, he has taught at the University of West Indies, Jamaica, and as a Fulbright lecturer at the University of Liberia, West Africa.

Gene Kerstiens (G.K.): Especially in the popular press, but also in faculty conversations and professional journals, we are inundated with complaints that today's students are woefully underprepared for engaging in the demands of college-level course work. Much of this criticism focuses on the declining basic skills of students. If these perceptions are valid, what areas of skills development are in most need of attention?

Walter Pauk (W.P.): Of course, by basic skills we usually mean reading, writing, and math. Being most familiar with reading and writing, I'll respond to these.

In the old days, reading meant the reading of the "100 best books" involving what is considered classical literature: novels, poetry, drama, and essays. Even then there weren't very many well-read students.

Although students were assigned Shakespeare, Wordsworth, Carlyle, and Sophocles, they hardly ever understood enough of these classic writings to discuss them or put their thoughts to use. So even though knowledge of classical literature was required, students in general got very little out of this exposure which was expected to involve volumes of material. Understandably, the amount a student read, and presumably assimilated, was the measure of his reading skill. Consequently, reading instruction comfortably and conveniently emphasized reading speed and all the hearsay and misinformation that process involved. But when we refer to reading today, we're usually talking about a rather different process and purpose.

G.K: Then what is the difference, and how are current reading competencies assessed?

W.P.: Today the emphasis is on reading from textbooks about content that is factual, practical, and descriptive, sometimes called study reading or reading in the content field. The required reading task places emphasis on comprehension and process rather than appreciation. This involves concentration, review, and then recitation or putting what you have read in your own words. The entire process requires a habit of reflection and rereading, demanding time and patience which is disallowed on the timed, multiple-choice tests typically used to measure student reading skills. To the extent that many students have not learned and practiced a study-reading method, they continue to enter college classes under-prepared, although not necessarily as assessed by the tests that evaluate them. But their competency in writing is a different matter.

G.K.: Please explain.

W.P.: Writing skills had deteriorated greatly until recently. Current improvement is largely due to application of advances in technology. For instance, TV bombards the student with a constant stream of words. Students now understand more words, although they may not have incorporated them fully into speech or written vocabulary. Television, then, has helped build a richer passive vocabulary capable of becoming an active vocabulary. But other newly emerging technical tools are having an even greater influence on writing improvement. The computer has probably had the strongest influence. Many students are comparatively computer literate. Some learned how to program a computer before they learned long division. Others have written only on a word processor. And this expertise facilitates writing in a number of ways. It makes the physical act of writing easier, faster, and more legible. Accessories like the spelling and grammar checkers as well as dictionary and thesaurus features also simplify otherwise time-consuming technical tasks. Perhaps more importantly, electronic mail accelerates the interchange of messages so that writing becomes interactive—faster if not instantaneous more like oral discourse which by nature is more personal. These conditions encourage students to practice writing. And practice promotes confidence and builds skills for those who would otherwise find writing tasks intimidating.

G.K.: Speaking of confidence, do you agree with the findings that students' academic confidence, their perception of their competencies or readiness, is substantially independent of their actual (or measured) abilities?

W.P.: In the case of actual abilities, I would say no. Most students are not unrealistic. They believe, and the research will confirm their optimism, that motivation can override most skill deficiencies a student may have. If the student is interested and is convinced that what he is studying is useful or eventually rewarding—and especially if he enjoys learning about the topic he can develop a level of skill that might be far above measured expectation as assessed by a testing or survey instrument.

G.K.: Then perhaps there is reason for some optimism concerning students' skills competencies. But given the growing body of information to be learned and mastered, are the curricular demands upon today's student greater than they were previously?

W.P.: Previously, the demands were traditional and often impractical. And if these conditions went against the grain of the student, the work was made tough. But compliance was simpler. Today, I think the demands in terms of quantity and the acquisition of new information are much greater and more complicated. For example, look at the biological sciences. We dissected earthworms, disemboweled frogs, and memorized phylogenetic taxonomies, but now you have to understand DNA and all its biochemical technical properties. The concepts are light-years ahead of what we had to learn. Also, the distractions and the pressures of day-to-day living that interfere with learning are more numerous.

G.K.: Are you saying that increased stress differentiates today's academic learning environment from that of, say, 4 decades ago?

W.P.: Certainly. Today's student is more likely to be older and probably lives off campus and has a job. This circumstance more than any other interferes with time and energy allocations that learning demands. Also, the student is more likely to be married and perhaps have children and other obligations, concerns that interfere with optimal conditions for learning. So the distractions connected with today's academic life are more numerous and intense. Having started my freshman year when I was 32 years old, I can understand these pressures.

G.K.: So far we have discussed conditions that enhance or impede learning. Related to that topic, what are the most significant research findings in learning theory that have appeared during the last 4 decades?

W.P.: There are two. But let me digress for a moment to give a personal account of how the earliest one affected me and my teaching.

While a graduate student at Cornell in 1953, I was also a teaching assistant in the Speed Reading Program. Almost nothing but speed reading was taught at that time. Briefly, a class consisted of a short talk on vocalization, then on eye fixations, then on skimming and scanning. But, no academic study skills. After the short talk, the Harvard Speed Reading Films were shown on a large screen; finally, for the balance of the session, the students worked on machines: the reading accelerators. What a barren course! That's all we knew, and I taught it with enthusiasm, but I didn't believe in it. We had nothing else. So when I heard about the SQ3R Method, I knew instantly that study skills, not speed reading, was the way to help students help themselves. As fast as I could prepare new materials, I changed the speed reading course into a study skills course, even without discussing the change with the professor in charge of the entire program.

G.K.: Obviously, the SQ3R method had a dramatic effect on your teaching. But how and why was it so influential in reading instruction at large?

W.P.: In 1941 Francis Robinson of Ohio State University published *Effective Study*, although the book was not to receive widespread recognition until its second edition in 1946. This publication stood out like a giant. And we, all of us who stood on the firing line—all of us who stood before class after class of students to teach them how to read and study more efficiently—had Robinson to thank. This imaginative innovation took study skills forever out of the misty realm of well-meaning, paternalistic advice and placed textbook reading and study skills into a sharp category where prescribed techniques were based on and backed by research and experimentation. It was a major breakthrough. It was to reading and study skills what the breaking of the four-minute mile was to track and athletics. And what exactly did he do?

He selected all of the learning theories he could find, particularly in the areas of short-term and long-term memory, and applied them in a formula to help students learn faster and retain what they have read longer. The method was designed with a deep understanding of human perception, cognition, and retention. It inspired much of what we have learned and practiced in the reading/study skills business. I suspect that the SQ3R Method is still taught in almost every college and university in the United States. I suspect, too, that it is taught in most secondary schools that have a reading program. The acronym stands for a method sequence familiar to virtually anyone involved in teaching reading/study skills: survey (preview what you will read), question (turn headings and subheadings into questions and decide what you want to learn), read (read the entire chapter or segment), recite (recite what you have learned), and review (review what you have learned at a later time). Probably because this acronymic formula looked scientific, sounded scientific, was easy to memorize, and implied precision, it caught on quickly. Also, it was taught because it was neat and tidy and even exciting to teach. And because this textbook reading method and variations of it have proved effective for so many students, it has been taught more widely than any other in study skills programs over the years and has had an enduring influence upon teaching and learning.

G.K.: And the second piece of research that has influenced how we teach . . .

W.P.: More lately, I think the research and writings on hemispheric specialization have and will continue to have a profound influence upon improving how we learn. We now know that verbal and conceptual knowledge is stored in the left side of the brain and that concrete events, which can be visualized easily, are stored in the right side. Interestingly, what is stored in the right side is much more durable than what exists in the left side, which would embody the knowledge we most likely need to learn in academic study. What we have discovered in this area has brought to the attention of teachers and students the use of mental visualization as an additional and efficient way to learn and remember. Which is to say that by attaching verbal meaning to concrete events, you'll have dual representation (verbal and visual). Then the verbal message or concept is more likely to be lodged in long-term memory and be available for recall. Therefore, by relating newly learned conceptual material that is stored in the left brain area to a visualized object stored in the right brain, you can efficiently affect long-term memory. The strategy is especially helpful in remembering newly encountered concepts. This knowledge is truly an important breakthrough.

G.K.: Could you give an example of how this visualization technique works?

W.P.: Yes. Kenneth Higbee explains how the right hemisphere of the brain works best with concrete events, objects, and words. For example, an apple can be imagined or visualized very easily. However, when exercising the left brain and verbally classifying the apple as a fruit, you can visualize a basket of fruit but not all of the varieties of fruit in the world.

We can carry the example of an apple two steps further: that is, classifying an apple as food and further, as nourishment. To sum up, the word *apple* can be handled visually by the right hemisphere, but once we move on to the abstract verbal material of fruit, food, and nourishment, the shift over to the left hemisphere should be automatic, natural, and inevitable, if understanding is to be achieved.

G.K.: Given that research can significantly influence our ability to learn, could you mention changes you have made in the new edition of *How to Study in College* and indicate research and/or innovation that has inspired them?

W.P.: Yes, but not all alterations are driven by formal research findings, although most revisions are consistent with the latest studies. Suggestions from students and the results of strong requests of colleagues have been incorporated in each edition. Responding to this constructive criticism, I've concentrated on changes that are practical, things the teacher in the trenches can use to make a difference at the following Monday morning class. I'll mention a few.

The "To the Student" introduction has been reoriented. It starts by bringing in the personal concept of "the will to learn" and there's a 10-item self-assessment inventory, which greatly aids students in identifying their basic learning style.

"Setting Goals: A Self-Management Skill" is a brand-new chapter on a vital subject, the importance of which is unarguable. This chapter includes about 20 question-and-answer paragraphs and illustrations to aid students in formulating their academic and lifetime goals.

The chapter "Improving Your Reading Speed and Comprehension" was brought back from the Fourth Edition. It is packed with new approaches based on recent research as well as many classical approaches to apply techniques that best fit a student's individual learning style.

"Understanding and Using Key Concepts" is not only a brand-new chapter; it is a brand-new concept. It incorporates elements of principles found in all sound learning systems to make learning understandable as well as components — recitation, reflection, and questioning — to make the material memorable. With a separate chapter to explain the importance of these principles, students gain a thorough understanding of them so that when the words *recite, reflect,* and *question* are mentioned in any system, understanding will be swift and complete.

Part IV, "Your Lecture Notes," comprises two chapters: "Listening to Take Good Notes" and "Taking Good Notes." Note taking is too important to discuss in one chapter; therefore, we have back-to-back chapters.

Three things are different in this edition regarding vocabulary development. First, I have reassembled the "Improving Your Vocabulary" chapter as a unit rather than distributing the topic throughout the book. Second, at the end of each chapter you will find a vocabulary exercise composed of 25 practical words taken from current publications. Third, the last component in "Vocabulary Development" features word origins, which creates in many students a permanent interest in words.

Each "Have You Missed Something?" chapter quiz includes questions to reinforce students' understanding of key concepts. The rationale for these questions is not to test but rather to teach.

Other revisions included to update this edition involve treatment of the "concept map" technique, the chapter on "Studying Mathematics," and the chapter on "Learning with the Computer."

G.K.: So far you've covered aspects of learning as they pertain to the demands made by the college-level experience. But beyond success in courses and degree attainment, what are the essential skills needed for lifelong learning?

W.P.: Of course, the skills and attitudes we have discussed so far are also those that are needed for learning beyond the classroom. But if we are looking at success as it relates to formal education as well as a profession or a vocation, then the most important factor is not a skill, per se, but attitude or mind-set—specifically goal setting. And goal setting is a hard thing to do.

G.K.: Why?

W.P.: I think because it has a deep emotional dimension. To set a life's goal, we must enter not only our minds but also our hearts. There is no SQ3R for setting goals, no cut-and-dried formula. A goal, to be a mainspring in your life, has to be internalized. By internalizing, I mean that you have thought about your goal over and over again. You have visualized it and have written out the steps you need to take to attain it.

Once you have decided on a destination, then motivation to reach that goal follows almost inevitably. And I believe that we, as teachers, can help students internalize by providing stories and incidents, especially those based upon our own experience, that students can take into themselves as an inspiration. Simply telling a student to have a goal is not enough.

G.K.: Shifting from matters that directly entail student learning, how do you rate the preparation of practitioners currently entering the profession?

W.P.: I haven't had many opportunities to observe them lately, but my brief exposure to them leaves me with the impression that they tend to talk about new concepts. I fear that many of these innovative notions are too esoteric and precious. Although they are interesting, perhaps entertaining, and even worthy of serious research, many of the new concepts are not of much practical help to the student who wants to know how to get the most out of textbooks and lectures and how to prepare for the exam next Thursday. Instructors are not getting down to the basics.

G.K.: Then what advice would you offer to a person preparing to enter the profession?

W.P.: I'd say, forget about the money or prestige. Largely, we are not nor have we ever been considered very acceptable to faculty who look upon underprepared students as problems rather than as opportunities. Even though some of our services now enjoy a permanent place in the budget and there is evidence that a substantial number of students are successful principally because of our efforts, there are those who look upon us as an academic underclass operating low-grade student support agencies. Therefore, you may need to be satisfied with your own expert competence rather than having emotional intimacy with faculty.

I'd also advise new professionals to become proficient, cultivate someone whose work you admire and believe in. Allow the person to mentor you, and work with him or her until your skills are developed. Then, continue to network with others in your field with whom you feel comfortable, especially those who do effectual and interesting things. Finally, systematically read the professional literature, and participate in at least one professional organization in order to keep you current on practice and policies that you might want to experiment with and perhaps incorporate in your own bag of tricks.

G.K.: Concerning these professional organizations, compared to their influence during the 50s and 60s, are today's organizations fulfilling a leadership function?

W.P.: During the very early years, there were only a few organizations that represented reading/study skills. Except for the National Reading Conference and the College Reading Association, they concentrated on primary/secondary concerns that had little relevance to the problems and programs we were dealing with. Essentially, we were isolated from others who were also helping students improve their learning skills. Probably only at annual conferences or in the publications of their yearbooks were we able to participate in professional dialogue. Today there are a number of organizations in which you can participate. Some of these provide opportunities to focus on aspects of student support that appeal to an individual teaching style or focus of study. Especially as these organizations publish or draw our attention to reports and research that promise to improve our strategies and methods, they are providing an invaluable service.

G.K.: Looking to the future, what recommendations would you make to professional organizations?

W.P.: First of all, keep membership participation inexpensive. You don't have to have big bucks to be effective. If the price is too high, you'll be limiting membership to those who probably need it the least and will be neglecting the majority who are in the trenches. Second, exert more time and energy on communicating via publication, whether in print or email. Listening to inspirational speeches at conferences is fine, but having the information you need at hand as a ready reference is more enduring.

Selected References of Historical Importance to the Field of College Reading and Learning

Norman A. Stahl

> The tenor of an age is usually indicated by the books that age produces. They objectify the thinking and voice the interests of the time.
> — Paul Leedy, 1958

For the past forty years, the field of college reading and learning has been situated on the fringes of the reading profession. Whether such marginalization has been real, imagined, or a combination of the two, one cannot argue that the big show for the nation has been the curriculum and instruction for emergent and elementary reading instruction. Those in postsecondary reading and learning instruction have been part of a sideshow at best. Yet it is vitally important for members of the college reading and learning community of practice to understand that we share a rich foundation of theory, research, and practice that dates back over a dozen decades. In fact, there was a period of time in the past decades when research with college students greatly informed the knowledge base for the entire profession.

Hence, it is the purpose of this component of *Teaching Developmental Reading* to provide you with a list of sources—journal articles, professional books, work-texts, monographs, or technical works—that serve as the most important texts produced for the field in the last century. In presenting the sources, I employ a simple decade-by-decade scheme. Indeed, historians would likely prefer lines of demarcation that correspond to watershed events. Nevertheless, this simple scheme works for the purposes of this text. I also must note that the collection of works was not based on a formal survey and rating by experts, but rather on historical knowledge of the profession.

All this said, I believe that these are the sources that all scholars in the field should read at some point in their career. Furthermore, I believe that this list will provide a valuable reference resource for the growing number of individuals enrolling in doctoral programs preparing the future scholars for the field. Finally, it is through knowledge of these works and the additional references contained within them that we are able to carefully evaluate the various proposals associated within the current redesign movement in the field.

Pre-1900

Abell, A. M. (1894). Rapid reading: Advantage and methods. *Education Review. 8,* 283–286.

Porter, N. (1877). *Books and reading; Or, what books shall I read and how shall I read them?* New York, NY: Scribner, Armstrong.

Todd, J. (1836). *The student's manual: Designed by: specific directions to aid in forming and strengthening the intellectual and moral character and habits of the student.* Northampton, MA: J. H. Butler.

Watts, I. (2005). *Improvement of the mind to which is added a discourse on the education of children and youth.* London, England: Elibron Classics, (original work published 1837).

1900–1909

Hinsdale, B. A. *The art of study.* New York, NY: American.

Huey, E. B. (1908). *The history and pedagogy of reading with a review of the history of reading and writing and methods, texts, and hygiene in reading.* New York, NY: Macmillan.

McMurry, F. M. (1909). *How to study and teaching how to study.* Cambridge, MA: Houghton Mifflin.

McMurry, C. A., & McMurry, F. M. (1905). *The method of the recitation.* London, England: Macmillan.

1910–1919

Adams, J. (1915). *Making the most of one's mind.* New York, NY: Doran.

Haggerty, M. E., & Thomas, J. M. (1917). Preliminary study of the reading attainments of college freshmen. *School and Society, 6,* 203–238.

Foster, W. F. (1917). *Should students study?* New York, NY: Harper & Brothers.

Kerfoot, J. B. (1916). *How to read.* Boston, MA: Houghton Mifflin.

King, I. (1917). A comparison of the efficiency of slow and rapid readers. *School and Society, 6,* 203–204.

Kitson, H. D. (1916). *How to use your mind.* Philadelphia, PA: J.B. Lippincott.

Koopman, H. L. (1913). How students actually read. *Education, 23,* 563–569.

Moore, E. C. (1915). An experiment in teaching college students how to study. *School and Society, 2,* 100–107.

Sandwick, R. L. (1915). *How to study and what to study.* Boston, MA: D. C. Heath.

Whipple, G. M., & Curtis, J. N. (1917). Preliminary investigation of skimming in reading. *Journal of Educational Psychology, 8,* 333–349.

1920–1929

Beyer, T. P. (1923). A college course in general reading. *English Journal, 12,* 377–383.

Book, W. F. (1926). *Learning how to study and work effectively.* Boston, MA: Ginn.

Book, W. F. (1927). Results obtained in a special how to study course given to college students. *School and Society, 26,* 529–534.

Book, W. F. (1927). *How to succeed in college.* Baltimore, MD: Warwick & York.

Crawford, C. C. (1928). *The technique of study*. Boston, MA: Houghton Mifflin.

Crawford, N. A. (1928). *How to study (Little blue book # 1319)*. Girard, KS: Haldeman-Julius.

Eurich, A. C. (1929). *An experimental study of the reading abilities of college students*. Unpublished doctoral dissertation. University of Minnesota, Minneapolis.

Garth, T. R. (1920). How college student prepare their lessons. *Pedagogical Seminary, 27*, 90–98.

Germane, C. E. (1920). The value of the controlled mental summary as a method of studying. *School and Society, 12*, 591–593.

Gilliland, A. R. (1920). The effect of the rate of silent reading on the ability to recall. *Journal of Educational Psychology, 11*, 474–479.

Good, C. V. (1925). An experimental study of the merits of extensive and intensive reading in the social sciences. *School Review, 33*, 755–770.

Jones, E. S. (1929). The preliminary course on how to study for freshmen entering college. *School and Society, 29*, 702–705.

Kornhauser, A. W. (1924). *How to study: Suggestions for high school and college students*. Chicago, IL: University of Chicago Press.

Lyman, R. L. (1924). *The mind at work in studying, thinking, and reading: A source book and discussion manual*. Chicago, IL: Scott Foresman.

O'Brien, J. A. (1920). Training in perception as a means of accelerating the silent reading rate. *Journal of Educational Psychology, 11*, 402–417.

Muse, M. B. (1929). *An introduction to efficient study habits according to the laws and principles governing economical learning*. Philadelphia, PA: W.B. Saunders.

Pressey, L. C. (1928). *A manual of reading exercises for freshmen*. Columbus, OH: Ohio State University Press.

Pressey, L. C. (1928). The permanent effects of training in methods of study on college success. *School and Society, 28*, 403–404.

Webb, L. W. (1920). Students' methods of studying a certain subject-Psychology. *Journal of Educational Psychology, 11*, 193–206.

1930–1939

Bird, C. (1931). *Effective study habits*. New York, NY: Century.

Buswell, G. T. (1939). *Remedial reading at the college and adult levels: An experimental study. Supplementary Educational Monographs, No. 50*. Chicago, IL: University of Chicago Press.

Crawford, C. C. (1930). *Studying the major subjects*. Los Angeles, CA: Author.

Crawley, S. L. (1936). *Studying effectively*. New York, NY: Prentice-Hall.

Dearborn, W. F., & Anderson, I. H. (1937). A new method for teaching phrasing and for increasing the size of reading fixations. *Psychological Record, 1*, 459–475.

Frederick, R. W. (1938). *How to study handbook*. New York, NY: Appleton-Century.

Gabriel, J. (1933). *Practical methods of study: A textbook for student nurses*. New York, NY: Macmillan.

Gray, W. S. (1936). Reading difficulties in college. *Journal of Higher Education, 7*, 356–362.

Imus, H. A., Rothney, J. W., & Bear, R. M. (1938). *An evaluation of visual factors in reading*. Hanover, NH: Dartmouth.

Laurer, A. R. (1936). An experimental study of the improvement in reading by college students. *Journal of Educational Psychology, 27,* 655–662.

Parr, F. W. (1930). The extent of remedial reading work in state universities in the United States. *School and Society, 31,* 547–548.

Robinson, F. P. (1930). *Analysis and treatment of reading inadequacies in college freshmen.* Unpublished master's thesis, State University of Iowa.

Robinson, F. P. (1934). An aid for improving reading rate. *Journal of Educational Research, 28,* 453–455.

Strang, R. (1938). *Problems in the improvement of reading in high school and college.* Lancaster, PA: Science Press.

Wrenn, G. G., & Cole, L. (1935). *How to read rapidly and well.* Stanford, CA: Stanford University Press.

1940–1949

Ammons, R. B., & Hierouymus, A. N. (1947). Critical evaluation of a college program for reading improvement. *Journal of Educational Psychology, 38,* 449–470.

Charters, W. W. (1941). Remedial reading in college. *Journal of Higher Education, 12,* 117–122.

Digna, S. M. (1944). An integrated program of remedial reading. *Journal of Higher Education, 13,* 209–211.

Henry, N. B., & Gray, W. S. (1948). *Reading in the high school and college. Yearbook of the National Society for the Study of Education, 47* (2). Chicago, IL: University of Chicago Press.

Laycock, S. R., & Russell, D. H. (1941). An analysis of 38 how to study manuals. *School Review, 49,* 370–379.

McCallister, J. M. (1942). *Purposeful reading in college.* New York, NY: Appleton-Century-Crofts.

McCaul, R. L. (1942). The cost of remedial reading programs in eighteen colleges. *School and Society, 56,* 361–364.

Perry, W.G., & Whitlock, C. P. (1948). *Selections for improving speed and comprehension.* Cambridge, MA: Harvard University Press.

Robinson, F. P. (1941). *Diagnostic and remedial techniques for effective study.* New York, NY: Harper.

Robinson, F. P. (1943). Study skills of soldiers in ASTP. *School and Society, 58,* 398–399.

Robinson, F. P. (1946). *Effective study.* New York, NY: Harper and Row.

Strang, R. M. (1947). The college personnel worker's responsibility for improvement of reading. *Educational and Psychological Measurements, 7,* 603–611.

Traxler, A. E. (1943). Value of controlled reading: Summary of opinion and research. *Journal of Experimental Research, 11,* 280–292.

Traxler, A. E. (1944). *The improvement of study habits and skills. Educational records bulletin No. 41.* New York, NY: Educational Records Bureau.

Triggs, F. O. (1941). Current problems in remedial reading for college students. *School and Society, 53,* 376–379.

Triggs, F. O. (1943). *Remedial reading: The diagnosis and correction of reading difficulties at the college level.* Minneapolis, MN: University of Minnesota Press.

Wilkins, S.V., & Webster, R. G. (1943). *A college developmental reading manual.* Cambridge, MA: Houghton Mifflin.

Witty, P. A. (1940). Practices in corrective reading in colleges and universities. *School and Society, 52,* 564–568.

Wrenn, C. G., & Larsen, R. P. (1941). *Studying effectively.* Stanford, CA: Stanford University Press.

1950–1959

Barbe, W. B. (1951). Reading improvement services in colleges and universities. *School and Society, 74,* 6–7.

Barbe, W. B. (1952). The effectiveness of work in remedial reading at the college level. *Journal of Education Psychology, 43,* 229–237.

Judson, H., & Baldridge, K. (1954). *The techniques of reading.* New York, NY: Harcourt, Brace and Co.

Leedy, P. D. (1958). *A history of the origin and development of instruction in reading improvement at the college level.* Unpublished doctoral dissertation, New York University. (University Microfilms No. 59–01016).

Miller, L. L. (1957). Evaluation of workbooks for college reading programs. In O.S. Causey (Ed.), *Techniques and Procedures in College-Adult Reading. 6th Yearbook of the Southwest Reading Conference for College and Adults.* Fort Worth, TX: Texas Christian University Press.

Miller, L. L. (1959). *Maintaining reading efficiency.* New York, NY: Holt.

Perry, W. G. (1959). Student use and misuse of reading skills: A report to the faculty. *Harvard Education Review, 29,* 193–200.

Wilcox, G. W. (1958). *Basic study skills.* Boston, MA: Allyn & Bacon.

Yearbooks issued by the Southwest Reading Conference during the 1950's. Fort Worth, TX: Texas Christian University Press.

1960–1969

Berger, A. (1966). *Effectiveness of four methods of increasing reading rate, comprehension, and flexibility.* Unpublished doctoral dissertation, Syracuse University, Syracuse.

Christ, F. L. (1966). *Studying a textbook.* Chicago: Science Research Associates.

Leedy, P. D. (1964). *College-adult reading instruction.* Newark, DE: International Reading Association.

Shaw, P. (1961). Reading in college. In N. B. Henry (Ed.), *Development in and Through Reading: Sixtieth Yearbook of the National Society for the Study of Education.* Chicago, IL: University of Chicago Press.

Smith, D. E. P., & Haag, C. (1961). *Learning to learn.* New York, NY: Harcourt, Brace & World.

Yearbooks issued by the North Central Reading Association during the 1960s.

1970–1979

Ahrendt, K. M. (1975). *Community college reading programs.* Newark, DE: International Reading Association.

Anderson, T. H. (1978). *Study skills and learning strategies. Technical report no. 104.* Urbana, IL: University of Illinois, Center for the Study of Reading.

Bahe, V. R. (1970). A content analysis of current college reading manuals. In G. B. Schick & M. May (Eds.), *Reading: Process and Pedagogy. 19th Yearbook of the National Reading Conference (Vol. 2)*. Milwaukee, WI: National Reading Conference.

Berger, A. (1970). A comparative study of reading improvement programs in industry and education. In G. B. Schick and M. M. May (Eds.), *Reading: Process and Pedagogy. Nineteenth Yearbook of the National Reading Conference*. Milwaukee, WI: National Reading Conference.

Cuomo, G. (1978). *Becoming a better reader and writer*. New York, NY: Harper & Row.

Fairbanks, M. (1974). The effects of college reading improvement programs on academic achievement. Interaction: *Research and Practice for College-Adult Reading. Twenty-third Yearbook of the National Reading Conference*. Milwaukee, WI: National Reading Conference.

Gerow, J. R., & Lyng, R. D. (1975). *How to succeed in college: A student guidebook*. New York, NY: Charles Scribner's Sons.

Grant, M. K., & Hoeber, D. R. (1978). Basic skills programs: Are they working? (AAHE- ERIC Higher Education Research Report No. 1). Washington, DC: American Association for Higher Education.

Kerstiens, G. (1971). *Junior-community college reading/study skills*. Newark, DE: International Reading Association.

Lagan, J. (1978). *Reading and study skills*. New York, NY: McGraw-Hill.

Maxwell, M. (1979). *Improving student learning skills*. San Francisco, CA: Jossey-Bass.

Pauk, W. (1974). *How to study in college*. (2nd Ed.). Boston, MA: Houghton Mifflin.

Raygor, A. (1970). *McGraw-Hill basic skills system*. New York, NY: McGraw-Hill

Roueche, J. E., & Snow, J. J. (1977). *Overcoming learning problems*. San Francisco, CA: Jossey-Bass.

Yearbooks issued by the Western College Reading Association during the 1970s.

1980–1989

Algier, A. S., & Algier, K. W. (1982). *New directions for college learning assistance: Reading and study skills. (No.8)*. San Francisco, CA: Jossey-Bass.

Anderson, T. H., & Armbruster, B. B. (1980). *Studying. Technical report no. 155*. Urbana, IL: University of Illinois, Center for the Study of Reading.

Bartholomae, D., & Petrosky, A. R. (1986). *Facts, artifacts and counterfacts: Theory and method for a reading and writing course*. Upper Montclair, NJ: Boynton Cook.

Brown, A. L. (1980). Metacognitive development and reading. In R. J. Spiro, B. C. Bruce, & W. F. Brewer (Eds.), *Theoretical issues in reading comprehension*. Hillsdale, NJ: Erlbaum.

Brozo, W. G., & Johns, J. L. (1986). A content and critical analysis of 40 speed reading books. *Journal of Reading, 30*, 242–247.

Day, J. D. (1980). *Teaching summarization skills: A comparison of training methods*. Unpublished doctoral dissertation, University of Illinois, Urbana.

Frager, A. M. (1989). *College reading and the new majority: Improving instruction in multicultural classrooms*. Oxford, OR: College Reading Association.

Harri-Augstein, S., Smith, M., & Thomas, L. (1982). *Reading to learn*. London, England: Methuen.

Heimichs, A. S., & La Branche, S. P. (1986). Content analysis of 47 college learning skills textbooks. *Reading Research and Instruction, 25*, 277–287.

Martin, D. C. (1980). Learning centers in professional schools. In K. Y. Lauridsen (Ed.), *New Directions for College Learning Assistance: Examining the Scope of Learning Centers*. San Francisco, CA: Jossey-Bass.

McWhorter, K. T. (1980). *College reading and study skills*. Boston, MA: Little Brown.

Nist, S. L., & Hynd, C. R. (1985). The college reading lab: An old story with a new twist. *Journal of Reading, 28*(4), 305–309.

Radencich, M. E., & Schumm, J. S. (1984). A survey of college reading/study skills texts. *Reading World, 24*, 34–47.

Smith, B. (1981). *Bridging the Gap*. Chicago, IL: Scott Foresman.

Stahl, N. A., & Henk, W. A. (1986). Tracing the roots of textbook study systems: An extended historical perspective. J. A. Niles & R. V. Lalik (Eds.). *Solving problems in literacy: Learners, teachers, and researchers, Thirty-fifth yearbook of the National Reading Conference*. Rochester, NY: NRC.

Stahl, N. A., Brozo, W. G., & Simpson, M. L. (1987). Developing college vocabulary: A content analysis of instructional materials. *Reading Research and Instruction, 26*, 203–221.

Trillin, A. & Associates (1980). *Teaching basic skills in college*. San Francisco, CA: Jossey-Bass.

1990–1999

Casazza, M. E., & Silverman, S. L. (1996). *Learning assistance and developmental education: A guide for effective practice*. San Francisco, CA: Jossey-Bass.

Flippo, R. F., & Caverly, D. C. (1991a). *College reading and study strategy programs*. Newark, DE: International Reading Association.

Flippo, R. F., & Caverly, D. C. (1991b). *Teaching reading and study strategies at the college level*. Newark, DE: International Reading Association.

Henry, J. (1995). *If not now: Developmental readers in the college classroom*. Portsmouth, NH: Boynton/Cook.

Maxwell, M. (1993). New insights about college reading: A review of recent research. *Journal of College Reading and Learning, 27* (1), 34–42.

Maxwell, M. (1994). *From access to success*. Clearwater, FL: H & H Publishing.

Maxwell, M. (1997). *Improving student learning skills: A new edition*. Clearwater, FL: H & H Publishing.

Nist, S. L., & Olejnik, S. (1995). The role of context and dictionary definitions on varying levels of work knowledge. *Reading Research Quarterly, 30*(2), 172–193.

Nist, S. L., Simpson, M. L., Olejnik, S., & Mealey, D. L. (1991). The relation between self-selected study processes and test performance. *American Educational Research Journal, 28*(4), 849–874.

Simpson, M. L., Hynd, C. R., Nist, S. L., & Burrell, K. I. (1997). College academic assistance programs and practices. *Educational Psychology Review, 9* (1), 39–87.

Stahl, N. A., Simpson, M. L., & Hayes, C. G. (1992). If only we had known: Ten recommendations from research for teaching high-risk college students. *Journal of Developmental Education, 16* (1), 2–11.

Traub, J. (1994). *City on a hill: Testing the American dream at City College.* Reading, MA: Addison-Wesley.

2000–2013

Arendale, D. R. (2010). *Access at the crossroads: Learning assistance in higher education. ASHE Higher Education Report*, 35(6).

Boroch, D., Hope, L., Smith, B., Gabriner, R., Mery, P., Johnstone, R., & Asera, R. (2010). *Student success in community colleges: A practice guide to developmental education.* San Francisco, CA: Jossey-Bass.

Caverly, D. C., Nicholson, S. A., & Radcliffe, R. (2004). The effectiveness of strategic reading instruction for college developmental readers. *Journal of College Reading and Learning, 35*, 25–45.

Flippo, R. L., & Caverly, D. C. (2000). *Handbook of college reading and study research.* Mahwah, NJ: Erlbaum.

Flippo, R. L., & Caverly, D. C. (2009). *Handbook of college reading and study research* (2nd edition). New York, NY: Routledge.

Grubb, W. N. (2012) *Basic skills education in community colleges: Inside and outside of classrooms.* New York, NY: Routledge.

Hodges, R., Simpson, M. L., & Stahl, N. N. (2012). *Teaching study strategies in developmental education: Readings on theory, research, and best practice.* Boston, MA: Bedford/St. Martin's.

Nist, S. L., & Holschuh, J. P. (2005). Practical applications of the research on epistemological beliefs. *Journal of College Reading and Learning, 35*, 84–92.

Nist, S. L., & Simpson, M. L. (2000). College studying. In M. L. Kamil, P. B. Mosenthal, P. D. Pearson, & R. Barr (Eds.). *Handbook of reading research: Volume III* (pp. 645–666). Mahwah, NJ: Erlbaum.

Paulson, E. J., Laine, M. E., Biggs, S. A., & Bullock, T. L. (2003). *College reading research and practices: Articles from the Journal of College Literacy and Learning.* Newark, DE: International Reading Association.

Perin, D. (2013). Teaching academically underprepared students in community colleges. In J. S. Levin & S. T. Kater (Eds.) *Understanding community colleges* (pp. 87–103). New York, NY: Routledge.

Simpson, M. L., & Nist, S. L. (2000). An update on strategic learning: It's more than textbook reading strategies. *Journal of Adolescent & Adult Literacy, 43* (6), 528–541.

Simpson, M. L., & Nist, S. L. (2001). Encouraging active reading at the college level. In M. Pressley & C. C. Block. *Comprehension instruction: Research based best practices.* New York, NY: Guilford Press.

Simpson, M. L., Stahl, N. A., & Francis, M. A. (2004). Reading and learning strategies: Recommendations for the 21st Century. *Journal of Developmental Education, 28* (2), 2–4, 6, 8, 10–12, 14–15, & 32.

Stahl, N. A., & Boylan, H. (2003). *Teaching developmental reading: Historical, theoretical, and practical background readings.* Boston, MA: Bedford/St. Martin's.

Zimmerman, B. (2004). Becoming a self-regulated learner. *Theory into Practice, 41,* 64.

2

Cross-Level Conversations

Introduction

I n the second decade of the twenty-first century, issues surrounding college and career readiness are the focus of literacy professionals' conversations at all educational levels. Of particular interest, especially since the widespread adoption of the Common Core State Standards (CCSS), is the transition from high school to college. It is clear that movement toward a better, stronger, and clearer alignment between these two educational levels is essential. To make this possible, however, requires that professionals not only have a clear sense of what happens at each level, but also a good idea of the differences as well as the similarities, especially with regard to literacy expectations. Thus, this chapter provides context, both historical and current, related to the secondary-postsecondary transition period.

Such conversations are not at all new to the field of college reading. In fact, this chapter's Historically Significant Work is the first chapter from Frances Triggs's (1943) book *Remedial Reading: The Diagnosis and Correction of Reading Difficulties at the College Level.* In this piece, Triggs provides a historical context for the rapid growth of "remedial reading programs" on college campuses between 1929 and 1942 that mirrors many of the conversations being had this very day about college readiness. Further, she acknowledges the responsibility of such programs not only to help students to be successful in college, but also to prepare them for what comes beyond college. Much of what she argues has continued relevance, particularly with the current renewed focus on college and career readiness.

Triggs's argument about educators' responsibility to prepare students for the literacy expectations they will face in college and beyond provides a perfect segue into larger theoretical conversations related to developmental reading. For this, we have included Patricia Alexander's seminal article outlining a developmental model of reading that is built upon a life span perspective; she posits that reading is developed in stages over a lifetime. Alexander's work serves as a much-needed reminder that we are all always developing as readers—that we are all, in a sense, *developmental* readers. This perspective allows for current conversations of the CCSS to be situated in a model that explicates the need for careful and purposeful scaffolding across all educational levels.

Another essential piece of these conversations about college and career readiness, especially those related to the ever-evolving CCSS, is the need for better alignment between educational contexts (specifically, high school and college). Following Alexander's article are two articles that provide insights needed for conversations focused on this issue of alignment. The first of these is from Lisa Schade Eckert, who tackles not only the secondary-postsecondary divide in her theoretical discussion, but also the literature-literacy divide. She argues that infusing literary theory into reading strategy instruction at the high school level can provide a scaffold into the types of critical thinking and reading practices expected of college students. Eckert's article reminds us that conversations related to college and career readiness need to be not only cross-level, but cross-disciplinary as well.

In the next selection, Rona Flippo acknowledges that the research and scholarship included in one of our field's defining texts, *The Handbook of College Reading and Study Strategy* (Flippo & Caverly, 2009), has been well-received and highly regarded not just by the postsecondary educators commonly thought to be the primary audience, but also by secondary-level literacy professionals. Like other scholars whose work is highlighted in this chapter, Flippo argues for more cross-level conversations and sharing in order to get at those important literacy questions that span educational levels, and, ultimately, to work toward closing the instructional gaps between high school and college.

This selection of works provides background, context, and ideas that should motivate postsecondary literacy specialists to initiate cross-level conversations about college and career reading readiness.

Additional Readings

ACT. (2011). *The condition of college & career readiness 2011*. Iowa City, IA: Author.

Barnett, E. A., Corrin, W., Nakanishi, A., Bork, R. H., Mitchell, C., Sepanik, S., Wathington, H. D., Pretlow, J., Hustedt, B., Edgecombe, N., Gardenhire, A., & Clabaugh, N. (2012). *Preparing high school students for college: An exploratory study of college readiness partnership programs in Texas.* National Center for Postsecondary Research Working Paper. New York, NY: National Center for Postsecondary Research.

Brown, R., & Niemi, D. (2007). *Investigating the alignment of high school and community college assessments in California* (National Center Report #07-3). San Jose, CA: National Center for Public Policy and Higher Education.

Conley, D. T. (2011). *Redefining college readiness, Vol. 5.* Eugene, OR: Educational Policy Improvement Center.

Conley, D. T. (2010). *College and career ready: Helping all students succeed beyond high school.* San Francisco, CA: Jossey Bass.

Conley, D. T. (2007). The challenge of college readiness. *Educational Leadership. 64*(7), 1–6.

Conley, D. T. (2005). *College knowledge: What it really takes for students to succeed and what we can do to get them ready.* San Francisco, CA: Jossey-Bass.

Flippo, R. L., & Caverly, D. C. (2009). *Handbook of college reading and study research* (2nd ed.). New York, NY: Routledge.

Moss, B., & Bordelon, S. (2007). Preparing students for college-level reading and writing: Implementing a rhetoric and writing class in the senior year. *Reading Research and Instruction, 46*(3), 197–221.

National Governors Association Center for Best Practices, Council of Chief State School Officers (2010). *Common Core State Standards.* Washington DC: Author. Retrieved from http://www.corestandards.org/

Sepanik, S. (2012). *Getting ready for success: Bridging the gap between high school and college in Tacoma, Washington.* New York, NY: MDRC.

Strayhorn, T. L. (2010). Bridging the pipeline: Increasing underrepresented students' preparation for college through a summer bridge program. *American Behavioral Scientist, 55*(2), 142–159.

Triggs, F. O. (1943). *Remedial reading: The diagnosis and correction of reading difficulties at the college level.* Minneapolis, MN: University of Minnesota Press.

Zygouris-Coe, V. I. (2012). Disciplinary literacy and the Common Core State Standards. *Topics in Language Disorders, 32*(1), 35–50.

Historically Significant Work

From Remedial Reading: The Diagnosis and Correction of Reading Difficulties at the College Level

Frances Oralind Triggs

In this selection, Frances Oralind Triggs argues that, in general, the American public, including college graduates, does not read widely, often, or critically. Students do not receive specialized training in reading after the early grades, despite the fact that reading expectations are more specialized in high school and college. Corrective instruction at the college level is there-

fore needed because students entering college are not prepared for the read-
ing demands at that level. Writing in the 1940s, Triggs posited that
postsecondary reading programming should focus on helping students
meet the reading demands of college, but could also encompass reading de-
mands beyond college as well as provide an avenue for raising the overall
literacy level of the entire nation. Such a statement seems to be quoted di-
rectly from the twenty-first-century reform movement. Yet Triggs's essay in-
forms us that such concerns are over sixty years old. There is much to learn
from the sage advice of our academic benefactors.

Even in this day of split-second communications, especially in this day of book-burnings overseas, there should be no need to labor the importance of reading to educated, civilized men. Through books and reading each succeeding generation is saved from having to accumulate its experience from scratch. Through books and reading man's horizons are extended, even while he is brought closer to all his fellows in understanding. We have not yet lost our faith that words and knowledge are better tools than bombs and guns for accomplishing the world's great tasks. But this assumes not merely man's ability to read; he must use his ability to discharge his vocational and cultural responsibilities, and at this point our faith is shaken.

The American public does not read critically. The average citizen is content to read his newspaper in desultory fashion, a popular magazine or two, and perhaps an occasional light novel. Beyond that he does not venture. Only about a fourth of the American people read books of any kind, and those who read nonfiction are a distressingly small proportion of that fourth. In recent years a number of studies have been made of the reading interests and activities of different segments of the American public, and the findings have been uniformly discouraging.[1] Americans read far less than might be expected for a nation that is wealthier than any other and has an unusually high standard of universal education—and far, far less than is healthy for a nation whose hope of betterment rests upon the opinions and decisions of its citizenry at large.

Especially disturbing is the fact that college graduates differ very little in the amount and kind of their reading from other, less highly educated members of the population. After an intensive comparative study of the reading interests of college graduates and those of students who stopped with a year or two of college, Pace of Minnesota concluded that there are no differences between the two groups in either the quantity or the quality of books, magazines, and newspapers they read.[2] Other evidence on this matter is less specific, but there can be little doubt that so far our schools have failed either to equip students with reading skills that can be used when the need arises or to broaden or elevate their reading tastes to anything approaching the degree we might reasonably expect.

school's
fault?

These facts constitute a major indictment of American educational methods. True, some of the responsibility for the want of wide reading among our people rests upon the home, where the child's formative years are spent. But parents are not likely to pass on to their children abilities or habits they do not themselves possess, and parents too are the product of home and school. It is to the schools we must look for education, and education does not deserve the name if it leaves no apparent impress on the individual's activities in the years after high school or after graduation from college. A child's years of schooling are of doubtful value if when they are over he cannot use or is not impelled to use his ability to read.

What are the causes of this widespread indifference to reading? One cause may lie in the fact that schoolteachers, like parents, are themselves part of the great nonreading American public. They can hardly develop mature and useful habits of reading in their pupils if their own reading skills and interests are undeveloped. And unfortunately, American schoolteachers are found to suffer in comparison with other professions in the depth and scope of their reading.[3] They simply hand on to those they teach the same inadequate reading standards they have themselves acquired. This vicious spiral must be broken.

Of major importance in the situation is the indisputable fact that a tremendous number of Americans do not know *how* to read well. They simply cannot tackle anything beyond the simplest and lightest of materials, not necessarily because they are unintelligent or mentally lazy, but often because they were never taught the techniques of mature reading. Their training in reading ceased when they passed from the early grades. Throughout high school and college they were assumed to have adequate reading ability, regardless of the fact that the work they were required to do called for more and faster reading, a much larger vocabulary, deeper understanding of quite different materials, and the ability to judge and evaluate what they read. These abilities they were expected to acquire for themselves.

Many students, it is true, either through native aptitude or because of superior home and school training, are able to develop the necessary skills for mature reading without difficulty, but there is evidence to show that approximately 20 per cent of the young people entering our colleges and universities read less efficiently than does the average eighth-grade pupil. Obviously these students do not have the reading skills necessary to handle the reading load of the standard college curriculum. In a given class one student may spend three or four hours plodding through an assignment that a skilled reader can master in an hour. Another student may be totally at a loss to distinguish between the main ideas and the lesser details in a reading assignment. Still another may attach an incorrect meaning or no meaning at all to more than half of even the nontechnical words he encounters. For all such students reading is a desperately laborious task. They are unable to keep up with their assignments or to separate the grain from the chaff in their reading, and consequently their grades begin to drop. Yet in many cases once their reading handicaps were overcome they would prove capable of doing entirely satisfactory work in their college courses.

The fact of great individual differences in reading ability has been confirmed over and over again. A series of investigations begun in the early 1920's showed definitely that many college students could not use silent reading efficiently as a study skill.[4] Later in a survey of freshmen at the University of Chicago, Booker found an amazing diversity in their reading skills.[5] Some students could read 18,000 more words, about 45 more pages, an hour than could others, and usually the faster readers read with greater comprehension as well. In another study Pressey of Ohio State University examined textbooks to determine the various types of reading commonly required of college students, then made up a test including these skills and gave it to a group of freshmen.[6] Their scores ranged all the way from 7 to 57 correct answers out of a possible 62, with the median at 30.

Such instances could be cited by the score, now that another decade of research has been added to the studies of reading deficiencies. It is becoming more and more evident that college students vary as greatly in their ability to read well as in their ability to skate or to play the piano.

There are several reasons for the growing recognition of the reading problem. Since the turn of the century far-reaching social changes have brought a much larger number of students into our schools and universities, and as a result the student bodies are no longer the more or less homogeneous groups they once were. Today they include students of widely divergent home backgrounds and degrees of native ability, largely because of the accepted philosophy that every young person has a right to an education commensurate with his ability. The means of paying, or of earning, the cost of an education is still one of the most powerful selective factors,[7] but these means are more widespread than formerly and, through the growth of state-supported universities, the cost has been greatly reduced.

It is probable also that present-day curriculums require more readings and in some cases more difficult reading than formerly. Furthermore, as methods for testing the abilities of students have increased in scientific accuracy and popularity, the differences in reading abilities have become more apparent, or at least more demonstrable. And differential testing has made it clear that a student's failure to measure up to college standards is by no means always due to general inaptitude; it may as easily be the result of a reading disability that can be remedied. Students themselves are usually keenly aware of their reading deficiencies and are often anxious for help in overcoming them.[8]

Our colleges and universities have only recently acknowledged this reading problem and formulated plans for dealing with it. Formerly educators were oblivious to the fact that a problem existed; they assumed that students admitted to college possessed adequate reading skills. It is true that authorities on reading believe that "by the sixth grade of the elementary school, children can master the basic factors of the reading process so well that, for material within their range of experience and within their vocabulary, they can read with as much speed and with as full understanding as adults can read the same kind of material."[9]

They *can* learn to do this, but many of them do not. Nonetheless they are passed on into high school and college, and there, plunged into new reading situations, they fail in their attempts to cope with them. Unable to read rapidly and without difficulty even when the vocabulary and content are simple, they naturally cannot adjust to the increased and varying demands of reading on the higher levels. Some are even without adequate facility in the mechanics of reading (word recognition); others possess this but have not acquired such skills as skimming, varying their rate with their purpose, and so on; still others may have acquired the fundamentals of such skills but have never had training or practice in the efficient use of them. For all these deficiencies remedial or corrective instruction is necessary.[10]

It is highly desirable that the major portion of the responsibility for reading instruction should rest with the elementary and secondary schools, and there is encouraging evidence that they are taking constructive steps toward discharging this responsibility. But until their reading program is further developed the colleges and universities must accept the task of supplying the necessary remedial instruction.

Nor are the institutions of higher education by any means guiltless in the matter themselves. In college the student is quite suddenly confronted with considerably more extensive reading requirements and with new vocabularies and new concepts. No matter how good his previous training in reading has been, he ought not to be left to sink or swim as he has been in the past. Development in reading should be a part of the instructional program in every content field. It is to be hoped that the time will come when college instructors in economics, sociology, zoology, psychology, and other fields will recognize it as part of their job to acquaint incoming students with the particular reading and study techniques required in their fields. But until then where such training is necessary for the individual's success in college, it must be provided as a supplementary program and largely by a specially trained personnel.

In response to the evident need more and more colleges throughout the country have instituted remedial reading programs of one sort or another. In 1929 only seven institutions reported such services, and most of these were state universities. By 1937 reports from 82 colleges and universities, both public and private, indicated that 64 per cent of them were making some attempt to meet their students' reading problems. In 1941 the *Journal of Higher Education* reported a quick survey in which inquiries were sent to 675 institutions, of which 172 replied. Of these 106 had established a remedial service of some kind on their campuses. And early in 1942 another survey, in which questionnaires were sent to 1,528 colleges and universities, revealed that of the 334 who replied 201 had already set up remedial reading services, while 74 more were planning to establish such a service in the coming fall. This represented an increase of 36.8 per cent in one year.[11] The movement is growing, and each new program, no matter how informal or experimental it may be, is at least a step toward the goal.

Beyond question, many of these efforts have been unorganized and uncertain gropings in the dark, for the problem is still a new one, and in spite of the growing interest in it neither the specific difficulties involved nor adequate techniques for overcoming them have been finally determined. It is easy for earnest enthusiasts in the cause to become discouraged at the slowness of development, and as late as 1940 an investigation by one of them led him to the gloomy conclusion that remedial reading at the college level had made dishearteningly little progress.[12]

If we analyze the reasons for the slow advance, however, we see that they are difficulties which hamper any new educational program in its early stages and are not insurmountable. There is first the insufficient number of well-trained persons to develop the field; second, the lack of inexpensive remedial material—tests, exercise manuals, and the like; third, a need for more valid and reliable methods of diagnosing reading difficulties; and fourth, the lack of clear-cut demonstrations that remedial programs really do improve students' reading abilities.[13]

It is the purpose of this book to help meet the first two of these difficulties. The third will no doubt be overcome as we gain knowledge and experience in the work. But before the fourth we must pause. Do the remedial programs really serve their purpose? The answer is no, if we expect them to work miracles. The most effective of remedial techniques could not turn every student into an expert reader. Improvement is closely related to the native ability of the individual, a fact that should be remembered whenever the results of remedial reading are evaluated. Good reading involves so much of active mental participation that it is absurd to expect a person of comparatively low intelligence to become as accomplished in the art as a person of superior intelligence is likely to be. Moreover, in some cases there may be factors involved in poor reading—poor vision or personality difficulties, for example—upon which remedial techniques alone can have little effect, or at least for which they would not be considered the most directly effective treatment.

But we ought not to conclude from this that there is no point in setting up a remedial reading program. Medical science has not given up its war on tuberculosis because some cases are incurable. Actually, there are few students with reading disabilities, even serious ones, who, given average ability, cannot overcome them sufficiently to make a real and important difference in their studies and in their enjoyment of reading as well. That fact has been confirmed again and again in the reports of workers in the field, notably in those of Booker and Bear,[14] and by the experience of the University of Minnesota reading clinic.

The main objective of any college remedial program should be to give the student proficiency in the reading skills he needs to do his college work satisfactory. It may also aim to broaden his use of reading to meet the responsibilities and problems he faces in college and afterward. It is hard to measure exactly the extent to which either of these objectives has been achieved when the remedial work is finished. For the first of them we can measure the student's improvement in the individual reading skills—comprehension, vocabulary, speed, and the like—and see how his course work and other activities are affected by that improvement. Such measurement can at best be only an approximate indication, for what we call individual reading skills may be, probably are, dependent on one another, and the student's course grades will be influenced by other factors in addition to his reading ability. But we can see the results of real improvement when it occurs, even though we cannot determine its precise degree.

The second possible objective of remedial reading, to encourage students to read ever more widely and intelligently, is the objective of much of education in general. How far the remedial program contributes to this objective can be determined only subjectively by the teachers as they watch their students' reading habits change and grow. But surely we shall come nearer attaining our goals if we keep them constantly in mind. Specific remedial techniques must deal mostly with the more tangible reading skills, and even these techniques are far from perfected or standardized. But along with exercises and practice, students must be encouraged to *use* their developing skills—to appraise the worth of what they read and to appreciate and enjoy the values that may come from reading. Thus our remedial programs may in some measure help to alleviate the poverty of reading in the nation at large, as well as to correct the academic difficulties of college students.

Notes

1. Harold A. Anderson, "Reading Interests and Tastes," in William S. Gray, ed., *Reading in General Education* (Washington, D.C.: American Council on Education, 1940), pp. 217–68. See also Douglas Waples and Ralph W. Tyler. *What People Want to Read About: A Study of Group Interest and a Survey of Problems in Adult Reading* (Chicago: American Library Association and the University of Chicago Press, 1931); R. L. Duffus, Books—Their Place in a Democracy (New York: Houghton Mifflin, 1930); and Louis R. Wilson, The Geography of Reading (Chicago: American Library Association and the University of Chicago Press, 1938).

2. C. Robert Pace, *They Went to College* (Minneapolis: University of Minnesota Press, 1941), p. 73. See also M. Lincoln Schuster, "Can College Graduates Read?" *Publishers' Weekly,* 125: 837–39 (Feb. 24, 1934).

3. Anderson in Gray, *Reading in General Education*, p. 233.

4. Ivan A. Booker, *The Measurement and Improvement of Silent Reading among College Freshmen* (Chicago: University of Chicago Libraries, 1934), p. 2.

5. *Ibid*., p. 112; William S. Gray, "Reading Difficulties in College," *Journal of Higher Education*, 7:357 (Oct. 1936).

6. Luella Cole Pressey, "College Students and Reading," *Journal of Higher Education*, 2:34 (June 1931).

7. Although at present the weight of evidence supports this statement, data collected by E. H. Finch may modify it. These data are summarized in the *Psychological Bulletin*, July 1942, p. 432.

8. Ruth Strang, *Problems in the Improvement of Reading in High School and College* (Lancaster, Pa.: Science Press Printing Co., 1938), p. 15.

9. Guy T. Buswell, *Remedial Reading at the College and Adult Levels: An Experimental Study* (Supplementary Educational Monographs, No. 50, University of Chicago, Nov. 1939), p. 6.

10. The word *remedial* is used in the title of this book in its generic sense derived from the verb "to remedy." In the term *remedial reading* as distinguished from *corrective reading* it has a more limited meaning. Reading disability cases may be grouped according to the degree of deficiency as: inefficient readers, corrective cases, and remedial cases. The inefficient reader usually has satisfactory reading skills but does not know how to apply them; in corrective cases some skills are lacking, but usually only those that can be supplied without a great deal of difficulty, though the student must also be taught to use them efficiently; in remedial cases the individuals lack even the basic skills of word recognitions.

 Authorities differ slightly in their use of these terms, but in general the distinctions just outlined are accepted. For instance, James M. McCallister in his *Corrective and Remedial Reading Instruction* (New York: Appleton-Century, 1936), p. 83, says: "Remedial measures differ from corrective measures only in the degree to which they are adapted to the needs of individuals. Throughout this book the term remedial implies individual instruction based on through diagnosis; the term corrective implies group instruction based on the common needs of a number of individuals. The general principles governing the selection of measures for the two forms of instruction are similar."

11. Robert M. Bear, "The Dartmouth Program for Diagnostic and Remedial Reading with Special Reference to Visual Factors," *Educational Record*, 20:69–88 (supplement 12, Jan. 1939); W. W. Charters, "Remedial Reading in College," *Journal of Higher Education*, 12:117–21 (March 1941). The 1942 survey was conducted by the University of Minnesota Press in preparation for the publication of this book and its accompanying manual of remedial exercises, *Improve Your Reading*. Further information about the results of this survey may be found in Triggs, "Remedial Reading Programs: Evidence of Their Development," an article soon to be published in the *Journal of Educational Psychology*.

12. Paul A. Witty, "Practices in Corrective Reading in Colleges and Universities," *School and Society*, 52: 564–66 (Nov. 30, 1940).

13. Triggs, "Current Problems in Remedial Reading for College Students," *School and Society*, 53: 376–79 (March 22, 1941).

14. Booker, *Measurement and Improvement of Silent Reading*, p. 175; Henry A. Imus, John W. M. Rothney, and Robert M. Bear, *An Evaluation of Visual Factors in Reading* (Hanover, N.H.: Dartmouth College Publications, 1938), p. 114.

The Path to Competence: A Lifespan Developmental Perspective on Reading

Patricia A. Alexander

Patricia A. Alexander presents a model of literacy development that accounts for reading growth from "womb to tomb." This framework notes six characteristics of reading development, each one accounting for changes that occur as readers develop over a lifetime. These characteristics, which emphasize readers' knowledge, personal interest, and motivation, were informed by Alexander's (1997) research on the Model of Domain Learning. The resulting developmental perspective calls for literacy instruction and support across the disciplines, across educational levels, and across the life span. From her seminal work, we have a strong research and theoretical foundation for the concept of developmental reading instruction.

Executive Summary

The purpose of this paper is to present a developmental model of reading that encompasses changes across the lifespan. Until we adopt this lifelong perspective, we continue to run the risk of turning out undeveloped, unmotivated, and uncritical readers unable to fulfill their responsibilities within a democratic society.

This framework of lifespan development in reading is grounded in the extensive research in expertise, particularly the research on the Model of Domain Learning (Alexander, 1997). Based on that research, I forward several characteristic of lifespan reading development:

- Readers' knowledge of language and knowledge of content domains are critical forces in developing competence.

- Readers' personal interest in reading becomes a driving force in their development as competence is achieved.

- Lifespan development involves systematic changes in readers' strategic processing.

- Reading development is a lifelong journey that unfolds in multiple stages.

- Profiles of successful and struggling readers are reflective of developmental forces.

- Readers in acclimation are especially vulnerable and in need of appropriate scaffolding.

The unique configuration of knowledge, interest, and strategic processing for each of the stages of lifespan reading development—acclimation, competence, and proficiency/expertise—is discussed. Further, educational implications and instructional recommendations for these stages and the varying profiles of more or less successful readers are considered.

The Path to Competence: A Lifespan Developmental Perspective on Reading

There is little question that educators, the general public, and policy makers perceive reading as one the most basic and essential abilities for an educated populace (Reinking, McKenna, Labbo, & Kieffer, 1998). The ability to read allows one to navigate a world in which so much of interest and importance is conveyed through written language. The ability to read opens avenues for self-exploration and self-enrichment that would otherwise be inaccessible (Marshall, 2000). Further, reading permits individuals to deepen their understanding of other critical domains of knowledge and allows them to experience feelings of pleasure, beauty, excitement, and more (Reed & Schallert, 1993; Wade & Moje, 2000).

Given the essential nature of reading, it is understandable why so much attention is paid to it. The ability to survive and to thrive in our world is strongly linked to achieving reading competence. For that reason, educators, the general public, and policy makers must do what they can to ensure a literate society—a society of competent readers, writers, speakers, and listeners.

If this goal of a literate society is to be achieved, we must take another look at what it means to read competently. We must consider what it takes to read well not just in the early years, as children struggle to unravel the mysteries and beauty of written and spoken language, but across the lifespan, as the purposes for reading and the character of written language change. In other words, we can do more to realize the goal of a literate society if we better understand the full nature of reading development.

Development and Reading

Within the literacy community, there are two distinct but complementary perspectives on reading development. The first, prevalent in several well-publicized documents and federal legislation (e.g., Adams, 1990; National Reading Panel, 2000; Snow, Burns, & Griffin, 1998), deals almost exclusively with the early period of reading development, what might be described as emergent literacy. This early period is unquestionably a critical time in reading development, and a great deal of research has focused on basic dimensions of reading acquisition, including phonological awareness, vocabulary, and fluency.

Yet there is another view of reading development that extends well beyond the initial period of basic skill and process acquisition. This perspective looks at reading as "a long-term developmental process," at the end of which "the proficient adult reader can read a variety of materials with ease and interest, can read for varying purposes, and can read with comprehension even when the material is neither easy to understand nor intrinsically interesting" (RAND Reading Study Group, 2002, p. xiii). This particular orientation does not discount the emergent literacy view but subsumes it as a first step in lifespan development.

It is this second, less-addressed perspective of reading development that I examine here. Specifically, my goal is to investigate how reading develops across the lifespan by building on the vast literatures in developmental psychology, cognitive psychology, expertise, motivation, and domain-specific learning, as well as reading research.

Viewing reading within a lifespan developmental framework has important educational benefits. For one, it helps to consider the changes and challenges students and adults face once they journey beyond the early elementary grades. Currently, there is an increased awareness that more must be done to understand the nature of adolescent literacy (Alvermann et al., 1996; Moje, 2000) and adult literacy (Kruidenier, 2002; Nist & Holschuh, 2000). The more we understand about adolescents' and adults' continued development as readers, the better we can provide for them. The approaches and interventions suitable for young readers taking their first steps toward reading competence are not likely to work for older children, adolescents, or adults, even if they are still struggling to make sense of print (Alvermann, 2002). Not only have these adolescents and adults changed cognitively, physically, and socially, but the in-classroom or at-work literacy demands they face have changed as well (Nist & Simpson, 2000). A lifespan developmental perspective would not stop in the early years or attend only to those who have yet to acquire the most basic skills or processes. Rather, it would consider reading from womb to tomb; that is, for all populations and for all phases of reading growth.

Another benefit of a lifespan developmental perspective on reading is that it would allow for the identification of forces that may contribute to students' waning performance as they progress through school. There is ample documentation that readers continue to encounter problems with written language even if they acquire basic linguistic abilities during the early years of schooling (Alvermann, 2002; Moje, 2000). For example, data from the National Assessment of Educational Progress (NAEP) indicate that in 1998, 74% of 8th graders and 77% of 12th graders could not perform beyond a basic level in reading (National Center for Education Statistics, 1999). That means that the majority of those 8th and 12th graders had not achieved competency in reading and could not perform such fundamental tasks as inferring meaning or drawing conclusions from grade-appropriate materials.

If educators understood the nature of changes that should occur in readers as they progress toward competence, and if educators had some idea of the problems that might arise during that journey, then they could better formulate interventions or craft educational materials that might circumvent problems or ameliorate their effects (Pressley, 2002). For example, students' motivations for reading are critical forces in sustaining their continued growth and development in the domain of reading (Guthrie & Wigfield, 2000). Thus, educational programs intent on supporting students' long-term reading development should give ample consideration to such motivational variables, including students' interests and goals.

Modeling the Development of Reading

A lifespan model of reading development would represent a significant advancement in the study and practice of reading. There is much to be learned about reading development from the expertise literature, especially the new generation of theory and research (Alexander, 2003a, 2003c). Here I draw on one of those research-based models from the expertise research to illuminate important factors and their transformations that should unfold as students move forward in their journeys toward competence or perhaps even expertise. The Model of Domain Learning (MDL) (Alexander, 1997, 2002) is particularly relevant to this topic of lifespan development in reading for several reasons. Specifically, it is concerned with academic domains; focuses on cognitive and motivational factors; and explores systematic changes in those factors across three stages of development: acclimation, competence, and proficiency/ expertise (see Figure 1). Text-based tasks are also routinely incorporated in MDL studies, which increase this model's relevance to discussions of reading development. Therefore, based primarily on the research on the MDL, as well as other relevant programs of expert/

Figure 1. Stages of Reading Development

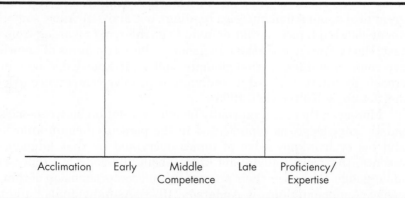

| Acclimation | Early | Middle | Late | Proficiency/ |
| | | Competence | | Expertise |

novice research (Newell & Simon, 1972), several conclusions about reading development can be derived.

Characteristics of Lifespan Reading Development

Readers' Knowledge of Language and Knowledge of Content Domains Are Critical Forces in Developing Competence

One of the potent findings of cognitive research is that knowledge is a significant predictor of developing competence (Alexander & Murphy, 1998b). This finding is also consistent with conclusions from reading research. Even if students have acquired the ability to decode print accurately, they need an understanding of the concepts or ideas those letters and sounds symbolize. In the MDL, two forms of subject-matter knowledge have relevance to reading development—domain and topic knowledge (Alexander, Schallert, & Hare., 1991).

Domain knowledge refers to the breadth of one's knowledge or how much one knows about reading. Topic knowledge represents the depth of knowledge about specific topics relevant to the domain and referenced in text. Because of the nature of reading, those topics may be reading-specific, as when students study main ideas, syllabication, sound-symbol relations, or text genres. However, because students are asked to read about a multitude of topics in reading classes and in their content courses, those topics can also run the gamut, from Harry Potter to Harry Truman. Consider the cases of Emma, a fourth grader reading about main ideas in her language arts class, and Jackson, a classmate reading a story about the Revolutionary War. In both instances, their grasp of the content will depend, in part, on their pre-existing knowledge of the domain (reading), as well as the specific concepts expressed in the text (e.g., main ideas, supporting details, Boston Tea Party, and "taxation without representation").

Both forms of subject-matter knowledge are important to understanding reading development, especially in the early stage. That is because those relatively new to an academic domain may not know a great deal about a domain (e.g., reading), but may still know something about selected topics in that domain (e.g., inferring meaning from context, Harry Potter, or turtles). In general, these two forms of knowledge are complementary, in that domain and topic knowledge become increasingly interconnected as individuals achieve competence (Alexander, Jetton, & Kulikowich, 1995).

Moreover, there is a mutually beneficial relation between one's linguistic knowledge, as represented in the person's domain knowledge, and his or her knowledge of topics encrypted by that language. In essence, the more individuals know about the concepts represented in language, the easier their processing and comprehension of that language (Anderson, Spiro, & Anderson, 1978). As individuals build their knowledge of language, they are also building their knowledge of the ideas those letters and sounds signify. For instance, reading "c-a-t" with meaning involves some understanding of what "cat" represents. Repeated encounters with texts about cats not only build readers' language facility but their conceptual knowledge as well. In effect, learning to read and reading to learn are cofacilitative processes that continue throughout development. Thus, as individuals move from being novices to more competent readers, their breadth of knowledge in the reading domain should increase along with their depth of knowledge about specific reading topics (see Figure 2).

Readers' Personal Interest in Reading Becomes a Driving Force in Their Development as Competence Is Achieved

Interest refers to the energizing of learners' underlying needs or desires (Ames, 1992; Dweck & Leggett, 1988). Two distinct and, at times, competing forms of interest have been supported by the expertise research—individual and situational interest. Individual interest pertains to one's long-term investment or deep-seated involvement in the target field (Hidi, 1990; Schiefele, 1991). By contrast, situational interest refers to the momentary arousal or temporary attention that is triggered by conditions in the existing context (Mitchell, 1993). Consider the following example:

> Samuel, Meredith, and Riley are ninth graders reading a chapter on genetics in their biology textbooks. Even though Samuel is not a particular fan of biology, he finds the subject of genes and gene-mapping intriguing. Meredith, by contrast, has long found the domain of biology personally relevant and engaging, in part because a number of family members suffer from certain biological disorders. Even as a young student, Meredith

Figure 2. Changes in Topic and Domain Knowledge by Stages

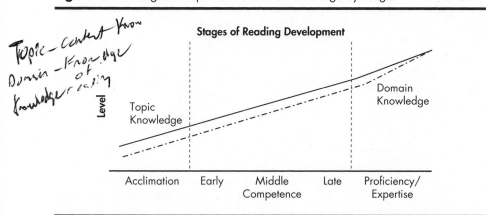

enjoyed reading about the human body and she hopes to become a pediatrician. Riley, however, finds all things biological to be dry and boring. It does not matter if the topic is genes or digestion.

Based on this description, we would say that Samuel shows situational interest in the topic, whereas Meredith is individually interested in the domain. Riley, however, appears to be neither situationally nor individually interested in reading about genetics.

Interest, in some manner, plays an essential role in reading development across the lifespan. For instance, situational interest is expected to play a stronger role in the early periods of reading development than individual interest. As with Samuel, something about the topic or the context grabs readers' attention and urges them onward. However, as individuals progress toward competence in the target domain, individual interest becomes increasingly more important, with the effects of situational interest leveling off. Individually interested readers like Meredith bring an internal excitement or passion to the reading task at hand. Of course, it may help if the biology text is well written or the teacher is highly motivating. However, Meredith's personal identification with the domain and her fascination with related readings would likely endure under less favorable conditions.

The relative importance of situational and individual interest to reading development shifts over time, as illustrated in Figure 3. This shifting relation between situational and individual interest is of particular significance to the development of reading competence. Over time, readers who become competent in reading must find an abiding connection between themselves and written language. A passion for the process of reading, or for encounters with specific forms of text (e.g.,

Figure 3. The Developmental Paths of Situational and Individual Interest

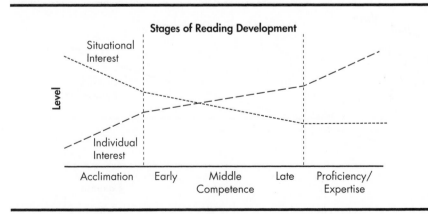

historical fiction or poetry), is necessary for the continued journey into competence or expertise.

Lifespan Development Involves Systematic Changes in Readers' Strategic Processing

Performing competently or expertly in any domain requires confronting the problems that inevitably arise and resolving those problems efficiently and effectively. Strategies are the tools we play during problem solving. In effect, strategies can be defined as the general cognitive procedures used in task performance (e.g., predicting, questioning, summarizing). Strategies also encompass the monitoring or regulation of learning and performance (e.g., Garner & Alexander, 1989; Weinstein & Mayer, 1986; Zimmerman, 1990), processes associated with metacognitive and self-regulatory strategies. Certainly, for the domain of reading, as with other complex academic domains, learning involves the strategic processing of written and oral texts (Alexander & Jetton, 2000).

Two forms of strategic processing play a role in reading development—surface-level and deep-processing strategies (Alexander, Sperl, Buehl, Fives, & Chiu, 2004; Murphy & Alexander, 2002; VanSledright & Alexander, 2002), as shown in Figure 4. Surface-level reading strategies promote initial access to and comprehension of written or oral text. Procedures such as rereading, altering reading rate, or omitting unfamiliar words fit within the category of surface-level strategies. As Emma, our fourth grader, reads the text on the topic of constructing a main idea, she occasionally pauses to reflect on what she read and to check her understanding. She might feel the need to reread certain

Figure 4. The Shifting Roles of Deep-Processing and Surface-Level Strategies

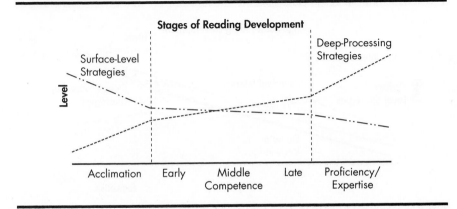

portions or go back to the sample exercises. These are surface-level strategies.

Deep-processing strategies, by comparison, involve the personalization or transformation of text. Examples of deep-processing strategies are cross-text comparisons, creating an alternative representation, or questioning the source. As Emma reads a story about whales as part of the main idea lesson, she makes comparisons between the author's descriptions and the information on whales she read in science class—a deep-processing strategy.

While surface-level strategies are particularly important in the early period of reading development, as individuals build a base of knowledge and interest in the domain, deep-processing strategies become increasingly more evident during competence and proficiency/expertise (Alexander et al., 2004). For example, an experienced biologist reading a high-school biology chapter may have little occasion to reread or paraphrase the text, as compared to high school students enrolled in introductory biology, but he or she may spend time questioning the importance or accuracy of the content or the clarity of the information in that chapter.

Reading Development Is a Lifelong Journey That Unfolds in Multiple Stages

Unlike early models that dichotomized expertise as a novice-to-expert process, the MDL represents reading development in three stages arising from distinct relations between readers' knowledge, interest, and strategic processing—acclimation, competence, and proficiency/expertise. Here, as shown in Figure 5, we consider the interplay of knowledge, interest, and strategic processing at each of these three stages as

Figure 5. The Interplay of Knowledge, Interest, and Strategies Across the Lifespan

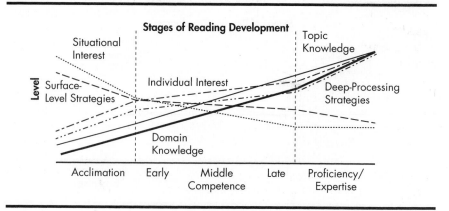

a way to better understand the nature of reading development and implications for reading instruction.

Although the stages of reading development correspond, to some degree, to years of schooling, the three stages of development—acclimation, competence, and proficiency/expertise—are not specifically age- or grade-related. That is, we would expect to encounter many more readers in acclimation in the early years of schooling, but readers in acclimation exist at all ages and in all grades. Yet, as would be expected, the longer it takes students to acquire the fundamental knowledge, seeds of interest, and strategic repertoire, the more problems they are likely to face in the future (Alexander, 2003b). Those problems can include limited background knowledge; negative beliefs about self or about school; and feelings of helplessness, apathy, and diminished engagement.

ACCLIMATION. Within the stage of acclimation, individuals are just beginning to get the sense of an unfamiliar academic terrain, reading. Thus, those in acclimation will understandably have a limited and fragmented base of reading knowledge (i.e., domain knowledge). Nonetheless, acclimating readers may have pockets of topic knowledge that can serve them well, as with young readers' knowledge of Hogwarts, witches, magic, and other topics from the Harry Potter novels. Further, the knowledge of readers in acclimation is not particularly cohesive or well integrated but more piecemeal. In essence, these acclimating readers lack "principled knowledge" (Gelman & Greeno, 1989). For example, even though Chet is performing above grade level in his third-grade reading class, he still does not have a clear understanding of what the domain of reading actually entails, such as how diverse genres within the domain (e.g., persuasive essay or folktale) may serve varied goals, have distinct structures, and require differential processes.

In part because of the fragmented and fragile state of their subject-matter knowledge, acclimating readers often experience difficulty distinguishing between information that is relevant versus irrelevant, accurate versus inaccurate, or important versus trivial (Jetton & Alexander, 1997). Moreover, acclimating readers encounter many text-based tasks that are novel and challenging, in large measure because of their limited and fragmented knowledge base. Thus, for those in acclimation, reading requires a great deal of strategic effort.

In addition, because those in acclimation are attempting to establish an initial foothold in the domain, a good portion of the strategies they use will be surface-level. Such strategies allow readers in acclimation to make sense of unfamiliar or demanding texts (Alexander et al., 2004). Even though there is a strong reliance on surface-level strategies in acclimation, there will be instances when the particular text, supporting context, or the readers' specific knowledge of or interest in a topic allows for deeper and richer processing.

Like the paths for surface-level and deep-processing strategies, the trajectories for individual and situational interest during acclimation are quite divergent. With limited domain or topic knowledge at their disposal, those in acclimation are expected to rely on situational interest to focus their attention, stimulate their engagement, and sustain their performance (Guthrie et al., 1998; Mitchell, 1993). In effect, acclimating readers need settings and materials that promote situational interest and sow the seeds of individual interest. Nevertheless, even as educators work to orchestrate situationally interesting learning environments, they must be careful to focus readers' attention on content and concepts central to the domain (Garner, Gillingham, & White, 1989; Jetton & Alexander, 1997). In effect, educators should not expect acclimating readers like Chet to discover the nature of the reading domain solely from the instructional tasks they encounter. Educators must help those in acclimation identify the core principles to which such language activities are linked. Alexander, Murphy, and Woods (1996) described this connection between reader and domain as rooted relevance.

COMPETENCE. The interrelations among knowledge, interest, and strategies evidenced in acclimation undergo significant transformation in competence. For one, there are shifts in individuals' knowledge bases (Alexander & Murphy, 1998a). Competent readers demonstrate more domain knowledge and topic knowledge than those in acclimation, and their knowledge is also more interconnected and cohesive in structure (i.e., more principled). Part of the competent readers' ability to grow in subject-matter knowledge results from a synergy between knowledge and strategies. That is to say, increased familiarity with the domain allows competent readers to be more efficient and effective in strategic processing of text (Alexander & Judy, 1988; Garner, 1990). There is more automaticity or fluidity of performance, so competent readers can delve into domain tasks via deep-processing strategies (Alexander, Graham, & Harris, 1998).

Along with the changes in their knowledge and strategies, competent readers evidence a rise in their individual interest and less dependence on situationally interesting characteristics of the immediate context (Alexander et al., 1995). Competent readers, in essence, are increasingly more motivated from within than from without (Dewey, 1913). The rise in individual interest during competence is significant because those seeking to reach higher levels of competence, or even expertise, must pursue experiences not required by the K–12 educational system (Csikszentmihalyi, 1985).

PROFICIENCY/EXPERTISE. For the transition from competence into expertise to occur, readers must not only display highly rich and principled knowledge but also effective and efficient strategy use, particularly deep-processing strategies and a personal identification with and investment in the domain (Alexander, 1997). Specifically, there is a distinct rise in subject-matter knowledge during proficiency/expertise. Experts continue to broaden and deepen their knowledge of reading. They are also actively engaged in problem finding (Alexander et al., 2004). That means proficient readers are well versed in the problems and methodologies of reading, such as evaluating the merits of primary and secondary sources in history. Proficient individuals have also achieved a high degree of fluency or automaticity in the performance of common reading tasks, allowing them to devote more time and mental energy to posing questions and instituting investigations that push the boundaries of the reading field.

Thus, what distinguishes proficient readers from those who are highly competent is that they add to the body of knowledge of the domain through their creative and analytic efforts. The National Reading Conference, for example, is a community of scholars immersed in the study of reading. Their investigations of basic and applied questions about the domain, such as questions about the developmental nature of reading, exemplify problem finding. The outcomes of such pursuits alter the very domain to which these experts are enculturated.

Experts' search for new and creative understandings within the domain is fueled by their abiding interest in the domain and facilitated by their strategic abilities (Csikszentmihalyi, 1990; Renninger, 1992). Consequently, the individual interest of experts is quite high, while their reliance on situational interest levels off. This personal identification and investment in reading allows proficient readers to maintain their level of engagement over time, even in the face of tremendous difficulties and frustrations. Finally, because of their pursuit of domain-transforming ideas, the level of strategy use among expert readers is quite high, although those strategies are almost exclusively deep-processing in form.

Profiles of Successful and Struggling Readers Are Reflective of Developmental Forces

When differences among readers are discussed in the literature, comparisons are often made in broad and oppositional terms, such as "good" versus "poor" or "successful" versus "struggling" (Snow et al., 1998). Yet the complexity of lifespan reading development and the interplay of knowledge, interest, and strategic processing that exists within each developmental stage suggest varied profiles of more and less successful readers. Based on the past decade of expertise research (e.g., Alexander & Murphy, 1998a; Murphy & Alexander, 2002), we can describe six reader profiles: highly competent readers, seriously challenged readers, effortful processors, knowledge-reliant readers, nonstrategic processors, and resistant readers. The highly competent and seriously challenged profiles represent the sharpest contrast in knowledge, interest, and strategic processing and more closely approximate the "good" versus "poor" dichotomy presented in the literature.

The remaining four profiles signify varying levels of reading success or difficulty, rooted in differing levels of knowledge, interest, or strategic ability. Individuals representing each of these profiles may be found in the acclimation or early competence stages of reading development. However, as the journey toward high competence and expertise continues, those with serious knowledge, interest, or strategic processing concerns will be increasingly less evident.

HIGHLY COMPETENT READERS. In effect, all forces in development are working well for highly competent readers (Alexander et al., 1995; Alexander et al., 2002). They have principled knowledge about language and a sufficient base of world knowledge relevant to the topics at hand. In addition, highly competent readers have a rich repertoire of surface-level and deep-processing strategies to apply to a range of text-based tasks they encounter (Paris, Wasik, & Turner, 1991). As important as their knowledge base and their strategic repertoire, highly competent readers display interest in the domain of reading or topics about which they are reading. Of course, not every text these highly competent readers encounter will cover content that is familiar or personally interesting to them. Yet in these situations, these more successful readers can draw on their well-honed strategic processes and their interest in reading to carry them forward.

Because of these salient attributes, highly competent readers are actively engaged readers (Reed, Schallert, & Goetz, 1993) who direct their various cognitive and motivational resources toward personal enrichment and academic success (Winne, 1995). Educators working with highly competent readers need to ensure that they have ample opportunities to participate in reading activities that are sufficiently challenging and relevant to their particular interests and goals (Csikszentmihalyi, 1990).

Although Chet, our third grader, is still just beginning his journey toward competence in reading, he still manifests the characteristics of a highly competent reader. He has not only used his knowledge of language well to process text, but he also has a solid base of world knowledge that he uses effectively to make sense of the concepts he encounters in his reading. Moreover, he performs strategically when he experiences a barrier to comprehension. Books and reading are also a routine part of Chet's life in and out of school, especially books dealing with space and space travel.

It is essential to recognize that young readers, like Chet, who appear highly competent in the early years of schooling are not assured of continued success as the journey toward competence or expertise in reading becomes more demanding and, thus, precarious. A failure of will or the onset of disengagement or apathy can stifle progress and halt movement toward increased competence. The motivational slump experienced by many middle-school students is evidence of just such an occurrence for many otherwise promising young readers (Wigfield, Eccles, & Pintrich, 1996).

SERIOUSLY CHALLENGED READERS. At the other end of this continuum are seriously challenged readers, who display a complex of reading problems (Alexander & Murphy, 1998a). Among the barriers to successful text-based learning these readers confront are language-processing difficulties, limited background knowledge, strategic insufficiencies, and negative motivational conditions (Curtis, 2002). Such challenged readers are frequently the target of educational and legislative initiatives, such as the No Child Left Behind Act (PL 107–110; Department of Education, 2001). The complexity of their difficulties puts these readers' continued development at great risk. Moreover, the multifaceted nature of their problems requires interventions and educational supports that are equally multifaceted.

Without significant attention to all aspects of reading development (e.g., knowledge, interest, and strategic processing), these seriously challenged readers may never be able to progress beyond the initial phases of acclimation. They may never be able to feel competent in reading, or experience the pleasure of reading that others do. They will be left behind as others continue their developmental journey.

EFFORTFUL PROCESSORS. Between highly competent and seriously challenged readers, there are effortful processors. These readers generally perform well at reading tasks and progress well in their development because they are goal directed and effortful (Alexander & Murphy, 1998a). Effortful processors are readers who engage in high levels of strategic effort for the purpose of achieving understanding. They maintain this level of effort even when they encounter linguistic difficulties or have limited topic knowledge. Thus, even though effortful processors experience success in the domain of reading, that success does not come easily but as a result of their determination and persistence.

Among the educational assistance that could be provided to effortful processors is guidance in how to work smarter rather than harder (Weinstein & Mayer, 1986). In other words, they need to learn how to maximize their strategic efforts. For example, they may find it more effective to spend more time planning their approach to a text-based task before immersing themselves in the reading (Schoenfeld, 1988; Winne, 1995). This planfulness, such as monitoring their level of performance during and after reading, may improve their strategic efforts (Paris & Winograd, 1990). Given their personal investment in the domain and apparent tenacity or will to succeed, some effortful processors may reach high competence or expertise. This likelihood is greater if these readers learn how to harness their strategic efforts in a way that maximizes knowledge gains.

KNOWLEDGE-RELIANT READERS. Others who can manage some level of success at text-based learning are knowledge-reliant readers (Alexander & Murphy, 1998a), so named because they rely heavily on their existing world or topic-related knowledge to bolster their reading performance. While some of that background knowledge was likely acquired through print, these individuals also gain knowledge through alternative means, such as direct experience or audio-visual channels. If these students continue to depend too heavily on their existing knowledge to promote reading performance, they may face difficulties later when they confront especially demanding or highly novel tasks. Without the linguistic knowledge or strategies required in those situations, it is unlikely that such learners will progress deeply into competence (Garner & Alexander, 1991). For knowledge-reliant readers, it may prove useful to incorporate alternative media in text-based presentations (Anderson-Inman & Horney, 1998; Reinking, 1998). This pedagogical strategy might appeal to these readers' processing approaches (Gardner, 1993), while still engaging them in reading.

NONSTRATEGIC PROCESSORS. Nonstrategic processors are among the readers whose developmental trajectories are somewhat precarious because they operate with few or faulty strategies for processing linguistic information (Alexander, Kulikowich, & Schulze, 1994; Alexander & Murphy, 1998a). Moreover, these readers often have limited understanding of task demands, which hampers their efficient and effective use of available strategies. They also demonstrate little self-monitoring or self-regulation of their text processing, or are not particularly good at judging the quality of their reading performance (Winne, 1995; Zimmerman, 1990).

As with effortful processors, the development of nonstrategic processors can be greatly aided by explicit instruction in general cognitive and self-regulatory strategies that can be applied in a variety of reading contexts (Harris & Graham, 1996; Rosenshine, 1997). Incorporating group activities into the culture of the classroom can also support readers who have limited strategic repertoires, because they can learn from peer models, as well as directly from teachers, how to judge performance or what compensatory steps seem viable (Palincsar & Brown, 1984). Because strategic processing takes time and effort, it is also essential that educators build in sufficient time for strategic processing and expressly reward such efforts in the classroom (Garner, 1990). As long as schools reward speed over reflection, assume that effective and varied strategies will be naturally acquired, or give little weight to process over product, there will be barriers to reading strategically.

RESISTANT READERS. Finally, for some readers, the barriers to growth and development reside more in their lack of investment in the domain or maladaptive goals than in other forces of development (Alexander, 2002; Alexander & Murphy, 1998a). These resistant readers apparently have the requisite knowledge and relevant strategies they need to reach competence or even expertise. However, they lack the desire or will to realize this potential (Garner & Alexander, 1991; Paris & Winograd, 1990). In effect, their failure to progress toward proficiency is principally of their own choosing. It is important to recognize that no one can become highly competent or expert in all or even many academic domains. Part of maturing as learners is to be selective as to the paths we pursue academically and in our careers. Yet ensuring that all students are given the experiences and support they require to reach competence in the critical domain of reading is a reasonable goal.

Support for resistant readers may come in the form of highly stimulating tasks and contexts (Mitchell, 1993) or personally relevant activities that draw them into the print experience (Wade & Moje, 2000). Ideally, the source of the motivation would come from within the reader (Alexander et al., 1996). This can be aided by allowing students some degree of choice or autonomy in their reading activities (Alexander & Jetton, 2000). Also, students who see the value of reading tasks and the merits of strategic effort will be more willing to exert the cognitive energy required (Palmer & Goetz, 1988; Schoenfeld, 1988).

Readers in Acclimation Are Especially Vulnerable and in Need of Appropriate Scaffolding

Although reading is a complex domain for which the developmental journey will encompass a lifetime, the first steps in that journey remain crucial. Because of their limited knowledge, strategies, and interest, those in acclimation are in need of thoughtful guidance from more knowledgeable others (Alexander, 2002). As is true of anyone in strange and complicated territory, acclimating readers require the care and guidance of more knowledgeable others (Vygotsky, 1978). Those more competent individuals guide readers in acclimation through the academic terrain by acquainting them with the routines and rituals that are part of the domain culture (Rogoff, 1990; VanSledright, 2002).

Competent or even expert readers benefit from more knowledgeable role models as well. However, the need for external guidance is particularly acute during the acclimation stage. Without such appropriate guidance, acclimating readers may encounter increased difficulties in building a base of domain and topic knowledge and a rich repertoire of surface-level and deep-processing strategies. Further, they may never discover the relevance of reading without others to illuminate the way or model their own passions and personal investment in the domain.

Conclusion

Viewing reading from a lifespan development perspective has many benefits. As we have seen, a developmental framework of reading can be forged from the extensive expertise research that chronicles the lifelong journey toward proficiency that begins with one's first engagement with written language. We recognize that there are other powerful forces and events in the lives of readers, outside those considered here, that can help determine the fate of developing readers. However, our focus here has been on the factors addressed in the expertise literature, particularly in the research on the Model of Domain Learning (Alexander, 1997).

Those factors—knowledge, interest, and strategies—should be elements of effective reading programs and school curricula. A commitment to this lifespan perspective would also result in certain programmatic emphases for teacher development. For instance, there would be explicit attention to the teaching of strategies that underlie reading performance. In that way, teachers would be better able to assist their students in the development of rich strategic repertoires. Further, we would expect professional development to target a range of narrative and expository reading materials of both a traditional (e.g., books) and alternative (e.g., websites) nature—materials that students are likely to confront both in and out of school. In addition, techniques for motivating readers and for incorporating their interests in reading instruction would be an integral part of teachers' professional development. Perhaps most significantly, a concern for the fostering of reading development would no longer be relegated to the early elementary grades. Rather, the development of reading would be seen as a responsibility of all teachers—from preschool through high school.

The bottom line is that the need for a lifespan development model of reading is great. Until educators, the public, and politicians come to view reading from this lifespan perspective, we continue to run the very real risk of turning out undeveloped, unmotivated, and uncritical readers from our educational institutions—readers without the skill to engage in the processing of challenging texts; readers who lack any passion for or investment in reading and who cannot fulfill their responsibilities within a democratic society that relies on an informed and involved populace. Until society accepts reading as a complex process of growth and development that continues from womb to tomb, reading instruction will not receive the attention it warrants throughout the educational experience. It will mistakenly be confined to the early years of schooling when readers are only learning to take their first steps toward competence. In light of these compelling factors, the National Reading Conference believes that it is time to commit fully to a lifespan development perspective on reading. Let the journey begin.

References

Adams, M. J. (1990). *Beginning to read*. Cambridge, MA: MIT Press.

Alexander, P. A. (1997). Mapping the multidimensional nature of domain learning: The interplay of cognitive, motivational, and strategic forces. In M. L. Maehr & P. R. Pintrich (Eds.), *Advances in motivation and achievement* (Vol. 10, pp. 213–250). Greenwich, CT: JAI Press.

Alexander, P. A. (2002, January). *The struggling adolescent reader: A new perspective on an enduring problem*. Keynote presented at the Adolescent Literacy Workshop sponsored by the National Institute of Child Health and Human Development, Washington, DC.

Alexander, P. A. (2003a). Can we get there from here?: Introduction to the special issue on expertise. *Educational Researcher, 32*(8), 3–4.

Alexander, P. A. (2003b). Profiling the developing reader: The interplay of knowledge, interest, and strategic processing. In C. M. Fairbanks, J. Worthy, B. Maloch, J. V. Hoffman, & D. L. Schallert (Eds.), *The Fifty-first yearbook of the National Reading Conference* (pp. 47–65). Oak Creek, WI: National Reading Conference.

Alexander, P. A. (2003c). The development of expertise: The journey from acclimation to proficiency. *Educational Researcher, 32*(8), 10–14.

Alexander, P. A., Graham, S., & Harris, K. (1998). A perspective on strategy research: Progress and prospects. *Educational Psychology Review, 10,* 129–154.

Alexander, P. A., & Jetton, T. L. (2000). Learning from text: A multidimensional and developmental perspective. In M. L. Kamil, P. B. Mosenthal, P. D. Pearson, & R. Barr (Eds.), *Handbook of reading research: Vol. III* (pp. 285–310). Mahwah, NJ: Erlbaum.

Alexander, P. A., Kulikowich, J. M., & Schulze, S. K. (1994). How subject-matter knowledge affects recall and interest. *American Education Research Journal, 31*. 313–337.

Alexander, P. A., Jetton, T. L., & Kulikowich, J. M. (1995). Interrelationship of knowledge, interest, and recall: Assessing a model of domain learning. *Journal of Educational Psychology, 87*, 559–575.

Alexander, P. A., & Judy, J. E. (1988). The interaction of domain-specific and strategic knowledge in academic performance. *Review of Educational Research, 58*, 375–404.

Alexander, P. A., & Murphy, P. K. (1998a). Profiling the differences in students' knowledge, interest, and strategic processing. *Journal of Educational Psychology, 90*, 435–447.

Alexander, P. A., & Murphy, P. K. (1998b). The research base for APA's learner-centered principles. In N. M. Lambert & B. L. McCombs (Eds.), *Issues in school reform: A sampler of psychological perspectives on learner-centered school* (pp. 25–60). Washington, DC: American Psychological Association.

Alexander, P. A., Murphy, P. K., & Woods, B. S. (1996). Of squalls and fathoms: Navigating the seas of educational innovation. *Educational Researcher, 25*(3), 31–36, 39.

Alexander, P. A., Schallert, D. L., & Hare, V. C. (1991). Coming to terms: How researchers in learning and literacy talk about knowledge. *Review of Educational Research, 61*, 315–343.

Alexander, P. A., Sperl, C. T., Buehl, M. M., Fives, H., & Chiu, S. (2004). Modeling domain learning: Profiles from the field of special education. *Journal of Educational Psychology, 96,* 545–557.

Alvermann, D. (2002). Effective literacy instruction for adolescents. *Journal of Literacy Research, 34,* 189–208.

Alvermann, D. E., Young, J. P., Weaver, D., Hinchman, K. A., Moore, D. W., Phelps, S. F., et al. (1996). Middle and high school students' perceptions of how they experience text based discussions: A multicase study. *Reading Research Quarterly, 31,* 244–267.

Ames, C. (1992). Classrooms: Goals, structures, and student motivation. *Journal of Educational Psychology, 84,* 261–271.

Anderson, R. C., Spiro, R., & Anderson, M. C. (1978). Schemata as scaffolding for the representation of information in connected discourse. *American Educational Research Journal, 15,* 433–440.

Anderson-Inman, L., & Horney, M. A. (1998). Transforming text for at-risk readers. In D. Reinking, M. C. McKenna, L. D. Labbo, & R. D. Kieffer (Eds.), *Handbook of literacy and technology: Transformations in a post-typographical world* (pp. 15–43). Mahwah, NJ: Erlbaum.

Csikszentmihalyi, M. (1985). Emergent motivation and the evolution of the self. In D. A. Kleiber & M. L. Maehr (Eds.), *Advances in motivation and achievement* (Vol. 4, pp. 93–119). Greenwich, CT: JAI Press.

Csikszentmihalyi, M. (1990). *FLOW: The psychology of optional experience.* New York: HarperCollins.

Curtis, M. E. (2002). *Adolescent reading: A synthesis of research.* Washington, DC: National Institute of Child Health and Human Development. Department of Education. Retrieved August 29, 2005, from http://216.26.160.105/conf/nichd/synthesis.asp

Department of Education. (2001). *No child left behind* (Public Law 107–110). Washington, DC: Author.

Dewey, J. (1913). *Interest and effort in education.* Boston: Riverdale.

Dweck, C., & Leggett, E. (1988). A social-cognitive approach to motivation and personality. *Psychological Review, 95,* 256–273.

Gardner, H. (1993). *Multiple intelligences: The theory in practice.* New York: Basic Books.

Garner, R. (1990). When children and adults do not use learning strategies: Toward a theory of setting. *Review of Educational Research, 60,* 517–529.

Garner, R., & Alexander, P. A. (1989). Metacognition: Answered and unanswered questions. *Educational Psychologist, 24,* 143–148.

Garner, R., & Alexander, P. A. (1991, April). *Skill, will, and thrill: The role of interest in text comprehension.* Presented at the meeting of the American Educational Research Association, Chicago.

Garner, R., Gillingham, M. G., & White, C. S. (1989). Effects of "seductive details" on macroprocessing and microprocessing in adults and children. *Cognition and Instruction, 6,* 41–57.

Gelman, R., & Greeno, J. G. (1989). On the nature of competence: Principles for understanding in a domain. In L. B. Resnick (Ed.), *Knowing, learning, and instruction: Essays in honor of Robert Glaser* (pp. 125–186). Hillsdale, NJ: Erlbaum.

Guthrie, J. T., Van Meter, P. Hancock, G. R., Alao, S., Anderson, E., & McCann, A. (1998). Does concept-oriented reading instruction increase strategy use and conceptual learning from text? *Journal of Educational Psychology, 90*, 261–278.

Guthrie, J. T., & Wigfield, A. (2000). Engagement and motivation in reading. In M. L. Kamil, P. B. Mosenthal, P. D. Pearson, & R. Barr (Eds.), *Handbook of reading research: Vol III* (pp. 403–422). Mahwah, NJ: Erlbaum.

Harris, K. R., & Graham, S. (1996). *Making the writing process work: Strategies for composition and self-regulation.* Cambridge, MA: Brookline.

Hidi, S. (1990). Interest and its contribution as a mental resource for learning. *Review of Educational Research, 60*, 549–571.

Jetton, T. L., & Alexander, P. A. (1997). Instructional importance: What teachers value and what students learn. *Reading Research Quarterly, 32*, 290–308.

Kruidenier, J. (2002). *Research-based principles for adult basic education: Reading instruction.* Portsmouth, NH: RMC Research.

Marshall, J. (2000). Research on response to literature. In M. L. Kamil, P. B. Mosenthal, P. D. Pearson, & R. Barr (Eds.), *Handbook of reading research: Vol III* (pp. 381–402). Mahwah, NJ: Erlbaum.

Mitchell, M. (1993). Situational interest: Its multifaceted structure in the secondary school mathematics classroom. *Journal of Educational Psychology, 85*, 424–436.

Moje, E. B. (2000). *"All the stories that we have": Adolescents' insights about literacy and learning in secondary schools.* Newark, DE: International Reading Association.

Murphy, P. K., & Alexander, P. A. (2002). What counts?: The predictive power of subjectmatter knowledge, strategic processing, and interest in domain-specific performance. *Journal of Experimental Education, 70*, 197–214.

National Center for Education Statistics. (1999). *NAEP 1998: Reading: Report card for the Nation and the States.* Washington, DC: U.S. Department of Education, Office of Educational Research and Improvement.

National Reading Panel. (2000). *Report of the National Reading Panel.* Washington, DC: National Institute of Child Health and Human Development.

Newell, A., & Simon, H. A. (1972). *Human problem solving.* Englewood Cliffs, NJ: Prentice-Hall.

Nist, S. L., & Holschuh, J. L. (2000). Comprehension strategies at the college level. In R. F. Flippo & D. C. Caverly (Eds.), *Handbook of college reading and study strategy research* (pp. 75–104). Mahwah, NJ: Erlbaum.

Nist, S. L., & Simpson, M. L. (2000). College studying. In M. L. Kamil, P. B. Mosenthal, P. D. Pearson, & R. Barr (Eds.), *Handbook of reading research: Vol. III* (pp. 645–666). Mahwah, NJ: Erlbaum.

Palincsar, A. S., & Brown, A. L., (1984). Reciprocal teaching of comprehension-fostering and monitoring activities. *Cognition and Instruction, 1*, 117–175.

Palmer, D. J., & Goetz, E. T. (1988). Selection and use of study strategies: The role of the studier's beliefs about self and strategies. In C. Weinstein, E. T. Goetz, & P. A. Alexander (Eds.), *Learning and study strategies: Issues in assessment, instruction, and evaluation* (pp. 77–100). San Diego: Academic Press.

Paris, S. G., Wasik, B. A., & Turner, J. C. (1991). The development of strategic readers. In R. Barr, M. L. Kamil, P. Mosenthal, & P. D. Pearson (Eds.), *Handbook of reading research: Volume II* (pp. 609–640). Mahwah, NJ: Erlbaum.

Paris, S. G., & Winograd, P. (1990). Dimension of thinking and cognitive instruction. In B. F. Jones & L. Idol (Eds.), *How metacognition can promote academic learning and instruction* (pp. 15–51). Hillsdale, NJ: Erlbaum.

Pressley, M. (2002). Effective beginning reading instruction. *Journal of Literacy Research, 34*, 165–188.

RAND Reading Study Group (2002). *Reading for understanding: Toward an R&D program in reading comprehension*. Santa Monica, CA: RAND Corporation

Reed, J. H., & Schallert, D. L. (1993). *The nature of involvement in academic discourse*. Journal of Educational Psychology, 85, 253–266.

Reed, J. H., Schallert, D. L., & Goetz, E. T. (1993, April). *Interest happens but involvement takes effort: Distinguishing between two constructs in academic discourse tasks*. Presented at the meeting of the American Educational Research Association, Atlanta, GA.

Reinking, D. (1998). Introduction: Synthesizing technological transformations of literacy in a post-typographic world. In D. Reinking, M. C. McKenna, L. D. Labbo, & R. D. Kieffer (Eds.), *Handbook of literacy and technology: Transformations in a post-typographical world* (pp. xi–xxx). Mahwah, NJ: Erlbaum.

Reinking, D., McKenna, M. C., Labbo, L. D., & Kieffer, R. D. (1998). *Handbook of literacy and technology: Transformations in a post-typographic world*. Mahwah, NJ: Erlbaum.

Renninger, K. A. (1992). Individual interest and development: Implications for theory and practice. In K. A. Renninger, S. Hidi, & A. Krapp (Eds.), *The role of interest in learning and development* (pp. 361–395). Hillsdale, NJ: Erlbaum.

Rogoff, B. (1990). *Apprenticeship in thinking: Cognitive development in social context*. New York: Oxford University Press.

Rosenshine, B. (1997, March). *The case for explicit, teacher-led, cognitive strategy instruction*. Presented at the annual meeting of the American Educational Research Association, Chicago.

Schiefele, U. (1991). Interest, learning, and motivation. *Educational Psychologist, 26*, 229–323.

Schoenfeld, A. H. (1988). When good teaching leads to bad results: The disasters of "well-taught" mathematics courses. *Educational Psychologist, 23*, 145–166.

Snow, C. E., Burns, M. S., & Griffin, P. (1998). *Preventing reading difficulties in young children*. Washington, DC: National Academy Press.

VanSledright, B. (2002). *In search of America's past: Learning to read history in elementary school*. New York: Teachers College Press.

VanSledright, B., & Alexander, P. A. (2002). *Historical knowledge, thinking, and beliefs: Evaluation component of the Corps of Historical Discovery Project* (#S215X010242). Washington, DC: U. S. Department of Education.

Vygotsky, L. (1978). *Mind in society*. Cambridge, MA: Harvard University Press.

Wade, S. E., & Moje, E. B. (2000). The role of text in classroom learning. In M. L. Kamil, P. B. Mosenthal, P. D. Pearson, & R. Barr (Eds.), *Handbook of reading research: Vol. III* (pp. 609–627). Mahwah, NJ: Erlbaum.

Weinstein, C. E., & Mayer, R. E. (1986). The teaching of learning strategies. In M. C. Wittrock (Ed.), *Handbook of research on teaching* (3rd ed., pp. 315–327). New York: Macmillan.

Wigfield, A., Eccles, J. S., & Pintrich, P. R. (1996). Development between the ages of 11 and 25. In D. Berliner & R. Calfee (Eds.), *Handbook of educational psychology* (pp. 148–185). New York: Macmillan.

Winne, P. H. (1995). Inherent details in self-regulated learning. *Educational Psychologist, 30*, 173–187.

Zimmerman, B. J. (1990). Self-regulated learning and academic achievement: An overview. *Educational Psychologist, 25*, 3–18.

Bridging the Pedagogical Gap: Intersections between Literary and Reading Theories in Secondary and Postsecondary Literacy Instruction

Lisa Schade Eckert

Lisa Schade Eckert provides a discussion of the pedagogical divide between the instructional practice of literacy and literature professionals, acknowledging further that this divide has contributed to some of the instructional gaps between secondary and postsecondary education. Eckert's examination of the theoretical intersections between literacy and literature therefore provides insights for educators teaching reading strategies, and also serves as a bridge between high school and college reading instruction.

On March 10, 2006, *The Chronicle of Higher Education* released the results of surveys commissioned to investigate the gap in perception between college professors and high school teachers regarding student preparedness for college in the United States (Sanoff, 2006, p. B9). In the area of reading comprehension, 41% of college professors indicated students are not well prepared for college-level demands, as opposed to only 15% of high school teachers. This discrepancy illustrates the pedagogical disconnect that exists between literacy and literature instructional practice. Literary scholars and reading researchers have historically been seen, and have viewed themselves as, entirely separate pedagogically, which has hindered the continuity of literacy instruction between K–12 and higher education classrooms.

My experiences during the 10 years I spent in secondary school classrooms before I became a teacher educator provide a unique perspective from both sides of the pedagogical divide. The problem is not the fault of either secondary or postsecondary educators, nor is it alleviated by an increased emphasis on remedial or compensatory classes.

Although a growing body of research and practice in reading strategy instruction in secondary education has identified specific and successful methods for encouraging metacognitive awareness (Block, Gambrell, & Pressley, 2002; Fisher & Ivey, 2006; Jetton & Dole, 2004), there remains little published research connecting these findings to postsecondary literacy education. As a result, there remains a gap between the conception and teaching of reading and interpretation.

In this article, I will examine intersections between teaching literary theory and teaching reading strategies as a means to bridge the pedagogical gaps between secondary and postsecondary, as well as between compensatory and mainstream literacy/literature instruction. To illustrate this intersection, I will highlight similarities in the research and theories of reading researcher Kenneth Goodman and literary theorist Wolfgang Iser, and I share ways that I draw upon both in teaching reading strategy instruction in my preservice English methods courses. While Iser remains an often-cited response theorist in literary research and interpretation, Goodman has profoundly changed the way educators view the teaching of reading throughout the K–12 curriculum.

Although this is not the only way to forge a connection between secondary and postsecondary content, I focus on English language arts content and literary literacy instruction (as opposed to, for example, science literacy or social science literacy) in comparing these points of convergence. This framework is instructive for educators at all levels and for literacy instruction in content areas other than English, and it provides impetus to identify similar theoretical connections in other disciplines. My ultimate goal is to suggest the inclusion of specific concepts in literary theory as a means for extending reading strategy instruction into secondary and postsecondary literature curricula and, consequently, bridging the pedagogical and ideological gap between "teaching reading" and "teaching literature" as components of comprehensive literacy curricula.

From Reading to Interpretation: What's the Difference?

As students progress from reading in primary- and intermediate-level language arts classes to secondary and postsecondary literature classes, textual content becomes increasingly complex, edging out instructional time devoted to active integration of reading and interpretive strategy instruction. Too often, secondary school teachers and college professors expect students to effectively use advanced reading strategies and interpretive approaches, requiring students to "read" with an understanding that this means critically engaging with textual material and assuming an interpretive stance, without explicitly teaching them how to do so (Orlando, Caverly, Swetnam, & Flippo, 2003). Because students have often been trained throughout childhood and young adolescence to understand that *reading* refers to the decoding of words (Underwood & Pearson, 2004), they do not speak the language of critical literary interpretation. Graff (2000) described this state as

> being alone with texts . . . bored and helpless, since I had no language with which to make them mine. On the one hand, I was being asked to speak a foreign language — literary criticism — while on the other hand, I was being protected from that language, presumably for my own safety . . . teachers cannot avoid translating the literature they teach into some critical language or other, [and] neither can students, for criticism is the language students are expected to speak and are punished for not speaking well. (pp. 45–47)

Zhang (2003) echoed this sentiment, arguing "the problem is not lack of ability, but lack of preparedness" (p. 14). Without the means of assuming an interpretive stance on their own, students come to class expecting—even requiring—teachers to explicate the nuances of the text for them.

In this way, literary literacy instruction can vacillate between two extremes. On one end of the spectrum are developmental or compensatory reading classes based on an unexamined definition of reading (Fishman, 2003; Smittle, 2003) designed to help struggling readers catch up, often by emphasizing repetitive skills-based instruction and underestimating what students are capable of doing (Johannessen, 2004; Lesley, 2004; Perin, 2002). On the other end are literature classes, which still have a large role as essential English courses in high school and college (Applebee, 1996), that are viewed as intellectually lofty, emphasizing highly theorized definitions of literary interpretation. Yet there is very little evidence-based practice specifically designed to scaffold student progress from one level to the next (Ehren, Lenz, & Deshler, 2004). The gap between learning reading strategies and practicing literary interpretation forces students to make a prodigious cognitive leap from *reading* to *interpretation* if they are to gain access to college, or college preparatory, English classes.

Simpson, Stahl, and Francis (2004) emphasized that reading strategy *transfer*, not merely skills instruction, should be a primary component of any compensatory or developmental academic program. Means and Knapp (1991) argued that such programs should "focus on complex, meaningful problems" and "global tasks" (pp. 10–11) to facilitate such transference.

Caverly, Nicholson, and Radcliffe (2004), in their research investigating reading instruction for developmental college students, found that linking developmental reading courses to "challenging core-academic" courses resulted in "significantly higher self-efficacy and systematic studying" on the part of students who participated when compared with students who completed a stand-alone reading course (p. 30). In this context, students are better able to transfer reading strategy instruction to disciplinary genres—the academic literacy tasks necessary to complete college-level course work. I argue that this transfer can be mediated by introducing students to critical theory as scaffolding for metacognitively constructing meaning from text; in other words, by explicitly teaching theoretical approaches to literature, English teachers better enable students to transfer reading strategy skills to literary analysis and interpretation.

Reading Processes and Interpretative Skills

Literary scholars have long used the term *reading* as a noun; a student is required to construct *a reading* of a text, somehow understanding that this really means a critical *interpretation* of the text. Used as a verb, however, *reading* is relegated to a lower, less scholarly, cognitive activity in which the reader has little agency in constructing meaning from text. For example, noted literary theorist Eagleton (1996) described the "state of reading . . . [as] one of intense attention . . . a state in which the text works on us, not we on it" (p. 32).

Similarly, Scholes (1985) in *Textual Power: Literary Theory and the Teaching of English,* a classic text in literature classrooms, clearly made a distinction between reading and interpretation, defining reading as "a largely unconscious activity [during which . . . a reader constructs a whole world from just a few indications . . . all without hesitation or difficulty" (pp. 21–22). He argued that interpretation, in contrast, "depends upon the failures of reading" and "is a higher skill than reading" (p. 22). Interpretation, according to Scholes, "can be the result of either some excess of meaning in a text or some deficiency of knowledge in the reader" (p. 22). In other words, the reader has to work harder to interpret, rather than merely to read, the words on the page.

But if we accept that interpretation is a higher skill, which implies it requires additional knowledge to assume an interpretive stance, it would seem more logical to argue that the reader should begin with *more* prior knowledge rather than with a deficiency of knowledge. This prior knowledge comes in the form of metacognitive reading strategies and knowledge of literary theory and conventions.

The fact that Scholes (1985) hoped reading "has been dealt with in secondary school—a hope that seems less and less well founded as we go on" (p. 3) emphasizes the gulf between high school and college English literacy instruction—a gulf that is partially the result of definitions of reading and the evidence-based assessments that are imposed on secondary English teachers by state and federal standards and assessments in the United States, and partially the result of a lack of curricular communication between educational institutions. His statement also implies that interpretation is a process reserved for higher education—high school English teachers should be more concerned with improving their practices for teaching reading as he defines it, which, unfortunately, they aren't doing very well. Nothing could be further from the truth, however, and Scholes offers little in the form of suggestions for ways in which educators can contribute to bridging the gap between educational levels.

In practice, there is little distinction between the cognitive processes involved in reading or interpretation; recognizing this provides a link between research on teaching reading and teaching literature. Fish (2001) made this point, arguing that reading is "a set of interpretive strategies, which, when they are put into execution, become the large act of reading . . . interpretive strategies are not put into execution after reading . . . they are the shape of reading" (p. 2085). McCormick (1996) also emphasized the need to recognize the similarities in teaching reading and literary interpretation, by stating the following:

> During the past two decades, work in literary and cultural studies . . . has accomplished such retheorizing of the reading subject and the text, but such work has only just begun to be translated into concrete pedagogies. By entering into a more active dialogue with other areas of reading that focus more specifically on pedagogy, literary and cultural studies can begin to locate reading within the complex cultural contexts in which it actually occurs. (p. 295)

Similarly, Crowley (1989), in *A Teacher's Introduction to Deconstruction*, pointedly stated "The practice of reading pedagogy [is] called 'teaching literature' in English departments" (p. 26). If reading strategies are defined as intentional plans that enable readers to construct meaning (Dunston, 2002; Keene, 2002; Tovani, 2000), then teachers of literature, English, and language arts at all educational levels are teaching literary theory and reading skills whether or not they clearly identify the underlying theoretical perspective or ideological approach they employ. Explicitly teaching the basic tenets of different schools of literary theory scaffolds literacy/literature instruction, encouraging students to consider using a theoretical approach to construct meaning from text as an intentional plan (Eckert, 2006).

Decades of Research

Clearly, the teaching of literary interpretation and the teaching of reading are not separate pedagogies: instead, crucial points of intersection between research in both fields provide the opportunity to link concepts of reading and interpretation for students and teachers. Indeed, connections between literary theory and the elementary reading curriculum were identified in the mid-1970s, beginning with the publication of research such as *The Child as Critic: Teaching Literature in the Elementary School* (Sloan, 1975), and Stott's (1981) report of research presented at the Children's Literature Association's Symposium on Teaching Literature Criticism in the Elementary Grades, at roughly the same time as many schools of literary theory were developing.

Both Sloan and Stott adapted Frye's (1957) concepts of structure and myth in teaching methods for reading strategy instruction in elementary classrooms; both researchers found that students readily internalized such reading strategies and became more critical readers when they applied these theories. Nodelman (1996) provided an extensive bibliography of scholarly research on the use of literary theory with children's literature in *The Pleasures of Children's Literature*, including ideological theory, feminist theory, and a review of Frye's work as well as of structuralist theory.

Other teachers and researchers continued to suggest the value of incorporating elements of literary theory and criticism with literacy/

literature instructional methods in secondary classrooms. Moore (1997) explored having middle school students apply theoretical perspectives to young adult novels in *Interpreting Young Adult Literature: Literary Theory in the Secondary Classroom.* Carey-Webb (2001) wrote of his experiences teaching high school students using a cultural studies approach informed by a range of theoretical perspectives. Appleman (2000) and Soter (1999) explored the results of teaching literary theory in the secondary English classroom. Appleman emphasized ideological and modern theories of literary interpretation to prepare students for taking the Advanced Placement exam; Soter focused on the pedagogical implications of introducing modern and postmodern approaches. I concluded, through my own investigation of the efficacy of teaching literary theory in general secondary English classrooms, that making diverse theories of literary interpretation explicit in the practice of teaching literature at all educational levels not only builds on students' prior knowledge of textual situations but also encourages them to expand their repertoire of reading strategies to comprehend increasingly complex and diverse material in a variety of media (Eckert, 2006).

This growing body of research indicates that when students become cognizant of using a theoretical lens as a strategy for constructing meaning from text, they can begin to further question the cultural and ideological influences at work in a text, as well as the influence of their own values and beliefs in this transaction. Teaching theory extends methods of reading and literature instruction by further expanding students' repertoire of strategies for analyzing dimensions of meaning and provides structure to help students clearly conceive and articulate a response to a text.

Because theory is present in every level of the English language arts classroom — whether or not a teacher acknowledges his or her theoretical perspective — also present is the implicit expectation that students will "catch on" to the teacher's theoretical stance. Methods for teaching reading or literature have traditionally ranged from objective (seeking to find the "correct" construction of meaning from text) to constructivist (constructing individual or "authentic" meaning from text) models of instruction. Explicitly teaching literary theory, from text-based to response-based approaches, provides balanced literacy curricula, similar to a balanced reading approach advocated by researchers in reading theory (Weaver, 1998).

The missing link in this research is the specific connection between literary theory and reading strategy instruction at the postsecondary level. There is little published research investigating the efficacy of literary theory as reading strategy in developmental or beginning college English studies, although studies have been conducted on teaching reading strategies to encourage academic literacy at this level (Simpson et al., 2004). If existing research provides evidence of success in both elementary and secondary English language arts classrooms, then it would seem pedagogically relevant and useful in postsecondary literacy/literature classrooms as well.

Explicit Strategy Instruction and Academic Literacy

Using literary theory as scaffolding for reading instruction essentially links cognitive reading instruction to concepts often taught in literature courses that are core academic requirements at most colleges and universities, engaging students in authentic reading situations and making the transfer of skills taught in remedial and prerequisite courses more likely. Comparing the points of convergence in the work of literary theorist Wolfgang Iser (1987, 2000) and reading theorist Kenneth Goodman (1996) clearly illustrates similarities between reading theory and literary theory, offering pedagogical suggestions for how the gap between reading instruction and literary interpretation instruction could be mediated. Iser espoused a phenomenological analysis of the reading process, the study of which is usually reserved for advanced college courses in literary theory and interpretation. Goodman engaged in psycholinguistic analysis of the reading process, an approach that has transformed reading instruction in the early grades and also provided diagnostic tools and instructional frameworks for secondary and postsecondary literacy instruction.

When the research of these scholars is closely examined, common themes emerge that clearly intersect, holding potential for a middle ground in literacy/literature instruction. Goodman (1996) and Iser (1987, 2000) both supported a response-based approach to literacy pedagogy, arguing that reading requires more than decoding textual signifiers and is a cognitive activity so complex that it is remarkable that we can do it at all. Both emphasize the ambiguities inherent in the written language that a reader must resolve; the reader must make the language of the text have a personal meaning. Words mean something because the reader expects them to. It is interesting that both scholars were drawing similar conclusions about the process of constructing meaning; they were contemporaries but there is no evidence that they were familiar with each other's work. Iser extended the discussion to a theoretical level, while Goodman developed the process of miscue analysis to identify, record, and analyze the specific strategies readers use to construct meaning, and, although this connection is never acknowledged by either researcher, clearly illustrated that Iser's theory is accurate in practice.

Iser (2000) explained the act of reading as "a product arising out the interaction between text and reader," describing "gaps" or "blanks" in the text and arguing that "whatever is present is marked by an absence . . . the task of interpretation is thus dual in nature . . . the absent and the present are made continually to point at each other" (p. 72). The text as it stands on the page is incomplete, it is simply a set of instructions for creating an imaginative work within the mind of the reader. This indeterminacy, however,

> stimulates the reader into filling the blanks with projections. He is drawn into the events and made to supply what is meant from what is not said . . . it is the implications and not the statements that give shape and weight to the meaning. But as the unsaid comes to life in the reader's imagination, so the said "expands" to take on greater significance . . . what is concealed spurs the reader into actions, but this action is also controlled by what is revealed. (Iser, 1987, p. 149)

Iser (2000) argued that the "real" text is an imaginative, fluid entity existing somewhere between the reader's expectations and the words on the page, and although those words provide guidelines for a reader's interpretation, "the reading process therefore cannot be mere identification of individual linguistic signs" (p. 120).

Goodman (1996) also argued that "reading isn't a linear process . . . the information [in the text] is sufficiently ambiguous that we are constantly leaping to conclusions while, at the same time, being tentative enough to look out for conflicting information" (p. 93). The diagnostic process of miscue analysis, an evaluative method creating what Goodman called a "window on the reading process" (Goodman & Goodman, 1998, p. 105), examines a reader's deviations from the text as he or she continuously predicts how these gaps should be filled. A miscue is a deviation made by the reader from the expected text on the page, and is a result of "not what the eye has seen but what the brain has generated for the mouth to report" (Goodman & Goodman, 1998, p. 105): it is the reader's construction of meaning based on what is perceived or predicted.

Analyzing a reader's miscues in light of his or her verbal reporting of what a text means documents how the reader is attempting to make sense of the text. The underlying reason for the use of the word *miscue* is the understanding that all reading is cued by the semiotic system of graphic symbols arranged on the page, but a reader's perception of those symbols is "controlled by [the] need to make sense" of the interrelationships between words, sentences, and paragraphs (Goodman, 1996, p. 26). Readers will correct only the miscues that cause a disruption in the construction of meaning as they read; the miscues that are left uncorrected are deemed unimportant by the reader because they are able to construct meaning even though the miscue has taken place. Perception, therefore, is not controlled by what a reader sees; instead, it is controlled by the reader's response to what he or she sees or doesn't see on the page.

Closely examining the terminology of both scholars illustrates not only the complementary nature of their research but also the ways in which Goodman's miscue analysis provides concrete data to support Iser's theory of gaps and segments in the interaction of reader and text.

Both describe the reader's process of organizing textual cues into a meaningful whole by building consistency within the linguistic structure, noted by Iser (2000) as "consistency building" (p. 16) and by Goodman (1996) as "building order out of ambiguous information" (p. 67) to make sense of text.

This is accomplished in a split second, as the reader processes the textual cues through the filter of prior knowledge or schemata and predicts what is coming next. At the same time, the reader is continually modifying that organization, monitoring for accurate meaning construction and perception of textual cues. When meaning breaks down, however, the reader has to dig more deeply into his or her repertoire of prior knowledge about genre and subject, modifying not only perceptions of the text itself but also expectations. In so doing, a reader will also modify the words on the page to fill in missing information and fulfill expectations. Iser (2000) called these "reciprocal modifications" (p. 124), again emphasizing the cyclical interaction of text and reader that Goodman identified as miscues.

Miscue analysis and Iserian phenomenology provide a foundation for developing reading strategy instructional plans in my course English 461: Integrative Teaching Methods, an English education capstone. I emphasize the similarities in theory and practice to model literary literacy instruction and activate, as well as bridge, the prior knowledge the students bring from their literature and education classes. Students have studied literary theory as English majors and have had basic reading strategy instruction course work in the Education department. I have found that designing miscue analysis projects based on Goodman's research helps students identify cognitive activities inherent in reading and interpretation, encouraging them to consider ways of extending reading strategy instruction to the secondary and postsecondary level (Hoge, 1983; Paulson, 2001; Worsnop, 1980). I am indebted to Weaver (2002) and Wilde (2000) for providing essential resources for conducting a miscue analysis for preservice and inservice educators and would strongly encourage teachers to consult these sources before designing miscue analysis projects for the classroom.

I have developed a project requiring students to conduct a miscue analysis with a secondary-level (grade 6–12) student subject, following these six steps:

1. Interview the subject about reading practices with prepared questions.

2. Record the subject's oral reading from an appropriate text chosen to match the reader's interests.

3. Record miscues on a miscue coding chart.

4. Analyze the miscues for syntactic, graphophonemic, semantic, and correction patterns.

5. Draw conclusions about the subject's reading strengths and weaknesses.

6. Design literary literacy instructional plans for encouraging the subject to progress (even if the subject is a proficient reader).

Once students have completed the miscue analysis project, I model ways to extend the strategies they have identified to include explicit instruction in literary theory by specifically linking concepts from Goodman and Iser, as I have discussed in this article. Students then reflect on the ways in which teaching literature is teaching reading and how instruction using the same classroom text can be differentiated for struggling and proficient readers by focusing on a combination of reading strategy instruction and explicit teaching of literary theory; essentially they consider how to help students of all levels create an "intentional plan" for constructing meaning from text. Connecting the theory of miscue analysis to Iser's theory of reader engagement with and construction of textual meaning provides a conceptual framework linking reading and literature pedagogies.

I also encourage students to draw similar connections between pedagogical theory and practice by linking additional perspectives on reading theory and literary theory. For example, objective instructional methods emphasizing phonemic decoding and grammar literacy skills can be extended to include text-based literary theory (structuralism, formalism, and New Criticism). Similarly, sociohistorical approaches to literary interpretation provide an opportunity to encourage students to more critically read historical fiction, biographical approaches provide a basis for reading multiple works from specific authors, and cultural theory can serve as a basis for a unit on literature in popular culture. The key is in explicitly teaching literary theory as a reading strategy to scaffold the transfer of reading skills to more advanced coursework, which is a pedagogical approach to literacy instruction that research has shown to be effective with students in a general English classroom.

Improved Strategy Use Leads to Critical Thinking

Teachers and teacher educators can learn much about teaching reading from the centuries of debate and experimentation in the field of literary and critical theory. Systematically introducing theory into the literature and reading classroom, beginning at least in the middle school, encourages students to consciously use everything they know to construct meaning from a text. Sloan (1975) in *The Child as Critic* argued that

> criticism begins in the experience of literature and in personal response to it. But it does not end there. It continues with study that aims to unify and integrate all of the students' literary experiences. (p. 45)

When students at any level become more cognizant of the strategies they use for constructing meaning from text, they can begin to further question the cultural and ideological influences at work in a text, as well as the influences of their own values and beliefs in this transaction. Teaching theory extends methods of reading and literature instruction by further expanding students' repertoires of strategies for analyzing dimensions of meaning and providing structure to help them clearly conceive and articulate a response to a text. The role of theory should not remain merely an intellectual point of reference for the experienced reader to use—in itself a separate subject of study—but rather should become a method for developing that experience by encouraging reading, inquiry, and engagement with text for all students, extending the literacy pedagogies that began with a student's first reading lesson.

References

Applebee, A. N. (1996). *Curriculum as conversation: Transforming traditions of teaching and learning*. Chicago: University of Chicago Press.

Appleman, D. (2000). *Critical encounters in high school English: Teaching literary theory to adolescents*. New York: Teachers College Press.

Block, C. C., Gambrell, L. B., & Pressley, M. (2002). *Improving comprehension instruction: Rethinking research, theory, and classroom practice*. Newark, DE: International Reading Association; San Francisco: Jossey-Bass.

Carey-Webb, A. (2001). *Literature & lives: A response-based, cultural studies approach to teaching English*. Urbana, IL: National Council of Teachers of English.

Caverly, D. C., Nicholson, S. A., & Radcliffe, R. (2004). The effectiveness of strategic reading instruction for college developmental readers. *Journal of College Reading and Learning, 35*(1), 25–43.

Crowley, S. (1989). *A teacher's introduction to deconstruction*. Urbana, IL: National Council of Teachers of English.

Dunston, P. J. (2002). Instructional components for promoting thoughtful literacy learning. In C. C. Block, L. B. Gambrell, & M. Pressley (Eds.), *Improving comprehension instruction: Rethinking research, theory, and classroom practice* (pp. 135–151). Newark, DE: International Reading Association; San Francisco, CA: Jossey-Bass.

Eagleton, T. (1996). *Literary theory: An introduction*. Malden, MA: Blackwell.

Eckert, L. S. (2006). *How does it mean? Engaging reluctant readers through literary theory*. Portsmouth, NH: Heinemann.

Ehren, B. J., Lenz, B. K., & Deshler, D. D. (2004). Enhancing literacy proficiency with adolescents and young adults. In C. A. Stone, E. R. Silliman, B. J. Ehren, & K. Apel (Eds.), *Handbook of language and literacy: Development and disorders* (pp. 681–701). New York: Guilford.

Fish, S. E. (2001). Interpreting the *variorum*. In V. B. Leitch (Ed.), *The Norton anthology of theory and criticism* (pp. 2071–2089). New York: W. W. Norton.

Fisher, D., & Ivey, G. (2006). Evaluating the interventions for struggling adolescent readers. *Journal of Adolescent & Adult Literacy, 50*(3), 180–189. doi: 10.1598/JAAL.50.3.2

Fishman, A. R. (2003). Reading, writing, and reality: A cultural coming to terms. In E. J. Paulson, M. E. Laine, S. A. Biggs, & T. L. Bullock (Eds.), *College reading research and practice: Articles from the* Journal of College Literacy and Learning (pp. 38–53). Newark, DE: International Reading Association.

Frye, N. (1957). *Anatomy of criticism: Four essays.* Princeton, NJ: Princeton University Press.

Goodman, K. (1996). *On reading: A common sense look at the nature of language and the science of reading.* Portsmouth, NH: Heinemann.

Goodman, K. S., & Goodman, Y. M. (1998). To err is human: Learning about language processes by analyzing miscues. In C. Weaver (Ed.), *Reconsidering a balanced approach to reading* (pp. 101–123). Urbana, IL: National Council of Teachers of English.

Graff, G. (2000). Disliking books at an early age. In D. H. Richter (Ed.), *Falling into theory: Conflicting views on reading literature* (2nd ed., pp. 41–48). New York: St. Martin's.

Hoge, S. (1983). A comprehension-centered reading program using reader selected miscues. *Journal of Reading, 27*(1), 52–55.

Iser, W. (1987). Interaction between text and reader. In D. Keesey (Ed.), *Contexts for criticism* (pp. 147–154). Mountain View, CA: Mayfield Publishing Company.

Iser, W. (2000). *The range of interpretation.* New York: Columbia University Press.

Jetton, T. L., & Dole, J. A. (2004). *Adolescent literacy: Research and practice.* New York: Guilford.

Johannessen, L. R. (2004). Helping "struggling" students achieve success. *Journal of Adolescent & Adult Literacy, 47*(8), 638–647.

Keene, E. O. (2002). From good to memorable: Characteristics of highly effective comprehension teaching. In C. C. Block, L. B. Gambrell, & M. Pressley (Eds.), *Improving comprehension instruction: Rethinking research, theory, and classroom practice* (pp. 80–105). Newark, DE: International Reading Association; San Francisco: Jossey-Bass.

Lesley, M. (2004). Refugees from reading: Students' perceptions of "remedial" literacy pedagogy. *Reading Research and Instruction, 44*(1), 62–86.

McCormick, K. (1996). Reading lessons and then some: Toward developing dialogues between critical theory and reading theory. In J. F. Slevin & A. Young (Eds.), *Critical theory and the teaching of literature: Politics, curriculum, Pedagogy* (pp. 292–315). Urbana, IL: National Council of Teachers of English.

Means, B., & Knapp, M. S. (1991). Introduction: Rethinking teaching for disadvantaged students. In B. Means, C. Chelemer, & M. S. Knapp (Eds.), *Teaching advanced skills to at-risk students: Views from research and practice* (pp. 1–26). San Francisco: Jossey-Bass.

Moore, J. N. (1997). *Interpreting young adult literature: Literary theory in the secondary classroom.* Portsmouth, NH: Boynton/Cook.

Nodelman, P. (1996). *The pleasures of children's literature* (2nd ed.). White Plains, NY: Longman.

Orlando, V. P., Caverly, D. C., Swetnam, L. A., & Flippo, R. F. (2003). Text demands in college classes: An investigation. In E. J. Paulson, M. E. Laine, S. A. Biggs, & T. L. Bullock (Eds.), *College reading research and practice:*

Articles from the Journal of College Literacy and Learning (pp. 118–125). Newark, DE: International Reading Association.

Paulson, E. (2001). Discourse of retrospective miscue analysis: Links with adult learning theory. *Journal of College Reading and Learning, 32*(1), 112–127.

Perin, D. (2002). *Literacy education after high school*. New York: ERIC Clearinghouse on Urban Education. (ERIC Document Reproduction Service No. ED467689; www.ericdigests.org/2003–2/literacy.html)

Sanoff, A. P. (2006). What professors and teachers think: A perception gap over students' preparation. *The Chronicle of Higher Education, 52*(27), B9. Retrieved June 30, 2008, from chronicle.com/free/v52/i27/27b00901.htm

Scholes, R. (1985). *Textual power: Literary theory and the teaching of English*. New Haven, CT: Yale University Press.

Simpson, M. L., Stahl, N. A., & Francis, M. A. (2004). Reading and learning strategies: Recommendations for the 21st century. *Journal of Developmental Education, 28*(2), pp. 2–4, 6, 8, 10–12, 14.

Sloan, G. D. (1975). *The child as critic: Teaching literature in the elementary school*. New York: Teachers College Press.

Smittle, P. (2003). Principles for effective teaching. *Journal of Developmental Education, 26*(3), 10–16.

Soter, A. (1999), *Young adult literature and the new literary theories: Developing critical readers in middle school*. New York: Teachers College Press.

Stott, J. C. (1981). Teaching literary criticism in the elementary grades: A symposium. *Children's Literature in Education, 12*(4), 192–206. doi:10.1007/BF01142764

Tovani, C. (2000). *I can read it, but I don't get it: Comprehension strategies for adolescent readers*. Portland, ME: Stenhouse.

Underwood, T., & Pearson, P. D. (2004). Teaching struggling adolescent readers to comprehend what they read, In T. L. Jetton & J. A. Dole (Eds.), *Adolescent literacy research and practice* (pp. 135–161). New York: Guilford.

Weaver, C. (1998). *Reconsidering a balanced approach to reading*. Urbana, IL: National Council of Teachers of English.

Weaver, C. (2002). *Reading process and practice* (3rd ed.). Portsmouth, NH: Heinemann.

Wilde, S. (2000). *Miscue analysis made easy: Building on student strengths*. Portsmouth, NH: Heinemann.

Worsnop, C. (1980). *A procedure for using the reading miscue inventory as a remedial teaching tool with adolescents*. Unpublished doctoral dissertation, Queen's University, Kingston, Ontario, Canada.

Zhang, J. (2003). In defense of college developmental reading education. In E. J. Paulson, M. E. Laine, S. A. Biggs, & T. L. Bullock (Eds.), *College reading research and practice: Articles from the* Journal of College Literacy and Learning (pp. 13–18). Newark, DE: International Reading Association.

Transcending the Divide: Where College and Secondary Reading and Study Research Coincide

Rona F. Flippo

Rona F. Flippo previews the contents and issues represented in one of the field's key texts, the Handbook of College Reading and Study Strategy Research *(Flippo & Caverly, 2009). This text has been well-received by literacy professionals at the postsecondary level. Flippo argues that many of the issues raised in the* Handbook *are relevant to literacy educators at multiple levels, not just the college level. Through an examination of some of the issues shared by literacy professionals at both the secondary and postsecondary levels, it becomes clear that far more cross-level scholarship and collaboration are needed to bridge the gap between high school and college.*

Those of us who teach literacy usually accept the idea that reading, writing, and study strategies are developmental. Youngsters develop their literacy from birth on, and, to some of us, dividing literacy education into steadfast designations such as early childhood, elementary, middle, secondary, and college learning (which may have pragmatic value) seems counterproductive or at least arbitrary.

Even so, many educators and others (e.g., parents, community leaders, writers and journalists, policymakers) think of learning as going from childhood through the college years and beyond, and that what happens in the early years informs the elementary years, what happens in the elementary years informs the middle school years, and so on. This, of course, is true, yet this linear way of conceptualizing literacy education appears to move in one direction. What if we take another view? What if we turn it around and see that we can be informed from both directions?

The focus of this commentary is just that: What if, using the findings of scholars reported in the *Handbook of College Reading and Study Strategy Research* (Flippo & Caverly, 2009), we see how this research can inform secondary-level teachers? I suggest that we take a backward look as well, instead of just the forward trajectory and level divisions to which we have become accustomed.

When several of the *Handbook* chapter authors and I presented our findings at International Reading Association's (IRA) Annual Convention (Flippo, Parker, Jackson, Alvarez, Risko, Becker, & Schumm, 2009), comments from attendees emphasized the need to share these findings with middle and secondary teachers "before it was too late for their students." In fact, they urged us to do this.

The related point of this commentary is to reinforce the idea that we are in this together: Whether we are elementary, middle, secondary, or college teachers, we are seeing that many of the issues, problems, and research in the field of reading literacy are common to all levels of education. An examination of the newest scholarship in publications certainly indicates this. And articles in *Reading Today* (Long, 2010a; 2010b), IRA's bimonthly newspaper, discuss legislation in Washington, DC, including issues and new standards that will affect teachers and students across all levels.

So where do we begin? A logical point is to briefly investigate the history of college reading to reveal the actual roots of the entire field of reading research, education, and practice, at all levels as we know them today.

History of College Reading

In the *Handbook*, the chapter by Stahl and King (2009) presented the history of college reading. Using this as my primary source, I summarize from their history to make the connection between college reading and various level divisions we currently see in U.S. schools.

Stahl and King (2009) indicated that college reading can be traced back to 1636, at the dawn of the United States' institutions of higher education. This was, they emphasized, also the beginning of the entire field of reading. Early historical foundations in college reading were representative of the field of reading for a long time. However, as education became more universal, and as secondary and grade schools developed, attention to reading at lower levels slowly emerged.

Moje (2008) noted that since the early 1900s, educational practitioners and researchers have grappled with questions about the role of instruction in reading and writing in secondary school, while Stahl and King (2009) emphasized the importance of realizing that our current understandings of basic reading processes still rest on work conducted by many early great researchers in the field of reading, who, even in the 1950s, did their original research with college readers. These include works of William S. Gray, Constance McCullough, Nila B. Smith, Ruth M. Strang, Miles A. Tinker, George Spache, and Francis P. Robinson. For those of us who teach at all levels, Stahl and King emphasized that our professional associations were founded with the major input of college reading researchers: IRA, National Reading Conference, College Reading Association, and the American Reading Forum.

That is an important point to stress no matter what levels we teach: Our foundations began with research about how college readers study, read, and learn. Although most of us recognize that certain developmental understandings or theories may be more operational and appropriate at certain levels, through my own research and professional experiences I suggest we should instead be thinking about issues and focusing on research, possible solutions, and understandings that will help us do a better job with more of the students we teach, regardless of their levels.

Therefore, I explore some of the common issues (and related learnings) affecting reading education at all levels, particularly college and secondary years. Similar insights can also be gleaned from the research reported in the *Handbook*, from Vacca, Vacca, and Mraz (2010), and from a wide sampling of articles from the *Journal of Adolescent & Adult Literacy (JAAL)* as well as other journals and literature that specifically speak to secondary audiences.

Universal Issues

What are some of the big issues common to both college and secondary reading literacy? What suggestions have been offered in the reviewed research that could be helpful to teachers and the students they teach?

Content, Academic, and New Literacies

The need to enhance content literacy in schools is more of an agreement than an issue. Literacy researchers at all levels have been calling for more content materials in our reading, writing, and dialoguing in school. Whether using traditional texts, electronic texts, content area trade books, newspapers, biographies, historical documents, or the many-faceted new literacies, the literature has suggested that students are interested in factual materials, can be highly engaged with these materials, and can enjoy researching, learning from, writing about, conversing about, and otherwise sharing or reporting their ideas based on these readings. However, although there is general agreement on the importance of content literacy across the field, as the saying goes, "the devil is in the details." Today, there are calls for more attention to academic literacy, disciplinary learning, and the new literacies in our schools.

Academic literacy has been receiving attention across grade-level designations. Many researchers who call for a focus on academic literacy indicate that this focus is appropriate to the work of college teachers and students (Pawan & Honeyford, 2009) who need to be successful within academia, and that academic literacy is inclusive of academic discourse skills and the newer literacies, including the visual, online, research, content area, and information skills so important to varied disciplines and life today.

In the *Handbook*, Pawan and Honeyford (2009) explored the idea that academic literacy can be thought of in three parts: first, the initial or entry-level literacy needed to access academia; second, the platform literacy that students need to participate and engage in the academic community; and third, the academic literacy that enables students to legitimize their individual differences so as to affect curricular direction. Researchers in secondary literacy (e.g., Moje, 2008) suggest that a focus on content reading or literacy alone may not be as appropriate as the focus on disciplinary learning. This is because students and their teachers tend to be much more interested in the discipline and topics they are studying than in the notion of learning how to read or to read better in a content area.

For this reason, the emphasis on content reading skills and strategies is often a turnoff to secondary students and their teachers who regard the academy and the content areas they are learning and teaching in the academy to be the purpose of their learning and teaching pursuits, not the learning and acquisition or teaching of reading. Many of the chapter authors in the *Handbook* indicate the same: Literacy and study strategy development is most successful when imbedded within the context and tasks of the actual reading, writing, research, and study at hand.

Focusing on academic literacy and disciplinary learning really achieves what most of us consider desirable and optimal literacy development in secondary and college courses, without the resistance to teaching or learning reading strategies to apply to content areas that often provokes teachers and students in colleges and secondary schools. Furthermore, Pawan and Honeyford (2009) indicated,

> Technology has made it much easier for all of us to be a part of the knowledge authorship and creative process; to engage in multi-modality, at multiple levels across disciplines; to have access to multiple perspectives; and to juxtapose our experiences in and out of school. However, unless students take the capabilities and opportunities created by the new media to cultivate a sense of who they are as students and what they bring to academic literacy communities, the students will be subject to the literacy judgment and agendas by others . . . how literacies are used is the determining factor between those who are successful and those who are left behind in academia. (p. 41)

Numerous others have also been focusing on the importance of the new literacies in college and secondary reading. These include many of the chapter authors in the *Handbook* (e.g., Alvarez & Risko, 2009; Caverly, Peterson, Delaney, & Starks-Martin, 2009; Jackson, 2009), as well as *JAAL* authors (e.g., Alvermann, 2008) and content literacy textbook authors (e.g., Vacca et al., 2010). "It simply is not possible," argued Vacca et al., (2010), "to adequately prepare students for reading and writing in the twenty-first century without integrating new literacies into the everyday life of today's classrooms. . . . New literacies are transforming the way we read and write" (p. 29).

The other authors cited concur, emphasizing that the scope and breadth of these new literacies are constantly growing and changing, which needs to be reflected in our classrooms. They offer thought-provoking ideas, discussions, strategies, materials, media, tools, software, websites, activities, and examples to help college and secondary teachers integrate new literacies into their classroom reading, writing, study, research, and instructional endeavors.

Policy, Testing, and Student Diversity

We have all seen firsthand and, unfortunately, continue to see, the politicization of education that has taken place at all grade-level designations. In the *Handbook*, Parker (2009) focused on the policy environment regarding reading and study and learning programs in the past as well as more recent developments in colleges today. Much of what she reports should be of great interest to secondary teachers who have students hoping for and considering entry into college, but whose future may be marginalized by the politics and policies of the day. She stated,

> Policy makers suggest that issues related to accountability, efficiency, educational quality, degree completion, and student success are at risk due to high levels of remedial education across the nation. . . . [However, she believes] definitions for underpreparedness and remediation are arbitrary; policies that reduce or eliminate remediation may unnecessarily exclude students who might benefit from a four-year college experience from pursuing a college degree. (p. 61)

In sum, Parker suggested more collaboration between high schools and colleges, and studies that might better inform the policy decisions regarding who benefits from remedial education and in what contexts and situations.

Student diversity is often mentioned as important in the policies we see in our colleges and schools, but the richness of our students' diversity and their importance to our school communities and society is an important issue that deserves more than passing mention. Many diverse students are not doing well in our colleges and secondary schools. Focusing on the appropriateness and quality of many of the tests we have been using, on nondiscriminatory alternative assessments that do not marginalize our diverse students' strengths and gifts, and on how we can work best with students who have not done well in our more traditional classroom settings and curricula will yield far more productive results than fixating on test scores. *Handbook* authors Abbate-Vaughn (2009) and Higbee (2009) addressed aspects of these questions and offered suggestions, including sources of assistance and guiding principle to help students and programs.

High-stakes testing remains a hot issue throughout education today. Youngsters and their teachers at all educational levels are being marginalized, suffering from the overuse of testing, overuse of testing preparation, and often inappropriate use and interpretation of test results. This is particularly true for black, Hispanic, and other language-diverse students who tend not to do as well on these tests as white and non–language diverse students.

Questions about why this marginalization occurs have never been adequately answered, although possibilities include taking tests in a language not one's own; attending schools in inner-city, low-income areas, where trips to the local library or school might be dangerous; and living in poverty or low-income situations where the adults are constantly working to buy food and pay rent, with little time available to read to children. Other disadvantages arise out of the possible bias of some high-stakes tests against certain test takers (e.g., Santelices & Wilson, 2010).

In one of my *Handbook* chapters (Flippo & Schumm, 2009), we discussed commercially available tests being used to evaluate reading in colleges and in secondary schools, and we found all of them lacking in one way or another. We provided in-depth reviews of each test, pointing out the information a college or secondary teacher would need to consider before using them, including weakness and strengths. Overall, we concluded we need better tests and offered recommendations for publishers who produce tests and recommendations for teachers and other users, including the following:

- A variety of assessments should be used.

- Reading programs should compile their own data and norms.

- New tests should be developed that more accurately reflect the genre, content, and length of required reading.

- Authentic assessments more appropriate for the populations of students should be used.

- The goals of the teacher or program should be consulted for compatibility before choosing testing instruments.

- Technical information should be in user-friendly and accessible formats.

- Tests should be developed that gauge the reading strengths and challenges of all students.

Reading, Writing, and Studying Practices

Several chapters in the *Handbook* report extensive research on vocabulary, comprehension, reading and writing, and study-reading development. The myriad of research findings, best practices, instructional ideas, and recommendations the chapters collectively provide could benefit both secondary and college teachers and students. The breadth and extent of this research limit me to sharing only some of the suggestions.

Francis and Simpson's (2009) review of vocabulary research yielded recommendations that include achieving a balance of approaches, teaching vocabulary from context, stimulating awareness of and interest in words, reinforcing word learning, providing language-rich environments, and wide reading by students (which supports word learning).

Holschuh and Aultman (2009) reported on comprehension research and recommended that every strategy presented to students should have the potential of becoming generative in nature, so that students can and will engage in strategies independently because they recognize the values of these strategies, not because they are required to do them.

Jackson (2009) reported on the connections and practices of reading and writing, and she emphasized that how one views reading and writing practices affects how one teaches them. Her research suggested that it is important for teachers to make everything explicit for students to facilitate their reading and writing development. She explained,

> At the research level, this means using think-aloud protocols and interviews. In the classroom, this means both teachers and students modeling their thinking to increase metacognition. Technology can aid in this by providing a multitude of ways authors and audiences can instantly interact and as a means to record these interactions for further study. (p. 167)

Mulcahy-Ernt and Caverly (2009) reviewed study strategies and provided insight on their usefulness. They, as well as other *Handbook* chapter authors, suggested that self-regulated learning holds great promise for developing strategic readers for reading both traditional and nontraditional texts. Other findings include that not all students benefit from the use of the same strategies when reading and learning from text; teachers should model use of strategies and make explicit their expectations (e.g., the relationship between lecture notes and future tests, so students can choose the study-learning strategies that will best prepare them for the exam); and text difficulty is a factor when using study-learning strategies.

Several other *Handbook* chapters also review research on study strategies, note-taking, and test taking that is just as applicable to secondary students as it is to college students. The Alvarez and Risko (2009) chapter focused on motivation and study strategies that engage students in their learning. These authors used electronic texts with literacy strategies to demonstrate how students' learning was enhanced.

They recommended teachers first address their students' motivations, drawing on out-of-school experiences and personal knowledge to form links to new concepts under study and to apply new knowledge to problems and situations that are meaningful to the students. Next, teachers must attend to students' goals in their courses, fostering engagement while encouraging the use of particular strategies to deepen learning as students strive to meet their goals. Teachers should give students time to elaborate on what they have learned, to help students see what they can do and cultivate feelings of self-efficacy.

Armbruster's (2009) chapter addressed the research on note-taking from lectures. Because the lecture method still dominates in U.S. classrooms from middle school through college, a review of this research is important information for teachers at all these levels. "Research has confirmed that the quantity and quality of the notes that students take is related to achievement . . . [but unfortunately, because of the complexity or cognitive demands of the task] students do not take very effective notes" (p. 243). Armbruster recommended that teachers provide lecture handouts; videotape their lectures, making them available for student viewing; and encourage cooperative review where students work together to ask and answer higher order, open-ended questions or generate lecture summaries.

Flippo, Becker, and Wark (2009) reviewed research on test preparation and test performance, test-wiseness, test-taking skills, and coaching. Because the findings are extensive, I highlight only a few that I believe are critical knowledge for middle, secondary, and college teachers: Special instruction in test preparation can improve performance and result in higher test scores. Strategies for helping students with essay and multiple-choice tests have been identified. Test-wise students can recognize cues within tests, and most can improve their scores by changing answers as they work through tests. Coaching can affect test performance under certain conditions.

Additionally, *Preparing Students for Testing and Doing Better in School* (Flippo, 2008)—developed for middle, secondary, and college teachers to use with their students and their particular content areas—provides a framework with many examples of preparing for and taking tests, with suggested exercises to help students become more test-wise.

Transcending the Divide

When we wrote our chapters for the *Handbook* and later reported some research findings at IRA in 2009, we were expecting a college reading audience. Although there were college reading practitioners at the symposium, we realized there were many secondary practitioners, too. When they suggested that this content was important for secondary and middle school teachers, we realized they were probably right.

After preparing for this commentary, reviewing literature addressed primarily to middle school and secondary audiences, and taking another look at our findings in the *Handbook*, I am even more cognizant of the mutual issues and concerns we all face. I strongly believe that we need to do much more between-level research and sharing, across all reading levels—we must transcend the divide in order to reap the benefits from all levels of reading research and scholarship.

References

Abbate-Vaughn, J. (2009). Addressing diversity. In R. F. Flippo & D. C. Caverly (Eds.). *Handbook of college reading and study strategy research* (2nd ed., pp. 289–313). New York: Taylor & Francis/Routledge.

Alvarez, M. C., & Risko, V. J. (2009). Motivation and study strategies. In R. F. Flippo & D. C. Caverly (Eds.), *Handbook of college reading and study strategy research* (2nd ed., pp. 199–219). New York: Taylor & Francis/Routledge.

Alvermann, D. E. (2008). Why bother theorizing adolescents' online literacies for classroom practice and research? *Journal of Adolescent & Adult Literacy, 52*(1), 8–19. doi:10.1598/JAAL.52.1.2

Armbruster, B. B. (2009). Notetaking from lectures. In R. F. Flippo & D. C. Caverly (Eds.), *Handbook of college reading and study strategy research* (2nd ed., pp. 220–248). New York: Taylor & Francis/Routledge.

Caverly, D. C., Peterson, C. L., Delaney, C. J., & Starks-Martin, G. A. (2009). Technology integration. In R. F. Flippo & D. C. Caverly (Eds.), *Handbook of college reading and study strategy research* (2nd ed., pp. 314–350). New York: Taylor & Francis/Routledge.

Flippo, R. F. (2008). *Preparing students for testing and doing better in school.* Thousand Oaks, CA: Corwin.

Flippo, R. F., Becker, M. J., & Wark, D. M. (2009). Test taking. In R. F. Flippo & D. C. Caverly (Eds.), *Handbook of college reading and study strategy research* (2nd ed., pp. 249–286). New York: Taylor & Francis/Routledge.

Flippo, R. F., & Caverly, D. C. (Eds.). (2009). *Handbook of college reading and study strategy research* (2nd ed.). New York: Taylor & Francis/Routledge.

Flippo, R. F., Parker, T., Jackson, J., Alvarez, M., Risko, V., Becker, M., & Schumm, J. (2009, May). *College reading and study strategies research.* Symposium at the 54th annual convention of the International Reading Association. Minneapolis, MN.

Flippo, R. F., & Schumm. J. S. (2009). Reading tests. In R. F. Flippo & D. C. Caverly (Eds.), *Handbook of college reading and study strategy research* (2nd ed., pp. 408–464). New York: Taylor & Francis/Routledge.

Francis, M. A., & Simpson, M. L. (2009). Vocabulary development. In R. F. Flippo & D. C. Caverly (Eds.), *Handbook of college reading and study strategy research* (2nd ed., pp. 97–120). New York: Taylor & Francis/Routledge.

Higbee, J. L. (2009). Student diversity. In R. F. Flippo & D. C. Caverly (Eds.), *Handbook of college reading and study strategy research* (2nd ed., pp. 67–94). New York: Taylor & Francis/Routledge.

Holschuh, J. P., & Aultman, L. P. (2009). Comprehension development. In R. F. Flippo & D. C. Caverly (Eds.), *Handbook of college reading and study strategy research* (2nd ed., pp. 121–144). New York: Taylor & Francis/Routledge.

Jackson, J. M. (2009). Reading/writing connection. In R. F. Flippo & D. C. Caverly (Eds.), *Handbook of college reading and study strategy research* (2nd ed., pp. 145–173). New York: Taylor & Francis/Routledge.

Long, R. (2010a, June/July). Common Core State Standards released: What comes next? *Reading Today, 27*(6), 26.

Long, R. (2010b, June/July). Literacy, education issues hold sway in Congress. *Reading Today, 27*(6), 26.

Moje, E. B. (2008). Foregrounding the disciplines in secondary literacy teaching and learning: A call for change. *Journal of Adolescent & Adult Literacy, 52*(2), 96–107. doi: 10.1598/JAAL.52.2.1

Mulcahy-Ernt, P. I., & Caverly, D. C. (2009). Strategic study reading. In R. F. Flippo & D. C. Caverly (Eds.), *Handbook of college reading and study strategy research* (2nd ed., pp. 177–198). New York: Taylor & Francis/Routledge.

Parker, T. L. (2009). Policy issues. In R. F. Flippo & D. C. Caverly (Eds.), *Handbook of college reading and study strategy research* (2nd ed., pp. 47–66). New York: Taylor & Francis/Routledge.

Pawan, F., & Honeyford, M. A. (2009). Academic literacy. In R. F. Flippo & D. C. Caverly (Eds.), *Handbook of college reading and study strategy research* (2nd ed., pp. 26–46). New York: Taylor & Francis/Routledge.

Santelices, M. V., & Wilson, M. (2010). Unfair treatment? The case of Freedle, the SAT, and the standardization approach to differential item functioning. *Harvard Educational Review, 80*(1), 106–134.

Stahl, N. A., & King, J. R. (2009). History. In R. F. Flippo & D. C. Caverly (Eds.), *Handbook of college reading and study strategy research* (2nd ed., pp. 3–25). New York: Taylor & Francis/Routledge.

Vacca, R. T., Vacca, J. L., & Mraz, M. E. (2010). *Content area reading: Literacy and learning across the curriculum* (10th ed.). Boston: Allyn & Bacon.

3

Student Population and Diversity

Introduction

A merican higher education has a long history in which each new academic generation reflects a greater degree of cultural, economic, social, national, and physical diversity. Within each generation there have always been new subgroups—some who were outwardly embraced, others who were begrudgingly acknowledged, and still others who were attacked by the members of the academic status quo. The college reading and learning movement, along with its later offshoots in the form of learning assistance centers and the like have been there to serve the increasingly diverse student body. As never before, postsecondary educators, including college reading and learning specialists, need to understand the diversity of the students who populate their classrooms.

The articles in this chapter begin by looking at the manner in which programs served students in the 1930s, when the concept of developmental reading was first introduced as an instructional paradigm opposed to remedial and corrective reading in postsecondary reading and study skills instruction. In this particular article we introduce the father of American reading instruction, William S. Gray, as he presents a developmental reading program for a Depression Era population.

The article that follows reports on the perceptions that a group of African American college students held about their secondary school literacy preparation for college. Joy Banks shows that, from the perspective of her study sample, many of the difficulties with text encountered in college can be traced back to secondary school experiences.

The next entry presents research on the literacy experiences encountered by a set of Latina and Latino students through the lens of identity negotiations. Holly Hungerford-Kresser presents sociocultural definitions of literacy as well as theory that focus on "identity as position" so as to discuss the ways that these particular students are positioned by the various discourses embedded in the academic literacies of a predominately white university.

Finally, Ellen Urquhart Engstrom presents an integrated developmental reading and writing program from Landmark College, which serves students with learning disabilities and attention disorders. The article presents a curricular approach to integrating instructional methods for improving reading comprehension, fluency, and accuracy along with writing instruction and assistive technology.

Additional Readings

Abbate-Vaughn, J. (2009). Addressing diversity. In R. F. Flippo & D. C. Caverly (Eds.), *Handbook of college reading and study strategy research* (2nd ed., pp. 289–313). New York, NY: Routledge.

Abreu-Ellis, C., Ellis, J., & Hayes, R. (2009). College preparedness and time of learning disability identification. *Journal of Developmental Education, 32*(3), 28–30, 32, 35–38.

August, G. (2011). Spelling facilitates good ESL reading comprehension. *Journal of Developmental Education, 35*(1), 14–16, 18, 20, 22, 24.

Avramidis, E., & Skidmore, D. (2004). Reappraising learning support in higher education. *Research in Post-Compulsory Education, 9*(1), 63–82.

Comeaux, E., & Harrison, K. C. (2011). A conceptual model of academic success for student–athletes. *Educational Researcher, 40*(5), 235–245.

DuPre, E. A., Gilroy, D., & Miles, T. R. (2007). *Dyslexia at college* (3rd ed.). New York, NY: Routledge.

Guillory, R. M. (2009). American Indian/Alaska Native college student retention strategies. *Journal of Developmental Education, 33*(2), 12–14, 16, 18, 20–21.

Hadley, W. M. (2006). L. D. students' access to higher education: Self-advocacy and support. *Journal of Developmental Education, 30*(2), 10–12, 14–16.

Hand, C., & Payne, E. M. (2008). First generation college success: A study of Appalachian student success. *Journal of Developmental Education, 32*(1), 4–6, 8, 10, 12, 14–15.

Higbee, J. L. (2009). Student diversity. In R. F. Flippo & D. C. Caverly (Eds.), *Handbook of college reading and study strategy research* (2nd ed., pp. 67–94). New York, NY: Routledge.

Higbee, J. L., Kwabena, S., & Bruch, P. L. (2007). Assessing our commitment to multiculturalism: Student perspectives. *Journal of College Reading and Learning, 37*(2), 7–25.

Jimenez, R. T., & Teague, B. L. (2009). Language, literacy, and content: Adolescent English language learners. In L. Mandel Morrow, R. Rudea, & D. Lapp (Eds.), *Handbook of research on literacy and diversity* (pp. 114–136). New York, NY: Guilford Press.

Kirby, J. R., Silvestri, R., Allingham, B. H., Parrila, R., & La Fonte, C. B. (2008). Learning strategies and study approaches of postsecondary students with dyslexia. *Journal of Learning Disabilities, 41*(1), 85–96.

Mandel Morrow, L., Rudea, R., & Lapp, D. (Eds.). (2009). *Handbook of research on literacy and diversity*. New York, NY: Guilford Press.

Moody, S. (2007). *Dyslexia: Surviving and succeeding at college*. New York, NY: Routledge.

Tatum, A. W. (2008). Toward a more anatomically complete model of literacy instruction: A focus on African male adolescents and texts. *Harvard Educational Review, 78*(1), 155–180.

Tatum, A. W. (2011). Diversity and literacy. In J. Samuels & A. Farstrup (Eds.), *What research has to say about reading instruction* (pp. 425–447). Newark, DE: International Reading Association.

Historically Significant Work

Reading Difficulties in College: The Nature and Extent of Reading Deficiencies among College Students

William S. Gray

Just as George Washington is rightly called the father of his country, the argument can be made that William S. Gray is the father of the modern field of reading pedagogy and research. Gray was interested in reading as it was taught, mastered, and then practiced across the life span. Yet, few individuals realize that he did have an interest in college reading. This article was authored during the golden age of college reading and provides us with what was likely the first call for developmental reading instruction for the college population. The value of this historical work is that it demonstrates how far the field has come in understanding students' reading skills and problems over eight decades; yet, it also shows that many of the concerns being voiced in the twenty-first century are similar to the concerns about those reading competencies brought to college at the time the article was published.

Two decades ago most college teachers took for granted that their students had acquired satisfactory reading habits. The assumption prevailed, therefore, that there were few or no reading problems at the college level. In the course of time, the fact was recognized that some students read so rapidly and well that they could easily do more than the usual amount of assigned work. In order to enable them to work at their maximum capacity, new opportunities were provided, such as reading for honors and pursuing independent study programs. Significant as these provisions were, they affected the welfare of only superior students.

During the last decade, the deficient reader also has been identified. As his achievements and needs have been studied, it has become increasingly clear that he is seriously handicapped in efforts to do successful college work. Indeed, the view has been expressed in many quarters that such students either should not be admitted to colleges or should be given training that will enable them, if possible, to do college work satisfactorily. In the discussion that follows, I wish to support the contention that colleges should provide both an adequate diagnostic and remedial program for deficient readers and such developmental instruction in reading for all as will insure a growing intellectual grasp of the various fields studied.

The method used most frequently in determining reading deficiencies at the college level is to check reading achievements by testing. In a survey made at Miami University, for example, Guiler found that 55 per cent of a group of 437 college Freshmen

> were below the standard for high-school Seniors when measured by the Shank reading test; . . . and one-fifth were unable to read as well as the average pupil in the last year of the junior high school.[1]

It is obvious that this college group was seriously deficient in reading habits.

Using separate tests of rate, comprehension, and meaning vocabulary, Booker secured evidence of striking differences in the reading achievement of 664 Freshmen at the University of Chicago. One student, for example, read more slowly than two words per second whereas other students read more than seven words per second. These records indicate that some students could read 18,000 more words per hour than other students. Allowing 400 words to the page, the most rapid readers could read 45 pages more per hour than the slowest. If the comprehension of the former was as good as that of the latter, their advantage was certainly great.

An examination of the comprehension scores showed that they varied from 20 to 66. In other words, the best reader responded correctly to more than three times as many test items as did the most superficial reader. Since the better readers, as a rule, were also among the most rapid, their advantage was tremendous. One explanation for poor comprehension scores lies in a meager meaning vocabulary. Three of the students tested made vocabulary scores lower than 10, while more than twenty made scores higher than 45. The former group attached no meanings or incorrect meanings to about four-fifths of the words in the test. As pointed out by Booker, they knew the meanings of only relatively few of the words included in the vocabulary of the "intelligent reader."[2]

A third type of evidence was secured by Pressey who gave tests at Ohio State University to find out how well students could read and interpret the different kinds of material usually assigned in their courses. As a preliminary step, she read all the textbooks used by the Freshmen and identified the various major types of reading required. A test was then developed including the various kinds that would be required by the average Freshman. From this test, six measures of reading efficiency were obtained:

> ... speed of reading typical paragraphs, comprehension of textual matter of various kinds, comprehension of common types of diagrams, comprehension of problems (not the working out of the problem), comprehension of formulas, that is, the reading of their meaning, and comprehension of directions.

When the test was given to about a thousand Freshmen, the scores ranged from 7 to 57, out of a possible score of 60, with a medial score of 30. When the 350 who ranked lowest in the test were later studied individually, it was found that not more than 10 per cent of them were able to read paragraphs taken from seventh- and eighth-grade materials well enough to "locate the main idea." Such findings indicate that college students not only differ widely in reading achievement, but that many of them have surprisingly immature and deficient reading habits.[3]

The foregoing statement is further supported by facts secured from photographic records of eye-movements. For example, Booker found pronounced individual variations in the reading habits of his subjects: "The average number of fixations per line ranged from 4.4 to 14.8; regressive movements, from .1 to 5.4; and duration of fixations, from 6.0 to 10.0 twenty-fifths of a second."[4] Even wider differences were revealed by records from more than two hundred students in three institutions secured by the writer during the current academic year through the use of the ophthalmograph, a portable instrument for photographing eye-movements. These records also showed that many college students are less mature in respect to fundamental habits of recognition than the average eighth-grade pupil. Even more significant is the fact that many students of average ability show clear evidence of a surprising amount of immaturity in habits of recognition. Such findings reinforce the conviction that colleges should make intensive studies of the reading achievements and needs of their students and provide appropriate corrective and remedial training for those who are deficient. They also support the recommendation that guidance in reading and study habits should be provided for many who are not potential failures. In fact, experiments show that the greatest improvement is usually made by those of average ability when appropriate guidance is provided.

. . .

Attention will be directed next to five factors or groups of factors that are closely related to poor achievement in reading at the college level. Analyses of the records of those who are most deficient in reading show that they also rank low, as a rule, in mental ability, or capacity to learn. Unfortunately, the group intelligence tests that have usually been used in diagnosing such cases involved reading. In such cases, the validity of the ranks assigned to intelligence may be questioned. On the other hand, clinical studies which have been made supply convincing evidence that limited mental ability is characteristic of college students whose percentile ranking on reading tests is fifteen or below. A large majority of them not only rank low on intelligence tests, but they make slow progress, as a rule, in response to remedial training. The fact that there are notable exceptions indicates either that other significant factors are involved or that students vary widely in respect to those components of mental ability which are most closely related to reading achievement. Undoubtedly, both assumptions are valid in many cases. Certainly, we are seriously in need of intensive studies of the relative significance to reading of various mental abilities and of more discriminating tests of capacity to learn.

A second cause of reading disability is a limited meaning vocabulary. With but few exceptions, college students who score low on comprehension tests rank low also in meaning vocabulary. The chief difficulty does not lie in the fact that they cannot recognize and pronounce words accurately; it is due rather to the fact that they often associate few or no relevant meanings with the key words of the passages read. Unless the sight of a word arouses clear, vivid, and appropriate meaning associations while in the act of reading, it is obvious that comprehension will be inadequate. Experiments reported by various writers show that a definite increase in word knowledge is usually accompanied by a corresponding improvement in silent-reading achievement. This is especially true in the case of students whose rank in comprehension is lower than their rank in intelligence.

A third cause of poor achievement in reading on the part of many students is inappropriate attitudes and ineffective habits of thinking while reading. Of primary importance is the fact that one should approach reading with a purpose and with an inquiring attitude of mind. Furthermore, a high degree of mental activity should accompany the reading act. For example, the reader should relate the various elements of meaning that comprise units of thought, he should grasp the author's arrangement of ideas and should relate them to personal experiences and problems, he should supplement the author's meaning from his own stock of ideas, he should raise questions concerning the facts included, he should judge the relative significance of the ideas presented and should critically evaluate them, and he should make use of the facts learned in the solution of problems or in the discovery of new interests. Furthermore, the mental steps or procedures used should vary with the purpose of reading. As shown by Ryder, there are notable differences between good and poor students in respect to such reading and study habits. He secured in a controlled experiment convincing evidence of the value of acquainting students with the nature of their weaknesses and with constructive suggestions for improvement.

A fourth cause of reading deficiency, particularly in respect to rate, is the persistence of immature and ineffective habits that frequently characterize the reading of children. For example, many college students are virtually word readers and have never acquired what Morrison has aptly called "the reading adaptation." Their span of recognition is narrow, their mental response to stimuli from the printed page is slow, and they persist in such immature habits as moving the lips or pointing with the fingers. Experience teaches that if such habits have become definitely established through long use, it is often difficult to modify them. On the other hand, the students of this group who rank relatively high in intelligence often make phenomenal progress as soon as they recognize the nature of their deficiency and receive appropriate guidance.

A fifth cause of unsatisfactory achievement in reading relates to visual defects of one type or another. The large percentage of college students who wear glasses supplies striking evidence of the reality of visual difficulties. During the last five years, both ophthalmologists and reading specialists have become increasingly concerned with problems in this field. As a result, facts have been discovered which indicate that the reading achievement of good, as well as of poor, readers may in many cases be improved through the use of properly adjusted lenses or through controlled practice which overcomes such difficulties as those resulting from poor habits of accommodation and co-ordination. To cite but one case, clinical examinations and diagnoses made at Harvard, Columbia, and Chicago revealed the following visual defects among others on the part of a highly intelligent student who was quite unable to cover the assigned readings because of extreme slowness in rate of reading: over-convergence of the right eye, lack of lateral control in the movements of the left eye, a significant difference in the visual acuity of the two eyes, unequal refractive errors of the two eyes, marked differences in the amplitude of accommodation of the two eyes, and a limited area of retinal sensitivity in the left eye. New lenses were secured to eliminate or relieve certain conditions. The student is now receiving training in prism reading in which use is made of a metronoscope which makes possible the presentation of material at any rate desired. These exercises are designed to condition co-ordination of accommodation and convergence at the same time that better control of the lateral eye-sweep is acquired. The results secured thus far are very promising.

Reference has been made in the foregoing discussion to only a few of the factors and conditions which are associated with poor reading habits among college students. The list is sufficiently extended, however, to supply clear evidence that many of them encounter genuine handicaps that could be removed if steps were taken to identify and correct them. Various institutions have recognized their opportunity and responsibility in this connection and have adopted more or less limited diagnostic and remedial programs in attacking the problem. Brief reference will be made to the work which is now in progress at one institution by way of illustrating possibilities in this field.

At the beginning of the current academic year, Central State Teachers College, at Mount Pleasant, Michigan, introduced diagnostic and remedial work as an essential phase of the reorganized curriculum which is being experimentally developed there. As a means of identifying poor readers and of diagnosing their difficulties, psychological, reading, and vocabulary tests were included in the battery given during freshman week. Use was made also of the ophthalmograph and the telebinocular in securing eye-movement records and evidence of visual defects. The analysis of the test records and of the personal data obtained, including the preparation of individual profiles, supplied striking evidence of reading deficiencies. In some cases, the students were weak in all phases of reading; in other cases, they were especially deficient in particular phases, such as power of comprehension and interpretation, meaning vocabulary, rate of reading, and habits of recognition.

Remedial work for an experimental group of about 35 students is provided during regular periods each week by an instructor who made preliminary preparation last summer for giving such instruction. Three types of activities have been organized which will extend throughout the year. The first includes individual conferences on specific defects. The purpose is to provide students with more detailed reports on their deficiencies than were possible at the time the scores on the tests and other items of information were tabulated. The interviews also provide opportunity to secure a clearer understanding of the students' difficulties, to suggest appropriate remedial steps, and to encourage the students to attack their problems vigorously. The second type of activity includes a series of group conferences concerning reading and study habits. In this connection, use is being made of the Ryder Check Lists[5] which identify numerous desirable reading and study procedures. Through their use, attention is directed to the fact that there are significant differences between good and poor reading and study habits and stimulus is provided for self-criticism. An effort is made during group conference in which various staff members participate to supply students with such facts and judgments as will enable them to revise their habits intelligently. The third type of activity includes the preparation of periodic reading reports by the students which are used as a measure of their reading interests and habits and which trace changes in them during the first year of college work.

A second general phase of the remedial program includes specific guidance and practice in reading to overcome difficulties and to secure improvement in achievement. Different types of training are planned for the three terms of the academic year. During the autumn term, individual use was made of published manuals, such as *Experiments in Reading* by McCall, Cook, and Norvell,[6] which provide exercises that promote growth in comprehension, speed, and related skills. During the winter term, those students who read slowly have been asked to engage regularly in the reading of simple material that is highly charged with interest in order to promote the development of fluent habits of recognition and the rapid grasp of meaning. During the spring term, group reading of selections of common interest followed by discussions of the reading problems involved will be provided as an aid in discovering and correcting difficulties in reading and interpreting various types of material. The fact is recognized that the mental processes involved in different kinds and purposes of reading differ significantly. Accordingly, vigorous effort will be made to acquaint students with appropriate differences in procedure and to provide opportunity for applying the facts learned under supervision.

The reading program which has been described is far broader in scope than has been provided in most institutions. It is based on a clear recognition of the fact that the average as well as the poor reader at the college level can greatly improve his reading efficiency. Those directing the curriculum reorganization at Mount Pleasant believe also that the ultimate program must include appropriate guidance of a developmental type in each subject or field taught. This includes the conscious building from time to time of a background for intelligent interpretation, the development of clear vivid meanings that attach to the essential vocabulary of a unit, the presentation of dominant motives that should guide the student in his reading, and the cultivation of those patterns of thinking in which pupils must engage while reading if they are to achieve the major objectives of study in particular fields.

As Judd and Buswell point out,

> the printed page is the source of a mass of impressions which the active mind of the good reader begins to organize and arrange with reference to some pattern which it has been trained to work out. If the mind is fitting together the impressions so as to bring into high relief grammatical relations or distinctions, the grouping of words and the distribution of emphasis will be according to one pattern. If the mind is intent on something wholly different from grammar, as for example, the experiences which the author is trying to picture, the whole mental and physical attitude of the reader will be very different.[7]

Unfortunately, a surprisingly large percentage of college students use little or no discrimination in the mental attitudes which they adopt in their various reading activities. This deficiency, in my judgment, can be overcome only as each instructor consciously develops and stimulates students to employ appropriate habits of thinking while engaged in assigned reading activities. This is but another way of saying that one of the basic aims of all good teaching is to cultivate those modes of intelligent interpretation, critical evaluation, and application which characterize efficient study in particular fields.

May I emphasize once more the fact that colleges face both a challenging opportunity and an obligation to provide an adequate diagnostic and remedial program for deficient readers. Even more significant is the possibility of promoting greater breadth and depth of scholarship on the part of all students through appropriate reading guidance of a developmental type.

Notes

1. Guiler, W. S. "Background Deficiencies," *Journal of Higher Education*, III (October, 1932), p. 369.
2. Booker, Ivan A. "The Measurement and Improvement of Silent Reading among College Freshmen." 1934. A Doctor's dissertation on file in the library of the University of Chicago.
3. Pressey, Luella Cole. "College Students and Reading," *Journal of Higher Education*, II (January, 1931), pp. 30–34.
4. Booker, *op. cit.*, p. 137.
5. Ryder, Stephen P. "An Experimental Study of Potential Failures in College." 1934. A Doctor's dissertation on file in the library of the University of Chicago.
6. McCall, William Anderson, Cook, Luella, Bussey, and Novell, George Whitefield. *Experiments in Reading to Accompany Hidden Treasures in Literature.* New York: Harcourt, Brace and Company, 1934. (Editor's note).
7. Judd, Charles H. and Buswell, Guy T. *Silent Reading: a Study of the Various Types.* Chicago: University of Chicago Press, 1922, p. 4. (Supplementary Educational Monographs, No. 23).

African American College Students' Perceptions of Their High School Literacy Preparation

Joy Banks

Joy Banks shows, by drawing from varied forms of national data, that a significant subset of African American students enrolling in postsecondary education is placed in developmental reading courses. She notes that the students have difficulty with textual analysis, problem solving, and critical thinking. Furthermore, these issues are not new but rather have their roots in the secondary education experience. To fully understand the problems these students bring to the higher education arena, the author utilized a phenomenological interview method to examine the high school experiences of eleven African American students who were newly enrolled in a four-year university. Through the interview process the students shared their perceptions of their literacy preparation, their instructors' assumptions of their competencies and the resultant influence on the students' academic self-perceptions, and the strategies employed by the students that promote academic success.

The National Center for Education Statistics (2001) found that after high school only 17% of African American students were able to demonstrate effective literacy skills as characterized by ability to find information and understand, summarize, or explain moderately complex texts. More alarming is that the National Assessment for Educational Progress (2002) reports the average reading proficiency score for African American twelfth-grade students has declined over the past decade. Upon entering college, these students exhibit lower literacy proficiency as implied by their average verbal Scholastic Achievement Test (SAT) score of 433, as compared to a score of 529 earned by average white students (NCES, 2001). In addition, 62% of all entering African American college students require remedial instruction in English as compared to 22% of the total college population (Hoyt, 1999; Roach & Finney, 2000).

Educators and researchers continue to identify factors that contribute to limited literacy proficiency among African American students. Issues such as language and communication style and culturally relevant teaching practices are dominant themes in research on African American literacy performance. However, few studies include the perceptions of students when determining the influence of language, school preparation, and culture on literacy performance. Focus on these factors without student input may hinder identification of factors that most significantly affect literacy performance of African American students.

Much of the research on literacy performance of African American students has centered on themes of language competence related to the acquisition of reading skills and school performance. According to Smitherman (1977) some linguists and historians have characterized the speech patterns of African Americans as imperfect imitations of Standard English. These claims have spurred a "deficiency" model of literacy performance. This model implies that if African American students are to enhance their academic standing they must first learn to speak Standard English. Farkas (1994) reinforced this notion when he concluded: "one begins to believe that African American students' relatively poor reading performance is due to their relatively meager exposure to standard English rather than because they are *not smart*" (p. 32).

Standard English

Other researchers have reasoned that the underperformance of African American and low-income students is a result of shortcomings in urban schools. For example, Oakes (1995) found that: (a) minority students are significantly under enrolled in advanced placement courses even when such courses are available; (b) minority students are referred less often to advanced courses although they may meet the necessary criteria; and (c) minority students are likely to exclude themselves from advanced courses to remain with social peers. This situation may inhibit attainment of literacy skills developed through advanced texts, dialogues, and critical thinking strategies.

A different perspective on school climate is presented by Delpit (2002), who suggests that African American students' under performance in literacy is due to a school atmosphere absent of meaningful cultural representation and a lack of general appreciation for diversity within many schools. This shortcoming creates in students an attitude of resistance and alienation toward the curriculum (Delpit, 1995; Fine, 1987; Harris, 1990). To overcome this attitude Lee (1995) found that classroom factors can promote students' literacy skills when students are able to (a) communicate and work in small groups, (b) integrate analogies from text that relate directly to prior knowledge, and (c) rely upon their own language styles and social knowledge to interpret text meanings. African American students must see themselves as intellectually capable and culturally valued if they are to succeed in literacy tasks (Perry, 2004). This is accomplished through deliberate curricula connections with real world experiences relevant to students.

The consequences of limited academic literacy among some African Americans is not only felt at the college level but is compounded when one considers that high levels of literacy are associated with gainful employment, advanced educational goals, and acquisition of quality of life (National Center on Education and the Economy, 1990). In a study of the relationship between post-high school employment and literacy, the National Center on Education and the Economy (1990) found 41% of adults who demonstrate low literacy proficiency are living in poverty. Given the importance of advanced literacy skills in African American students in higher education and the workforce it is necessary to strengthen literacy preparation in high school and college contexts. While researchers have suggested intervention strategies at both levels, approaches that bridge the two experiences for African American students are overlooked. The students, themselves, are key to resolving this issue. Their perceptions might influence how school preparation can be transformed to promote language and literacy development.

To better understand the implications of this context, eleven African American first-year students were interviewed using a qualitative phenomenological approach. The students' perceptions and assumptions about literacy preparation were documented as they grappled with literacy requirements in Freshmen English. The following research questions were addressed: How do African American first-year college students perceive their high school literacy preparation? What factors do African American first-year college students perceive as necessary for college literacy success? How do African American students develop strategies to cope with the transition from high school to college English classrooms? By questioning the students' perceptions of literacy preparation, the findings can (a) add to our understandings of African American students' experience in the college-level English classroom, and (b) improve upon the current theory and instruction used in both high school and college English classrooms to more effectively assist African American students in reading and writing development.

Method

The study was conducted at a large four-year Northeastern university. The freshmen class at the university consisted of 3,233 students, 5.4% of whom were African American. African American students graduate from the university at an expected rate of 17% after four years, compared with 40% of white students. Because of a high attrition rate as well as other factors such as: low family income, first generation college student, ethnic minority status, or low standardized test scores, African American students were considered at-risk.

Students were identified by faculty in the English Department and through the office of Student Support Services. Faculty and students were provided with written consent forms which offered an overview of the study. Criteria used for student-participants were that students had to be African American, first-time freshmen students from urban high schools who were enrolled in Freshmen English.

The two courses in which students were enrolled were *English Through Writing* and *English Through Literature*. Each course was designed according to the university's curriculum for freshmen English seminar. Courses were designed to focus on the development of students' writing skills through revision and reflection, an understanding of themselves as writers and thinkers, thus instructional methods encouraged students to become more powerful and self-aware writers, readers, and thinkers. The ethnic backgrounds of the student population in the English courses were representative of those within the entire university. That is, each of the ten classes used in the study consisted of approximately 1 African American, 2 Asian, 1 Hispanic, and 21 European American students. Two students in the study were enrolled in the same class.

Participants

The African American students in this study brought different experiences to the college environment. Four of the students were African

American males and seven were African American females. All of the students attended urban high schools that were predominantly African American and Hispanic. Two of the students attended public charter schools, one student attended a public magnet school, and the remaining eight students attended local public schools. Students' high school grade point averages ranged from 2.7 to 3.5 Verbal SAT scores of the students ranged from 428 to 490. Eight of the eleven students completed a university remedial English course due to their low SAT score. Despite their diverse backgrounds students shared a similar desire to have their experiences acknowledged. One of the students explained that she "want[ed] people to know that the transition from high school was difficult." She continued by stating, "Some students don't think about their educational experience. They just accept what's given to them."

Data Collection

Phenomenological interviewing "assum[es] that through dialogue and reflection the quintessential meaning of [participants'] experiences will be revealed" (Rossman & Rallis, 1998, p. 72). This approach was employed to engage eleven African American first-year college students in in-depth conversations about their perceptions of high school literacy preparation. Each student participated in three individually scheduled interviews and one focus group session. Interviews began with a cohort of five students during the fall semester and continued with six students during the spring semester. Each interview engaged students in three 90 minute interviews (Seidman, 1998). The first interview engaged students in a guided conversation in which they reflected on their high school reading and writing experiences. The second interview focused on the student's current attitudes and perceptions of their transition into college level English courses. Specific focus was given to their academic preparation. The third interview included a self-assessment of their perceived ability to meet the demands of the college English course. The final interview also included students' perceptions of factors that contribute to literacy success in college. Twenty-five open-ended questions were developed prior to the interview; however, not all questions were asked of all students.

Data Analysis

Data collection and analysis occurred throughout the study. Consequently, information gathered during the interviews, field notes, and a focus group influenced classroom observations and visa versa. Each interview was audiotaped and transcribed. Prior to the analysis of readings and coding multiple listenings of the interviews were conducted by the researcher (Brown & Gilligan, 1992). The purpose of the four listenings was similar to those of the three interviews, to establish the participants' personal history, develop details on their interactions in literacy environments, and allow for reflection upon those details.

Phenomenological methods of narrative analysis began with broad patterns and themes (Rossman & Rallis, 1998). Themes related to African American students' literacy success formed the basis for the analytic framework. This framework guided the analysis and organization of emergent themes, such as social attitudes toward literacy, general social supports, perceived ability to become literate, and efforts to seek assistance. Emergent themes were retained or eliminated based upon the recurrence of each theme. After each interview, an analytic memorandum was completed to summarize the interview, identify emergent themes, assign initial coding, and identify areas for further investigation.

Trustworthiness

Students' written assignments, interviews, and classroom observations were used to triangulate the findings, thus developing converging lines of inquiry through the data (Lincoln & Guba, 1985; Yin, 1994). Additionally, member checking was used during the second and third interviews. Students reviewed the analytic memos to ensure that emergent themes were accurately identified and to ensure the initial analysis of their experiences.

Results

The comments of African American students in this study provide guidance to teachers and others who aspire to improve the literacy performance of African American students in urban high schools and colleges. Themes resulting from the interviews were divided into three categories: (a) influence of teacher expectation; (b) influence of social comparison; and (c) coping strategies.

Teacher Expectations

Teacher expectation greatly contributed to students' perceptions of literacy preparation. Students reported that teachers in their urban high schools had low expectations of them, did not encourage critical thinking, and used only passive-receptive instructional styles. According to several students, teachers' low expectations resulted in a teaching approach which promoted rote memorization, explicit retelling of comprehension details, and over emphasis on product completion instead of the development of style and voice in written assignments. Tracy, a second semester freshman, elaborated:

In high school all you had to do was read the story. The teacher would go over what she was looking for so when you took the test you just had to remember what she told you earlier. It was so simple! You didn't have to analyze anything. All you had to do was remember what she said in class.

Students attributed their high school academic success to the lack of challenge presented by teachers. As a consequence, students did not think their high school grades were valid. Nicole, a student from an urban charter school, discussed the frustration of receiving inaccurate evaluation from high school teachers and principals:

It's really frustrating when you're in high school and all the teachers and principals said, "You're smart." I didn't feel that smart. I don't know why they felt that way, maybe because I was getting good grades, but it wasn't challenging. So I didn't feel smart. It's when you're challenged and you're doing a good job and then you feel like you've done something.

Another student attributed his college literacy frustration directly to high school teachers' misperceptions and low expectations, "I don't think my high school prepared us enough [for college.] I don't feel like I got the same education, as students in other schools. My high school was just basic."

The students frequently mentioned that race may have influenced the high school teachers' evaluation of their literacy performance. Family members and teachers with high expectations assisted students in developing a more accurate view of their literacy performance and overall capability. Tracy and Mark attended the same high school. Mark made the following comment:

I don't think they (teachers) compared me to other students in my high school. I think they compared me to other minorities at my high school, but if I compared myself to everybody else, I would say I was average. My teacher's would say "Your grades are perfect," but I remember when my grades slipped to a 2.9, my parents lost it!

Tracy agreed that some teachers in their high school had lower expectations for African American students:

Most of my teachers thought my writing skills were great. I got an A on every single paper. It was real easy. But once I had a southern black woman [English teacher]. She took no mess from anyone. She was preparing us for college. All the other teachers were very lax, but she wasn't. If you didn't read, she knew you didn't read. Very few people got A's in her class.

Many students commented on the level of teacher expectation in college, which was notably higher than that experienced in high school.

Students reported differences in teachers' level of academic expectation, instructional styles, and use of course content. The texts introduced in the students' college English classrooms often incorporated various genres, historical time periods, and multiple perspectives of ethnically diverse writers. Students were required to utilize multiple frameworks to analyze implicit themes within complex texts. Teacher-student interactions were also unique in that students were expected to provide individual perspectives of the texts, as opposed to repeating teacher-directed responses.

Students experienced low levels of teacher expectation during high school literacy preparation. In college, the students were forced to reconcile the tension between their high school preparation and college expectations. The literacy experiences of which the students spoke highly were those in which teachers and parents provided students with academically challenging tasks and valued their potential to excel.

Social Comparison   2 — Level of AP, over prep

Social comparison worked as both a hindrance and source of motivation as students began to view literacy as a series of complex interactions that require text analysis, consideration of historical perspectives, and incorporation of personal background. The students indicated that more European American students came to college more prepared to handle the English material. In addition, students often reported frustration with the limited literacy success they experienced in college as compared to the success experienced in high school. They believed themselves to be above average when compared to their high school peers, but low average when compared to college peers.

All students discussed how various high school academic placements can affect college literacy performance. The students perceived high school Advanced Placement (AP) courses as most effective for college literacy preparation. Advanced Placement courses were believed to provide students with reading and writing experiences that paralleled those in college. Increased levels of teacher expectation, additional focus on written assignments, exposure to social and cultural topics, and scaffolding of critical thinking skills were attributes believed to increase the college literacy performance of AP students. Starr, Janet, and Demetrius reflected on the influence AP courses had on high school peers presently enrolled in college:

> I was in a good English class, but it wasn't AP. So I feel that they are a bit more advanced than me. I know AP was the same thing as college English, as far as analyzing stories.

> I had a few friends that were in AP English. That class was more similar to the college structure. I see most of those people, who were in AP classes,

doing a lot better than students who weren't. I think they were pushed more. More was expected of them.

In AP classes they teach you critical thinking. I didn't think about that until now, AP students are more prepared and have more of an advantage.

While students did believe that AP students were better prepared, they also believed that college literacy success is a combination of school district affluence, teacher expectations, and social stereotypes. Students who attributed their literacy development to these factors generally believed they had the intellectual ability but were not provided with the high school resources necessary for college success. Jalil's comment emphasized the impact of teacher stereotypes and student outcomes:

I think money changes the teachers' frame of mind. It's more about spending, and that's related to higher expectations. In my school, teachers might not feel we have the potential to learn and they let it be known to the students. The students might not feel that they have the potential either. So it goes back and forth. But in suburban schools, their schools are better, because it's a fact their students are better prepared for college. I don't think I was prepared for college. Students from Green Valley (affluent school district) come prepared. I have a little more catching up to do. I'm not saying they're brighter, I just know that they know a little bit more than I do.

Some other students internalized their lack of preparation. For students who internalized their lack of preparation, peers who were better prepared for college were believed to be more academically confident and competent. Students also reported that better prepared students were able to negotiate the assignments more easily. As a consequence, these students were often reluctant to participate in peer editing sessions or during classroom discussions for fear that others would believe they did not belong in college. Michelle and Octavia commented:

The other people in my English class seem very confident. When I read their papers I always think, "Oh my, my paper does not compare to this." That's why I hate sending my papers out [for peer editing]. I don't want them to think I don't belong in college, because I feel so much less advanced.

Some of the students read better than I do, at least they sound pretty smart in class. When they read the story, doors open to them that explain it better than when I read it. They just understand it better than I do.

Students struggled to complete assignments with the same level of academic success as their college peers. Many of the students mentioned feeling angry and short-changed by their high schools, but remained motivated to achieve. Matthew explained:

> I feel like I learned absolutely nothing in high school. This is so different from what they actually teach in high school. So, I'm going to have to do a lot of work. I feel like I'm behind and you don't want to feel that you have to catch up to everyone else. I just get so overwhelmed.

Nicole also reflected on the sense of being cheated.

> I feel cheated! In high school you have to take all preparatory and academic classes for college. It's supposed to help you. Then you do well in those classes and you think college is going to be easy. It's so different here. It's nothing like what they taught you in high school.

Interestingly, students did not compare themselves to other African American students. Moreover, students did not discuss their academic performance with other African American peers. The students were able to recognize characteristics of high school preparation that contributed to the academic success of their peers. Students remained frustrated that they were not able to maintain the same academic status that they achieved in high school. Students also capitalized on this frustration to remain motivated to increase their literacy performance.

Coping Strategies in the College Classroom

Despite the frustration of limited high school preparation, once experienced in the college English setting, the students developed a variety of academic and personal strategies to compensate for lack of literacy preparation and to negotiate college teaching styles. Students developed specific strategies based upon their evaluation of personal strengths and weaknesses. Many of these strategies included spending more time on reading and writing assignments. Janet and Matthew noted spending more time on assignments:

> When I read I take a lot more notes. I used to just read. Now I look for the main ideas and write in the margins. I make pencil markings, circles, and stars as I read the text. I write little notes in my notebook. For assignments, I pick out quotes. I analyze [the text] a little more.
>
> In high school I didn't proof read. I used to do my papers in one night. That's how easy I thought they were. I could write a paper in one night and expect to get a good grade on it. Now [in college] I go to the Writing Center. I access other people's opinions.

In-class strategies implemented by students included active listening. Gilbertson (2002) described active listening as a method of "listening-in" on discussion, or classroom dialogue, so that the learner may gain new understanding of the topics. Students who were most apprehensive about their participation in classroom discussions used this technique. Most of the students used active listening to enhance vocabulary and increase knowledge of topic-centered classroom dialogues. Nicole and Tracy explained:

> I think that my vocabulary isn't as advanced as other students. When I talk out loud it doesn't sound as good compared to when I write on paper. When I hear other people talk and use words I pick up on their language. That's the way I learn. I can read a book and look up the words and I still won't learn them. I'll look up a word and two sentences later I'll lose it, but if I hear someone use it out loud I'll understand it. That is very important to me, hearing other people talk.

> You have to be more cautious [in college English]. So, I don't say anything. I don't want to come off looking like I don't know anything. So I don't really participate in class because I'm not sure of myself. I'm not sure if what I'm doing is correct. Of course, the teacher says everyone has their own interpretation of the reading, but if you say something that the other students disagree with they'll jump all over you. So I don't say anything. I just listen.

Conversely Starr and Mark employed verbal participation as a primary strategy to increase their reading and writing skills.

> In high school I never talked. I think that's a big part of being literate being able to express how you feel. In order to do that in English you have to speak up in class, so I do that. I do that more in college since more is expected.

> I question the teacher a lot. If I don't believe in something somebody is explaining in the text I'll question him or her about it. [In high school] I just went along with it because I thought the teacher was always right. Now since I have a variety of books and resources I take a different perspective or a different point of view.

Some students who used active listening as a primary strategy elected to participate in class discussions when the focus was on the African American experience. Tracy stated that she participated during these class discussions because she believed that other students would not challenge her:

> If I feel strongly about something then I'll participate, but for the most part I just listen. I was most confident in class when we were discussing Langston Hughes and the [college] instructor asked should we have black history month. Most of the students in the class said no. They were just being really ignorant. So, I told them how I felt. Of course, they weren't going to argue with me. That was the one time I said something in class.

Starr also spoke about how the choice of classroom text influenced their contribution to classroom dialogue and reading and writing performance:

> [I'm interested in] books that are about trying to change situations. There is one essay we read in freshmen English the author was Alice Walker, *In Search of Our Mothers' Gardens*. I got a B on that paper! I was able to relate to the topic and that helps me bring out more points. If I can't relate to a reading then I don't really see a point in writing about the topic.

As evidenced in these comments, students developed strategies that varied according to their perceived academic strengths and weaknesses. All students reported spending more time on reading and writing assignments than they did in high school. They believed that verbal participation is necessary to remain successful in the college classroom. Most students, however, believed they did not have the verbal skills to participate during class discussion therefore they actively listened. In addition, culturally relevant course content enhanced their participation and confidence.

Discussion

The purpose of the study was to explore literacy experiences contributing to African American college students' reading and writing success. It is likely that some African American first-year college students have dissimilar experiences. For example, the students in this study established strong connections with university-sponsored programs intended to support African American students' success in academic and social endeavors. Additionally, nine of the students participated in a 6-week summer program that required weekly contact with supportive university staff and other underrepresented students. It is possible that African American students who do not have a similar network of support would have different experiences. Nevertheless, the results of this study have implications for educators who teach African American students.

Experiences described by the students reveal that they understand the magnitude of high school literacy preparation and its contribution to literacy performance in college. One of the convincing themes related by the students was the negative consequence of low expectations that some high school teachers have held. The students' perspectives of teacher expectation support the claims that it is not African American students' lack of capacity to learn that limits their academic success, rather it is the quality of instruction that most influences academic outcomes (Hilliard, 2002; Texeira & Christian, 2002).

Students also acknowledged a difference in literacy preparation based on high school English placement and the affluence of various school districts. Participation in AP courses was believed to better prepare students for success in the college classroom because of AP assignments that nurture critical thinking on a variety of topics. Students believed peers from affluent school districts did not suffer from negative stereotypes which hinder exposure to complex texts, critical thinking, and challenging curricula. The students' experience with high levels of anxiety and self-doubt in the belief that faculty and peers may question their legitimacy as college students is consistent with findings of other studies (Nora & Cabrera, 1996; Smedley, Myers, Harrell, 1993; Steele, 1997). Regardless of their limited high school literacy experiences, students remained confident of their ability to achieve literacy success in the college classroom. Student awareness of the difference in preparation and the benefits of high school AP courses is important for improving African American students' literacy performance in the college classroom.

Students' anxieties also influenced their academic strategies in the college classroom. A few students used their verbal skills to demonstrate their understanding of the written assignments. Other students focused their effects on listening to peers during class discussions in hopes of enhancing their literacy skills. Students reported verbally participating during classroom discussion on topics that related to the experience of African Americans. If students are to develop more effective strategies, it is important that they understand the influence of ethnicity, schooling, and teacher expectation on their college performance. Study groups which provide learning strategies, challenging discussions on the expandability of intelligence, and on the historical under preparation of students in urban schools might help students to cope with the anxieties created from lack of adequate literacy preparation provided in many urban schools.

Implications

The perceptions of African American students regarding their high school preparation are critical elements in addressing the literacy crisis of African American students as they enter the college classroom. The data suggest that some high school and college teachers may need to develop instructional strategies which explicitly acknowledge and enhance African American students' literacy potential. Also, curricular changes are needed to provide African American students with equitable levels of expectation, culturally rich text experiences, increased classroom dialogue in which students may include their personal experiences, as well as opportunities to develop critical thinking skills related to reading and writing. It is ultimately the combination of teachers' levels of expectation and curricular modifications that will appropriately prepare African American students for literacy success.

The data suggest that African American students in urban high school settings may not be receiving literacy preparation equal to their peers who attend schools in financially affluent school districts. Despite limited high school literacy preparation, the first-year African American college students in this study used their triumphs and frustrations as motivators to remain academically successful. Educational opportunities made available to students in urban high school and college settings must exemplify a commitment to equal and equitable access to knowledge, skills, and information. African American students must perceive, and know, that their literacy preparation appropriately provides them with the vital skills that lead to endless possibilities toward academic and professional goals. Accomplishing this goal may require uncomfortable dialogues between teachers and students to improve teacher expectation, selection of curricula, and classroom dialogues which enhance critical thinking.

References

Brown, L. M. & Gilligan, C. (1992). *Meeting at the crossroads: Women's psychology and girls' development.* Cambridge, MA: Harvard University Press.

Delpit, L. (1995). *Other peoples' children: Cultural conflict in the classroom.* New York, NY: The New Press.

Delpit, L. (2002). No kinda sense. In L. Delpit & J.K. Dowdy (Eds.), *The skin that we speak: Thoughts on language and culture in the classroom* (pp. 31–48). New York, NY: The New Press.

Farkas, G. (1996). *Human capital or cultural capital: Ethnicity and poverty groups in an urban school district.* New York, NY: A. de Gruyter.

Fine, M. (1987). Silencing in public schools. *Language Arts, 64,* 157–174.

Gilberston, B. (August, 2002). Intake before output: Active listening a key way to reach mutual understanding on issues. *Estate Gazette.*

Harris, V. J. (1990). African American children's literature: The first one hundred years. *Journal of Negro Education, 59,* 540–553.

Hilliard III, A. G. (2002). Language, culture, and the assessment of African American children. In L. Delpit & J. K. Dowdy (Eds.), *The skin that we speak: Thoughts on language and culture in the classroom* (pp. 87–106). New York, NY: The New Press.

Hoyt, J. E. (1999). Remedial education and student attrition. *Community College Review, 27,* 51–72.

Lee, C. D. (1995). Signifying as scaffolding for literacy interpretation. *Journal of Black Psychology, 21,* 357–381.

Lincoln, Y. S., & Guba, E. G. (1985). *Naturalistic inquiry.* Thousand Oaks, CA: Sage.

National Assessment of Educational Progress (2002). *Reading report card for the nation and the states.* Office of Educational Research and Improvement, Washington, D. C.: U.S. Department of Education.

National Center on Education and the Economy. (1990). *America's choice: High skills or low wages!* Rochester, NY: Author.

National Center for Education Statistics (2001). *Digest of Educational Statistics.* Washington, DC: U.S. Government Printing Office.

Nora, A., & Cabrera, A. F. (1996). The role of perceptions of prejudice and discrimination on the adjustment of minority students to college. *Journal of Higher Education, 67,* 119–148.

Oakes, J. (1995). *Keep tracking: How schools structure inequity.* New Haven, CT: Yale University Press.

Perry, T. (2003). Up from the parched earth: Toward a theory of African-American Achievement. In T. Perry, C. Steele, & A. G. Hilliard III (Eds.), *Young, gifted, and black: Promoting high achievement among African-American students* (pp. 1–108). Boston, MA: Beacon Press.

Roach, R., & Finney, K. (2000). Remediation reform. *Black issues in higher education, 17*(12), 16–18

Rossman, G. B., & Rallis, S. F. (1998). *Learning in the field: An introduction to qualitative research*. Thousand Oaks, CA: Sage.

Seidman, J. (1998). *Interviewing as Qualitative Research: A Guide for researchers in education and the social sciences* (2nd ed). New York, NY: Teachers College Press.

Smedley, B.D., Myers, H.F., & Harrell, S.P. (1993). Minority-status stresses and the college adjustment of ethnic minority freshmen. *Journal of Higher Education, 64*, 434–451.

Smitherman, G. (1977). *Talkin and testifyin: The language of Black America*. Boston: Houghton Mifflin.

Steele, C.M. (1997). A threat in the air: How stereotypes shape intellectual identity and performance. *American Psychologist, 52*, 613–629.

Texeira, M. T., & Christian, P. M. (2002). And still they rise: Practical advice for increasing African American enrollments in higher education. *Educational Horizons*, 117–124.

Yin, R. K. (1994). *Case study research: Design and methods*. Thousand Oaks, CA: Sage.

Navigating Early College: Literacy Experiences and Identity Negotiations of Latina/o Students

Holly Hungerford-Kresser

Holly Hungerford-Kresser describes her research on the relationship between student identity development and literacy competencies. She employed a case study approach with five Latina / o students to investigate how these two factors can empower Latina / o students as they transition into the postsecondary environment and negotiate the academic literacies encountered during the first two years of college. In this selection, the author outlines implications from her work and provides suggestions for both college readiness preparation and college academic literacy support.

I spent the last four years of my public school teaching career working with a predominately Latina/o population in an urban high school, and was fortunate to loop with them as their English and AVID (Advancement Via Individual Determination) teacher for the majority of their high school careers. My desire to learn what happened as they left high school and entered college became the fuel for a year-and-a-half-long research study into their early college literacy experiences. During the 2006–2007 school year, I studied five of my former Latina/o students as they graduated and enrolled in college. All of my participants were in the top 10% of peers (e.g., Kirst, 2004). Only 46% of Latina/o students who enroll in college attain a bachelor's degree, and only 10% in the 24–64 year-old age range graduate from four-year institutions (Oseguera, et al., 2009). Statistics tell part of the story, but equally important to understanding the early college literacy negotiations of Latina/os are the lessons to be learned from stories these students tell about their experiences (González, 2002; Solórzano, 1998; Villalpando, 2003).

Background and Need

There are numerous studies that look at connections among identities and literacies, particularly with students. For example, Leander (2002) focused on the stabilization of identities through the production and configuration of identity artifacts. Broughton and Fairbanks (2003) studied connections between middle school girls' literacy practices and identity negotiations, finding that schools did little to focus on the links between the two. Jimènez (2000), in his year-long study of four bilingual classrooms, found that students' literacy knowledge and their construction of biliterate identities had noticeable influence on one another. Schultz (1999) reinforced connections between identity and literacy with her study of urban adolescent females' transition from high school to university. Her work demonstrated the ways in which the girls' identity enactments simultaneously positioned them in and against school. Her conclusions were not unlike those of other literacy researchers—it is imperative that schools (and literacy research) pay attention to the myriad shifting identities students bring with them to school (Broughton & Fairbanks, 2003; Moje, 2004; Schultz, 1999). Scholars such as Bronwyn Williams (2006) highlight similar connections among literacies and identities in students' academic literacies at the university, while others have studied the contexts of academic literacy, in particular college writing, highlighting issues of power and discourse in the ways universities teach students to compose and organize text (Bartholomae, 2003; Bizzell, 2003; Elbow, 1998).

At the same time, the scholarship involving Latina/o students and university contexts highlights the difficulties in adjustment for Latina/os to the culture of the university and offers insights into possibilities for assistance. Meta-analyses of the educational pipeline demonstrate the countless opportunities for exit for Latina/o college students in the current system (Oseguera, et al., 2009; Solórzano, et al., 2005), while more intimate case studies indicate that Latina/os often find the university to be a hostile and alienating environment (González, 2002; Solórzano, 1998; Villalpando, 2003).

In this study, I draw on scholarship that argues for an inclusion of identity in the study of students' literacy development and scholarship that argues for more detailed case studies of Latina/o student experience in university contexts in the hopes of offering implications that might impact the experiences of Latina/o students as they learn the academic literacies associated with the university.

In the field of literacy there are few case studies that look specifically at Latina/os, literacy, and early college, although there is a burgeoning body of work in a variety of fields that focuses on Latina/os in higher education. This qualitative case study, focused on five Latina/o first-generation college students, attempts to fill that gap. Because successful navigation of early college is connected to a navigation of multiple academic literacies (Zamel & Spack, 1998), it is imperative to highlight the early college literacy experiences of Latina/o students.

In addition, the inextricable connections between literacy experiences and identity constructions (Gee, 2000–2001; McCarthey & Moje, 2002; Moje, 2004; Moje, Luke, Davies, & Street, 2009) offer valuable insight for educators and researchers concerned with the preparation of Latina/o urban-schooled students and the retention of these students once they enter the university. As such, this study focused on the following questions: In what ways did participants demonstrate newly acquired academic literacies as they navigated early college experiences? How did these literacies impact their personal identity negotiations?

Conceptual Framework

Sociocultural Views of Literacy

This study draws upon sociocultural theories of literacy (Heath, 1983; Wells, 1999, 2001; Wertsch, 1991), coupled with an additional critical stance, in order to emphasize issues of power embedded in the contexts of literacy learning and identity development (Lewis, Enciso, & Moje, 2007; Moje, Overby, Tysvaer & Morris, 2008). Access and the ability to navigate the cultural codes of a community ultimately determine an individual's place or power within it. Sociocultural theories do not situate literacy within the individual person, making it simply about reading and writing skills; instead, they situate literacy in society so as to emphasize connections between the inter-workings of literacy and power (Gee, 1996). Many use the term *literacies* rather than *literacy*, and often, this broader view of literacies encompasses much more than listening, speaking, reading, and writing. Based on this literature, this study defines literacies as socially situated, and often contested, ways of knowing, valuing, and being in the world (Gee, 2000–2001; New London Group, 1996; Street, 1995, 2003). This study attempts to highlight issues of power associated with students' learning of multiple new literacies as they enter college. Literacy learning does not occur in a vacuum, but in the complex contexts embedded in the many facets of university life. Students learn multiple literacies, both academic and personal, as they strive to find success at the university.

Academic Literacies

Academic literacies are more than an ability to read and write college-level texts; the definition includes multiple approaches to knowledge. Zamel and Spack (1998) argue, "College classrooms have become sites where different languages and cultures intersect, including the various discourses of students, teachers, and researchers. In our experience, the result of this interaction, even when (perhaps because) it involves struggle and conflict, is most often intellectual growth, for these different languages and cultures build on and give shape to one another" (p. ix).

Academic literacies (Zamel & Spack, 1998), are a type of literacy practice, defined by Brandt and Clinton (2002) as "socially regulated, recurrent, and patterned things that people do with literacy as well as the cultural significance they ascribe to those doings" (p. 342). For students to survive or be deemed successful at the university level, they must learn the ins and outs of the university and the multiple discourses that encompass the cultural world of the university—discourses that change from class to class and group to group (Bartholomae, 2003; Bizzell, 2003; Elbow, 1998; Rose, 1998). Arguably, the navigation of these discourses at the university level can lead to a (re)negotiation of various identities, including, but not limited to, the identities associated with being a student. However, it is important to recognize that often these discourses are also mainstream, White, and culturally alienating for many students as they enter the university (Solórzano, et al., 2005; Urrieta, 2007).

Literacies and Identities

Scholars point to clear connections between studies of literacy and studies of identity (McCarthey & Moje, 2002; Moje, 2004). Moje and her colleagues (2009) recently called for an increased theorizing of identity and literacy and the ways in which "the two breathe life into each other" (p. 416). In the field of literacy, it is commonly acknowledged that viewing "literacy practices as social has led many theorists to recognize that people's identities mediate and are mediated by the texts they read, write, and talk about" (Moje, et al., 2009, p. 416). In this study, I draw on the metaphor of "identity as position" as a means of including discourses, narratives, and the power imbedded in these sorts of literacy practices (Moje, et al., 2009). Identities are multiple, fluid, and contingent, based in part on how individuals see themselves as well as how others view the individual; they are continuously being constructed and reconstructed (Gee, 2000–2001; Holland, Lachicotte,

Skinner, & Cain, 1998). Individuals enact particular identities based on their interactions with the literacies of a particular community.

However, at the same time students are positioning themselves, they are also being positioned in particular ways by the discourses they are exposed to at the university. These manifest themselves in conversations, academic assignments, and the university culture, to name a few. Individually answering to the ways they are positioned is not a choice for students because all identity work happens in collectivity, and literacies are profoundly sociocultural; however, the form that response takes is not predetermined. This is where identity work finds agency—in the individual's ability to author himself/herself (Holland, et al., 1998). This give and take contributes to the continuous (re)negotiation of identities; identity enactments are constantly being shaped by the practices of literacy.

Thus, identity matters to a study of literacies because students' literacies shape their identities and their identities shape their literacies (McCarthey & Moje, 2002). The academic literacies students learn and/or use in college are going to shape their identities as students and more importantly, as college-going students. At the same time, these new identities may contradict former identities (e.g., those of student, family member, or friend), which may in turn cause conflict or cause identities to be reevaluated or renegotiated. The ways in which students utilize the literacies of the university position them in particular ways. For example, students might be considered "good" or a "bad" students, "successful" or "struggling," based on their perceived ability to navigate the academic literacies they are exposed to in the university context.

Method

Case Study Research

In this study, I used qualitative research methods (Merriam & Associates, 2002; Mertens, 2005), and specifically case study research (Merriam, 1998; Stake, 1995). Case study is best suited for phenomena that cannot be separated from the context—specific, contextualized, and not able to be understood without the inclusion of rich description. In addition, case studies are meant to resonate with the reader's experience, and it is acknowledged that each reader will bring his/her own knowledge and generalizations to the reading of the case (Merriam, 1998; Stake, 1995).

I believe the data in this study offer an "answer" to Stake's (1995) question: What can be learned from the single case? The participants in this study articulated powerful connections between literacies and identities in their early college lives. Such portraits are imperative to individualizing literacy research (Rubenstein-Avila, 2003). In addition, their relationships, forged through multiple interactions as friends and focus group participants, added depth and breadth to the individual cases, subsequently offering connections across cases. Case studies offer researchers a means of detailing participant journeys, highlighting their unique stories while making beneficial connections for educators. Therefore, while using case study for my own research, I also argue its usefulness as a powerful research framework for analyzing connections between literacies and identities.

Participants

Participants for this study included five (three female, two male) urban-schooled youth who personally identified as Latina/o and enrolled in a four-year college after graduating high school. Four of these students are bilingual and two are biracial. All participants were freshmen and attending school full time. Prior to attending State University (all school and participant names are pseudonyms), they attended Roland High School, a statistically "typical" low-performing urban high school: 79% eligible for free and reduced lunch, 63% Latina/o, 34% African American, and 2% White, with 23% of the student body designated Limited English Proficient. The school did not perform well on state-mandated tests and there was a high turnover of both teachers and administrators. They were my students when I taught high school, and were willing to participate in the study and meet regularly to talk about their early college experiences. In addition, these students also participated in detracking and college-readiness programs in secondary school provided to assist them as they transitioned to the university. For instance, they participated in AVID (Advancement Via Individual Determination), a well-known detracking initiative popular in many school districts nationwide.

Context: State University

State University (SU) is a large university in the Southwest. It is a highly ranked public university and competition for admission to a freshman class is intense and largely impossible for students who rank outside of the top 10%. The number of enrolled students at SU at the start of the 2006/2007 school year was 49,697. According to the university's online *Statistical Handbook*, 56.6% of the students were identified as White, .5% as American Indian, 14.4% Asian American, 8.9% Foreign, .7% Unknown, 3.9% African American, and 15% "Hispanic."

Data Collection and Data Sources

I spent a year and a half with these participants, both informally and formally. We were in contact at least once a week and often daily. As part of my formal research protocol, I conducted case study research

(Merriam, 1998; Stake, 1995), facilitating five focus groups (2–3 hours in length and spread out over the course of two semesters), five impromptu individual interviews with each participant, and detailed individual life history interviews for each student (2–3 hours each in length). Artifacts were collected and included written classroom work, syllabi from all classes, emails, text messages, and access to MySpace and Facebook accounts. Students all used cameras to take photographs of important landmarks and experiences in lieu of keeping journals. A separate interview was conducted with each participant in which he/she described all of the photographs chosen for the photo journal. All focus groups and individual interviews were transcribed in their entirety. Student interactions with professors and teaching assistants were studied through comments on student work, occasional classroom observations, and professor interviews. Additionally, I kept a research journal throughout the process (Merriam & Associates, 2002). All of these data informed my analysis. For this study, I have chosen to focus on recurrent themes I recognized in all types of data, but to use focus group data to illustrate them. The focus group data allow all of the participants' voices to be heard, and thus, makes the most sense for presenting themes.

Data Analysis

Using constant comparative analysis, I examined both individual and focus group interviews throughout the process, allowing categories to emerge from the data (Lincoln & Guba, 1984). Initial codes included categories like "typical difficulties," one I used to label comments about trouble getting out of bed to get to class and knowing how to manage their free time. I also initially used the code "lack of diversity" to indicate instances where participants noted SU was a predominately White university.

After summarizing thoughts across interviews, artifacts, and observations, I conducted member-checking, asking each participant to review my summaries (Merriam & Associates, 2002; Mertens, 2005). For this paper, I was particularly interested in conversations where students used the language they were learning in school, and in the ways they chose to critique their new environment. Initial categories centered in these two areas: "using new academic language" and "critiques of SU." At times these categories overlapped and excerpts were given multiple categorical labels. For instance, often when being critical of SU, participants were simultaneously referencing a lack of diversity. Once I had found all notable examples, I extracted a few examples that seemed indicative of conversations we regularly had about their experiences. I offered these examples to participants in a second member-checking interview, allowing them to clarify, elaborate, and/or choose new examples to study. I then attempted to complicate my understandings gleaned from the constant comparative method—fleshing out details through more complicated analyses using Fairclough's levels of discourse (Fairclough, 1995). When applicable, I analyzed portions of data on local, institutional, and societal levels (Fairclough, 1995; Rogers, 2004).

Fairclough's model is three-tiered on multiple levels: there is always description, interpretation, and explanation of discourse and social practices at three domains of analysis—the local, institutional, and societal (Rogers, 2004). These domains do not exist separately, but are constantly in conversation with the others (Fairclough, 1995; Rogers, 2004). I considered participants' experiences on campus to be emblematic of the local level of discourse, and I specifically looked for evidence of institutional and societal discourses in the transcripts I analyzed. These analyses ultimately provided a means for looking at power and knowledge in the literacies students chose to use in order to articulate their identity negotiations. As a White female researcher working with young Latina/os, a critical level of analysis is mandatory for creating an ethical study that does not ignore power/knowledge relationships at work in the lives of my participants and in our relationships (Frankenberg, 1993; Greene & Abt-Perkins, 2003; McIntyre, 1997).

Findings and Discussion

Data suggest that even early in their first semester, students began to appropriate academic terminology as a means of articulating their thoughts on a variety of topics. They were learning to navigate a variety of academic literacies at the university, and this apprehension of new literacies impacted their identity developments. In addition, data suggest two seemingly contradictory findings with regard to students' identity (re)negotiations: (1) participants developed critical perspectives based on the ways they were positioned by interactions with classmates, professors, and early college literacies. However, they also (2) appeared to internalize some of the very deficit perspectives (Moll, Amanti, Neff, & Gonzalez, 1992; Ronda & Valencia, 1994) they were attempting to argue against. I argue that these two findings are particularly important when considering implications for Latina/os enrolled at the university. Evidence of these findings, which appear throughout focus group and interview transcripts, are highlighted in the following samples.

Positioned by "Others": Critical and Deficit Perspectives

Excerpts from a focus group highlight the findings outlined above. The first provides an example of students developing critical perspectives; it shows them speaking from the voice of a collective "other" when articulating institutional discourses of race and discrimination. When I asked about the major issues affecting Latinos at the university, participants responded:

> *Manuel:* "We're viewed as not making it because of our race."
>
> *Monique:* "Discrimination."
>
> *Manuel:* "Oh well you'll drop out by the end of the semester."

These students realized that deficit perspectives, situated in institutional discourses, exist about Latina/os, negatively position them, and subsequently shape their university experiences. But, rather than allow these discourses of failure, underpinned by deficit thinking, to simply position them, these participants acted with agency by making the discourses visible. Manuel's comment, "You'll drop out by the end of the semester," exemplifies how these students used their developing critical perspectives to work against the discourses that set Latina/os up for attrition rather than matriculation.

In our focus groups, we also discussed participant responses to the negative statements and incidents to which they were exposed. The conversation excerpted below highlights the language participants were learning to help give their ideas credence and structure. This excerpt also shows that issues at the university were discussed in terms of the new academic literacies they were apprehending, including terminology from content area courses (Bartholomae, 2003; Bizzell, 2003; Elbow, 1998). At the same time, this conversation highlights participants' ongoing development of critical perspectives in relation to their new experiences at the university (Delgado Bernal, 2001; Villalpando, 2003):

> *Monique:* "It makes you work harder."
>
> *Manuel:* "What it does to me is it makes me want to prove them wrong. Prove to them that I can make it. I can really make it like they can. You know, it's a way of me being pushed along."
>
> *Idalia:* "Well, supposedly in our sociology class, we're learning that it's basically society that puts all these things on you. This creates self-consciousness. Then you think you can't do it because of what other people, because of what society says."
>
> *Manuel:* "You're influenced basically."
>
> *Monique:* "Yeah, we're brainwashed."
>
> *Aurelo:* "Not only that but . . ."
>
> *Idalia:* "It becomes a part of you supposedly. Like Tom's Theory or whatever . . ."

Looking at this conversation as a local level of discourse, participants mentioned a need to prove people wrong. The group's assumption was that others have presuppositions about what they are capable of achieving because of their race and class. Data suggest that participants perceived these assumptions as deeply engrained in the academic literacies of the university; however, they chose to use the university's discourse to explain their own thoughts. They specifically borrowed the language from the university (academic literacies), to talk about the societal level of discourse they regularly encountered. Idalia clearly articulated what she believed to be a societal discourse when she said, "what society says" (Fairclough, 1995). Not surprisingly, repeated exposure to societal discourses—racialized and classed—caused them to reinterpret success and failure as brainwashing. Literacy learning is not free from issues of power. Identity formations occur in collectivity; students learn who they are by participating in a community (Holland, et al., 1998). Literacy experiences positioned participants in particular ways. In response, students began to position themselves in a variety of ways based on their personal and collective interpretations of their literacy experiences. While attempting to position themselves differently from others' perceptions, they inadvertently began to internalize some of the deficit perspectives they were trying to resist.

A third excerpt from this transcript reinforces the finding that students were developing critical perspectives, in particular a healthy suspicion of others' motives and actions, but simultaneously shows that students often articulated the same deficit perspectives they argued against. Monique, one of two biracial members of the group, noted a personal experience: "I noticed last week, I went with my TA for math, and there was a Hispanic girl beside me. It was me, a Hispanic girl, and another Asian girl. And the TA didn't really talk to the Hispanic girl. He talked mainly to me and the Asian girl and he ignored the Hispanic girl. But, I didn't really think much of it until I got out . . . Was he not paying attention to her because she didn't ask questions? Or was it because he didn't think she would understand it because she doesn't really know that much English? She knows more Spanish and when she talks you can hear her accent really bad. Maybe he didn't really talk to her because of that?"

As they developed increasingly critical perspectives, once seemingly innocuous incidents were no longer thought of as neutral. Monique's comments demonstrated how these Latina/o participants critically reflected upon the interactions they had with professors and peers. Not only did these students speculate about possible reasons for the actions of others, they importantly speculated about how others' perceptions position students, which in turn, assists in shaping their student identities.

The previous excerpt also suggests that participants unwittingly adopted some of the dominant discourses they seemed to be attempting to resist. For instance, Monique, in her discussion of what might be a racist practice, appeared to be perpetuating a deficit perspective that placed more value on her biracial, Latina identity and less value on the identity of the girl, whom she repeatedly referred to as Hispanic. Indeed, she borrowed a racialized, colonial term to discuss her interpretations of a possible racist act. While the term *Hispanic* remains widely used in popular discourse, especially in the Southwestern U.S., it is connected to the U.S. Census and to Spanish Colonizers, rather than the population to which it refers. In contrast, the term *Latina/o*, although not without its own critiques (e.g., MacDonald, 2004), emerged from activist groups within the population. What is perhaps more problematic than the use of terms themselves was Monique's hierarchical distinction between who is Hispanic and her own identity, which she constructs as more privileged. In fact, during interviews, Monique frequently referenced her ability to "pass for White." Despite being raised in both Mexico and Texas, Monique assumed her instructor has placed more value on her position as a White student, and articulated this instance through that perception.

used system to her advantage

Comparisons to "Others": Critical and Deficit Perspectives

Deficit perspectives were often made evident in conversations about differences between their group (my focus group from Roland High School) and the other students on campus. Exposure to students of a different class, especially those who had grown up in the same Central Texas town, led participants to articulate elaborate assumptions and comparisons about their secondary educations and those of their classmates at SU.

Manuel:	"It's so competitive."
Idalia:	"You have to like keep on track."
Manuel:	"But I don't know their grades. I'm assuming they have better grades than me, but I don't actually know."
Holly:	"Why do you assume that?"
Manuel:	"Because they look smarter."
Holly:	"What makes a kid look smarter?"
Idalia:	They are always reading.'
Alex:	[laughing] "They are blondehaired and blue-eyed. Nah, I'm just playing. No, I'm just saying you assume."
Manuel:	"Yeah, it's just like a stereotype I guess."
Holly:	"So the stereotype is that White kids will do better?"
Manuel:	"Yes, and they usually do."

Alex:	"They look like they come from richer schools."
Idalia:	"And they have the background, better training, and more experience."
Manuel:	"Their educational backgrounds are more . . ."
Alex:	"The curriculum they come from was more challenging."
Idalia:	"And their parents who can hire like . . . in high school they probably had like mentors or tutors or whatever. Tutors who taught them how to do things in college, like college work."

The conversation moved quickly from competition to a seemingly light-hearted reference to privilege. Additionally, the participants verified the purported stereotypes, based on their ideas about those students' secondary educations. Though mentioned jokingly, "blonde-haired and blue-eyed" was equated with others "looking smarter." Next, even though they admitted it was a stereotype that White kids do better in school, participants drew conclusions about others' success in early college based on the presumed resources available to them prior to attending SU. Because of wealth and location, these students were positioned to succeed at SU before ever arriving, and if that thought is taken to its logical completion, then conversely, students who did not attend those schools were not positioned to succeed at SU (Holland, et al., 1998; Leander, 2002). Data highlight that new academic literacies were initially difficult for participants to learn, and they assumed, under the guise of competition, that other students who came from "better" high schools did not have the same difficulties (Zamel & Spack, 1998).

In many interviews, participants both reflected and refuted the widely held institutional and societal belief that urban-schooled students are underprepared for the rigors of university academics. Manuel said the following about his high school experience: "I guess at Roland, we focus too much on how to get students out of there, rather than on what we learn." Though he and the others then explained that their education at Roland was not inferior, Manuel then stated:

"The curriculum I think is like the same in all schools, you know, the faculty and teachers try and teach us the same things. It's just that, I guess, the ethnicities, you know Black and Hispanic, the kind of school Roland is, so we don't strive. The teachers, they're there. They can teach you something. But we choose not to. I guess because all our lives we have been knowing, or I guess people have been telling us, you know, just because we are Hispanics, Mexicans or whatever, and Blacks, we can't succeed. But we can be better than Westforest but I think we choose not to because of that."

While arguing that the curriculum at his urban high school was "the same" as the curriculum at other schools, Manuel also placed the blame for a perceived lack of student success squarely on the shoulders of the students themselves. He articulated a societal discourse of minority youth being lazy when he said, "we don't strive," but at the same time, he was aware of being positioned this way by these same discourses. He then spoke of Westforest (a local, wealthy predominately White high school near the lake) and argued that Roland students could "be better" than the students at Westforest at being successful in college, but that they made a choice not to be. Again, there is the apparent contradiction of a developing critical perspective and an articulation of deficit perspectives. The following excerpt was in response to Manuel's statements:

Alex: "Yeah, and they tell us to succeed *even though* we're minorities . . ."

Manuel: "They make us feel inferior."

Alex: "Yeah."

Idalia: "Oh, that's bad."

Again, data suggest that a local instance brought out deep-rooted feelings about racialized and classed societal discourses regarding success and failure (Fairclough, 1995; Rogers, 2004). In this dialogue, the participants also recognized the ability of others to "make" them "feel inferior." As they often did throughout the course of my study, they attempted to interrupt these notions. Their responses, though often couched in the same deficit language to which they had grown accustomed, demonstrates possibility and agency in the lives of Latina/o students. Despite the great resistance they perceived in widely held beliefs about their previous education, participants still focused on authoring themselves in very specific ways at SU. They attempted to position themselves as students capable of using academic literacies and able to identify as college students (Holland, et al., 1998). It is in this agency that I find hope for impacting Latina/o student matriculation at the university.

Implications

This research affirms Latina/o students are both subjects and agents; identities are not stagnant (Urrieta, 2007). They change, shift, and alter (Holland, et al., 1998), and they can be complex and contradictory (Villenas, 2006). At the same time, the literacies that students attempt to navigate at the university are just as complex and contradictory as the identity negotiations they experience. Though this research was conducted with college students, the implications for postsecondary education cannot be neatly separated from implications for secondary education. The early college years are a unique time in young adults' lives, and these issues need to be addressed at both levels. At the secondary level, this research offers insight into the preparation of

Latina/o youth for the academic literacies and cultural issues they will face as they attempt to become members of a new community. At the postsecondary level, it offers possibilities for assisting Latina/o students once they successfully enter the university to be positioned for success, not failure. While a number of studies in a variety of fields have focused on Latina/o youth in secondary contexts (e.g., Valenzuela, 1999), little attention has been paid to the navigation of academic literacies and subsequent identity (re)constructions of Latina/o youth as they struggle to navigate early college life. The ways in which students are positioned affects how they view themselves. There are issues of power attached to students' learning, and the subsequent impact of their university literacy experiences on their identity development affects their ability to be successful in a variety of university contexts.

Throughout their early college literacy experiences, participants in this study could point to discourses (Foucault, 1977) they encountered in university life, including those of race, class, and Whiteness (Frankenberg, 1993; Greene & Abt-Perkins, 2003; McIntyre, 1997). Their conversations frequently highlighted an understanding of the ways in which their positionings impacted their college careers. The semiotic mediators of the university, in the form of academic literacies, "adopted by people to guide their behavior . . . serve to reproduce structures of privilege and the identities, dominant and subordinate defined within them" (Holland, et al., 1998, p. 143) were both underscored and utilized as improvisational tools in the experiences of these students.

However, even with this awareness, through the course of their educations they adopted some of the racist language and ideas they were arguing against. It was common for their conversations to be peppered with anti-Mexican or anti-urban school rhetoric, often subtly inserted into discussions of race and class. In addition to a critical awareness of the discourses that both surround and impact them, this study suggests that students would benefit from tools to analyze their *own* discourses. At times, it appeared they had internalized various societal discourses related to issues such as race and class. While they often seemed capable of recognizing these discourses in their encounters with others, they repeatedly failed to recognize their own internalizations of discourses. It appeared they stopped short of recognizing their own unintentional use of such language, though they were clearly able to point to society's perceptions of them as urban-schooled Latina/os. An emancipatory pedagogy steeped in issues of critical literacy (Freire & Macedo, 1987; Lewison, Flint, & Van Sluys, 2002) would assist both students and teachers. Students would have the opportunity to learn to interrogate their own literacy practices as well as those of the people around them. A framework of critical literacy at both the high school and university levels could offer instruction to educators in how to incorporate critical discussions into multiple content areas and encourage critical questioning as a regular part of students' daily academic lives.

Data suggest that students' ability to acquire the various literacies of their early college experiences regularly figured into their identity constructions. In this study, the university, steeped in issues of power and knowledge, quickly became a difficult cultural world for participants to navigate. As such, their unique perceptions of their own identities altered based on their positionings within the university. These positions were often connected to their perceived successes and failures with new academic literacies encountered at SU. They chose various ways of authoring themselves as students, as Latina/os, as similar and/or different from their classmates, as they were exposed to the new literacies of SU. There was a constant battle between participant perceptions of self and the perceptions dictated by those in positions of power within the cultural world of the university. These were inextricably tied to academic literacies.

Identity ongoing w/ performance

Implications: Secondary Schooling

The data from this study suggest that exposing students to a variety of academic literacies (Zamel & Spack, 1998), the mediating tools of the discourses of the university (Holland, et al., 1998), can be vital to student participation in this new world. This instruction is crucial throughout Latino/o students' schooling, but seemingly more important throughout adolescence (Garcia, 2001). Thus, in secondary education, as neighborhood schools become less and less ethnically and economically mixed (Kozol, 2006), it remains imperative to assist students in negotiations of race and class issues, even when these negotiations exist only as hypothetical situations. These critical thinking skills, along with critical lenses through which they can view the world, are an important piece of adolescent literacy development. Students' exposure to critical literacies provides them with opportunities to interrogate societal practices and positions afforded them within institutions (Freire & Macedo, 1987; Van Sluys, Lewison, & Flint, 2006).

The experiences of these participants at State University suggest that college as we have come to "know" it is about more than academic achievement; it is also about issues of race, class, and disconnect, especially for students not of the dominant culture. The curriculum spaces (Cary, 2006) of the high school, which are epistemological spaces of the production of discourse, knowledge, and power, not merely places where students learn a particular value-free curriculum, offer a place where students might begin this initial exploration, an opportunity for them to develop into more critically minded individuals before entering the university. Thus, the field would benefit from more research that studies the implementation of critical literacy in teacher education classrooms and in on-going staff development practices. Additionally, research that highlights student responses to critical pedagogy would help to inform our practice.

Implications: Postsecondary Education

The university, as an institution, is steeped in issues of power. The discourses inherent in the daily functioning of the university system are deeply ingrained (Cary, 2006; Foucault, 1977; Holland, et al., 1998; Usher & Edwards, 1994). Therefore, this study's findings provide evidence that students, particularly those whose educational backgrounds differ dramatically from the majority of students enrolled at a university, could benefit from an educational philosophy that takes into account the impact college life has on students' personal development and the ways in which the daily interactions within the university impact the identities of students (Holland, et al., 1998). This could be achieved partially through programs already in existence, such as the transition programs available to students at the university, as long as the philosophies of the programs were extended and grounded in a theory of critical literacy (Lewison, et al., 2002; Van Sluys, et al., 2006) or emancipatory education (Freire & Macedo, 1987). The needs of students at the university are connected to issues associated with the culture of power (Delpit, 1995) and the hidden curriculum (Apple, 1990), but these need to be made more transparent to students and include practical techniques for assisting both students and educators in understanding the complexities of student identity transformations.

Therefore, data highlight the possibility of university programs similar to those suggested for secondary schools. In addition to tools for teaching academic literacies, university curricula could offer elements of a critical pedagogy throughout. This focus on university campuses would not just help urban-schooled students learn to navigate the new and difficult literacies of university life. Other students from more privileged backgrounds would also benefit from an ongoing exposure to difference and a forthright conversation confronting and complicating understandings of diversity. The culture of the university could be greatly impacted by such exposure. At the same time, data suggest that professors and other university staff could benefit from similar staff development practices in critical pedagogy advocated for by Lewison, Flint, and Van Sluys (2002).

Implications: Literacy Research

This study, limited in scope to students at one university, has several implications for future research. However, I feel it is important to highlight some limitations of my study. While participants participated in transition programs that surely had an impact, it was beyond the scope of this study to analyze those programs. More analyses that look at these programs are needed. Additionally, the focus of this study was young adult students. Future research might offer portraits of professors and other actors as a means of further developing the field. Finally, this study focuses on a group of Latina/o students at one large, public, competitive state university. Student experiences vary based on a number of factors, including context. More research is needed to understand how student experiences differ in a variety of postsecondary contexts.

While previous literacy research has demonstrated the importance of contextualized, complex accounts that highlight the deep connections between literacies and identities, data from this study suggest that the field would be enhanced by more studies that focus on this link after students' secondary school experiences and throughout the first two years of their college lives. Between research on students' secondary literacy experiences and the literature on adult literacy lies an untapped area of study—young adulthood. For many individuals, this time marks one of the most difficult transition periods in both the literacies of their lives and in the myriad identities negotiated in the various figured worlds in which they participate (Holland, et al., 1998). Additionally, research has shown this to be a time when many minority students leave the university system (Kirst, 2004; Valle, 2007). Findings suggest that students could benefit from a deeper understanding of access and places to negotiate issues of power at the university. This study maintains that a focus on student identity development, coupled with literacy development, as a way to deepen understandings of what is typically understood as "transition" to the university, could help with the retention and matriculation of Latina/o students. Research that highlights what students face on a daily basis as they struggle to navigate the academic literacies of the university is imperative to improving the early college experiences of Latina/os.

References

Apple, M. W. (1990). *Ideology and curriculum.* New York: Routledge.

Bartholomae, D. (2003). Inventing the university. In V. Villanueva (Ed.), *Cross-talk in comp theory: A reader* (2nd ed., pp. 623–653). Urbana, IL: National Council of Teachers of English.

Bizzell, P. (2003). Cognition, convention, and certainty: What we need to know about writing. In V. Villanueva (Ed.), *Cross-talk in comp theory: A reader* (2nd ed., pp. 387–411). Urbana, IL: National Council of Teachers of English.

Brandt, D., & Clinton, K. (2002). Limits of the local: Explaining perspectives on literacy as social practice. *Journal of Literacy Research, 34*(3), 337–356.

Broughton, M. A., & Fairbanks, C. M. (2003). In the middle: Seventh-grade girls' literacy and identity development. *Journal of Adolescent and Adult Literacy, 46*(5), 426–435.

Cary, L. J. (2006). *Curriculum spaces: Discourse, postmodern theory and educational research*. New York: Peter Lang.

Delgado Bernal, D. (2011). Learning and living pedagogies of the home: The mestiza consciousness of Chicana students. *Qualitative Studies in Education, 14*(5), 623–639.

Delpit, L. (1995). *Other people's children*. New York: New Press.

Elbow, P. (1998). Reflections on academic discourse: How it relates to freshmen and colleagues. In V. Zamel & R. Spack (Eds.), *Negotiating academic literacies: Teaching and learning across languages and cultures* (pp. 145–170). Mahwah, NJ: Lawrence Erlbaum.

Fairclough, N. (1995). *Critical discourse analysis: The critical study of language*. New York: Longman.

Frankenberg, R. (1993). *The social construction of Whiteness: White women, race matters*. New York: Routledge.

Freire, P., & Macedo, D. (1987). *Literacy: Reading the word and the world*. South Hadley, MA: Bergin & Harvey Publishers.

Foucault, M. (1977). *Discipline and punish: The birth of the prison*. New York: Vintage.

Garcia, E. E. (2001). *Hispanic education in the United States: Raìces y alas*. Lanham, MD: Rowman & Littlefield Publishers.

Gee, J. P. (1996). *Social linguistics and literacies: Ideology in discourses*. New York: Routledge Falmer.

Gee, J. P. (2000–2001). Identity as an analytic lens for research in education. *Review of Research in Education, 25*, 99–125.

González, K. P. (2002). Campus culture and the experiences of Chicano students in a predominately white university. *Urban Education, 37*(2), 193–218.

Greene, S., & Abt-Perkins, D. (Eds.). (2003). *Making race visible: Literacy research for cultural understanding*. New York: Teacher's College Press.

Heath, S. B. (1983). *Ways with words: Language, life, and work in communities and classrooms*. New York: Cambridge University Press.

Holland, D., Lachicotte, J., Skinner, D., & Cain, C. (1998). *Identity and agency in cultural worlds*. Cambridge, Massachusetts: Harvard University Press.

Jimènez, R. T. (2000). Literacy and the identity development of Latino/a students. *American Educational Research Journal, 37*(4), 971–1000.

Kirst, M. W. (2004). The high school/college disconnect. *Educational Leadership. 62*(3), 51–55.

Kozol, J. (2006). *The shame of a nation: The restoration of apartheid schooling in America*. New York: Crown Publishers.

Leander, K. M. (2002). Locating Latanya: The situated production of identity artifacts in classroom interaction. *Research in the Teaching of English, 37*, 198–250.

Lewis, C., Enciso, P., & Moje, E. (2007). *Reframing sociocultural research on literacy: Identity, agency, and power*. Mahwah, NJ: Erlbaum.

Lewison, M., Flint, A. S., & Van Sluys, K. (2002). Taking on critical literacy: The journey of newcomers and novices. *Language Arts, 79*(5), 382–392.

Lincoln, Y. S., & Guba, E. G. (1984). *Naturalistic inquiry*. Thousand Oaks, CA: Sage.

MacDonald, V. M. (2004). *Latino education in the United States: A narrated history from 1513–2000*. New York: Palgrave Macmillan.

McCarthey, S. J., & Moje, E. B. (2002). Identity matters. *Reading Research Quarterly, 37*(2), 228–238.

McIntyre, A. (1997). *Making meaning of Whiteness: Exploring racial identity with White teachers.* New York: SUNY Press.

Merriam, S. B. (1998). *Qualitative research and case study applications in education.* San Francisco: Jossey-Bass.

Merriam, S. B., & Associates (Eds.). (2002). *Qualitative research in practice: Examples for discussion and analysis.* San Francisco: Jossey-Bass.

Mertens, D. M. (Ed.). (2005). *Research and evaluation in education and psychology: Integrating diversity with quantitative, qualitative, and mixed methods* (2nd ed.). Thousand Oaks, CA: Sage.

Moje, E. B. (2004). Powerful spaces: Tracing the out-of-school literacy spaces of Latino/a youth. In K. Leander & M. Sheely (Eds.), *Space matters: Assertions of space in literacy practice and research* (pp. 15–38). New York: Peter Lang.

Moje, E. B., Luke, A., Davies, B., & Street, B. (2009). Literacy and identity: Examining the metaphors in history and contemporary research. *Reading Research Quarterly, 44*(4), 415–437.

Moje, E. B., Overby, M., Tysvaer, N., & Morris, K. (2008). The complex world of adolescent literacy: Myths, motivations, and mysteries. *Harvard Educational Review, 78*(1), 107–154.

Moll, L. C., Amanti, C., Neff, D. & Gonzalez, N. (1992). Funds of knowledge for teaching: Using a qualitative approach to connect homes and classrooms. *Theory into Practice, 31*(2), 132–141.

New London Group. (1996). A pedagogy of multiliteracies: Designing social futures. *Harvard Educational Review, 66,* 60–92.

Oseguera, L., Locks, A. M., & Vega, I. I. (2009). Increasing Latina/o students' baccalaureate attainment. *Journal of Hispanic Higher Education, 8*(1), 23–53.

Rogers, R. (Ed.). (2004). *An introduction to critical discourse analysis in education.* Mahwah, NJ: Erlbaum.

Ronda, M.A., & Valencia, R.R. (1994). "At-risk" Chicano students: The institutional and communicative life of a category. *Hispanic Journal of Behavioral Sciences, 16*(4), 363–395.

Rose, M. (1998). The language of exclusion: Writing instruction at the university. In V. Zamel & R. Spack (Eds.), *Negotiating academic literacies: Teaching and learning across cultures* (pp. 9–30). Mahwah, NJ: Erlbaum.

Rubenstein-Avila, E. (2003). Facing reality: English language learners in middle school classes. *English Education, 35*(2), 122–136.

Schultz, K. (1999). Identity narratives: Stories from the lives of urban adolescent females. *The Urban Review, 31*(1), 79–106.

Solórzano, D. G. (1998). Critical race theory, race and gender microaggressions, and the experience of Chicana and Chicano scholars. *Qualitative Studies in Education, 11*(1), 121–136.

Solórzano, D. G., Villalpando, O., & Oseguera, L. (2005). Educational inequities and Latina/o undergraduate students in the United States: A critical race analysis of their educational progress. *Journal of Hispanic Higher Education, 4*(3), 272–294.

Stake, R. E. (1995). *The art of case study research.* Thousand Oaks, CA: Sage.

Street, B. (1995). *Social literacies: Critical approaches to literacy development.* New York: Longman.

Street, B. (2003). What's "new" in New Literacy Studies? Critical approaches to literacy in theory and practice. *Current Issues in Comparative Education, 5*(2), 77–91.

Urrieta, L., Jr. (2007). Identity production in figured worlds: How Mexican Americans become Chicano/a activist educators. *The Urban Review, 39*(2), 117–144.

Usher, R., & Edwards, R. (1994). *Postmodernism and education*. New York: Routledge.

Valenzuela, A. (1999). *Subtractive schooling: U.S.-Mexican youth and the politics of caring*. New York: State University Press.

Valle, F. (2007). Closing the achievement gap. *Polimemos: UTSA Leadership and Policy Studies* [On-line]. Available: http://utsa.edu/PoliMemos/thepolimemo.htm

Van Sluys, K., Lewison, M., & Flint, A.S. (2006). Researching critical literacy: A critical study of analysis of classroom discourse. *Journal of Literacy Research, 38*(2), 197–233.

Villalpando, O. (2003). Self-segregation or self-preservation? A critical race theory and Latina/o critical theory analysis of a study of Chicana/o college students. *Qualitative Studies in Education, 16*(5), 619–646.

Villenas, S. (2006). Latina/Chicana feminist postcolonialities: Un/tracking educational actors' interventions. *International of Journal of Qualitative Studies in Education, 19*(5), 659–672.

Wells, G. (Ed.). (1999). *Dialogic inquiry: Toward a sociocultural practice and theory of education*. Cambridge, MA: University Press.

Wells, G. (Ed.). (2001). *Action, talk and text: Learning and teaching through inquiry*. New York: Teachers College Press.

Wertsch, J. V. (1991). A sociocultural approach to socially shared cognition. In L. B. Resnick, J. M. Levine, & S. D. Teasley (Eds.), *Perspectives on socially shared cognition* (pp. 85–100). Washington, DC: American Psychological Association.

Williams, B. T. (2006). Pay attention to the man behind the curtain: The importance of identity in academic writing. *Journal of Adolescent & Adult Literacy, 49*(8), 710–715.

Zamel, V., & Spack, R. (Eds.). (1998). *Negotiating academic literacies: Teaching and learning across languages and cultures*. Mahwah, NJ: Erlbaum.

Reading, Writing, and Assistive Technology: An Integrated Developmental Curriculum for College Students

Ellen Urquhart Engstrom

Ellen Urquhart Engstrom describes a unique offering at Landmark College, which is known nationally for its supportive and innovative programming for students with special needs. Engstrom provides details of a developmental course that integrates reading and writing as augmented by assistive technology. She also presents the curricular model and instruc-

*tional design that are intended to improve each learner's reading compre-
hension, fluency, and accuracy as well as writing competencies.*

In the United States, educators are increasingly concerned about the
numbers of students in secondary schools who do not read well. The
findings of the National Reading Panel (National Institute of Child
Health and Human Development, 2000) encouraged educators and legislators to address the gaps in school curricula and teacher training
in order to effect substantial change in reading outcomes for elementary school-age children. While educators and lawmakers debate the
merits of code-based versus meaning-based instruction for beginning
readers, vast numbers of children continue to move through the schools
and are often placed in remedial reading classes that teach skills in
isolation. As important as it is to address the needs of young children
entering the schools, their older counterparts leave secondary school
without the skills necessary for stable and satisfying employment and
often encounter failure. Ideally, these students should make the leap
from learning to read to reading to learn and should be capable of reading to solve complex and specific problems. In fact, numbers of students
arrive at middle school, high school, or even college unable to access the
complex texts they encounter. Recent National Assessment of Educational Progress (NAEP) test results indicated that few American
students gain the literacy knowledge and skills that would allow them
to successfully engage in higher level problem solving required in
an information age economy (Donahue, Voekl, Campbell, & Mazzeo,
1999).

Failure to acquire academic literacy has many causes. The following are some of them:

- Reading instruction stops once students move into middle school,
  even if students had elementary school instruction that included
  phonics, fluency training, and comprehension strategies. Instead,
  middle school teachers are focused on teaching subject area content (Greenleaf, Schoenbach, Cziko, & Mueller, 2001).

- Some reading difficulties are characterized by slow and halting
  processing of text, but they are not captured on tests of single-word
  decoding. As a result, these students go undiagnosed and receive
  no remediation (Berninger, Abbott, Billingsley, & Nagy, 2001).

- Students with poor single-word decoding skills or poor fluency read
  far less than their reading-enabled peers, which results in a depri-
  vation of background knowledge. Comprehension research has
  shown that background knowledge provides a scaffold for the acquisition of new knowledge (Mastropieri & Scruggs, 1997). Poverty
  of background knowledge limits future learning.

- A lack of prior reading experience affects a student's ability to learn academic writing. Expressing concepts in writing requires the coordination of multiple language systems. Poor decoding leads to poor spelling, which becomes a barrier to fluent writing. Lack of experience with texts deprives students of the models they need to organize and structure their writing.

The recent emergence of assistive technology encourages researchers and educators to explore its possible benefits for students who lack the reading and writing skills necessary for success in higher education (Anderson-Inman & Szymanski, 1999; Higgins & Raskind, 1997). Two major reviews of the research in assistive technology (MacArthur, Ferretti, Okolo, & Cavalier, 2001; Okolo, Cavalier, Ferretti, & MacArthur, 2000) confirmed the utility of computer-assisted instruction and synthesized speech feedback to improve students' phonemic awareness and decoding skills, as well as the benefits of electronic texts to enhance comprehension by compensating for reading difficulties. Assistive technologies include text-to-speech software, word-processing programs, voice-recognition software, and software for organizing ideas. While these technologies are relatively new, they hold the promise of bridging the gap between a student's needs and abilities. They may let a student with relatively low decoding skills access course texts through a text reader. A student with very low writing output but good oral language can use voice recognition software. Technology offers students the opportunity to access higher education that their previous school experience had denied them.

Research on the outcomes of developmental education in community colleges has indicated that developmental reading and writing courses improve student achievement in postsecondary courses (Napoli & Hiltner, 1993). A study of a collaborative effort between English and reading courses at a California community college suggested that integrating these two developmental courses had a positive effect on student academic outcomes in subsequent semesters (Office of Institutional Research and Planning, 1995). In their comprehensive review of the literature on teaching comprehension strategies, Mastropieri and Scruggs (1997) documented the positive benefits of multipass reading strategies on students' reading comprehension.

This article explains how a combination of sound instructional strategies for improving reading comprehension, accuracy, fluency, and writing with assistive technology helped students make gains beyond what they had achieved previously.

The Context

At Landmark College, a college designed exclusively for students with learning disabilities and attentional disorders, many students are able and motivated to get a college education, but they lack the fundamental reading and writing skills necessary for success. Thus, the education program that they receive at Landmark College includes a precredit developmental skills program, where students learn academic skills in small classes that teach specific strategies for active reading, note taking, and writing. The developmental skills curriculum is designed to develop a broad range of skills in students whose learning profiles vary. Some students have weaknesses in comprehension or decoding. Students with attention-deficit disorder may have gaps in their decoding, encoding, and comprehension performance due to inconsistent focus or poor executive coordination of multiple language processes (Berninger et al., 2001). Some students in the precredit curriculum are limited by inaccurate or slow reading. Students entering the developmental skills program frequently have reading scores between grade levels 5.0 and 8.0, as measured by the Gray Oral Reading Test (GORT–3). In addition, the reading rate of these students frequently falls below grade level 5.0. It is common for students to express frustration about their problems with reading, and how these problems have limited their prior academic progress. Although students receive intensive instruction in reading and study skills strategies as well as the writing process, direct instruction in word-level skills (decoding) and selective use of assistive technology could be expected to help students increase their reading accuracy, speed, and comprehension of the course material.

The Curriculum

The purpose of the integrated curriculum was to address the multifaceted task of building language skills through three strands of instruction. Students needed access and experience with a variety of texts in order to build background knowledge and improve their comprehension skills. Also, they needed to develop further their understanding of text structures through writing. Students with poor decoding or fluency skills needed the opportunity to use text-to-speech software to assist their reading. Learning technology to support their study skills could remove the typical barriers to writing and organization that plague students with language-based learning disabilities. Students whose test results indicated specific deficits in phonological awareness, decoding, and fluency needed direct instruction to address these difficulties. The precredit curriculum consisted of a developmental reading course, a developmental writing course, and skills support sessions (tutorials).

The Reading Course

A primary objective of the reading course was teaching the strategy of active reading (Arieta, 2001). Active reading combines a series of

Table 1. Reading Course Elements

Active Reading	Assistive Technology
Paragraphs	Kurzweil 3000
• Paragraph unity	• Highlighting
• Topic sentences	• Extracting highlights
• Supporting details	• Adding notes
Textbooks	• Extracting notes
• Previewing a textbook chapter	• Reading the web
• Setting up a note-taking system	• Spelling prediction
• Reading for content	• Write/speak feature
Multiparagraph articles	Inspiration
• Extracting main ideas and supporting details	• Brainstorming
• Extractions (using Kurzweil 3000) to create an outline	• Concept mapping
• Recognizing essay patterns	• Sorting and organizing ideas
Longer articles	• Note taking
• Recognizing topic shifts within the article	• Exporting outlines to a word-processing program
• Chunking	
• Creating a summary	

strategies into a process for comprehending and retaining information in written text. The active reading process mirrors the brain's memory process, offering the reader an effective system for comprehending and remembering text. Active reading steps include prereading, reading, highlighting, margin noting, chunking sections of text, and summarizing the text. By strategically combining a text reader with a visual organizer and a word processor, the software helps a student to accomplish active reading by eliminating the need for word-by-word decoding, freeing active working memory for comprehension. Students have the benefit of (a) hearing and seeing their texts, (b) visually organizing the concepts within the reading in a concept map, and (c) transferring those concepts into essay form.

Students were able to use Kurzweil 3000, a text-to-speech software program, for prereading, reading, highlighting, and margin noting. They used Inspiration software for mapping or outlining key elements of the text. Exporting these elements into a word processor facilitated drafting of a summary, while the word processor, combined with Kurzweil 3000, assisted in editing and proofreading the summary. The reading course taught the reading and study skills described in Table 1.

Table 2. Writing Course Elements

Writing	Assistive Technology
Sentence structure	Word-processing program
• Basic parts of speech	• Spell checker
• Sentence expanders	• Reduce the need for handwriting
Paragraph structure	• Use of revision toolbar to assist revisions and
• Paragraph unity	proofreading
• Topic sentences	Inspiration
• Supporting details	• Brainstorming
Writing process	• Sorting and organizing ideas
• Generating ideas	• Export feature to aid in drafting
• Sorting ideas	
• Drafting	
• Revising	
• Proofreading	
Rhetorical patterns	

The Writing Course

The purpose of the developmental writing course was to teach explicitly the writing skills and strategies that students need to know in order to read and write more effectively in academic settings (see Table 2). The course was designed to incorporate thematic connections from one unit to another, as well as to include the forms, structures, and process strategies introduced in the reading course.

The Integration of the Reading and Writing Courses

The reading and writing courses were organized so that students would learn text patterns simultaneously. Therefore, while students learned how to write a narrative essay, they also learned how to read narrative essays for content and structure. The timeline of the two courses were coordinated as shown in Table 3.

The Skills Support Systems

Finally, the skills support sessions provided a menu of practices individualized to fit student profiles and skills needs. This menu included word recognition; fluency; spelling; and activities to reinforce sentence, paragraph, and essay writing. The *Wilson Reading System* (Wilson, 1988) provided the materials for instruction in word

Table 3. Integrated Writing and Reading Curriculum

	Writing	*Reading*

Weeks 1–3	Syllabus terms
	• Parts of speech
	• Sentence structure —
	  isolated and short
	  paragraphs
		Decoding
		• Establish procedures
		Comprehension
		• Paragraph unity
		Kurzweil 3000 basics

Weeks 4–5	Description and narration
	• Writing descriptive
	  paragraphs
	• Writing personal
	  narratives
		Paragraph structure
		• Main ideas
		• Supporting details
		Reading
		• Personal narratives
		• Finding the central idea of a
		  passage

Weeks 6–7	Process
	• Writing: "How to"
		Paragraph structure
		• Major and minor details
		• Transition words
		Reading
		• Process articles
		• Textbooks: previewing and
		  setting up a note-taking
		  system
		Technology
		• Inspiration software

Weeks 8–10	Definition • Writing: "What is . . . .?" • Summary writing	Reading • What is terrorism? • Active reading • Margin noting • Summarizing Study skills • Test preparation
Weeks 9–11	Argument	Introduction to critical reading • The elements of reason Reading • Persuasive essay
Weeks 12–15	Shared topic: Stem cell research • Final essay Portfolio revision	Shared topic: Stem cell research • PowerPoint presentation Final exam

recognition, spelling, and fluency. In addition, *Great Leaps Reading* (Campbell, 1998) was used for students who needed to increase their reading rate.

The Lessons

Lessons to improve reading skills were designed to be multifaceted. Because the active reading strategy was taught at the beginning of the course, its use was reinforced with every reading that was assigned. In addition, the characteristics of each text pattern needed to be emphasized. All of the readings were available in both hard copy and digitized form so that students could access them through either means. In order for a screen reader to read text, the text must be scanned and saved as a graphic. The great advantage of offering texts in both hard copy and digitized form is that students who have difficulty reading accurately and fluently have the opportunity to read the same text that students with more fluent reading skills have. The availability of digitized text and screen readers makes it possible for students with reading difficulties to keep up with and work together with students without those difficulties.

One example of a text used in the curriculum is the narrative essay, "The Dyslexic CEO" (Mathewson, 2001). In this short narrative, the author tells the story of how he became a writer despite his dyslexia. The author's message is that the use of technology was crucial to his success. Before students read this essay, they learn that an author of a narrative has a purpose, a message (or central idea), and a story to support the message. While reading personal narratives in their reading class, students were composing their own personal narratives in their writing class, taking care to include their purpose, their central idea, and their story to bear out their purpose and message. While highlighting and annotating the text of "The Dyslexic CEO" helped students to see where in the essay the author states his central idea and how he organizes his story, the use of an accompanying graphic organizer made those connections even clearer. As an aid to understanding and summarizing, students completed the graphic shown in Figure 1.

An important feature of Inspiration software is that as the user completes a graphic organizer such as that in Figure 1, he or she simultaneously creates an outline, which can be viewed by toggling to the outline side of the program. Therefore, once students completed the organizer they had also created an outline of the summary. Working in a visual mode enables many students to identify and understand the concepts and structure of their reading. Toggling between the diagram and outline views helps students learn and understand outlining, and it also prepares them for drafting a written summary. Table 4 is a sample outline of the graphic in Figure 1 that shows how ideas can be expanded and organized. By expanding and exporting this outline to a

Figure 1. Graphic Organizer Used in Writing Class

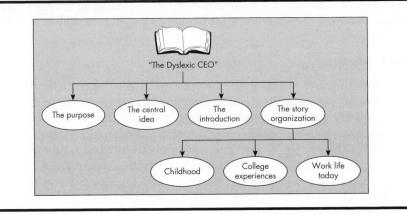

word processor, each student had a draft of a succinct paragraph summary of the narrative essay, "The Dyslexic CEO." The features of the word-processing program, including spell check, grammar check, and the use of the revision toolbar to aid in editing, completed the active reading process.

Tracking the Students

Eight students enrolled in this integrated curriculum. In order to track their progress, all students were given the following battery of reading tests at the beginning of their first semester and again at the end of their participation in the curriculum: the GORT–3, the Comprehensive Test of Phonological Processing (C-TOPP), the Wilson Assessment of Decoding and Encoding (WADE; Wilson, 1998), and the word-attack subtest of the Woodcock–Johnson Psycho-Educational Battery–Revised (WJ–R). In addition, students participated in a structured interview to track the confidence they had in their comprehension over time (Stone, 1994). While the size of the student cohort that piloted this curriculum was too small to draw definitive conclusions about the efficacy of integrated instruction, the positive outcomes for these students suggest the importance of combining reading and writing strategy instruction with assistive technology support and word-level instruction in a way that scaffolds the students' total written language development.

The Students

The eight students enrolled in this project were all new students to Landmark College. Of the eight students, four enrolled in Landmark

Table 4. Outline of "The Dyslexic CEO"

"The Dyslexic CEO"

I. The purpose
To educate others about dyslexia and how to overcome it with technology.

II. The central idea
If you work very hard on your weakness and use technology, you can be successful.

III. The introduction
The article starts by telling about John Chambers, the CEO of CISCO.

IV. The story organization
A. Childhood
The author worked with his mom on spelling for five years. He didn't get better. He spent hours on spelling with no improvement.
B. College experiences
He didn't have enough technology, but he had some. He had to use a dictionary.
C. Work life today
Now James Mathewson uses lots of technology strategies to help him in his work as a writer and editor.

College in the fall following their high school graduations; the other four students had attended other post-secondary institutions before coming to Landmark College. All of the students identified some area of reading as being problematic for them. All had completed the fall semester, while seven of the eight returned for the spring semester. One student left Landmark College for financial reasons. The other seven students continued in the precredit curriculum for another semester. Following that semester, one student chose not to pursue college and left. Therefore, six of the original eight students entered the credit program at Landmark College. One of the six transferred to another college after four semesters at Landmark College, while five remained at Landmark College. Three of these students have graduated from Landmark College, while two others are near graduation at this writing. What follows are accounts of two of the students' experiences in the curriculum.

Case Study 1: Mark

Mark (pseudonym) was extremely motivated, but he had a history of struggling in school. He had attended a public high school, where he had received special education services that consisted of spending time each day in a resource room. He never received any extra help or tutoring in decoding or encoding. On his application for admission, Mark stated that he had difficulty with reading comprehension and that his goal was to improve his reading. Mark's testing showed that he had difficulty with decoding and his reading rate was slow. On the GORT–3, Mark tested below the first percentile in rate and at the second percentile in accuracy. Mark's rapid-naming score on the C-TOPP fell in the low range, but his phonological awareness and phonological memory fell within the average range. His WADE scores indicated that he had an inconsistent pattern of word attack as well as much hesitation before reading the words. Mark's grade-level score on the word-attack subtest of the WJ–R was 4.4. On his initial comprehension confidence interview, Mark ranked his comprehension as "fair," and he stated that his primary comprehension strategy was to read the passage multiple times.

Mark was an enthusiastic, motivated student throughout his participation in the curriculum. He embraced highlighting for main ideas, paraphrasing to make margin notes, and using visual organizers to help him see patterns in various texts, including his own writing. Once he began instruction in the *Wilson Reading System,* he realized that he had gaps in his decoding ability. The scaffolded approach to learning word, text, and writing patterns seemed to allow Mark to make the functional connections between these areas of language instruction. He also found that the use of a text reader was extremely helpful for longer reading assignments, because it saved him time and it gave him confidence that he was able to read every word. In his final comprehension confidence interview, Mark listed his confidence in understanding the passage he read as a 10 (highest rank). He said he always uses a pen or highlighter when he reads in order to highlight keywords or phrases, make margin notes, or break up longer words into syllables for decoding. When asked how he knew if he understood the passage, Mark said, "My brain absorbs the information. I can relate to each concept. If I can get an overall sense of the reading, I feel I understand." Despite the well-known difficulty of improving fluency in older students, Mark's rate of reading improved by the end of the yearlong curriculum. His GORT–3 rate rose from <1% to 5% from September to May. His accuracy and comprehension scores improved as well: accuracy rose from 2% to 5%, while comprehension rose from 5% to 37%. Mark chose to continue his *Wilson Reading* instruction for an additional year while he pursued his associate's degree. Mark achieved honors grades, and he plans to finish his BA at a four-year college.

Case Study 2: Bob

Bob (pseudonym) was admitted to Landmark College directly after graduating from high school. Like Mark, Bob had experienced difficulty with academic tasks in high school, notably reading. However, Bob's profile differed substantially from Mark's. Bob was diagnosed with attention-deficit hyperactivity disorder, and his hyperactivity, combined with his inattention, resulted in a learning profile that was not characterized by the systematic errors typical of students with language-based learning disabilities. Bob exhibited a more random pattern of errors likely brought about by inattention and distractibility. Nonetheless, Bob's initial testing reflected the academic difficulties he described on his application for admission. On the GORT–3, Bob's rate was 25%, while his accuracy was 9%. His comprehension score was 2%. On the word-attack subtest of the WJ–R, Bob scored at grade level 5.5. Bob's C-TOPP scores placed him above 50% on phonological awareness, phonological memory, and rapid naming. When asked, "How well do you think you understood this passage?" Bob replied, "Good." When asked, "On a scale of 1 to 10, how sure are you that you understand this passage?" Bob rated his understanding at 7. Asked, "How can you tell you understood the passage that well?" Bob replied, "I have to be tested to be sure. I find I think I did well, then I can't do the test."

Like Mark, Bob was a highly motivated student who came to Landmark College to find ways to ensure his academic success. Like Mark, Bob attended his classes and his skills support sessions regularly. Though less enthusiastic than Mark, Bob agreed to use the study skills and writing strategies he learned in his developmental reading and writing classes. He made rapid progress in both reading and spelling using the *Wilson Reading System*. Bob identified himself as a visual learner, and he responded well to using concept maps as a way to make sense out of text patterns. He also identified visualization as a powerful comprehension tool. Bob's fluency work was highly successful, but his success was the direct opposite of Mark's. Bob began the year with a rapid reading rate but a high number of errors on the *Great Leaps Reading* fluency passages. As the academic year wore on, Bob's rate remained high while his errors decreased dramatically. At the year's end, Bob showed improvement in his ability to read and spell real and nonsense words on the WADE, his word-attack score on the WJ–R jumped to grade level 11.9, and his GORT–3 scores improved in accuracy (from 9% to 25%) and in comprehension (from 2% to 50%). His GORT–3 rate score dropped from 25% to 16%, which may reflect his efforts to slow down and be more accurate. In his final comprehension confidence interview, Bob explained that he felt confident that he could get the broad concepts in his reading without highlighting and margin noting, but to grasp the more technical details, he needed to use the active reading and note-taking strategies.

Assistive Technology Aids Comprehension

Introducing assistive technology support into an integrated reading and writing skills curriculum was an attempt to address a broad range of difficulties that young adults face in their effort to become skillful readers and students. Mark and Bob entered the program with low reading levels that arose from their distinct learning profiles. While it is possible to individualize a curriculum in a small, structured class of eight, the purpose of the study was to explore how to build reading proficiency in a diverse group of students while engaging them in academically challenging work that makes the structure of language more transparent. By introducing students to a variety of text structures through reading and writing, we can scaffold the learning experience so that students gain a deeper understanding of the conceptual base of written language. By supporting text structure instruction with a text reader and the software to visually represent the concepts and patterns in the text, we expand the ways in which students can understand and process text. By giving students of diverse learning profiles the opportunity to learn word structure through exposure to sounds, syllable patterns, and word analysis, we give them the tools to automatize their word recognition and to free them to focus on understanding written language.

Students' reading skills and capabilities significantly affect what they can accomplish when faced with the complex demands of academic reading. Successful comprehension of various texts requires mastery of a complex set of interpretive mental activities as well as a solid foundation for rapid and accurate single-word recognition. To make progress toward this end, we must give our students opportunities to participate in a variety of reading and writing experiences, understand the multifaceted process of reading, and be active observers of their own reading styles so that they can develop the skills, strategies, and confidence to be successful students.

References

Anderson-Inman, L., & Szymanski, M. (1999). Computer-supported studying: Stories of successful transition to postsecondary education. *Career Development for Exceptional Individuals, 22,* 185–212.

Arieta, C. (2001). College active reading skills. In S. Strothman (Ed.), *Promoting academic success for students with learning disabilities* (pp. 83–104). Putney, VT: Landmark College.

Berninger, V., Abbott, R., Billingsley, F., & Nagy, W. (2001). Processes underlying timing and fluency of reading: Efficiency, automaticity, coordination, and morphological awareness. In M. Wolf (Ed.), *Dyslexia, fluency, and the brain* (pp. 383–414). Timonium, MD: York Press.

Campbell, K. (1998). *Great leaps reading.* Micanopy, FL: Diarmuid.

Donahue, P. L., Voekl, K. E., Campbell, J. R., & Mazzeo, J. (1999). *The NAEP 1998 reading report card for the nation and the states.* Washington, DC: National Center for Education Statistics.

Greenleaf, C., Schoenbach, R., Cziko, C., & Mueller, F.(2001). Apprenticing adolescent readers to academic literacy. *Harvard Educational Review, 71*(1), 79–129.

Higgins, E., & Raskind, M. (1997) The compensatory effectiveness of optical character recognition/speech synthesis on reading comprehension of post-secondary students with learning disabilities. *Learning Disabilities, 8*(2), 75–87.

MacArthur, C. A., Ferretti, R. P., Okolo, C. M., & Cavalier, A. R. (2001). Technology applications for students with literacy problems: A critical review. *Elementary School Journal, 101*, 273–301.

Mastropieri, M. A., & Scruggs, T. E. (1997). Best practices in promoting reading comprehension in students with learning disabilities: 1976 to 1996. *Remedial and Special Education, 18*, 197–214.

Mathewson, J. (2001, July). The dyslexic CEO. *Computer User.* Retrieved March 16, 2005, from http://www.ComputerUser.com/articles/2007,3,1,1,0701,01 .html

Napoli, A.R., & Hiltner, G. (1993). An evaluation of developmental reading instruction. *Journal of Developmental Education, 17*(1), 14–16, 18, 20.

National Institute of Child Health and Human Development. (2000). *Report of the National Reading Panel. Teaching children to read: An evidence-based assessment of the scientific research literature on reading and its implications for reading instruction.* (NIH Publication No. 00–4769). Washington, DC: U.S. Government Printing Office.

Office of Institutional Research and Planning. (1995). *Project Success: An examination of a collaborative effect in English course work.* Retrieved March 17, 2005, from http://www.gccc.net/research/reports/projsux.pdf

Okolo, C. M., Cavalier, A. R., Ferretti, R. F., & MacArthur, C. A. (2000). *Technology and literacy for students with disabilities: A synthesis of 20 years of research.* Paper presented at the annual meeting of the American Educational Research Association, New Orleans, LA.

Stone, N.R. (1994). Self-evaluation and self-motivation for college developmental readers. *Research and Teaching in Developmental Education, 10*(2), 53–62.

Wilson, B. (1988). *The Wilson reading system.* Milbury, MA: Wilson Language Training.

Wilson, B. (1998). *Wilson assessment of decoding and encoding.* Milbury, MA: Wilson Language Training.

4

Structuring Postsecondary Reading

Introduction

Since the first edition of *Teaching Developmental Reading* was released a decade ago, the American education scene from the earliest grades through graduate school has become enmeshed in a reform movement unlike any seen before. College reading instruction has not been immune to these reform efforts. Within this ever-changing context we are able to share program and class designs that demonstrate great promise for the years ahead.

The chapter begins with a historically significant work by James R. King, Norman A. Stahl, and William G. Brozo that examines a model from the early 1980s in which the authors built upon a "language experience" theory to integrate college reading and study skills instruction within the university context. The course drew on models from the 1960s and 1970s, which were precursors to current models such as academic contextualized instruction and FYE courses. The article shows, in a sense, that rather than having radically new programs emerge in the college reading and learning strategy field, we have been building upon over a century of pedagogical theory, research, and practice.

Next is an article by Sonya L. Armstrong and Mary Newman proposing that the model of intertextuality provides a theoretical construct for the design of college reading courses and programs in both university and community college settings. Moving beyond the theoretical underpinnings of the model, the authors describe two exemplar course designs for this scaffolded, schema-building approach that employ the power of intertextuality.

The article that follows, by Katie Hern, highlights the work being undertaken and the resultant successes through acceleration efforts supported by the California Acceleration Project. Hern explains the rationale for acceleration by describing the levels of attrition that have plagued developmental education programs over the years, and then demonstrates how the acceleration model is a viable answer to the problem. It is important for developmental reading professionals to stay abreast of current work being done on acceleration regardless of the discipline; because developmental mathematics has been doing this work for some time, program descriptions for both fields are provided here.

Next, Sugie Goen-Salter's article describes another reform initiative, San Francisco State University's Integrated Reading and Writing (IRW) Program. She positions her description of the program's development in the context of a long-standing effort to reduce the need for developmental coursework. IRW programming has a long history, beginning with its roots at the University of Pittsburgh, but is currently attracting new attention as a form of acceleration. Goen-Salter provides details on the program's successes, and provides insights on the need for resources to ensure the successes of such programming.

The concept of integrated learning communities can be traced back to several West Coast universities in the late 1960s and early 1970s. Yet even as the concept was brought into the field of developmental education and college reading and learning instruction, there has been a dearth of high-quality research on the impact of the model. The work of Michael Weiss, Mary Visher, Heather Wathington, Jed Teres, and Emily Schneider as presented here in the research brief of a larger technical report highlights the findings of a rigorous study at the community college level that examines the results of pairing a developmental reading course with a college success course.

Finally, the chapter concludes with an abstracted version of a technical report that highlights the foundation for contextualized teaching and learning as well as the description of three community college reading programs that are formulated upon the model. Elaine Baker, Laura Hope, and Kelley Karandjeff also highlight considerations for the implementation of Contextualized Teaching and Learning (CTL) programs.

Additional Readings

Bartholomae, D., & Petrosky, A. (1986). *Facts, artifacts and counterfacts: Theory and method for a reading and writing course*. Upper Montclair, NJ: Boynton Cook.

Beyer, T. P. (1923). A college course in general reading. *English Journal, 12*, 377–383.

Bosley, L. (2008). "I don't teach reading": Critical reading instruction in composition courses. *Literacy Research and Instruction, 47*(4), 285–308.

Edgecombe, N., Jaggars, S. S., Baker, E. D., & Bailey, T. (2013). Acceleration through a holistic support model: An implementation and outcome analysis of FastStart@CCD. New York, NY: Columbia University, Teacher's College, Community College Research Center.

Goen, S., & Gillotte-Tropp, H. (2003). Integrating reading and writing: A response to the basic writing 'crisis.'" *Journal of Basic Writing, 22*(2), 90–113.

Greenleaf, C. L., Litman, C., Hanson, T. L., Rosen, R., Boscardin, C. K., Herman, J., Schneider, S. A., Madden, S., & Jones, B. (2011). Integrating literacy and science in biology: Teaching and learning impacts of reading apprenticeship professional development. *American Educational Research Journal, 48*, 647–717.

Henry, J. (1995). *If not now: Developmental readers in the college classroom*. Portsmouth, NH: Heinemann.

Hilton, J. L., Wilcox, B., Morrison, T. G., & Wiley, D. A. (2010). Effects of various methods of assigning and evaluating required reading in one general education course. *Journal of College Reading and Learning, 41*(1), 7–27.

Hodges, R., & Agee, K. S. (2009). Program management. In R. F. Flippo & D. C. Caverly (Eds.), *Handbook of college reading and study strategy research* (2nd ed., pp. 351–378). New York, NY: Routledge.

Laufgraben, J. L. (2006). *Common reading programs: Going beyond the book* (Monograph No. 44). Columbia, SC: University of South Carolina, National Resource Center for the First-Year Experience and Students in Transition.

Nadelson, S. G., & Nadelson, L. S. (2012). In search of the right book: Considerations in common read book selection. *Journal of College Reading and Learning, 43*(1), 60–66.

Nodine, T., Dadgar, M., Venezia, A., & Braco, K. R. (2013). *Acceleration in developmental education*. San Francisco, CA: West Ed.

Rey, V. M., & Karstadt, R. (2006). Strategies in teaching paired reading with content courses. *NADE Digest, 2*(1), 29–33.

Simpson, M. L., Hynd, C., Nist, S. L., & Burrell, K. (1997). College reading and learning academic assistance programs. *Educational Psychology Review, 9*, 39–87.

Simpson, M. L. (2002). Program evaluation studies: Strategic learning delivery model suggestions. *Journal of Developmental Education, 26*, 2–10.

Historically Significant Work

Integrating Study Skills and Orientation Courses

James R. King, Norman A. Stahl, and William G. Brozo

James R. King, Norman A. Stahl, and William G. Brozo begin with two questions that still concern postsecondary educators more than a quarter century after this article was published. How can we "ready underprepared freshmen for the rigors of college work"? How can we keep these students long enough for them to adapt to this new academic environment? With the model as it evolved at several institutions, campus units cooperated so that a group of incoming freshmen who had previously selected a section of

College Reading and Study Skills would be designated simultaneously as an orientation group. Using this model for structuring instruction, skills and strategies were taught in a manner that immersed students in the "university milieu and surroundings of the campus community."

Many college students of the 1980s, like their predecessors of the 1960s and 1970s, require additional academic preparation and training before they are ready for college level courses; hence, postsecondary educators must overcome two interrelated challenges. One pressing issue is how to ready underprepared freshmen for the rigors of college work. A current approach is teaching the requisite skills in a developmental or remedial course. A second challenge schools face is how to keep these new students in college long enough for them to adapt to the new environment. The traditional solution to this problem is the freshman orientation course. Both of the solutions to the foregoing problems can work: reading and study-skills classes do help students, and orientation type coursework is generally rated as a worthwhile activity.

Poor study habits and new environments, however, are not the exclusive causes of students leaving school (Lemming, Beal, & Saner, 1980; Ramist, 1981). Many students leave colleges because of finances. Others drop out because of the rigors of advanced coursework. Still others drop out because of emotional or psychological factors. Most frequently, a combination of problems is the basis for students' decisions to discontinue higher education. A successful plan for dealing with such an interrelated group of causes may require an integrated teaching approach for stabilizing "at-risk" students, both in social-emotional and in academic-study contexts.

Customarily, orientation groups are formed by one university agency (e.g., the Office of Student Affairs, the Orientation Office), while another campus unit such as the reading education, psychology, English, or developmental studies departments develops and maintains reading and study skills coursework. In this integrated course approach, campus units cooperate so that a group of incoming freshmen, who would have previously selected a section of College Reading and Study Skills would also be designated simultaneously as an orientation group. In effect, freshmen are oriented to the university through the context of a reading and study-skills course that itself focuses on a reality-based approach to instruction. While students assigned to such a course may be from divergent backgrounds, course leaders can also draw enrollees from specific populations (e.g., dorm students, athletes, commuters, adults) and then "customize" the course content to the group's special social and academic needs.

The content of this integrated course does not differ markedly from usual college reading and study-skills offerings, as the curriculum includes (1) a systematized notetaking method, (2) a reading-study approach for textbooks, (3) a testwiseness unit, (4) a vocabulary development component, and (5) reading rate work. In addition, the basic structure of the course is also standard; meeting for three fifty-minute sessions each week for a semester. What is different, what appears to be unique is the context in which the curriculum is taught. Every attempt is made to teach the skills in a way that also immerses the student in the university mileau and surroundings of the campus community. Hence, the course-required projects distinguish this student-university centered approach from the traditional college reading and study-skills course. In designing the different course projects to teach and reinforce the curriculum, the authors consciously require students to gain university-wide experience in order to complete the projects. Thus, notetaking simulations occur in campus classrooms, of different sizes, disciplines, and locations. Vocabulary development stresses not only the structural-analytic approach found in most vocabulary development texts (Stahl, Brozo, & Burk, 1984), but also learning both discipline specific language (Hopper & Wells, 1981; Sartain et al., 1982) and campus specific vocabulary (Johnson, 1976), whether it is slang, in-group jargon, or university "bureaucratese." In all, assignments are tailored to both the students' immediate needs and long term goals. The following projects are illustrative of learning experiences generally utilized with this approach to reading and study-skills instruction.

A Notetaking Sequence

Students are required to record notes using an organized approach in a lecture style class. Early in the semester, we establish a method for notetaking. As a basic foundation, we teach and train the Cornell Method (Aiken, 1953; Pauk, 1984), but believe students should eventually adapt the method to their particular needs and their future academic endeavors. Initial training for notetaking occurs in the classroom when students (1) listen to a taped lecture on the history of the university, (2) take notes with their own best method, (3) review their notes after the presentation, and (4) take a short quiz on the lecture material. Next notes are evaluated by peers using the Notetaking Observation and Training Scale—NOATS (Stahl, King, & Henk, 1984). Students then compare their scores on both the quiz and evaluation scale during a class discussion that points out the relationship between accurate, concise notes and efficient recall for testing. The second session on notetaking involves a guided demonstration of the Cornell Method with an overhead projector. As the lecture proceeds the instructor takes notes on transparencies for all to see. While the lecture is based on introductory principles and concepts generally covered in a lower division sociology class, psychology, political science, or other introductory courses in the social sciences could be used. The demonstration occurs in a large lecture hall, with the class dispersed throughout the hall. Following the lecture, a comparison of students' recorded notes leads to conclusions about optimum seating in a large lecture hall. Although the students may have previously been told of the benefits of sitting near the front of a class for a lecture, they are still surprised by their own "hard data" obtained in this demonstration. A brief discussion of the relevant literature on listening in college classes closes the session. In the third training class, students listen to and take notes on a presentation on emotional and psychological stress that often accompanies the freshman year. At the next class session students review their notes and take a short quiz. Subsequent discussion centers on effective notetaking techniques and information from the speaker's presentation. At this point students select one social science or science course (hereafter referred to as the content study course) in which they regularly record class notes in the trained manner throughout the remainder of the semester. Periodic instructor and peer evaluation, two or three times each month, with the NOATS scheme leads students to a uniform, yet flexible, notetaking style. In addition, the evaluation system provides the course instructor with criteria to monitor student growth in notetaking ability.

Textbook Reading Study Skills

Over the semester students are gradually introduced to a systematic method of textbook study. The training begins with analyzing the university bulletin for examples of textual aids, and then students create a structured overview of the bulletin. In a follow-up assignment, students investigate the required books from their content study courses for evidence of text structure. During the second training session, students in similar content study courses form cluster groups (e.g., psychology, chemistry, biology). These groups analyze and discuss their required texts and report findings to the class. As a homework activity, the entire class prereads selected sections of the university bulletin and/or the student handbook to practice the prereading activities such as surveying, raising questions, and setting objectives of studying.

In a follow-up session a text chapter is provided by the instructor, and the students are guided through the steps of SQ3R (Robinson, 1970) or a similar approach (see Stahl, 1983, for a listing of 100 systems). Students then practice with the sample chapter and in their cluster groups discuss the positive and negative aspects of a structured reading/study approach. The general psychological principles and research based rationale for the method (as well as all other methods suggested in the course) are highlighted to the class. Students undertake additional regular practice throughout the term with their course texts and the college bulletin. When students are not enrolled in subject matter courses, the instructor can assign text from a college outline series (e.g., *United States to 1877*, Krout, 1971) to facilitate practice with content field material.

As an extension of SQ3R, a subsequent class session centers on both inductive and deductive mapping strategies (Baldridge, 1977; Bird, 1931; Frederick, 1938; Hauf, 1971; Merritt, Prior, Grugeon, & Grugeon, 1977; Miller, 1980) as post-reading organizers. Students are introduced to different mapping techniques with a handout and on an overhead transparency. In small groups, students read a short passage on the academic organization and hierarchy of the institution. After this reading, each cluster group completes a different type of map (e.g., radial, hierarchial, pyramidal, inductive outline, flow chart). These maps are then drawn on large sheets of butcher paper for whole class inspection and comparison.

Future class sessions on textbook reading and study are scheduled regularly throughout the term since analyses of the literature on study reading (Anderson & Arbruster, 1980; Stahl, 1983) point out that successful utilization of textbook-study methods appears to be based on long term training. During these sessions students read simulated chapters on topics such as student support services or grading policies. Using these chapters, students suggest notetaking abbreviations, short cuts, and organizational techniques they have adopted in personalizing the previously introduced reading and study systems. The long term goal is to lead each student to develop a highly individualized method of textbook study based on a foundation of sound principles and personal commitment.

Testwiseness

Shortly before the midterm period the class begins a unit on test-taking skills. As with the other projects, student-university interaction is stressed. The initial session on testing is a combination of discussions designed both to elicit the students' prior knowledge about tests and to present the instructor's comments supplementing the students' basic understanding of the subject. Students describe and then comment on different test formats and test-taking skills. As a summary for the discussion, the cluster groups draw graphic organizers or retrieval charts depicting each format. Students then read assigned selections from materials like Millman and Pauk (1969) or Woodley (1978) for the next class session. During that next session students discuss the test formats and the techniques for taking tests presented in the readings. The discussion is followed by a simulation of an essay examination. Students are given an essay question that tests mastery of the content covered in reading assignments on test taking. The completed essays are then scored by peers. Discussion of what makes a "good answer" should lead to class developed principles of answering essay questions. The following class meeting deals with objective test items. Students brainstorm objective test-taking techniques (Brozo, Schmelzer, & Spires, 1984; Gordon, 1982). Sample objective test items that demonstrate key words, educated guessing techniques, and format cues are completed by students.

During the next class session students complete an instrument such as the *Test Anxiety Inventory* (Spielberger, 1980) while visiting the university counseling center. While administration of the TAI does not require specially trained personnel, the field trip introduces the whole class to an academic support service that could be perceived as potentially threatening when students need it most. When on site they hear about different counseling services that are available to students. One of these services, found commonly at postsecondary institutions, is the Test Anxiety Workshop, and students, identified as at-risk by the TAI, can sign up for the sessions at that time. Through the test-taking unit, students not only learn of the recognized "tricks of the trade," but also interact with the trained professionals who can provide in-depth services for test anxious students.

Vocabulary Development

Students work on vocabulary building in two separate but interactive ways. The first method is through a personal vocabulary collection. Over the semester, students collect interesting words from their comprehension "twilight zones" (O'Connor, cited in Pauk, 1984) encountered in class lectures and readings, heard during conversations with professors and peers, or encountered within the overall university environment. To educators interested in student survival, both slang and socially oriented words are as important as academic vocabulary, because such words promote ease of assimilation into the campus culture. These words are collected daily and recorded in a 5" by 7" looseleaf binder. Students define the words, jot down the phonetic spelling, use the words in sentences, and note the prefixes or suffixes. In order to get maximum benefit from the collection, students can categorize their daily entries by subject area, social contexts, or other categories during in-class group work. Each week the classmates quickly review the new entries in the other student's collections. Interesting and/or potentially useful words are nominated for the distinction of "Word of the Week."

An additional source for words are those specific to the college environment. Students record some of these new words in their collections. To insure that they have been introduced to the majority of these specialized word selections from Stahl and King (1981) or Johnson (1976) are assigned and discussed. As with any vocabulary learning, limited numbers of new terms should be introduced at a given time. Small groups of specialized college and university terms are presented and reinforced over the course of the semester as students are likely to require knowledge of them (e.g., terms related to financial aid procurement when next year's application forms are due).

The second method of on-going vocabulary development may take one of several avenues. Students may complete specified sections of a vocabulary workbook independently and then progress to the next section with ninety percent mastery on each section test. If several forms of each mastery test exist, students can self-pace learning and score their own work. Initial placement in any of several texts can be based upon scores on a standardized vocabulary measure such as the *Basic Word Vocabulary Test* (Dupay, 1975). The authors have found that assigning three vocabulary texts in one class is possible without undue confusion. A second avenue for vocabulary development is to key in on words previously used on the *SAT*. A publication like the one by Norback and Norback (1979), contains such words. Students often believe that mastering such a set of words is a valid assignment since it appeals to their "fix up my problem" view of college reading. In other words, they understand that had they known these words previously, they might have scored higher on the verbal section of the *SAT* and hence not needed a college reading course. Finally, a third avenue places emphasis on technical words and primary concepts underlying introductory, lower division coursework. Several authors (Hopper & Wells, 1981; Sartain et al., 1982) have specified problematic vocabulary from the various college disciplines. Students can be introduced to these terms before entering a course or, if already enrolled in a course, can carefully monitor their mastery of the terms. The students learning the content vocabulary also serve as resource specialists to the members of the reading class not enrolled in the content course.

Field Trips

Since an important part of this course is acclimatizing the new students to the university environment, getting them around campus is essential. Several class meetings occur outside the classroom. Meetings in a large lecture hall for notetaking practice and testing in the counseling center were already mentioned. In addition, the class meets in several of the university libraries for guided tours, library scavenger hunts (designed with the cooperation of the institution's librarians), term paper clinics, and information gathering for the group projects. Another site the class visits is a writer's workshop sponsored by the English department. Over the course of the semester, students read either an auxiliary novel required by an outside class or elect to read another novel as a group. The selected novels (usually no more than five different titles per section) are used for a writing catalyst as well as reading rate training. Short reaction papers to these novels are evaluated by group members for content and mechanics. Rewritten papers are subsequently taken to the English department's writing workshop by the individual students for a final critique. An additional campus trip focuses on the services offered students by the Learning Skills Center. Students listen to staff members detail the different tutorial and academic support services available at the center and then record the information in their college survival manual.

Students finalize their acculturation to the institutional setting toward the end of the semester. Students previously self-selected content fields such as psychology, chemistry, or political science which they consider potential majors. Small groups of students with like interests are formed to thoroughly review the methods and techniques on reading/study, vocabulary development, testing, and notetaking for that discipline. Next, each group shares its expertise through presentations that take place in classrooms generally assigned to the selected content departments. For example, the student presentation on efficient studying in psychology would take place in a large psychology lecture hall. A chemistry presentation may occur in a chemistry lab. A humanities presentation might be held in a seminar room. Each group develops and distributes to their peers a guide to studying in the chosen area.

College Survival Manual

Throughout the term the students develop college survival manuals comprised of their own writings and those of their classmates. Specifically, the manual contains (1) a "how-to" section on registration procedures, on and off campus housing information, financial aid procedures, and various other important details and procedures essential for college survival; (2) an academic referral section with information on the learning assistance center, the writing lab, the counseling center, and other campus services; (3) a vocabulary section with self-selected vocabulary terms drawn from the class text, the university environment, and selected courses; (4) a content field section that consists of the guidelines developed by each of the student cluster groups for reading and studying in the common undergraduate disciplines; (5) a section on notetaking which includes the student's class notes and NOATS evaluation material. In addition, the journal process encourages each student to make comments about the personal adjustments one must make in crossing the bridge from the world of high school to that of higher education. Comments generally include frank discussions on the need for and value of a personal time management approach and methods for monitoring and assessing the effectiveness of personal study procedures used in one's content study course as well as other classes. Finally, the journal contains pre and post assessments of reading comprehension, vocabulary knowledge, reading rate, study-skills knowledge and attitudes, and notetaking skills. In essence then, the journal is an organized collection of work for the entire course that becomes a reference manual for the student's college years.

In a day and age when institutional resources are stretched to the limits and "economize" is the watch word, many varied academic support services may be in danger of losing full or partial funding. One highly plausible and potentially cost effective method of continuing to offer college reading and study-skills classes as well as college orientation coursework is based on the model which integrates the content of the two courses into a single course designed to immerse the students in the campus environment. Of course, each institution considering the implementation of such a model would need to adapt it to their existing setting.

References

Aiken, D. J. (1953). *You can learn how to study.* New York: Rinehart.

Anderson, T. H., & Armbruster, B. B (1980). *Studying* (Technical Report No. 155). Urbana: University of Illinois, Center for the Study of Reading. (ERIC Document Reproduction Service No. 157–037)

Baldridge, K. P. (1977). *Seven reading strategies.* Greenwich, CT: BRIM, Inc.

Bird, C. (1931). *Effective study habits.* New York: Century.

Brozo, W. G., Schmelzer, R. V., & Spires, H. A. (1984). *The frequency of test-wiseness clues in college teacher-made multiple choice tests with implications for academic assistance centers* (College Reading and Learning Assistance Technical Report 84–01). Atlanta: Georgia State University, Division of Developmental Studies. (ERIC Document Reproduction Service No. pending)

Dupay, H. J. (1975). *Basic word vocabulary test.* Highland Park, NJ: Dreier Educational Systems.

Frederick, R. W. (1938). *How to study handbook.* New York: Appleton-Century.

Gordon, B. (1982). Teaching them to read the questions. *Journal of Reading, 26,* 126–132.

Hauf, M. B. (1971). Mapping: A technique for translating reading into thinking. *Journal of Reading, 14,* 115–230, 270.

Hopper, J., & Wells, J. C. (1981, April). *The specific vocabulary needs of academic disciplines.* Paper presented at the meeting of the Western College Reading Association, Dallas. (ERIC Document Reproduction Service No. ED207000)

Johnson, S. W. (1976). *The freshman's friend.* Woodbury, NY: Barron's.

Krout, J. A. (1971). *United States to 1877* (7th ed.). New York: Barnes & Noble.

Lemming, O. T., Beal, P. E., & Sauer, K. (1980). *Retention and attrition: Evidence for action and research.* Boulder, CO: National Center for Higher Education Management Systems.

Merritt, J., Prior, D., Grugeon, E., & Grugeon, D. (1977). *Developing independence in reading.* Milton Keynes, England: The Open University Press.

Miller, C. F. (1980). Flow chart organizational training and its effect on reading comprehension and retention. (Doctoral dissertation, University of Pittsburgh, 1980). *Dissertation Abstracts International, 41,* 611A. (University Microfilms No. 80–18, 319)

Millman, J., & Pauk, W. (1969). *How to take tests.* New York: McGraw-Hill.

Norback, C, & Norback (1979). *The must words.* New York: McGraw-Hill.

Pauk, W. (1984). *How to study in college* (3rd ed.). Boston: Houghton Mifflin.

Ramist, L. (1981). *College student attrition and retention* (College Board Rep. No. 81–1). New York: College Entrance Board.

Robinson, F. P. (1970). *Effective study* (4th ed.). New York: Harper & Row.

Sartain, H. W., Stahl, N. A., Ani, U. A., Bohn, S., Holly, B., Smolenski, C. S., & Stein, D. W. (1982). *Teaching techniques for the languages of the disciplines.* Pittsburgh, PA: University of Pittsburgh and the Fund for the Improvement of Postsecondary Education. (ERIC Document Reproduction Service No. 234–653)

Spielberger, C. D., & collaborators. (1980). *Test anxiety inventory.* Palo Alto, CA: Consulting Psychologists Press.

Stahl, N. A. (1983). A historical analysis of textbook-study systems. (Doctoral dissertation, University of Pittsburgh, 1983). *Dissertation Abstracts International*, listing pending.

Stahl, N. A., Brozo, W. G., & Burk, B. (1984). *A content analysis of adjunct vocabulary used in college reading programs* (College Reading and Learning Assistance Technical Report No. 84–3). Atlanta: Georgia State University, Division of Developmental Studies.

Stahl, N. A., & King, J. R. (1981, October). *A language experience model for teaching college reading, study, and survival.* Paper presented at the meeting of the College Reading Association, Louisville, KY.

Stahl, N. A., King J. R., & Henk, W. (1984, March). *Training students to be effective notetakers with notetaking observation and training scales.* Paper presented at the meeting of the National Association for Developmental Education, Philadelphia.

Woodley, K. K. (1978). *Test wiseness: Test-taking skills for adults* (2nd ed.). New York: McGraw-Hill.

Teaching Textual Conversations: Intertextuality in the College Reading Classroom

Sonya L. Armstrong and Mary Newman

Sonya L. Armstrong and Mary Newman present a model for structuring developmental reading instruction that provides students with experiences making connections across texts. This model emphasizes intertextuality as an approach that explicitly teaches students to link unfamiliar texts or ideas with prior knowledge. In the context of developmental reading classrooms at both community college and university levels, Armstrong and Newman explain that this model accounts for academic text situations in which students may not have relevant schemata to draw upon. By providing a carefully structured design of purposefully linked supplemental and core texts that mirrors the multiple-text expectations of postsecondary reading, students come to recognize this process of linking texts as a comprehension strategy that results in their increased involvement with and understanding of academic texts.

F or most first-year students the transition to college is not easy. There are obvious adjustments to be made, socially, culturally, personally, and emotionally. In the midst of all these various types of transitions, most beginning college students also face some form of literacy transition (e.g., Armstrong, 2007; Curry, 2003; Sanchez & Paulson, 2008; Shaughnessy, 1977). Especially as students begin to realize that the academic literacy practices expected of them in postsecondary contexts are vastly different from those they are familiar with from their primary schooling, this literacy transition often requires conceptual change related to their views of reading and writing.

Misconceptions about Learning and Reading

Beginning college students often hold on to deeply ingrained misconceptions about learning (e.g., Holschuh, 2003; Simpson & Nist, 2003). For example, Simpson and Nist have argued that "Most college freshmen believe learning is simple, can be accomplished quickly, and that knowledge and learning occur when someone else 'does something to you'" (p. 172). In other words, many students seem to understand their role as learners to be passive recipients of information rather than active constructors of knowledge (e.g., Perry, 1970). Students' epistemological views are particularly relevant for those of us who teach developmental literacy courses, including reading, writing, and study strategies, because it is in these courses that these literacy transitions need to be facilitated.

Not surprisingly, many students also tend to view reading as a passive activity that involves determining a single, correct meaning that is "in" the text, but that they often can't seem to retrieve. According to El-Hindi (2003), "Students tend to read on 'automatic pilot,' and do not realize when they have trouble comprehending or truly digesting text" (p. 360). In terms of the models of reading outlined by Schraw and Bruning (1996), many students hold more of a transmission model than a transactional model (see also Rosenblatt, 1994).

A transmission model of reading is limiting indeed, especially when reading for academic purposes. For one, a link between reader conceptualizations and strategy usage has been well-documented (e.g., Goodman & Marek, 1996; Holschuh, 2003; Schraw & Bruning, 1996). In short, readers whose conceptualizations of reading are transmission-oriented tend to choose surface-level strategies (or none at all) rather than deep-level, active reading strategies (e.g., Newman, 2008). Additionally, a transmission model of reading does not allow for a view of reading as engaging in dialogic conversations with texts, which is more like the view of reading embedded in the expectations of most college-level instruction. Finally, a transmission view implies a universal reading approach to texts, rather than an understanding of the need for strategic, situation-specific approaches to text. Given the variety of text types, purposes, and goals students will face in academia, such a misconception of reading can be detrimental to their success in college.

In addition to the problem of student misconceptions about academic literacy practices, a related transmission model also persists in the field of postsecondary developmental literacy instruction. Such pedagogically based transmission models generally involve a deficit or remediation approach that translates into skill-drill-type instruction; because this type of instruction encourages, rather than dispels students' passive views of reading, it usually serves to further complicate their literacy transitions. In fact, the intertextual model we describe in this article was born from our frustrations with such approaches, and, on some level, was created as a reaction against skill-drill-type teaching approaches, which we view as ineffective models for preparing students for their academic goals. We came to develop our respective instructional approaches, separately and at different institutions, as a means to help students develop the necessary reading and learning strategies that represent, more realistically, what students will be doing in their college courses. To be fair, we are beginning to see publishers move toward offering more strategies-based developmental reading textbooks such as *Read to Succeed* (Rothman & Warsi, 2010) and *Efficient and Flexible Reading* (McWhorter, 2011); however, we still see few that focus on intertextual reading and writing.

With skill-drill, deficit approaches, generally, the focus is on a single text, and students tend to take what they read in the classroom text as "the truth" (Wineburg, 1991) or the only version of a particular topic. They may not have been trained to consider the fact that what they read is just one author's perspective, or bias, on the matter. Here, students read at a literal level. They read only one source, only one version, take it as truth, then work to gather and memorize facts (Seixas, 1993; Wineburg, 1991). This kind of single-text approach does not adequately reflect the types of reading/studying/writing/thinking requirements that students face in college-level coursework (Hynd, 1999). It is challenging, indeed, to think of a single academic discipline that does not involve intertextual materials and cross-textual synthesis on some level. For that reason, this article introduces intertextuality as an approach to teaching college reading in environments that aim to facilitate and support students' literacy transitions. In the next section, we begin with a brief background on the concept of intertextuality before proceeding to a presentation of our model.

Introduction to Intertextuality

The idea of intertextuality was first introduced by Swiss linguist Ferdinand de Saussure (1857–1913), who is credited with theories of language as a structured system or relationship between the sign (word), the signified (thought), and the signifier (sound). Saussure focused on the role of language in understanding text. Later, the French post-structuralists (e.g., Kristeva, 1967 / 1986; 1968) discussed the term "intertextuality" as referring to the relationship between the text, the writer, and the reader. With this view, language itself is central. Here, meaning is found in the constantly changing textual relationship, not in an author or a reader. With the poststructural view of intertextuality, little consideration is given to the reader or to the intertextual relationships among texts that occur without the reader. Consequently, intertextual relationships exist within and between texts alone—apart from the reader.

In addition, many literary definitions of intertextuality tend to be rather narrowly focused on the text itself. For example, one common usage of the term is for situations where a well-known canonical work is retold, usually with a twist (for example, Jane Smiley's *A Thousand Acres*, 1991, is a modern retelling of *King Lear*, 1997). Another common usage occurs in situations where one author's words are directly used in another author's work. Again, for most literary uses of this term, the focus is limited to texts alone, not the reader's interaction with texts.

Spivey (1997) discussed a view of intertextuality that contradicted the poststructural and more literature-specific views. She understood this interaction as a

> constructivist emphasis on human agency, [and thus she] considers intertextuality in terms of intertextual cues made and discerned by people and in terms of intertextual knowledge used by people as individuals and as social groups. Intertextuality is implication on the part of authors and inferences on the part of readers. (p. 86–87)

Building from this definition, in this article we conceptualize intertextuality as an instructional approach where instructors offer multiple texts and materials of a wide variety of genres to give students the opportunity to increase background knowledge; make connections across and among texts; develop multiple perspectives, interpretations, and a broader picture of a topic; and develop their critical thinking skills (Lenski, 1998).

An Intertextual Model for College Reading Instruction

Intertextuality, as we conceptualize it and discuss it in class, involves an analogical process of simultaneously building—and immediately applying—schemata that are introduced by supplemental texts. One metaphor that may be useful in understanding this concept is a block foundation (see Figure 1), which represents a learner's conceptualizations and comprehension of a particular content (this can include a concept, a text, a topic, etc.). When this foundation is strong enough, it can allow a learner a support upon which to continue to build.

Figure 1. Foundation Metaphor for the Schema-Building Process

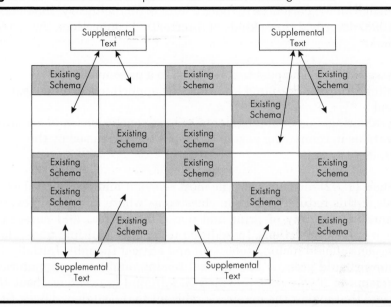

A learner's comprehension of a particular text is rarely completely supported by existing schema and prior knowledge (the blocks). For that reason, supplemental texts (understood broadly as including multimedia, ideologies, events, etc.) brought into the discussion at appropriately timed moments anticipate students' gaps in prior knowledge. These supplemental texts provide additional knowledge needed to fill in some of the gaps in a learner's foundation of comprehension. Although this foundation may not be completely blocked in, even with the support of the supplemental texts, it becomes stronger and sturdier with each additional block of schema.

Intertextuality as an Instructional Approach

Using intertextuality as an instructional approach in a reading class allows students to practice the process of making connections or relationships between what is being read and what has previously been read on a topic. Intertextuality involves the connection — the analogical linking — of one's prior knowledge on a topic to the new knowledge or experience (Allen, 2000; Alvermann, Moon & Hagood, 1999; Bloome & Egan-Robertson, 1993; Hartman, 1991, 1995; Short, 1992). It is also the synthesis of information among various texts on the same topic (Breiter, 1990; Hartman & Hartman, 1995).

Instructors can teach students that they should make associations (Hartman, 1991) to their existing knowledge, and that they should make mental pictures or maps of a topic and make connections to prior knowledge and experiences (Crouch Shinn & Shaughnessy, 1984). Lenski (1998) described three kinds of intertextual connections the reader can make:

A. Associating: Some past text is linked to a present text;
B. Integrating: Background knowledge is applied to a present text; and
C. Evaluating: Personal judgments, values, conclusions, and generalizations in comparing past and present texts are used by the reader.

Short (1992) reported that the most relevant and meaningful experiences of this nature happen in classrooms where instructors expose students to a variety of print and non-print sources and encourage them to make connections. In addition to reading multiple texts, class discussions should include reflection and critical thought. Initially, instructors should present intertextual reading and learning materials to students in a way that provides background knowledge about the topic and that makes the materials relevant to the students' lives. Students become engaged in the topic when instructors use various pre-reading strategies, such as previewing and predicting, that help students think about what they already know about the topic. During reading, the instructor could allow students time to talk with the class about what they have read. This discussion gives students time to think about their ideas as well as hear ideas they may not have taken into account. And, after reading, students can write about and discuss the ideas presented in the various texts. In this manner, students become more actively engaged in the reading and learning experience (Newman, 2008).

Intertextuality involves a scaffolded, schema-building approach to teaching college reading. The purpose is to facilitate the building of a knowledge base on topics associated with a core text or content topic. Through this method, which is scaffolded over the course of an academic term, students come to recognize this process of linking texts as a comprehension strategy that results in their increased involvement and understanding of the conversations central to the core text. For example, in the next section, we describe a history unit as part of a developmental reading course; in this unit, students are expected to compare and contrast various and often conflicting views on a particular topic, synthesize that information, and then provide their own interpretation and contribute it to the existing conversation. These practices are not unlike what students would experience in philosophy, literature, biology, psychology, or most other college courses. However, very few professors provide explicit instruction on how to do this kind of reading (Hynd-Shanahan, Holschuh, & Hubbard, 2004; Simpson &

Nist, 2002). Developmental reading courses are, in theory, designed to help students transition into the literacy practices of the academy. An intertextual approach allows for beginning college students to gain practice that realistically prepares them for the tough reading tasks ahead of them throughout their academic careers.

Research shows that students must learn to direct and control their own cognitive processes if they are to be successful with academic reading and learning. Hadwin and Winne (1996) propose that "it is the element of intent to manipulate one's cognitive processes that distinguishes self regulating from merely using a study tactic" (p. 693). Studies show that to reach their academic goals, students need to learn a variety of reading and learning strategies, or tactics, to learn to adapt those strategies to various tasks and settings, and to transfer such tactics appropriately to other disciplines (Butler & Winne, 1995; Rasnak, 1995; Stahl, Simpson, & Hayes, 1992). Strategic learning occurs when students learn to use the appropriate learning strategies or tactics necessary for the successful completion of a particular academic task (Newman, 2008).

Description of Intertextuality in Two Classroom Exemplars

What follows are descriptions of two practical applications of intertextuality in developmental reading courses, one in a community college setting, and another in an alternative-admission setting at a public university.

Community College Context

The first illustration of intertextuality in a developmental reading course is at a large, Midwestern community college with an open-admissions policy. The college admits all students with a high school degree, but those students who demonstrate unpreparedness for college-level work, based on placement scores received on the Compass Reading Placement Test (ACT, Inc.), are required to take developmental coursework before taking courses for college-level credit. Developmental reading coursework offerings range from courses designed for those demonstrating a very low level of skills to courses for those who test just below the college level. The highest level of these courses, Preparation for College Reading II, is the focus of this discussion.

COURSE CONTEXT. Preparation for College Reading II is a strategies-based course developed around the concept of intertextuality. A strategies-based text is used during the semester as a core text for explicit instruction in basic reading strategies. At the beginning of the semester, students focus on learning reading strategies such as how to read actively, how to identify the main idea and major supportive detail, and how to develop stronger vocabulary skills. Such instruction helps develop a stronger foundation upon which to incorporate deeper-level reading strategies. By the third or fourth week of the semester, students receive instruction on a strategy developed by Hynd (1999) and Hynd-Shanahan, Holschuh, and Hubbard (2004) based on the work of Wineburg (1991), which teaches students domain-specific reading and learning strategies. This deeper-level reading strategy involves using multiple, conflicting historical texts and engaging students in intertextuality to learn to read and think critically (Newman, 2008). Table 1 includes a listing of the specific texts and materials used during this course.

These materials include a variety of primary and secondary sources of information on the topic of the Tonkin Gulf Incident of the Vietnam War, such as an autobiography from a former Secretary of State, a history book, a book published by a high-ranking military official about the U.S. involvement in Vietnam, an editorial written by a history professor published in the *Christian Science Monitor* on the 20th anniversary of the Tonkin Gulf Incident, and a rebuttal to that editorial written by an archivist of historical documents from Indochina. During this unit, students read about the Tonkin Gulf Incident from a variety of perspectives, discuss their views on the various texts in class in small groups paragraph and then as a whole write multiple short essays designed to help them form their own interpretation of the historic event.

Additionally, a teaching method suggested by Nist and Simpson (2000) helps students develop discipline-specific knowledge and deeper-level strategy use. This method includes modeling the processes involved in using these strategies by showing examples on the overhead projector and the board, providing examples of these strategies, building in class time to practice using the strategies, and offering feedback to students on their use of the strategies through teacher evaluation. Students discuss difficult concepts and vocabulary in class discussions and share their responses in class. Moreover, students begin completing various charts and graphic organizers to help them interpret each author's position on the issues related to the Vietnam War and the Tonkin Gulf Incident.

The charts and graphic organizers encourage students to use these intertextual learning materials to practice using Wineburg's (1991) heuristic, which includes sourcing, contextualization, and corroboration to arrive at their responses (see Newman, 2008 for a full description of this teaching method as well as the charts and graphic organizers used during this unit). This heuristic teaches students to consider the source of the information (the text), the context in which the text was written (time, space, political and social issues of that time, etc.), and collaboration (the agreement or disagreement among the various authors and texts about issues related to the topic).

Table 1. Texts and Materials Used for Preparation for College Reading II

Source	Context Information
• Dean Rusk (1990), *As I Saw It*	• Former Secretary of State during the Johnson Administration; professor of international law, University of Georgia
• Berkin, Miller, Cherny, & Gormly (1990), *Making America: A History of the United States*	• Historians, a college textbook
• Gareth Porter (1984), "Tonkin *Gulf Incident Editorial*"	• Professor, City University of New York, a column in the *Christian Science Monitor*
• Phillip B. Davidson (1990), *Secrets of the Vietnam War*	• Former chief of intelligence for the United States Army, later publishing several texts on the Vietnam War; however, this information was withheld from students as part of the lesson on establishing an author's credibility when no information is available
• Douglas Pike (1984), response to Gareth Porter's editorial	• Archivist in the Indochina Archive at the University of California, Berkeley, citing evidence from *Military Events,* a work published by the People's Army of Vietnam Publishing
• Video: "Vietnam Lecture" (Steuck, 1990)	• A lecture on the Tonkin Gulf Incident given by Dr. William Steuck, a history professor at the University of Georgia
• Video: *The American Experience: LBJ* (1991)	• A PBS documentary on Lyndon B. Johnson and the Vietnam War

University Setting

The second context provided here as an exemplar is a decentralized alternative-admissions developmental program (Johnson & Carpenter, 2000) housed within a Midwestern public university. The program consists of four components, each of which is housed in its respective academic unit: Literacy, English, Communications, and Math.

Students enrolled through this program are typically recruited through target high schools, which are selected based on student populations high in minority and low socio-economic status backgrounds. Typically, these students are identified as being ineligible for "traditional" admission to the university due to high school GPA or ACT scores. Once accepted into the alternative-admission program, students take a battery of placement exams for each area; placement for the Literacy courses includes a combination of ACT Reading Subtest and ACCUPLACER reading comprehension scores. For the literacy component, there is a two-course sequence: College Reading, and Reading and Study Strategies. The focus of the description that follows is on the first course, College Reading.

COURSE CONTEXT. College Reading is a text-based course developed around the theme of intertextuality. Because most students in the program enroll in this course during their first semester, novels are used as the primary, or core, texts as a way to scaffold students into academic reading practices using text genres that are familiar to them. The two core texts serve as the centerpiece and main conversations of the course. Currently, the core texts used in the course are a fictional novel, Jonathan Safran Foer's (2005) *Extremely Loud & Incredibly Close*, and an auto-biographical graphic novel, Marjane Satrapi's (2003) *Persepolis: The Story of a Childhood*. In addition to these core texts, numerous supplemental texts are incorporated throughout the course (see Table 2 for examples of supplemental texts used in this course). These supplemental texts connect in some foundational way to the conversations of the core texts; are typically expository and more academic texts; and include college-level textbook chapters, scholarly journal articles, historical chronologies, and primary sources, as well as pop-culture media texts such as songs, video clips, and film.

An illustration of the core-supplemental text relationships may be useful. Within the Foer (2005) novel, there is a textual conversation on the topic of the Dresden fire bombings; this conversation has a high expectation for background knowledge as very little is provided by the novel's author. At the same time students are being introduced to this conversation within the core text, they are also assigned to read a supplemental text—a brief excerpt from a college-level world history textbook—that provides fundamental information and context on the Dresden fire bombings. As this conversation continues in the core text, students are also assigned to read an excerpt from a scholarly chapter on the use of air attacks in World War II.

The goal is to provide students with exposure to and experience with a variety of text genres, all the while ensuring that the course doesn't become too focused on literary texts, terms, or concepts. Further, the course is designed to welcome discussion about other texts students have read (cultural texts like movies, music, and art, for example). For example, students do usually have some schema related to the events of 9/11; they use their own understanding of the situation to interpret the *New York Times* article from September 12, 2001, as well as the related textual conversation within the core novel.

Table 2. Texts and Materials Used for College Reading

Source	Context Information
• Introductory chapter from Stephen Hawking's *A Brief History of Time*	• The main character in one of the core texts is a fan of Stephen Hawking
• The lead story of *The New York Times* from September 12, 2001	• A major event of one of the core texts is the September 11 tragedy
• An excerpt from a college-level history textbook on Hiroshima	• Another event mentioned in one of the core texts is Hiroshima
• A scholarly chapter on air attacks related to World War II	• Yet another key event in one of the core texts is the Dresden fire bombings
• Music from the Beatles	• The main character in one of the core texts is a fan of the Beatles
• CNN footage from the Long Island Ferry crash	• This event is mentioned briefly in one of the core texts
• An excerpt of any film version of *Hamlet*	• The main character in one of the core texts is playing Yorick in a school play

It is important to note, too, that in order to introduce the concept of intertextuality for first-year students, it is often necessary to first define texts. Some students have a very narrow definition of the term (just textbooks, for example), rather than a definition that includes written texts, cultural experiences, events, people, ideas, and so on. It helps sometimes to also introduce the metaphor of conversations, which we have used throughout this article, to explain intertextuality. That is, a text can be defined as a conversation that is informed by other conversations. The key idea to convey is that, often, if we aren't familiar with certain external conversations, our reading of conversations within a text will be qualitatively different and, potentially, far less rich. Intertextuality is a pedagogical approach to college reading that allows students to recognize when they might need additional information in order to have a richer conversation with a given text.

Final Thoughts

As stated previously, beginning college students often view reading—and learning—as a very passive process. Indeed, they often view reading as something akin to hearing (as distinguished from listening), as though the text author is *telling* and they, as readers, are supposed to sit back and just receive the information. An intertextuality-based course, however, challenges this analogy as students are asked to reconceptualize reading as a conversation—one in which they are active participants.

Future Directions

We have identified three specific foci for future consideration of intertextuality related to both research and practice. First, we are interested in looking at how students use intertextuality when it is introduced as a reading and studying strategy. Specifically, we are interested in exploring whether and how students transfer this strategy to different learning situations and contexts. Perhaps a longitudinal study that investigates students' use and transfer of intertextual reading and learning strategies—over time and in other academic contexts—would be one way to approach this issue. In addition, we are interested in the writing aspect of intertextuality. We wonder if students who learn with intertextual materials write stronger essay responses and whether they are better able to talk about such texts in class. It would be useful to measure evidence of intertextuality in students' essays and responses to discussions in class. Discourse analysis may be useful in such a situation. Finally, we are interested in continuing to explore intertextuality as a philosophical model beyond the context of developmental reading and writing. For example, we have both incorporated this model in other contexts as well—in writing courses, in graduate-level teaching methods courses, and more.

In the end, through research and classroom-based developments we are looking for a change in the way developmental reading is approached, including the materials being used as well as the instructional philosophy. Intertextuality can help those responsible for curriculum development move toward a more meaningful experience for students. We advocate a curriculum designed to include multiple texts on a variety of topics, intertextual reading and writing about such texts, and authentic practice with critical analysis. In addition, discussion of texts is essential to developing the types of thinking involved when synthesizing, interpreting, and analyzing texts, as this is what is expected of college students at all levels. If the goal of developmental literacy instruction is, as we have argued in this article, to facilitate students' literacy transitions by helping them to reconceptualize academic literacy practices and better prepare them for the types of literacy practices they will be using in their college coursework, we have to move beyond the skill-drill models so widely used in our field.

References

ACT, Inc. (2009). *Compass/ESL test*. Iowa City, IA: Magna Publications Inc.

Allen, G. (2000). *Intertextuality*. New York, NY: Routledge.

Alvermann, D. E., Moon, J. S., & Hagood, M. C. (1999). *General culture in the classroom: Teaching and researching critical media literacy*. Newark, DE: International Reading Association.

American experience: LBJ. (1991). WGBH Educational Foundation, Boston, MA: David Grubin Productions, Inc.

Armstrong, S. L. (2007). *Beginning the literacy transition: Postsecondary students' conceptualizations of academic writing in developmental literacy contexts* (Unpublished doctoral dissertation). University of Cincinnati, Cincinnati, Ohio.

Berkin, C., Miller, C. L., Cherny, R. W., & Gormly, J. L. (1990). *Making America: A history of the United States, Vol II. Since 1865*. Boston, MA: Houghton Mifflin.

Bloome, D., & Egan-Robertson, A. (1993). The social construction of intertextuality and classroom reading and writing. *Reading Research Quarterly, 28*(4), 303–333.

Breiter, J. C. (1990). Using a multi-text/cooperative learning approach in a methods course [Part 1]. Iowa State University of Science and Technology. Ames, Iowa: Research Institute for Studies in Education.

Butler, D. L., & Winne, P. H. (1995). Feedback and self-regulated learning: A theoretical synthesis. *Review of Educational Research, 65*(3), 245–281.

Crouch-Shinn, J., & Shaughnessy, M. F. (1984). *Brain research: Implications for education* [electronic version]. Retrieved from ERIC database. (ED271707)

Curry, M. J. (2003). Skills, access, and basic writing: A community college case study from the United States. *Studies in the Education of Adults, 35*(1), 5–18.

Davidson, P. B. (1990). *Secrets of the Vietnam War*. Novato, CA: Presidio.

El-Hindi, A. E. (2003). Connecting reading and writing: College learners' metacognitive awareness. In N. A. Stahl, & H. Boylan (Eds.). *Teaching developmental reading: Historical, theoretical, and practical background readings* (pp. 350–362). Boston, MA: Bedford/St. Martin's.

Foer, J. S. (2005). *Extremely loud & incredibly close*. New York, NY: Houghton Mifflin.

Goodman, Y. M., & Marek, A. M. (1996). *Retrospective miscue analysis: Revaluing readers and reading*. Katonah, NY: Richard C. Owen Publishers, Inc.

Hadwin, A. F., & Winne, P. H. (1996). Study strategies have meager support: A review with recommendations for implementation. *Journal of Higher Education, 67*(6), 692–715.

Hartman, D. K. (1991). *Eight readers reading: The intertextual links of able readers using multiple passages*. (Unpublished doctoral dissertation). University of Illinois, Urbana.

Hartman, D. K. (1995). Eight readers reading: The intertextual links of proficient readers reading multiple passages. *Reading Research Quarterly, 30*(3), 520–561.

Hartman, J. A., & Hartman, D. K. (1995). *Creating a classroom culture that promotes inquiry-oriented discussions: Reading and talking about multiple texts*. (Technical Report No. 621). Urbana, IL: Illinois University, Urbana Center for the Study of Reading.

Hawking, S. (1998). *A brief history of time*. New York, NY: Bantam.

Holschuh, J. P. (2003). Do as I say, not as I do: High, average, and low-performing students' strategy use in biology. In N. A. Stahl, & H. Boylan (Eds.).

Teaching developmental reading: Historical, theoretical, and practical background readings (pp. 316–329). Boston, MA: Bedford/St. Martin's.

Hynd, C. R. (1999). Teaching students to think critically using multiple texts in history. *Journal of Adolescent and Adult Literacy, 42*(6), 428–436.

Hynd-Shanahan, C., Holschuh, J. P., & Hubbard, B. (2004). Thinking like a historian: College students' reading of multiple historical documents. *Journal of Literacy Research, 36*(2), 141–176.

Johnson, L. L., & Carpenter, K. (2000). College reading programs. In R. F. Flippo & D. C. Caverly (Eds.), *Handbook of college reading and study strategy research* (pp. 321–363). Mahwah, NJ: Lawrence Erlbaum Associates.

Kristeva, J. (1968). *Problemes de la structuration du texte, dans: Theorie densemble.* Paris, France: Seuil/Tel Quel.

Kristeva, J. (1967/1986). Word, dialogue, and novel (A. Jardine, T. Gora, & L. S. Roudiez, Trans.). In T. Moi (Ed.), *The Kristeva reader* (pp. 34–61). New York, NY: Columbia University Press. (Original work published in 1967).

Lenski, S. D. (1998). Intertextual intentions: Making connections across texts. *Clearing House, 72*(2), 74–80.

McWhorter, K. (2011). *Efficient and flexible reading.* New York, NY: Pearson Longman.

Newman, M. C. (2008). *Disciplinary knowledge, intertextuality, and developmental readers: A study of community college students* (Unpublished doctoral dissertation). Northern Illinois University, DeKalb, IL.

Nist, S. L., & Simpson, M. L. (2000). College studying. In M. L. Kamil, P. B. Mosenthal, P. D. Pearson, & R. Barr (Eds.), *Handbook of reading research* (Vol. III, pp. 645–666). Mahwah, NJ: Erlbaum Associates.

Perry, W. G. (1970). *Forms of ethical and intellectual development in the college years.* San Francisco, CA: Jossey-Bass.

Pike, D. (1984, August 22). Fact or fiction? *Christian Science Monitor*, p. 15.

Porter, G. (1984, August 9). Lessons of the Tonkin Gulf crisis. *Christian Science Monitor*, p. 15.

Rasnak, M. A. (1995). *Metacognitive dimensions of the election and use of learning strategies by adult college students and traditional-age college students.* (Unpublished doctoral dissertation). Northern Illinois University, DeKalb, IL.

Rosenblatt, L. M. (1994). The transactional theory of reading and writing. In R. B. Ruddell, M. R. Ruddell, & H. Singer (Eds.), *Theoretical models and processes of reading* (4th ed., pp. 1057–1092). Newark, DE: International Reading Association.

Rothman, D. & Warsi, J. (2010). *Read to succeed: A thematic approach to academic reading.* New York: Pearson Longman.

Rusk, D. (1990). *As I saw it.* New York, NY: W. W. Norton.

Sanchez, D., & Paulson, E. J. (2008). Critical language awareness and learners in college transitional English. *Teaching English in the Two-Year College, 36*(2), 164–176.

Satrapi, M. (2004). *Persepolis: The story of a childhood.* New York, NY: Pantheon Books.

Schraw, G., & Bruning, R. (1996). Readers' implicit models of reading. *Reading Research Quarterly, 31*(3), 290–305.

Seixas, P. (1993). Historical understanding among adolescents in a multicultural setting. *Curriculum Inquiry, 23*(3), 301–327.

Shakespeare (1997). King Lear. In S. Greenblatt, W. Cohen, J. E. Howard, & K. E. Maus (Eds). *The Norton Shakespeare* (pp. 2307–2479). New York, NY: W. W. Norton.

Shaughnessy, M. (1977). Some needed research on writing. *College Composition and Communication, 28*(4), 317–320.

Short, K. G. (1992). Researching intertextuality within collaborative classroom learning environments. *Linguistics and Education, 4,* 313–333.

Simpson, M. L., & Nist, S. L. (2002). Encouraging active reading at the college level. In M. Pressley & C. Collins Block (Eds.), *Comprehension instruction: Research-based best practices* (pp. 365–379). New York, NY: Guilford Press.

Simpson, M. L., & Nist, S. L. (2003). An update on strategic learning: It's more than textbook reading strategies. In N. A. Stahl, & H. Boylan (Eds.). *Teaching developmental reading: Historical, theoretical, and practical background readings* (pp. 157–178). Boston, MA: Bedford/St. Martin's.

Spivey, N. M. (1997). *The constructivist metaphor: Reading, writing and the making of meaning.* San Diego, CA: Academic Press, Inc.

Stahl, N. A., Simpson, M. L., & Hayes, C. G. (1992). Ten recommendations from research for teaching high-risk college students. *Journal of Developmental Education, 16*(1), 2–4, 6, 8.

Steuck, W. (1990). *Vietnam lecture: The Tonkin Gulf Incident.* Unpublished film of a class lecture. University of Georgia, Athens, GA.

Wineburg, S. S. (1991). Historical problem solving: A study of the cognitive processes used in the evaluation of documentary and pictorial evidence. *Journal of Educational Psychology, 83*(1), 73–87.

Acceleration Across California: Shorter Pathways in Developmental English and Math

Katie Hern

Acceleration, as a model for structuring postsecondary reading, is gaining widespread attention. In this selection, Katie Hern presents a rationale for acceleration as well as an overview of the acceleration efforts supported by the California Acceleration Project. Hern also describes the principles that underlie the acceleration model presented: a reduction in the number of stacked courses in order to move students into college courses sooner; a reduction in the use of high-stakes standardized placement assessments; and contextualized, authentic, and supported developmental reading curricula.

Developmental courses in English, math, and reading have an important purpose in higher education, especially in the open-access world of community colleges. These classes—also referred to as "remedial"—are intended to give less-prepared students a chance to catch up and meet the challenges of college-level coursework.

And yet, despite these noble intentions, remedial course sequences have become the place where college dreams go to die.

Nationwide studies have shown that the more semesters of remediation a student is required to take, the less likely that student is to ever complete a college-level math or English course, never mind reach a longer-term goal such as earning a degree or transferring to a four-year college or university. In a multi-state study of 57 community colleges, the Community College Research Center found that among students who are placed three or more levels below college math, fewer than 10 percent ever go on to complete a college-level math course. Put differently, community colleges weed out more than 90 percent of these students before they get through the first gate.

This bleak reality has motivated a growing number of California community colleges to re-think their approach to remediation. Joseph Gerda is now the vice-president of instruction at College of the Canyons, but in spring 2011 he was a mathematics instructor who was looking for a solution to what he calls the "tremendous blood loss" in remedial math. He and a group of colleagues attended a workshop organized by the California Community Colleges' Success Network (3CSN), where they heard Myra Snell talk about a new developmental course she'd developed at Los Medanos College.

Instead of accepting the traditional curriculum as a given, Snell set out to design an alternative, accelerated pathway for students who would go on to take statistics as their college-level math requirement. The solution: Path2Stats, a one-semester developmental course leading to college statistics, with no pre-requisites or minimum placement score. Rather than enrolling in up to four semesters of remedial arithmetic and algebra review, Path2Stats students begin learning statistics on day one, with "just-in-time remediation" of relevant arithmetic or algebraic skills along the way (e.g., reviewing how to calculate percentages or convert ounces to grams when they need these skills to analyze data).

In developing Path2Stats, Snell wanted to address an issue math educators have quietly recognized for years: the disconnect between the traditional developmental sequence and college statistics. The vast majority of what elementary and intermediate algebra courses cover is geared toward calculus, the track students will pursue in science, technology, engineering, and math (the STEM fields) and a few other majors.

Most of the knowledge and skills picked up in these classes are never used in the study of statistics; they are not, in fact, "pre-requisite knowledge" for that course. Despite this, community college placement tests assess all students based on their recall of their previous knowledge of algebra and—regardless of the student's intended major—force those determined to be "not college ready" into the algebra sequence.

Gerda says that seeing how Myra approached her class gave him "a sense of possibilities" he didn't have before, and he began working with his College of the Canyons colleagues to develop their own version of the course. "This is a solution to the one of the biggest problems in the community college system. It felt like a wonderful gift."

The College of the Canyons is one of 17 community colleges supported by the California Acceleration Project in offering over 100 sections of new accelerated math and English courses in 2011–12. The Project is an initiative of the state-funded California Community Colleges' Success Network (3CSN), with additional private support from the Walter S. Johnson Foundation, Learning Works, and the Scaling Innovation project of the Community College Research Center.

In 2011–12, seven colleges offered accelerated pre-statistics courses and received coaching from Myra Snell, while I coached the ten that offered accelerated English courses. The Project will support a second round of colleges in offering accelerated pilots in 2012–13.

Why Acceleration? The Basic Math of Long Sequences

The California Acceleration Project began in the summer of 2010, when Myra Snell and I published an article in *Perspectives*, the newsletter published of the California community college system's Research and Planning Group. We argued that the high attrition rates in developmental sequences are attributable to the length of the sequences. "The problem," we wrote, "is fundamentally structural. Attrition is high in developmental sequences, but more important, attrition is exponential. As students fall away at each level, the pool of continuing students gets smaller and smaller until only a fraction of the original group remains to complete the sequence."

In that article—and in a series of 3CSN workshops offered throughout California in 2010–11—we demonstrated that low completion rates can be explained by the number of "exit points" in students' path. Students starting two levels below college math or English face five exit points before completing the college-level course. They must (1) pass the first course, (2) choose to enroll in the next course, (3) pass the second course, (4) choose to enroll in the college-level course, and (5) pass that course. The specific reasons for student attrition vary, but community college students peel off at every exit point—and at higher rates when facing semester after semester of classes that earn no credit toward a longer-term goal.

Here's a thought experiment to illustrate what is occurring: Imagine you have a cohort of students starting out two levels below college English/math. Now imagine that 80 percent of them pass each course in the sequence and that 80 percent of the successful students persist to each subsequent course (a fairly optimistic assumption for many colleges). As your cohort makes its way through the exit points, the pool of continuing students shrinks: 80 percent of the original group pass the first course, and 80 percent of *those* students enroll in the second remedial course. Now you've got 80 percent *of the 80 percent*, or 64 percent of the original group. After you've made it through all five exit points, you end up with just 33 percent of the original group completing the college-level course. It's simple multiplication: .80 multiplied by itself five times = .33.

What this means, the article argues, is that to increase the number of developmental students who complete college-level gatekeeper courses in English and math, we must "step outside the prevailing assumption that multi-level sequences are the best way to support under-prepared students for the rigors of college. We will never increase completion rates for College English and Math—and therefore increase the numbers of students becoming eligible for transfer and degrees—unless we shrink the length of our sequences."

Also, It Works

The laws of multiplication alone wouldn't be enough, though, to convince faculty to dramatically overhaul their curricula. For acceleration to spread across the state, faculty needed to believe that shorter, redesigned pathways could actually lead to student success.

On the reading and writing side, evidence from Chabot College has helped to make that case. Since the mid-1990s, Chabot has offered an accelerated, integrated reading and writing class one level below college English. Students who don't qualify for college English can choose this four-unit course (English 102: Reading, Reasoning, and Writing—Accelerated), or a two-semester, eight-unit developmental sequence (English 101A and 101B: Reading, Reasoning, and Writing I and II). Both the accelerated course and the first non-accelerated course are open access, with no pre-requisite or minimum placement score.

Despite the absence of a minimum placement score, students from Chabot's accelerated course complete college-level English at substantially higher rates than students who start in the longer sequence.

Chabot's developmental curriculum is based on the principle that what under-prepared students need to be ready for college English is not grammar workbooks or assignments that ask them to write a paragraph about making a tamale. They need practice in the same kinds of reading, writing, and thinking they'll be asked to do in the college-level course, with more guidance and support than needs to be given to better-prepared students.

Developmental students at Chabot read full-length books, mostly nonfiction, and they integrate ideas and information from these books in their essays. This approach guides both the accelerated and non-accelerated paths at Chabot. The difference is simply pacing and

Figure 1. Completion of English 1A within 3 Years, Chabot College

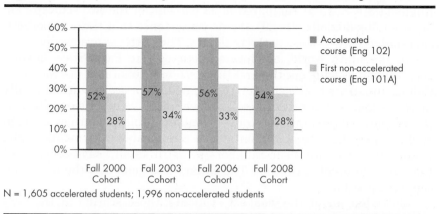

N = 1,605 accelerated students; 1,996 non-accelerated students

Data from the Basic Skills Progress Tracker, Data Mart, California Community Colleges Chancellor's Office. Students were followed for three years from their first enrollment in a developmental English course (English 101A or 102) and tracked for all subsequent enrollments in English. Completion rates include students who passed 1A at any point within the timeframe (first attempts and repeats).

whether students have one or two semesters to demonstrate sufficient academic literacy to move into college English.

What's striking about the Chabot data is that the trend has remained so consistent over the last decade. During this time, the college significantly increased its offerings of the accelerated course. In fall 2000, Chabot offered 24 sections of English 101A (the first non-accelerated course) and just 13 sections of English 102 (the accelerated course). By fall 2007, the balance had shifted, with 25 sections of the accelerated course and 18 sections of the first non-accelerated course on offer. The number of accelerated sections has further increased since then. In fall 2011, the ratio of accelerated to non-accelerated sections was three to one.

The accelerated class now serves a majority of developmental students rather than the minority who enrolled when fewer sections were available. And yet, English 1A completion rates have barely moved. This is important to keep in mind when skeptics hypothesize that accelerated students complete college English at higher rates because of differences in student characteristics: they are presumed to be self-selected, better motivated, better skilled, etc. If that were true, the completion rates would be expected to decline as most students were channeled into the accelerated path and the population became, presumably, *less* self-selected, motivated, skilled, etc. But that has not happened.

Accelerated students face just three exit points in their path through college English instead of five. Continuing the earlier thought experiment where 80 percent of students pass and persist at each level, we end up with 51 percent of the accelerated cohort completing college English (.80x.80x.80), compared to 33 percent for the two-semester sequence (.80x.80x.80x.80x.80). It's no coincidence that these hypothetical numbers are so close to the real data. The patterns are predictable.

In the math world, accelerated courses like Path2Stats haven't been around as long, but the first three student cohorts at Los Medanos College illustrate that a shorter, redesigned sequence can dramatically increase completion rates in college-level math. Students enrolling in the accelerated pre-statistics course completed college math at as much as 4.5 times the rate of students with comparable placements in the traditional sequence. "The numbers are still small," says Snell, "But they provide proof of concept. The canary has gone into the mine and come out just fine."

But what about the weakest students, those scoring at the very bottom of placement tests? [Figure 2] shows that students placing into pre-algebra or arithmetic have performed less well in the accelerated pathway than students with higher placement scores. However, these students do not have better results in the slower sequence, where they complete college math at a rate of just 9 percent.

At Chabot, we see a similar pattern among students with the bottom 20 percent of scores on the Accuplacer reading and sentence-skills tests. These students are much less likely to pass the accelerated class than students with higher scores (45 percent vs. 65 percent). However, their pass rates are equally low in the first course of the slower sequence.

The pattern holds true even for students scoring in the bottom 7 percent of Accuplacer scores: their pass rates are lower than those of higher-scoring students, but they see no gains from enrolling in the slower sequence: they pass the accelerated course at a rate of 48 percent, compared to 45 percent for the first non-accelerated course. At both Chabot and Los Medanos, we can see that although low-scoring students are at higher risk than other students, they are not better served by a slower, multi-semester sequence.

Shared Principles for Acceleration

In addition to providing training and coaching to the pilot colleges working closely with us, the California Acceleration Project does a lot of outreach to make a wider case for acceleration. By the end of 2011, our workshops and conference presentations had reached more than 90 of California's 112 community colleges, along with community colleges from more than 30 other states. In these workshops, we talk about our campuses' experience with acceleration, and we share video footage and materials from our own classrooms. But we do not intend for colleges to adopt the Chabot and Los Medanos models off the shelf.

Figure 2. Los Medanos College

Student placement in math sequence	Path2Stats % of students successfully completing college statistics in one year	Traditional Path % of students successfully completing college-level math course in three years
Transfer level	100% (3 of 3)	
Intermediate Algebra	82% (18 of 22)	33% (215 of 651)
Elementary Algebra	78% (25 of 32)	17% (102 of 598)
Pre-algebra or Arithmetic	38% (21 of 55)	9% (45 of 507)
Unknown placement	57% (4 of 7)	
Overall Completion Rate	60% (71 of 119)	21% (362 of 1756)

Path2Stats data include only students' first attempts at courses within one-year timeframe (no repeats). Data for Traditional Path include first attempts and repeats within a three-year timeframe.

Instead, we're trying to provide a concrete vision of the possible. We want faculty and administrators to leave with the sense that students are capable of more than low-level courses typically ask of them, as well as with ideas for how they can help more students make it to and through college-level courses. Rather than strict models to adopt, we offer principles for curricular reform.

- *Increasing completion of college-level English and math requires shorter developmental pathways and broader access to college-level courses*

   The length of developmental sequences must be significantly reduced to eliminate the many points at which students are lost by not passing or not enrolling in courses in the sequence. Colleges should also experiment with lowering the barriers blocking student access to college-level courses.

- *We must reduce our reliance on high-stakes placement tests*

   Standardized placement tests are notoriously poor predictors of student performance. We need to stop using these tests to separate students into rigid "levels" and instead allow them to demonstrate their capacity in challenging, supportive, streamlined pathways.

- *Streamlined developmental curricula should reflect three key principles:*

Backwards design. Rather than requiring all students to go through a single generic English, reading, or algebra curriculum, literacy and math instruction should be aligned with students' educational pathways. For students pursuing technical credentials, this might involve contextualized literacy and quantitative skills embedded in a vocational program. For students in academic, transfer-oriented paths, it might include pre-statistics and "practice English 1A" classes like those at Los Medanos and Chabot.

Just-in-time remediation. Current models of developmental education often break down complex skills and ways of thinking into discrete sub-skills, then deliver these skills up front to students in a linear, step-by-step curriculum. We argue instead for immersing students in challenging, authentic literacy and quantitative tasks and providing targeted reviews of foundational skills at the moment they are relevant to the higher-order work at hand.

Intentional support for affective issues. When developmental students aren't successful in their classes, the core issue is often *not their ability to handle the course content.* They may well have the capacity to write a good essay or solve a particular math problem. But when they encounter a difficult task, or receive critical feedback, or start to feel hopeless about their prospect of success, many of them will disengage, withdraw effort, and even disappear from class. Successful accelerated instruction involves classroom policies and practices that keep these dynamics from derailing students, such as intervening early with struggling students, grading policies that allow students to recover from a weak start, and building in time for one-on-one work with students.

In the California Acceleration Project, we argue that these are the necessary conditions for stopping the blood loss from our developmental arteries. If we leave our long sequences unchanged, we will never see meaningful progress in student completion. We can't address the problem simply by increasing tutoring, or adding a student success course, or linking classes through learning communities. As valuable as these interventions can be, the problems in developmental education are structural and fundamental. Our solutions must be as well. The good news: there are many, many ways to go about this.

Local Adaptation

Across California, colleges are considering these principles and making changes they think will work locally. Not every math department is ready to implement something like Path2Stats, but many colleges have implemented "compression" models of the standard developmental math sequence, such as combining previously separate courses in elementary and intermediate algebra into one, more intensive course, thereby eliminating the redundancy and the exit point between the two classes.

Another approach to acceleration: Chaffey College offers a three-week math review to students who place into arithmetic (four levels below college-level math), then allows students to retest. The majority of students completing the review have re-tested into intermediate algebra (one level below); Chaffey then offers late-start sections of the course so that students can complete four levels in one term.

Another acceleration strategy involves "mainstreaming" students who might otherwise have been placed into developmental courses directly into college-level English and math. Sometimes these approaches provide additional support, as in the highly successful Accelerated Learning Project at the Community College of Baltimore County, where upper-level developmental English students enroll in a regular college composition class along with a simultaneous small-group support class taught by the same instructor. Tennessee's Austin Pea State University has also seen impressive results from replacing remedial courses with mainstreaming models.

Other versions of mainstreaming qualify students for enrollment in a regular college-level course through mechanisms other than the placement exam, such as recognition of high school coursework. Fresno City College, for example, reviews students' high school transcripts and allows those who have passed Algebra II to enroll directly in statistics.

In San Diego's Grossmont-Cuyamaca district, students who had passed high school courses aligned with the college curriculum were allowed to enroll in the college English course regardless of their placement scores. Brad Phillips described the program in an online article for *Good Education*:

> Like many of their fellow freshmen nationally, a whopping 95 percent of high school graduates from West Hills [High School] who received As and Bs in their senior English courses did not "pass" the placement test. Yet when allowed to enroll in college-level courses instead of remedial classes, 86 percent successfully completed college-level English, lost no time in their progress, and stayed on course toward earning a degree.

Berkeley City College has developed its own unique approach to accelerating developmental English students. The college's traditional curriculum had—depending upon how you interpreted it—either two or four levels of developmental courses. There were officially two levels, but each level had an "A" and "B" course to allow for easy repeatability by unsuccessful students. Many faculty—particularly those juggling part-time work at multiple colleges—mistakenly believed that students were required to take the A and B courses in sequence, so the two levels often became four. English 1A completion rates were predictably low.

More recently, the English department has been retooling their classes using backwards design, giving developmental students assignments similar to the kinds they'll see in the college-level class. Then, near the end of the semester, faculty get together for a blind portfolio review to assess students' work against a rubric of competencies required for exiting college English. When assessing the portfolios, instructors don't know the students' names or the course in which they were enrolled. Based upon the quality of the work, a student officially placed two levels below can be advanced directly to college English, and a strong developmental student can even earn credit for the college-level course through the credit-by-examination process.

"Our department chair Jenny Lowood has been *on fire* about this work," says Cleavon Smith, a Berkeley City College faculty member and network coordinator for 3CSN. One of the issues spotlighted in the portfolio reviews is the arbitrariness of the line between students placed two levels below and one level below. The department responded quickly, piloting an open-access, one-semester developmental course that leads directly to college English. The class is four units of regular class time, with an additional three hours of scheduled lab in a computer class-room, where students work with the instructor and several tutors and receive individualized guidance on their writing. The college started small, with Smith teaching the first section in spring 2012, but plans for fall 2012 include replacing most sections of the two-levels-below course with this high-support accelerated model.

Among the 17 pilot colleges participating in the California Acceleration Project, there is a lot of variation in how the principles of acceleration are being implemented. In math, all seven colleges are offering new pre-statistics classes that provide a shorter alternative to the traditional algebra sequence, but some are doing open-access courses with no pre-requisites, while others have arithmetic or pre-algebra pre-requisites. Some use fairly traditional approaches to math pedagogy, others have built their curriculum around online statistical materials, and others have adopted the project-based learning and statistical software programs used at Los Medanos.

Some colleges have started with just one or two sections per semester, whereas the College of the Canyons is offering 11 sections in spring 2011, including an extra-accelerated version that compresses the pre-stats and college-level classes into a single semester. Gerda says they anticipate expanding to 20 sections of pre-stats per semester within a year.

Of the ten colleges piloting accelerated English in the project, several are implementing a model similar to Chabot's—an open-access, one-semester course that integrates attention to reading and writing and serves as a "practice 1A" class. Solano College's cumbersome traditional curricular structure had several different levels and required lab co-requisites plus departmental finals—and students had been getting stuck and never getting out. "We were tweaking and tweaking and tweaking an English program that was set up maybe 10 years ago," instructor Melissa Reeve explained. "I was at the point where I said, I'm not putting my energy into any more tweaking. There's something fundamentally wrong with what we're doing. If I'm going to do something, it needs more be more radical."

Los Angeles Trade Tech adapted Chabot's model for their own population by pairing it with specific vocational programs, so that students are part of a cohort. Reading and writing skills are now contextualized within students' chosen fields.

Other colleges were interested in Chabot's approach but did not feel they could implement it on their own campuses, at least not initially. Yuba College, for example, had four different levels of reading and writing classes below college English, or eight remedial courses in all. It felt like a big leap to go from this curriculum to a single, open-access, integrated course. What they did instead was to pilot integrated reading and writing courses at different levels of their existing sequence, along with a course that combined the bottom two levels (four courses, 16 units total) into a single 6-unit course.

Kyra Mello was the instructor who piloted the latter model. Using backwards design from college English, she gave students challenging readings and essay assignments, and she was impressed with the quality of the work they produced. At the end of the semester, Mello used Yuba's pre-requisite challenge process to enable many successful students to skip the next one to two levels of the sequence. She believed that *all* of these students could have handled moving directly into the college course, but she put most of them into the course one level below because she felt concerned about jeopardizing the new acceleration effort if her colleagues teaching English 1A said, "This student shouldn't have been in my class."

Teaching with an emphasis on acceleration and backwards design makes a lot more sense to Mello than traditional skill-and-drill approaches to remediation. She came to Yuba after completing the master's in composition program at Chico State University, where she says the focus was on main-streaming under-prepared students rather than remediating them: "My professors and my mentors always taught us that students were highly capable and intelligent," Mello said.

She struggled to adapt to the long sequences in the community college world, with classes on how to write a sentence and assignments like, "Write a paragraph about your favorite room." Before officially teaching an accelerated course in fall 2011, she did her own version of acceleration: "I just expected more, and they always delivered."

Yuba's early pilots paved the way for more significant changes to the curriculum. The English department decided to eliminate the bottom two levels of developmental courses entirely, and all full-time faculty agreed to teach the new open-access course two levels below college

English. Mello says that the faculty are planning to work as a cohort—meeting once or twice a month, teaching a common book, and organizing their classes using backwards design.

They will also share some of the affective-level interventions that Mello and her team learned in the California Acceleration Project, such as reaching out to students when they show signs of struggle, having a "'fess-up" routine that holds students accountable for doing the reading, and using class time to have students collaboratively make sense of the assigned readings. Mello says the college is also moving away from offering separate reading classes, considering instead one-unit reading courses linked to challenging classes across the curriculum, such as biology.

Other approaches piloted in the California Acceleration Project: Pasadena City College created special sections of its course one level below college English, reserving 10 out of the 25 seats for students who had officially placed two levels below. Fullerton College took several sections of its course two levels below college English and taught them to the outcomes of the course one level below. Students who demonstrate sufficient mastery at the end of the term can jump directly to college English through the pre-requisite challenge process; those who don't can still advance to the class one level below.

All of these approaches illustrate how creatively faculty have implemented the principles of acceleration: shortening sequences, reducing reliance on placement tests, redesigning curricula, and giving students access to more challenging tasks. The statewide movement also illustrates the power that can be generated when colleges work together in collaborative networks like the California Community Colleges' Success Network (3CSN). "It's hard to do things without a community," says Gerda, recalling the 3CSN workshop he attended where he first heard about Path2Stats. "What I saw that day was the chance to do this in a community. You didn't have to do it alone."

Next Steps: More Colleges, More Research, and a National Movement

As a second group of colleges joins the California Acceleration Project in summer 2012, we will also be conducting research into outcomes from the first 17 colleges. 3CSN is partnering with California's Research and Planning Group to track how many students from the accelerated pilots complete college-level gatekeeper courses in English and math, compared to students with similar placements in the traditional sequences. The Community College Research Center is also studying the initiative in its Scaling Innovation project, funded by the William and Flora Hewlett Foundation to understand what it takes to spread curricular and pedagogical innovations in developmental education.

We have worked as well with the Research and Planning Group and the state chancellor's office to create a new cohort tracking tool that enables all 112 California community colleges to see how many students complete college-level English and math from different starting points in their sequences. Yuba College, for example, can go online and see that in fall 2006, 55 students began its developmental writing sequence four levels below college composition. Five years later, at the end of spring 2011, just two of those 55 students had completed college English—3.6 percent of the original group. This kind of data mobilizes faculty to rethink their approach to remediation, as Yuba did when it cut its developmental sequence in half.

The California Acceleration Project is also linking up with community colleges in other states to build a national acceleration movement. The Accelerated Learning Project of the Community College of Baltimore County (CCBC) is one of the other major players in this movement, having inspired more than 30 colleges in multiple states to implement main-streaming models of acceleration in English.

Each June, CCBC hosts the national conference on acceleration; this year the event (June 6–8, 2012 in Baltimore) will be co-sponsored by the California Acceleration Project. Together, CCBC and the Project have made the case for acceleration to the 29 states participating in Complete College America, the American Association for Community Colleges, the National Association for Developmental Education, and the colleges participating in the multi-state Achieving the Dream initiative.

It's a promising time for community colleges. Research from the Community College Research Center has provided a much clearer sense of the problems we face, as well as promising solutions for these problems. Buoyed by the Obama administration's emphasis on college completion and investments by national philanthropic organizations such as the Hewlett, Gates, and Lumina Foundations, the movement to reform developmental education is gaining momentum, and accelerated courses are being piloted around the country. Some states—Virginia and Arkansas, for example—have even made accelerated learning models the centerpieces of statewide reform efforts.

It is also a precarious time for community colleges. We know that our current multi-level remediation systems are not working and that change is imperative. But we need to ensure that we don't end up compromising our commitment to at-risk students in the process. We cannot simply cut the bottom levels of our existing sequences and deny access to the students placed there, as some states are contemplating in the form of a "floor" for remediation.

In this time of constrained state budgets, we must be vigilant to protect the broad-access mission of the community college and the students that developmental education was intended to serve. We need to cut levels, not students. The results from Chabot and Los Medanos make clear that the "lowest-level" students are much more capable than we have believed. It's time to unleash their capacity through challenging, supportive accelerated courses and fulfill the promise of a more level playing field for under-prepared students.

Resources

Accelerated Learning Project, Community College of Baltimore County. Retrieved from http://alp-deved.org/

Basic Skills Progress Tracker. Management Information Systems Data Mart. California Community Colleges Chancellor's Office. http://datamart.cccco .edu/Outcomes/BasicSkills_Cohort_Tracker.aspx

California Acceleration Project. Retrieved from http://cap.3csn.org

Hern, K. (2011). *Accelerated English at Chabot College: A synthesis of key findings*. Hayward, CA: California Acceleration Project. Retrieved from http:// cap.3csn.org/developing-pilots/integrated-reading-and-writing/

Hern, K., with Snell, M. (2010). Exponential attrition and the promise of acceleration in developmental English and math. *Perspectives*. Berkeley, CA: Research and Planning Group. Retrieved from http://www.rpgroup.org /resources/accelerated-developmental-english-and-math

Phillips, B. (2011, Sept. 18). *How to break the cycle of remedial college classes*. Retrieved from www.good.is/post/how-to-break-the-cycle-of-remedial-college -classes/

Critiquing the Need to Eliminate Remediation: Lessons from San Francisco State

Sugie Goen-Salter

Sugie Goen-Salter describes a model of structuring developmental reading programming that has a long history, and has taken many different forms over the years, but is now gaining attention as Integrated Reading and Writing (IRW). She describes how this model was implemented as a reform effort at San Francisco State University. In closing, she acknowledges the need for additional faculty training and professional development for those teaching in postsecondary developmental contexts.

Ever since the California State University (CSU) first authorized remedial instruction in the mid-1970s, it has been waging an expensive, but losing, battle to eliminate the need for it. In the 1980s, students deemed to be in need of remediation (as determined by a system-wide English Placement Test) numbered somewhere around 42% of the incoming class. This, in turn, caused the California Postsecondary Education Commission to declare that remediation was careening out of control at California's colleges and to call on the California State University and the University of California to prepare comprehensive plans for reducing the amount of remedial instruction at their institutions (California Postsecondary Education Commission, *Promises to Keep*).

The CSU Board of Trustees responded with a set of initiatives aimed chiefly at high schools to reduce the number of incoming first-year students who would need remediation to no more than 12% by 1990. Among other things, the CSU added four years of high school English to its admissions criteria, a requirement that at the time was even more stringent than that of the University of California. It also beefed up its teacher education programs with new minimum entry and exit requirements, including maintenance of higher grade-point averages, an "early field experience," and more rigorous assessments of "professional aptitude" (California Postsecondary Education Commission, *Segmental Actions* 6). The plan included a 4.4 million dollar program to improve the clinical supervision of student teachers. And, in the event that this impressive array of high school course requirements and toughened standards for teacher credentialing did not help stem the tide of remediation, the CSU's plan also called for a number of cooperative school-college partnerships to ensure that the high schools clearly understood what would be expected of students when they arrived at college. Among the chief results of these partnerships was the joint publication by the Academic Senates of the California Community Colleges, the CSU, and the University of California of the "Statement on Competencies in English and Mathematics Expected for Entering Freshmen."

To ensure that the "Statement on Competencies" was not simply shipped out in the mail and forgotten, it was featured at a number of statewide and regional articulation gatherings sponsored by the CSU, the University of California, and the California Community Colleges. Also, it became the centerpiece of the High School Diagnostic Testing Program in Writing, sponsored in part by the CSU-funded California Academic Partnership Program. Starting in 1984, the Diagnostic Testing Program focused on 11th-grade students of underrepresented minority backgrounds, inviting them to write a "mock" CSU English Placement Test (or UC Subject A test) on which they would receive a score based on the university rubric as well as comments from university writing program faculty. These students were also invited to attend Saturday workshops on academic writing. CSU and UC faculty and high school teachers collaborated on the reading and scoring of the essays in the hopes that the high school teachers would adopt the university standards in their curriculum.

A story of the obstinacy of remediation emerges from these efforts, for while they were being put into practice, the percentage of CSU incoming students who needed remediation in English (as determined by the English Placement Test) was steadily creeping upward to an all-time high. By 1990, the year the CSU had set as its goal to reduce the need for remediation in English to no more than 12% of the incoming class, 45% were assessed as needing remediation, and that figure was climbing.

Undeterred by this failure, or as Mike Rose put it in "The Language of Exclusion," suffering from the institutional amnesia endemic to higher education when it comes to writing instruction, a new Board of Trustees decided in 1997 to mandate yet another set of initiatives to reduce remediation to no more than 10% of the incoming class by 2007. Following in the footsteps of the City University of New York, which banned remedial instruction from CUNY's four-year colleges and moved it—as well as the students deemed in need of it—to its two-year community colleges, the CSU plan called first for a one-year limit on remedial instruction in English and mathematics available to any given student. Students who failed to complete their remedial course work during their first year were subject to disenrollment from the university. Disenrolled students would be able to return to the university only after completing their remedial course work at a community college. The second, more ambitious, part of the plan called for a 10% reduction each year in the number of students entering the CSU who were in need of remediation, putting the State University system finally on track for eventually eliminating remediation from its campuses.

I open with this brief history because, as Mary Soliday argues in *The Politics of Remediation*, basic writing suffers from a lack of historical consciousness that renders it vulnerable to efforts to eliminate it. This is especially dangerous because "proponents of downsizing often rely upon a particular version of the remedial past to bolster their arguments in the present" (10). Far too often, concerns about curriculum, pedagogy, and basic writing theory are left out of administrative policy discussions about remediation. Just as often, however, scholars and teachers in the field of basic writing are content to ask questions only about curriculum and pedagogy while ignoring basic writing's complex history and the ways it interacts with vested institutional, economic, and political interests. In the remainder of this article, I provide an update on San Francisco State University's Integrated Reading/Writing (IRW) program. By locating the IRW reform project in the context of the California State University's history of remediation, I am better able to question these vested interests, most notably the institutional need to claim that remediation is being eliminated.

The Integrated Reading/Writing Program

As Helen Gillotte-Tropp and I first reported in our 2003 article in the *Journal of Basic Writing* (Goen and Gillotte-Tropp, "Integrating Reading and Writing"), San Francisco State's Integrated Reading/Writing program developed in response to two concerns directly related to the CSU's latest attempt to reduce the need for remediation. The first was that substantive reductions to the population of students who test into remediation would threaten CSU access and equity goals.[1] The second was that efforts to eliminate remediation are implicitly linked to a persistent tendency in literacy education to treat reading and writing as distinct and separate processes. Postsecondary institutions have stubbornly enacted policies based on the belief that learning to read should have been accomplished by third grade, and learning to write by twelfth. Accordingly, there remains a prevailing attitude at many institutions that any postsecondary instruction in reading and writing is *de facto* "remedial," and, thus, vulnerable to political and educational forces aimed at its removal.

Even if we hadn't faced these remedial policy imperatives, we had good reasons to want to integrate instruction in reading and writing. Informed by lessons from the past, we knew that students were systematically placed into basic writing classes disproportionately on the basis of the reading portion of the CSU's English Placement Test, regardless of the fact that these courses may offer little or no instruction in reading. We were also convinced by empirical research demonstrating the crucial connection between learning to read and learning to write. Sandra Stotsky summarized this research as follows: better writers tend to be better readers, better writers tend to read more than poorer writers, and better readers tend to produce more mature prose than poorer readers (16). We knew that particular kinds of reading experiences, for example, Mariolina Salvatori's "introspective reading" (446), have a stimulating and generative effect on writing, and, as Vivian Zamel notes, the corollary is also true: particular writing experiences teach students to be more effective readers (470).

We took seriously as well Kathleen McCormick's warning that when reading and writing are taught as separate subjects, these beneficial effects are all but lost (99). Since reading instruction has historically had no place in the postsecondary curriculum—and basic writing instruction a rapidly diminishing place—we could only wonder how at-risk students were to successfully negotiate the literacy tasks that await them in college. And, while some of the research findings on the reading-writing connection have informed instructional practice, Nancy Nelson and Robert Calfee remind us that instruction itself is still far from integrated, but is rather "a collection of separate components, each with its own traditions, theoretical underpinnings and terminology" (36). By way of example, they cite the "integrated language arts" teacher who teaches students about "main ideas" when teaching reading, but refers to "topic sentences" when teaching writing without pointing out, or perhaps even noticing, any overlap (35–36).

Our reasoning in designing the IRW program was fairly straightforward: if the link between instruction in reading and writing is as crucial as we hypothesized, then it follows that students would reap demonstrably greater benefits from an approach that integrates the two. And if this hypothesis proved true, we wondered if students deemed least prepared for college-level reading and writing could also achieve these benefits effectively and swiftly enough to enable them to move into the academic mainstream in less time than the one-year institutional limit on remedial instruction. Could we, in other words, eliminate the "need for remediation" by providing students with an enriched literacy experience during their first, crucial year of college?

The IRW program provides an alternative to San Francisco State's traditional approach to English remediation. Students who scored in the lowest quartile on the English Placement Test (two levels below first-year composition) used to complete a full year of developmental-level course work. In their first semester, they took a 3-unit basic writing course concurrently with a 1-unit reading course. In their second semester, they took another 3-unit basic writing course concurrently with another 1-unit reading course. To meet this remedial English requirement, students had two different writing instructors, two different reading instructors, and four different groups of classmates by the time they entered their first-year composition course in their third semester of enrollment. The curriculum of the reading and writing courses was mostly separate. The texts students read in the reading course, and the strategies they learned to guide their reading, were rarely used in the writing course. Similarly, the topics students wrote about in the writing class and their growing understanding of the writing process and of discourse structures were not explicitly used to help students decide how and what to read in the reading course.

Rather than requiring students to complete two basic writing classes concurrent with two reading classes before becoming eligible for first-year composition, the IRW program (like Arizona State's *Stretch Program* [see Glau]) enrolls them in a single year-long course; students who successfully complete this course will have met not only the CSU remediation requirement, but also the first-year college composition requirement, in effect completing in one year what would ordinarily have taken three semesters to accomplish.

In 1999, Helen Gillotte-Tropp and I began working with five instructors to develop an integrated curriculum (for more specific information on the IRW course, see Goen and Gillotte-Tropp; Baldwin, Gillotte-Tropp, Goen-Salter, and Wong). During our deliberations and planning, we realized that in order for our course to be truly integrated, it could not be a course in which reading always precedes writing, reducing writing to something that is done after the reading is complete as a way to check comprehension rather than a way to work through, analyze, and arrive at an understanding of a text. Neither could it be a course that reduces reading to a supporting role, one that provides information and lends authority to bolster the writing.

Accordingly, a primary goal of the IRW course is to provide students with an explicit understanding of the complex ways that reading and writing intersect, to make visible to them the choices they make as readers, and how those choices inform the decisions they make when writing, and vice versa. At some point in the reading of any text, students are asked to examine the text not just for what meaning they derived from it, but for how the author constructed the text and the effect of those formal decisions on how students made sense of the text. In short, the course tries to break down the barrier between text reception and text production, by inviting students to look at a text they read for clues to its production, and a text they produce for clues to how it might be received.

Helping students attain awareness and knowledge of their own mental processes such that they can monitor, regulate, and direct themselves to a desired end are key components in the IRW curriculum. The course accomplishes this through a variety of self-reflective activities. For example, at various junctures, students write a modified version of Mariolina Salvatori's difficulty paper. In the IRW version of the difficulty paper, students are asked to explore in writing their surprises, hunches, puzzlements, and difficulties with a reading, to articulate an action plan for how to address those difficulties, and then put that action plan to work. In the final part of the assignment, students reflect on any new insights they gained, or new questions that arose, as a result of putting into action their strategic plan. They also reflect on the efficacy of their plan, how well it worked to guide them to a different, perhaps more satisfying, experience with the text. Finally, students consider how their experiences as readers, as recorded in the difficulty paper, might inform decisions they make as writers. We have found that the difficulty paper teaches students to become conscious of their mental moves and to revise or complicate those moves as they become aware of what those moves did or did not make possible, thereby encouraging recursion and self-monitoring in both reading and writing. Perhaps most importantly, this assignment makes "difficulty" a generative force in student learning, something to be critically engaged rather than avoided or ignored. And we have discovered it helps create important bridges between academic learning and students' lived experience in the world beyond school as they discover that their experience with reading is shaped not only by the formal properties of a text or their comprehension and interpretive skills, but also by their social and cultural location.

Our intent in designing the IRW curriculum was not to radically alter the content of either the basic writing or reading course, but to redesign the curriculum so that what students learned about reading would function as an explicit scaffold for learning about writing, and vice versa. By necessity, we created some new writing topics to correspond to texts assigned in the reading class, and we added some new readings to help students think through topics assigned in the writing class. Otherwise, our emphasis was not on curricular change so much as it was on strategic double-duty—using what had traditionally been considered reading heuristics to aid students in the act of writing, and using writing strategies to help students better understand their roles as readers.

One example of a strategy that we use extensively is K-W-L+. It represents a four-step procedure that begins by accessing students' prior knowledge, explicitly attaching new learning onto what students already know (K). We then invite students to ask questions. Given what they know, what would they like to know (W)? What curiosities do they have or what puzzlements would they like to explore? Teachers then introduce a learning activity, which can be anything from reading a text, watching a film, listening to music, looking at visual stimuli, to analyzing data collected as a class. The next step is to gather what they've learned (L) from the activity. Which of their questions got answered? How has this new learning amplified or modified what they knew before? In the final stage, students pose new questions (+). Given what they knew, and what they have now learned, what new questions do they have or what new avenues of inquiry would they like to explore? While K-W-L+ has traditionally been considered a reading strategy only, we have found it to also be an excellent idea-generating strategy for writing essays. Students brainstorm and generate categories for ideas (K), develop interests and curiosities by asking questions (W), write on what has been learned (L), and use this as a guide for additional reading and inquiry (+), which can then form the seeds of a new writing project. As used in the IRW program, K-W-L+ is a strategy that students can use to not only comprehend a text, but to shape and organize ideas for a written product, and finally, use in peer response groups to give or receive feedback (what do I know about my peer's essay? what do I want to know about my peer's essay? what did I learn from reading my peer's essay? what do I still want to know now that I've read my peer's essay?). Through instruction and experience in using strategies such as K-W-L+, the IRW program instills in students a sense that reading and writing are complementary processes of meaning making—whether meaning comes from their transaction with text or their production of text.

Bolstered by their direct experience with the reading-writing connection, students are encouraged through a series of reflective activities to consider how reading and writing work reciprocally to help them discover meaning, not only in the IRW course, but in courses across the college curriculum, and in their own lives. And, we added a powerful incentive: Students who successfully complete the IRW course have met not only the CSU remediation requirement, but also San Francisco State's first-year college composition requirement, in effect completing in their first year what would ordinarily have taken them three semesters to accomplish.

We began by piloting 5 experimental sections of the IRW course. Then in 2001, with a three-year grant from the U.S. Department of Education's Fund for the Improvement of Postsecondary Education (FIPSE), we expanded to 10 sections and an enrollment of 169 students. In 2002–2003, we offered 11 sections with 190 students, and in 2003–2004, we again offered 11 sections and enrolled 193 students. At the conclusion of the grant, the program expanded to include over 30 sections enrolling more than 500 students.

Project Results

To measure how well the IRW program was meeting its goal to provide students with an enriched literacy experience that would facilitate their entry into mainstream college courses, we used a number of outcome measures to compare students enrolled in the IRW program to a control group enrolled in the traditional sequence of separate reading and writing courses. In our 2003 article (Goen and Gillotte-Tropp), we published results on the first year the program was funded by FIPSE. These first-year results showed that students in the IRW group had higher retention rates, completed the remediation requirement sooner and in greater numbers, scored similarly to or higher on measures of reading comprehension and critical reasoning, received higher ratings on their writing portfolios, and exited the program better able to pass the next composition course in the required sequence. More importantly, the IRW group was able to accomplish these goals in one semester less of instruction than students in the control group. We noted at the time that while these first-year findings painted "a promising portrait of literacy development, the extent to which the integrated program can prove to be a viable response . . . will be more fully determined by corroborating data from the second and third years" (109). As described below, the results from the first year held steady over the next two years.

Retention Rates

Many students enrolled in the IRW program work full or part time, come from families with low incomes, and/or have family responsibilities caring for younger siblings or their own children. In designing their "Enrichment" program at CUNY,[2] Mary Soliday and Barbara Gleason noted that "forming communities is vitally important" for under-prepared students (66). The IRW program, with its year-long cohort structure, provides a place on a large urban commuter campus for students to form a community of peers and provides vital skills and strategies to help students negotiate this crucial first year. Students enrolled in the IRW program had retention rates of 88% in the first year, compared to 83% for students in the traditional sequence. In the

Table 1. Comparison of Remediation Pass Rates, IRW v. Control

Year	IRW	Control Group (n = 221)	Percent Difference
2001–2002	97% (N = 136, n = 132)	84% (N = 204, n = 173)	+13%
2002–2003	97% (N = 171, n = 166)	87% (N = 212, n = 184)	+10%
2003–2004	99% (N = 181, n = 179)	89% (N = 221, n = 201)	+10%

second year, IRW retention had increased to 90%. By the third year, the IRW retention rates improved to 94%, while the rate for the traditional sequence remained relatively stable at around 85% over this same two-year period.

Remediation Pass Rates

Across all three years of FIPSE funding, the IRW students passed the integrated course at a higher rate than students in the traditional two-semester sequence of remediation. These higher pass rates have significant consequences in the context of the CSU's one-year limit on remediation. The penalty for not passing the remediation requirement in the first year is dis-enrollment from the university. Each year between 1997, when the remediation rule went into effect, and 2007, the CSU as a whole had on average dis-enrolled 11% of its first-year students. In the first three years of the remediation rule, San Francisco State dis-enrolled 16%; after the IRW program was implemented, that percentage decreased to an average of slightly more than 12%. In the third year of the IRW program, 99% of students in the IRW course passed (and thereby met the CSU remediation requirement). By comparison, 89% of the students in the traditional sequence passed, leaving 11% subject to dis-enrollment under the CSU policy. Table 1 shows a comparison of remediation pass rates across all three years.

Reading Comprehension and Critical Reasoning

To assess reading outcomes, we used the Descriptive Test of Language Skills. The DTLS is a widely used and reliable measure of reading comprehension and critical reasoning. Scores from the DTLS are normed against those of an ethnically diverse sample of students enrolled in regular and developmental courses, including a proportionate number

Table 2. Summary of DTLS Posttest Results, IRW v. Control

		IRW Group	*Control Group*	*Difference Between Groups*	*Significance of Difference*
Reading Comprehension Mean Score	Year 1: 2001–02	29.20	27.0	2.20	0.005
	Year 2: 2002–03	28.78	27.57	1.21	0.038
	Year 3: 2003–04	28.43	28.73	-.30*	ns
Critical Reasoning Mean Score	Year 1: 2001–02	20.2	18.6	1.6	0.002
	Year 2: 2002–03	19.41	18.62	0.79	ns
	Year 3: 2003–04	18.90	19.85	-0.95*	ns

*These inverse figures for Year 3 are not entirely surprising. By the third year, the traditional reading course had come under heavy influence of the IRW program. In fact, most of these traditional courses were taught by instructors who readily conceded that they approached their traditional courses in much the same way as they approached their IRW courses.

of ESL students, from 11 two-year colleges and 24 four-year colleges across the U.S. As shown in Table 2, between 2001 and 2004, students in the IRW courses performed similarly or showed significantly higher gains on both the reading comprehension and critical reasoning measures. At least as important, the IRW students achieved these gains after one semester of instruction, compared to the control group whose gains were assessed after one year. See Table 2.

Essay Portfolios

We collected essay portfolios from both groups of students. The portfolios contained essays from students in the IRW group collected during the first semester (one essay from early in the first semester, one from the mid-point, and one towards the end of the semester). These portfolios were labeled "Developmental-level" and compared to portfolios from the control group (one essay collected early, one at mid-point, and one near the end of the year of the traditional two-semester sequence of developmental courses).

Table 3. Year 1 (2001–2002) Student Essay Portfolios, IRW v. Control

	Measure	IRW Group	Control Group	Difference Between Groups	Significance of Difference
Developmental Level Mean Score	1. R/W Integration	2.71	2.68	0.03	ns
	2. Thesis	2.69	2.58	0.11	ns
	3. Org	2.65	2.59	0.06	ns
	4. Syntax	2.67	2.50	0.17	0.05
	5. Mechanics	2.47	2.30	0.17	0.05
	6. Audience*	n/a	n/a	n/a	n/a
	7. Overall	2.71	2.51	0.20	0.01
First-Year Comp Level Mean Score	1. R/W Integration	3.05	2.8	0.03	0.025
	2. Thesis	2.82	2.65	0.11	ns
	3. Org	2.8	2.76	0.06	ns
	4. Syntax	2.69	2.57	0.17	ns
	5. Mechanics	2.48	2.50	-0.02	ns
	6. Audience*	n/a	n/a	n/a	n/a
	7. Overall	2.83	2.59	0.24	0.044

*In Year 1, we used an evaluation checklist with only six measures. The checklist was modified in Years 2 and 3 to include the measure "Audience Awareness."

We also collected three essays from the IRW group during the second semester of the integrated course. These portfolios were labeled "First-Year Composition (FYC)-level." These portfolios were compared to those collected from the control group during their third semester, when they were enrolled in the first-year written composition course.

The portfolios were assessed in blind and normed scoring sessions using two independent raters (any discrepant scores were resolved by a third independent reader). Experienced external readers assessed each portfolio using a modified version of the checklist used by Soliday and Gleason in their "Enrichment" program ("From Remediation to Enrichment"). Portfolios were assessed on a four-point scale across six

Table 4 Year 3 (2003–2004) Student Essay Portfolios, IRW v. Control

	Measure	IRW Group	Control Group	Difference Between Groups	Significance of Difference
Developmental Level Mean Score	1. R/W Integration	2.73	2.64	0.09	ns
	2. Thesis	2.75	2.51	0.24	0.0045
	3. Org	2.66	2.47	0.19	0.042
	4. Syntax	2.52	2.26	0.26	0.005
	5. Mechanics	2.82	2.50	0.32	0.0011
	6. Audience	2.82	2.74	0.08	ns
	7. Overall	2.74	2.46	0.28	0.0011
First-Year Comp Level Mean Score	1. R/W Integration	2.7	2.5	0.2	ns
	2. Thesis	2.8	2.6	0.2	ns
	3. Org	2.6	2.6	0	ns
	4. Syntax	2.5	2.5	0	ns
	5. Mechanics	2.9	2.7	0.2	ns
	6. Audience	2.9	2.8	0.1	ns
	7. Overall	2.8	2.6	0.2	ns

subcategories, and were given an overall rating (see Appendix). Over the three years, students in the IRW group consistently outperformed the control group, but with varying levels of statistical significance. In the interest of space, Tables 3 and 4 summarize the comparative results for the first and third years only.

Second-Year Composition Pass Rates

Students who successfully complete the year-long IRW course have met two of San Francisco State's written English proficiency requirements. They have not only complied with the one-year remediation rule, but also have met the first-year composition requirement and are now eligible to enroll in the mandatory second-year composition course. Since students coming out of the IRW program arrive in this second-year course a full semester earlier than students in the control group, we were especially interested to see how the IRW students fared in this second-year course. As Table 5 shows, across all three years, students

Table 5. Comparison of Pass Rates in Second-Year Composition*

	Year 1: 2001–2002		Year 2: 2002–2003		Year 3: 2003–2004	
Pass Rates of Students Eligible via IRW	97%		93%		95%	
	N = 76	(n = 74)	N = 124	(n = 115)	N = 181	(n = 172)
Pass Rates of Students Eligible via Traditional Pathways	90%		88%		92%	
	N = 1967	(n = 1740)	N = 1964	(n = 1728)	N = 1883	(n = 1732)

*We compared pass rates in second-year composition of students from the IRW program to aggregate pass rates of students who arrived in second-year composition by (a) testing directly into it; (b) testing into and completing first-year composition; (c) testing into and completing the traditional remedial sequence followed by successful completion of first-year composition; or (d) transferring in coursework equivalent to first-year composition from a community college.

who arrived in the second-year course via IRW passed the course at consistently higher rates than students who arrived by other pathways.

Taken as a whole, the evidence seems clear. The IRW program allows students deemed most at-risk for not succeeding and/or dropping out, who begin San Francisco State with a full year of high-stakes remediation as their welcome mat, to enter the academic mainstream during the crucial first year and to move on to more advanced composition courses—in short, to thrive as college students.

Eliminating the Need for Remediation

During the time that the IRW program was being implemented, the clock was steadily ticking on the CSU's policy to reduce the need for remediation to no more than 10% of the incoming class by the year 2007. In 1997, when the reduction plan went into effect, 47% of all incoming first-year students were assessed as needing remediation in English. Not unlike the initiatives in the 1980s, this new plan called for comprehensive strategies, most of which were aimed at creating joint partnerships between the CSU and public schools to strengthen the preparation of high school graduates. One strategy introduced in 1999 was the Collaborative Academic Preparation Initiative (CAPI), a partnership between various CSU campuses and local high schools, whose purpose was to strengthen the mathematics and English preparation of college-bound high school students. When the CSU eliminated funding for this program, it was replaced in 2003 with a new flagship initiative, the Early Assessment Program (EAP). Jointly administered by the State Board of Education, the California Department of Education, and the California State University, the Early Assessment Program's goal is to identify students not yet proficient in English before they arrive at a California State University campus.[3] The aim is to identify these students by the end of their high school junior year, and then provide them with an amplified course of instruction in their senior year, thus relieving the CSU of the need to remediate these students in their first year of college. Since it was first put into practice, the number of high school students volunteering to take the EAP has grown to more than 300,000 in 2007 alone.

Two primary initiatives accompany the EAP plan. The first is an 80-hour course of study for high school teachers called Reading Institutes for Academic Preparation (RIAP). The stated goal of these reading institutes is to help teachers "learn the expectations for college-level work in English . . . and practice specific strategies for building academic reading competency . . . including content-specific reading demands, critical thinking, and academic reading/writing connections" ("Pilot Study" 6). More than two thousand high school teachers have participated in these reading institutes since their inception.

The second initiative is the twelfth grade Expository Reading and Writing Course (ERWC). Developed in collaboration with CSU faculty and high school teachers, it consists of fourteen assignment modules. Each module contains a sequence of "integrated reading and writing experiences" that take between two to three weeks to teach ("Pilot Study" 7). High school teachers are offered four days of professional development led by CSU faculty, high school teachers, and county office of education language arts specialists. Since the introduction of the ERWC in 2004, more than 2,200 teachers have participated in these workshops and adopted the ERWC modules for students in their schools.

Anecdotal evidence suggests that these efforts are doing much good, that many students are finding higher education accessible as a direct result of the collaborative efforts of dedicated university and high school teachers. And I would argue that increased collaboration between high school and university faculty is having a beneficial effect on both, providing a forum for a rich exchange of ideas, expertise, and resources, not to mention professional support and encouragement. But offered as a comprehensive plan to reduce the need for remediation, these strategies belie the historical record. In implementing this expensive EAP initiative, the CSU is operating from a persistent but flawed belief that if it only sets its standards high enough, and articulates them clearly to the secondary schools, the result will be fewer under-prepared students seeking admission and, eventually, complete elimination of the need for remedial courses at the university level.

Despite these well-intentioned and well-implemented programs in the high schools, in 2007—the target year for reducing the number of new students needing remediation to 10%—the remediation figures for that year remained at the recalcitrant rate of 46.2%.

In light of these disappointing results, the CSU has looked for alternative ways to reduce educational spending on remedial programs, most directly by declaring that as of 2007 there would be no more general funding for remediation. Campuses across the CSU were in a tough bind: they would receive no more general funding to support basic writing, yet they would be admitting just as many students as ever in need of these programs. Initially, the San Francisco State administration was considering two options in lieu of continuing to fund the almost $700,000 annually to provide remedial instruction in English. The first option was to remand all remediation to the College of Extended Learning (where SFSU houses its program of adult continuing education courses); the second was to outsource remedial instruction to the community colleges. Of these two plans, the San Francisco State administration preferred the former, despite the prohibitive premium students would have to pay to register for these courses through Extended Learning ($220 per unit compared to regular full-time tuition of $127 per unit); some other CSU campuses have opted for the latter option—sending students in need of remediation to the community colleges.

Around the time of these budget deliberations, the IRW program began to receive national and statewide attention[4] for its documented success and its cost effectiveness,[5] and the San Francisco State administration saw a solution to its problem. Gone were the extended learning and outsourcing plans, and in their place the IRW program became fully adopted and was approved as a first-year composition equivalent course, permanently replacing the traditional sequence of separate developmental-level reading and writing courses. As of 2006, all incoming first-time students who score at the remedial level on the English Placement Test (approximately 1,100 each year) enroll in a credit-bearing integrated reading/writing course in a vastly expanded IRW program.

History Lessons

We can take many lessons from this story. The most obvious one is that despite institutional efforts to say it isn't so, many students will continue to arrive on college campuses deemed under-prepared to engage in the various literacy practices of the university.[6] I'd like to argue for a different lesson though, one that more directly calls into question the institutional need to claim that remediation is being eliminated. If we accept this need as a realistic one, we subscribe to the amnesiac logic that better efforts might eventually yield the as-yet elusive result of a

high school graduating class in which all students are adequately prepared for college-level reading and writing. Instead, I suggest we read
this history to critique the fundamental notion that college remediation is a problem in need of a solution.

On the homepage of the California State University website, the
CSU describes itself in bold letters as "a leader" in both accessible and
high-quality education. Obscured in this claim is the fact that remediation sits at the intersection of these twin goals, between the democratic
ideal of equal educational opportunity on the one hand, and high academic standards on the other. In my search through two decades worth
of policy documents, I saw repeated instances where higher education
in California has tried to have it both ways, to authorize remedial programs in the name of equal educational opportunity even as it calls for
elimination in order to preserve high standards. As institutions of
higher education perform this delicate balancing act, expensive efforts
to reduce remediation, however unsuccessful they might be, serve the
institutional need to convince state legislatures and the tax-paying
public that democratic ideals are being met, while reassuring them
that their dollars are not being wasted teaching students what they
should have learned in high school. As long as remediation sits at this
intersection, institutions like the CSU will need initiatives such as the
Early Assessment Program. While they may fail to reduce the need for
remediation, as public policy they succeed perfectly.

In a certain sense, the success of the IRW program embodies this
dilemma. On the one hand, the insoluble problem of how to curtail remediation created the opportunity that gave rise to the IRW program.
On the other hand, the IRW program offered a face-saving solution to
the dismal results of the CSU's latest efforts to reduce remediation.
The IRW program maintains access for students who would otherwise
be sent elsewhere, and it helps them successfully negotiate the literacy
values and practices of the university while mitigating the risk of dis-
enrollment. It does so without any obvious erosion of academic standards, as measured by comparative pass rates in the second-year
composition course, and it does so in a cost effective way. But it also
suggests that if we cease to think of remediation as a problem to be
solved, and think of it as an opportunity to practice what Soliday refers
to as "translation pedagogy"—if we envision first-year courses where
students can negotiate the discourses they bring with them to college
and those they will encounter across the university curriculum—then
the problem of remediation goes away (17).

New Possibilities

Imagine what could happen if the CSU embraced this reading of its remedial past. No longer would it have to invest millions of dollars trying
to get high schools to perform a function that is, by necessity, rooted in

the college experience. To perform its democratic function, basic writing sits not at the point of exit from high school, but at the *entry* point to higher education. Historically, basic writing has served to initiate students to the discourses of the academic community, which may be far distant from and even alien to those of their home communities.[7] But basic writing doesn't just initiate students to a more privileged language; it also offers them the opportunity and instructional practice to critically reflect on a variety of discourses, of home, school, work, and the more specific public discourses of the media, the law, the health care system, and even of the college writing classroom itself. By reading its history this way, the CSU could stop playing the elimination game and argue instead for its campuses as the appropriate location for basic writing instruction. If the CSU ceased having to claim that it can reduce remediation in order to justify the existence of its basic writing programs, it might also be persuaded to dedicate sorely needed funding for faculty development and two- and four-year college partnerships commensurate to what it currently earmarks for programs like the EAP. Without doubt, one of the biggest challenges basic writing faces is a woeful lack of graduate programs to help prepare new generations of basic writing faculty. California has 109 community college campuses, serving some 2.5 million students. The University of California stopped offering remedial instruction in English back in the 1990s, and now with more CSU campuses following suit, these community colleges have already become the primary site for basic writing instruction. A majority of the thousands of basic writing classes offered on community college campuses in California are taught by instructors who receive their graduate degrees from a CSU campus. In California, a discipline-appropriate master's degree is the minimum qualification to teach at a community college. According to the American Association of Community Colleges, more than 70% of full-time community college faculty nationwide have terminal master's degrees. Given that there are so few master's programs in composition and/or programs that focus on teaching basic writing, it's safe to presume that these instructors most likely have degrees in English or related fields, but not necessarily in composition, let alone basic writing. Noting a study indicating that only "20% of institutions nationwide reported requiring full-time faculty to possess specific training in developmental education before teaching remedial courses," the California Community Colleges are developing strategic plans to recruit and hire faculty who are both "knowledgeable and enthusiastic" about teaching basic writing and who "choose to teach remedial classes as opposed to being assigned to them." They even went so far as to cite a study recommending that any instructor who teaches a remedial-level course should possess a terminal degree in a discipline relevant to developmental education (Center for Student Success 20).

This faculty recruitment goal, however laudable, is sure to be hamstrung, for even though an important mission of CSU graduate programs is to prepare California community college teachers, only a handful of the 23 CSU campuses (3 by my latest count) offer a true MA degree in composition (or comp/rhetoric), and an equally small number offer graduate course work, in teaching basic writing. Even fewer of these already-too-few graduate courses offer any preparation in teaching postsecondary reading.

With FIPSE funds, the IRW program intended, albeit modestly, to help fill this gap through a series of regularly scheduled workshops to prepare San Francisco State and local community college faculty to teach IRW courses. We also videotaped the workshops for use with new teachers in San Francisco State's graduate teacher education program. While these workshops provided a venue to exchange ideas, we quickly learned that teaching integrated reading/writing is not something that even experienced teachers can absorb in one or two half-day workshops. Accordingly, we made several modifications to our approach to faculty development. To help prepare new faculty to teach integrated reading/writing, my colleague Helen Gillotte-Tropp and I created a year-long graduate seminar ("Seminar in Teaching Integrated Reading/Writing") as part of the San Francisco State's MA and graduate teaching certificate programs in Postsecondary Reading and Composition. Since we first began offering this graduate course in 2002, we have seen more than twenty community college instructors, representing some fifteen different campuses, come to our campus to take the course so they could begin to develop integrated reading/writing courses at their home institutions.

While these new efforts are helping to prepare basic writing teachers who live or work in close proximity to the San Francisco State campus, they remain hampered by certain constraints. A typical sabbatical leave for community college teachers is a single semester only, so they cannot feasibly complete a year-long course of instruction. For those not on leave, it is very difficult to take graduate courses while teaching full-time. As such, our efforts have fallen well short of meeting this growing need, even at this very local level. But if the CSU could read its history to legitimize the place of developmental English in the higher education curriculum, it might authorize new and expanded graduate programs to help prepare a new generation of community college faculty "knowledgeable and enthusiastic" about teaching basic writing and reading. Since it's not likely that graduate education alone can meet the challenge of preparing a new generation of faculty or effectively address the needs of already-degreed community college teachers, the CSU might also offer similarly comprehensive faculty development programs and collaborative partnerships between community college and university faculty similar to the ones it currently provides in the Early Assessment Program, perhaps something along the lines of the California Writing Project, but directed towards community college teaching.

My goal in this article is not merely to wish some utopian vision on the California State University. Rather, it is to raise historical consciousness by using the story of San Francisco State's IRW program to critique the particular ways the California State University has institutionalized basic writing. This is a local example, admittedly, but one I hope sheds light on more global challenges facing basic writing. I hope we can find in this story the grounds to advocate for higher education as *the* appropriate location for basic writing and to advocate, in turn, for the resources necessary to theorize, develop, and sustain a rich variety of approaches to basic writing instruction — instruction that might justifiably focus on reading as well as writing. I hope as well that we use this story to call for more graduate programs and faculty development to help prepare a new generation of basic writing teachers and scholars to meet the new basic writing students who will inevitably continue to arrive on our college campuses.

Notes

1. While not necessarily the case at all institutions, at San Francisco State, basic writing is inextricably linked to ethnic and cultural diversity. As recently as 2007, two-thirds of all African American, Mexican American, and "other Latino" students admitted to the CSU placed into remedial English. Over the last decade, African American students have consistently placed into remedial courses at higher relative percentages than any other group (CSU Division of Analytic Studies).

2. Not coincidentally, the Enrichment Program at City College of New York was embedded in its own institution's effort to eliminate remediation. Despite its documented success, the program was fatally compromised when the CUNY Board of Trustees and the New York State Board of Regents voted to eliminate remediation in the system's senior colleges, housing it exclusively on the two-year college campuses as part of a new master plan that created a tiered system, not unlike ours in California. See Gleason for further details.

3. Developed in 2001, the EAP identifies not-yet proficient high school students by their scores on an expanded California Standards Test in English (augmented by the addition of 15 multiple choice items and an essay, both of which are retired items from the CSU English Placement Test).

4. In addition to being awarded the FIPSE grant, the IRW program has also been the recipient of the 2005 Conference on Basic Writing Award for Innovation, and at its Spring 2005 meeting, the California State University English Council passed a resolution designating San Francisco State's IRW program as a model to be used throughout the CSU system. At the January 2008 meeting of the CSU Board of Trustees, the IRW program was cited as an example of "effective practices" that provide an alternative to remediation.

5. Because students who successfully complete the IRW course do not have to take the mandatory first-year composition course, the university can offer as many as 50 fewer sections per year of first-year composition. San Francisco State's traditional three-semester progression from Developmental Writing/Reading through first-year composition carried an annual cost of $672,100. The year-long IRW program reduces that annual expenditure to $286,000, for a net savings of $386,100.

6. One could also question the validity of the English Placement Test. If significant reforms to the high school curriculum appear unable, both historically and currently, to budge the percentage of students placing into English remediation, then perhaps the test is assessing skills that are of an altogether different nature than what even the most rigorous and comprehensive high school courses are teaching. I leave that critique for another day.

7. I make this claim aware that BW's initiation function is a contested one. See for example, Bizzell, Harris, Horner and Lu, and Soliday.

Works Cited

Academic Senates of the California Community Colleges, The California State University, and the University of California. *Statement on Competencies in English and Mathematics Expected of Entering Freshmen.* Sacramento, CA: The California Roundtable of Educational Opportunity, 1982.

Baldwin, Patty, Helen Gillotte-Tropp, Sugie Goen-Salter, and Joan Wong. *Composing for Success: A Student's Guide to Integrated Reading and Writing.* Boston: Pearson Custom Publishing, 2007.

Bizzell, Patricia. *Academic Discourse and Critical Consciousness.* Pittsburgh: U of Pittsburgh P, 1992.

California Postsecondary Education Commission. *Promises to Keep: Remedial Education in California's Public Colleges and Universities.* Sacramento, CA: California Postsecondary Education Commission, 1983.

___. *Segmental Actions Regarding Remedial Education.* Sacramento, CA: California Postsecondary Education Commission, 1983.

California State University Division of Analytic Studies. *Proficiency Reports of Students Entering the CSU System.* <http://www.asd.calstate.edu/performance/proficiency.shtml>. Accessed 21 Aug. 2008.

Center for Student Success and The Research and Planning Group for California Community Colleges. *Basic Skills as a Foundation for Student Success in California Community Colleges.* Sacramento, CA: California Community Colleges, 2007.

Glau, Gregory R. "*Stretch* at 10: A Progress Report on Arizona State University's *Stretch Program.*" *Journal of Basic Writing* 26.2 (2007): 30–48.

Gleason, Barbara. "Evaluating Writing Programs in Real Time: The Politics of Remediation." *College Composition and Communication* 51.4 (2000): 560–88.

Goen, Sugie, and Helen Gillotte-Tropp. "Integrating Reading and Writing: A Response to the Basic Writing 'Crisis.'" *Journal of Basic Writing* 22.2 (2003): 90–113

Harris, Joseph. "Writing Within and Against the Academy: What Do We Really Want Our Students to Do?" *Journal of Education* 172.1 (1990): 15–16.

Horner, Bruce, and Min-Zhan Lu. *Representing the "Other": Basic Writers and the Teaching of Basic Writing.* Urbana, IL: NCTE, 1999.

McCormick, Kathleen. *The Culture of Reading and the Teaching of English.* New York: Manchester UP, 1994.

Nelson, Nancy, and Robert Calfee, eds. *The Reading-Writing Connection.* Chicago: National Society for the Study of Education, 1998.

"Pilot Study Evaluation of the Early Assessment Program's Professional Development in English." Sacramento, CA: California County Superintendents Educational Services Association, October 2005.

Rose, Mike. "The Language of Exclusion." *College English* 47.8 (1985): 341–59.

Salvatori, Mariolina. "Conversations with Texts." *College English* 55.4 (1996): 440–54.

Soliday, Mary. *The Politics of Remediation.* Pittsburgh: U of Pittsburgh P. 2002.

Soliday, Mary, and Barbara Gleason. "From Remediation to Enrichment: Evaluating a Mainstreaming Project." *Journal of Basic Writing* 16.1 (1997): 64–78.

Stotsky, Sandra. "Research on Reading/Writing Relationships: A Synthesis and Suggested Directions." *Composing and Comprehending.* Ed. J. Jensen. Urbana, IL: ERIC Clearinghouse on Reading and Communication Skills and NCRE (1984): 7–22.

Zamel, Vivian. "Writing One's Way into Reading." *TESOL Quarterly* 26.3 (1992): 463–85.

Appendix

Portfolio Evaluation Checklist
San Francisco State University
Integrated Reading/Writing Program

Portfolio Number _____   Reader Number _____

Directions to Readers: Each portfolio contains three essay "sets" written by the same student, one written near the beginning of the term (but not a diagnostic), one written near the mid-term, and one essay written near the end of the semester. Read through each portfolio, then considering the body of work **as a whole**, complete the following checklist. For each category listed below, place a check mark clearly on one point of the 4-point rubric. Based on your evaluation, please also indicate as "**Category Seven**" whether you think the portfolio indicates that the student has met the learning objectives of the course and is eligible to proceed to the next level course. Completing the space for comments on the portfolio as a whole is encouraged, but optional.

Category One: Formulating/Supporting a Thesis

The writer has a clear purpose/controlling idea/thesis that is supported by thoughtful analysis. The complexity of ideas is recognized and the thesis is substantiated through personal insights and appropriate references to assigned or chosen texts.

_____ 4	_____ 3	_____ 2	_____ 1
Above Average	Average	Below Average	Poor

Category Two: Organization

The writer makes appropriate organizational choices. Paragraphs are coherent internally and the writer uses transitions between paragraphs. Introductions and conclusions function purposefully within the text.

_____ 4	_____ 3	_____ 2	_____ 1
Above Average	Average	Below Average	Poor

Category Three: Sentences

The writer writes sentences that are both well-focused and employ a variety of syntactic structures such that he/she is able to develop ideas at the level of the sentence, rather than by mere accretion of sentences.

_____ 4   _____ 3   _____ 2   _____ 1
Above Average   Average   Below Average   Poor

Category Four: Grammar and Mechanics

The essay is well-proofread and mainly free of significant errors in usage, spelling, and mechanics.

_____ 4   _____ 3   _____ 2   _____ 1
Above Average   Average   Below Average   Poor

Category Five: Reading/Writing Integration

The writer is able to use readings to inform his/her understanding and discussion of the topic. The writer comprehends the texts he/she reads (that is, he/she is able to distinguish between major [gist] and minor [evidentiary] propositions of the texts) but also evaluates and employs textual information to inform his/her own discussions/arguments.

_____ 4   _____ 3   _____ 2   _____ 1
Above Average   Average   Below Average   Poor

Category Six: Audience Awareness

The writer shows a conscious awareness of the reader's needs. The writer orients the reader by employing word choice and tone appropriate to his/her purpose and audience (for example: providing background information in the introduction and defining or modifying key terms.)

_____ 4   _____ 3   _____ 2   _____ 1
Above Average   Average   Below Average   Poor

Category Seven: Overall Evaluation

Meets Learning Outcomes   _____
Does Not Meet Learning Outcomes   _____

Comments:

Learning Communities for Students in Developmental Reading: An Impact Study at Hillsborough Community College

Michael J. Weiss, Mary G. Visher, and Heather Wathington, with Jed Teres and Emily Schneider

Michael J. Weiss, Mary G. Visher, Heather Wathington, Jed Teres, and Emily Schneider report on a study sponsored by the National Center for Postsecondary Research that focused on learning communities. The introductory section that appears here is excerpted from a much larger report about the efficacy of learning communities as yet another model for structuring programming toward student success.

Executive Summary

Over the last 40 years, community colleges have played an increasingly vital role in American postsecondary education. Since 1963, enrollment in these institutions has increased by more than 700 percent, with enrollment reaching 6.2 million students in 2006–2007. Each fall, community colleges enroll 35 percent of all postsecondary education students.[1] This dramatic growth is largely due to the fact that community colleges are open-entry institutions and are generally more affordable than four-year colleges and universities. Unfortunately, while enrollments are increasing, overall success rates in community colleges are disappointingly low. Among students who enroll in community colleges with the intention of earning a credential or transferring to a four-year institution, only 51 percent fulfill these expectations within six years.[2] While the rates of degree or certificate attainment are low in general, rates are even lower for students who need developmental education, who comprise a significant proportion of the community college student body.[3]

Given these statistics, community college stakeholders are searching with increasing urgency for approaches with the potential to bolster success rates for community college students, particularly for those who need developmental education. One popular strategy is to create "learning communities," an idea that has come to describe an array of programs and services offered at community colleges. The most basic learning community model simply co-enrolls a cohort of students into two classes together. Proponents believe that when students spend time together in multiple classes they are more likely to form social and academic support networks that in turn help them persist and succeed in school. More comprehensive learning communities include additional components: They co-enroll a group of students in multiple classes, the courses have thematically linked curricula, instructors collaborate closely both to align their curricula and to support students, teaching includes project-based and experiential learning experiences, assignments and readings are integrated, and student services such as enhanced advising and tutoring can be embedded.

This report presents results from a rigorous study of a basic learning communities program operated at Hillsborough Community College in Tampa Bay, Florida. Hillsborough is one of six community colleges participating in the National Center for Postsecondary Research's (NCPR) Learning Communities Demonstration.[4] The demonstration's focus is on determining whether learning communities are an effective strategy for helping students who need developmental education.

Hillsborough's basic learning community model linked a developmental reading course and a "college success" course with the intention of improving the outcomes of academically underprepared students in particular. Hillsborough developed this program as part of its involvement in Achieving the Dream: Community Colleges Count, an initiative designed to help community colleges make better use of their own data to help students succeed. Hillsborough came up with the model after seeing low success rates for students in developmental courses and higher success rates for students who took a college success course. Learning communities offered the possibility of leveraging the skills acquired in the college success course to assist students who were doing poorly in developmental courses.

The learning communities study at Hillsborough is based on an experimental design in which, from fall 2007 to fall 2008, three cohorts of students in need of developmental education were randomly assigned to either a program group, whose 709 members had the opportunity to participate in learning communities, or to a control group, whose 362 members received the college's standard services. The impact of the learning communities program is estimated by comparing the outcomes of program and control group members using student transcript data collected during the year after random assignment. This report is the first in a series of reports presenting impact findings from the Learning Communities Demonstration.

In summary, the key findings from this report are:

- **The most salient feature of learning communities implemented at Hillsborough was co-enrollment of students into linked courses, creating student cohorts.** Faculty and students suggested that this course structure and the formation of student cohorts increased social linkages among students, a key element of the learning community experience.

- **The learning communities program at Hillsborough became more comprehensive over the course of the study.** Curricular integration and collaboration between faculty members teaching in paired courses are considered a key element of comprehensive, strong learning communities. At Hillsborough, curricular integration and faculty collaboration were generally minimal at the start of the study (as planned), but increased over time.

- **Overall (for the full study sample), Hillsborough's learning communities program did not have a meaningful impact on students' academic success.** With respect to total credits earned, students in the program group and the control group performed about the same during the program semester and the first postprogram semester. In addition, during the two semesters following the program, students in the program group and the control group registered for courses at around the same rate (that is, their rates of persistence were similar).

- **Corresponding to the maturation of the learning communities program, evidence suggests that the program had positive impacts on some educational outcomes for the third cohort of students.** During the program semester, the program group students who enrolled in learning communities in fall 2008 (the third and final cohort) earned more credits than their control group counterparts. In the semester following the program, the third cohort's program group students registered at a higher rate than their control group counterparts. Readers are advised that when the impacts of the third cohort of students are compared with the impacts of the first and second cohorts, the differences generally are not statistically significant. This indicates that the results for the third cohort should be viewed with caution. Since program maturation was observed at several learning community demonstration sites, analyses will be conducted in future reports to see if there is common improvement in later cohorts.

Notably, this report presents findings from only one of the colleges in the demonstration, which operated one learning communities model. The six colleges taking part in the national Learning Communities Demonstration were selected, in part, because they represent various learning community models. Hillsborough's model was more basic than some of the other colleges' models in the demonstration. In order to better understand the effectiveness of learning communities more broadly, it will be essential to see whether more comprehensive, robustly implemented learning communities yield positive impacts. In addition, the growth and improvement of Hillsborough's program as it scaled up was a pattern exhibited at the other Learning Communities Demonstration colleges. It will also be interesting to see whether more mature versions of the programs tested at the other colleges will similarly yield more positive impacts.

In designing the Learning Communities Demonstration, NCPR was seeking to better understand whether learning communities are an effective strategy to help improve students' chances at succeeding in community college. During the next several years, NCPR will report impact findings from the other five colleges as they become available. The result will be a significant body of experimental research on the effectiveness of learning communities in the community college setting.

Notes

1. Provasnik, S., & Planty, M. (2008). *Community Colleges: Special Supplement to The Condition of Education 2008.* Statistical Analysis Report. NCES 2008–033. Washington, DC: U.S. Department of Education, Institute of Education Sciences, National Center for Education Statistics.
2. Hoachlander, G., Sikora, A. C., & Horn, L. (2003). *Community College Students: Goals, Academic Preparation, and Outcomes. Postsecondary Education Descriptive Analysis Reports.* Washington, DC: U.S. Department of Education, Institute of Education Sciences, National Center for Education Statistics.
3. Adelman, C. (2004). *Principal Indicators of Student Academic Histories in Postsecondary Education, 1972–2000.* Washington, DC: U.S. Department of Education, Institute of Education Sciences.
4. MDRC, in partnership with the Community College Research Center at Columbia University's Teachers College, the Curry School of Education at the University of Virginia, and faculty at Harvard University, created the NCPR through a grant from the U.S. Department of Education. Several foundations provided additional support to the Learning Communities Demonstration: the Bill & Melinda Gates Foundation, the Ford Foundation, the Kresge Foundation, Lumina Foundation for Education, and the Robin Hood Foundation.

Contextualized Teaching and Learning: A Faculty Primer

Elaine Delott Baker, Laura Hope, and Kelley Karandjeff

Elaine Delott Baker, Laura Hope, and Kelley Karandjeff provide background and examples of an increasingly popular model for structuring instruction at the postsecondary level: contextualized teaching and learning (CTL). CTL is associated with both learning theory and a growing body of literature advocating the method for assisting college students in developing basic skills. This article, which is abstracted from a larger report, provides a discussion of existing models and the elements of each model and then presents descriptions of several programs that employ CTL in the teaching of college reading.

A Case for Contextualized Teaching and Learning

What Is Contextualized Teaching and Learning?

In *Basic Skills as a Foundation for Student Success in the California Community Colleges,* Contextualized Teaching and Learning (CTL) is identified as a promising strategy that actively engages students and promotes improved learning and skills development. CTL has been defined in different ways, based on the intent of the group championing its use. Most recently, the United States Department of Education Office of Vocational and Adult Education (2001) characterized CTL as a "conception of teaching and learning that helps teachers relate subject matter content to real world situations" (Berns & Erickson, 2001, p. 2). Chris Mazzeo (2008) broadened the definition, describing CTL as a "diverse family of instructional strategies designed to more seamlessly link the learning of foundational skills and academic or occupational content by focusing teaching and learning squarely on concrete applications in a specific context that is of interest to the student" (p. 4).

While much of the research on CTL is fairly recent, student engagement in contextual learning has deep roots. John Dewey introduced experiential learning at the turn of the century as the most sensible and effective way to make learning meaningful for students. In 1916, Alfred North Whitehead told the Mathematical Association of England that "the second-handedness of the learned world is the secret of its mediocrity"—hitting on a central feature of contextual learning: the best learning is that which can be used. In the 1970s, functional context education entered the education and training community and served as a pre-cursory to what is now known as CTL. Based on lessons learned from the U.S. military's efforts to raise the skill levels of its soldiers (Sticht & Kern, 1970), functional context education is defined as "an instructional strategy that integrates the reaching of literacy skills and job content to move learners more successfully and quickly toward their education and employment goals" (Wider Opportunities for Women, 2009).

At that time, several proponents of this strategy introduced a curriculum development tool to integrate academic and vocational competencies termed "literacy task analysis" (Mikulecky, 1985). Piloted by the U.S. military and widely adopted in customized training, literacy task analysis profiles the specific reading, writing, computational, and communication competencies required for different occupational positions. These competencies are then incorporated into a contextualized curriculum, with literacy skills taught in the context of specific job applications. In the 1980s, Wider Opportunities for Women began promoting functional context as a tool to strengthen intergenerational literacy in *Six Strategies for Family Economic Self-Sufficiency* (Wider Opportunities for Women, 2009). Literacy task analyses also became part of the standard toolkit for customized training and the workplace education programs of the 1990s. Latter-day example of the functional context approach can be seen in WorkKeys customized training applications.

In 1990, the Department of Labor formed the Secretary's Commission on Achieving Necessary Skills (SCANs) to identify the skills young people would need to succeed in the future workforce. Key principles identified by the Commission included: "join knowledge and skills; learn abstract concepts by doing practical activities; connect schoolwork with the real world" (Hull, 1993). In 1998, the Commission's primary publication *Learning a Living: A Blueprint for High Performance* specifically highlighted contextualization as a key instructional strategy. According to Johnson (2002),

> [The word] "contextual" naturally replaced "applied" academics because the word "applied" was simply too small to encompass the startling innovations achieved by this grassroots reform movement. The more comprehensive contextual—in context—implies the interrelatedness of all things. Everything is connected including ideas and actions. Contextual also directs our thinking toward experience. When ideas are experienced, in context, they have meaning (p. 10).

The recommendations of the SCANs Commission aligned with the concurrent passage of the national School-to-Work Initiatives Act at the secondary level and the intensified focus in the Carl D. Perkins Career and Technical Education Act[1] on creating intentional connections between students' academic preparation and workforce readiness. Perkins legislation began requiring that community colleges specifically integrate academic and vocational education for improved student performance and outcomes. The legislation only deepened its focus on issues of integration in its 1998 and 2006 renewals. In turn, secondary and community college educators have been experimenting with some form of contextualized teaching and learning for several years. Researchers have performed extensive investigation of these approaches and have developed standards and frameworks for this kind of integration as well as identified the benefits and limitations from view of these practitioners (Grubb & Kraskouskas, 1992; Grubb, 1995; Grubb & Badway, 1999).

One of the goals and effects of a contextualized approach is to capture a student's attention by illustrating the relevance of the learning experience. CTL helps students find and create meaning through experience, drawing from prior knowledge in order to build upon existing knowledge. A primary principle of CTL is that knowledge becomes the students' own when it is learned within the framework of an authentic context. In CTL, the traditional curriculum is ". . . placed in a broader framework that integrates other subject content into the learning process for the students. Learning goals are elevated to higher order thinking skills in the process of learning to find information, adapt to change, and communicate effectively while relating to others" (Berns & Erickson, 2001, p. 5). In the traditional classroom, students often struggle to connect with abstractions. An authentic context helps the learner see the relevance of information and creates a pathway for them to understand the material.

The SSE Instructional Design Series (2007, p. 2) articulates several characteristics of contextualized learning frameworks including: (1) problem-solving within realistic situations, (2) learning in multiple contexts, (3) content derived from diverse work and life situations, and (4) authentic assessment. More broadly, Johnson describes CTL as a "holistic system" (2002, p. 24) with several components working together to create a systemic learning approach—suggesting that instruction and learning derives from the whole and not from a discreet part. She argues that together, these components create a network by which students are better able to create meaning and retain information. These components include: (1) making meaningful connections, (2) doing significant work, (3) self-regulated learning, collaborating, (4) critical and creative thinking, (5) nurturing the individual, (6) reaching high standards and (7) using authentic assessment.

All of these features point to the importance of relevance and authenticity, which resonate with the objectives of the SCANs Commission. Instructors routinely ask students to "apply" a concept at the end of a lesson as a demonstration of the student's understanding of the concept, but the application of a concept to a real situation is different than a learning process that is structured around an authentic context. Svinicki defines the authentic situation in this way: "an authentic situation is similar to the situation in which the skills will really be used eventually, or it can be a real life situation in which the skills are needed but not necessarily representative of the learners' future use of them" (Svinicki, 2004, p. 69). Moreover, learning that takes place within authentic situations is also more likely to engage the student as a participant rather than an observer.

Another concept often incorporated into CTL is "cognitive apprenticeship," which also distinguishes contextual teaching and learning from mere application. Cognitive apprenticeship refers to the acquisition of academic knowledge and/or skills in ways that are similar to those employed by craftsmen in technical occupations (Bond, 2004). In cognitive apprenticeship, the instructor models the skills necessary to complete a task, but also helps students articulate the thinking that accompanies the completion of the task. Cognitive apprenticeship differs from the more traditional instructional models, where the instructor explains the concepts and models the application, after which students attempt to imitate what they have just seen. Raelin harkened back to Dewey in support of this strategy, stating "Dewey warned educators that merely doing an activity was not enough to produce learning; rather, doing should become a trying, an experiment with the world to find out what it is like" (Raelin, 2008, p. 72).

Using a cognitive apprenticeship model, students do more than just "practice" the skill in an application process. The entire task is explored within the parameters of a real-life situation, with the instructor coaching students through the mental thought process that accompanies the completion of the task and helping them create an internal dialogue or narrative of the process. Raelin (2008, p. 13) calls this "externalizing the process" for the learner.

What Learning Theory Supports CTL?

A wide range of learning theories relate closely to contextualized teaching and learning as a strategy for improving students' basic skills acquisition, particularly in relationship to under-represented and adult learners. Recent breakthroughs in brain research lend additional support. The following section provides a brief summary of several relevant learning theories and highlights their implications for a CTL practice.

MOTIVATION THEORY

Contemporary theoretical approaches to helping adults learn, or "andragogy" (Harris, 2003, p. 38), acknowledge students' role as an agent in the learning process. In this paradigm, learners are assumed to be: (1) self-directed, (2) enriched by a diversity of personal experience, (3) ready to learn, (4) life-centered, task-centered and problem-centered, and (5) motivated by internal factors. According to Harris, "The basic format of the andragogical model is a process design that uses life experiences" (2003, p. 38). Mezirow (2000) describes this in terms of "meaning systems" which act as filters for information as students attempt to make connections to new information. He also underscores the necessity of the learners to "become critically aware of [their] own tacit assumptions and expectations and those of others and [assess] their relevance for making an interpretation" (p. 4). Inherently, this idea emphasizes the importance of the learners' experiences and maturity, which is central for the success and motivation of adult learners.

To that end, Svinicki suggests that the instructor address the following issues:

- Increase the value of the learning to the learner. . . . It is important to get the learner to believe that the choices being made [during the learning process] are under the [learner's] control, if possible. Otherwise, motivation will be damaged.

- Increase the learner's self-efficacy with regard to the task . . . focusing on smaller more immediate goals [to help students] make success more likely and believe in the eventual success of the whole task. (2004, p. 245)

Additionally, when students feel that they can influence the learning through their own volition, as well as accept responsibility for the impact of learning, their motivation to learn is also increased. In this framework, setting clear goals, providing students options, and providing constant and meaningful feedback are also essential roles for the instructor.

Implications for CTL. Many instructors are accustomed to addressing questions from students like "Why do I need to know this?" or "When am I going to use this?" or "Will this be on the test?" Students who learn in a contextual environment are simultaneously introduced to the relevance of the learning content, which commensurately improves motivation. Predmore asserts, "Students are learning material within a concrete, memorable context. . . . Once they see the real-world relevance of what they're learning, they become more interested and motivated" (2005, pp. 22–23). In turn, contextual learning has the potential to motivate and effectively engage students who view school as boring or non-essential, or who have struggled to make the connections between the demands of the classroom and their own personal goals and aspirations.

PROBLEM-CENTERED LEARNING

Known as problem-centered or problem-based learning (PBL), this theory addresses students' engagement with real-world problem solving to develop a "deep foundation of factual knowledge and understand that knowledge in the context of a conceptual framework . . . , and finally to facilitate the development of metacognitive skills" (Massa, 2008).

Merrill and Gilbert (2008, p. 207) assert five components to an effectively designed problem-centered learning experience including: (1) engagement of students in a progression of tasks leading to a logical conclusion, (2) activation of existing cognitive structures of recall and experience, enhanced through collaboration and demonstration, (3) learner observation of skills and connection to concepts being learned, including peer discussion and demonstration, (4) application of new knowledge followed by "intrinsic or corrective" feedback, and (5) integration of new information with an everyday life skill and demonstration of that new knowledge.

Implications for CTL. Problem-centered learning closely relates to contextualized learning in its active involvement of students in a networked context to make learning more effective and relevant. This approach also frequently calls for students to work in teams, direct their own learning, and develop creative solutions to real-world problems. Often a central component of contextualized learning, PBL deemphasizes knowledge for its own sake and capitalizes on the utility of skills and information.

SOCIAL LEARNING THEORY

The research on the effectiveness of CTL strategies is well supported by theories involving collaborative learning. Collaborative learning rests on social cognitive theories suggesting that students' learning can be facilitated and enhanced by connectivity to peers. "Collaborative learning is based on the idea that learning is a naturally social act" (Gerlach, 1994, p. 8). This model assumes that students create learning within this social context rather than within the solitary confines of their own studying or by just listening to the instructor. This approach is also distinct from "cooperative learning" which many theorists deem more appropriate for children; collaborative learning is more closely aligned with the needs of adult learners and adult education (Clardy, 2005; Van Hook, 2008; Merriam, Caffarella, & Baumgartner, 2006).

According to this theory, students and instructors need to understand each other's roles and further, students must learn collaborative skills in order for this approach to be successful. Bosworth (1994) asserts that teachers should train students to learn what skills will be necessary, ask students to demonstrate those skills, model those skills in their instruction, provide feedback about students' collaborative skills, and give students an opportunity to reflect on the collaborative experience. In the traditional classroom setting, where students compete for grades and academic standing, cooperation and collaboration are usually not rewarded. While collaboration models vary, the ultimate goal of social learning approaches is increased involvement.

Barkely, Cross, and Major (2005, p. 4) argue that collaborative learning strategies are particularly effective for diverse populations. The evidence strongly confirms that non-traditional students greatly benefit from the opportunity to participate in group settings: "women, members of under-represented racial and ethnic groups, adult and re-entry students, commuters, and international students have all been identified as students for whom peer and group learning seem especially valued and valuable" (2005, p. 4).

Implications for CTL. Despite the challenges of structuring effective collaborative learning experiences, Johnson (2002, p. 88) asserts that "collaboration is an essential component of the CTL system." She further states, "the collaboration process removes the mental blinders imposed by limited experience and narrow perfections. . . . Working together, members of small groups are able to overcome obstacles, act independently and responsibly, rely on the talents of team members, trust others, speak up, and make decisions," which are all skills necessary to promote effective learning, as well as appropriate workplace behavior (p. 89).

LEARNING STYLES

While learning is at once social, instruction must also account for the differences in students' individual learning styles. The research on learning styles is voluminous, with varying, and sometimes contradictory classification systems for learning dispositions. What is commonly agreed upon is that because students present such a wide variety of traits, experiences, and preferences to the learning task, effective instruction must include some considerations of the different ways in which students learn.

Researchers tend to agree that there are some specific differences among learners that significantly impact the learning process. First and foremost is the role that prior knowledge and experience play in that process. According to Svinicki (2004), "prior knowledge impacts what learners pay attention to, how they perceive and interpret what they are experiencing, and how they store new information based on what they already know" (p. 185). This prior knowledge is not limited to what students bring to the particular discipline, but also their cultural orientation and personal view of themselves and the world.

In addition, differences in motivational factors also shape learning. According to Alexander and Murphy (1998), student interest is one of the most essential factors in producing the best learning. And yet, it is one of the most common questions for classroom faculty: how can students be motivated to learn? Goal orientation, self-efficacy and the students' interpretation of the relevance of the learning all contribute to develop student motivation (Svinicki, 2004, pp. 205–07).

Finally, personality differences may cause learners to prefer a specific set of learning modalities. Indicators like the Myers-Briggs point to varying factors that influence a learner's tendency to gravitate to particular experiences. Kolb's learning style indicator is yet another tool commonly used to make similar determinations. All of these tools assist the instructor in designing experiences that will lead to deeper understanding and easier comprehension for the students.

Implications for CTL. Kolb indicates that in the most effective learning situations, learners "must be able to involve themselves fully" in the process. He asserts that no matter what style the learner prefers, students must have the opportunities to "learn from feeling," "learn by watching and listening," "learn by thinking," and "learn by doing" (Jacoby et al., 1996, p. 69). Predmore (2005) argues that "CTL can be a highly effective means of accommodating students' different learning styles" because an instructor has the ability to utilize a number of divergent instructional models within the contextual framework including collaborative pairs, hands-on demonstration and inquiry groups, to name a few (p. 23). In keeping with the philosophy of CTL and learning styles sensitivity, Brown also suggests "personalizing the learning environment, having the students relate personal experiences to content" helps learners engage the material and makes learning more powerful and significant (Silverman & Casazza, 2000, p. 190).

BRAIN RESEARCH

Research on how the brain processes information adds a new dimension to our understanding of the learning process. In the language of brain research, effective instruction creates changes in the brain: that change is "learning."

Recent studies challenge the assumption that the brain is fixed at maturity and suggest that the brain is more like "plastic"—"changing its own wiring, almost continuously" (Zull, 2004, p. 68). The most current research is especially compelling in relationship to adult learners, stating that "the neurological nature of learning strongly suggests that there is no age of finality for any learning" (Zull, 2006, p. 8). In fact, some research implies that the neurological complexity of the adult brain may actually improve conditions for learning, since the adult learner has a more extensive associative foundation from which to make new knowledge.

Zull asserts that two conditions create these changes: practice and emotion. According to Zull (2004), when neurons are active, they create biochemical pathways to other neurons. Repeated firing encourages neurons to reach out more frequently. When neurons connect and communicate as a result of this extension, synapses are created. This activity then leads to the development of networks within the brain that create the physical demonstration of knowledge or learning (p. 68). Similarly, emotion creates a chemical reaction in the brain initiated by adrenaline, dopamine, or serotonin. These chemicals fortify the network connections within the brain, deepening the learning experience and entangling emotion and learning (p. 70). These emotions, Zull argues, then play a role in motivation as students strive to recreate the sensations associated with the chemical reaction. It gives a theoretical basis to one of the foundations of effective practice: success in learning motivates students to learn, which leads to further success, which leads to a confidence in the ability to learn.

In addition to emotion and practice, experience and the environment also appear to significantly impact learning. The human brain is highly responsive to association and sensory experience. New stimuli are connected to associations or memories that the brain already comprehends, creating an electrical network of new and known information. The ability of this network to result in long-term understanding and knowledge depends on how many regions of the neocortex are engaged. Zull suggests that this leads to "four pillars" of learning (inspired by Kolb's learning process): gathering data, reflection, creating, and testing (2006, pp. 5–7). Brain-based education emphasizes "the individual as an active learner in control of his [or her] learning situation, with the teacher facilitating student planning, self-evaluation, and self-monitoring skills" (Frith, 2005, p. 10). Cognitive research also emphasizes the importance of including sensory interaction. According to Johnson, "significant activities such as preparing projects, solving real world problems, conducting interviews, creating graphs and designing multimedia presentations place students in a rich learning environment that have the potential to appeal to an array of senses, address a variety of learning styles, and awaken many interests" (2002, p. 15).

Implications for CTL.   Neuroscience adds another voice in support of contextual learning. From this perspective, contextual teaching and learning stimulates the students' brain to develop patterns and create meaning by linking experience and sensory stimuli to new knowledge through a convergence in real-life application.

What Does the Research Say about the Impact on Student Outcomes?

With these theories as support, a growing number of researchers and practitioners increasingly agree that contextualization has a positive impact on the learning experience. Contextual teaching and learning advocates believe that through this strategy, learners can develop foundational knowledge (understanding specific ideas or concepts), application (the ability to engage this information in action), integration (understanding the relationships between the knowledge learned), and human dimension (the capacity to understand one's self or others), promoting significant learning by engaging students at every stage.

The issue of transferable skills, or the students' ability to demonstrate the competencies learned through one context in another, has become a more explicit goal in many contextualized programs. The measure of transferable skills can be evidenced by performance in placement tests or by the ability to function successfully in the next level of coursework or training. From a metacognitive perspective, transferable skills can be seen as the end product of "learning to learn," meaning that the student has developed into a better learner by becoming more aware and self-directed as well as increasingly capable of constructing more effective inquiry and transferring that knowledge to other fields.

Program evaluation and research assessing the effectiveness of CTL is continuing to expand and include a more detailed analysis of specific outcomes. Earlier assessments of contextual learning in traditional vocational programs, and more recently in U.S. Department of Education's workplace education grants, focused on the effectiveness of this learning strategy in preparing workers for specific jobs. As the expectations and demands of the workforce have changed, the focus of these investigations have expanded from traditional workforce outcomes, such as reduced errors, Return on Investment (ROI), reduced turnover, and employee advancement to include the research and evaluation of more traditional learning outcomes such as the ability of students to apply the skills learned in a vocational context to an academic context, persistence, success, and certificate and degree completion.

Because of the relatively recent implementation of contextual learning models in community colleges, there are few examples of programs with longitudinal data on student success. Washington State's I-BEST program, featured in the next section of the primer, offers the most extensive evaluation to date. This model integrates ESL and basic skills education with training in specific career pathways. Students in the ten original I-BEST programs piloted in 2004 earned five times more college credits on average and were 15 times more likely to complete workforce training than were traditional ESL students during the same amount of time.

Another recent study performed by the National Research Center for Career and Technical Education (NRCCTE) looked at imbedded math instruction in five high school career and technical education programs including: agriculture, auto technology, business/marketing, health and information technology (Stone et al., 2006). Teachers in these content areas worked with math instructors to design integrated lessons and activities. After one year, students in the intervention showed significant math gains on both the ACCUPLACER and the TerraNov (Mazzeo, 2008, p. 5). Students also performed equally well on assessments of their technical knowledge, suggesting that the integration of vocational and academic competencies results in higher outcomes in academic skills without a reduction in applied knowledge. A smaller-scale investigation of the impact of contextualizing developmental math with allied health examples on community college nursing students showed learners in experimental groups achieving higher results on course exit exams than those in control groups (Shore, Shore, & Boggs, 2004).

An additional benefit cited by the research is the positive impact on students' learning behavior. Richard Lynch, a professor of occupational studies and the principal investigator of the University of Georgia's study of CTL, states that "94% of the students said that they learned a lot more in CTL strategy classes than in traditional courses in that same subject area" (Predmore, 2005, p. 23). Similarly, a recent study utilizing CTL indicated that as a result of their experience "more than 80% of the participants expressed that they were able to think more deeply about the topics and were able to participate more actively in the learning" (Choo, 2007, p. 198). Raelin asserts that through this deep engagement, a learner may be able to demonstrate knowledge without articulating the aspects or dimensions of that knowledge, distinguishing knowing how to do something from knowing something (Raelin, 2008, p.68). While the data in these studies is self-reported, they point to areas for potential further research.

Grubb and Kraskouskas (1992) suggest that other benefits to a contextualized curriculum or integrated learning model are more indirect. They assert that "integration efforts provide natural ways for faculty to collaborate, and particularly, to break down the isolation between occupational and academic instructors. . . . Integration can help bridge the distinct islands of activity within the community college, providing a way of moving toward a true community of learners" (p. 5). Grubb and Kraskouskas's assertion bears out as a key characteristic of CTL practice, as evidenced by the descriptions of faculty and staff that follow in the next section of this document.

Contextualized Teaching and Learning in Practice

As outlined in the previous section, contextualized teaching and learning is connected to a number of learning theories as well as a growing discourse on strategies to promote adult learners' acquisition of basic skills. Contextual learning in practice is also becoming more visible as an effective learning strategy and as a focus of developmental education. To better understand what contextualized basic skills instruction looks like in practice, the RP Group interviewed faculty and staff implementing an array of models both in California and other states. The following section looks at common themes that emerge from these models and addresses some of the topics that faculty and administration might consider in plans to adopt or expand CTL practices in their colleges.

What Are the Existing Models for Implementation?

As noted by Mazzeo (2008), CTL practices can assume a number of forms and are found in a broad range of settings. The 11 practices featured vary in scale of implementation ranging from individual classrooms to program models; in the type of context utilized, from personal goals and experiences to workplace applications; and in the focus and the intensity of contextualization, from specific applications to comprehensive career preparation. **These examples represent only a small fraction of the entire breadth of models available**; rather, these practices were selected to offer a sampling of the continuum of possibilities for using contextualization as a strategy for improving students' acquisition of basic skills.

At a fundamental level, all of the featured practices fall into two broad categories: stand-alone classroom practices and linked courses or learning communities.

STAND-ALONE CLASSROOMS. These models focus on a single classroom and offer a flexible format. While faculty might work with peers in other disciplines to develop the course content, the primary locus of control rests with the individual instructor. Drawing on the work of Mazzeo, Perin, and others, stand-alone classroom models can include infused academic and infused occupational delivery modes (Mazzeo, 2008; Perin, 2001).

Infused academic classrooms are individual courses focused on academic skill building. The context serves as a vehicle for enhancing the relevance of those skills to students and provides them opportunities to engage in active learning. Examples range from the exploration of students' cultural or ethnic background and personal experiences (Los Medanos College, mathematics) to the incorporation of service-learning (College of San Mateo, English).

Infused occupational classrooms are organized around the teaching of specific occupational content. Academic skills are taught in the context of the vocational competencies, or "embedded" within the curriculum. Examples include colleges that offer a single career technical education course that incorporates the development of basic skills such as reading, writing, or mathematics (Ivy Tech, Shifting Gears Project, El Camino College's Basic Math Skills for Statistical Control Processes). The primary goal is to teach occupational content; academic skill development is the tool that advances this goal. In some models, an important secondary goal is for students to be able to demonstrate academic skills in different contexts. The ability to transfer skills from a vocational setting to an academic setting is particularly important in colleges where "cut-off scores" are used to screen students who wish to enroll in higher level courses.

LINKED COURSES/ LEARNING COMMUNITIES. Mazzeo (2008) describes contextual learning communities as a cohort of students taking two or more courses that are linked in content. While learning communities take many formats and may or may not contextualize curriculum, the examples selected for this primer are ones that exhibit a high degree of collaboration and that utilize a specific context for delivery. These learning communities contextualize their basic skills instruction according to a variety of organizing principles, such as students' occupational goals, social justice interests, or cultural and community experiences. Some are delivered in short-term intensive formats (Los Angeles Trade Technical College's Utilities and Construction Prep Program), while others take place over the course of one to two semesters (Cabrillo College's Digital Bridge Program, City College of San Francisco's Bridge to Biotech

Program, Chabot College's Daraja Program, Community College of Denver's FastStart, Pierce College's I-BEST) or multiple years (Southwestern College's Spanish to English Associate Teacher Program).

While each course retains it own objectives, learning community courses connect to mutually reinforce a set of shared goals. Faculty who implement these communities collaborate to ensure that the content of each course complements and supports the others. In deeply integrated curriculum, the boundaries between courses disappear, and students learn both disciplines and skill sets simultaneously within a shared context.

What Elements Link These Models?

While the 11 featured practices represent a broad diversity of delivery modes, several key themes emerged across the courses and programs. Moreover, the design features of every model are consistently connected to the learning theories outlined in the previous section. The instructors either implicitly or explicitly operationalize the theoretical understanding that any significant learning experience requires the motivation and engagement of the learner, that it is often socially constructed, that it must be individualized, and that it must be framed as a transferable process. These learning theories thread throughout the key common elements in the following section.

FACULTY COLLABORATION. All of the faculty members who were interviewed discussed the importance of collaboration—with their peers, other divisions of their college, administration, employers, community partners, and/or funders. In many cases, cross-discipline and cross-function partnerships fueled faculty innovations. The importance of collaboration was referenced in a number of activities including: program design and course curriculum development; engagement of services or the development of community experiences for students; professional development; evaluation and improvement of one's practice; and the acquisition of resources to support instructional innovation. While collaboration varied in intensity by model type, it remained a central element of all practices. Reflective of contextualized instruction itself, collaboration across disciplines and functions of the college and with members of the community advanced faculty's ability to serve students in the classroom.

CURRICULUM/INSTRUCTIONAL MATERIAL DEVELOPMENT. Most faculty cited the need to develop appropriate instructional materials to support their CTL practice, pointing to the artificial nature of the applications in traditional texts as well as the lack of relevance of these applications to students' interests or experience. Several of the featured practices have invested significant time, effort and funds into developing and documenting lessons, assignments, instructional handbooks and texts for their coursework. In some cases, faculty performed this work on their own, but more often faculty worked with their peers in their own department, across disciplines or with the support of external partners. Underscoring the importance of authenticity to CTL, practitioners often acquired instructional materials or based their materials on resources from employer and community partners, or from students' experiences in the workplace or their communities.

Relevant Context.   All faculty and program directors noted the critical importance of employing a relevant context in curriculum design and delivery. Contexts varied by practice from the personal to the professional. In some cases, the instructor chose a context they believed would interest students, like service-learning or real-world problem solving; or, instructors engaged students in developing the context, identifying the issues and concerns most relevant to their lives, cultures, and communities. In other instances, students chose a course or program for the context in which basic skills were being taught (e.g., workforce development, social justice). In describing the dynamics of the classroom, all of the faculty interviewed noted how use of a relevant context helped students recognize the purpose and utility of the reading, writing, and math skills to their personal or career development. Many indicated that the motivational aspect of these connections enhanced the efficiency of the learning process and facilitated students' mastery of the material.

Interactive Teaching.   Faculty regularly referenced use of interactive teaching in their course and program implementation. Whether it was students interacting with the instructor, with one another, or with the hands-on applications of the coursework itself, faculty noted that interactive teaching played a prominent role in how they delivered curriculum. Use of an authentic context facilitated strong student engagement, often calling for team work, peer to peer review, real-world data collection and problem solving, experiences with employers or community organizations, authentic assessments, and reflective essays. While interactive teaching is an overall aspect of quality instruction, working with contextualized curriculum provided instructors with a multiplicity of opportunities to construct complex and engaging interactive activities. Echoing the social learning and learning styles theories discussed earlier, this interactive teaching allowed faculty to both accommodate different educational needs and leverage the power of faculty-to-student and student-to-student collaboration.

PROFESSIONAL DEVELOPMENT.   Instructors and program directors noted the role of professional development in CTL course and program design, curriculum development and implementation, and learning assessment. In some cases, professional development focused on helping faculty clarify the learning outcomes afforded by an integrated curriculum.

Some activities concentrated on better understanding and developing course content, while other training targeted how to teach in a contextualized manner. For example, some academic faculty teaching in career-focused learning communities cross-trained in occupational courses, often taking coursework alongside the students they would ultimately teach contextualized basic skills. In another case, two occupational faculty partnered with their academic peers to identify the natural opportunities to teach basic math in their CTE curriculum as well as develop an understanding of how an academic instructor might teach those skills. Several instructors and program directors pointed to ongoing professional development as vital to maintaining the quality of their CTL practice.

INSTITUTIONAL SUPPORT   Several faculty and program directors highlighted the critical importance of institutional support to the success of their CTL practice. This support came in a multiplicity of forms including administrative backing of new course creation and experimentation, release time for professional and curriculum development, sharing of faculty across departments, flexible scheduling, and use of facilities and staff dedicated to program coordination for interaction with community and employer partners. For all program models (excluding the stand-alone classroom practices), linkages with student services or dedicated staff providing intensive support such as individual case management, academic and career advising, or job placement was of particular importance. Many practices also pointed to the critical nature of institutional support in their ability to move beyond initial grant funding or pilot stages to the ongoing sustainability and true institutionalization of these CTL innovations.

CONTINUOUS IMPROVEMENT.   While a focus on continuous improvement tends to accompany any instructional innovation, the integrated nature of CTL seemed to heighten the importance of reflection and ongoing revision while the practice is evolving. Nearly all faculty interviewed noted significant learning in the initial semester of the course or program implementation, such as realizations about how to effectively blend academic and occupational and foundational content, whether the time allotted was feasible for developing desired competencies, and how to best coordinate curriculum with other instructors and coursework. Many instructors talked about their curriculum "gelling," their instruction improving, and their overall understanding of contextualization deepening after multiple semesters of implementation. Several practitioners have altered the design of their model since inception to address both students' needs and logistical challenges. Faculty referred to student feedback and input as a significant driver of the continuous improvement process. In some cases, the analysis of student achievement data during and/or persistence and performance indicators drove significant adaptations.

IMPROVED OUTCOMES. Despite the limited duration of most of the programs highlighted in this primer, nearly all report on some qualitative or quantitative data that demonstrate promising preliminary outcomes. The most consistent evidence of impact across all programs is in qualitative measures, such as student engagement, motivation, increased self-esteem and confidence, and employer satisfaction. Some of this data is self-reported, or compiled from a comparison of Community College Study of Student Engagement (CCSSE) data. In addition to these broad qualitative measures, many program models collected some quantitative measures. These measures spanned a broad range both in time and topics, from course completion, grade point average (GPA), employment, and certificate completion, to measures of academic gains and subsequent performance in college-level classes. While the data points are inconsistent across outcome measures, what is consistent in them all is the belief of faculty that contextualization is a key to success, and that a more extensive evaluation will both support what they have observed in their classes and help them refine their practice.

What Do Faculty Say about CTL?

The next section summarizes 11 different practices as told from the perspective of the faculty and program directors involved in their implementation. These practices are presented according to the type of delivery mode (stand-alone classroom, learning community) and along a continuum of scale which takes into account the commitment and resources required for implementation. The summaries outline the following for each practice: background; program organization; faculty roles and collaboration; key components of instruction; impact on/outcomes for students; and the challenges to and supports for implementation.

In reviewing the examples below, readers are likely to identify elements that are already part of their own classroom practice, even though they might not have viewed these practices as "contextualized learning." Indeed, the examples identified here as CTL appear in many different formats in several different classroom settings. The goal of this section is to help faculty think more intentionally about ways to implement or further advance CTL in their own classrooms or departments as part of their efforts in improving basic skills instruction. When reading the summaries, faculty may consider the following:

- What are you thinking about doing (or are already doing) that can be informed by these practices?

- Which practice(s) may be appropriate for your own courses, department, or college?

- Who can you collaborate with (in your own department, across disciplines and functions of the college) to develop your CTL practice?

- What kind of professional development might be needed, at what stage in the process, and who could provide it?

- What type of institutional support do you need to advance your engagement with CTL?

- What leadership in your college can champion CTL as an approach to basic skills instruction?

- What relationships can you leverage outside your institution to support CTL in your classroom?

While some readers may select to review those practices associated with their particular discipline, faculty may find elements in all the practices that can relate to and be adapted in their own instruction.

NOTE: The following section has been abridged to present only programs related to literacy.

Intensive Introduction to Composition Reading and Writing

Daniel Keller
College of San Mateo (CSM)

Model Type: infused academic course

Description: intensive basic skills composition and reading course one level below transfer; incorporates service learning

Target population: students who place low-middle percentiles on college placement test

Requirements: placement test or prior coursework in basic skills sequence

Type of Assessment: English Placement Test (EPT)

Length: 1 semester/course

Credit/Noncredit: credit

Program status: in progress since 2001

BACKGROUND. English instructor Daniel Keller read an article on service learning during his graduate studies that motivated him to pursue this instructional strategy at College of San Mateo. The article described a service learning model that engaged college athletes in mentoring elementary school students in reading. The results of this model showed powerful reading and academic gains for both the elementary school students and the athletes. Excited by this research, Keller decided to try a similar approach in his own instruction. At the time, the college offered support to instructors interested in service learning through a campus organization called "CSM Connects" and Keller jump-started his practice utilizing these resources.

PROGRAM ORGANIZATION. Keller teaches a five-unit, stand-alone basic skills English course called *Intensive Composition and Reading.* He describes this course as targeting those students who place in the low to middle percentiles on the college's English Placement Test. At the same time, because this course falls one level below transfer, students must have the potential to get to college level within one semester. Keller has independently chosen to incorporate a service-learning approach into the one to two sections of the course he teaches each semester with a focus on critical community issues such as hunger and the environment. Coursework includes "intensive practice in reading, writing, listening, speaking, and thinking to develop and refine composition proficiency" in the context of a community issue as well as a voluntary service day in a related organization or agency.

FACULTY ROLES AND COLLABORATION. Keller currently works on his own to implement this course. At the onset, Keller benefited from support from CSM Connects which provided a small stipend and a series of four trainings with colleagues on how to incorporate a service-learning approach into course curriculum. At this time, CSM Connects is no longer an active function of the college. Keller arranges his own service-learning opportunities and works on his own to select readings, develop and deliver assignments, and arrange the service experience.

KEY COMPONENTS OF INSTRUCTION. A community issue and service experience serves as the context for a portion of Keller's course. Keller notes that for his students "reading and writing is unfamiliar . . . it's not a regular part of their lives. They see it strictly as a school activity. They don't read at home, didn't grow up reading . . . they don't see reading and writing as having anything to do with real world activities." By connecting assignments to a real world issue, Keller aims to actively engage students in experiencing how what they are reading and writing plays out in their communities. He selects topics that he believes will be interesting and relevant to students and that are "complex, requiring lots of critical thinking, where they have to advocate a lot of different solutions . . . anything that involves them debating what works."

For example, Keller may focus a part of his course on the issue of hunger. He starts with students reading *Growing Up Empty*—a book that claims America is experiencing a hunger epidemic. He then engages students in a class debate on food stamps and other potential solutions to hunger. Using an additional reading that focuses on the use of food stamps as an intervention, they are required to work in teams to develop positions for and against making food stamps more accessible. Following, students write an essay based on these readings that describes issues of hunger in America and then argues for a solution to the problem. Keller requires the same composition components he would of an equivalent essay delivered in a non-service-learning course: four dependent clauses, four appositive phrases, four short quotations from the book using MLA citations, a clear introduction and thesis, etc. To add further perspective, students subsequently read and discuss *Fatland: How Americans Became the Fattest People in the World.*

Building on these hunger-focused reading and writing assignments, Keller then engages his students in a voluntary service project on a Saturday. For example, students have volunteered at Samaritan House, a local food distribution center. Students can participate in the service project and write a reflection paper in lieu of a final exam. Over multiple semesters of implementation with hundreds of students, he can only recall one individual opting out of participation. The final essay involves students informing the reader about the nature of the problem of hunger and reflecting on their own service experience. Keller requests an introduction that frames the problem based on the semester's readings and additional research on the issue locally; he also requires students to reflect their observations from the service experience through "strong descriptive writing [that] follows the principle of 'show and don't tell.'" These assignments can comprise up to 27% of a student's grade (including the final reflective essay).

Keller indicates the relatively low impact this approach has on his curriculum. He reflects that during his first semester of implementation, he "probably spent more time than I needed researching organizations and creating materials that weren't necessary." While it requires him to select different readings and tweak writing assignments, Keller says it does not impact the reading and composition skills or competencies he teaches.

IMPACT ON/OUTCOMES FOR STUDENTS. At the same time, Keller highlights the positive impact engaging with a real-world issue, and the service experience in particular, has on students' performance. "It doesn't really impact what I can or can't cover . . . it's just that students are more excited and interested." He observes that experiencing the context allows students to comprehend their reading and express themselves in writing in a deeper way. "It is revealing that even though [*Growing Up Empty*] stresses the diversity of those with hunger, they are shocked when they go to Samaritan House and see working people, people who don't look like they're starving, needing food. It's as if what they had read didn't make an impact until they see it in person."

In describing how the service experience effects the final reflective writing assignment, Keller notes the richness of detail and description he receives from students. He asks students to reflect back to their initial position paper on how to solve the issue of hunger and consider how their impressions and opinions on the issue have changed. In doing so, he reports that students voluntarily ask to write well beyond the three page minimum—something he remarks is rare in his developmental students. Ultimately, Keller finds these essays elicit students' best writing.

Additionally, Keller notes the bonding that takes place among students through the service experience and the satisfaction they feel at doing physical work in their communities. Students self-report in final course evaluations that the lessons and assignments that utilize the service context are the most interesting and engaging parts of the semester. They also note the pragmatic value of the experience—including the service on their resumes and in cover letters. In a few cases, students have chosen new majors or courses of study based on their service.

CHALLENGES AND SUPPORTS. While Keller states that this particular practice requires minimal additional effort on his part, particularly after multiple semesters of implementation, he does acknowledge the value of having a function like CSM Connects available to support selection of and engagement with community organizations. He felt this function signified the institution's investment in service learning and an encouragement of faculty taking on this approach in their classroom. "Knowing the organization was there and that I had institutional encouragement, particularly when I was starting out and not totally confident about what I was doing, was helpful. It's not that I really needed the stipend; it was just nice to know the institution was supporting service learning."

He also acknowledges a few logistical challenges, such as selecting a topic that leads to service in an agency or organization that can accommodate large groups of students at one time. In some cases, transportation can be a challenge for students but they tend to work together to carpool or arrange rides. Keller expresses these as minor, surmountable obstacles. Ultimately, he and his students have great enthusiasm for the experience: "It's exciting, it's fun, it's something different . . . it makes students like the class more." . . .

FastStart@CCD

Lisa Silverstein, Kristin Cutaia, Rosalinda Martinez, Ruth Brancard, Elaine Baker
Community College of Denver

Model Type: learning community

Description: basic skills instruction contextualized with career exploration in an accelerated learning community format

---

Target population: first-time students who test at least two levels below college skills in English/reading or Math

Requirements: assess into two levels of developmental coursework

Type of Assessment: Accuplacer

Length: 1 semester

Credit/Noncredit: credit

Program status: in progress since Fall 2005

BACKGROUND. The FastStart program at Community College of Denver (FastStart@CCD) began with lessons learned from two successful career pathway programs. The first, the Essential Skills Program (ESP), was a response to the work-first focus of the 1997 welfare reform legislation. ESP offered a one-semester certificate (with concentrations in different areas such as business services, early childhood, phlebotomy, medical clerical, etc.) that gave participants access to jobs. ESP was able to move welfare participants into entry-level jobs within a short time span; however, over the next few years it became evident to program staff that if students left the ESP without the foundation skills needed for success in the next level of training, their career options were seriously limited. ESP was successful in reducing caseloads, but not in moving under-prepared students toward long-term economic self-sufficiency. As Elaine Baker, former ESP Program Director and current CCD Director of Workforce Initiatives remarked, "When students leave us before they've had the opportunity to develop strong basic skills, we haven't really given them entrance to a career pathway. We've just given them access to a slightly higher-level, dead-end job."

The second effort that informed FastStart@CCD was the CNA to LPN program, a workforce development partnership with the City and County of Denver, long-term care providers, and the college, which gave certified nurse assistants an opportunity to move up the career ladder to a licensed practical nurse position. The CNA to LPN program began with a six-month accelerated remedial curriculum delivered at the work site. The program demonstrated that with contextualized curriculum and appropriate student support, students could accelerate through multiple levels of the remedial sequence. The program successfully moved CNAs who tested into the lowest levels of developmental math and the mid-range of developmental English through the remedial sequence and into the LPN program.

The successful integration of vocational context and the acceleration of basic skills instruction led to a new set of questions: "What about the broader population of developmental learners who struggle through multiple levels of developmental courses? How could faculty utilize the powerful strategies of acceleration and contextualization to promote learning in the larger population of students who hadn't already made vocational choices, or whose goal was transfer?" To answer these questions, Baker and Ruth Brancard, Senior Chair of the Center for Educational Advancement (developmental studies) joined efforts to design FastStart@CCD, a developmental education learning community that uses acceleration and contextualized learning as its core strategies.

PROGRAM ORGANIZATION.   Instead of contextualizing specific vocational curriculum, FastStart draws its content from the career exploration and educational planning processes. The program is structured around the principle that academically under-prepared students can accelerate to college-level skills through a blend of high academic challenge, a supportive academic structure, and enhanced advising with a career exploration emphasis. FastStart students have the option to accelerate in two levels of developmental math or two levels of an integrated developmental English and reading course in one semester. Classes are offered twice a week in three-hour blocks. Daytime students are required to enroll in a linked college experience course that emphasizes career exploration and academic planning. Participants receive tutoring through the college's learning labs, with student support delivered by an educational case manager specifically dedicated to the program.

FACULTY ROLES AND COLLABORATION.   The program is coordinated by an English faculty member through a .4 release position. Faculty observe each other's classes and provide feedback to each other, convene monthly to discuss program effectiveness and student issues, and work in sub-groups on the development of contextualized curriculum and in the planning of new learning community combinations. Stipends for adjunct faculty and release time for full-time faculty support additional curriculum development. In many ways, the FastStart instructors, coordinator, and the educational case manager operate as a faculty learning community. Other critical collaborations include chairs of the math and English departments, deans, and different divisions in student services, such as the testing center, recruitment, and career services.

KEY COMPONENTS OF INSTRUCTION.   The goals of FastStart are to reduce the time spent in developmental classes, to help students develop the habits, attitudes and skills of successful learners, and to help students make informed career decisions. FastStart staff believe that the achievement of these goals requires the integration of instruction, student services, and career planning. Key components are acceleration, a learning community/cohort model, case management, contextualized curriculum, student support services integrated with academic instruction, and professional development.

For students, acceleration provides motivation; for instructors, acceleration provides a block of time that promotes the development of community. Acceleration creates opportunities for efficiency, eliminating the duplication of content that characterizes traditional remedial sequences, and reduces the time students spend in developmental coursework.

The learning community model provides a vehicle to integrate academic, career, and social support. According to Baker, "The learning community gives student the opportunity to get to know each other and creates an environment where students support each other to achieve their individual academic and personal goals."

A key instructional tool of the FastStart learning community is active learning. FastStart Coordinator and instructor Lisa Silverstein describes:

> Students are actively engaged in their learning and are a part of a classroom community where questions are encouraged and critical thinking is infused in every lesson. Students are an integral part of the learning and discovery process. The class, including the instructor, operates as a team, learning through doing, experiencing, and discussing. Relevant content provides many layered opportunities for "ahas," for both the class and the individual student.

Career exploration is delivered in three complementary formats. The accelerated developmental English/reading course employs career exploration as its organizing content. Silverstein continues, "First we accelerate so we can retain students, but it has to be more than just getting through classes. We have to make it more meaningful. That's where career exploration comes into play." Class activities and assignments begin with personal reflection and the clarification of aptitudes and interests and move to a structured investigation of careers, which includes labor market research, an informational interview with someone in the selected profession, a written evaluation of the career and a presentation to the class. Products include the "I-Search" paper (a personal investigation), a gallery walk, and exhibit of what students have learned, and oral presentations.

In the one-credit college success course required for all daytime FastStart students, the instructor works with a more focused career investigation, which feeds into the final class product, the student's education plan. Career specialist Kristin Cutaia describes how the college success curriculum parallels the career development work in the English/reading class:

> In the beginning we offered workshops on different careers, but we realized early on that most of our students work and were too busy to attend workshops, and that if we thought the material was important, we had to

find a way to incorporate it into class. We began to integrate career assessments, then students went on to other investigations such as informational interviewing, job shadowing, putting together a job outlook with wages and individual goals. All this is directed toward what we call a "career decision," which culminates in a career investigation project, and finally, in an individual education plan.

The third prong of the contextualized career exploration is the Career Majors Fair. Through the Career Majors Fair, students meet with college program advisors and former students who have graduated and are working in different professions. Cutaia continues:

> We needed to give students some additional exposure to community and advisors in a more informal way than in a classroom, so we put together a Career Majors Fair with real industry people, employers, and former students. We wanted to give students confidence in their goals and a sense of what is expected. . . . Informed career planning is a developmental skill. It begins by looking at who you are, first as a student, then as a professional, then as a member of the community. . . . Who are you? Why are you here (in college)? When we get students to answer those questions, we can direct them to the path and connect them with the resources that will help them become that professional.

While the learning community creates bonds among participants, career planning creates a bond between students and the college experience. As former FastStart co-director Ruth Brancard states in her doctoral dissertation:

> For most FastStart students, attending college is not the expected trajectory of their lives. They come to college with the idea that they want to improve their lives . . . , but in many ways the decision is a tentative one, fraught with doubt. We need to give students the opportunity to answer the burning question of whether college will help them reach their goals. . . . Career exploration helps students answer that question.

FastStart strategies emphasize the integration of student-focused instruction, academic support services, and student support services. The FastStart educational case manager is the first point of contact for students, helping them evaluate whether their schedules and goals fit the accelerated format. The case manager remains a key person for students throughout the semester and is the ongoing point of contact for faculty, who notify the case manager if students stop coming to class or need additional help with either personal or academic issues. The case manager works with two work-study students (called ambassadors) in outreach, helping students learn the processes for financial and enrollment procedure, as well as providing referrals to community agencies and support services. Additional academic support is available through CCD's learning labs, which provide computerized learning support and individual tutoring.

IMPACT ON/OUTCOMES FOR STUDENTS. Results from a 2007 study of Fast-Start students showed statistically significant differences between students in the intervention and a matched comparison in rates of completion in developmental math, overall course completion of developmental courses, and first semester GPA. In addition, longitudinal tracking of accelerated math cohorts showed statistically significant differences between the intervention and comparison groups in completion of college-level math. Because of a growing awareness of the negative impact of multiple levels of remedial courses on certificate and degree completion, there is considerable interest in the program's outcomes. A more comprehensive longitudinal study of the program by the Community College Research Center is scheduled for completion in Fall 2009.

CHALLENGES AND SUPPORTS. FastStart was initially funded by the Lumina Foundation and was continued with funding provided by the Charles Stewart Mott Foundation to the Breaking Through initiative, a joint project of the National Council of Workforce Education and Jobs for the Future. CCD has institutionalized FastStart positions, including the project co-coordinator and case manager positions. Funding to expand the program is being provided through "Scaling Up," a continuation of the Mott Foundation's efforts in Breaking Through, with additional support from the Bill and Melinda Gates Foundation. With the institutionalization of core positions, the ongoing program challenges include those of logistics, such as scheduling and space, professional development for existing and new faculty, ongoing curriculum development, and continued reflection and evaluation of the program.

FastStart staff successfully adapted the model for GED completers in 2007 as a component of its Breaking Through project. The eight-week summer intensive, called College Connection, was the basis of a 2007 grant from the US Department of Education, Office of Vocational and Adult Education (OVAE), which is replicating the intensive at seven Colorado community colleges.

Digital Bridge Academy

Diego Navarro
Cabrillo College

Model Type: learning community
Description: social justice curriculum delivered in a learning community format

Target Population: full-time students who test below transfer-level in math and English

Type of Assessment: CTEP Reading Assessment

Length: one semester

Credit/Noncredit: credit

Requirements: 7th–9th grade reading, math at any level, ability to attend full-time

Program Status: in progress since Fall 2002

BACKGROUND. The Digital Bridge Academy (DBA) began in response to a deep concern with gang activity among high-risk 18–25 year olds in Watsonville, California, and consideration of the role the local community college could play in addressing this issue. Diego James Navarro, a former Hewlett Packard (HP) employee, was exploring how he could bring his business skills to assist the Santa Cruz community and Cabrillo College during these initial conversations about local youth involvement in gangs in 2000–2001. As a social science researcher at HP Laboratories, Navarro had been involved in empowering workers to make decisions and creating more efficient work environments. He believed that the same tools industry employed to empower their workers could be used to engage Watsonville's high-risk young adults in their own education and future. Navarro worked with Cabrillo faculty to create DBA—a strength-based program that would address both students' academic needs and the behavioral changes necessary for them to succeed in the knowledge economy.

PROGRAM ORGANIZATION. DBA is a one-semester program that serves as a bridge to college-level coursework. The program recruits from the pool of students enrolled in basic skills classes before census date, through extensive presentations at high schools and through referrals from probation officers, homeless shelters, rehabilitation centers, and other community agencies. DBA requires students to enroll full-time. In this "bridge semester," participants attend a foundation course from 9:00 A.M. to 5:30 P.M. for the first two weeks, followed by six courses delivered 9:00 A.M. to 3:00 P.M., Monday through Thursday for 13 weeks.

FACULTY ROLES AND COLLABORATION. DBA addresses a dual challenge: designing a strength-based behavioral curriculum that will help students understand and overcome the unconscious patterns of behavior that stand between them and success in the knowledge works economy; and integrating this behavioral curriculum with basic skills instruction. The result is a contextualized curriculum that bolsters students' sense of belonging in the college community and improves their academic readiness for transfer-level coursework.

To develop and adapt the program, Navarro engaged experts from the natural and behavioral sciences and formed partnerships with student services providers, employers, other community colleges, foundations, advisory committees, community agencies, and intermediaries. According to Navarro, the most important ongoing role of faculty is the delivery of the curriculum. He calls faculty "the countervailing force" in changing the counter-productive behaviors of the DBA youth. Faculty receive training in curriculum delivery through a structured professional development experience led by Navarro and other DBA master mentors. To date, DBA has trained more than 150 faculty from over 20 California community colleges.

KEY COMPONENTS OF INSTRUCTION.   Navarro sums up his pedagogy as a self-management approach that utilizes multiple modalities, contextualized curriculum of high value and relevance to students and problem-based experiential learning. The DBA program involves two primary components including (1) student self-growth and support and (2) academic acceleration. The student self-growth and support component is comprised of the Foundation course and the Team Self-Management course. The academic acceleration component consists of a project-based social justice course and just-in-time feeder courses that academically prepare students for successful completion of the project-based course.

According to Navarro, this curriculum has dual purposes with an academic goal of preparing students for transfer-level English and beginning algebra and a "cultural education" aim of readying students with the affective skills needed to succeed as knowledge workers. He describes the curriculum as having four organizing areas:

> The first is purpose and direction. It's critical for students to figure out what their purpose and direction is because the students of today are going to have multiple jobs in their lifetime; getting to know yourself and knowing what drives you is the first thing. The second is self-discipline. Self-discipline has to do a lot with self-regulation; self-management falls into that area. The third organizing area is collaborative leadership skills. This has to do with team self-management, recording and facilitating meetings, and project management. The fourth is academic skills, which is the traditional focus of community colleges.

DBA finds that unprepared students are capable of making rapid academic progress once they have hope that they can succeed and a clear sense of who they are as students. Navarro explains that the Foundation course—an intensive, immersion-style experience early in the semester—rekindles students' "fire for learning" by teaching them how to recognize their strengths and change their approach to learning. The program delivery incorporates a range of techniques drawn from corporate executive training and social service models as well as more traditional educational methods. Navarro highlights that over 90% of students who have entered have completed the course and he observes that these students emerge confident and motivated to learn. "The deep bonds of community created within the cohort and with the program create a 24/7 support environment for the students, ameliorating the centripetal force of distractions in their complex lives."

In creating the Team Self-Management course, program designers adapted a social system model of addressing counter-productive social behavior. Navarro talks about three "buckets of skills" students develop through this course. The first bucket includes academic competencies focused on helping students reach transfer-level English and beginning algebra. The second group includes "knowledge worker skills," a learning process intended to move students from hierarchical workers to self-managed professionals. The third "bucket" includes the behavioral system that teaches participants how to focus, show up on time, recognize the unwritten rules of the middle class and develop the overall behaviors needed to succeed in the knowledge economy.

To achieve development of these skills, the Team Self-Management course engages students in scenario planning, a strategic planning process commonly used in business to envision possible future scenarios. Navarro explains:

> Scenario planning is not about predicting the future; it's about capturing possible futures. . . . understanding possible futures and looking at the forces, events, and behaviors that would drive these possible futures. Then, we help them (students) look at the tactics that will get them to the future they want . . . we help them think about cause and effect regarding behavior, and to see possible futures, depending on their goals and behaviors.

In DBA's project-based social justice component, students work in teams to choose a research topic that has personal meaning and relevance to their community. Students administer 150 surveys with 35 to 45 questions, which are then tabulated and presented to a broad audience that includes the mayor, community members, family and friends, college administrators, and staff from public agencies. Examples of past topics include the effects of poverty on education in Watsonville, gang activity, domestic violence, child abuse, and the impact of war on the community. The primary research and the final presentation of their findings helps students develop academic competencies and engage with each other and the community.

In addition to the instructional experience, student services are another critical program component. While support is provided by the student services division at Cabrillo, Navarro points to the student cohort as the key mechanism for providing support:

> We use the cohort to provide support, to tap into the under-utilized potential of the cohort itself. We have students review what's blocking them from being successful and share with each other in class, which gives them practice for the final presentation. Having the students in one cohort full-time allows the creation of pedagogies of support to take advantage of the intensity of the experience.

The program continues to adapt, integrating just-in-time curriculum to the core approach. In addition to a college-level English course that was added to the original DBA model, now called the "Accelerated Digital Bridge," a just-in-time course in numeracy is scheduled to be added in Fall 2009. Cabrillo will also pilot a second semester science and math program in Fall 2009 which will include a contextualized science course supported by several just-in-time science and math feeder courses.

IMPACT ON/OUTCOMES FOR STUDENTS. A National Science Foundation evaluation of DBA showed that community college students who participated in the experience demonstrated higher rates of course completion, accumulation of credits, and completion than students who did not participate. A recent quantitative analysis by the Community College Research Center at Columbia University's Teaching College of the DBA program had significant positive effects for participation in both the accelerated and non-accelerated versions of the DBA, although the effects for the accelerated model were generally greater than for the non-accelerated one. To the extent that colleges are seeking strategies for increasing the rate at which academically unprepared students complete "gatekeeper" courses such as college-level English and earn college credits, the accelerated version of the DBA program seems to hold particular promise. The CCRC study evaluated nine semesters of DBA cohorts and was limited to outcomes over four semesters including the initial DBA intervention.

CHALLENGES AND SUPPORTS. Navarro observes several challenges, institutional and cultural, in DBA implementation. From an institutional perspective, he views the linear, industrial model of education (divisions, silos of resources, scheduling blocks, etc.) as lacking the flexibility necessary to meet the needs of under-prepared students. From a cultural perspective, Navarro articulates the challenge of bridging between the cultural and behavioral patterns of non-traditional students and the real-world expectations of habits and behaviors that will lead students to success. "Students come in with behaviors and responses that were very successful for being on the street, that were adapted to survival in the violent world of poverty, but those behaviors are counter-productive in the knowledge economy."

An additional challenge includes the project's sustainability. Several different funding streams, including the National Science Foundation, the Irvine Foundation, Lucille Packard Foundation, and the William and Flora Hewlett Foundation have contributed to the development and adaptation of DBA. While the process of replication and the costs associated with DBA have yet to be tested on a larger scale, Navarro is confident that the essential design and preliminary outcomes place replication within reach.

Daraja Project

Tom deWit
Chabot College

Model Type: learning community

Description: intensive basic skills composition and reading course followed by English 1A—each paired with a college success course; focus on African-American curriculum

Target population: first-time freshmen, 18–20 year-old at-risk students

Requirements: college placement test, application, in-take interview and writing sample

Type of Assessment: Descriptive Test of Language Skills (DTLS)

Length: two semesters

Credit/Noncredit: credit

Program status: in progress since 1988

BACKGROUND.   In 1988, a team of administrators and faculty at Chabot College initiated the Daraja program to increase the retention and transfer rate of under-represented African American students. Daraja, which means steps, set of steps or stepping-stone in Swahili, focuses on African American literature and culture (Daraja Program, 2009). Since that time, like-minded community college programs across California have formed the Umoja Community—a network of programs committed to enhancing the cultural and educational experiences of African American and other students (deWit and Colondres, 2007). Daraja serves as a key inspiration for and has taken leadership in developing core curricular principles and resources with Umoja colleges.

PROGRAM ORGANIZATION.   Daraja offers students a year-long learning community experience that links English and college success coursework with student services and supports. First semester coursework includes English 102, an intensive reading and composition class one level below transfer. Coursework is organized as follows.

Semester 1	Semester 2
English 102 — Accelerated Reading/Reasoning/Writing	Psychology/Counseling 20 — The College Experience
English 1A — Critical Reading & Composition	Psychology/Counseling 7 — Contemporary Issues in Psychology/Counseling

While the curriculum focuses on African American culture, literature, and experience, the program welcomes all students—primarily targeting 18–20 year-old, first-time freshman who may be at-risk of dropping out of college. In addition to Chabot's assessment and placement process, participants submit an application, take part in an intake interview and complete a short writing sample. Faculty utilize information gathered through this application process to advise students and tailor curriculum. Approximately 40 students annually enroll in the program.

FACULTY ROLES AND COLLABORATION Tom deWit is both an English faculty with Chabot's Daraja program and co-chair of the state-wide Umoja Community. He has taught with Daraja since its second year and before that, with the Puente Project—a related model, also originated at Chabot, focused on increasing the academic achievement of Latino students. deWit describes the intense collaboration that still occurs among program instructors, counselors, and staff. In addition to bi-weekly meetings, faculty attend summer and winter retreats, collaboratively assess student work, and develop shared mid-term and final progress reports. While he observes they are "not fine-tuned synchronized by any means," he notes faculty co-develop curriculum, read one another's books, and share assignments to reinforce them in one another's courses. Daraja staff also benefit from instructional materials, program design tools, and professional development offered through Umoja. One significant focus of training includes learning "everybody's business" such that anyone delivering the Daraja model can address students' needs on the spot—even if outside one's expertise.

KEY COMPONENTS OF INSTRUCTION. deWit explains that while his Daraja's English 102 course outline is the same for all of Chabot's *Accelerated Reading/Reasoning/Writing* classes, emphasis and approach to coursework is flavored by a focus on African-American literature and culture. Most importantly, deWit describes Daraja's context as one based unequivocally on the communities and experiences of participating students. "The students are our context. Our teaching, content and student services are provided directly inside of where they're coming from and what they're bringing to the classrooms. We're intentional about knowing students' situations and their stress points in any given year and adapting curriculum, thematics, discussions, assignments, and even learning goals to the community in the room." Initial classroom activities are designed for faculty to quickly understand students' experiences, families and communities and to adjust curriculum accordingly from there.

Daraja's *Accelerated Reading / Reasoning / Writing* course outcomes include those focused on developing critical thinking and doing sustained reasoning and representative writing; others specifically address developing students' positive identities as learners and increasing their capacity for integrating in writing the ideas of class texts with their own experiences. "We're very much trying to make linkages across a whole span of history, voices and themes so our students' community, language and experience are accepted and dignified in a college setting."

To illustrate, deWit discusses a language assignment designed to address the tension between "standard" and "Black" English. He explains that students often bring many associations about language to the classroom and stresses about the difference in how they and their families and communities communicate versus that which is called for in school. In addition to reading articles and texts on the issue, such as James Baldwin's "If Black English Isn't a Language, Tell What Is," students develop what they call a "Black-tionary"—a dictionary of their own language. Students work in teams choosing and defining 20 to 40 terms, complete with examples of words in context. Students then present the terms in both writing and in presentations to show real world uses of the words and to ultimately demonstrate the power and beauty of language.

Another series of assignments focuses on *Manchild in the Promised Land*—an autobiography written by Claude Brown about his coming of age in mid-century Harlem. Students read the book and complete related assignments over the course of the semester. Discussions and writings include connecting the ideas about the text to their own lives as well as interpreting and analyzing the work of their peers. For example, one of students' first experiences with textual analysis includes reviewing written responses to a key passage from *Manchild* produced by former Daraja participants. Students must underline the analytical or interpretive sentences in those responses, write about how the responses are connected, select an analytical statement from one of the responses and rewrite it as their own "clean punchy thesis" as well as write a thesis of their own that arises from the assignment.

Referencing the *Manchild in the Promised Land* assignments, deWit remarks on a current concern among English faculty about rising students' inability to engage with literature analytically and critically—only having been asked to study it through their personal experience. He clarifies that assignments are "not a bunch of personal writing . . . it's a way for students to try abstract language and reasoning on to their own lives and then back through the text . . . it's a high level of textual analysis and thesis-driven, evidence-driven argumentation." Ultimately, deWit emphasizes a heavy focus on developing Daraja students' transferable skills and knowledge to the point where instruction in English 102 includes conscious, metacognitive training around abstracting ideas, applying them to their own situation and transferring them to another setting.

> Ideas and abstractions, which are the standard fare of college, are what take center stage. So at the same time they're applying an idea to their own lives, it's the ability to abstract and transfer that is absolutely the learning goal. We need them to be comfortable learning abstractions in other disciplines like Psychology or Philosophy where they don't see an immediate relevance to their lives; [we prepare them] to deal with abstract ideas and do some applying back to themselves.

IMPACT ON/OUTCOMES FOR STUDENTS. deWit alludes to several anecdotal stories of success and impact on students' motivation and notes the extreme rarity of a student voluntarily leaving the Daraja program. He prefers to reference longitudinal data showing the impact of Daraja participation on students' performance, persistence, and success in following transfer-level coursework. According to data compiled by the Chabot Office of Institutional Research, between 1994–2004, Daraja students (age 21 or under) successfully completed the Basic Skills to Freshman Composition sequence at a rate 19% higher than African American students (age 21 or under) not in Daraja. Furthermore, between 1995–2005, Daraja students (age 21 or under) successfully completed the second semester critical thinking course which follows freshman composition at a rate 11% higher than African American students (age 21 or under) not in Daraja. deWit notes that this critical thinking course is not part of the Daraja learning community and the higher success rate underscores the quality of academic preparation students receive in the Daraja Project.

CHALLENGES AND SUPPORTS. deWit acknowledges the need to treat development of one's contextual practice as an iterative process and a "work in progress." He cautions against developing an instructional design that is too rigid; "I've seen folks work super hard to put things in place and if a few things fall apart, they feel like the whole thing is falling apart." He comments on the evolution of the Daraja program over time, in particular through student feedback and evaluation. As is done in Daraja, deWit encourages instructors trying on CTL to incorporate an intentionally reflective process with students in small, focused ways whether it be through classroom assessment techniques or engaging an outside evaluator or hosting a focus group with students. He also notes the benefits of making such a practice public. While deWit says faculty can try a contextualized unit or two without significant administrator approval, he still strongly encourages instructors to share their work with colleagues and students to get their feedback on what does and does not work. For a full-scale program like Daraja, administrative support has been critical and believes this support is vital for other like programs.

Driving home Daraja's intense focus on its participants' personal and academic goals and needs, deWit cites students' ambitions, experience and sense of self as a key element to designing any context for learners.

> The students should define and inform the context, not just the field or the subject matter. There are ways of inviting students in and dignifying their fears, ambitions and stresses so these are part of the context in which students are learning, without becoming a therapist or missing time needed to cover the content. Students have to feel grounded, comfortable and confident in this setting, or they very well might leave . . . and say I can't do college and it's not for you either. Even if students don't stay in [Daraja] but share with their peers that college is great and it's definitely for you, then we've been successful.

. . .

I-BEST (Integrated Basic Skills and Skills Training) Certified Nurse Assistant Program

Jon Kerr
Lower Columbia College (formerly Pierce College)

Model Type: infused occupational

Description: pairs Adult Basic Education/ESL with professional-technical training in a CNA certificate program

Target Populations: mid-range ESL or ABE learners

Requirements: level four ABE or ESL, as defined by reading assessments

Type of Assessment: CASAS

Length: two quarters

Credit/noncredit: credit for college-level courses

Program status: in progress since 2005

BACKGROUND. I-BEST evolved from a pilot career pathway program integrating ESL instruction with workforce training to a statewide effort of 70 programs in 32 community colleges, serving approximately 1,000 students each year. I-BEST challenges the traditional notion that students must complete all levels of developmental education before they can begin college-level workforce training. Israel Mendoza, Director of Adult Education with the Washington State Board of Community and Technical Colleges (WSBCTC), conceived and championed the program in response to the state's critical workforce needs and the growing number of immigrants and non-native speakers in the state, whose numbers doubled in the decade between 1990 and 2000.

Washington launched I-BEST with 10 pilots in five colleges and expanded the program after an initial analysis of outcomes found that I-BEST participants were "substantially more likely than similar basic skills students to advance to college-level work and to reach the "tipping point" of at least one year of credits and a credential (Bloomer, 2005; WSBCTC, 2005). The importance of the "tipping point" emerged from a study of Washington's low-skill adult community college students (Prince & Jenkins, 2005), which found that completing a year's worth of college credits and earning a certificate created a "tipping point" which resulted in an average wage gain of $7,000 per year for ESL learners, $8,500 per year for Adult Basic Education (ABE) students, and a gain of $2,700 and $1,700 per year respectively for students who entered college with only a GED or high school diploma.

Based on the initial success of I-BEST pilots and an analysis of its potential economic impact, WSBCTC approved a funding formula that represented an increase of .75 FTE over traditional funding. Current I-BEST offerings include programs that prepare students for employment in Allied Health, early childhood education, business technology, corrections, automotive, para-educator, and other entry-level positions that lead to careers. Most I-BEST programs are one semester, with all credits applying to two-and four-year programs (with the exception of Allied Health).

In addition to the general description of I-BEST, this example includes a profile of the Certified Nursing Assistant (CNA) program at Pierce College (WA), which provides an operational view of how the program functions at the college level.

PROGRAM ORGANIZATION. According to Jon Kerr, former I-BEST Director at Pierce College, "I-BEST is not a special program; I-BEST is a delivery method," based on a team teaching model that pairs a content instructor and a basic skills instructor, along with additional instructional and student support. ESL faculty and technical-professional instructors work together in the classroom. The content instructor is responsible for delivering the content and the basic skills instructor is responsible for providing the basic skills support needed for students to succeed in content coursework. In some colleges, both instructors are present for the instructional content, and in others, there is a 50% overlap. The basic skills instructor is contracted for an additional credit, called an "educational interview," which provides time for instructors to work with students and connect them to additional academic and non-academic resources. Additionally, most colleges have an I-BEST coordinator and assistant; however, the primary responsibility for the program rests with the Basic Skills division.

The Pierce CNA program was targeted, in part, to meet the goals of ESL learners who had worked as health care professionals in their native countries and were seeking ways to re-enter the field; however the program is not limited to ESL learners. All instruction is delivered in English. The eight-credit certificate program spans two quarters. The first quarter, Foundations of Allied Health, is structured around the required certifications in CPR, HIPPA, First Aid, AIDS training, and hand-washing. The second semester covers the related didactic and clinical requirements. The clinical component is a five-credit class that runs from 7:30 A.M. till 3:30 P.M. on Wednesdays. On Thursdays, students attend a support class from 1:00 till 4:00 P.M. and a didactic class from 5:00 till 9:00 P.M. The total time is 50 contact hours, 30 for the didactic content, 40 for the clinical and approximately 50 hours for academic and non-academic support.

FACULTY ROLES AND COLLABORATION. Since Washington State delivers both Adult Basic Education and ESL through the community and technical colleges, I-BEST has been able to involve adult education and college-level vocational instructors in all levels of collaboration, curriculum development and leveraged funding. Instructors regularly attend workshops and are involved in curriculum development for new offerings. Faculty collaborate on all aspects of the program, which includes advising students on further education and training and program adaptations. I-BEST faculty development begins with a clearly stated hypothesis on team teaching: "In order for instructional teams to function effectively, as equal partners working in the same classroom, they must be trained in, investigate, and analyze various types of team teaching, views of experienced team teachers, and issues effecting team teaching."

KEY COMPONENTS OF INSTRUCTION. I-BEST programs have two strands: traditional content coursework and support class where students are given help in mastering the content class. While content classes may include both I-BEST and traditional students, I-BEST participants engage in an additional 30 hours of instruction to review and prepare for the next class. Support classes are led by the basic skills instructor, with participation of the content instructor based on need. In Pierce's CNA program, this arrangement translates into 30 hours of content in allied health topics, with an additional 30 hours of support in basic skills/ESL.

Since I-BEST relies on a combination of existing certificate programs and additional academic support, the principal instructional component is the integrated faculty approach to team teaching, which pairs basic skills and content faculty in planning, delivery of instruction and continuous improvement. According to Kerr, professional development is critical to program success. "Training is ongoing . . . I bring in teams once a quarter and review the different kinds of models and require them to . . . demonstrate a fifteen minute lesson, and so it's a kind of 'learn by what we are doing.' . . . The essential piece is the team."

IMPACT ON/OUTCOMES FOR STUDENTS. In assessing the impact of contextualization on outcomes, Kerr remarked, "When students are learning something in the context of something they are interested in, they can immediately apply it and understand it. For ESL students, their reading scores go way up. Instead of reading about things that aren't part of their lives, they are reading about things they need to know and they can actually apply them, so it's that whole thing about experiential learning."

I-BEST also benefits from a substantive evaluation component that provides quantitative data on the program's success. In the first four cohorts of Pierce's CNA program, 54 students enrolled, with a 70% program completion rate; students showed a 93% course completion rate with a GPA of 3.3, which was higher than for non-participants. Learning gains, using federal and state measures for adult learning, were also substantial. Of the 38 students who post-tested after 80 hours of instruction, there were 19 federal reading gains, 74 state reading gains; 6 federal math reading gains, 23 state math reading gains; 9 federal reading gains and 40 state listening gains.

CHALLENGES AND SUPPORTS. In addressing a core assumption of I-BEST, that students do not necessarily have to complete all levels of developmental work before they can begin college, Kerr comments, "I don't think the concern that these students aren't at a high enough academic level is really a concern, because they do just fine!" Instead, he identifies the logistical challenges of working across disciplines and the ongoing need for professional development to reinforce effective practice and continuous improvement.

I-BEST is noted for its pioneering state funding formula that provides fiscal support for team teaching, professional development, student support and coordination. While the program's strong outcomes make the case for its continuation, Kerr does not expect that I-BEST will be immune to cutbacks in funding in the current fiscal crisis. This will likely result in closer scrutiny of plans for expansion, but according to Kerr, the strong and consistent program outcomes from multiple evaluations position will be an important factor in its continuation.

Considerations for Implementing CTL

Today's learners must be engaged differently in order to prepare them for life and work in the 21st century — as argued in the case statement and made tangible in the narratives above. Students' unique challenges and needs present an imperative for transformation of community college practice, particularly as related to basic skills instruction. The experiences of the faculty and program directors featured in this primer as well as a growing body of related research indicate that CTL is an alternative strategy that holds promise for moving students towards self-sufficiency and life-long advancement.

As evidenced by the highlighted practices, faculty can take many approaches to CTL. Implementation can vary significantly depending on an instructor's interests and subject matter, students' needs and motivations, and/or a college's educational and workforce development priorities. Development of one's CTL practice can take shape in small ways through a series of activities in a stand-alone classroom or through more comprehensive approaches in learning communities and cohort models. The modest number of practices presented in this primer coupled with a growing number of models developing in California community colleges and across the nation present a myriad of possibilities for how faculty can move forward with CTL in their own classrooms.

Whatever the implementation approach, the clear commonality among the examples featured is the choice of practitioners to use a context relevant to students' lives, communities and/or career goals in basic skills instruction. As highlighted in the previous section, faculty identified several other distinguishing features of their practice that connect to this decision. Engagement with CTL encouraged faculty collaboration on a range of activities and involvement in related professional development. The choice to contextualize led to the creation of original curriculum and instructional materials and the utilization of interactive teaching to involve students with that material. In many cases, employment of CTL called for leveraging a range of institutional supports. Moreover, these practitioners noted that use of CTL meant a commitment to continuous improvement and a focus on how the strategy could impact students and improve their outcomes.

In addition to these common elements for CTL implementation, four key considerations emerge out of the practices featured. These considerations have implications for faculty, colleges, funders, and policy makers alike interested in supporting CTL as an instructional innovation: resources, research, replicability, scalability, and sustainability.

Resources

Many of the common elements that characterize the featured CTL practices have unique resource implications. To design a new practice, faculty often need release time for collaboration and curriculum and instructional material development. To implement a new strategy, instructors might require funds for small items like instructional materials or more significant expenses like team teaching. Support from and partnership with student services divisions of the college may also be vital to the success of the model. To sustain a CTL innovation, faculty are likely to need access to support in the form of program coordination, ongoing professional development or facilitated data collection for and discussions about continuous improvement of their practice.

These resource implications vary according to the scope and scale of the CTL practice. A small infusion of funds can help fuel individual or small teams of faculty interested in trying CTL in their own classrooms. More holistic interdisciplinary or cross-functional models likely call for significant and long-term investments. All of the featured practices benefited from some form of direct or in-kind support from their institution and/or an external funder.

In California community colleges, faculty and institutions can leverage Basic Skills Initiative funding. Carl Perkins Career and Technical Education Act grants and an increasing number of foundation-funded initiatives offer other opportunities for faculty experimentation with contextualization of basic skills instruction. Based on the current research and interest in CTL, there are likely to be additional opportunities for fiscal support, such as short-term mini-grant opportunities for individual faculty as well as investments in larger-scale, sustained funding efforts focused on comprehensive program development.

Research

As seen in the review of the literature and as demonstrated in the faculty stories, there is an abundance of anecdotal evidence and a growing body of outcome data that point to the positive impact of CTL on student behavior, performance, persistence and achievement in subsequent coursework and employment. However, experimental designs utilizing random assignment are few. An ongoing multi-college study of contextualized learning in allied health programs is currently underway through the Community College Research Center (Perin, in progress). Recent experimental studies also include the National Research

Center for Career and Technical Education (NRCCTE), which looked at high school math outcomes in five states (Stone et al., 2006), and the National Center for Postsecondary Research (NCPR) study of learning community outcomes in Kingsborough Community College (Visher et al., 2008). The outcomes of both studies are positive, although the NCPR study has a broader unit of analysis (the learning community) than the NRCCTE study, which looks at the pedagogy that facilitates the transferability of math competencies.

Because of the limited institutional research capacity of most community colleges, evaluation is often an afterthought rather than an integral part of program design. This makes it difficult to compare program effectiveness across colleges as well as to make consistent data-based statements on the impact of CTL innovations. Going forward, it is recommended that new programs pay more attention to the role of initial assessment and ongoing evaluation as an integral component of CTL design.

To accomplish this, faculty should partner with institutional researchers before the program has been implemented to identify which questions they are addressing in their inquiries and the type of data that could answer these questions. Campus-based student learning outcomes coordinators or initiatives can also offer another source of support for developing related outcomes, choosing appropriate assessments and engaging in an analysis focused on continuous course or program improvement. As mentioned previously, practices like the Bridge-to-Biotech, Los Medanos Mathematics Department, the Career Advancement Academies/ Career Ladders Project, Daraja, Digital Bridge, and I-BEST all provide examples of a formal program evaluation targeting continuous improvement. At both the institutional level and beyond, developing the conditions for longitudinal tracking, the agreement on common data collection, and the capacity to determine a valid comparison or control group will all contribute to a more in-depth understanding of program effectiveness.

Finally, practitioners, policy makers and funders alike would benefit from further research related to the range of rationales behind and ways for using contextualization in teaching and learning. For example, the majority of practices in this primer focus on developing students' basic skills in career contexts with the purpose of improving their readiness for related college-level coursework or entry into a particular occupation. At the same time, a few examples specifically connect basic skills development to students' personal identities and experiences in their neighborhoods, schools, and communities and serve as an arena for developing their capacity to pursue social change. As these kinds of practices grow, they offer an additional lens through which to view CTL and beckon for additional research on how such strategies work to develop students' foundational skills and promote equity in CA community college instruction.

Replicability / Scalability

Intimately tied to resources and research are issues of replicability and scalability. Faculty often respond to discussions on contextualization with the comment, "I already do that in my classroom." Yet documentation, dissemination and expansion of CTL models beyond individual classroom and college practice remain a challenge. With appropriate resource allocation for effective implementation and a clear plan for collecting and analyzing student outcomes, faculty will be better positioned to expand their efforts in effective CTL practice.

Documentation of curriculum and materials development, a description of the collaborations that were critical to the success of the venture, a detailed understanding of the resources required and an overview of the initial and ongoing professional development needed to implement and continue innovation will allow faculty and staff to share substantive examples of their work with peers. Several featured practices, including the Bridge-to-Biotech, the Spanish to English Assistant Teacher Certificate, and FastStart@CCD have all documented their models and developed relationships with peers in related colleges to explore replication. Developing communities of practice around a particular CTL model, as exemplified by the Career Advancement Academies and the Umoja Community, offers another way to disseminate effective practices, work collaboratively on issues of program improvement, identify opportunities for program extension to a larger population, and develop a substantive body of evidence about the efficacy of CTL as an instructional strategy.

Programs like I-BEST show how conscious policy and diversified private and public funding can support measured, thoughtful scaling of CTL across an entire community college system. As noted by Mazzeo (2008) "many of the leading edge states implementing community college reforms have found creative ways to use a mix of state, federal and private dollars to support innovative practices" (p. 11). Models such as I-BEST, the Detroit Bridge Project and Ivy Tech Community College's embedded skill programs are examples of private foundations' interest in supporting the development of CTL as part of their agenda on increasing student success.

Sustainability

Sustainability is an increasingly significant aspect of the discussions around innovation. While foundations and other grant making organizations have the capacity to fund innovation, their concerns go beyond an initial proof of concept to the likelihood that successful programs will be institutionalized. Two recent publications give programs and colleges a way to evaluate the long term fiscal impact of innovation through a cost benefit analysis. In both *Basic Skills as a Foundation for*

Student Success in California Community Colleges and *Calculating the Productivity of Innovation,* the authors introduce a methodology that calculates the costs and revenues of specific practices (CSS, 2007; Corash & Baker, 2009). These methodologies give institutions and policy makers a way to calculate the time it will take to recoup an initial investment in program improvement, as well as a way to project the long term fiscal benefit of the innovation to the institution. "There are real, college-level economic reasons that alternate approaches to basic skills at the very least go a long way towards paying for themselves, and in many cases may very well result in a net economic benefit to the college" (CSS, 2007, p. 7).

While grants or a special allocation may seed a project, funds alone will not maintain innovation. Faculty interest and leadership are necessary elements of the sustainability of any effort, irrespective of its scale. Initiatives that contribute to institutional change at the programmatic level must be integrated into the campus culture, as Rose Asera has noted with the SPECC projects sponsored by the Carnegie Foundation. A change effort develops "sustainability" as it becomes part of the institutional narrative and is woven into the framework of institutional evaluation and review (2008, p. 21). In addition, a sustainable programmatic effort that has the support of the administrative leadership who "repurpose structures" or develop ways of crossing campus boundaries is likely to develop roots (p. 22).

Notes

1. The Carl D. Perkins 1990 legislation was titled the Vocational and Applied Technology Act; the reauthorization of 1998 renamed the legislation the Vocational and Technical Education Act; the most recent 2006 reauthorization revised the title yet again to the Career and Technical Education Act.

References

Adelman, C. (2004). *Principal indicators of student academic histories in post-secondary education, 1972–2000.* Washington DC: U.S. Department of Education, Institute of Educational Sciences.

Andersson, F., Holzer, H., & Lane, J. (2005). *Moving up or moving on: Who advances in the low-wage labor market?* New York, NY: Russell Sage Foundation.

Alexander, P. A., & Murphy, P. K. (1998a). A test of cognitive and motivational dimensions of domain learning. *Journal of Educational Psychology, 90,* 435–447.

Alexander, P. A., & Murphy, P. K. (1998b). The research base for APA's learner-centered psychological principles. In N. Lambert & B. McCombs (Eds.), *Issues in school reform: Sampler of psychological perspectives on learner-*

centered schools (pp. 33–60). Washington, DC: American Psychological Association.

Asera, R. (2008). *Change and sustainability: A program director's reflection on instutional learning.* A report from the Carnegie Foundation for the Advancement of Teaching and Learning.

Attewell, P., Levin, D., Domina, T., & Levey, T. (2006). New evidence on college remediation. *Journal of Higher Education, 77*(5), 886–924.

Bailey, T. (2009). *Rethinking developmental education in community college.* (CCRC Brief No. 40). New York, NY: Columbia University Teachers College, Community College Research Center.

Barkley, E., Cross, P., and Major, C. H. (2005). *Collaborative learning techniques: A handbook for college faculty.* San Francisco, CA. Jossey-Bass.

Berns, R. G., & Erickson, P. M. (2001). *Contextual teaching and learning: Preparing students for the new economy. The Highlight Zone: Research @ Work, 5,* 2–9. (ERIC Document Reproduction Service No. ED452376)

Bond, L. (2004). Using contextual instruction to make abstract learning concrete. *Techniques: Connecting Education and Careers.* Association for Career and Technical Education.

Bosworth, K. (1994). Developing collaborative skills in college students. In K. Bosworth & S. J. Hamilton (Eds.), *Collaborative learning: Underlying processes and effective techniques. New Directions for Teaching and Learning, No. 59* (pp. 25–32). San Francisco, CA: Jossey- Bass.

Center for Student Success. (2007). *Basic skills as a foundation for success in California community colleges.* Sacramento, CA: California Community Colleges Chancellor's Office.

Center for Student Success. (2005). *Environmental scan: A summary of key issues facing California community colleges pertinent to the strategic planning process.* Sacramento, CA.

Choo, C. B. (2007). Activity-based approach to authentic learning in a vocational institute. *Educational Media International, 44*(3), 185–205.

Clardy, A. (2005, August 1). *Andragogy: Adult learning and education at its best?* Online Submission (ERIC Document Reproduction Service No. ED492132). Retrieved March 24, 2009, from ERIC database.

Corash, K., & Baker, E. D. (2009). *Calculating the productivity of innovation: Using a simplified cost-benefit analysis to promote effective practice.* Prepared for the Ford Foundation Bridges to Opportunity Project and the Lumina Foundation for Education. Retrieved on March 30, 2009, from http://www.communitycollegecentral.org/StateInitiatives/Colorado/Colorado Cost_Benefit.pdf

Crosley, A., & Roberts, B. (2007). *Strengthening state policies to increase the education and skills of low-wage workers.* Chevy Chase, MD: Working Poor Families Project.

Daraja Program. (2009). *What is daraja?* Retrieved on March 31, 2009, from http://daraja.pyuple.com

Frith, U. (2005). Teaching in 2020: The impact of neuroscience. *Journal of Education for Teaching, 31*(4), 289–291.

Gerlach, J. M. (1994). "Is this collaboration?" in Bosworth, K., and Hamilton, S. J. (Eds.), *Collaborative learning: Underlying processes and effective techniques.* New Directions for Teaching and Learning No. 59.

Grubb, N. (1995). *Education through occupations in American high schools.* Williston, VT: Teachers College Press.

Grubb, N., & Badway, N. (1999). *Integrating academic and occupational education among California community colleges: Current practice and future opportunities.* Prepared for the Chancellor's Office of California Community Colleges Education Services and Economic Development Division, Vocational Education Unit.

Grubb, W. N., & Kraskouskas, E. (1992). *A time to every purpose: Integrating occupational and academic education in community colleges and technical institutes.* Washington, DC: Office of Vocational and Adult Education. (ERIC Document Reproduction Service No. ED50405)

Harris, L., & Ganzglass, E. (2008). *Creating postsecondary pathways and good jobs for young high school dropouts: The possibilities and the challenges.* Washington, DC: Center for American Progress.

Harris, S. (2003). Programs in practice. *Kappa Delta Pi Record,* 38–41.

Holzer, H., & Lerman, R. (2007). *America's forgotten middle-skills jobs: Education and training requirements in the next decade and beyond.* Retrieved on March 10, 2009, from http://www.skills2compete.org/atf/cf/%7B8E 9806BF-4669-4217-AF74-26F62108EA68%7D/ForgottenJobsReport%20 Final.pdf

Hull, D. (1993). *Opening minds opening doors. The rebirth of American education.* Waco, TX: Center for Occupational Research and Development.

Jacoby, B., Albert, G., Bucco, A., Busch, J., Enos, S., Fisher, I., et al. (1996). *Service-learning in higher education.* San Francisco, CA: Jossey-Bass.

Jenkins, D. (2002) *The potential of community colleges as bridges to opportunity for the disadvantaged: Can it be achieved on a large scale?* Chicago, IL: Illinois University, Chicago, Great Cities Institute. (ERIC Document Reproduction Service No. ED466244)

Johnson, E. B. (2002). *Contextual teaching and learning: what it is and why it's here to stay.* Thousand Oaks, CA: Corwin Press, INC.

Kirsch, I., Braun, H., Yamamoto, K., & Sum, A. (2007). *America's perfect storm.* Princeton, NJ: Educational Testing Service.

Kuh, G. D., Kinzie, J., Cruce, T., Shoup, R., & Gonyea, R.M. (2006). *Connecting the Dots: Multi-faceted analysis of the relationships between student engagement results from the NSSE, and the institutional practices and conditions that foster student success.* Lumina Foundation for Education Grant #2518. Bloomington, IN: Center for Post-Secondary Research.

Massa, N. M. (2008). Problem-based learning: A real-world antidote to the standards and testing regime. *The New England Journal of Higher Education,* 19–20.

Mazzeo, C. (2008). *Supporting student success at California community colleges.* Prepared for the Bay Area Workforce Funding Collaborative Career by the Career Ladders Project for California Community Colleges.

Merriam, S., Caffarella, R., & Baumgartner, L. (2006). *Learning in adulthood: A comprehensive guide* (3rd ed.). San Francisco, CA: Jossey-Bass. (ERIC Document Reproduction Service No. ED499592)

Merrill, M. D., & Gilbert, C. G. (2008). Effective peer interaction in a problem-centered instructional strategy. *Distance Education, 29*(2), 199–207.

Mezirow, J. (2000). *Learning as transformation: Critical perspectives on a theory in progress.* San Francisco, CA: Jossey Bass.

Mikulecky, L. (1985). *Literacy task analysis: Defining and measuring occupational literacy demands.* Paper presented at the National Adult Educational Research Association, Chicago, IL.

Perin, D. (2001). Academic-occupational integration as a reform strategy for the community college: Classroom perspectives. *Teachers College Record, 103*(2), 303–335.

Perin, D. (in progress). Columbia University Teachers College Community College Research Center, National Science Foundation study in progress.

Prince, D., & Jenkins, D. (2005). *Building pathways to success for low-skill adult students: Lessons for community college policy and practice from a statewide longitudinal tracking study.* New York, NY: Columbia University Teachers College, Community College Research Center.

Predmore, S. R. (2005). Putting it into context. *Techniques.* Retrieved January 31, 2009, from http://www.acteonline.org

Raelin, J. A. (2008). *Work-based learning.* (T. J. Elliot, Ed.). San Francisco, CA: Jossey-Bass.

Shore, M., Shore, J., & Boggs, S. (2004). Allied health applications integrated into developmental mathematics using problem based learning. *Mathematics and Computer Education, 38*(2), 183–189.

Silverman, S. L., & Casazza, M. E. (2000). *Learning and development: Making connections to enhance teaching.* San Francisco, CA: Jossey-Bass.

SSE Design Series. (2007). *The importance of contextualized learning: An instructional design perspective.* Retrieved February 1, 2009, from http://www.sselearn.net/assets/pdfs/WhitePaperContextualizedLearning.pdf

Sticht, T. G. & Kern, R. P. (1970). Project realistic: determining literacy demands of jobs. *Journal of Reading Behavior, 2*(3), 191–212.

Stone, J. R., Alfeld, C., Pearson, D., Lewis, M. V., Jensen, S. (2006). *Building academic skills in context: Testing the value of enhanced math learning in CTE.* National Research Center for Career and Technical Education, University of Minnesota.

Svinicki, M. D. (2004). *Learning and motivation in the postsecondary classroom.* San Francisco, CA: Jossey-Bass.

Van Hook, S. (2008). *Theories of intelligence, learning, and motivation as a basic educational praxis.* Online Submission. (ERIC Document Reproduction Service No. ED501698)

Visher, M., Wathington, H., Richburg-Hayes, L., Schneider, E., Cerna, O., Sansone, C., et al. (2008). *The learning communities demonstration: Rationale, sites and research design.* Retrieved on March 30, 2009, from http://www.mdrc.org/publications/476/full.pdf

Wider Opportunities for Women. (2009). *Strategies for family economic self-sufficiency.* Retrieved on March 25, 2009, from http://www.wowonline.org/ourprograms/fess/sfess.asp

WSBCTC [Washington State Board for Community and Technical Colleges]. (2005). *I- BEST: A program integrating adult basic education and workforce training.* Olympia, WA: Author. Retrieved from http://www.sbctc.ctc.edu/college/d_basicskills.aspx

Zull, J. E. (2004). The art of changing the brain. *Educational Leadership,* 68–72.

Zull, J. E. (2006). Key aspects of how the brain learns. *The Neuroscience of Adult Learning, 110,* 3–9. doi: 10.1002/ace.

5

Disciplinary Literacy Instruction

Introduction

Disciplinary literacy instruction is an important topic right now for literacy professionals at all educational levels. To fully understand what a disciplinary literacies approach is, though, one has to first understand the shift in focus away from traditional approaches and content area literacy. This chapter traces that transition and provides some exemplars of the work that should inform college reading professionals who are developing and delivering instruction to prepare students for the various literacy demands of college careers.

We begin this chapter with a historically significant work: a 1983 *Reading Research Quarterly* article by David W. Moore, John E. Readence, and Robert J. Rickelman that takes us all the way back to the pre-1900s roots of content area literacy. Their historical overview of content area literacy, including the theoretical and practical roots of that movement, outlines five main issues of continued relevance: locus of instruction, reading demands of various subjects, study, reading materials, and age focus. These issues continue to be relevant as we shift into the more current focus on disciplinary literacy instruction.

Within the scholarly literature, a new way of approaching literacy in the disciplines has gained wide momentum, one that emphasizes the particular ways of reading, writing, and thinking in a discipline that impact how learners are apprenticed into these disciplines. Timothy and Cynthia Shanahan define a disciplinary literacy approach and explain the critical differences between content area literacy and disciplinary literacy. Whereas traditional content area literacy instruction was focused on imposing reading/literacy strategies generically and universally across subject areas, a disciplinary literacy approach instead focuses on the development of literacy strategies from within a discipline and is specifically tied to the cognitive and metacognitive demands of that particular discipline area.

As one illustration of this disciplinary approach to literacy instruction, Cynthia Hynd, Jodi Patrick Holschuh, and Betty P. Hubbard's article focuses on the ways of reading like a historian. With specific disciplinary literacy instruction provided, the college students who participated in their study were able to shift from traditional memorization-based strategies to more critical thinking and multiple text-oriented strategies.

And finally, we close this chapter with an example of a classroom-tested strategy that is discipline driven. Note launchers is an active-reading strategy created specifically for textbook reading and studying in mathematics. Josh and Kimberly Turner Helms address the particular difficulties many students have with mathematics textbooks, and acknowledge the typical approach to reading such texts. Using note launchers, they write, is a way of making such reading tasks more accessible to students because the strategy is grounded in an understanding not only of the specific text expectations of mathematics as a discipline, but also of students' cognitive stages.

The tracing of reading in the disciplines, from early content area reading approaches to the more current disciplinary literacies perspective, is an important one for developmental reading professionals, as we are always preparing students for the next course, the next level, and the next context. As you read this chapter, consider ways to help students understand that context matters with reading.

Additional Readings

Alexander, P. A., & Kulikowich, J. M. (2006). Learning from physics text: A synthesis of recent research. *Journal of Research in Science Teaching, 31*(9), 895–911.

Beyeler, J. (1998). Reluctant readers: Case studies of reading and study strategies in Introduction to Psychology. *The Learning Assistance Review, 3*(1), 5–19.

Chaplin, S. (2007). A model of student success: Coaching students to develop critical thinking skills in introductory biology courses. *International Journal for the Scholarship of Teaching and Learning, 1*(2), 1–7.

Eades, C., & Moore, B. (2007). Ideas in practice: Strategic note taking in developmental mathematics. *Journal of Developmental Educational, 31*(2) 18–26.

Glynn, S. M., & Muth, K. D. (1994). Reading and writing to learn science: Achieving scientific literacy. *Journal of Research in Science Teaching, 31*(9), 1057–1073.

Gurung, R. A. R., Chick, N. L., & Haynie, A. (Eds.). (2009). *Exploring signature pedagogies: Approaches to teaching disciplinary habits of mind.* Sterling, VA: Stylus Publishing.

Holschuh, J. P. (2000). Do as I say, not as I do: High, average, and low-performing students' strategy use in biology. *Journal of College Reading and Learning, 31*(1), 94–107.

Hynd, C., & Alvermann, D. E. (1986). The role of refutation text in overcoming difficulty with science concepts. *Journal of Reading, 29*(5), 440–446.

Hynd, C., Holschuh, J., & Nist, S. (2000). Learning complex scientific information: Motivation theory and its relation to student perceptions. *Reading & Writing Quarterly, 16*, 23–57.

Langer, J. (2010). *Envisioning knowledge: Building literacy in academic disciplines*. New York, NY: Teachers College Press.

McConachie, S. M., Petrosky, T., Petrosky, A. R., & Resnick, L. B. (2009). *Content matters: A disciplinary literacy approach to improving student learning.* Hoboken, NJ: John A. Wiley & Sons.

Newman, M. C. (2008). *Disciplinary knowledge, intertextuality, and developmental readers: A study of community college students* (Unpublished doctoral dissertation). Northern Illinois University, DeKalb, Illinois.

Nokes, J. D. (2013). *Building students' historical literacies: Learning to read and reason with historical texts and evidence.* New York, NY: Routledge.

Norris, S. P., & Phillips, L. M. (1994). Interpreting pragmatic reading when reading popular reports of science. *Journal of Research in Science Teaching, 31*(9), 947–967.

Pawan, F., & Honeyford, M. A. (2009). Academic literacy. In R. F. Flippo & D. C. Caverly, (Eds.), *Handbook of college reading and study strategy research* (2nd ed., pp. 26–46). New York, NY: Routledge.

Rey, V. M., & Karstadt, R. (2006). Strategies in teaching paired reading with content courses. *NADE Digest, 2*(1), 29–33.

Shanahan, T., & Shanahan, C. (2008). Teaching disciplinary literacy to adolescents: Rethinking content-area literacy. *Harvard Educational Review, 78*(1), 40–59.

Shanahan, C., Shanahan, T., & Misischia, C. (2011). Analysis of expert readers in three disciplines: History, mathematics, and chemistry. *Journal of Literacy Research, 43*(4), 393–429.

Shepherd, M. D., Selden, A., & Selden, J. (2011). *Possible reasons for students' ineffective reading of their first-year university mathematics textbooks* (Technical Report No. 2011–2). Cookeville, TN: Tennessee Technological University.

Siebert, D., & Draper, R. (2012). Reconceptualizing literacy and instruction for mathematics classrooms. In T. Jetton & C. Shanahan (Eds.), *Adolescent Literacy in the Academic Disciplines* (pp. 172–198). New York, NY: Guilford Press.

Simpson, M. L., & Nist, S. L. (1993). A case study of academic literacy tasks and their negotiation in a university history course. In C. Kinzer & D. Leu (Eds.), *Literacy research, theory, and practice: Views from many perspectives* (pp. 253–260). Chicago, IL: National Reading Conference.

Simpson, M. L., & Nist, S. L. (1997). Perspectives on learning history: A case study. *Journal of Literacy Research, 29*, 363–395

Simpson, M. L., & Rush, L. (2003). College students' beliefs, strategy employment, transfer, and academic performance: An examination across three academic disciplines. *Journal of College Reading and Learning, 33*, 146–156.

Wilkins, J. (2010). Modeling quantitative literacy. *Educational and Psychological Measurement, 70*(2), 167–190.

Wineburg, S. S. (1991). Historical problem solving: A study of the cognitive processes used in the evaluation of documentary and pictorial evidence. *Journal of Educational Psychology, 83*(1), 73-87.
Wineburg, S. S. (2001). *Historical thinking and other unnatural acts: Charting
the future of teaching the past.* Philadelphia, PA: Temple University Press.

Historically Significant Work

An Historical Exploration of Content Area Reading Instruction

David W. Moore, John E. Readence, and Robert J. Rickelman

*In this selection, David Moore, John Readence, and Robert Rickelman pro-
vide a historical examination of recommendations for content area reading
instruction. Such recommendations proliferated during the first half of the
twentieth century as modern education emerged from the tradition of mental discipline. The writings of humanists, developmentalists, and scientific
determinists were utilized by influential educators to demarcate the field of
content area reading instruction. Five issues that confront educators today
are rooted in these early writings: (1) locus of instruction, (2) reading demands of various subjects, (3) study, (4) reading materials, and (5) age
focus.*

C urriculum histories clarify the origin and development of instructional practices in order to define the conditions which educators
inherit. Such histories deepen understandings of the knowledge base
underlying the teaching profession. Furthermore, history makes evident the gaps in knowledge which a field possesses. Identifying gaps
supplies researchers and curriculum developers a point of departure
into present-day concerns for which the past provides little guidance.
Thus, new knowledge can be constructed. This paper begins an historical investigation of content area reading instruction in the United
States.

The specialty of content area reading instruction came about in
recognition of the fact that readers require various strategies when
they study particular subject areas and read many kinds of materials
for different purposes. Content area reading instruction is designed to
deliver those strategies. To date, the primary mission of this instruction is to develop students' reading-to-learn strategies. This focus seeks
to help students locate, comprehend, remember, and retrieve information that is contained in various styles of writing across the curriculum. Another mission is to help students in reading-to-do situations.
Students who read-to-do perform actions such as completing laboratory experiments, assembling mechanical devices, and following

recipes. Essentially, content area reading instruction attempts to enable students to cope with the special reading materials and tasks encountered during the study of school subjects. Methods textbooks devoted to this specialty area include those by Herber (1978), Readence, Bean, and Baldwin (1981), Robinson (1978), Singer and Donlan (1980), and Vacca (1981), to name a few.

With the above description as a basis, we will define more specifically the parameters of this field by presenting its beginnings. We also will present historical background on five current issues which deal with how best to deliver this instruction. By doing so, we hope to clarify and deepen understandings of the goals of content reading instruction and identify gaps in the knowledge about instruction in this field.

It is important to realize that this presentation is of published discourse. It traces the prominent opinions and research findings that were reported in journal articles, conference proceedings, and textbooks. The foundations of current published writings on content area reading instruction are reported here. As such, this presentation is a history of ideas; it is not a history of school practices. Questions about the "lived" curriculum (Hazlett, 1979) of past schools and classrooms regarding content area reading instruction remain for future investigations.

In order to start the historical research reported here, primary documents were identified using three main reference sources: (a) the Summary of Investigations Relating to Reading from 1925 to the present (see Johns, 1982), (b) *An Index to Professional Literature on Reading and Related Topics* (Betts & Betts, 1945), and (c) the bibliographic information contained in the primary documents themselves. Some sources that were invaluable for guiding this inquiry were the following early, major publications that, at least in part, dealt specifically with content area reading instruction:

1. three yearbooks of the National Society for the Study of Education (Henry, 1948; Whipple, 1925, 1937);

2. two conference yearbooks from the University of Chicago (Gray, 1947, 1952);

3. the first reading education textbook to include separate chapters on reading tasks and instructional procedures for particular content areas (McCallister, 1936);

4. two textbooks devoted to elementary school reading that frequently are cited as major contributions to content area reading instruction (McKee, 1934, 1948); and

5. one of the first textbooks devoted entirely to reading instruction beyond the elementary and intermediate grades (Bond & Bond, 1941).

Hypotheses about the beginnings of content area reading instruction, which we discuss in the first section of this paper, were derived from the above publications and then investigated further to determine their consistency. In historical research, consistency is one of the best available criteria for substantiating hypotheses (Cook, Note 1). Thus, our hypotheses about the beginning of content area reading instruction were verified by virtue of their being discussed regularly and in the same way throughout the professional and research literature that was directed to this topic. The five issues about how to deliver instruction, which we present in the second section, were selected by professional judgment, although background on them was verified again on the basis of consistency.

The Beginnings of Content Area Reading Instruction

In order to understand content area reading instruction, one needs to understand the larger context in which it emerged. The predominant tradition in American schools prior to the 1900s consisted of mental discipline. This tradition emphasized imitation and rote learning. Following these emphases, early U.S. reading instruction consisted mainly of elocution and memorization. Students at all grade levels were drilled so that they could declaim a text with correct articulation, inflection, accent, emphasis, and gesture. And in order to demonstrate that they had "learned" the information, students went through class periods of reciting verbatim portions of the text. For instance, typical questions of the time began with "What is said of . . . ?" Oral reading and rote learning became the accepted goals of such instruction.

At the turn of the century, mental discipline declined as the primary mission of American schools. New goals came to the forefront as the result of different interest groups and educational philosophies. Modern American education in general, and content area reading instruction specifically, emerged largely as the result of three forces, humanists, developmentalists, and scientific determinists. At the same time, certain educators tailored the general curricular thrusts to fit their particular field, reading. As a result, those educators carved out content area reading instruction as a distinct specialty.

Humanists

Among other things, humanist educators championed the cause that the central functions of the schools were to develop students' abilities to learn information meaningfully and think independently. Humanist thought set the stage for current beliefs about reading-to-learn.

Humanist concerns can be traced to the Greeks in earliest times, and those concerns were shaped by a plethora of educators such as Erasmus, Comenius, and Pestalozzi. In the middle 1800s in America, Horace

Mann championed the humanist cause of reading for meaning: "to suffer children to read without understanding is one of the most flagrant cases of incompetent teaching" (Mann, 1845, reprinted in Caldwell & Courtis, 1925). However, Mann's influence was realized more in the area of public support for schools. It was the Progressive Movement, which derived its theoretical base in part from humanist thought, that contributed substantially to an emphasis on meaningful reading. John Dewey was a compelling force as he nudged American education toward this goal.

Dewey placed children at the center of the curriculum. He criticized past educational practices which promoted rote learning, and he stressed plans that connected school activities with children's experiences, interests, and problem-solving abilities. This humanist concern for meaningful processing is typified by William James' (1923) anecdote wherein a friend was dismayed to find students who knew that "The interior of the globe is in a condition of igneous fusion" (p. 150) but who did not know whether the bottom of an extremely deep hole would be warmer or colder than the top.

The additional humanist concern of helping students think and make inferences on their own surfaced intermittently throughout the history of education with appeals to reasoning. This concern reached a high point during the 18th century French Enlightenment. John Dewey emphasized the need for helping students learn to reason independently in his classic text, *How We Think* (1910). In this text, Dewey presented his theory of how reflective thought operated, and he suggested instructional practices to promote it.

The humanist, Progressive emphases on meaningful, assimilative learning and independent thinking carried clear implications for reading instruction. For instance, Colonel Francis Parker (1894), a dominant figure in American education and Progressivism at the turn of the century, connected reading directly to meaningful learning: "Reading shall be used from the beginning to the end in the enhancement of intrinsic thought" (p. 219). In an explanation of reading comprehension, Parker stated,

> A reader does not think the thought of an author, he simply thinks his own thought. By the action of words upon the mind, ideas arise above the plan of consciousness; individual concepts and judgments that have formerly been in consciousness reappear, and are recombined and associated . . . the mental results of written or printed words upon the mind are predetermined by the mind itself. (p. 189)

This definition exemplifies the active role which Progressives attributed to readers during the reading act. It was a role which denied passive, verbatim attention to text information.

Progressive educators strongly advocated the humanist belief that students should be able to independently transform ideas contained in text rather than to only reproduce their surface forms. This belief is accepted today by writers concerned with reading-to-learn in the content areas, although different beliefs exist about the best reading materials and teaching methods.

Developmentalists

Developmentalism became an influential force in education at the turn of the century. Psychologists such as G. Stanley Hall and Arnold Gesell were in the forefront of this field as they studied patterns of growth among children. Child study added to the emergence of content area reading instruction mostly by pointing out that children at various degrees of development demonstrated various strategies for coping with their worlds. Thus, developmentalists helped sensitize educators to the need for reading instruction that was tailored to individuals' requirements at all grade levels with a variety of texts and tasks (Gray, 1939).

By making clear the fact that children progressed through different stages, developmental studies caused reading educators to consider how best to promote growth at stages beyond the primary grades. Reading educators tackled the question of how to deliver reading instruction that helped students attain high-level abilities with complex materials and assignments. To be sure, graded reading series were available in the U.S. before the 1900s, but educational emphases varied little from one grade level to another. Developmental thought brought about shifts in what educators expected students to be able to accomplish. For instance, calls to extend developmental reading programs to high schools (Bond & Bond, 1941; Strang, 1938) were based on beliefs that young people required guidance as they refined and extended their reading abilities.

Along with sensitizing educators to children's age-stage progressions, the developmental influence focused instructional attention on children as individuals in their own right rather than as units of society to be treated in preconceived ways. Child study reports pointed out that children differed substantially among each other; consequently, educators began calling for differentiated instruction and readiness activities. This call helped stimulate content area reading instruction by focusing attention to what each student needed in order to cope effectively with his or her subject matter reading assignments. Developmentalists' attention to individuals clarified the pitfalls of teachers simply assuming that all students could handle all tasks and materials that were assigned at particular grade levels.

Scientific Determinists

The use of scientific principles in education also attuned educators to the need for content area reading instruction. Scientific determinists believed that decisions about school affairs could best be made through empirical methods. Educators caught up with this movement divided between two groups, social efficiency educators who ran the schools and reading researchers. These two groups helped focus educators' attention on reading comprehension.

SOCIAL EFFICIENCY. Social efficiency educators sought to identify and implement the most productive approaches to education (Callahan, 1962). And in order to identify which approaches worked best, educators needed trustworthy, scientific methods of comparison. Following the lead of Rice, Binet, Cattell, and Thorndike, test developers produced standardized tests that provided the needed, comparable measures of students' academic abilities. Reading comprehension was one of the abilities that was measured in order to assess the outcomes of the schools.

The new, standardized reading comprehension tests required students to demonstrate their understanding of never-before-seen passages by completing never-before-seen tasks. This test format differed from earlier ones in the United States wherein town officials conducted reading recitations in place of the teacher or else students wrote out definitions of terms. Standardized reading comprehension test formats required students to comprehend passages without the benefit of prior, direct instruction about their contents. This technological advance, which focused on comprehension, fit well with humanist emphases on training reasoning abilities. As a result, American students for the first time were expected to independently derive meaning from what they read (Resnick & Resnick, 1977). Educators soon came to realize that students required help doing that.

READING RESEARCH. Mental measurements designed to promote efficiency in schools' curriculums also were used to investigate reading processes, and research in reading processes directed educators to comprehension. Between 1890 and 1910 basic research in reading surged (Venezky, 1977). The best thinking at that time about the basis of the reading act was originated as well as summarized by Huey (1908). Huey devoted an entire chapter to the nature of reading for meaning in his frequently cited text, *The Psychology and Pedagogy of Reading*. He claimed that thinking was vital to reading, and he outlined the reading process with a meaning emphasis. Following the impetus of basic research, applied reading studies continued to address passage comprehension, but most basic research efforts turned to a reductionistic paradigm that focused on words in isolation. The emergence of cognitive psychology in the 1970s rekindled basic research interest in comprehension.

Specific early studies that gave rise to content area, reading-to-learn instruction included those that reported the superiority of silent reading over oral reading (Mead, 1915, 1917; Pinter, 1913) and E. L. Thorndike's famous "Reading as Reasoning: A Study of Mistakes in Paragraph

Reading" (1917). Indeed, the continuing impact of Thorndike's early study is revealed by the Social Science Citation Index which shows that it was cited 44 times in the professional literature between 1969 and 1981. "Reading," stated Thorndike, "is a very elaborate procedure, involving the weighing of many elements in a sentence, their organization in the proper relations one to another, the selection of certain of their connotations and the rejection of others, and the cooperation of many forces to determine final response" (p. 323). Thorndike used quantitative means to outline the reasoning processes in reading which Progressive educators wanted to develop. He maintained that readers needed to predetermine purposes for reading and construct a "mind-set" for subsequent reading. To help students accomplish this process, he called for educators to replace oral reading with exercises in silent reading and to have students answer questions, ask questions about what they read, and summarize material. Interestingly, he concluded that "Perhaps it is in their outside reading of stories and in their study of geography, history, and the like, that many school children really learn to read" (p. 282).

Additional studies that focused attention on content area reading instruction included investigations of the correlation between reading achievement and overall achievement in school subjects. Researchers investigating this topic compared reading achievement with subject matter achievement as measured either by course grades or standardized tests. An early study of this type was by Smith (1919), who compared students' scores on four reading tests with their school grades in English and algebra. Discrepant but high correlations among the measures were obtained. As a result, Smith concluded that reading ability was related to school achievement.

Eva Bond Wagner's 1938 thesis at Teachers College, Columbia University was a wide-ranging study of students' reading abilities and scholastic success that was cited frequently in later writings. Wagner administered a test battery that measured seven reading skills and nine areas of subject matter achievement, and she found various positive relationships. Her principal conclusion was that ability in composite reading comprehension was related strongly to composite ninth-grade achievement. Many other correlational studies supported the conclusions reached by Smith and Wagner and contributed to educators' beliefs that content area reading instruction was required for students' success in the content areas.

Reading Educators

Several influential educators contributed to the origin of content area reading instruction through their essays, research, and influence on students. The three key figures who helped set apart reading instruction as a distinct professional area, Arthur I. Gates at Columbia University,

William S. Gray at the University of Chicago, and Ernest Horn at the University of Iowa, also contributed to the emergence of content area reading instruction as an identifiable component. The dominant curricular forces of the time influenced these men as they demarcated this field. Of the three, William S. Gray was the predominant individual in this area.

Gray published several essays and edited two monographs on content area reading instruction, he conducted a seminal study on developing meaning vocabulary in American history, and he repeatedly included separate attention to content reading studies in his annual summaries of reading investigations. Indeed, in Gray's (1927) second annual summary of reading research, he reported that "Reading as it relates to the various school subjects and activities is now challenging some of the attention that it has long deserved" (p. 464).

In an early paper presented to the National Education Association, Gray (1919) called for educators to focus attention on specific reading skills that were necessary for successful study. In addition, Gray was chairman of the National Committee on Reading, a group within the National Society for the Study of Education, which emphasized reading across the disciplines in its classic report in the 24th NSSE Yearbook (Whipple, 1925). This report distinguished "recreational" reading from "work-type" reading, and Chapter Five, "The Relation of Reading to Content Subjects and Other School Activities," provided guidelines and sample lessons to develop students' work-type reading abilities. Work-type reading, which was to be addressed in the content areas, included skills such as "finding answers to questions, following directions, selecting big points, remembering, and relating what is read to experience" (p. 104). Suggested lessons to help students acquire these skills called for activities such as self-questioning, identifying key words, and making notes. The recommendations of Gray's committee were consistent with the major curricular forces' recommendations of the time. For example, the committee emphasized reading for meaning and attention to individual differences.

Gray also played a key role in popularizing the content area reading instruction slogan, "Every teacher a teacher of reading." Gray again chaired the National Committee on Reading when it issued its second report in the 36th NSSE Yearbook (Whipple, 1937). This report formally proclaimed that all teachers should include reading instruction as part of their curriculum, and it detailed how this instruction should be provided. The two NSSE reports dealing with work-type reading helped specify methods whereby educators could go beyond concerns with decoding and understanding narrative passages. These two yearbooks quite likely were the most influential books about content area reading instruction published during the first half of this century.

Ernest Horn also played a dominant role in establishing and developing content area reading instruction. Horn set in motion some of the first studies that addressed ways to enhance learning from text (Germane, 1921; Yoakam, 1922), and he published one of the first descriptions of work-type reading tasks (Horn, 1923). Horn published relatively few articles on this topic, although his text, *Methods of Instruction in the Social Studies* (1937), contains a first-rate discussion of it. He especially emphasized wide reading in the subject areas in order to enhance meaningful learning and accomodate individual differences. Two of his students, Paul G. McKee and Gerald A. Yoakam, contributed substantially to his field and bear witness to Horn's influence.

Paul McKee's contribution to this field mostly consisted of his professional textbooks. McKee's texts, *Reading and Literature in the Elementary School* (1934) and its revised version *The Teaching of Reading in the Elementary School* (1948), generally were considered to be the most practical presentations of reading in the content areas when they first were published (Durrell, Note 2). McKee presented a compelling rationale for the necessity of developing students' reading-to-learn abilities, and he provided general suggestions and specific exercises for such development at various grade levels. Four chapters centered about teaching the abilities to (a) locate information, (b) select and evaluate material, (c) organize material, and (d) remember material.

Gerald A. Yoakam also studied under Horn, and in 1992 he reported an empirical investigation of the retention of various materials. Two conclusions from his research were especially noteworthy: (a) although the effects of a single reading varied individually, the average subject retained fewer than half the total ideas, and (b) a single reading coupled with review was a more powerful means of learning than a single reading alone. Earlier research into readers' recall of text had been reported by Binet (see Thieman & Brewer, 1978), but Yoakam's research was more available and frequently cited by educators who dealt with reading and learning content materials. Yoakam published one of the first textbooks on the relations among reading, learning, and subject matter instruction (Yoakam, 1928), and he continued producing work in this area during four decades (Yoakam, 1936, 1945, 1955).

The third key figure in reading instruction, Arthur I. Gates, contributed to content area reading instruction mostly through his landmark study on retention (Gates, 1917). Although Gates focused his professional career mainly on measuring and diagnosing reading achievement, he and his Columbia University colleagues such as Percival Symonds and Allan Abbott either helped stimulate or directed numerous learning from text dissertations. These dissertations included investigations of study techniques (Barton, 1930; Newlun, 1930), comprehension difficulties presented by specific subjects (Ayer, 1926; Irion, 1925), the value of wide reading for subject matter learning (Coryell, 1927; Curtis, 1924), and the relation between reading and scholastic achievement (Bond, 1940; Wagner, 1938). The early textbooks and journal articles on content area reading instruction frequently cited these research reports.

Summary

In the early 1900s, educators devoted unprecedented attention to the help that students required while learning and acting on subject matter reading materials. Humanist emphases on reasoning processes and meaningful learning, developmentalist attention to individual growth, scientific assessments conducted to promote efficient schooling and gain insight into reading, and university-level reading educators' influences resulted in the specialty of content area reading instruction. Although research attention to this field blossomed in the first half of this century, it waned in the middle years because of the shift in basic studies to a reductionistic, behavioristic viewpoint. Reading education textbooks, articles, and applied research continued to deal with learning from text, but few innovative theories or practices emerged. Most writings reflected the information contained in the 24th NSSE Yearbook. Content area reading instruction re-emerged in the 1970s with the cognitive revolution in psychology and with the publication of Herber's (1970) text, *Teaching Reading in Content Areas.*

Recurring Issues about Content Area Reading Instruction

Several issues in the professional literature to date confront educators concerned with delivering content area reading instruction. This section presents an historical perspective on five such matters. We seek to clarify these issues and identify points that require additional inquiry.

Issue 1: Locus of Instruction

A compelling issue in content area reading instruction regards the locus of instruction. This problem centers about the appropriate teacher, location, and materials for instruction. To illustrate, strategies for organizing information can be taught in content classrooms by content area teachers or in reading classroom by reading teachers. The teaching materials can consist of subject matter textbooks or reading instruction texts. In essence, there are two choices: direct, skills-centered instruction, or functional, content-centered instruction (Herber, 1970).

DIRECT, SKILLS-CENTERED INSTRUCTION. Skills-centered instruction occurs when teachers identify a set of skills and present them to students regardless of the tasks currently being faced during subject matter lessons. For example, teachers may present a lesson on interpreting line graphs even though such graphs are not included in students' current subject matter assignments. The point is that reading skills are taught separately from the content being studied.

Separate instruction in content area reading skills during reading lessons with provisions for later opportunities for transfer to content areas was recommended by Gray (1919), Gates (1935), and McKee (1934). For instance, McKee proposed three types of teaching activities: "(1) the initial or introductory teaching of an ability to be taught; (2) the use of drill exercises as a means of establishing the ability through practice; and (3) the prevision of opportunities in other school work by which the pupil may utilize the ability taught" (p. 85).

The main argument for such an approach was based on concerns about systematic reading instruction. The influential educators listed above pioneered scope and sequence skill charts so that students were sure to receive instruction in all the skills deemed important. Those educators favored intentional, rather than incidental, skills instruction. As a result, learning skills was placed over learning subject matter. Text content was seen mainly as a vehicle that allowed direct and systematic presentation of skills.

Another argument for direct skills instruction, which secondary-school educators emphasized, was that content area teachers would not assume reading instruction responsibilities. Subject matter specialists tended to emphasize their content rather than students' processes for acquiring that content, so implementing reading programs across the disciplines was seen to be futile. Pragmatic considerations led to this argument.

FUNCTIONAL, CONTENT-CENTERED INSTRUCTION. Functional instruction occurs when teachers identify skills which are prerequisite for completing certain tasks and then present those skills along with the subject matter learnings. Functional, content-centered reading instruction was espoused by Progressive educators in the early 1900s. For example, Parker (1894) stated that "in the school all the reading should be a direct means of intensifying, enhancing, expanding and relating the thought evolved by the study of the subjects" (p. 19). Parker further added that "The reading in botany, in zoology, in history,—in fact, all reading—should be concentrated upon the study of the central subjects" (p. 220). Progressives did not favor setting aside time for isolated skills instruction; instead, reading was to be "organically bound up" with all the other work of the school (Thorne-Thomsen, 1901, p. 227). Other educators not closely affiliated with the Progressive Movement also recommended combining reading and subject matter instruction (Horn, 1937; McCallister, 1936; Monroe & Mohlman, 1924; Yoakam, 1928). And research support for this practice was provided by studies conducted in the 1930s and 1940s (Blank, 1932; Jacobson, 1932; Leggitt, 1934; Rudolf, 1949; Simon, 1934).

The Progressive tradition does not separate reading instruction from subject matter instruction (Zirbes, 1928). However, educators in this tradition do distinguish between no attention to language forms and some attention to forms. The first group claims that students automatically develop reading and study abilities while investigating subject matter topics. The statement by J. L. Meriam (cited in Harris, 1964), "Let children read to learn, incidentally they will learn to read," summarizes this position. Students are thought to gain content acquisition skills naturally as they solve content-related problems.

In contrast to no attention to language forms, other educators in the Progressive tradition claim that students always should be directed toward content but that lessons which emphasize specific aspects of written language occasionally should be conducted (Goodman & Goodman, 1981). For instance, if a social studies passage contains a mixture of fact and opinion, then teachers might present a reading strategy lesson that helps students induce the differences between facts and opinions in order to help those students cope with that form of language. Content still is paramount, but students' attention occasionally is directed toward how that content is presented.

The two main arguments for helping students improve their reading abilities while they study content materials centered about motivation and transfer. Progressive educators followed developmentalist insights and placed a high premium on children's interests and activities as a prerequisite to learning. Consequently, reading improvement was thought to occur best when students became motivated enough to satisfy "felt needs" brought about by the purposeful study of compelling topics.

Concern for transfer of training was another reason for welding content to skills instruction. Educators worried that reading-to-learn and reading-to-do skills acquired during official reading periods would not carry over to content area situations. That is, students might become adept at outlining materials provided during reading periods yet remain unable to outline their social studies materials.

Determining whether students were better served by reading instruction in separate reading periods or during the presentation of subject matter was addressed by Harold L. Herber in *Teaching Reading in the Content Areas* (1970). This text was the first one devoted exclusively to content area reading instruction, even though that specialty had been explored for at least 45 years. As the title of his text indicated, Herber unequivocally called for functional instruction, with content teachers addressing reading abilities while presenting subject matter. His contention received some empirical support from a series of investigations which he stimulated at Syracuse University (Herber & Barron, 1973; Herber & Riley, 1979; Herber & Sanders, 1969; Herber & Vacca, 1977). However, research efforts conducted to date on content-free, metacognitive skill training have produced results which favor skills-centered instruction (Brown, Bransford, Ferrara, & Campione, in press). The following statement by the National Committee on Reading aptly summarized this complex locus of instruction issue in content reading instruction:

> The difficulty which constantly confronts the teacher is to keep the reading skills sufficiently in the foreground that they may be improved and refined, yet at the same time make them subservient to the real interests and larger purposes for which pupils read. (Whipple, 1925, p. 140)

Issue 2: Reading Demands of Various Subjects

Textbooks that deal with content area reading instruction such as those by Burmeister (1977), Hafner (1977), Robinson (1978), and Singer and Donlan (1980) devote individual chapters to reading in individual subjects such as English, mathematics, and social studies. On the other hand, texts such as those by Estes and Vaughan (1978), Herber (1978), and Readence, Bean, and Baldwin (1981) deal with content area reading in a more general manner, as no special chapters address each discipline. The issue, then, is whether content area reading instruction should concentrate on content-dependent skills or on generic skills.

The various reading demands which the disciplines placed on readers were investigated empirically a number of ways during the first half of the 1900s. The numerous studies of this problem and their frequent citation reveal the impact scientific determinism had on this field. The studies fall into four categories: eye movement analyses, vocabulary frequency counts, reading achievement test correlations, and observational research.

EYE MOVEMENT ANALYSES. Judd and Buswell (1922) observed that readers' eye movements varied with the type of material that was encountered. In one part of the study, readers were presented seven types of content that ranged from *Annabel Lee* to a section of *Paradise Lost* to prose extracts taken from fiction, geography, rhetoric, French grammar, and algebra. Inspection of each reader's eye movement patterns with the various materials led Judd and Buswell to conclude that "Different types of material induce different types of reading attitudes" (p. 22). These attitudes were characterized by average numbers of eye fixations per line, durations of fixations, and numbers of regressions that differed appreciably according to the material being read. Judd and Buswell's frequently cited basic research report admonished educators to provide reading instruction across the curriculum:

> There ought, for example, to be a technique of teaching high school students to read algebra fluently and intelligently. There ought to be

teaching of methods of reading science. These higher applications of reading ability are not to be ignored or thought of as automatically provided for by training given through the reading of fiction or poetry. (p. 26)

VOCABULARY FREQUENCY COUNTS. The vocabulary load of the content areas received a great deal of attention in the 1920s and 1930s, and the identification of technical vocabularies within the separate disciplines contributed substantially to calls for special instruction. Vocabulary studies were stimulated by E. L. Thorndike's *Teacher's Word Book* (1921) and by the prevailing demands for objective, scientific measurements of school materials as well as school children. Word frequency lists were common as researchers assessed vocabularies from sources such as adults' personal letters, children's spontaneously written compositions, children's literature, children's speech, and lists of words which children could produce in 15 minutes (Dolch, 1928). Against this backdrop, Louella Cole Pressey (1923) produced *The Special Vocabularies of the Public School Subjects*. Pressey and her associates identified 15 groups of school subjects and collected more than 200 school books in this project. These investigators then subjectively judged which words in the textbooks comprised the technical vocabulary of the subjects, and they estimated the relative importance of each term. Pressey's report is flawed, but it points out the focus on technical vocabulary at that time. Indeed, other extensive word counts were conducted in fields such as arithmetic (Buswell & John, 1931), history (Barr & Gifford, 1929), and science (Curtis, 1938). These studies provided evidence that each discipline presented at least one characteristic reading demand, its technical vocabulary, which deserved special attention.

READING ACHIEVEMENT TEST CORRELATIONS. Research into the relationships among students' comprehension test scores over various types of materials also contributed to concerns about the different reading demands of the subjects. Researchers following this line obtained test scores on general tests of reading comprehension and compared them with scores on reading tests drawn from specific disciplines. In an ambitious, early study, Ritter and Lofland (1924) measured student's answers to questions following short passages and related them to students' solutions of tasks resembling riddles. Because the correlations varied considerably among grade levels and because many individuals obtained widely discrepant scores between the two types of tasks, Ritter and Lofland concluded that different types of reading abilities existed. In their interpretation of results they stated, "Reading can never be learned except in connection with some content, but the technique of interpreting one type of content is probably very different from that required in another" (p. 546).

Later researchers such as Artley (1943), Aukerman, (1948), Bond (1940), Shores (1943), Swenson (1942), and Wagner (1938) also compared students' comprehension of a variety of materials to comprehension of specific subject matter materials. Although these reports indicated various degrees of similarity between "general" and "specific" comprehension, all concluded that the subjects presented distinct reading demands.

OBSERVATIONAL RESEARCH. James M. McCallister (1930, 1932) reported an observational study that was fundamentally different than the studies of eye movements, vocabulary frequencies, and reading test correlations. Rather than assessing only content reading differences due to materials, McCallister assessed differences due to classroom teachers' daily assignments. He used research procedures such as classroom observations, subjective analyses of students' written reports, and interviews in order to identify reading activities required in the subjects and the reading difficulties students experienced during the various activities. His main conclusions were that differences existed among the types of reading activities assigned in various content areas and that students required help coping with those differences. McCallister's conclusions were highlighted in his 1936 textbook, *Remedial and Corrective Instruction in Reading,* wherein he claimed that "It is generally recognized that reading activities essential to effective study differ notably in various subjects" (p. 200). In his text, McCallister included five chapters on guiding students' reading. Two chapters presented general principles for guiding reading, and three chapters covered reading in history, mathematics, and science. As far as can be determined, this was the first reading education textbook to devote separate chapters to reading in separate content areas.

In summary, researchers during the first half of this century investigated whether the content areas presented reading demands that were content-specific or generic. Practically all the studies concluded that different reading demands existed due either to different texts or different tasks. The assertion that content area texts differed fundamentally was supported more recently by Smith (1964), who reported that the disciplines contained distinctive rhetorical patterns, and by Bruner (1960), who contended that the structures of the disciplines varied according to their perspectives on the world and their methods of constructing knowledge. Additionally, more recent writers have argued that content area reading methods texts actually provide only superficial overviews of the reading processes that are appropriate for specific content areas (Hoetker, 1982; Peters, 1982). For instance, there is a substantial quantity of knowledge currently available on responding to English literature that is virtually ignored in content area reading methods texts. And reading educators often refer to the social studies without specifying which conceptualization of social studies education they mean (e.g., social inquiry, moral education, clarifying public issues).

Despite the legacy that views reading skills as content-dependent, many content area reading methods texts present skills in generic terms. This practice seems to be based on three considerations. One, the generic treatment is based on the idea that a common set of strategies underlies all content area reading texts and tasks but that the strategies are adjusted to handle specific demands. For example, students need to monitor their understanding, but the monitoring of a math word problem may differ from that required for a piece of fiction. Thus, the underlying strategy remains constant, but its application is adjusted. Generic skills advocates do not point out each and every specific adjustment. What remains to be determined is whether the nature of those adjustments differ by amount or by fundamental quality.

A second reason for presenting generic skills is that each traditional content area encompasses diverse specialties. After all, social studies encompasses specialties such as geography, economics, and sociology, and those areas can be divided into even finer sets. At what point does a collection of knowledge constitute a content area? Moreover, specialty areas each contain various styles of writing and purposes for reading within their fields. The study of geography entails reading expository, narrative, and technical styles of writing for broad overviews as well as for specific, detailed information. Consequently, the reading demands within each content area are seen to differ more drastically than those between each area.

Finally, presenting specific chapters on "Reading in Home Economics," "Reading in Science," and "Reading in English" is thought to reflect only persuasive writing techniques rather than substantive differences between the fields. Some authors maintain that content specialists attend only to suggestions that deal with their particular specialties. Because of this, reading methodology is presented only with examples from particular fields as a persuasive tactic. Those who present generic skills apparently do not consider that tactic worthwhile.

The well known tetrahedral model for designing and interpreting research provided by Jenkins (1979) may help reduce the confusion regarding the various reading demands among the content areas. Jenkins' model calls for researchers to specify the nature of their texts, tasks, learners' characteristics, and learners' strategies while reporting outcomes. If this model is adhered to, educators may obtain a more lucid view of what students require in order to learn or act on specific information. The issue about content-dependent versus generic skills mostly was popularized by research; at present, refining research through Jenkins' model offers much promise.

Issue 3: Study

Helping students study is a long-standing concern. Philosophers since antiquity have suggested proper ways to help students acquire information, and early American writers such as Watts (1793) and Todd (1850) recommended appropriate practices. Interest in this area among professional educators was intense in the early 1900s.

At the turn of the century, little attention was devoted to improving students' study of specific reading passages; instead, attention was devoted to studying general course content. Woodring and Flemming's 1935 text, *Directing Study of High School Pupils*, illustrates this diffuse attention. This book is a compilation of the 14 articles which the two authors published between 1928 and 1935 in Columbia University's *Teachers College Record*. The articles consisted of annotated bibliographies and elaborated treatments of the process and pedagogy of study. With one exception (Flemming & Woodring, 1929), the articles treated study as a general concern with little mention of special reading abilities. Moreover, many early investigations of study (Butterweck, 1926; Monroe, 1924; Strang, 1928) compared the performance of control groups with the performance of experimental groups who received instruction on general procedures such as planning a daily schedule, reviewing for exams, and concentrating upon assignments. And supervised study (Brownell, 1925; Hall-Quest, 1916), which received a great amount of attention, included diverse general features, also. Administrative techniques were suggested such as providing and maintaining order in study halls and lengthening class periods, and instructional techniques were offered such as giving students how-to-study rules.

William S. Gray laid the foundation for distinct attention to reading abilities in relation to study as he fashioned the field of content area reading instruction. In an early address, Gray (1919) stated that it is "a matter of the first importance that pupils be trained to study effectively as they read" (p. 580). This statement was based on research wherein Gray had teachers at the University of Chicago High School list pupils' uses of reading while preparing class assignments. On the basis of this rather crude investigation, 29 uses of reading during study periods were listed. "To determine the main outline of a story or article" and "To follow directions with accuracy and reasonable speed" represent the uses which Gray described. This 1919 report helped distinguish reading activities from global classroom activities.

When educators and researchers in the first half of this century focused on study specifically in relation to reading, they followed two points of departure which were inherited from the earlier attention to general, supervised study. That is, reading-study instruction was separated between directing students to knowledge and training students to acquire knowledge on their own. As a result, the legacy to educators on how to help students learn from text is problematic: some teaching procedures focus on arranging conditions so that students acquire desired information, while other procedures emphasize helping students learn independently.

DIRECTING STUDENTS. Directing students' study differed from the traditional recitation method which called for teachers simply to "hear" what students had memorized. Directed study focused students' attention to specific learnings. Teachers planned activities to regulate what students learned through methods such as holding individual conferences, providing printed directions about how to acquire certain information, and guiding learning through questions. These procedures consisted mostly of arranging classroom situations so that efficient learning could occur.

The early research on methods of studying text indicates the attention paid to efficiently directing students to information. Although the methodology of the first research contains many flaws, that research was cited frequently in articles and textbooks which dealt with learning information from content area materials. The early research on studying text centered around two general areas, questioning (Distad, 1927; Golden, 1942; Gray, 1929; Holmes, 1931; Washburne, 1929) and organizing information through notetaking, underlining, outlining, and summarizing (Arnold, 1942; Crawford, 1929; Dynes, 1932; Germane & Germane, 1922; Greene, 1934; Mathews, 1938; Newlun, 1930). Mixed results emerged from these studies, so educators were left with unclear directions to follow. But the point about these studies which is important for this discussion is that they investigated how best to lead students to information. The questioning research compared the short-term effects on learning of different amounts and placements of questions; similarly, the research on organizing material compared the short-term effects of different ways of transforming information. In a manner similar to most of the general study literature, these early, scientific studies focused on efficiently delivering facts and generalizations. As Tierney and Cunningham (1980) recently pointed out, practically no studies investigated how to train students to comprehend and remember on their own.

TRAINING STUDENTS. Helping students become independent learners is a traditional concern of the humanist force in education. In a frequently cited text, *How to Study, and Teaching How to Study*, McMurry (1909) claimed that eight factors comprised the essential studying components: (a) setting specific purposes, (b) supplementing information, (c) organizing ideas, (d) judging the worth of statements, (e) memorizing, (f) using ideas, (g) maintaining a tentative attitude, and (h) relying on self-directed learning. These components indicate the book's strong emphasis on developing independence. Indeed, McMurry affiliated himself with the Progressive educators of his time who advocated teaching students to solve problems and learn how to learn through their own efforts. Other educators who clearly addressed the need to produce independent learners include Kilzer (1931) and Pitkin, Newton, and Langham (1935).

The role which independent reading abilities eventually assumed in educators' perceptions of study is demonstrated in Laycock and Russell's (1941) analysis of how-to-study manuals. Laycock and Russell analyzed 38 manuals published between 1926 and 1939. They found that the manuals discussed 3,743 topics dealing with study, and they formed 24 general categories, from these topics. After analyzing their categories, Laycock and Russell reported that "a large number refer to various forms of habits and skills in reading" (p. 371). These reading habits and skills included strategies such as using one's own questions, shifting rates according to purposes for reading, knowing parts of a book, and interpreting pictorial aids. Those who intended to help students become independent learners had available a number of specific "reading-study" suggestions by 1941.

The well known Survey-Question-Read-Recite-Review (SQ3R) technique, originated by F. P. Robinson (1946), is devoted solely to learning from text, and it is an independent strategy. Robinson intended his strategy to help students focus on the quality of their study rather than just the amount. He based his recommendations upon the research guidelines available at his time, but he adjusted their focus by placing learners in charge of manipulating their own mental operations. Robinson recommended previewing, to get a general idea of the material, and questioning, to set purposes. His final two steps were meant to control the amount of forgetting that typically occurred after a single unaided reading. He claimed that SQ3R would be self-motivating and help students improve their independent processing of text. This strategy influenced content area reading instruction recommendations as numerous variants (e.g., PQ4R, EVOKER, PANORAMA) have been offered throughout the years.

As noted earlier, the beginning research on studying text mainly compared the efficiency of certain study interventions. During this historical exploration, only two investigations from the first half of this century (Salisbury, 1934; Simpson, 1929) were located that attempted to train students to learn from text independently. Current educators and researchers who are involved with developing students' independent learning-from-text strategies have little prior research information to direct their efforts. Recognition of the problem of developing independent learning abilities is not new, but research-based solutions will be. For instance, the distinctions among blind, informed, and self-control study training (Brown, Bransford, Ferrara, & Campione, in press) are fresh perspectives on old problems. Of course, refining the techniques that efficiently direct students to specific information always will remain a researchable topic. Moreover, a perplexing task currently before content area reading educators, which is part of the locus of instruction issue, is to determine the exclusivity of directing and training activities. That is, how does directing students to information affect their independent comprehending and remembering abilities?

Issue 4: Reading Materials

Classroom teachers regularly confront the task of providing their students appropriate reading materials. Two main stumbling blocks involve balancing the type and amount of students' reading selections.

The type divides roughly between informational and literary passages, and the amount typically is discussed in terms of a single text versus multiple materials.

Content area reading educators consistently complain about the literary type of passages which students encounter during basal reading instruction. But this emphasis is a somewhat recent phenomenon in the U.S. The first elementary school reading texts in this country primarily included informational selections (Robinson, 1930; Smith, 1965). These selections emphasized religion and consisted of materials such as the Lord's Prayer, the Ten Commandments, the Psalms, and other pieces of scripture. Strictly religious content eventually gave way to content that emphasized morals and nationalistic virtues. Industry, good manners, and patriotism were exalted. In general, readers of the early 1800s contained didactic lessons on how to conduct one's life.

By the middle 1800s, most basal reader passages provided information about the world rather than about morals. These passages included topics such as nature and American history. At the end of the century, materials for reading instruction emphasized English literature, and students were expected to appreciate and gain an interest in fine writing. For example, the popular McGuffey Readers were billed as containing "Selections in Prose and Poetry from the Best American and English Writers." Finally, school readers since the early 1900s fluctuated in their balance between informational and literary passages, although the latter type predominated. Young students mostly worked with narratives during formal reading instruction, even though those students encountered objective, detached explanations of the world in their content area materials.

Along with the type of reading materials, the amount that was presented to young students posed a problem. Early reading and subject matter instruction typically utilized single textbooks because few supplementary reading materials were published. Furthermore, teachers in the 18th and 19th centuries were poorly educated and received little training in pedagogy, so those teachers relied heavily on textbooks as the sole basis of the curriculum. Thus, educators at the beginning of the 20th century faced the issue of getting appropriate materials into the hands of young readers. The most common recommendation to this end was to provide students trade books, periodicals, and other supplemental materials during reading and subject matter instruction.

Humanist, developmentalist, and scientific influences are evident in calls for wide reading of supplementary materials. Such an approach included problem-solving activities as students sampled information from various sources and determined what was relevant. Students read materials that were personally rewarding and appropriately difficult. The difficulty of the materials was controlled through vocabulary frequency counts and readability formulas. Comprehension was the goal. Indeed, the idea to include extra reading materials during reading and subject matter instruction constituted a fundamental change in American education.

Educators recommended several ways to use supplementary reading materials. The Progressive's implementation of purposeful reading through the project method was one of the first to emphasize wide reading and was an influential suggestion. Projects involved students in formulating questions, obtaining information from various sources to answer the questions, and then reporting what was learned (Kilpatrick, 1919). Many variations on project methods soon developed and became subsumed under unit planning. Indeed, the 19th NSSE Yearbook (Whipple, 1920) presented numerous unit approaches that were developed within a few years of the project method's introduction. Wide reading is a common feature of those approaches.

Research into the value of wide, project-type reading indicates the attention educators paid to this concern. For example, C.V. Good (1927), in *The Supplementary Reading Assignment*, reported investigations, conclusions, and suggested practices regarding intensive reading of a single textbook and extensive, wide reading. In general, Good recommended extensive reading to obtain a range of information and intensive reading to obtain text information most accurately.

Implementation perhaps is the main issue regarding the use of supplementary materials during reading and subject matter instruction. Obtaining materials that are appropriate for a particular unit can be quite a chore. Teachers must spend a great deal of time planning activities and then managing them. Young readers frequently lose their focus if someone is not available to keep them on the right line of inquiry. The challenge, then, is to engineer projects that keep students on task yet allow flexibility.

Issue 5: Age Focus

Practically every reading education text-book devoted to content area reading instruction focuses on middle-school and senior-high students. The books imply that only older students encounter reading materials while studying subject matter. This age focus is curious because elementary-age students regularly read content area materials, too. In fact, the majority of the early writings in this field dealt with elementary school instruction, and most elementary reading methods texts include at least one chapter on content area reading concerns. An historical perspective on remedial and developmental reading instruction at the secondary level helps explain why elementary-age students currently are neglected in content area reading instruction methods texts.

Standardized measurement of students' school achievement in the early 1900s substantiated the fact that school children at all grade levels exhibited wide ranges of reading levels. And developmentalist thought advocated instruction to meet the needs of students regardless of their grade placement. The dominant response to these forces at the secondary level was to implement remedial reading programs. Indeed, practically all reading instruction that was provided by secondary schools during the first half of this century consisted of remedial instruction. In general, the remedial programs followed the well known pull-out model of large-scale testing, identification of students with reading problems, instruction in special classes, and then posttesting. That large numbers of older students were candidates for such instruction is confirmed by the reports of Center and Persons (1937), Gray (1937), Hunt and Sheldon (1950), Kottmeyer (1944), and Witty (1948).

The connection between remedial reading instruction at secondary levels and content area reading instruction is that educators faced the necessity of transfer of skills across disciplines. For example, the remedial program described by Center and Persons (1937) included the provision that "all teachers in the school should help the pupils make the application of reading skills to all subjects" (p. 139). This admonition can be found in varying levels of prominence in most available descriptions of secondary school remedial programs. As educators came to realize that older students needed help in developing adequate reading abilities, those educators further realized that reading adequately in secondary schools actually meant being able to read in the content areas.

Concerns for remedial programs helped focus content reading instruction at the upper age groups, and the notion that older, average readers required help learning to read contributed to that focus. School testing programs indicated that growth in reading did not stop after the elementary grades. Consequently, reading abilities were seen to have no upper limit, and reading instruction was determined to be important in intermediate and secondary grades. A key book on reading instruction for older students was *Developmental Reading in High School* by Guy Bond and Eva Bond (1941). The authors established a rationale for the development of reading skills in every subject area. This book was unusual for its time in that it outlined the responsibilities of administrators, supervisors, and teachers in the coordination of a total school reading program at the secondary level. This text and the work of Ruth Strang (1937, 1938, 1962) were instrumental in establishing professional awareness of the need to provide reading instruction in high schools and to integrate it with subject matter instruction. In fact, the predominant attention to content area reading instruction during the 1940s and 1950s consisted of pointing out the necessity for it at secondary and college levels. As a result, that specialty was assumed by educators concerned with secondary school reading.

The issue educators face with regard to age focus involves the developmental nature of reading-to-learn and reading-to-do abilities. For instance, do the organizational processes of 10-year-olds differ from those of 18-year-olds? Are those processes amenable to different forms of instruction? Should instruction be delivered in fundamentally different ways to students in the different grades? Research and curriculum development in content area reading instruction from the middle of the century to the present neglected youngsters in the early grades as educators turned to the reading needs of older students. But young students require attention, too.

A Final Word

The purpose of this paper was to clarify the foundations of content area reading instruction as it currently is treated in the professional literature. The context in which recommendations for such instruction emerged and the reasons for fundamental differences between the recommendations make up essential features of this field's knowledge base. Clear understandings of that context and those reasons provide starting points for implementing and innovating teaching practices that meet present demands.

References

Arnold, H. F. The comparative effectiveness of certain study techniques in the field of history. *Journal of Educational Psychology*, 1942, *33*, 449–457.

Artley, A. S. A study of certain relationships existing between general reading comprehension and reading comprehension in a specific subject matter area. *Journal of Educational Research*, 1943, *37*, 464–473.

Aukerman, R. C., Jr. Differences in the reading status of good and poor eleventh grade students. *Journal of Educational Research*, 1948, *41*, 498–515.

Ayer, A. M. *Some difficulties in elementary school history* (Teachers College Contributions to Education, No. 212). New York: Columbia University, Teachers College, 1926.

Barr, A. S., & Gifford, C.W. The vocabulary of American history. *Journal of Educational Research*, 1929, *20*, 103–121.

Barton, W. A. *Outlining as a study procedure.* (Teachers College Contributions to Education, No. 411). New York: Columbia University, Teachers College, 1930.

Betts, E. A., & Betts, T. M. *An index to professional literature on reading and related topics.* New York: American Book Company, 1945.

Blank, K. J. Improving reading in Biology. *School Science and Mathematics*, 1932, *32*, 889–892.

Bond, E. A. *Tenth-grade abilities and achievements.* (Teachers College Contributions to Education, No. 813). New York: Columbia University, Teachers College, 1940.

Bond, G. L., & Bond, E. *Developmental reading in high school.* New York: Macmillan, 1941.

Brown, A. L., Bransford, J. D., Ferrara, R. A., & Campione, J. C. Learning, remembering, and understanding. In J.H. Flavell, E.M. Markman (Eds.), *Carmichaels' manual of child psychology*, Vol. 1. New York: Wiley, in press.

Brownell, W. A. *A study of supervised study* (Bulletin No. 26). Urbana, IL: University of Illinois, Bureau of Educational Research, 1925.

Bruner, J. *The process of education*. Cambridge, MA: Harvard University Press, 1960.

Burmeister, L. E. *Reading strategies for middle and secondary school teachers* (2nd ed.). Reading, MA: Addison-Wesley, 1978.

Buswell, G. T., & John, L. *The vocabulary of arithmetic* (Supplementary Educational Monographs, No. 38). Chicago: University of Chicago Press, 1931.

Butterweck, J. S. *The problem of teaching high school students how to study* (Teachers College Contributions to Education, No. 237). New York: Columbia University, Teachers College, 1926.

Caldwell, O. W., & Courtis, S. A. *Then and now in education: 1845–1923*. Yonkers-on-Hudson, NY: World Book, 1925.

Callahan, R. *Education and the cult of efficiency*. Chicago: University of Chicago Press, 1962.

Center, S. S., & Persons, G. L. *Teaching high school students to read: A study of retardation in reading*. New York: Appleton-Century, 1937.

Coryell, N. C. *An evaluation of extensive and intensive teaching of literature: A years experiment in the eleventh grade* (Teachers College Contributions to Education, No. 275). New York: Columbia University, Teachers College, 1927.

Crawford, C. C. Relative values of reading and outlining as methods of study. *Educational Method*, 1929, *8*, 434–438.

Curtis, F. D. *Some values derived from extensive reading of general science* (Teachers College Contributions to Education, No., 163). New York: Columbia University, Teachers College, 1924.

Curtis, F. D. *Investigation of vocabulary in textbooks of science for secondary schools*. Boston: Ginn, 1938.

Dewey, J. *How we think*. Boston: D. C. Heath, 1910.

Distad, H. W. A study of the reading performance of pupils under different conditions on different types of materials. *Journal of Educational Psychology*, 1927, *18*, 247–258.

Dolch, E. W. Combined word studies. *Journal of Educational Research*, 1928, *17*, 11–19.

Dynes, J. J. Comparison of two methods of studying history. *Journal of Experimental Education*, 1932, 1, 42–45.

Estes, T. H., & Vaughan, J. L. *Reading and learning in the content classroom: Diagnostic and instructional strategies*. Boston: Allyn & Bacon, 1978.

Flemming, C. W., & Woodring, M. N. Training high school pupils in study procedures, with emphasis on reading. *Teachers College Record*, 1929, *30*, 589–610.

Gates, A. I. Recitation as a factor in memorizing. *Archives of Psychology*, 1917, *6*, 1–104.

Gates, A. I. *The improvement of reading: A program of diagnostic and remedial methods*. New York: Macmillan, 1935.

Germane, C. E. Outlining and summarizing compared with re-reading as methods of studying. In G.M. Whipple (Ed.), *Report of the society's committee on silent reading* (Twentieth Yearbook of the National Society for the Study of Education, Part II). Bloomington, IL: Public School Pub., 1921.

Germane, C. E., & Germane, E. G. *Silent reading*. Chicago: Row Peterson, 1922.

Golden, M. L. Reading guided by questions versus careful reading followed by questions. *Journal of Educational Psychology*, 1942, *33*, 463–468.

Good, C. V. *The supplementary reading assignment.* Baltimore, MD: Warwick & York, 1927.

Goodman, K. S., & Goodman, Y. M. *A whole-language, comprehension-centered reading program* (Position Paper No. 1). Tucson, AZ: University of Arizona, Center for Research and Development, 1981.

Gray, C. T. A comparison of two types of silent reading as used by children in different school grades. *Journal of Educational Psychology*, 1929, *20*, 169–176.

Gray, W. S. *The relation between study and reading* (Proceedings of the Annual Meeting of the National Education Association). Washington, DC: National Education Association, 1919.

Gray, W. S. Summary of reading investigations: July 1, 1925 to June 30, 1926. *Elementary School Journal*, 1927 *27*, 456–466, 495–510.

Gray, W. S. The nature and organization of basic instruction in reading. In G.M. Whipple (Ed.), *The teaching of reading: A second report* (Thirty-sixth Yearbook of the National Society for the Study of Education, Part I). Bloomington, IL: Public School Pub. Co., 1937.

Gray, W. S. Reading. In G.M. Whipple (Ed.), *Child development and the curriculum* (Thirty-eighth Yearbook of the National Society for the Study of Education, Part I). Bloomington, IL: Public School Pub. Co., 1939.

Gray, W. S. (Ed.). *Improving reading in content fields* (Supplementary Educational Monographs, No. 62). Chicago: University of Chicago Press, 1947.

Gray, W. S. (Ed.). *Improving reading in all curriculum areas* (Supplementary Educational Monographs, No. 76). Chicago: University of Chicago Press, 1952.

Greene, E. B. Certain aspects of lecture, reading, and guided reading. *School and Society*, 1934, *39*, 619–624.

Hafner, L. E. *Developmental reading in middle and secondary schools: Foundations, strategies, and skills for teaching.* New York: Macmillan, 1977.

Hall-Quest, A. L. *Supervised study.* New York: Macmillan, 1916.

Harris, A. J. Progressive education and reading instruction. *The Reading Teacher*, 1964, *18*, 128–138.

Hazlett, J. S. Conceptions of curriculum history. *Curriculum Inquiry*, 1979, *9*, 129–135.

Henry, N. B. *Reading in the high school and college* (Forty-seventh Yearbook of the National Society for the Study of Education, Part II). Bloomington, IL: Public School Pub. Co., 1948.

Herber, H. L. *Teaching reading in content areas.* Englewood Cliffs, NJ: Prentice-Hall, 1970, 1978.

Herber, H., & Barron, R. (Eds.). *Research in reading in the content areas: Second year report.* Syracuse, NY: Syracuse University, Reading and Language Arts Center, 1973.

Herber, H., & Riley, J. (Eds.). *Research in reading in the content areas: Fourth report.* Syracuse, NY: Syracuse University, Reading and Language Arts Center, 1979.

Herber, H., & Sanders, P. (Eds.). *Research in reading in the content areas: First Year Report.* Syracuse, NY: Syracuse University, Reading and Language Arts Center, 1969.

Herber, H., & Vacca, R. (Eds.). *Research in reading in the content areas: Third report.* Syracuse, NY: Syracuse University, Reading and Language Arts Center, 1977.

Hoetker, J. A. A theory of talking about theories of reading. *College English*, 1982, *44*, 175–181.

Holmes, E. Reading guided by questions versus careful reading and re-reading without questions. *School Review,* 1931, *39*, 361–371.

Horn, E. The objectives in reading as a guide to remedial and prophylactic work. In J. L. Bracken (Ed.), *The problem of the elementary school principal in the light of the testing movement* (The Second Yearbook, Bulletin of the Department of Elementary School Principals). Washington, DC: National Education Association, 1923.

Horn, E. *Methods of instruction in the social studies*. New York: Charles Scribners Sons, 1937.

Huey, E. B. *The psychology and pedagogy of reading.* New York: Macmillan, 1908.

Hunt, L. C., Jr., & Sheldon, W. D. Characteristics of the reading of a group of ninth grade pupils. *School Review*, 1950, *58*, 348–353.

Irion, T. W. H. *Comprehension difficulties of ninth grade students in the study of literature* (Teachers College Contributions to Education, No. 189). New York: Columbia University, Teachers College, 1925.

Jacobson, P. B. The effect of work-type reading instruction given in the ninth grade. *School Review*, 1932, *40*, 273–281.

James, W. *Talks to teachers on psychology: And to students on some of life's ideals.* New York: Henry Holt, 1923.

Jenkins, J. J. Four points to remember: A tetrahedral model of memory experiments. In L.S. Cermak & F.I.M. Craik (Eds.), *Levels of processing and human memory*. Hillsdale, NJ: Erlbaum, 1979.

Johns, J. L. Research in reading: A century of inquiry. In S. Weintraub, H. K. Smith, G. P. Plessas, N.L. Roser, W.R. Hill, & M.W. Kibby (Eds.), *Summary of investigations relating to reading: July 1, 1980 to June 30, 1981.* Newark, DE: International Reading Association, 1982.

Judd, C. H., & Buswell, G. T. *Silent reading: A study of the various types* (Supplementary Educational Monographs, No. 23). Chicago: University of Chicago Press, 1922.

Kilpatrick, W. H. *The project method.* New York: Teachers College Press, 1919.

Kilzer, L. R. *Supervised study.* New York: Professional and Technical Press, 1931.

Kottmeyer, W. Improving reading instruction in the St. Louis Schools. *Elementary School Journal*, 1944, *45*, 33–41.

Laycock, S. R., & Russell, D. H. An analysis of thirty-eight how-to-study manuals. *School Review,* 1941, *49*, 370–379.

Leggitt, D. Measuring progress in working skills in ninth-grade civics. *School Review*, 1934, *42*, 676–687.

Mathews, C. O. Comparison of methods of study for immediate and delayed recall. *Journal of Educational Psychology,* 1938, *29*, 101–106.

McCallister, J. M. Reading difficulties in studying content subjects. *Elementary School Journal*, 1930, *31*, 191–201.

McCallister, J. M. Determining the types of reading in studying content subjects. *School Review,* 1932, *40*, 115–123.

McCallister, J. M. *Remedial and corrective instruction in reading: A program for the upper grades and high school.* New York: Appleton-Century, 1936.

Mckee, P. G. *Reading and literature in the elementary school.* Boston: Houghton Mifflin, 1934.

Mckee, P. G. *The teaching of reading in the elementary school.* Boston: Houghton Mifflin, 1948.

McMurry, F. M. *How to study, and teaching how to study.* Boston: Houghton Mifflin, 1909.

Mead, C. D. Silent versus oral reading with one hundred sixth-grade children. *Journal of Educational Psychology*, 1915, *6*, 345–348.

Mead, C. D. Results in silent versus oral reading. *Journal of Educational Psychology*, 1917, *8*, 367–368.

Monroe, W. S. *Training in the technique of study* (Bulletin No. 22). Urbana, IL: University of Illinois, Bureau of Educational Research, 1924.

Monroe, W. S., & Mohlman, D. K. *Training and the technique of study* (Bulletin No. 20). Urbana, IL: University of Illinois, Bureau of Educational Research, 1924.

Newlun, C. O. *Teaching children to summarize in fifth grade-history* (Teachers College Contributions to Education, No. 404). New York: Columbia University, Teachers College, 1930.

Parker, F. W. *Talks on pedagogics: An outline of the theory of concentration.* New York: E. L. Kellogg and Co., 1894.

Peters, C. W. The content processing model: A new approach to conceptualizing content reading. In J. P. Patberg (Ed.), *Reading in the content areas: Application of a concept.* Toledo, OH: University of Toledo, College of Education, 1982.

Pintner, R. Oral and silent reading of fourth-grade pupils. *Journal of Educational Psychology*, 1913, *4*, 333–337.

Pitkin, W. B., Newton, H. C., & Langham, O. P. *Learning how to learn, with special emphasis on improving reading ability.* New York: McGraw-Hill, 1935.

Pressey, L. C. *The technical vocabularies of the public-school subjects.* Bloomington, IL: Public School Pub. Co., 1923.

Readence, J. E., Bean, T. W., & Baldwin, R. S. *Content area reading: An integrated approach.* Dubuque: Kendall/Hunt, 1981.

Resnick, D. P., & Resnick, L. B. The nature of literacy: An historical exploration. *Harvard Educational Review*, 1977, *47*, 370–385.

Ritter, B. T., & Lofland, W. T. The relation between reading ability as measured by certain standard tests and the ability required in the interpretation of printed matter involving reason. *Elementary School Journal*, 1924, *24*, 529–546.

Robinson, F. P. *Effective study.* New York: Harper and Brothers, 1946.

Robinson, H. A. *Teaching reading and study strategies: The content areas* (2nd ed.). Boston: Allyn & Bacon, 1978.

Robinson, R. R. *Two centuries of change in the content of school readers* (Contributions to Education of George Peabody College for Teachers, No. 59). Nashville, TN: George Peabody College for Teachers, 1930.

Rudolf, K. B. *The effects of reading instruction on achievement in eighth grade social studies* (Teachers College Contributions to Education, No. 945). New York: Columbia University, Teachers College, 1949.

Salisbury, R. A study of the transfer effects of training in logical organization. *Journal of Educational Research*, 1934, *28*, 241–254.

Shores, J. H. Skills related to the ability to read history and science. *Journal of Educational Research*, 1943, *36*, 584–593.

Simon, D. L. Developing desireable reading habits in studying citizenship. *School Review*, 1934, *42*, 447–458.

Simpson, R. G. The effect of specific training on ability to read historical materials. *Journal of Educational Research*, 1929, *20*, 343–351.

Singer, H., & Donlan, D. *Reading and learning from text*. Boston: Little, Brown & Co., 1980.

Smith, B. M. Correlation of ability in reading with the general grades in high school. *School Review*, 1919, *27*, 493–511.

Smith, N. B. Patterns of writing in different school subjects. *Journal of Reading*, 1964, *8*, 31–37, 97–102.

Smith, N. B. *American reading instruction*. Newark, DE: International Reading Association, 1965.

Strang, R. Another attempt to teach how to study. *School and Society*, 1928, *28*, 461–466.

Strang, R. The improvement of reading in high school. *Teachers College Record*, 1937, *39*, 197–206.

Strang, R. *Problems in the improvement of reading in high school and college*. Lancaster, PA: Science Press, 1938.

Strang, R. Progress in the teaching of reading in high school and college. *The Reading Teacher*, 1962, *16*, 170–177.

Swenson, E. J. A study of the relationships among various types of reading scores on general and science materials. *Journal of Educational Research*, 1942, *36*, 81–90.

Thieman, T. J., & Brewer, W. F. Alfred Binet on memory for ideas. *Genetic Psychology Monographs*, 1978, *97*, 243–264.

Thorndike, E. L. Reading as reasoning: A study of mistakes in paragraph reading. *Journal of Educational Psychology*, 1917, *8*, 276–282.

Thorndike, E. L. *The teacher's word book*. New York: Columbia University, Teachers College, 1921.

Thorne-Thomsen, G. Reading in the third grade. *The Elementary School Journal and Course of Study*, 1901, *2*, 227–229.

Tierney, R. J., & Cunningham, J. W. *Research on teaching reading comprehension* (Tech. Rep. No. 187). Urbana, IL: University of Illinois, Center for the Study of Reading, 1980.

Todd, J. *The student manual* (14th ed.). Northampton, MA: Hopkins, Bridgeman, 1850.

Vacca, R.T. *Content area reading*. Boston: Little, Brown & Co., 1981.

Venezky, R. L. Research on reading processes: A historical perspective. *American Psychologist*, 1977, *32*, 339–345.

Wagner, E. *Reading and ninth grade achievement* (Teachers College Contributions to Education, No. 756). New York: Columbia University, Teachers College, 1938.

Washburne, J. N. The use of questions in social science material. *Journal of Educational Psychology*, 1929, *20*, 321–359.

Watts, I. *The improvement of the mind: Or a supplement to the art of logic. In two parts*. Boston: Exeter, Lamson, & Odinone for West, 1793. (In C.K. Shipton (Ed.), *Early American Imprints, 1639–1800*. Worcester, MA: American Antiquarian Society. Readex Microprint No. 26440)

Whipple, G. M. (Ed.). *New materials of instruction* (Nineteenth Yearbook of the National Society for the Study of Education, Part I). Bloomington, IL: Public School Pub. Co., 1920.

Whipple, G. M. (Ed.). *Report of the National Committee on Reading* (Twenty-fourth Yearbook of the National Society for the Study of Education, Part I). Bloomington, IL: Public School Pub. Co., 1925.

Whipple, G. M. (Ed.). *The teaching of reading: A second report* (Thirty-sixth Yearbook of the National Society for the Study of Education, Part I). Bloomington, IL: Public School Pub. Co., 1937.

Witty, P. A. Current role and effectiveness of reading among youth. In N. B. Henry (Ed.). *Reading in the high school and college* (Forty-seventh Yearbook of the National Society for the Study of Education, Part II). Bloomington, IL: Public School Pub. Co., 1948.

Woodring, M. N., & Flemming, C. W. *Directing study of high school pupils.* New York: Columbia University, Teachers College, 1935.

Yoakam, G. A. *The effects of a single reading: A study of the retention of various types of material in the content subjects of the elementary school after a single silent reading* (University of Iowa Studies in Education, 2, No. 7). Iowa City: University of Iowa, 1922.

Yoakam, G. A. *Reading and study: More effective study through better reading habits.* New York: Macmillan, 1928.

Yoakam, G. A. Research studies in work type reading: A summary of work done at one university. *Journal of Educational Research,* 1936, *29*, 532–543.

Yoakam, G. A. Essential relationships between reading and the subject field or areas of curriculum. *Journal of Educational Research,* 1945, *38*, 463–469.

Yoakam, G. A. *Basal reading instruction.* New York: McGraw-Hill Book Co., 1955.

Zirbes, L. *Comparative studies of current practice in reading, with techniques for the improvement of teaching* (Teachers College Contributions to Education, No. 316). New York: Columbia University, Teachers College, 1928.

Reference Notes

1. Cook, W. D. *The historical study: A legitimate child of reading research.* Paper presented at the meeting of the International Reading Association, New Orleans, April 1981.
2. Durrell, D. D. Personal communications, October 16, 1981.

What Is Disciplinary Literacy and Why Does It Matter?

Timothy Shanahan and Cynthia Shanahan

Timothy and Cynthia Shanahan's discussion of disciplinary literacy instruction distinguishes it from more traditional content-area literacy instructional models, and provides an overview of the background and history on the move away from such traditional models, along with a review of relevant research across several disciplines. They also present an argument for why a disciplinary literacy model is appropriate, and posit that explicit instruction is needed to help students recognize the specific literacy practices inherent in various disciplines. Although their argument tends to be focused on middle and high school students, the implications and possible applications for postsecondary literacy venues are many.

Lately, educators have been turning their attention to the reading that is done in the content areas, such as mathematics, history, and science. The idea of focusing on reading within those subjects is not new, but it has gained new life as public attention has shifted from the problems of beginning reading to those of reading in adolescence. Education for young children has long accepted explicit and separate reading instruction as one of the basic three Rs (along with 'riting and 'rithmetic). However, with older students, the educational circumstances are different—middle and high schools do not usually assign a reading class to all students; many secondary schools do not even have remedial reading classes; and the idea of a core reading program and extensive professional development in literacy for teachers, both common practices in elementary education, are unusual.

Despite limited infrastructure and application, the idea of infusing literacy teaching into content subjects has complex roots and wide support. Yet, there is much confusion over what would constitute a sound content area literacy curriculum for middle school and high school students and what preparation their teachers need to receive. A fundamental premise of content area reading has been that, in secondary schools, reading should be "taught mainly in the subject fields with regular content materials and regular daily lessons" (Niles, 1965, p. 36). Educators have not yet reached this idyllic future, but content area literacy textbooks used for teacher education continue to promote the idea of content literacy as "the ability to use reading and writing to learn subject matter in a given discipline" (Vacca & Vacca, 2002, p. 15). As such, pre- and in-service training in content area reading education tends to emphasize the teaching of a generalizable set of study skills across content areas for use in subject matter classes.

More recently, the notion of disciplinary literacy has emerged (Shanahan & Shanahan, 2008). Although disciplinary literacy is a different construct from content area reading, its meaning has been confused to a great extent by those who erroneously use the terms interchangeably or who think that disciplinary literacy is just a new fad name for content area literacy. This is unfortunate because eliding these differences may lessen the likelihood that disciplinary literacy will gain a foothold in secondary education. Some might ask, "Why bother, if we are already teaching content area reading?" Our response is that failure to differentiate disciplinary literacy from content area literacy may mean that when schools do try to emphasize disciplinary literacy, teachers may struggle to support an ill-understood concept.

Given the potential for such confusion, the purpose of this article is to provide a brief introduction to the concept of disciplinary literacy. In this article, we explain what disciplinary literacy is, how it is different from traditional content area reading, where it comes from, and why it matters.

Distinguishing Disciplinary Literacy
From Content Area Literacy

Content area literacy focuses on study skills that can be used to help students learn from subject matter specific texts. Disciplinary literacy, in contrast, is an emphasis on the knowledge and abilities possessed by those who create, communicate, and use knowledge within the disciplines. The difference is that content literacy emphasizes techniques that a novice might use to make sense of a disciplinary text (such as how to study a history book for an examination), whereas disciplinary literacy emphasizes the unique tools that the experts in a discipline use to engage in the work of that discipline.

But would these approaches not overlap, at least, with regard to what middle school and high school students need to learn? Will the reading techniques of content area literacy not be the same as resources that disciplinary experts employ? Surprisingly perhaps, the answer to these questions is often, "No." Content area reading *prescribes* study techniques and reading approaches that can help someone to comprehend or to remember text better (with little regard to type of text), whereas disciplinary literacy emphasizes the *description* of unique uses and implications of literacy use within the various disciplines.

The major premise of content area reading proponents has been that the cognitive requirements of learning and interpreting any kind of text are pretty much the same, no matter what the subject matter. In some cases, research in this area has evaluated student learning using texts drawn from particular disciplines, but despite this, nothing has been particularly specialized or discipline-specific about the guidance provided to the students.

Examples of reports in which differences among disciplines have been ignored or elided include research on early study techniques such as SQ3R (survey, question, read, recite, review), which was recommended for use with content area textbooks (Robinson, 1961). Other examples include early content area reading approaches, such as three-level guides (Herber, 1970); general reading comprehension strategies (e.g., summarizing, questioning, monitoring, visualizing), such as those considered by the National Reading Panel (National Institute of Child Health and Human Development, 2000); and electronic tutoring tools and guidance systems aimed at supporting readers' metacognition and interpretive interactions with disciplinary texts (Graesser, McNamara, & VanLehn, 2005; Magliano et al., 2005).

Consequently, content area reading proponents tend to treat content differences as the major distinction among the disciplines. Although such proponents may acknowledge that one reads about mathematics in a mathematics book and history in a history book, they (along with many others who study reading comprehension) emphasize that what readers need is a common set of reading strategies that could be applied, perhaps with some minor adjustments, to varied content area texts. Thus, although researchers may examine the use of a comprehension strategy, such as the use of paraphrasing, within the context of science text, the effectiveness of such a strategy within science reading would not make paraphrasing a discipline-specific reading strategy. There is nothing about paraphrasing itself that is special to reading science texts; rather, one would find paraphrasing to be as useful in the reading of any text of similar difficulty and correspondence with readers' background knowledge.

For the past couple of decades, research has been revealing that disciplines differ extensively in their fundamental purposes, specialized genres, symbolic artifacts, traditions of communication, evaluation standards of quality and precision, and use of language. With regard to language use, different purposes presuppose differences in how individuals in the disciplines structure their discourses, invent and appropriate vocabulary, and make grammatical choices.

Contrasts in Vocabulary Learning

A major assumption of content area reading approaches is that students learn vocabulary similarly in different schools subjects. It is easy to identify sets of words or terms that are associated with each content area. Mathematics, for example, might focus on terms such as *minuend, rational, quotient*, and *rhombus*; science on *acid, adaptation, buoyancy, nucleus*, and *fermentation*; social studies/history on *affirmative action, Middle Ages, melting pot, Jim Crow*, and *migration*; and literature on terms such as *frugal, prosaic, wary*, and *mundane*. According to textbooks aimed at teacher education in content area reading, the study skills that one would use to learn such terminology should be pretty much the same, no matter which set of words is targeted. Content reading textbooks, therefore, recommend that teachers guide students to make connections among concepts, construct graphic organizers, brainstorm, create semantic maps, sort words, rate knowledge of words, analyze semantic features of words, categorize or map words, develop synonym webs, and so on, for all subjects. But such strategies would not adequately recognize discipline-specific distinctions.

For example, an examination of the earlier presented science vocabulary terms reveals that the list is rife with words constructed from Greek and Latin roots. This structure is not unique to science words, of course, because most English words have such roots. Because science uses such words extensively and for a purpose, however, analyzing the Greek and Latin derivatives can provide particularly effective support in understanding science concepts. The purpose of constructing (and analyzing) words in this way is to offer a more complete and precise description of concepts than is possible with vernacular terms. Furthermore, such words are considered more resistant to meaning changes and to the morphological shifts that occur across time and across languages (Nybakken, 1959).

Generic, content area reading activities that encourage students to organize words, to use mnemonics, and to rehearse or repeatedly match words with their meanings can be effective study aids with science words, but they would be insufficient. The perspective of disciplinary literacy, in contrast, would emphasize that students should focus on how and why scientific terminology is created and how to use tools such as analysis of Latin and Greek roots to unpack often dense, but precise and recoverable, meaning. It would emphasize, for example, that relations among concepts are often signaled by the vocabulary of classificatory sciences, such as botany (e.g., *annual, biennial, perennial*) or biology (e.g., *mammal, carnivore, herbivore*). General study techniques, such as repetition and mnemonics, are the province of content area literacy in science. In contrast, the nature of scientific vocabulary and the specialized tools to construct and analyze vocabulary used within the sciences are the forte of disciplinary literacy.

History, in contrast to the sciences, does not focus so heavily on a Greek- and Latin-based, based nomenclature. Unlike science, history is rife with openly metaphorical terms. Attempts at analysis of these words will not usually allow the reader to recover the meaning of the words, so a different approach would be more appropriate for studying history vocabulary. Technical terms in history are meant less to carry precise definitions than to unify extensive collections of weakly interwoven groups and events (the *Gilded Age*) or to express a particular perspective on a particular event or action (*Dark Ages* vs. *Middle Ages*). Such insights do not arise within a content area reading approach, but they are essential to a disciplinary approach to teaching subject matter.

As these examples show, although content area literacy might, quite reasonably, guide students to organize the vocabulary in a hierarchical manner that shows the relations among terms, a disciplinary approach might alternatively organize the vocabulary in terms of the authorial perspectives that it conveys. Both content area reading and disciplinary literacy may be able to support vocabulary learning, but they do so in different ways. It is our position that it is essential to understand these differences. To summarize differences in the area of vocabulary, although content area reading often does recommend the teaching of roots and combining forms, it is no more likely to tout this approach for science vocabulary than for the vocabulary of any other discipline. Significantly, no treatment of content area reading encourages teaching students the reasons why science vocabulary (in contrast to history vocabulary) is constructed in the ways that it is.

Other Language Differences

Similarly, functional linguistics has identified subtle, but profound, differences in the language used in the various disciplines (Fang &

Schleppegrell, 2008; Halliday & Martin, 1993). "Secondary-level science, social studies, language arts, and mathematics use patterns of language that enable these disciplines to develop theories, engage in interpretation, and to create specialized texts" (Fang & Schleppegrell, 2008, p. 4). These patterns of language, or grammars, include differences not only in the nature of the technical vocabulary but also in points of view, attribution of causation and agency, passive and active voice, and other linguistic differences that undergird the nature and purpose of the disciplines.

As examples of linguistic analysis, Fang and Schleppegrell (2008) traced the use of nominalization within science; that is, the rendering of verbs and adjectives into nouns. For example, water may *evaporate* (verb) but scientists study and write about the process of *evaporation* (noun). Fang and Schleppegrell claimed that, by helping students to unpack this kind of noun, teachers can provide them with a better understanding of science text. Furthermore, Fang and Schleppegrell noted that such effort makes the text less abstract while giving students valuable insights into the nature of science and scientific communication. One of the major benefits attributed to nominalization is that it shifts the emphasis from social agents to natural agents in the consideration of causation, which is a central premise in most scientific concepts.

In contrast, history texts and literary texts are less likely to focus on nominalized subjects. Although they, too, address causation, understanding human agency (rather than physical cause–effect) is more central to their purposes. Again, as students examine varied disciplinary choices or relatively specialized patterns of language use, they may become better equipped to deal with the learning demands of the particular disciplines. Variations occur, of course, within social and scientific studies. For example, in most sciences, human agency is attenuated; whereas in ecology and environmental sciences, human causation is more important. In fields such as physics, biology, and chemistry, human agency is not a central concern, whereas in the environmental sciences, there is increasing interest in the role that is played by human actions and how they influence aspects of the environment.

Contrasts in Levels of Author Awareness

Language differences revealed by linguistic analysis are only a part of what distinguishes the disciplines. Another example of a disciplinary difference with profound implications for literacy is the reader's awareness of the author.

Research has shown (Shanahan, 1992; Shanahan, Shanahan, & Misichia, 2011) clear differences in how those in the various disciplines think about the author during reading. For example, in history reading, author is a central construct of interpretation (Wineburg, 1991, 1998).

Historians are always asking themselves, "Who is this author and what bias does he or she bring to the text?" This is somewhat analogous to the lawyer's common probe, "What did he know and when did he know it?" Consideration of author is deeply implicated in the process of reading history, and disciplinary literacy experts have hypothesized that "sourcing," that is, thinking about the implications of author during interpretation, is an essential history reading process (Wineburg, 1991, 1998). Furthermore, studies show that author awareness can, at least under some circumstances, be taught to students in a way that improves their learning (Hynd-Shanahan, Holschuh, & Hubbard, 2004; see full text in this chapter).

Although historians and history students must consider a text's authorial source to understand context, research has revealed a different pattern of reading for scientists (Shanahan et al., 2011). Our interviews with chemists have shown that they do rely on author but more as a topical or quality screen when determining which texts to read. In our research, chemists admitted that they consider that laboratory with which an author may be associated to determine whether a text would be worth the time to read. Once reading begins, unlike the historians, however, scientists try to focus their attention specifically on the text. Considerations of author, according to chemists, should play no part in the interpretation of text meaning, something revealed in their think-alouds both during reading and in postreading interviews. In our research, this pattern of intentionally ignoring the author was even more evident in the reading done by mathematicians, who explained, almost stridently, that thinking about author would only be a distraction and that it could help in no way within the process of making sense of the text.

To bring the discussion of author full circle, whether the author should be considered interpretively has been a matter of great controversy within the field of literary criticism (English) for more than 50 years. Literary theorists have worked long and hard to minimize or discount entirely the author during interpretation (Brooks & Warren, 1938; Fish, 1980; Foucault, 1979; Gadamer, 1975; Rosenblatt, 1978; Wimsatt & Beardsley, 1946). Thus, some literary critics argue for the close reading of "authorless" texts, much in the fashion of the scientific or mathematical readings described earlier, whereas other critics allow for some consideration of the author, at least for making sense of the author's ideological stance, as in the historical reading already described.

These differences suggest that students must always read history with an eye to the author, while never reading mathematics that way. Students should reflect on authorship sparingly in science reading, though never to make sense of the text. When reading literature, they should sometimes interpret the author along with the text and, at other times, focus on the words of the literature with no consideration of the author at all.

The aim of disciplinary literacy is to identify all such reading-and writing-relevant distinctions among the disciplines and to find all ways of teaching students to negotiate successfully these literacy aspects of the disciplines. It is an effort, ultimately, to transform students into disciplinary insiders who are able to approach literacy tasks with some sense of agency and with a set of responses and moves that are appropriate to the specialized purposes, demands, and mores of the disciplines.

Summary

In this section, we have described the newer ideas of disciplinary literacy in some detail. Content area literacy, on the contrary, has been around longer and is the focus of dozens of teacher education textbooks. We should, therefore, be able to summarize the agenda of content area literacy proponents more efficiently.

It is evident from examining several decades of content area reading/literacy textbooks that the largely agreed-upon purpose of content area reading approaches is to provide students with a collection of generic reading strategies and study skills that will boost learning in all disciplines. For example, these approaches teach students to preview books through examination of tables of content and indices, preview of chapters through use of subheadings, and use of various print devices (e.g., italics, bold, font and point variations) to make sense of text. They promote the use of purpose setting and predicting, along with a rich collection of reading processes or strategies (e.g., visualization, summarization, clarification, questioning), and the use of particular study or study or teaching devices (e.g., Cornell note-taking, three-level guides, advance organizers).

A distinguishing feature is that the content area reading agenda aims not so much to help students to read history as an historian might but rather to read history with grasp of the information, using a set of generic learning or study tools that may be implemented in any subject. Thus, the focus of content area instruction is less on providing students with an insider's perspective of a discipline and ways of coping with the unique properties of particular disciplines than on providing students with tools to better remember the information regardless of the nature of the discipline.

Sources of Disciplinary Literacy

Basically, disciplinary differences in literacy exist because of differences in the disciplines themselves. These differences are inherent in the varied phenomena that are the focus of each of the disciplines. Historians study past events through an examination of primary documents and secondary sources; whereas scientists analyze, especially, exacting experimental and observational evidence and logic. Mathematicians focus on the implications of a set of axioms or self-evident truths or givens; whereas literature explores fictional or imaginational representations of human relations or development. These foundational differences in the disciplines require differences in texts and language and therefore differences in approaches to reading and writing.

The roots of the disciplinary literacy concept are threefold. They can be found in the historical development of content area reading, cognitive analyses of expert readers, and functional linguistics. The history of content area reading has been described in detail by Moore, Readence, and Rickelman (1983), and we rely heavily on that treatment. Moore et al. traced the history of content area reading research to the 1920s, when recognition of the importance of reading in content subjects began.

History of Content and Disciplinary Literacy

From the beginning, the emphasis of content area reading was on instructional applications of the relation of reading to content subjects. For instance, the National Committee on Reading explored this topic in the classic *24th Yearbook of the National Society for the Study of Education* (Whipple, 1925), which provided guidelines and sample lessons emphasizing how to find answers to questions, follow directions, select major ideas, remember content, identify key words, self-question, and make notes.

As a result of the recognition of the importance of reading in school subjects accorded by the National Committee of Reading, researchers began exploring the issue. According to Moore et al. (1983), the early studies focused on the identification of important vocabulary in textbooks from various subjects, the availability and effectiveness of various instructional procedures, and correlations of comprehension measures based on general and subject specific texts. Moore et al. concluded, "Although these reports indicated various degrees of similarity between 'general' and 'specific' comprehension, all concluded that the subjects presented distinct reading demands" (p. 429). Thus, despite the fact that their methods of research did not permit differences to be discerned, content area reading researchers typically promoted the notion that reading proficiency would be subject distinct. Furthermore, this idea of specialized reading has long been rhetorically honored in pedagogical treatments of content area reading, despite the fact that authors of content area reading textbooks for teachers have mainly endorsed general approaches to reading that were applicable generically across all subject matters.

Thus, the role that content area reading has played in the development of disciplinary literacy has largely been aspirational. It has pointed toward a theoretical conception of literacy processes specialized to particular discipline while fostering a fundamentally different approach, based upon highly generalizable learning strategies or processes that could be easily adapted and used across different school subjects.

Expert Reader Studies

A more empirical source supporting disciplinary literacy approaches has emerged from expert reader studies completed over the past three decades in various disciplines (summarized by Shanahan et al., 2011). Drawing on the expert-novice paradigm from the cognitive sciences, these studies have used observations and think-aloud protocols to identify performance differences.

In this paradigm, the individuals who are particularly proficient in some skill, such as the literacy of a particular discipline, are identified. Then, these experts are asked to perform their skill (e.g., reading a science text) while thinking aloud. Less skilled individuals, perhaps students of the discipline, are observed in the same way, and differences are noted. A permutation on that approach is to compare the relative performances of experts from different fields of study. Such studies have focused on the reading of science (Bazerman, 1985; Latour & Woolgar, 1979; Shanahan et al., 2011); history (Rouet, Favart, Britt, & Perfetti, 1997; Shanahan et al., 2011; Wineburg, 1991); and poetry (Peskin, 1998). They have gone a long way toward establishing the idea that disciplinary experts read differently from novices in their fields and, equally important, differently from experts in other fields.

For example, studies of the reading of physicists (Bazerman, 1985) revealed that they tended to pay particular attention to information that they did not already know and information that violated their expectations. The physicists separated reading to learn from critical reading, reserving the latter for work that was directly applicable to their own work. Historians were found to engage in sourcing (paying attention to the author), contextualization (connecting texts to the circumstances of the time), and corroboration (making comparisons across texts). Furthermore, unlike scientists, historians did not suspend their critical stance when they read information about which they knew little (Wineburg, 1991). As would be expected from studies using such an approach, this body of research identified strategies, perspectives, choices, and tendencies used by experts that involved a sense of self-awareness.

Functional Linguistics

Another approach, and the third source for differentiating disciplinary literacy, arose from functional linguistics (Halliday & Matthiessen, 2004). Functional linguistics is concerned with the choices made available to language users by a grammar. The choices associate speakers' and writers' intentions with the grammar. Thus, analyses of functional linguists can reveal important insights about the nature and conduct of the language users of particular disciplines. Although functional linguistics focuses on grammar, it does so by considering contextualized and practical uses of language, making it useful for considering differences across disciplines.

The tools of functional linguistics have been used to analyze the discourses of science and history (Halliday & Martin, 1993; Schleppegrell, 2004; Veel, 1997; Wignell, 1994). Earlier, we described how and why science texts employ nominalization; studies also have considered how such texts classify and describe phenomena (Halliday, 1994). History, in contrast, does not focus heavily on classification but, instead, construes actions and events, verbal and mental processes, descriptions, and background information (Schleppegrell, 2004). This means that verbs carry much of the meaning in history texts. Sciences texts, on the contrary, may be more tentative about conclusions than is history. This is because, in science, it is essential to be explicit about the degree or extent to which phenomena occur and scientists are more likely to present a mélange of mathematical equations, graphics, and prose. The reason for this explicitness and precision is that scientific claims are used to predict future reactions under similar conditions; even life and death can turn on the accuracy of scientific information. Because historians interpret events from partial documentation collected after the fact, the claims historians make often are not precise enough to determine the degree to which they are accurate. Historians strive instead to make claims plausible, given the evidence, and have different evidentiary constraints and standards from scientists.

Disciplinary literacy, then, is drawn from the largely unrealized aspirations of content area reading and, more substantively, from a growing body of cognitive and linguistic research that examines how disciplinary experts read and how language is structured in disciplinary texts. As such, the empirical roots of disciplinary literacy are not focused specifically on teaching, though many insights drawn from these studies are proving to be useful to literacy and disciplinary teaching. For example, Fang and Schleppegrell (2008) have developed several strategies on the basis of functional linguistics analyses for guiding students to make better sense of their textbooks. Shanahan and Shanahan (2008) have translated some of the expert reader analyses into practical classroom applications as well.

Why Disciplinary Literacy Matters

At this stage, the body of scientific research evidence is not yet sufficient for demonstrating the effectiveness of disciplinary literacy instruction at improving either literacy achievement or subject matter success. Only a few studies testing the efficacy of such methods have been undertaken so far and with mixed results (De La Paz & Felton, 2010; Hynd-Shanahan et al., 2004; Nokes, Dole, & Hacker, 2007). Nevertheless, the approach is promising and needed for several reasons.

First, although content area reading methods have been successful in a plethora of research studies over a long history, they have not made great headway in the schools (O'Brien, Stewart, & Moje, 1995). This is despite the fact that most secondary level teachers are required to have some training in content area reading (Romine, 1996). Various reasons have been proposed for this, none more important than the idea that content area reading approaches have not appealed to most content area teachers. The resistance of pre- and in-service teachers to these methods, however, is well documented (Lesley, Watson, & Elliot, 2007; Moje, 1996; O'Brien & Stewart, 1990; Reehm & Long, 1996; Simonson, 1995; Stewart, 1990; Stewart, & O'Brien, 1989).

One explanation is that issues of affiliation and identity are important in the development of young teachers (Britzman, 1994; Varghese, Morgan, Johnston, & Johnson, 2005). Someone who aspires to be a science or mathematics teacher is much more interested in replicating what science or math educators usually do rather than appropriating routines from reading education. Also, even when subject matter teachers do attempt to use procedures and activities drawn from content area reading, they often find these approaches to be ill-fitting with regard to the purposes of their disciplines or the nature of the texts to be read. In addition, reading strategies are not usually integrated into the subject matter curriculum; thus, teachers are left to determine how they can fit them on top of an already full agenda of instruction. Finally, teachers are usually motivated by the success of their students. The effectiveness of instructional procedures that often foster improvements only among the lowest performing students (Bereiter & Bird, 1985) may not be sufficient to be noticed or valued by content teachers.

Prior researchers have often interpreted the finding that strategies are more supportive of less skilled readers as evidence that readers are already using the strategies in question. However, this conclusion is not entirely consistent with the findings of think-aloud studies conducted with good readers. It also ignores the possibility of multiple routes to reading success. Nevertheless, instructional procedures that are only beneficial for some students are not as attractive to content teachers as would be approaches with more general benefit.

On the contrary, disciplinary reading approaches hold the promise of being more appealing than traditional content area reading approaches to content area teachers. Because the insights and strategies of disciplinary literacy are drawn from the disciplines themselves, a focus on this information does not pose the same challenges to teachers whose self-actualization is tied to their identities as mathematics, science, English, or history educators. If anything, the insights drawn from disciplinary literacy help these teachers to better understand the practices of their their respective disciplines. Instructional practices that have been drawn from examinations of disciplinary texts and studies of disciplinary texts and studies of successful-reader interactions with such texts seem more likely to produce procedures that facilitate the authentic learning demands of the disciplines than those practices that have been true of traditional content area reading routines.

The use of the so-called "generalizable" strategies of content area reading pose fundamental problems to learners, who must not only learn the strategies but must also recognize when they would be sensible to use in a particular discipline and then must adjust them to fit to the actual demands of the disciplinary texts. Such generalization can be very difficult in any learning situation. If disciplinary reading procedures require less stretching of strategies to texts, it stands to reason that these procedures would be more useful and more effective for secondary students to learn.

An open question with regard to the value of disciplinary literacy strategies has to do with whom these new approaches will be effective. As has been noted, traditional reading comprehension strategies and content area reading approaches have tended to be most beneficial for the lowest-proficiency readers, with lesser impact on result with average- and higher-proficiency readers. Perhaps, disciplinary strategies would have the same pattern of results, although given the specificity of disciplinary reading strategies and their emphasis on higher levels of thinking, this might not be the case. Further research is needed to make these determinations.

Many content area reading procedures seem to focus most heavily on getting students to engage with a text and to pay attention to the ideas expressed in the text. Less proficient readers are easily distracted and often do not think much or well about what they are reading; their focus often seems to be more on getting through the reading than trying to gain anything from the reading. Having students summarize what they are reading, ask themselves questions about the information in the text, and set purposes for their reading all offer the possibility that the students will, through the use of these tools, focus to a greater extent on what a text says and consequently, would benefit their learning. Proficient readers tend not to have the same problems with concentrating on the text information or trying to make meaning from it, though they do not always demonstrate the highest levels of interpretation. Strategies that guide one to think more effectively in a discipline-specific manner could guide such students to go beyond a superficial understanding and to grasp deeper and more sophisticated ideas. Thus, a student who could retell the basic story in a piece of literature might be better able to construct a theme or to interpret multiple perspectives or points of view in short stories or novels as a result of applying insights drawn from that discipline. Similarly, a student who could retell many facts from a history book but fail to grasp the author's underlying argument might, through disciplinary strategies, be able to analyze such reasoning or even to construct his or her own arguments from the information. If subject matter teachers see their average and advanced students improving, gaining better purchase on the content of the class, it is possible that they would be more likely to sustain their efforts at using such approaches in instruction.

What about the lowest performing students who struggle to gain even the most basic information from their content texts? Will disciplinary strategies benefit the better readers while casting aside the basic needs of their less proficient peers? Again, it is impossible to answer such questions without empirical study. But there is a very real possibility that disciplinary literacy approaches would be successful even with less proficient readers. As we have indicated, instructional procedures that have usually been successful with such students have done so by stimulating them to engage with text. There is no reason to believe that encouraging more disciplinary engagements would be any less successful in that regard. Thus, disciplinary strategies might be more attractive to content area teachers because it is possible that such procedures will be facilitative of the learning of a wider distribution of students.

Conclusion

We believe that teaching disciplinary literacy will provide learning advantages to middle school and high school students. Various assessments have shown that secondary school students in the United States are not reading well enough to succeed in careers or college, with particular concerns about their readiness to participate in the so-called STEM (Science-Technology-Engineering-Mathematics) professions.

We also believe that students would make greater progress in reading the texts of history, science, mathematics, and literature if instruction provided more explicit guidance that helped them to understand the specialized ways that literacy works in those disciplines. This approach stands in stark contrast with the more widely espoused content area reading approaches, which promote reading strategies that can be used in all disciplines rather than facilitating students' awareness of the specialized nature of literacy in each discipline.

Supporting our position, we have presented evidence from expert–novice comparison studies and analyses of texts using the tools of functional linguistics. These sources have increasingly revealed the unique properties of the disciplines. Insights from those studies, we believe, hold important implications—and potential promise—for supporting more effective instructional approaches for teaching all students to read disciplinary texts. The importance of realizing this promise is now recognized in the new, aptly named "common core state standards for

English language arts and literacy in history/social studies, and science/ technical subjects," which have been adopted as the basic curriculum by more than 40 U.S. states (National Governors Association/Council of Chief State School Officers, 2010). Greater focus on disciplinary literacy is needed to help secondary level students achieve these standards.

References

Bazerman, C. (1985). Physicists reading physics: Schema-laden purposes and purpose-laden schema. *Written Communication, 2*, 3–23.

Bereiter, C., & Bird, M. (1985). Use of thinking aloud in identification and teaching of reading comprehension strategies. *Cognition and Instruction, 2*, 131–156.

Britzman, D. P. (1994). Is there a problem with knowing thyself? Toward a post-structuralist view of teacher identity. In T. Shanahan (Ed.), *Teachers thinking, teachers knowing* (pp. 53–75). Urbana, IL: National Council of Teachers of English.

Brooks, C., & Warren, R. P. (Eds.). (1938). *Understanding poetry*. New York: H. Holt.

De La Paz, S., & Felton, M. K. (2010). Reading and writing from multiple source documents in history: Effects of strategy instruction with low to average high school writers. *Contemporary Educational Psychology, 35*, 174–192.

Fang, Z., & Schleppegrell, M. J. (2008). *Reading in secondary content areas*. Ann Arbor: University of Michigan Press.

Fish, S. (1980). *Is there a text in this class?* Cambridge, MA: Harvard University Press.

Foucault, M. (1979). What is an author? In J. V. Havari (Ed.), *Poststructuralist criticism* (pp. 141–160). Ithaca, NY: Cornell University Press.

Gadamer, H. (1975). *Truth and method* (J. C. B. Mohr, Trans.). New York: Seabury Press.

Graesser, A. C., McNamara, D. S., & VanLehn, K. (2005). Scaffolding deep comprehension strategies through Point&Query, AutoTutor, and iStart. *Educational Psychologist, 40*, 225–234.

Halliday, M. A. K. (1994). *Introduction to functional grammar* (2nd ed.). London: Edward Arnold.

Halliday, M. A. K., & Martin, J. R. (1993). *Writing in science: Literacy and discursive power*. Pittsburgh, PA: University of Pittsburgh Press.

Halliday, M. A. K., & Matthiessen, C. (2004). *An introduction to functional grammar* (3rd ed.). London: Hodder Education.

Herber, H. L. (1970). *Teaching reading in content areas*. Englewood Cliffs, NJ: Prentice-Hall.

Hynd-Shanahan, C., Holschuh, J., & Hubbard, B. (2004). Thinking like a historian: College students' reading of multiple historical documents. *Journal of Literacy Research, 36*, 141–176.

Latour, B., & Woolgar, S. (1979). *Laboratory life: The social construction of scientific facts*. London: Sage.

Lesley, M., Watson, P., & Elliot, S. (2007). "School" reading and multiple texts: Examining the metacognitive development of secondary-level preservice teachers. *Journal of Adolescent & Adult Literacy, 51*, 150–162.

Magliano, J. P., Todaro, S., Millis, K., Wiemer-Hastings, K., Kim, H., & McNamara, D. S. (2005). Changes in reading strategies as a function of reading training: A comparison of live and computerized training. *Journal of Educational Computing Research, 32,* 185–208.

Moje, E. B. (1996). "I teach students, not subjects": Teacher-student relationships as contexts for secondary literacy. *Reading Research Quarterly, 31,* 172–195.

Moore, D. W., Readence, J. E., & Rickelman, R. J. (1983). An historical exploration of content area reading instruction. *Reading Research Quarterly, 18,* 419–438.

National Governors Association/Council of Chief State School Officers. (2010). *Common Core State Standards for English language arts & literacy in history / social studies, science, and technical subjects.* Retrieved January 2, 2012, from http://www.corestandards.org/assets/CCSSI_ELA%20Standards.pdf

National Institute of Child Health and Human Development. (2000). *Report of the National Reading Panel. Teaching children to read: An evidence-based assessment of the scientific research literature on reading and its implications for reading instruction: Reports of the subgroups.* Washington, DC: U.S. Government Printing Office.

Niles, O. S. (1965). Developing essential reading skills in the English program. In J. A. Figurel (Ed.), *Reading and inquiry* (pp. 35–43). Newark, DE: International Reading Association.

Nokes, J. D., Dole, J. A., & Hacker, D. J. (2007). Teaching high school students to use heuristics while reading historical texts. *Journal of Educational Psychology, 99,* 492–504.

Nybakken, O. E. (1959). *Greek and Latin in scientific terminology.* Ames: Iowa State University Press.

O'Brien, D. G., & Stewart, R. A. (1990). Preservice teachers' perspectives on why every teacher is not a teacher of reading: A qualitative analysis. *Journal of Reading Behavior, 22,* 101–129.

O'Brien, D. G., Stewart, R. A., & Moje, E. B. (1995). Why content literacy is difficult to infuse into the secondary school: Complexities of curriculum, pedagogy, and school culture. *Reading Research Quarterly, 30,* 442–463.

Peskin, J. (1998). Constructing meaning when reading poetry: An expert-novice study. *Cognition and Instruction, 16,* 235–263.

Reehm, S. P., & Long, S. A. (1996). Reading in the mathematics classroom. *Middle School Journal, 27,* 35–41.

Robinson, D. (1961). Study skills for superior students in secondary schools. *The Reading Teacher, 25,* 29–33.

Romine, B. G. (1996). Reading coursework requirements for middle and high school content area teachers: A U.S. survey. *Journal of Adolescent & Adult Literacy, 40,* 194–198.

Rosenblatt, L. (1978). *The reader, the text, and the poem.* Carbondale, IL: Southern Illinois Press.

Rouet, J.F., Favart, M., Britt, M.A., & Perfetti, C.A. (1997). Studying and using multiple documents in history: Effects of discipline expertise. *Cognition and Instruction, 15,* 85–106.

Schleppegrell, M. J. (2004). *The language of schooling: A functional linguistics perspective.* Mahwah, NJ: Erlbaum.

Shanahan, C., Shanahan, T., & Misichia, C. (2011). Analysis of expert readers in three disciplines: History, mathematics, and chemistry. *Journal of Literacy Research, 43,* 393–429.

Shanahan, T. (1992). Reading as a conversation with an author. In M. Pressley, K. R. Harris, & J. T. Guthrie (Eds.), *Promoting academic competence and literacy in school* (pp. 129–148). San Diego, CA: Academic Press.

Shanahan, T., & Shanahan, C. (2008). Teaching disciplinary literacy to adolescents: Rethinking content area literacy. *Harvard Education Review, 78,* 40–59.

Simonson, S.D. (1995). A historical review of content area reading instruction. *Reading Psychology, 16,* 99–147.

Stewart, R. A. (1990). Factors influencing preservice teachers' resistance to content area reading instruction. *Reading Research and Instruction, 29,* 55–63.

Stewart, R. A., & O'Brien, D. G. (1989). Resistance to content area reading: A focus on preservice teachers. *Journal of Reading, 32,* 296–401.

Vacca, R. T., & Vacca, J. L. (2002). *Content area reading* (7th ed.). Boston: Allyn & Bacon.

Varghese, M., Morgan, B., Johnson, B., & Johnson, K. A. (2005). Theorizing language teacher identity: Three perspectives and beyond. *Journal of Language, Identity, and Education, 4,* 21–24.

Veel, R. (1997). Learning how to mean—scientifically speaking: Apprenticeship into scientific discourse in the secondary school. In F. Christie & J. R. Martin (Eds.), *Genre and Institutions: Social processes in the workplace and school* (pp. 161–195). London: Cassell.

Whipple, G. M. (Ed.). (1925). *Report of the National Committee on Reading* (Twenty-fourth Yearbook of the National Society for the Study of Education, Part I). Bloomington, IL: Public School Publishing.

Wignell, P. (1994). Genre across the curriculum. *Linguistics and Education, 6*(4), 355–372.

Wimsatt, W. K., & Beardsley, M.C. (1946). The intentional fallacy. *Sewanee Review, 54,* 468–488.

Wineburg, S. S. (1991). On the reading of historical texts: Notes on the breach between school and academy. *American Educational Research Journal, 28,* 495–519.

Wineburg, S. S. (1998). Reading Abraham Lincoln: An expert/expert study in the interpretation of historical texts. *Cognitive Science, 22,* 319–346.

Thinking Like a Historian: College Students' Reading of Multiple Historical Documents

Cynthia Hynd, Jodi Patrick Holschuh, and Betty P. Hubbard

Cynthia Hynd, Jodi Patrick Holschuh, and Betty P. Hubbard report on a study that investigated students' history-specific disciplinary literacy practices, including their strategy usage and epistemological beliefs about history. After explicit training in disciplinary strategies and how historians interact with texts, students demonstrated the ability to approach a topic and multiple texts in the manner of professional historians and process the text so as to develop a critical level of understanding rather than simply meeting the goals of task completion and memorization. This study's findings may provide some important insights on best practices for developmental reading courses.

This study examines how students think about multiple historical documents after receiving explicit instruction in strategies for approaching them. It was designed in response to research showing that students, without instruction, are particularly naïve in their attempts to interpret and make decisions about multiple historical texts (e.g., Afflerbach & VanSledright, 1998; Perfetti, Britt & Georgi, 1995; Wineburg, 1991). Our study focused on students' development of disciplinary and strategic knowledge and their beliefs about history.

Wineburg's (1991) study of historians and high school students as they read original source documents showed that the historians engaged in different processes than did the high school students. The historians used three unique processes: sourcing (an evaluation of the source of information), contextualization (placing the text's arguments in a particular time period and context), and corroboration (looking for corroborative evidence across different sources). The students, on the other hand, merely read the documents to collect the facts, a finding replicated by others (Afflerbach & VanSledright, 1998; Perfetti et al., 1995). In other words, the students read the documents as if they were historical truth, whereas the historians read them as if they were arguments. Other studies have found that, when students read multiple texts, they learn the information in common across the texts and ignore the disparate information (Britt, Rouet, & Perfetti, 1996; Stahl, Hynd Britton, McNish, & Bosquet, 1996). These studies confirm findings that students view history reading as fact collecting.

We attribute these findings to two possible explanations: a lack of disciplinary knowledge and/or a lack of appropriate strategies. The first explanation is that students may not have sufficient disciplinary knowledge. By disciplinary knowledge, we mean knowledge of the field of history and the tasks in which historians engage. Individuals with high levels of disciplinary knowledge know how knowledge is created and reported. They know how power relations are structured to determine "what counts." But in most high school history classes, there is a single textbook, and students learn the "story" of history. Despite excellent teaching of the story, students may never realize that there is more than one version of it, or that historians have biases that, often unwittingly, determine what information is privileged in the writing of history textbooks. A historian operates in a particular time frame and social/political/economic milieu, has certain beliefs, and is influenced by schooling and experience. These influences are often hidden from students. The tradition in history textbook writing is to write a coherent, seemingly true story, even though the story relies on hypothesized cause/effect relationships and other interpretations of data. Thus, when students read conflicting accounts of the same events, they understand there are different interpretations of history that are influenced by authors' perspectives and sources.

However, even when students are presented with conflicting sources, they do not automatically read them as arguments the way historians do. A second possible explanation, then, is that students do not have appropriate strategies for reading history texts. From our work teaching learning strategies, we know that students usually do not read informational texts in a critical way, the way disciplinary experts do. They rarely think about the authors of informational texts or about the processes that authors use in order to write within their disciplines. Students also rarely engage in intertextual comparisons and contrasts of their texts and other materials, and they do not fully synthesize information across sources.

Strategy use, we believe, is tied to disciplinary knowledge, becoming more specific as knowledge grows. In which strategies do they engage? Students in various studies conducted with multiple documents (Afflerbach & VanSledright, 1998; Britt et al., 1996; Perfetti et al., 1995; Stahl et al., 1996) mostly used general strategies, such as memorizing the dates of important events. Students with more disciplinary knowledge might realize that events are related and interconnected through case and effect. Historians deem cause and effect relationships to be important, and understanding them would change students' ideas about appropriate strategies (e.g., they might make a cause/effect chart or map). As students gain knowledge about the discipline, they may become aware that historians engage in research to advance theories about the way events are related. At that point, students may use strategies to help them identify areas where controversy about interpretations exists or where interpretations are incomplete (e.g., they may make a comparison/contrast chart of different historical interpretations). As knowledge of the discipline increases, strategies become more focused and sophisticated, especially if history teachers expect outcomes in line with students' growing disciplinary knowledge.

In our *Learning to Learn* classes, we attempted to address the lack of disciplinary knowledge and lack of high-level strategy use by instructing students about what it means to engage in historical research and writing. We taught students not only to read texts for factual information, but also to engage in sourcing, contextualization, and corroboration, the strategies that Wineburg (1991) found historians using. We used multiple, conflicting sources as texts, and told students it was their task to come up with their own interpretations of the event after using the three strategies. Through that instruction, we hoped that students would be encouraged to understand history the way historians do. In so doing, they would experience shifts in beliefs about history learning that accompanied the gain in disciplinary knowledge. That is, their views of the nature of historical knowledge would become more mature. They would begin to see the "truth" in history as contextual and relational. In addition, we expected that the gains in historical knowledge would also positively affect their strategy use; they would use fewer general and more specific strategies. The purpose of our study, then, was to examine shifts in disciplinary knowledge, beliefs, and strategies that students made as they learned how historians read and as they themselves read conflicting texts about a single historical event.

Theoretical and Research Background

We drew on theory and research from social psychology and educational psychology to understand three important aspects of this phenomenon: epistemological beliefs, belief change, and intertextuality. Our decision to focus on these areas was in response to our idea that students who came to believe that they were in charge of their own interpretation of texts (within the tradition of historical interpretation) would be more likely to engage in intertextual strategies and, hence, a more critical reading of text than those who did not. We explain these in turn and relate them to disciplinary knowledge and strategy use.

Epistemological Beliefs

To examine epistemological beliefs, we used Perry's (1968, 1970) theory. Perry examined how college students' beliefs about the nature of knowledge and about themselves as learners develop over time. Through interviews and survey responses, he found that many students enter college thinking that knowledge is handed down by authority. As they progress through college, however, the majority of students come to believe that knowledge is more tentative and is derived through reason.

According to Perry (1970), epistemologies are a system of complex beliefs; individuals progress through a series of nine developmental positions, beginning with a naïve position and moving toward a mature cognitive understanding. As individuals progress through the nine-position model, they pass through four delineated stages: dualism, multiplicity, relativism, and commitment within relativism. In the initial stage, dualism, students view the world in polar terms—right or wrong, good or bad. Right answers exist for every question, and a teacher's role is to fill students' minds with those answers. Because of their experiences in school or normal maturation, students then move through a series of middle positions to a stage of multiplicity, in which they begin to understand that answers may be more opinion than fact and that not all answers can be handed down by authority. Students at this stage range from expecting teachers to adjudicate truth for them to believing that truth is not yet known. They also may believe that all views are equally valid. From this position, students move to a stage of relativism, in which they understand that truth is relative and depends on the context and the learner.

Students who have moved to the stage of relativism are able to believe that knowledge is constructed, and they perceive themselves as active constructors of meaning. Students also begin to shift from a belief that knowledge resides externally to a belief that knowledge resides internally. In the final stage, commitment within relativism, students affirm their identity and commitment to a belief, realizing that they can make judgments based upon the quality of evidence for certain positions. In Perry's study, many students did not reach this final stage.

Perry's theory helped us explain students' beliefs about the nature of historical knowledge represented in the multiple texts they were asked to read. We believed that changes in the disciplinary knowledge of how historians create, share, and evaluate history would be accompanied by epistemological changes.

Belief Change

We chose a persuasion theory from social psychology based upon the reasoning that historians process historical documents as attempts to persuade (arguments). The Elaboration-Likelihood Model, also referred to as the Heuristic-Systematic Processing Model (Chaiken, 1980; 1987; Petty & Cacioppo, 1986; Sinatra & Dole, 1998), hypothesizes two routes, to persuasion—the central route and the peripheral route. By the central route, we mean becoming persuaded by a systematic processing of the text itself. We would call corroboration, finding likenesses and differences across sources, an example of central processing (although the social psychologists who studied these processes did not study multiple texts and their agreements and disagreements). Another example of central processing would be an evaluation of the quality of the evidence presented in the text rather than an evaluation of the way the evidence is structured or the amount of evidence presented. Central processing makes it likely that elaborative understandings of the ideas in the text will result from reading.

By the peripheral route, we mean becoming persuaded by a processing of the noncentral aspects of the texts based upon heuristics or rules. Historians engage in peripheral processing when they evaluate the source and context of the text they are reading. Peripheral processing includes evaluating a text's credibility based upon the heuristic that an author's close involvement in an event would bias her to tell the story in a way that makes her look good. Another example of peripheral processing includes the evaluation of a text based upon the heuristic that two-sided arguments are more believable than one-sided arguments. Our work with high school and college students has helped us to understand that one's heuristics may or may not be well-articulated and may or may not represent mature thinking (Hynd, 2001). Thus, high school students' peripheral processing of an argument is less mature than historians'. Further, we have come to believe that the level of disciplinary knowledge one has plays a role in the quality of the heuristics that are used. A practicing historian is more capable of evaluating the education and scholarship of an author of history than is a high school or college student, for example.

Sinatra and Dole (1998) believe that central processing of arguments is superior to peripheral processing because central processing signals a deeper engagement with the ideas in the text. We concur. When a person is unfamiliar with a topic, however, he is more likely to engage in peripheral processing than in central processing. Sinatra and Dole (1998) also say that a reliance on peripheral processing detracts from a reliance on the arguments in the text. But, even under conditions where individuals have a high level of knowledge and engage in primarily central processing, they can engage in peripheral processing as well. Hynd (2003) argues that when individuals have to make up their minds, processing information both centrally and peripherally is superior to engaging in central processing alone and will more likely lead to belief change. Indeed, experts may engage in both processes automatically. For example, an individual might read an argument calling for segregation and, through central processing, understand the argument fully. But that individual may be less than impressed with the argument if he notes that a member of the Ku Klux Klan wrote the text. Thus, central processing is necessary for understanding, but it may not be sufficient for analysis or for belief change. If multiple, conflicting documents are the information sources, then using a combination of central and peripheral processing leads to more informed decisions about what to believe than using either central or peripheral processing alone.

In this study, we examined the reasons students make decisions about what to believe. The central and peripheral processes that students use are an important part of our understanding. For example, if a student decided one text was more credible than another, we would want to know what process he or she was using to judge credibility. We also believed that an examination of central and peripheral processing could help us more fully understand the reasons historians choose to evaluate texts using the strategies of sourcing, contextualization, and corroboration.

Intertextuality

Because this is a study of multiple text processing, in addition to beliefs and strategy use, we also focused on the role of intertextuality on knowledge. In many theories of text processing, a single text is assumed. Reading more than one text complicates the processing that occurs. Or does it? Intertextuality has to do with the linking of texts, whether those texts include linguistic or nonlinguistic signs; whether they are tangible, such as those located on a written page, or intangible, such as experiences or memories (Rowe, 1987; Worton & Still, 1990). Intertextuality seems to be a consequence and cause of engaged reading, and so is a complication only in the sense that it is not always a part of instruction or text-based research. Engaged readers negotiate textual understandings by linking information both within and outside of the text(s), broadly defined, that they are reading (Hartmann, 1995). These sorts of discrepancies may motivate or trigger epistemological shifts.

In this study, we tried to discover ways to facilitate readers' intertextual moves—the linking of text across sources to construct mental representations. We also wanted students to recognize that writers create texts using similar intertextual moves—they select, connect, and organize information from various sources to construct mental representations that they use in their writing. We were especially interested in how students constructed understandings of historical events when presented with conflicting evidence. Our focus was on movements across the written texts rather than within or outside of them. These other kinds of intertextual linkages took place, to be sure, but our intent was to encourage the occurrence of cross-textual links (comparisons and contrasts of sources, contexts, and arguments).

Students can make cross-textual links if prompted; otherwise, they may need instruction and guidance. Hartmann (1995) studied eight advanced-level high school students as they read five historical passages that provided a rich intertextual environment. He found that students, when asked to do so, were capable of making exogenous links (to personal experiences or knowledge), primary endogenous links (within text), and secondary endogenous links (across text) to create textual meaning. However, even though the students were prompted to create links across the text, the data showed that they made fewer of these links than they did exogenous and primary endogenous ones. This is important to our study, because we wanted students to increase the quantity and quality of the cross-text links.

Stahl et al. (1996) studied high school students' reading of conflicting historical documents and noted that students who were not prompted to make cross-textual links failed to make them. The students tended to focus on the "facts" rather than to note agreements and disagreements across texts or to make sourcing and context comparisons. Students remembered the facts that existed in common across texts, but this remembering seemed more a function of repetition than a sense that the facts represented corroboration of evidence.

In this study, we hoped to have students engage in comparing and contrasting information in the texts they read, and thus make cross-textual links. That is, we decided to explicitly encourage the use of cross-textual links by showing students that historians make such links and by showing students a strategy for making them (a comparison/contrast chart). The instruction in disciplinary knowledge and strategy use, then, would help students engage in intertextuality.

Overview of Our Theoretical Orientation

Suppose a student in a history class is struggling to learn the course material. She believes she is studying hard, yet she has failed the first essay exam— an exam that required the synthesis, analysis, and evaluation of various materials. One might examine the theories on epistemology, the elaboration-likelihood model, intertextuality, discipline knowledge, and strategy use to understand the difficulties she is experiencing. For example, this student might have naïve beliefs about what it means to learn in history. (She may be in the stage of dualism where she is looking for truth or right answers, reflected mainly in names, dates, and places). These naïve beliefs represent her epistemology. If she didn't understand what historians did, then her lack of discipline knowledge might contribute to her belief that the authors of her textbook and other readings were simply recording what happened, and were not engaged in presenting a particular perspective or interpretation of history. This (mis)understanding of historians' work would influence her to believe the *heuristic* that "if it's in a history text, it must be true," a heuristic of poor utility that might actually discourage her from a more elaborative, critical reading of her texts, in line with the elaboration-likelihood model. Indeed, her processing of the text would proceed centrally, and she would not be engaging in the peripheral processing that might signal a belief change. An uncritical surface reading of history to gather the facts would mean that she would not only lack a deep understanding of historical interpretation, but would not be likely to change her beliefs or her strategies. Her reliance on surface-level strategies (such as memorization of events) that match her heuristics and beliefs about history would deter her from grasping the big picture. She would gain only disjointed knowledge, and would find it difficult to draw inferences across texts, typical of the majority of high school students who pay less attention to cross-textualties than to within-text or outside-of-text ties, as shown in Hartmann's (1995) intertextuality study. Thus, as depicted by this case, these theories can work in concert to explain an individual's approach towards making sense from text. The student's beliefs, strategy use, and disciplinary knowledge are intertwined to affect her ability to recognize and interpret ties across texts. The quality of each dimension reciprocally affects the quality of other dimensions. See Table 1 for a representation of how these theoretical perspectives intersect. In this study, we were interested in documenting their reciprocity.

Table 1. Relations Among Knowledge, Strategy Use, and the Three Theoretical Perspectives

Disciplinary knowledge	Strategy use	Epistemology	Intertextuality	Elaboration-Likelihood
Low knowledge: Historians are documenters (they find truth)	Students read for "the facts"	Dualism: There is truth	Not evident: Texts are separate entities	Central and peripheral processing are implicit and there is minimal engagement in text reading
Intermediate knowledge: Historians are synthesizers (they pull together information about what is true through their research)	Students read for corroboration	Multiplicity: Authorities don't have all the answers	Low level: Texts can be compared	Central and peripheral processing are implicit and there are low levels of engagement
Transitional knowledge: Historians construct historical interpretations (using sourcing, contextualization, corroboration) that are influenced by their biases	Students use sourcing contextualization, and corroboration to understand positions taken by authors of text	Relativism: Individuals, including authorities, act under different contextual and interpersonal positions	Transitional level: Texts can be compared and contrasted	Central processing and peripheral processing are explicit and actively engaged
High knowledge: Historians construct interpretations of history, influenced by biases, that are evaluated by peers	Students use sourcing, contextualization, and corroboration in decision-making	Commitment within relativism: Individuals are responsible for evaluating positions to decide what to believe	High level: Students connect texts to background knowledge of context and source and to their own experiences and beliefs	Central and peripheral processing are explicit and are at high levels of quality (students know what counts)

Method

Context

We conducted this study in three *Learning to Learn* classes at a large southeastern university. Students take *Learning to Learn* as an elective in order to learn effective reading and study strategies. Typically, the class draws a wide range of students, from freshmen to seniors, from students with 4.0 GPAs seeking entrance to law or medical school to students who are at risk of failing school. All majors are represented, although the business college so highly recommends the class that business majors are often in the majority. Approximately 20 students were enrolled in each of the classes during the semester of the study, as is typical. In the course, instructors teach students study strategies in relation to three content areas: psychology, history, and biology. Students read texts, listen to lectures, use supplementary materials, and take content-based tests while they are learning the strategies. The course had been developed in consultation with faculty members in psychology, history, and biology, but the classes were taught by two of the authors of this study, a faculty member and graduate teaching assistant in an Academic Assistance Unit of the university.

The history unit, the topic of this study, followed a psychology unit in which students had learned to annotate their textbooks, make concept cards of key vocabulary, organize materials using charts and maps, predict questions and answer them, and conduct "talk-throughs" in which they verbally elaborated on the information they would need to know for the test. The psychology unit exam consisted of a combination of short answer, multiple choice, and true/false items. The history unit was somewhat different, in that the tasks required identifying, evaluating, and discussing the significance of key events. The exam was a long essay in which students were required to take a position on the Tonkin Gulf Incident (see Appendix A for a brief explanation of the Tonkin Gulf Incident) and provide evidence for that position after reading from multiple sources. The emphasis on significance and taking a position was consonant with the emphasis placed on these elements in the introductory history classes at the university. Faculty members in the history department, themselves practicing historians, were unanimous in their decision to require that students read history from multiple perspectives and take part in interpretive arguments about events.

Procedures

Two of the researchers presented the history unit to three *Learning to Learn* classes over a three-week period. Before students began the history unit, they answered questionnaires about their knowledge, strategy use, motivation, and beliefs about history (see Appendix B). After reading each text, listening to a lecture, or watching a video, students summarized what they learned and reflected on their thinking. In addition, students engaged in conversations with their teacher about the development of their thinking via weekly e-mail journals; made comparison/contrast charts reflecting the different perspectives of four target texts; and had class discussion sessions with their classmates about the texts, lecture, and video.

After students had read and viewed all of the material in the history unit, they responded to an essay question in which they were asked to take a position on whether or not the United States provoked the North Vietnamese in order to increase U.S. involvement in the Vietnam Conflict. During the essay exam, students were given an additional text, an excerpt from Robert McNamara's (1996) book, *In Retrospect*, to reflect upon and incorporate into their understanding and stance on the issue. After answering the essay question, students completed a second set of questionnaires assessing knowledge, strategy use, motivation, and beliefs about history.

When students had completed the first questionnaire, we read their responses and chose 13 (7 females, 6 males) to participate in two open-ended interviews, one prior to instruction and one after instruction. We sought to recruit students who were either early or late in their college careers and whose responses to the questionnaires suggested a range of naïve to mature beliefs about learning. Of the 16 students initially approached to participate, 14 agreed to be part of the study and 13 participated in both interviews (one student dropped out for unknown reasons). Five students came from one of the classes, and four students each came from the other two classes. Five of the students were freshmen, one was a sophomore, one was a junior, and six were seniors. Their majors included sociology and pre-law, finance, elementary education, public relations management, accounting, and undeclared. Students' average reported GPA was 3.0 (range = 2.1–3.8). Their average reported SAT was 1168 (range = 950–1290). Table 2 provides a summary of this information and categorizes these students into "naïve" and "mature" regarding their epistemologies and strategy use. These categories were assigned after a researcher read the pre-questionnaire responses. Students who suggested that memorization or other low-level strategies were appropriate preparation for an essay test requiring critical thinking and evaluation endorsed naive strategies. Students whose answers reflected naïve beliefs about knowledge and learning endorsed naïve epistemologies. Epistemology and strategy use coincided, so that only one evaluation (naïve or mature) was used in the table.

The interviews of the 13 students allowed researchers to get more in-depth information about students' predispositions, their processing of the texts, and the development in their thinking. The students' *Learning to Learn* instructor/researcher and an additional researcher conducted the interviews. Thus, in each interview session, students

Table 2. Interview Participants

Name	Yr.	Major	GPA/SAT	Race	Strategy/epist.*	Hist. cls.**
Carey	Fr.	Business	3.8/1220	E-A	N	0
Dan	Fr.	Undec.	2.4/DK	E-A	N	0
Bob	Fr.	Undec.	3.2/1200	Asian/ Braz	N	0
Alice	Fr.	Undec.	3.5/1110	E-A	M	0
Leslie	Fr.	Education	2.75/DK	E-A	M	0
Anna	Soph.	Undec.	2.3/1190	E-A	M	2
Doby	Jr.	Mgmt.	3.2/DK	E-A	N	0
Jenny	Sr.	Mgmt.	2.6/950	E-A	N	1
Cory	Sr.	Finance	3.6/1200	E-A	N	0
Althea	Sr.	Finance	3.0/1290	E-A	M	0
Colin	Sr.	Acc.	2.7/1000	Korean	M	1
Jessie	Sr.	Sociology	2.1/1260	E-A	M	1
Shelly	Sr.	Public Rel.	3.3/1260	A-A	NA	2

*Naïve or mature epistemology/strategy use, as determined by answers to prestudy questionnaire
**Number of history classes taken in college

talked to an instructor they knew and a researcher they did not know. Because we believe students construct meaning in unique ways (Merriam, 1998), questions were arranged in a semistructured, open-ended, exploratory format (Kvale, 1996). Less structured interviews have greater potential for creating situated understandings grounded within the interactions between individuals (Denzin & Lincoln, 2000). Keeping the interviews conversational, and thus less like a testing situation, was also important to our efforts to equalize, as much as possible, the power relations students might perceive because one of the interviewers was their instructor. In addition, we explained to students, consistent with human participants' protection procedures, that their interviews would have no bearing on their grades and that they could choose not to participate at any time. The two instructors believed they had developed relationships with students that encouraged open discussion, and their openness was explicitly solicited. For these reasons, we believed that students would not merely say what they thought we wanted them to say.

In the first interview, we asked what historians did and how they did it, what students' strategies were for studying history, and what students' background in history was. In the second interview we again asked what historians did and how they did it, but we also asked what students were thinking about as they read, how they decided what to believe (how they knew what information was credible), what they thought their task was for learning the material, and what strategies they employed. We followed up these general questions with more specific clarifying questions depending upon their responses. Each interview lasted between 25 and 40 minutes, and transcriptions ranged from 3 and 9 pages per interview. Each interview was somewhat idiosyncratic, because the direction depended upon how students responded.

The Tonkin Gulf Incident

The study focused on students' reading and thinking about the Tonkin Gulf Incident of the Vietnam Conflict, considered by historians to be a disputed yet pivotal event leading to the expansion of United States involvement in America's longest war. A description of this event is in Appendix A. Students in the study read this description as background material. Disputes concern what happened on August 4, the second day of the event, and on whether or not Johnson and his staff were duplicitous in using the event to widen the war.

The materials included a number of resources. Some of them were considered background material because they provided a rich context for interpreting the Tonkin Gulf Incident even though they did not specifically discuss it. Students read the background text referred to previously about the Tonkin Gulf Incident, a text explaining sourcing, contextualization, and corroboration (see Appendix C), and a text arguing that students in history classes are interpreters of history. They saw a videotaped lecture on the Vietnam Conflict and a video on the Johnson years. See Table 3 for a more detailed description of these resources.

The documents specifically about the Tonkin Gulf Incident consisted of four conflicting texts. The four texts had commonalities and differences. For example, participants in the Vietnam Conflict wrote two of the texts; two of the texts were by historians. They represented a range of perspectives on the central questions: what happened during the Tonkin Gulf Incident, and whether the United States and President Johnson were culpable in instigating the attack and in using it to pass the Tonkin Gulf Resolution—legislation that led to increased U.S. involvement in Vietnam. These texts are more throughly described and characterized in Table 4.

Data Sources / Evidence

The data sources consisted of the interviews and students' e-mail reflections, with the interviews being the primary source of data. We used questionnaires primarily for choosing students to interview and

Table 3. Background Materials

Title	Author(s)	Type of Material	Summary
"The Tonkin Gulf Incident"	Researchers	Background summary	The text described the two alleged attacks and the subsequent passage of the Southeast Asia (Gulf of Tonkin) Resolution.
Instruction in corroboration, contextualization, and sourcing	Researchers	Instructional material	Explained that historians use the strategies and describes what they are.
"Self Defense for Your Mind"	Bryant Simon, university history professor	Article in university magazine	Simon discussed the way that songwriters, novelists, and other participants in pop culture use a variety of sources to make sense of events and communicate their interpretations to the public. In his view, they are engaging in historical interpretation. He believes it is the task of students to engage in historical interpretation, as well.
"Vietnam"	William Stueck, university history professor	Videotaped lecture	Stueck provided a chronology of the conflict, beginning in the 1940s and ending with the election of Nixon in 1968. The Tonkin Gulf Incident was not mentioned. The lecture focused on strategic, political, psychological, and economic factors that lead to the conflict. He expressed no personal opinion about Johnson's actions, although he contended that the policies in Vietnam were influenced by a European bias as well as by issues of credibility both nationally and internationally.
"LBJ: The American Experience"	PBS	Video documentary	This documentary portrayed Johnson in both positive and negative lights and discussed his belief that he had no choice but to escalate the war. The documentary presented Johnson as a man who was deeply concerned about the war, and emphasized how LBJ hid the costs of the war to pursue his domestic agenda. The documentary argued that Johnson believed that the U.S. had to appear strong to the rest of the world. The Tonkin Gulf Incident was, again, not mentioned.

Table 4. Target Materials

Author	Source	Personal involvement	Description	Aug. 4, 1964, attack was Real	U.S. provoked the attack	Johnson acted in good faith
Dean Rusk, Secretary of State during incident	Published auto-biography	Yes	Memoir. Rusk argues that the U.S. was acting defensively in passing the Southeast Asia Resolution in response to threats.	Most likely	No	Yes
Philip Davidson, former Secret Service agent/ military historian	Privately published book	Yes	Two-sided argument. Davidson argues that an intercepted North Vietnam-ese telegram indicated a hostile approach and that the U.S. was in international waters at the time of the attack on a non-hostile intelligence-gathering mission.	Yes, at least initiated	No	Yes
Berkin et at., historians	College-level textbook on American history	No	Johnson had been planning to escalate the War. The U.S. had been aiding South Vietnamese raids of North Vietnamese Islands. Johnson used the "attack" to pass the already formulated Southeast Asia Treaty.	No	Yes	No
Gareth Porter, historian	*Washington Post* editorial	No	U.S. did provoke an attack, and acted too hastily when errant reports of the attack came in.	No	Yes	Yes, but too hastily
Archivist at Berkeley	Rebuttal to *Washington Post* editorial	No	The attack had to have happened, because the North Vietnamese celebrate it	Yes	No	—
Robert S. McNamara, former U.S. Secretary of Defense during Vietnam	Excerpt from *In Retrospect,* an auto-biographical account of the Vietnam War written 20 years later	Yes	The attack probably didn't happen, but we believed that it did. We were wrong to get so involved in Vietnam, but, at the time, we believed we were doing the right thing in using the incident to pass the Southeast Asia Resolution.	Probably not	—	Yes

did not use them in the first analysis of data. After the first pass through the data, we used the written interview questions in the questionnaires to corroborate findings from other data sources. The data were used to look for patterns in students' decision making and thinking (signals of changes in disciplinary knowledge and strategy use), for shifts in historical thinking, and for shifts in strategies used for understanding the material. We made several passes through the data in order to elicit those patterns, using Constant Comparison methodology (Glaser & Strauss, 1967). On the first pass, we identified categories of responses. On subsequent passes, we identified patterns within those categories, looked for nonexamples, and discussed all categories and patterns until we reached consensus. Once patterns and categories were determined, we analyzed the data for common themes.

For example, on deciding that beliefs about historians were evident in the responses (category), we first read the data several times, then hypothesized a pattern of responses representing distinct views of historians: as documenters, synthesizers, and arbiters. We then reread the data for students' initial comments, sorted the comments into the views, and agreed that, in initial statements (questionnaires and at the beginning of the interviews), six of the students espoused the view that historians documented, three said they synthesized, and four said they arbitrated. (Students did not use these actual terms, but their comments were interpreted as representing those views.) Next, we looked for changes in the students' thinking and slotted these changes into the same categories. However, we found that some students went beyond viewing historians as arbiters. They actually began to think of historians as biased. So we used the comments of these students (the nonexamples) to add another category, "biasers." We continued through the data in this way until we could fit all statements into the categories. When we finished categorizing the pertinent comments made by students, we discussed the idea that these comments demonstrated an increase in students' level of disciplinary knowledge. That is, a change from the view that historians are documenters to a view that historians may be biased in their interpretation of historical events reflects a deeper knowledge about how historians do their work and about the nature of recorded history. Thus, our first theme emerged: thinking about a historian's job increases disciplinary knowledge. We produced two other themes using similar analytical strategies.

Results

Our analysis of the data suggested three themes: (a) Thinking about a historian's job increases disciplinary knowledge; (b) Students struggle with subjectivity/objectivity and relativism; and (c) Students change their strategies and their ideas about what it means to read about historical events. These themes are discussed in turn. We offer students' talk and e-mail as evidence for our themes. The student quotes are representative of the typical range of answers.

Theme 1: Thinking about a Historian's Job
Increases Disciplinary Knowledge

IDEAS BEFORE INSTRUCTION ABOUT WHAT HISTORIANS DO. Typically, students began the history unit having not thought deeply about what historians did. Students expressed their lack of knowledge and engaged in lengthy pauses before answering. However, when we pressed them to consider that question, their answers ranged from thinking that historians document what happened to the idea that historians arbitrate what happened.

Students also had not thought about the strategies that historians use in their work. However, as they thought about the answer to that question, they began to consider that historians would read various documents, evaluate them for credibility, and compare and contrast them. They mentioned these strategies despite the fact that we had not yet mentioned them to students in class and they had not yet read the background text on sourcing, contextualization, and corroboration. In other words, the process of thinking about the work of historians helped these students construct some of the ideas we were planning to teach them. We discuss these observations in the following paragraphs, providing quotes from students that represent typical answers.

Before beginning the history unit, students answered questions such as, "What do historians do?" and "What strategies do historians use?" Six students were categorized as viewing historians as documenters. Cory (Senior, Finance, no history classes) said historians

> give a description for other people. It's an important thing to do so everyone can have the knowledge of the past who doesn't have the time to do all that research on what happened. We need to know that so we won't make the same mistakes.

Doby (Junior, Management, no history classes) had the same idea: "To keep us up to date about what's happened so we don't make so many mistakes about what's happening." And Leslie (Freshman, Education, no history classes) said, "To study history and then to tell from what's going on the things we could do to avoid past mistakes." Bob (Freshman, undecided major, no history classes) explained, "I think historians just look at the past to see the decisions people have made and hope that we can make a better future."

These students believed that finding out about history could guide policy decisions and avoid future mistakes. Yet, that belief rests on the assumption that what historians tell us is, indeed, documented truth. From the prestudy questionnaire, we had rated most of these students as low on strategy use with rather naïve epistemologies, except for Leslie, who was rated as having a more mature epistemology and more sophisticated strategy use. These comments confirm that. However, their view of historians is a common one. Three of the students said they learned from their parents and high school teachers that knowledge of history helps people avoid future mistakes.

Three students had a view of historians as individuals who tried to find out about cause and effect and put the pieces together (synthesizers). For example, Dan (Freshman, undecided major, no history classes) said, "I'm sure they know all of the basics. They go into detail about stuff, why it happened, why it didn't happen, what could prevent it happening in the future." Alice (Freshman, undecided major, no history classes) said, "[T]hey are looking for why it occurred or motivations—why they did what they did." Two of the students were rated as high in strategy use and epistemology, yet had taken no history classes in college. They did have a more mature view of historians than did those who thought of historians as documenters. They understood, for example, that historians bring together the causes and effects of history and look for "why it occurred."

However, the emphasis is still on the idea of historians as uncovering truth.

Four students viewed historians as arbiters. For example, Jessie (Senior, Sociology, one history class) said a historian's job was "to tell things like they happened so to get rid of bias." He went on to explain that historians had to look at different perspectives and take a position after "looking for the different sides of it to find out as accurately as they can what took place." He said that historians interviewed people in order to find out "if there's a different story." Carey (Freshman, Business, no history classes) began talking about historians' need to document history, but she then decided, when asked to elaborate, that in order to do that right, they needed to get "multiple views." They have to incorporate that into "not what they think is correct but what they see is the consensus." They decide by

> getting lots of information and getting broad consensus if there is conflict—there is in everything—there are many takes in the same thing—sometimes you don't know who wrote it or what their background is. I think that makes it harder. They are looking for different views, factual info, and then tie it together.

Colin (Senior, Accounting, one history class) said,

> They have to look at things differently. . . . We perceive something happened, and there is some proof, but there could be new proof of other things. That is their job—to find new evidence to support different ideas. A historian researches information found through documents, letters, interviews, etc., of people who were involved during a period of time or

event. . . . They would use that information to objectively decide what really happened and they would want to publish their findings so that other historians could share their views about what was found.

We had rated more of these students than the students categorized as synthesizers as relatively mature in strategy use with more mature epistemologies on the prequestionnaire. They had gone somewhat beyond the idea of historians finding truth to the idea of history as a construction. However, they did not consider the idea that the selection of evidence reflects the biases of the historian. Their view was that historians were objective in their selection and interpretation process or that their reliance on consensus made it likely that their interpretations were true.

STUDENTS EXTEND THEIR VIEWS DURING THE INTERVIEWS.   Talking about how historians engaged in strategies led six students who had initially given a documenter or synthesizer explanation of historians' work to a different view. For example, Bob (Freshman, undecided major, no history classes) began by saying that historians "just look at the past to see the decisions people have made." But when he was asked to consider how they did this, he said, "They interview people, they create hypotheses, assumptions, and they investigate some more and look further back—I guess they try to cross-reference history with a lot of history to see if it's valid or not" (Arbiter). Cory (Senior, Finance, no history classes) started out saying that they just "read history books more carefully." But as he considered it, he continued, "They compile it together and try to make rational sense of it" (Synthesizer). And Alice (Freshman, undecided major, no history classes), after saying that she didn't know, said, "They go back and examine all the records and see where they conflict and are the same. They take their time and read it closely. In different documents they are looking for similarities and differences" (Synthesizer). Dan (Freshman, undecided major, no history classes) had originally depicted historians as synthesizers, but when he had to describe what they did, he said,

> I think they look at whether or not it's an article or a documentary. They have to take into account that person's bias. . . . There are a lot of processes you have to go through to try to piece things together. It takes a lot to get to a point where most everyone agrees. I think they look at whether or not it's an article or a documentary. They have to take into account that person's bias. . . . Biases can alter what's really right. A historian wants to know exactly what and why it happened. . . . so you don't want it to be biased (Arbiter).

The students who extended their ideas about what historians can do moved from documenter to synthesizer positions and from synthesizer to arbiter positions. Students mentioned evidence-based interpretation, comparison and contrast of different documents (corroboration) and consensus. Those who believed that historians were arbiters also mentioned sourcing.

These students changed their ideas about historians even before instruction began, just by talking about it. Evidently, prompting students to explain what they meant or to say everything they thought of ("Is that all you want to say?") or to consider how they figured out history led many to reason that historians engaged in some type of synthesis activity that required taking into account various perspectives and multiple sources of information. It did not seem to matter whether students were freshmen or seniors, or whether they had previously taken any college-level history courses.

CHANGES AFTER INSTRUCTION: STUDENTS FOCUS ON DIFFERENT PERSPECTIVES AND BIAS. During and after instruction, students' ideas about what historians do continued to shift towards the view of historians as arbiters and towards the idea that historians have to consider various perspectives and make decisions. They also became more concerned about inherent biases in historical documents and in the historians who write about history. That is, they came to see historians as biasers—unwitting creators of biased interpretations of events.

After instruction, three students continued talking about historians as arbiters or creators of history, and four more started to do so. These students referred to sourcing, contextualization, and corroboration. Dan (Freshman, undecided major, no history classes), who had originally depicted historians as synthesizers, said, "[Historians] check people's background. See where they were coming from. See if they have any previous writings. They have to do a little detective work, I guess." He began to see historians as having to engage in sourcing. Jenny (Senior, Management, one history class), who previously had said that historians' jobs were to look for "very important events that happened and that occurred in chronological order," after instruction said that they "write their own theories or agree with whatever they're reading or not. . . . Just think, and just over time, try to approach an idea that they believe," Leslie (Freshman, Education, no history classes), who previously had said that historians study history so we could avoid mistakes later, said that historians should evaluate the sources of documents (sourcing) because people had different perspectives based upon their backgrounds (contextualization). Cory (Senior, Finance, no history classes) said that historians had to look at a source's past and see whether or not they had done research or had good schooling (sourcing): "What is their schooling and background?"

Six students who had at one time depicted historians as synthesizers or arbiters became more concerned about bias on the part of historians as a result of their instruction. Shelly (Senior, Public Relations, two history classes) said,

Yeah, after reading certain things, I'm not sure they're aware of their biases, but after, like reading, for instance, articles in the Vietnam packet, they make, if you experience the war in a certain way or you interact with certain people and you talk to them and they may form opinions about certain things and they may interpret them, they may, I don't know whether they're aware of it or not, but you know, just like, for regular people, it's natural to form biases.

Bob (Freshman, undecided, no history classes), who originally thought of historians as documenters, said that he had changed his mind as a result of instruction and wondered about his own bias as a historian/reader. He focused on contextualization. That is, he saw that the time period in which a historian or a reader of history lives makes a difference in how one might interpret an event:

> I think history is not so much how we keep from making mistakes now as it is a tool. You need to know how to use it to interpret what is important. You use the knowledge and incorporate it. . . . But the flaw in that is that you may have a different mentality than the author or professor. It depends on the time they lived. Maybe 1990s is way different than 1920s but if I interpret the 1920s in a negative way because of the way we think now, I would be wrong.

Jessie (Senior, Sociology, one history class) originally believed that historians tried to "get rid of bias." After instruction, he believed that historians really tried to portray events as they happen but that "some do it in an unbiased manner and some don't."

Colin (Senior, Accounting, one history class) commiserated with historians, focusing on the context of the historian's life as a biasing element.

> I guess it is a tough task for historians to do. I think historians, even though they try to be as neutral as possible, there's some bias that is there as a human being. I guess you could try, but it's hard. When historians research a topic, that topic interests historians to begin with, and that interest comes from their parents, maybe. They're unaware of it. They may not be directly affected, or he or she may be influenced by it. . . . Not even having good solid reasons, you automatically have some stance. And I guess that influences partially what they research on and the stance they take. I don't think there's 100% neutrality. That's impossible.

Only one of the 13 students maintained essentially the same ideas about the work of historians across the interviews. This individual was Doby (Junior, Management, no history classes). Unlike other students, he never actually became interested in the materials and described himself as the kind of student who "just likes to get through." The rest of the students, however, changed their views. The nine students who originally saw historians as documenters and synthesizers later saw historians as arbiters or biasers. All of the four students who originally saw historians as arbiters later saw that historians had their own biases. Two students explicitly mentioned bias in the original interviews, and that bias had to do with the documents that historians read. Seven students explicitly mentioned bias after instruction (including the two who originally had mentioned it), and in six of those cases, students discussed the biases of the historian as well as the biases inherent in the documents. In all of the other cases, even though biases were not explicitly mentioned, students mentioned that historians had to somehow decide what took place and why after reading about an event from various perspectives. Whereas no students in the first interview mentioned contextualization as a strategy that historians, used, three students later mentioned contextual elements that could cause potential bias. These changes occurred somewhat independently of how we rated their strategy use and the maturity of their epistemology prior to the study.

Theme 2: Students Struggle with Subjectivity / Objectivity and Relativism

In their reading of the conflicting accounts of the Gulf of Tonkin Incident, students began to struggle with issues of credibility. We uncovered these struggles as we began to question their decisions about what happened in the Gulf of Tonkin during the second interview. In 11 of the 13 cases, students wanted to side with the sources with direct experience with Vietnam (Dean Rusk and the military historian, Philip Davidson) rather than the historians. But when we questioned them about why those sources would be more credible, nine students acknowledged that personal experience did not guarantee objectivity and in fact might discourage it. Althea (Senior, Finance, no history classes) said,

> I don't really know that any of them would be more credible than the others. You would think the textbook, but you find errors in them. Textbooks are aimed at states and stuff like that. And Dean Rusk would have to defend his own position. And then the private book. I thought he seemed like he knew what he was talking about. The retired general—now that might be credible too because of his occupation. But he might be biased as well because he is an army guy. Newspapers are like tabloids with the way they cover things. But I'm sure they have to have facts checked out in order to be published.

Colin (Senior, Accounting, one history class) struggled as well:

> I thought the Rusk one was pretty credible because he was there and he had experience with Johnson. All of the others, they didn't really have

actual experience other than the third one—the newspaper article—he may have studied for a long time, but he didn't have first-hand experience.

(Researcher: So being there makes it credible?)

I think so, but you also have to consider potential bias. Because they were involved, they may be dealing with emotions.

Jessie (Senior, Sociology, one history class) summarized the dilemma this way:

> The person who is there with that first-hand experience might be concerned with defending their actions, but they're also in a situation to describe what happened, whereas historians would or should take a more neutral stance, but they wouldn't have the, they couldn't actually portray the in-depth happenings. Except for Porter. He was the only one to divulge the meeting that he (Johnson) had with his staff.

Shelly (Senior, Public Relations, two history classes) thought about it in this way.

> (I take into account) who they are and what role they had and who they know in Vietnam and if they had any involvement because one of them was involved, so you have to take that into consideration. I think experience gives you more of an edge about what's going on. You know it happened if you're there, but I don't know . . . I don't know . . . That gives you a first hand thing. I don't know. . . . People who have involvement, they're going to make themselves or the people who are affiliated with them look, you know, not look as bad, so they're a little sketchy in terms of reading what they put down so I don't know. Historians, they can have biases too. . . .

How did students come to a decision about which texts were more credible? Not easily, and in varying ways. Jessie (Senior, Sociology, one history class) discussed taking into account a combination of the sources and the actual factual evidence in the texts. He said that he made a comparison/contrast chart, looked at all of the relevant facts, and, rather than just go with what the sources said, tried to construct his own interpretation of the events. Five students said they looked for stylistic concerns that signaled bias ("the little things they say") or they looked for evidence of neutrality. Davidson's text was written as a two-sided argument, and two of the students mentioned that it seemed less biased, more "neutral." It seemed evident that they had thought little about issues of subjectivity and objectivity before, and that this unit caused them to feel somewhat lost in relativism. Students used both central and peripheral processing of the texts.

We are not sure that all students would have struggled with the issues had we not engaged them in interviews. Students only entertained the idea that their bias towards experience might be wrong as a result of our asking questions such as, "So, are you saying that being there makes a person credible?" In one instance, we presented the student the following example and asked him to state who was more credible: a witness to an accident or a reporter who talked to several witnesses but who did not see the accident. Thus, we do not believe that the struggle was merely a product of reading the various sources, but also may have been a product of our questioning.

Theme 3: Students Change Their Strategies and Their Ideas about What It Means to Read about Historical Events

As students became engaged in the unit, they commented on two phenomena: (a) they saw themselves as needing to engage in the same strategies that historians used; and (b) they saw themselves as becoming more skeptical about accounts of historical events.

STRATEGY USE. Prior to the history unit, students typically discussed reading material once, and sometimes twice, sometimes with highlighting, for history classes. If their instructors gave study guides they would complete them. No students mentioned doing comparison/contrast charts, and only one mentioned engaging in any deep thinking. They largely saw the task as one of memorization, even though they often described the tests as consisting of higher-level questions. Jenny's (Senior, Management, one history class) account of her strategy use is typical:

> I usually have to read it a couple of times. The first couple of times I'll read it, then I'll go to class and we'll discuss it. I only annotate slightly, but only because a lot of class stuff in the text isn't really necessary and some is. Some I need to scan and some I need to focus on.

After instruction, students reported liking the idea of a comparison/contrast chart. They mentioned using the chart as well as annotating. In addition, they described how they changed their thinking about the materials they were reading. At the first interview, Anna (Sophomore, undecided, two history classes) had said that she "approached reading the world history text like any other text, read the prequestions, read the sections and put the book down." In describing how she approached the history unit, however, she explained:

> I like the way I am thinking as I am reading. I'm reading and analyzing all these things I've read before and comparing them while I'm reading. It's kind of weird, but it's cool. My brain is working overtime and extending its capabilities so that's good. I like things that really make you think, and this subject does just that. There is no real answer, so you have to analyze everything yourself and come up with your own conclusions.

Leslie (Freshman, Education, no history classes) originally said that to read the text in history, she would do, "Nothing but just read it. And he'd give us questions and I'd do those. But I didn't really read it as much as I should have." After the history unit, she said that she would approach history classes by using, "probably flashcards and charts and that sort of thing. And I wouldn't be focusing on dates but what I believe and don't believe and how they coincide with each other. I'd be focusing on what they have in common and what they differ on."

After telling us that she was going to make a chart to compare and contrast the ideas that disagreed and agreed, Althea (Senior, Finance, no history classes) commented that historians "do the same." Anna (Sophomore, undecided, two history classes) also recognized that she was doing the same thing that historians do. "I am reading a lot, analyzing all the data, determining who is more credible and why, and what they truly believe. [Historians do] the same thing I am doing."

Colin (Senior, Accounting, one history class) said he tried to keep an open mind while he read, and to compare and contrast the ideas. So did Cory (Senior, Finance, no history classes) and Bob (Freshman, undecided, no history classes). All but one of the 13 students reported that they would engage in deeper strategy use for similar tasks, and six students identified tasks other than the current history unit where those deeper strategies could be applied. One student, Shelly (Senior, Public Relations, two history classes), for example, was taking an African-American studies class in which she had to compare three biographies. She mentioned that the activity was nearly the same and that she could use the same strategies:

> I may use that chart we had in this class, because, in a way, it's similar to the paper we have to do in this class. . . . Because you're kind of taking the ideas, and also in this class you can make your own judgments about who's better, and so it's similar, in a way. So I'll probably use that towards the end.

STUDENTS CHANGE THEIR IDEAS ABOUT HISTORY. Six students commented on the ways in which the unit had changed their thinking in response to the question, "Tell us your thoughts about the history unit," or as part of the conversation initiated by other questions. Althea (Senior, Finance, no history classes) said:

> Life isn't like school; there usually isn't a textbook that tells you what to think, so learning how to come to conclusions when presented different sides of the same story will be useful. I do like having different points of view to read. I never liked having information spoon fed to me in grade school. It's nice to be able to form my own opinion about something.

Jessie (Senior, Sociology, one history class) commented:

> Viewing this assignment in the context of history in general, it makes you think of things, like about what I use to make a determination. It was informative. It makes you think about things like that. Like during the Gulf War, you didn't hear about a lot of the casualties when the U.S. was doing the bombing showing its military targets and now you have articles on civilian casualties, the portion that hit civilians, so it makes you think more about it.

Leslie (Freshman, Education, no history classes) made a similar comment.

> I thought it was a lot different than when I had history before, and I've never been given multiple things before. In some ways I liked it better but in some ways I didn't because I had to decide for myself. I think of the stuff I've been reading. And I don't believe it as much.

Shelly (Senior, Public Relations, two history classes) thought about it in a different way as well. "I'm learning more that you can form your own interpretations. Because this unit has a lot of different people who think different ways . . . you have to make up your own mind."

A difficult high school history class in which she had been expected to form her own opinion had frustrated Alice (Freshman, undecided, no history classes). About her teacher she now said, "I didn't realize then that he was really doing it right. I can see now what he was trying to do. I understand things better now."

In summary, the students evidenced changes in their beliefs about historians and history. By engaging in the reading of multiple, conflicting documents and understanding that historians engaged in the same kinds of activities, they were impelled, sometimes reluctantly, to take responsibility for making sense of history. As result, they became more engaged, enlisted deeper levels of thinking, and improved their strategic approach to learning.

Discussion

This study was undertaken to consider two explanations for the differences in how students and historians read historical texts: differences in availability of disciplinary knowledge and awareness of appropriate strategies. Results revealed the relevance of knowledge and strategy use to history reading, but more importantly, they suggest a potentially valuable hypothesis about how to effectively stimulate more suggest a potentially valuable hypothesis about how to effectively stimulate more sophisticated history reading routines for students. The students we interviewed appeared to increase their disciplinary knowledge and use more specific strategies as a result of: (a) discussing issues about historians and reading history during interviews; (b) learning about sourcing, contextualization, and corroboration; (c) reading multiple documents;

and (d) engaging in comparison-contrast strategies. These shifts were accompanied by shifts in beliefs about historians (epistemology) and more overt attention to central and peripheral processes. Future experimental studies could explore the dimensions of this hypothesis.

In Table 1, we summarized various theories we used in framing our study. Each of these theories posits particular variables central to history reading. This investigation highlighted the value of these variables, but suggests that they might best be thought of as a network of interrelated features within history reading. During the course of these interviews, the students evidenced clear changes from low knowledge to higher knowledge; from reading for facts to using sourcing, contextualization, and corroboration to make decisions; from dualism to relativism; from seeing texts as separate entities to comparing and contrasting them; and from implicit use of peripheral and surface-level central processing to explicit use of peripheral and deeper levels of central processing. However these improvements were not solely the result of "history teaching" or any kind of specific intervention aimed at improvement in any of these specific variables.

So what was the stimulus for this complex system of improvement? It appears that dialogue aimed at understanding what historians do, how they do it, and what their texts represent helped these students take responsibility for reading at deeper, more critical levels, as historians do. The role of reflection was a central element in this study. As noted, students made their first shifts in disciplinary knowledge not through instruction, but through reflection that had been encouraged by our probing questions. We believe that this kind of reflection helped students integrate the various elements of instruction so that they made more sense and may have encouraged multidimensional movement (i.e., simultaneous improvement in the variables described by the various theories).

The simultaneity of movement across the variables from these diverse theoretical perspectives suggests that the theories are related in fundamental ways. Developmental improvements in disciplinary reading appear to be highly multidimensional, and these dimensions seem to be embedded within the discourse of the discipline—particularly with regard to issues of participation within the social and intellectual aspects of the discipline, including ideas of what it means, for instance, to be a historian, to think like a historian, to grapple with the issues of history. Reflection on and participation in dealing with such issues may lead to more mature beliefs about what it means to learn in history. This understanding of historians' work would influence a student to examine the quality of the historian's preparation, the conditions under which data were gathered and the text written, and agreements and disagreements of the historian's stance with other historians. Strategies that encourage an elaborative, critical reading of text would encourage a shift to commitment within relativism. A critical, deep reading of history to decide what to believe would mean that the student would not only gain a deeper understanding of history but would also be likely to alter her beliefs or strategies for learning. She would rely on the strategies of contextualization, sourcing, and corboration that match her beliefs about history and help her gain her own perspective of the big picture. The theories would act in concert to explain an individual's approach and process in making sense from text.

Conclusion

This study, because of its qualitative nature and the small group of participants, cannot be generalized. Moreover, since our participants were college students, the responses that they made to our request that they consider the discipline of history might not be made by younger, less epistemologically mature high school students. Further, these students cannot be compared to students experiencing reading or severe achievement difficulties. Finally, because our data relied on self-report, students may have attempted to provide the responses they believed we wanted to hear. Although we were careful to not to prompt students toward a particular stance, as with any self-report data, this limitation must be considered.

Despite these limitations, this study is encouraging to teachers who are concerned with students' critical thinking and strategy use applied to subject matter material. Our findings suggest that students' reflections about what it means to engage in discipline-specific activities and their subsequent engagement in those activities can bring about epistemological and strategic development. Students used sophisticated strategies, thought deeply about issues such as subjectivism versus objectivism, and wrestled with the responsibility of making their own sense. We surmise that reflection coupled with authentic activity was the key to this development.

In the future, the impact of materials and activities such as these should be studied with high school students and with students of different achievement levels. In addition, we should experimentally test the notion that students who engage in these activities will perform in a more sophisticated manner on tests that measure their knowledge and thinking than students who do not employ such activities. We are interested in the role of reflection in fostering epistemological shifts, as well, and think that its causative nature should be tested under controlled conditions.

References

Afflerbach, P., & VanSledright, B. (1998, December). *The challenge of understanding the past: How do fifth grade readers construct meaning from diverse history texts?* Paper presented at the annual meeting of the National Reading Conference, Austin, TX.

Berkin, C., Miller, C., Cherny, R. W., & Gormly, J. (1990). *Making America: A history of the United States*. Boston: Houghton Mifflin.

Britt, M. A., Rouet, J. F., & Perfetti, C. A. (1996). Using hypertext to study and reason about historical evidence. In J. F. Rouet, J. F. Rouet, J. T. Levonen, A. Dillon, & R. Spiro (Eds.) *Hypertext and cognition* (pp. 43–72). Mahwah, NJ: Erlbaum.

Chaiken, S. (1980). Heuristic versus systematic information processing and the use of source versus message cues in persuasion. *Journal of Personality and Social Psychology, 39,* 752–766.

Chaiken, S. (1987). The heuristic model of persuasion. In M. P. Zanna, J. J. Olson, & C. P. Herman (Eds.), *Social influence: The Ontario symposium* (Vol. 5, pp. 3–39). Hillsdale, NJ: Erlbaum.

Davidson, P. (1990). *Secrets of the Vietnam War*. Novato, CA: Presidio.

Denzin, N. K., & Lincoln, Y. S. (Eds.) (2000). *Handbook of qualitative research* (2nd ed.). Thousand Oaks, CA: Sage.

Glaser, B. G., & Strauss, A. L. (1967). *The discovery of grounded theory*. Chicago: Aldine.

Hartmann, D. K. (1995). Eight readers reading: The intertextual links of proficient readers reading multiple passages. *Reading Research Quarterly, 30,* 520–560.

Hynd, C. (2001). Refutational texts and the change process. *International Journal of Educational Research, 35,* 699–714.

Hynd, C. (2003). Conceptual change in response to persuasive messages. In P. Pintrich & G. Sinatra (Eds.), *Intentional conceptual change* (pp. 157–169). Mahwah, NJ: Erlbaum.

Kvale, S. (1996). *Interviews: An introduction to qualitative research interviewing*. Thousand Oaks, CA: Sage.

McNamara, R. S. (1995). *In retrospect: The tragedy and lessons of Vietnam*. New York: Random House.

Merriam, S. B. (1998). *Qualitative research and case study applications in education*. San Francisco: Jossey-Bass.

Perfetti, C. A., Britt, M. A., & Georgi, M. C.(1995). *Text-based learning and reasoning: Studies in history*. Hillsdale, NJ: Erlbaum.

Perry, W. T., Jr. (1968). *Patterns of development in thought and values of students in a liberal arts college: A validation of a scheme* (ERIC Document Reproduction Service No. ED024315). Cambridge, MA: Harvard University Press.

Perry, W. T., Jr. (1970). *Forms of intellectual and ethical development in the college years: A scheme*. New York: Holt, Rinehart and Winston.

Petty, R. E., & Cacioppo, J. T. (1986). *Communication and persuasion: Central and peripheral routes to attitude change*. New York: Springer-Verlag.

Public Broadcasting System (1998). *LBJ: The American experience*. PBS Home Video. http://www.pbs.org.

Rowe, D. W. 1987. Literacy learning as an intertextual process. In J. E. Readence & R. S. Baldwin (Eds.), *Research in literacy: Merging perspectives: Thirty-sixth yearbook of the National Reading Conference* (pp. 101–102). Rochester, NY: National Reading Conference.

Rusk, D. (1991). *As I saw it*. Penguin.

Simon, B. (1999). Self defense for your mind. *Georgia Magazine, 78,* 35–40.

Sinatra, G., & Dole, J. (1998). Case studies in conceptual change: A social psychological perspective. In B. Guzzetti & C. Hynd (Eds.), *Perspectives on conceptual change: Multiple ways to understand knowing and learning in a complex world* (pp. 52–71). Mahwah, NJ: Erlbaum.

Stahl, S., Hynd, C., Britton, B., McNish, M., & Bosquet, D. (1996). What happens when students read multiple source documents in history? *Reading Research Quarterly, 31,* 430–457.

Wineburg, S. S. (1991). On the reading of historical texts: Notes on the breach between school and academy. *American Educational Research Journal, 28,* 495–519.

Worton, M., & Still, J. (1990). *Intertextuality: Theories and practices.* Manchester, England: Manchester University Press.

Appendix A

Background Text

The Tonkin Gulf Incident

The Tonkin Gulf Incident is actually a reference to two separate events that took place on August 2 and 4, 1964. On August 2, three North Vietnamese PT boats fired shots toward the *U.S.S. Maddox* while the *Maddox* was on patrol off the North Vietnamese coastline in the Gulf of Tonkin. Two days later, while the *Maddox* and a companion ship, the *C. Turner Joy*, were again on patrol, there were reports of another attack. President Johnson ordered a retaliatory strike and asked Congress to pass the Southeast Asia Resolution (also known as the Tonkin Gulf Resolution) to give him the authority to "take all necessary steps, including the use of armed force, to assist any member or protocol state of the Southeast Asia Collective Defense Treaty requesting assistance in defense of its freedom." This resolution was passed. Johnson used this approval to commit the U.S. to heavy involvement in the Vietnam War. "Hawks" (those who were supporters of the war) and "Doves" (those who were against the war) disagreed about what actually happened and about President Johnson's motivations in handling the incident. The disagreement still exists.

Appendix B

Questionnaires

Pre-Instruction Questions:

1. What do you plan to do after graduation?

2. How often do you use the Internet to access the World Wide Web?
   Often — several times a week or more
   Occasionally — several times a month
   Rarely — several times per year
   Never.

3. Describe how you use the World Wide Web (if applicable)? Circle your answer to the following questions.

4. Which viewpoint best describes your belief?

   a. We should be involved in other countries to help their people drive back aggression.

   b. We should generally avoid involvement in other countries' affairs.

   c. We should get involved in other countries only if U.S. interests are involved.

5. How would you rate your knowledge of the Vietnam Conflict?

   a. High, I have studied about the war and am familiar with many of the facts.

   b. Somewhat high, I have studied about the war.

   c. Moderate, I know a little about the war.

   d. Low, I have heard about the war.

   e. Very low, I know nothing about the war.

6. Tell what you know about the Vietnam Conflict.

7. How would you rate your knowledge of the Tonkin Gulf Incident of the Vietnam Conflict?

   a. High, I have studied about the incident and am familiar with many of the facts.

   b. Somewhat high, I have studied about the incident.

   c. Moderate, I know a little about the incident.

   d. Low, I have heard of the incident.

   e. Very low, I know nothing about the Incident.

8. Tell what you know about the Tonkin Gulf Incident.

9. Name the history classes you have taken in college and your grade in each class.

10. What strategies did you use to help you learn the material in history and to prepare yourself for tests?

11. Rate your <u>expertise</u> in history. Circle one.
    Low   **Medium**   **High**
    1   2   3   4   5   6
    Explain:

12. Rate your <u>interest</u> in history. Circle one.
    Low   **Medium**   **High**
    1   2   3   4   5   6

    Explain:

13. Rate the <u>usefulness</u> of studying history. Circle one.
    Low   **Medium**   **High**
    1   2   3   4   5   6

    Explain:

14. Is it important to study history? If so, why? If not, why not?

15. Which activities do you think historians find important?

    Not at all   Very Important   Important
    a. Uncovering and describing the facts of history
       1   2   3   4   5   6
    b. Using historical evidence to interpret history
       1   2   3   4   5   6
    c. Promoting social or political actions on the basis of history
       1   2   3   4   5   6
    d. Providing informed perspectives about current events
       1   2   3   4   5   6
    e. Explaining what really happened
       1   2   3   4   5   6
    Explain:

Scenario (Students read a scenario of a student who faced multiple sources of information and would have to write an essay on what he believed)

16. Whose responsibility is it that Pat understand what strategies to use to learn? Pat's? The Professor's? Explain.

17. Whose responsibility is it that Pat makes sense of what he reads? Pat's? The Professor's? Explain.

18. What should Pat focus on while reading?

19. What strategies should Pat use while reading?

20. How should Pat study for the essay exam?

21. How will Pat decide which claims to believe?

Post-Instruction Questions (only the question that is different is reported here. Other questions were the same as the pre-questionnaire)

22. What strategies do you think you would use if you enrolled in a history class at this university in which you engaged in similar tasks

as in the history unit for part of the class? (Assume essay answers to higher level questions and several books to read and apply to material in the textbook for the rest of the class).

Why?

Appendix C

Instruction in Corroboration, Contextualization, and Sourcing

Unlike historians, many students read history books as if they contained the one true account of events and their meaning. In short, students don't think at all like historians who approach history like detectives piecing together what really happened and why it happened. Historians read the texts that historians write, not as "truth," but as interpretations or arguments, just as they do the sources of evidence they use to create history, such as personal accounts, newspaper editorials, or military reports. They make judgments about the worthiness of texts.

It is not that hard for students to begin to read like a historian once they understand some basic things that historians do when they read. These strategies are: (1) Sourcing, (2) Context, (3) Corroboration.

Sourcing

When evaluating sources, consider the following:

(1) **Experience 1.** If a source is working for the President, the State Department, or the military at the time of a historical event, then he may have first-hand experience of that event. However, he may also need to justify an "official" point of view, and may not be objective in his assessment of the event. The benefit of experience needs to be weighed against the possibility of non-objectivity.

(2) **Experience 2.** People who are historical scholars develop their scholarship through research which includes the gathering of evidence to support their claims. It is important to look at the kind of evidence that has been gathered to determine the scholars' perspective. Have they looked at a broad range of evidence (military, political, social) or a narrow range?

(3) **Books.** A privately published book may have less credibility than one published by a known publisher. The book that has been published by a known publisher has had to survive a review process. Privately published books may be excellent works of scholarship but have not been judged by the authors' peers as being so.

(4) **Newspapers.** A newspaper such as the *New York Times* and the *Washington Post* pride themselves on the quality of their editorials and their in-depth reporting. Thus, a newspaper editorial from one

of these papers is not necessarily unscholarly just because it is in a newspaper. To determine the scholarship of the author of an editorial, you need to look at the author's qualifications and the arguments themselves.

Context

Pay Attention to the Context (Contextualizing): Historians note the time frame in which the text was written, the audience for whom the text was intended, the political and social events that may have been occurring while the text was being written, the type of writing that was used, and so forth. Thinking about the context of the writing can help determine an author's viewpoint and intentions and the reasons for certain interpretations as opposed to others.

Corroboration (Agreement / Disagreement)

Historians determine the likelihood of an event or an interpretation by noting the level of agreement that various authors may have. That is, they are more likely to believe an interpretation of history that is shared by a number of people than one that is not generally mentioned or that is discounted by others. The texts you are reading now agree or disagree on the following points:

- Whether the United States was provoked into a retaliatory attack on the North Vietnamese on August 4–5, 1964.

- If the crew on the U.S. warships were certain of an actual attack by the North Vietnamese when Lyndon B. Johnson ordered the retaliation.

- If President Johnson ordered the attack based more on his wish to show force and to intimidate North Vietnam into ceasing their support for the war in the South than on his belief that an actual attack had occurred.

- If the U.S. warships provoked North Vietnam to attack by breaking agreements with them.

When texts disagree, that disagreement tells us that authors are interpreting history in different ways. They may have paid attention to different sources, looked at history from different perspectives (a political versus a military perspective, for example), or operated from conscious or unconscious biases. Noticing the differences across texts can help readers develop a deeper understanding of historical events and the range of interpretations that might accompany them. When readers analyze the sources of evidence and the perspectives that are taken, they are more capable of making informed decisions about which interpretations to support.

Note Launchers: Promoting Active Reading of Mathematics Textbooks

Josh W. Helms and Kimberly Turner Helms

Josh W. Helms and Kimberly Turner Helms present an active reading strategy—note launchers—that was developed specifically for reading in mathematics texts. The authors also explain a classroom study undertaken to investigate student response to the use of the strategy. They found that students mostly reported that note launchers assisted them in reading their mathematics texts carefully and in preparing for class assignments.

In the past several decades, the teaching of mathematics has been influenced by the constructivist philosophy in which students are challenged to "learn to think mathematically" (Schoenfeld, 2006, p. 334). Part of the process of learning to think mathematically is being able to read mathematically, "to take the global meaning from the page, not just to be able to read a few sentences" and to recognize that "the reading of a mathematics text is far more complex than simply being able to read the words on the page. It is about comprehending the mathematical idea being put forward" (Noonan, 1990, p. 79). For college students studying mathematics, a source of difficulty is often mathematical language and notation, manifested in students' inability to restate definitions and concepts in their own words (Moore, 1994). Indeed, the densely-packed technical material within mathematics textbooks may be prohibitive for students who are not quantitatively literate. Incoming college students' customary passive reading strategies such as memorizing, reading, and "looking over" (Simpson & Nist, 1990) undercut their abilities to understand the discussions that are to follow in the classroom. Failure to grasp even the first few lessons has serious implications for success throughout the course.

Becoming active readers may help students make their way through this potential mathematical fog. Note launchers, an instructor-designed reading guide, model how to select, decide, and focus upon what textbook material is important to learn. Reading guides are specially-designed study aids that can steer students through difficult parts of assigned readings (Bean, 1996) while encouraging advance preparation. Part of a broader group of pedagogical content tools (Rasmussen & Marrongelle, 2006) or advanced organizers (Ausubel, 1960), reading guides facilitate students' abilities to make sense of complex material.

The idea of using reading guides as a textbook reading strategy is not new. Five decades ago, Ausubel (1960) noted that advanced organizers can help students comprehend and retain mathematical content better compared to standard pedagogical methods like memorizing formulas and procedures, which merely serve to enforce rote learning. Clements and Wright (1983) later recognized the effectiveness of "guided reading" in their mathematics courses, acknowledging that while textbooks include valuable mathematics information, the ability to learn mathematics from a printed page is quite difficult. Like "partial" notes provided to students during lectures that can increase recall and higher order learning (Armbruster, 2000), reading guides bridge the time between when students read and when they are accountable for that reading during subsequent class meetings.

Study Rationale

The purpose of this classroom research project was to create reading guides to engage students in critical and active reading of mathematics textbooks and to analyze how students used this tool. After observing that students were intimidated by Greek letters, mathematics notations, and equations placed within paragraph structure, the instructor in the present study took a proactive approach to help students change their reading strategies. Named *note launchers* in an effort to engage users, these reading guides introduced students to concepts in the chapter and provided a template of how students could approach new material and make sense of it themselves. This type of active learning prompted students to interact with printed text and selectively identify and record the key elements of what was just read, such as key words, phrases, definitions, and formulas.

Method

During the fall semester of the 2008 academic year, the instructor conducted this project with 50 students enrolled in three sections of Mathematical Modeling and Introduction to Calculus, generally the first mathematics course for students at this four-year postsecondary institution. The note launcher for each lesson required about an hour of the instructor's time to create; over the course of the semester, the instructor created 45 note launchers. The instructor distributed note launchers on each topic at least one class meeting ahead; note launchers were also available on the course website. Note launchers corresponded to approximately 10 pages of reading material.

While note launchers at the beginning of the course were quite prescriptive and formulaic, later in the semester, note launchers included more open-ended prompts for students to write concepts in their own words, rather than simply render a list of fill-in-the-blank definitions. Early in the semester, Stage 1 of note launchers included fill-in-the blank quotes from the textbook to help students learn to identify the definitions, rules, and assumptions that support the lesson objectives. For example, a note launcher prompt for the function properties lesson specified to students: *The two parameters for a linear function are: m = _____ or rate of _____ and b = y − _____* . About halfway through the semester, Stage 2 of note launchers evolved into prompts that still helped identify the key concepts, but put more of the note-taking responsibility on the student. In the linear polynomial lesson sequenced halfway through the course, for example, one note launcher prompt asked students: *How does the exponential function differ from the power function? (Hint: Where is the independent variable?)* to guide them to the best answer. For the last month of the semester, Stage 3 of note launchers only included the lesson objectives, placing the entire responsibility on the student to actively read and summarize key concepts based upon those objectives. The instructor intended that this "evolution" of note launcher format would develop the students' note-taking skills and build confidence in their ability to comprehend a mathematics textbook over time. Note launchers comprised a portion of students' participation grade; however, in terms of the overall course grade, note launchers were worth a minimal percentage so that students who chose not to complete them would not be unduly penalized.

In order to assess the effectiveness of note launchers, the instructor evaluated each student's notebook and note launcher completion rate. At each note launcher evolutionary stage, the instructor evaluated course notebooks in an effort to assess the growth of the students' note-taking skills. As the difficulty in completing note launchers increased, the point value doubled. Additionally, to assess their perspectives of note-taking using note launchers, students completed anonymous mid-course and end-of-course surveys.

Results

As note launchers evolved throughout the semester, the instructor assessed the students' note launcher completion rates. Table 1 summarizes the results of note launcher completion statistics for each stage.

The first question on the mid-and end-of-course survey asked students to rate the statement, "Completing note launchers helped me understand the lesson objectives" on a 5-point Likert scale. Figure 1

Table 1 Note Launcher Completion Rate as a Function of Stage

	Stage 1	Stage 2	Stage 3
Median	72%	83%	63%
Mean	66%	66%	60%
Standard Deviation	23%	33%	29%

Figure 1. Student responses to "Completing the Note Launchers helped me understand lesson objectives."

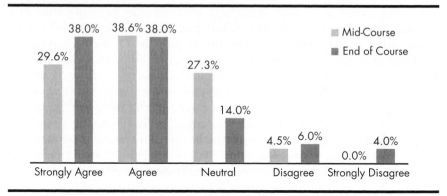

displays the students' responses, showing that more than 75% of the students ultimately felt that note launchers helped them understand the lesson objectives. There was little change in the students' responses from the mid-course survey to the end-of-course survey. An equal number of students from the neutral category changed their mind to favorable and dissenting opinions.

Students often perceive something as beneficial if it helps them get a better grade, so the next question asked students to rate the statement, "Completing note launchers helped me prepare for graded events" on a 5-point Likert scale. As seen in Figure 2, approximately the same percentage of students were favorable, neutral, or dissenting towards this statement during the mid-course survey as were during the end-of-course survey.

Figure 2. Student responses to "Completing the Note Launchers helped in preparation for graded events."

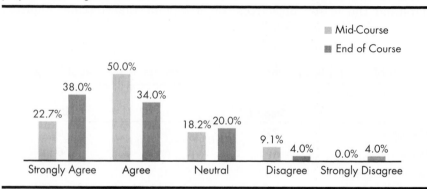

Figure 3. Student responses to "I appreciate the effort I put into Note Launchers."

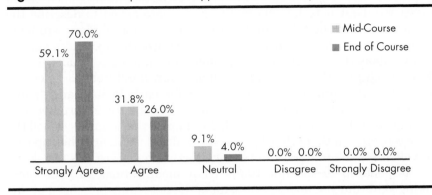

Similarly, the next question asked students to rate the statement, "I appreciate the effort I put into preparing the note launchers" on a 5-point Likert scale. Figure 3 shows evidence that the students appreciated whatever level of effort they put into note launchers.

Ideally, better note-taking skills in one course are transferrable to other courses. As seen in Figure 4, at the end of the semester, after seeing the benefits of how taking notes on reading assignments can assist in learning lesson objectives, more than 75% of the students said that note launchers encouraged note-taking in other classes.

Lastly, students were asked if the instructor should continue offering note launchers as part of course assignments. Figure 5 shows that more than 80% of the students agreed that note launchers should continue being offered.

Figure 4. Student responses to "Note Launchers encouraged note-taking in other classes."

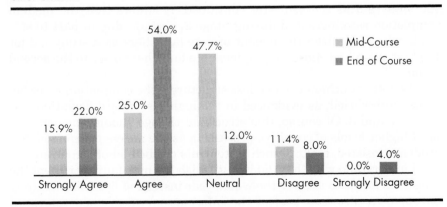

On the end-of-course survey, students could also answer open-ended questions about note launchers. Students were asked to describe the impact note launchers had on their course experience. Many students appreciated note launchers as a tool to recognize the textbook's signals for key ideas that the instructor planned to emphasize. Students said things such as, "Most importantly, [note launchers] help me pick out what the most important concepts are for each lesson" and "[Note launchers] provided guidance for what specifics the instructor was looking for us to know for class each day. I knew that if I understood the basic concepts on them that I was going to do all right, and the opposite as well, if I didn't understand I knew exactly what questions to ask."

Responding to the question, "What modifications to your note-taking skills did you make as a result of the note launchers used in this course?" students alluded to efficiency as a skill inherent in this method. For example, one student said, "I learned to sort through what was most relevant and important rather than take down everything and remember nothing." Similarly, another said, "The note launchers helped me focus on the important details of the material being covered. Otherwise I would proably [sic] be prone to take pages and pages of notes."

Discussion

The intent of the study was to encourage students who were intimidated by mathematical textbooks to engage actively with the material. As seen in Table 1, the mean note launcher completion rate was always lower than the median completion rate; moreover, there was little difference in the mean completion rate among the three stages. The authors posit that the median completion rate was a more representative descriptive statistic because it mitigated outliers, whereas the mean completion rate was negatively skewed by students who never completed note launchers and therefore was less reflective of students who did not complete some of the early note launchers, but elected to utilize the study aid as the semester continued. It follows that the median completion rate increased during Stage 2, perhaps due in part to students who recognized the benefit of note launchers as a study aid for the first exam and chose to complete note launchers prior to the second exam.

As note launchers became less structured, the completion rates became more varied, as evidenced in the higher standard deviations for Stages 2 and 3. Of course, this structural change should have encouraged higher levels of cognitive processing as the course progressed, but students resisted, making such statements on the end-of-course survey as, "I understand why they did it, but I wish the note launchers kept the questions for us to answer the whole year instead of becoming entirely on our own disection [sic] of the information we deemed relevant."

Moreover, these results show that the completion rate dropped off drastically when note launchers only included lesson objectives in Stage 3, although the results for Stage 3 might not be very accurate, as the instructor only evaluated note launcher completion and did not review other papers in the notebooks. Because note launchers did not include much information in Stage 3, students may have preferred to take notes on other papers or in the textbook. Nevertheless, as first- and second-year students are generally not independent, self-regulatory learners (Cukras, 2006), it is not surprising that they prefer more structure, and likely benefit more from Stage 1 and Stage 2 type note launchers. As such, the instructor has since developed note launchers for all lessons that include fill-in-the blank type questions as well as open-ended prompts, to meet students at their learning levels.

After 16 weeks, students felt more strongly about whether or not note launchers helped them understand lesson objectives and helped in preparation for graded events than they did at the mid-course point. On the end-of-course survey, more students strongly agreed or strongly disagreed that note launchers were useful. The group of students who strongly disagreed may not have given much effort and were satisfied with little effort, perceiving note launchers as not useful. This finding is supported by the evidence in Figure 3, in which a majority of the students in the end-of-course survey appreciated their own efforts put into note launchers; the actual quality and quantity of time is not a variable, only the students' perceptions of their efforts. Still, the students' agreement as to whether or not the instructor should continue offering note launchers (Figure 5) shows a substantial number of students perceived note launchers as useful.

Figure 5. Student responses to "The instructor should continue offering Note Launchers."

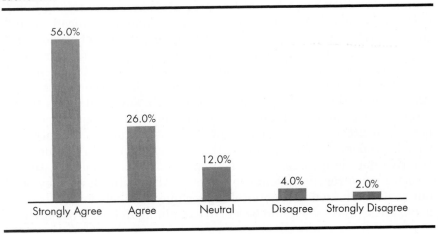

The most impressive student responses were to the statement, "The benefits gained from completing note launchers encourage me to take notes in other courses," rated on a 5-point Likert scale. While the scope of other course notes was not a variable in this study, 76% of the students agreed or strongly agreed that note launchers had indeed encouraged note-taking in other classes. Such skill transfer suggests that note launchers were an example of a teachable self-regulatory learning aid, something that students could practice in one discipline and then apply on their own in other academic situations. This finding was well worth the effort and time the instructor devoted to developing note launchers and grading course notebooks.

This research supports the instructor's intent to make mathematics texts more accessible, and as a result, the instructor has continued using note launchers in subsequent courses and has discovered that the time to create or update note launchers lessens with each iteration. Remarkably, students have written, unprompted, on the usefulness of note launchers in the overall course survey; one student commented that the "note launcher is also a very good thing, with . . . fill in the blanks for notes" and another noted that note launchers "were very valuable in WPRs and Writs" [institution-specific terminology for tests]. Observed another student, "I really liked the course note launchers that my class had because it helped me figure out what was important from the lesson and I learned more from that than I would have from simply taking notes on the readings." One student had the valuable suggestion to make note launchers available online to students in other sections of the course as well.

There were limitations to this study. First, to prevent fear of retribution, the surveys had to be anonymous; therefore, the instructor could not correlate note launchers with survey results, note launchers with final grades, or survey results with final grades. The authors recommend a research study that would allow for such correlations, the findings of which could be used to promote active note-taking habits early in the semester. Second, the instructor could not dedicate enough time to formative assessment, given the other amounts of graded work in the course and institutional requirements. The instructor would have preferred to evaluate note launchers with more detailed individual feedback, but frequently settled for a few brief comments and a general discussion of observations to the class. Third, although the instructor gave minimal grade weight to complete the assignment, he perhaps overestimated students' intrinsic motivation, as the incentive was disproportionate to the effort that students spent to produce substantive note launchers. Last, to supplement note launchers, the instructor encouraged students to annotate the textbook as they read, but never evaluated that note-taking technique. Likely mutually beneficial, these processes would be worth examining in future research.

In future applications of note launchers, the authors suggest instructors have a solid understanding of their students' cognitive stages, so as to provide the appropriate amount of challenge within the assignment. Note launchers should have just enough structure to engage students in active reading without appearing burdensome to students, or too elementary for learning to begin. Additionally, when introducing the concept, making available an exemplary completed note launcher would demonstrate what right looks like. Finally, to aid the unconvinced, instructors can share written comments from pleased former students about the value of note launchers.

As an example of a reading guide, note launchers can be a useful technique for facilitating mathematics textbook comprehension and getting students to read carefully and critically. In this study, although students sometimes grumbled about the amount of extra effort *at the outset*, many of them eventually recognized that note launchers make them more efficient studiers. At the very minimum, note launchers compel students to stay active during the reading process. Moreover, they provide students a framework for the kind of information—objectives, fundamental concepts, vocabulary, examples—they should seek in their textbooks, a skill that students can transfer to reading assignments in other courses.

References

Armbruster, B.B. (2000). Taking notes from lectures. In R.A. Flippo & D.C. Caverly (Eds.), *Handbook of college Reading and study strategy Research* (pp. 175–199). Mahwah, NJ: Erlbaum.

Ausubel, D.P. (1960). The use of advance organizers in the learning and retention of meaningful verbal material. *Journal of Educational Psychology, 51*, 267–272.

Bean, J. C. (1996). *Engaging ideas*. San Francisco, CA: Jossey-Bass.

Clements, R. A., & Wright, J.R. (1983). The use of guided reading in an engineering mathematics degree course. *International Journal of Mathematics Education in Science and Technology, 14*(1), 95–99.

Cukras, G. G. (2006). The investigation of study strategies that maximize learning for underprepared students. *College Teaching, 54*(1), 194–197.

Moore, R. C. (1994). Making the transition to formal proof. *Educational Studies in Mathematics, 27*, 249–266.

Noonan, J. (1990). Readability problems presented by mathematics text. *Early Child Development and Care, 54*, 57–81.

Rasmussen, C., & Marrongelle, K. (2006). Pedagogical content tools: Integrating student reasoning and mathematics in instruction. *Journal for Research in Mathematics Education, 37*, 388–420.

Schoenfeld, A. H. (2006). Learning to think mathematically: Problem solving, metacognition, and sense making in mathematics. In D.A. Grouws (Ed.), *Handbook of Research on Mathematics Teaching and Learning* (pp. 334–370). New York, NY: Macmillan.

Simpson, M. L., & Nist, S. L. (1990). Textbook annotation: An effective and efficient study strategy for college students. *Journal of Reading, 34,* 122–129.

Note: The views expressed in this article are those of the authors and do not necessarily reflect the official policy or position of the U.S. Army, the United States Military Academy, the Department of the Army, the Department of Defense, or the U.S. government.

6

Instruction: From Vocabulary to Comprehension

Introduction

In the long run it all comes down to the teacher and the instruction. Educational researchers and reading specialists have known this for so many years, but never before has it been more important. In this chapter we share five articles that offer different vantage points on instruction in the college reading classroom. We admit that we cannot do justice to such a topic in one chapter; hence, we remind all postsecondary reading specialists that we must always be attuned to the current scholarship that takes theory and research to best practice.

The chapter begins with a landmark article by one of the most important figures in reading pedagogy for the latter twentieth century, Steven A. Stahl. Stahl provides a historical framework for vocabulary instruction that considers the levels of processing necessary to master a word from both the definitional and the contextual perspectives. In addition, he clearly demonstrates the power of teaching our students generative strategies of vocabulary development.

The next article by Donna Willingham and Debra Price examines recent theoretical frameworks and research perspectives for vocabulary instruction with college developmental reading students. The authors also present successful strategies to integrate vocabulary instruction into college developmental reading classes.

In the article that follows, Marty Frailey, Greta Buck-Rodriguez, and Patricia Anders extend Nancy Atwell's groundbreaking work with literary letters for building elaboration competencies to the developmental reading classroom. Atwell's research focused on a literature-based component designed to improve both comprehension and attitude toward reading.

Dolores Perin next presents an extensive literature review on contextualization that aims to incorporate authentic content from courses across the disciplines into purposeful practice in developmental education courses. Perin describes two forms this instruction can take—contextualized and integrated—and explains the theoretical basis for these instructional approaches. The six practical recommendations at the close of this article offer direction that will be of interest to reading professionals considering the implementation of such an approach.

Finally, Eric J. Paulson proposes that if providing students with a foundation for lifelong reading is a goal for college developmental reading instruction, then courses must focus on encouraging and instilling in students the belief that reading has intrinsic value. It is through such an approach that reading competencies and academic growth can also be fostered.

Additional Readings

Conley, M. W., & Wise, A. (2011). Comprehension for what? Preparing students for their meaningful futures. *Theory into Practice, 50,* 93–99.

Elder, L., & Paul, R. (2003). Critical thinking . . . and the art of close reading, part I. *Journal of Developmental Education, 27*(2), 36–39.

Elder, L., & Paul, R. (2004). Critical thinking . . . and the art of close reading, part II. *Journal of Developmental Education, 27*(3), 36–37.

Elder, L., & Paul, R. (2004). Critical thinking . . . and the art of close reading, part III. *Journal of Developmental Education, 28*(1), 36–37.

Elder, L., & Paul, R. (2004). Critical thinking . . . and the art of close reading, part IV. *Journal of Developmental Education, 28*(2), 36–37.

Francis, M. A., & Simpson, M. L. (2003). Using theory, our intuitions, and a research student to enhance our students' vocabulary knowledge. *Journal of Adolescent and Adult Literacy, 47,* 66–78.

Francis, M. A., & Simpson, M. L. (2009). Vocabulary development. In R. F. Flippo & D. C. Caverly (Eds.), *Handbook of college reading and study strategy research* (2nd ed., pp. 97–120). New York, NY: Routledge.

Harri-Augstein, S., Smith, M., & Thomas, L. (1982). *Reading to learn.* London: Methuen.

Holschuh, J. P., & Aultman, L. P. (2009). Comprehension development. In R. F. Flippo & D. C. Caverly (Eds.), *Handbook of college reading and study strategy research* (2nd ed., pp. 121–144). New York, NY: Routledge.

Hsu, H., & Wang, S. (2011). The impact of using blogs on college students' reading comprehension and learning motivation. *Literacy Research and Instruction, 50,* 68–88.

Jackson, J. A. (2009). Reading/writing connection. In R. F. Flippo & D. C. Caverly (Eds.), *Handbook of college reading and study strategy research* (2nd ed. pp. 145–173). New York, NY: Routledge.

McGrath, J., & Hamer, A. (2007). Facilitating strategy transfer in college reading courses. *NADE Digest, 3*(1), 11–16.

Poole, A. (2008–2009). The relationship of reading proficiency to online strategy use: A study of U.S. college students. *Journal of College Literacy and Learning, 35,* 3–11.

Simpson, M. L., Stahl, N. A., & Francis, M. A. (2004). Reading and learning strategies: Recommendations for the 21st century. *Journal of Developmental Education*, *28*(2), 2–15, 32.
Stahl, S. A. (1999). *Vocabulary development*. Cambridge, MA: Brookline Press.
Wolf, A. A. (2005). Using discussion groups and engagement strategies to support reading comprehension. *NADE Digest, 1*(1), 27–31.

Historically Significant Work

To Teach a Word Well: A Framework for Vocabulary Instruction

Steven A. Stahl

*The late Steven A. Stahl offers literacy educators a cognitive processing
framework for vocabulary instruction that has stood the test of time. In his
seminal work, "To Teach a Word Well," Stahl theorizes that effective instruction will lead students to develop both definitional and contextual
knowledge of each word. In addition, he argues that students need to undertake deeper levels of processing to fully master a word. Corresponding
assessment and instructional recommendations are provided as well.*

D oes vocabulary instruction directly improve reading comprehension skill? Some researchers have found that it does (Kameenui,
Carnine, & Freschi, 1982; Stahl, 1982, 1983), while others were unable
to find such an effect (Ahlfors, 1978; Jackson & Dizney, 1963; Jenkins,
Pany, & Schreck, 1978; Tuinman & Brady, 1974).

Reviewing these studies, Stahl (1982) suggested that two factors
influence whether a vocabulary teaching program has an effect on comprehension. First, enough words must be taught. When small percentages of words appearing in passages were pretaught, researchers were
unable to find an effect on comprehension. When larger percentages of
passage words were taught, students given vocabulary instruction
showed significantly higher comprehension than those not given such
instruction. This could be because students can tolerate not knowing
some words in a passage and still comprehend the major ideas (Goodman, 1976). When this percentage gets too high, comprehension breaks
down (Freebody & Anderson, 1983). Second, the words must be learned
well, or students must know the words thoroughly and be able to get
the meanings automatically during reading. The purpose of this paper
is to discuss a framework, grounded in research in cognitive psychology, psycholinguistics, and other disciplines concerned with the meanings of words, which can be used to interpret the results of past research
and to design more effective vocabulary instruction.

Effective Vocabulary Instruction

Definitional and Contextual Information

The first aspect of this framework concerns the type of information a vocabulary teaching method provides about the words it teaches. Some programs expose students only to synonyms, others to full definitions, and others to words used in sentences. What types of information would a program have to provide to give a student a *full* sense of a word's meaning? A review of research indicates that a person who knows a word has two types of information about that word, definitional knowledge and contextual knowledge (Stahl, 1983).

Definitional knowledge can be defined as the knowledge of the relations (synonymic, superordinate, subordinate, etc.) between a word and other known words, as in a dictionary definition. This type of knowledge has been formally represented in network models of semantic memory (e.g., Collins & Loftus, 1975; Glass & Holyoak, 1975) and tested in that form. (See Figure 1 for an example of such a semantic network). In a network model, when a word is understood, activation spreads along the links between concepts, so that not only the node representing the word is activated but also nodes representing related words. Therefore, in this model, a word is understood totally by its relations to other words.

A complete review of research on semantic networks is beyond the scope of this paper (see Lachman, Lachman, & Butterfield, 1979; Smith & Medin, 1981, for such reviews). Some researchers have found support for this model, and thus for the necessity of the definitional view of word meaning (e.g., Meyer & Schvaneveldt, 1975). Others have found that network models do not describe all of our knowledge about the meanings of words. Most damaging to the network view are the findings that one does not ordinarily decompose a word into its definitional parts while understanding a word in context (Fodor, Garrett, Walker, & Parkes, 1980; Kintsch, 1974; Thorndyke, 1975). Another type of knowledge—contextual knowledge—seems to be necessary to fully account for word meaning.

Contextual knowledge can be defined as knowledge of a core concept and how that concept is realized in different contexts. The different types of knowledge can be demonstrated with the verb *smoke*. To smoke is to draw the smoke of tobacco, etc. into the mouth, and often lungs, and blow it out again. This would be an example of definitional knowledge of the concept. However, the word means slightly different things in different sentences, such as:

1. The man smoked the cigarette.

2. The psychologist smoked his pipe.

3. The hippie smoked his marijuana cigarette.

4. The 13-year-old smoked his first cigarette.

Figure 1. Piece of semantic memory as represented in network model of Collins and Loftus (1975)

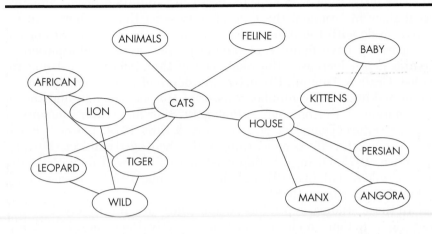

In all these sentences, the definition of *smoke* would be the same. However, the actions described by this definition vary from the puffing of the psychologist to the deep inhaling of the hippie. While the core meaning of *smoke* remains constant, this core meaning is realized differently in the different sentence contexts. A series of studies by Anderson and his associates (Anderson & McGaw, 1973; Anderson & Ortony, 1975; Anderson, Pichert, Goetz, Schallert, Stevens, & Trollip, 1976) demonstrated that the meanings of words can change in different contexts. For example, Anderson and Ortony (1975) found that people understood the word *nurse* differently in the sentences "Nurses have to be licensed" and "Nurses are often beautiful," even though the core concept of *nurse* is the same in both sentences. (These contexts need not be limited to sentences. Some words, notably concrete nouns and adjectives are best contextualized through a physical or pictorial context.)

Therefore, in order to know a word fully, one must have both definitional and contextual knowledge of that word; and to teach a word well, a vocabulary teaching program must at least provide both types of knowledge. Methods that do this, which can be called *mixed* methods of vocabulary instruction, do generally produce significantly better vocabulary learning and have greater effects on measures of reading comprehension than do purely contextual or definitional approaches (e.g., Gipe, 1979; Gray & Holmes, 1983).

Student Processing

Another factor, however, appears necessary to fully describe effective vocabulary instruction, the type of processing that students are required to do with the information they learn about words. Studies of list learning have found that having people process information at greater _depth_ increases the likelihood of that information being recalled (Craik & Tulving, 1975). Greater depth of processing, defined as either making a larger number of associations between new and known information (J. R. Anderson & Reder, 1978) or as greater amounts of cognitive effort (Tyler, Hertel, McCallum, & Ellis, 1979), has been found to have powerful effects on learning with school aged children (Murphy & Brown, 1975; Owings & Baumeister, 1979) as well as with adults (e.g., Craik & Tulving, 1975; Hyde & Jenkins, 1973; Johnson-Laird, Gibbs, & deMowbray, 1978).

In these studies, depth has been defined only intuitively. This is a very vague notion, and hard to measure exactly (Baddesley, 1978; Lockhart & Craik, 1978). But even with this vague definition, subjective judgments of the depth of processing required by a task have been found to correlate with the task effectiveness (Seamon & Vironstek, 1978). Applying our intuition to vocabulary learning tasks, it might be possible to define three broad levels of processing requirements, which might be useful in planning instruction:

1) *Associative processing* or having a child learn an association between a word and its synonym or definition, or with a particular context. A child who learns a list of synonyms may not comprehend them, since list learning can be accomplished without any consideration of the meanings of the words on the list. Similarly, a child who finds a particular word in a context may not think about the meaning of a particular word, since attention would be focused on the meaning of the whole context. Mere exposure to words in context, even multiple exposures, does not necessarily lead to learning the meanings of those words (Gray & Holmes, 1938; Sachs, 1943).

2) *Comprehension processing* or having the child apply an association. This generally involves having the child do something to demonstrate comprehension of an association, such as matching a word to its antonym, placing a word in the correct sentence blank, choosing the correct usage of a word in a group of sentences, etc.

3) *Generative processing* or having the student generate a novel context or definition for a word. The process of generation seems to involve more mental effort than comprehension, possibly because it is a more active process (Slamecka & Graf, 1978). Generation could involve having students produce their own sentences for

words, having them put definitions in their own words, having them create their own categories for words in lists, etc. The product does not have to be written; in fact, my experience suggests that discussion may force children to engage in deeper processing than written work (Barron & Melnik, 1973).

Table 1 lists a variety of common vocabulary teaching techniques, broken down by type of information provided and the type of processing required. This is only intended as a rough guide, since individual task and student variations may change information and processing requirements drastically. For example, sentence contexts vary greatly in difficulty, so that a sentence context such as "An onager is a wild African ass" may require only associative processing, rather than comprehension processing, and may also provide only definitional information, even though the word is presented in a sentence. (Humes, 1978, provides discussion of the cognitive processes involved in deriving the meanings of words in different contexts). Similarly, variations in student diligence and teacher demands may also change processing requirements. For example, for one vocabulary assignment, one of my students tried to hand in a list of sentences starting with "This is a _____." This is an extreme example, but it does point out the need for teachers to be aware of the ways students complete assignments as well as their finished products.

Methods Comparisons Studies

If association, comprehension, and generation represent three successively deeper levels of processing, and that deeper processing leads to better learning in vocabulary as it does in list learning, then we might expect that a method requiring comprehension processing to be more effective than one requiring only associative processing, and a method requiring generative processing to be more effective than one requiring comprehension processing, given that both methods provide similar types of information. As discussed earlier, one would also expect that mixed methods would be more effective than purely definitional or contextual methods, given equivalent levels of processing.

The recent vocabulary methods comparisons studies reviewed in Table 2 support these general predictions. Crist and Petrone (1977) and Johnson and Stratton (1966) both found that mixed methods requiring comprehension processing were more effective than definitional methods requiring associative processing. Crist and Petrone (1977) found that having subjects derive the meaning of each word from context produced significantly higher vocabulary learning than having subjects read each definition five times. Johnson and Stratton (1966) compared five vocabulary teaching methods—a synonym association task, a definition task, a classification task, a word in context

Table 1. Methods Comparison Studies in Vocabulary Instruction*

Study	Grade(s) Studied	Methods Compared (author's names)	Information Provided	Processing Requirements		
				ASSOCIATION	COMPREHENSION	GENERATION
Ahlfors (1978)	6th Grade	Definition	Definitional	X	X	X
		SENTENCE CONTEXT	Mixed*	X		
Anderson and Kulhavy (1972)	Undergraduate	Definition	Definitional	X	X	
		DEFINITION PLUS SENTENCE	Mixed	X		
Crist and Petrone (1977)	Undergraduate	Definitional	Definitional	X	X	
		CONTEXT	Mixed*	X		
Gipe (1979)	3rd and 5th	Association	Definitional	X		
		Category	Definitional	X		
		Definition	Definitional	X		
		CONTEXT	Mixed	X	X	X
Johnson and Strallon (1966)	Undergraduate	Synonym	Definitional	X		
		Definition	Definitional	X		
		Classification	Definitional	X		
		Sentence	Contextual	X		
		MIXED	Mixed	X	X	
Margosein, Pascarella, Pflaum (1982)	Junior High	Context (from Gipe)	Mixed	X	X	
		SEMANTIC MAPPING	Definitional	X	X	X
Stahl (1982, 1983)	5th	Definitional	Definitional	X	X	X
		MIXED	Mixed	X	X	X

*Note: Most effective method is in capital letters.

* In Crist and Petrone's and Ahlfor's studies, students were given words in sentence contexts and asked to derive definitions. Therefore, these could be classed as *mixed* methods.

Table 2. Sample Vocabulary Study Methods, by Type of Information Provided and Processing Requirements

		Definitional Methods	*Contextual Methods*

Processing Requirements	*Associative*	Association
		  Announce — say in Public
		
		Dictionary or Glossary study
		  Announce — to tell in public about;
		  proclaim
			Wide Reading

	Comprehension	Antonyms
		  What word means the opposite of
		  announce?
		  a. shout b. keep secret c. a pound
		
		Word Parts
		  What does *announcement* mean?
		  announcer?
		
		Categorization
		  Put these words in the correct
		  categories
		  ways of talking *ways of walking*
		  announcing loping striding
		  proclaiming verbalizing stepping
		
		Analogies
		  Announce: whisper: public: _____
		
		Word Groups (exclusion)
		  Circle the word that does not belong
		  announce walk speak orate
		
		Word Groups (inclusion)
		  Circle the word that best includes
		  the others
		    announce speak
		    proclaim converse
			Sentence Reading
			  What does *announce* mean in the
			  sentence:
			  "The boy announced his engage-
			  ment to his parents."
			
			Sentence Cloze
			  The winner was _____ at
			  midnight.
			
			Rewriting Sentences
			  Use *announce* in this sentence:
			  His name was *told publicly* today.
			
			Choosing Correct Usage
			  In which of these sentences is
			  announce used incorrectly?
			  a. The man announced his choice.
			  b. The store announced that it was
			    going out of business.
			  c. The little girl announced her
			    ABCs correctly.

	Generative	Restatement of Definitions
		  Tell me what *announce* means in
		  your own words
		
		Semantic Mapping
		  Discuss *tell* and *whisper*, then discuss
		  how *announce* is similar and
		  different.
			Writing Own Sentences
			  Write a sentence using the word
			  announce.

task, and a mixed method which amalgamated the other four, and found the mixed method produced significantly higher vocabulary learning.

Ahlfors (1978), Anderson and Kulhavy (1972), and Gipe (1979) found mixed methods requiring generative processing to be more effective than definitional methods requiring associative processing. Ahlfors compared a technique in which students were drilled on dictionary definitions to one in which students had to derive the meanings of target words from sentences and write their own sentences containing each target word. Anderson and Kulhavy (1972) found that having students create their own sentence for each defined target word produced significantly higher vocabulary learning than having them repeat each sentence three times. Gipe (1979) found that having students read target words in paragraphs which contained explicit definitions as well as the word in context and then generate sentences containing each word produced significantly higher vocabulary learning than having students study synonyms, study dictionary definitions, or classify target words in provided categories.

In these studies, it is hard to separate the different effects of type of information provided and processing requirements. Other studies appear to indicate that both produce important effects on vocabulary learning and reading comprehension skill. Pany and Jenkins (1977, Jenkins, Pany, & Schreck, 1978), in a series of studies, found that having students practice the association between a word and its synonym produces better vocabulary learning than merely giving the student the definition during reading. Presumably, the effect of the practice would be to force the students to deeper processing. Margosein, Pascarella, and Pflaum (1982) compared a definitional method requiring generative processing to a mixed method requiring comprehension processing and found that the definition method produced significantly higher results than the mixed method. In their mixed method, modeled after Gipe's (1979) context method discussed above, students had to read a paragraph for each target word. In each paragraph, the word was explicitly defined twice and put in a sentence context. The students were supposed to discuss the meaning of the word in the paragraph. (Unlike Gipe's treatment, the students did not have to generate a novel sentence.) In Margosein et. al.'s definitional method, semantic mapping after Pearson and Johnson (1978), students first discussed how two near synonyms known to the students such as *lonely* and *alone* were similar and how they differed. Next, a target word, such as *solitude*, was discussed in relation to the first two words, resulting in a semantic map of the relations between the three words. This semantic mapping could be expected to lead to more elaborate connections between the new information (the meaning of *solitude*) and known information (the general concepts of loneliness), resulting in deeper processing and presumably better learning.

Also, it is likely that some contextual information about each word entered in the discussions (see Stahl, 1982). These factors may have contributed to the overall superiority of the semantic mapping technique.

In the Stahl (1982, 1983) study, a deliberate attempt was made to equate the processing requirements of the two vocabulary treatments studied. Both mixed and definitional treatments required generative processing—the mixed method by having students generate sentences for each word and the definitional method by having students restate definitions in their own words. An equal amount of discussion was generated in both treatments. With processing level held equal, the mixed method produced significantly higher comprehension of passages and sentences using the taught words, but both methods were equally effective on a multiple choice synonym test.

Therefore, in the Pany and Jenkins (1977), Jenkins et. al. (1978), and Margosein et. al. (1982) studies, deeper or more elaborate processing seemed to produce significantly better vocabulary learning, regardless of the type of information provided. In the Stahl (1983) study, when processing requirements were roughly equal, the mixed method produced better vocabulary learning than a definitional method. This seems to indicate that both aspects of the framework are necessary to describe effective vocabulary learning. It should also be noted that subjects in these studies ranged from third grade to college and that the framework seemed to fit at each grade level. Also, in most of these studies, competing treatments were given for equivalent amounts of time, so that time on task seems not to be as important here as what is done during that time.

Instructional Implications

The concepts described in this paper can be used both to describe vocabulary teaching methods and to suggest ways of making vocabulary instruction more effective. For example, in the fourth grade level of basal reading series B, seven to ten words are to be put on the board in sentences. The meaning and pronunciation of each word is to be discussed. In addition, about ten other glossary words are given, with a suggestion that the teacher "may want to have the students look them up." In the fourth grade reader in basal reading series C, the teacher is directed to put about ten words on the board and lead the class in a discussion about the meaning of those words, either using a glossary or relying on the students' knowledge. After this discussion, an exercise is given which either involves another drill of the definitions or the use of the words in context. Following the lesson, the words are further reviewed using worksheets.

These three programs show a marked contrast. In basal A, the teacher is more likely to mention the meanings of the words, rather than teach them. Basal B's instruction can be classified as a mixed method requiring comprehension processing, as can that of Basal C. However, from this framework, it would appear that the activities in basal C would involve a greater number of connections between new and known information, and thus more elaborate processing. Of these three, it might be suggested that Basal C would produce higher vocabulary learning.

The framework also suggests that all three basal reading programs might be improved by inclusion of generative activities. One might add a second context sentence to the sentences used in basals B and C and discuss how each word's meaning differs in the two sentences. Or one might have students generate their own sentences for each word, either in a group or on paper. Such activities need not take any more time, since they might substitute for worksheet activities. As noted earlier, Barron and Melnik (1973) found that discussion was more effective than worksheets alone for vocabulary learning. In addition, some of the activities listed in Table I might be used for follow up to reinforce the initial instruction.

In the content areas, it is usually more important for students to learn the definitional relations between new concepts than it is for them to understand the words in context. This framework would suggest that techniques which require students to process this definitional information to greater depth would be more effective. Indeed, techniques developed to teach vocabulary in the content areas, such as the structured overview which graphically relates new concepts both to known concepts and to each other, would be expected to require deeper processing than giving students a list of terms and having them learn them (Herber, 1978; Vacca, 1981).

What has been suggested here is a hypothesis regarding vocabulary instruction. This hypothesis is grounded in cognitive science and supported by the results of vocabulary methods comparisons studies, but it is a hypothesis none the less. More direct tests of its implications are needed to refine the framework, but, in its present form, it may be useful in designing effective vocabulary instruction.

References

Ahlfors, G. (1978) *Learning word meanings: a comparison of three instructional procedures.* Unpublished doctoral dissertation, University of Minnesota.

Anderson, J. R., & Reder, L. M. (1978). An elaborative processing explanation of depth of processing. In L. S. Cermak & F. I. M. Craik (Eds.) *Levels of processing and human memory.* Hillsdale, NJ: Erlbaum.

Anderson, R. C., & Kulhavy, R. W. (1972). Learning concepts from definitions. *American Educational Research Journal, 9,* 385–390.

Anderson, R. C., & McGaw, B. (1973). On the representation of meaning of general terms. *Journal of Experimental Psychology. 101,* 301–306.

Anderson, R. C., & Ortony, A. (1975). On putting apples into bottles—a problem of polysemy. *Cognitive Psychology, 7,* 167–180.

Anderson, R. C., Pichert, J. W., Goetz, E. T., Schallert, D. L., Stevens, K. V., & Trollip, S. (1976). Instantiation of general terms. *Journal of Verbal Learning and Verbal Behavior, 15,* 667–669.

Baddesley, A. (1978). The trouble with levels: An examination of Craik and Lockhart's framework for memory research. *Psychological Review, 85,* 139–152.

Barron, R. F., & Melnik, R. (1973). The effects of discussion upon learning vocabulary meanings and relationships in tenth grade biology. In H. L. Herber & R. F. Barron (Eds.) *Research in reading in the content areas: Second year report,* Syracuse: Reading and Language Arts Center, Syracuse University.

Collins, A. M., & Loftus, E. E. (1975). A spreading activation theory of semantic processing. *Psychological Review, 82,* 407–428.

Craik, F. I. M., & Tulving, E. (1975). Depth of processing and the retention of words in episodic memory, *Journal of Experimental Psychology: General, 104,* 268–294.

Crist, R. & Petrone, J. (1977). Learning concepts from contexts and definitions. *Journal of Reading Behavior, 9,* 301–303.

Fodor, J. A., Garrett, M. F., Walker, E. C. T., & Parkes, C. H, (1980). Against definitions. *Cognition, 8,* 263–367.

Freebody, P., & Anderson, R. C. (1983). Effects of vocabulary difficulty, text cohesion, and schema availability on reading comprehension. *Reading Research Quarterly, 18,* 277–294.

Gipe, J. (1979). Investigating techniques for teaching word meanings. *Reading Research Quarterly, 14,* 624–645.

Glass, A. L., & Holyoak, K. J. (1975). Alternative conceptions of semantic theory. *Cognition, 3,* 313–339.

Goodman, K. S. (1976). Behind the eye: What happens in reading. In H. Singer & R. Ruddell (Eds.), *Theoretical models and processes of reading.* Newark, DEL: International Reading Association.

Gray, W. S., & Holmes, E. (1938). *The development of meaning vocabulary in reading.* Chicago: Publication of the Laboratory Schools of the University of Chicago.

Herber, H. L. (1978). *Teaching reading in content areas* (2nd ed.). Englewood Cliffs, NJ: Prentice-Hall.

Humes, A. (1978). Structures, signals, and cognitive processes in context clues. *Research in the Teaching of English, 12,* 321–334.

Hyde, T. S., & Jenkins, J. J. (1973). Recall for words as a function of semantic, graphic, and syntactic orienting tasks. *Journal of Verbal Learning and Verbal Behavior, 12,* 471–480.

Jackson, J. R., & Dizney, H. (1963). Intensive vocabulary training. *Journal of Developmental Reading, 6,* 221–229.

Jenkins, J. R., Pany, D., & Schreck, J. (1978). Vocabulary and reading comprehension: Instructional effects (Tech. Rep. No. 100). Urbana, IL: Center for the Study of Reading, University of Illinois.

Johnson-Laird, P. N., Gibbs, G., & deMowbray, J. (1978). Meaning, amount of processing, and memory for words, *Memory and Cognition, 6,* 372–275.

Johnson, D., & Stratton, P. (1966). Evaluation of five methods of teaching concepts. *Journal of Educational Psychology, 57,* 48–53.

Kameenui, E. J., Carnine. D. W., & Freschi, R. (1982). Effects of text construction and instructional procedures for teaching word meanings on comprehension and recall. *Reading Research Quarterly, 17,* 367–388.

Kintsch, W. (1974) *The representation of meaning in memory.* Hillsdale, NJ: Erlbaum.

Lachman, R., Lachman, J. L., & Butterfield, E. C. (1979). *Cognitive psychology and information processing: An introduction.* Hillsdale, NJ: Erlbaum.

Lockhart, R. S., & Craik, F. I. M. (1978). Levels of processing: A reply to Eysenck. *British Journal of Psychology, 69.* 171–175.

Margosein, C. M., Pascarella, E. T., & Pflaum, S. W. (1982). The effects of instruction using semantic mapping on vocabulary and comprehension. Paper presented at annual meeting of American Educational Research Association, New York City.

Meyer, D. E., & Schvaneveldt, R. W. (1975). Meaning, memory structure, and mental processes. In C. Cofer (Ed.) *The structure of human memory.* San Francisco: Freeman.

Murphy, M. D., & Brown, A. L. (1975). Incidental learning in preschool children as a function of level of cognitive analysis. *Journal of Experimental Child Psychology, 19,* 509–523.

Owings, R. A., & Baumeister, A. A. (1979). Levels of processing, encoding strategies, and memory development, *Journal of Experimental Child Psychology, 28,* 100–118.

Pany, D., & Jenkins, J. R. (1977). Learning word meanings: A comparison of instructional procedures and effects on measures of reading comprehension with learning disabled students (Tech. Rep. No. 25). Urbana, IL: Center for the Study of Reading, University of Illinois.

Pearson, P. D., & Johnson, D. D. (1978) *Teaching reading comprehension.* New York: Holt, Rinehart, and Winston.

Sachs, H. J. (1943). The reading method of acquiring vocabulary. *Journal of Educational Research, 36,* 457–464.

Seamon, J., & Vironstek, S. (1978). Memory performance and subject-defined depth of processing. *Memory and Cognition, 6,* 283–287.

Slamecka, N. J., & Graf, P. (1978). The generation effect: Delineation of a phenomenon. *Journal of Experimental Psychology: Human Learning and Memory, 4,* 592–604.

Smith, E. E., & Medin, D. L. (1981). *Categories and concepts.* Cambridge, MA: Harvard University Press.

Stahl, S. A. (1982). Differential word knowledge and reading comprehension. Unpublished doctoral dissertation, Harvard University.

Stahl, S. A. (1983). Differential word knowledge and reading comprehension. *Journal of Reading Behavior, 15,* 33–50.

Thorndyke, P. (1975). Conceptual complexity and imagery in comprehension and memory. *Journal of Verbal Learning and Verbal Behavior, 14,* 359–369.

Tuinman, J. J., & Brady, M. E. (1974). How does vocabulary account for variance on reading comprehension tests: A preliminary instructional analysis. In P. Nacke (Ed.) *Interaction: Research and practice in college-adult reading.* Clemson, SC: National Reading Conference.

Tyler, S. W., Hertel, P. T., McCallum, M. C., & Ellis, H. C. (1979). Cognitive effort and memory. *Journal of Experimental Psychology: Human Learning and Memory, 5*, 607–617.

Vacca, R. T. (1981). *Content area reading.* Boston: Little, Brown.

Theory to Practice: Vocabulary Instruction in Community College Developmental Education Reading Classes: What the Research Tells Us

Donna Willingham and Debra Price

Donna Willingham and Debra Price explore key theoretical constructs as well as extant research on vocabulary instruction for college reading students. Over the years both theory and research have suggested that vocabulary mastery is a key to student success and that those college students with vocabulary deficits are apt to be at risk particularly when coupled with other academic issues. The authors discuss strategies to promote mastery of vocabulary knowledge, which should be integrated in college reading courses.

A person who knows more words can speak, and even think, more precisely about the world. A person who knows the terms *scarlet* and *crimson* and *azure* and *indigo* can think about colors in a different way than a person who is limited to red and blue . . . words divide the world; the more words we have, the more complex ways we can think about the world (Stahl & Nagy, 2006, p. 5).

Community college developmental education students face numerous obstacles as they begin and proceed through their years of higher education. Some of these students find themselves in an academic setting for the first time in many years, and those who have recently graduated from high school often had marginal educational experiences at best. Consequently, developmental reading students have a variety of academic weaknesses, including deficient oral and written communication skills. Not surprisingly, some of these weaknesses are a direct reflection of students' limited vocabularies. Advanced communication skills are an integral part of higher education, so students may be at an academic disadvantage if these skills are not well developed. Overall, developmental students' inadequate oral and written vocabularies may negatively influence their abilities to excel when giving class presentations and writing essays (Simpson & Randall, 2000).

Due to the large amount of material presented in a sixteen week semester, vocabulary instruction is often either eliminated from developmental education curriculum or taught on a limited basis. The question is not whether vocabulary instruction is important (Stahl & Shiel, 1992), but how vocabulary instruction can be effectively added to what is already being taught. The following paragraphs discuss the primary types of vocabulary instruction.

Research on vocabulary acquisition typically falls into one of three categories: (a) predominantly supportive of indirect instruction, (b) predominantly supportive of direct instruction, (c) and those calling for *authentic word experiences,* defined as "teaching vocabulary words within context of literature study after the selection is read" (Dixon-Krauss, 2001, p. 312). Studies that focus on indirect vocabulary instruction discuss the importance of extensive reading, the significance of a student's prior knowledge, and word saliency (DeRidder, 2002; Freebody & Anderson, 1983a; Nagy, Anderson, & Herman, 1987; Tekman & Daloglu, 2006). Direct instruction studies include self-learning strategies, dictionary use, morphology, and mnemonics (Laufer, 2003; Pulido, 2003; Rott, Williams, & Cameron, 2002), and researchers that promote authentic word experiences (Blachowicz & Fisher, 2006; Dixon-Krauss, 2001; Francis & Simpson, 2003; McKeown, 1993) emphasize word awareness for vocabulary acquisition.

Vocabulary instruction is a critical component of developmental reading instruction (Simpson & Randall, 2000). Thus, the purpose of this article is to present theoretical frameworks and research perspectives surrounding vocabulary instruction with the intent to encourage developmental educators to continue examining a variety of vocabulary instructional methods. Additionally, studies exploring a variety of successful strategies for vocabulary growth are presented for developmental educators looking for ways to effectively integrate vocabulary instruction into a developmental reading class.

Theoretical Framework

Although numerous theories support vocabulary instruction, four closely intertwined theories particularly seem applicable. One significant theory related to effective vocabulary growth is *schema theory* since students with limited schemas, or prior knowledge, have more difficulty learning new words (Jenkins & Dixon, 1983). Developmental instructors must take this concern into account when contemplating appropriate vocabulary instruction for their students. When learning new words, the lack of schema, often due to limited reading, proves a common problem for developmental education students (Willingham & Price, 2008; Willingham, 2009).

Stahl, Jacobson, Davis, and Davis (1989) stated, "According to schema theory, the reader's background knowledge serves as scaffolding to aid in encoding information from text" (p. 29). The concept of scaffolding has foundations in Vygotsky's (1978) theoretical work on *Zone of Proximal Development* (ZPD), described as the distance between students' actual developmental level and potential level with direct instruction or peer collaboration. This theory suggests that as students' experiences with words grow, it becomes easier to learn new words.

Stanovich's (1986) theory of the *Matthew effect* also applies to students with limited vocabularies. He proposed that students who do not read well do not read, leading to a deficit of vocabulary building opportunities. Consequently, students' oral and written vocabularies suffer. Essentially, when students have limited word experiences, students will have limited vocabularies.

Saliency of words, or the concept that words are learned because they are deemed relevant, may explain why students learn some words they read and not others (Freebody & Anderson, 1983a). DeRidder's (2002) research showed students noticed and learned words they deemed important or useful. Freebody and Anderson (1983b) also demonstrated that word saliency plays a chief role in whether or not a student exerts any effort to learn a new word.

The theoretical framework presented provides the instructor with a justification and basis for the literature review and instructional suggestions that follow. It is the belief of the authors that good instruction is theoretically supported.

Literature Review

Duin and Graves (1987) said that "words embody power, words embrace action, and words enable us to speak, read, and write with clarity, confidence, and charm" (p. 312). Few would argue that college students need an extensive, expressive vocabulary in order to write essays, research papers, and make oral presentations in class (Simpson & Randall, 2000). Thus, college vocabulary development instruction rarely focuses on a student's receptive vocabulary, or the vocabulary needed for comprehension (Pearson, Hiebert, & Kamil, 2007), but on a student's productive, or expressive, vocabulary—the words a student uses for speaking and writing (Graves & Duin, 1985).

Stahl and Nagy (2006) proposed that a comprehensive vocabulary program includes learning the meanings of individual words, extensively reading rich texts, and developing the student's ability to learn new words independently. Designing such a program requires multiple strategies because both indirect instruction and direct instruction are important to a student's vocabulary growth (Herman & Dole, 1988; Nagy & Anderson, 1984).

Knowing a word involves an understanding of the word's definition as well as the word's approximate contextual usage (Stahl & Fairbanks, 1986). Researchers agree knowing a word is an incremental process that takes time and repeated exposures (Graves & Prenn, 1986; Stahl, 1986; Stahl & Nagy, 2006). Zimmerman (1997) was even more specific when she indicated this process includes three primary aspects: understanding (a) the subtleties of a word's various meanings, (b) the ranges of those meanings, and (c) the suitability of the word in context. Thus, a student will often not understand a word after only one or two experiences with the word.

Most articles that discuss vocabulary expansion include the idea of knowing a word (Stahl & Nagy, 2006; Wallace, 2007). Wallace (2007) specifically stated that knowing a word, or word *depth*, requires the understanding of a word's definition as well as the varied usages of the word. Yet, many times vocabulary instruction primarily focuses on vocabulary *breadth*, or how many words a student knows. Instruction should focus on both aspects.

Although most researchers believe both types of instruction are important, most remain entrenched in one of two camps: advocates for indirect instruction or advocates for direct instruction. However, proponents of direct instruction usually mention the need for wide reading in addition to direct word-learning methodologies (Laufer, 2003; Pulido, 2003; Rott, Williams, & Cameron, 2002) while indirect instruction proponents are less likely to address the need for directly teaching specific word-learning strategies (DeRidder, 2002; Freebody & Anderson, 1983a; Nagy, Anderson, & Herman, 1987; Tekman & Daloglu, 2006).

One significant issue in this debate is how many incidental exposures a student must have with a word before he or she truly learns the word. Research indicates word learning may result from only a few exposures (Herman, Anderson, Pearson, & Nagy, 1987); however, generally the more exposure, the more quickly a person will learn the word. The reason the number of exposures to words for contextual understanding proved so vital to proponents of direct instruction is because as a student reads, numerous incidental exposures to low-frequency words (words that rarely appear in a passage) does not usually happen (Laufer, 2003). For example, in a reading passage, the word *drone* will most likely occur only once and thus, not result in a contextual understanding of the word. Without a contextual understanding, the student is less likely to remember *drone*'s meaning the next time he or she encounters the word.

Indirect Instruction

Indirect instruction of vocabulary may be viewed as incidental in nature. Proponents of indirect instruction do not advocate for specific instruction or attention to vocabulary before or after a passage is read. While engaged in indirect instruction, a student might read a text, discuss the text, make connections to past learning experiences and even mention words they found compelling, without an instructor explicitly mentioning the vocabulary he or she would like the student to learn. Many educational experts support incidental word learning and reading extensively as a way to increase one's vocabulary (Nagy, Anderson,

& Herman, 1987). Indirect instruction includes several components: (a) extensive reading, (b) a student's background knowledge (schema), (c) word saliency, and (d) listening.

WIDE READING. Numerous vocabulary acquisition studies confirm the value of wide reading. The more the student reads, the more the student's vocabulary expands (Nagy & Scott, 1990). Specifically, Tekman and Daloglu (2006) stated that extensive reading "can help students to deepen their knowledge of a word's different meanings and contexts" (p. 236).

Nagy et al. (1987) suggested the amount of word knowledge gained while reading relies on three main factors: (a) the frequency of word exposure, (b) the text quality, and (c) the student's ability to infer meaning and recall the new words learned while reading. Thus, the most important factor in vocabulary development is the amount of reading that takes place. Word acquisition occurs by reading. Therefore, in order to realize substantial vocabulary expansion, a student must read extensively (Nagy et al., 1987).

An interesting part of the Nagy et al. (1987) study is that researchers statistically determined the probability of a reader advancing his or her vocabulary by reading. Their research reported that a student has a .05 percent chance of learning a new word from context while reading. This percentage was based on testing completed six days after the initial exposure to the new word. Thus, including both school and outside reading, the researchers determined a typical fifth grade student could learn 800–1,200 new words a year by reading alone. In the same study, the researchers found approximately one third of a student's yearly vocabulary increase was accounted for by broad reading, a much larger percentage increase than any reported by direct instruction studies.

A student has three choices when exposed to a new word while reading: (a) ignore the word if there is no loss of comprehension, (b) consult a dictionary or another person, or (c) infer the meaning from context (Fraser, 1999). When asked what they do when faced with an unfamiliar word, 56% of a surveyed group of developmental reading students indicated they tried to infer the meaning from context, 21% said they consulted a dictionary, and 16% responded that they usually skipped the word completely (Willingham, 2009). Although the largest percentage of students indicated they determined word meanings from context, Herman and Dole (1988) and Jenkins, Matlock, and Slocum (1989) emphasized the importance of teachers demonstrating or instructing how to actually use contextual clues. This skill does not come naturally but must be modeled.

Researchers are, however, divided on the actual advantages of readers using contextual clues when deciphering a word's meaning. The most divergent views seem straightforward: a word's context is significantly useful for determining the word's meaning (Gipe, 1979; Stahl & Nagy, 2006), or contextual clues are not substantially helpful in determining a word's definition (Juel & Deffes, 2004; Schatz & Baldwin, 1986). Those researchers in the middle, like Eeds and Cockrum (1985), found using contextual clues alone to establish a word's meaning was not as helpful as learning a word's meaning through teacher-led discussions.

SCHEMA OR BACKGROUND KNOWLEDGE. Another component of effective incidental or indirect word learning is the usefulness of a student's background knowledge (Jenkins & Dixon, 1983; Pulido, 2003). However, the value of schema, or background knowledge and experience in word learning, remains difficult to quantify. A number of schemata proponents commented on the significance of a reader's background knowledge when trying to infer a word's meaning. Nist and Olejnik's (1995) study found using the context to determine a word's meaning was only beneficial if the text was rich with clues. Nagy et al. (1987) felt contextual clues were helpful if three factors were in place: (a) the student had extensive exposure to written text, (b) there were adequate clues, and (c) the student was able to make inferences while reading and remember words acquired during reading.

SALIENCY. Saliency is also an important component of word learning (DeRidder, 2002; Freebody & Anderson, 1983a). DeRidder's research indicated students attend to and learn words they deem important or that are somewhat familiar to them already. Freebody and Anderson (1983b) also hypothesized that the saliency of a word plays a chief role in whether or not the student exerts any effort to learn the unfamiliar word. The authors propose that "salience of unfamiliar words may cause the reader to skip such words or even whole propositions containing such words . . . which are judged to be difficult or not vital to the progress of the theme" (p. 37). While the idea that readers will pay attention to words they deem important and ignore those they do not may seem elementary, too often educators assume that because we inform students about the importance of terms or concepts, the students take us at our word. The above cited research indicates it is critical to find ways to motivate students to learn the necessary vocabulary.

While many would attest to the importance of reading, the process often proves taxing for struggling readers. Zimmerman (1997) stressed that "although reading a good book can indeed be an engaging experience for the proficient reader, the process can be slow and painful for many . . . learners" (p. 135). Krashen (1989) recommended using light, low-risk, and pleasure reading to help inspire students to read more. These types of literature serve as a way to help unmotivated readers increase their vocabularies in a non-threatening atmosphere. Nagy, Herman, and Anderson (1985) summed it up well when they reported that their results suggested the most effective way to produce large scale vocabulary growth was through an activity that was all too often left out of reading instruction: *reading*.

Direct Instruction

Even though there are numerous proponents who wholeheartedly believe indirect instruction is the best, or only, way for students to develop their vocabularies, the research studies supporting direct instruction out number those supporting indirect instruction. The reason may be that most educators and researchers already perceive extensive reading as an effective way to acquire vocabulary, and thus, they want to test the value of direct instruction.

Though often debated, research shows that direct instruction has a place in vocabulary expansion. Direct instruction is commonly known as instruction that is teacher led, student practiced, and tied to a specific objective. It often follows the lesson plan format: introduction, modeling, guided practice, independent practice, and assessment. While the effectiveness of direction instruction has been debated because of its formulaic nature, Stahl and Shiel (1992) asserted that direct instruction can and should be quality instruction. Specifically they stated that while "good readers thrive on quality instruction, poor readers require it" (p. 239). Others agreed that direct instruction was especially beneficial for weak readers (Pulido, 2003; Rott, Williams, & Cameron, 2002).

Laufer (2003), an advocate for direct instruction, asserted that direct vocabulary instruction is necessary for vocabulary development. Specifically, word-focused tasks are beneficial for vocabulary expansion. She indicated several assumptions must be made when following the *reading for acquisition is better* philosophy: the student must (a) notice an unfamiliar word when he or she sees it, (b) choose to infer the word's meaning, and (c) remember the word and its perceived definition later. She contended that it is unlikely that all these steps take place when a student encounters an unfamiliar word. The next paragraphs discuss the need for self-learning strategies as well as examine the basic types of direct instruction: (a) dictionary use, (b) morphology, and (c) mnemonics.

Self-learning strategies are an important construct of direct vocabulary acquisition. Strategies should be explicitly taught, so students will choose to employ the strategies when engaged in independent reading. Because college students need to be in control of their own learning (Stahl, Simpson, & Hayes, 1992), the goal is for learning to continue when students leave the classroom (Nagy & Anderson, 1984; Stahl & Nagy, 2006). Instructors do not need to try to reinvent the wheel—just teach researched, self-directed word learning strategies on a regular basis. Several word learning strategies are discussed here.

DICTIONARY STRATEGIES. Dictionary use has certain limitations in the discussion of effective vocabulary acquisition. Primarily using dictionary definitions when learning unfamiliar words has fallen out of favor with teachers, and there are justifiable reasons for this occurrence. Scott and Nagy (1997) stated that word and dictionary definition exercises, without extra support, do not provide enough information when it comes to learning new words. Eeds and Cockrum (1985) and Marzano (2004) indicated that for dictionary strategies to work there must be some sort of contextual support or mental scaffolding (providing a sentence or a connection to other words or experiences) in order for a student to actually determine a word's meaning and subsequent usage. Dictionary definitions tend to be generic, thus, students find it difficult to use new words correctly if they do not understand the underlying concept and how the word is similar or dissimilar to related words. Dictionary definitions may be used initially, but the learning of a word's meaning should not stop there (Eeds & Cockrum, 1985; Marzano, 2004).

MORPHOLOGY INSTRUCTION. Morphology instruction is another potential vocabulary instructional strategy (Bromley, 2007; Nagy, Anderson, Schommer, Scott, & Stallman, 1989). In morphology study, the focus is on words' roots, suffixes, and prefixes. The term morphology comes from the word *morpheme* which refers to the meanings carried by the smallest units of a word (Nilsen & Nilsen, 2002). Advocates (Bromley, 2007; Graves, 1986; White, Power, & White, 1989) of this instructional method suggest that if a student understands a word's basic root, predominately Latin or Greek, the student has a greater opportunity to determine the word's meaning—especially if context clues are also used.

If students learn a small number of bases, suffixes, and prefixes, many words and families of words can be unlocked and learned more easily (Graves, 1986). Students break the unfamiliar word into smaller parts, examine for meaning, and then combine again. The word should then have an understandable meaning (White, Power, & White, 1989). Morphology and the use of contextual clues are the two most commonly direct instructional strategies included in developmental reading textbooks.

MNEMONICS. Mnemonics, or the key word method, is also an effective way for students to learn low-frequency, unfamiliar words through direct instruction (Simpson, Nist, & Kirby, 1987). The only method of explicit vocabulary instruction specifically mentioned and recommended by the report of the National Reading Panel is mnemonics (2000). The strategy is primarily used in two ways: drawings and cartoons (Burchers, Burchers, & Burchers, 1997), or mental visualization (Simpson & Randall, 2000; McCarville, 1993).

Both strategies depend on teacher instruction and interaction. An example of the use of drawings and cartoons can be found in the book

Vocabutoons (Burchers, Burchers, & Burchers, 1997). After students view a picture of a rabbit rapidly rowing a boat as a shark is in earnest pursuit, illustrating the meaning of the word *harrowing*, teachers lead students in forming sentences that use the word *harrowing* appropriately. For example, *being chased by a shark would be a harrowing experience*.

In mental visualization, the student concentrates on a word and its dictionary definition and then tries to concoct a mental image of the word that will be memorable. For example, if a student were trying to remember the word *acrophobia*, the fear of high places, the student might produce a mental image of an acrobat high in the air (Simpson & Randall, 2000). McCarville (1993) explains that it is imperative the student choose the visual image, not the instructor. The student must connect a mental picture to previous knowledge in order for this memory method to work effectively. Furthermore, this method typically brings humor and creativity to the task as it demands action and thinking. However, a downside to this self-strategy is that a mental image cannot be produced for every word, thus restricting this method's use to only certain words (Simpson et al., 1987).

Direct vocabulary instruction seems "to require a lot of time and energy" (Jenkins & Dixon, 1983, p. 243) which may be why so few instructors choose to include it in their curriculum. Developmental education reading instructors must recognize and understand the value for students before they are going to allot the time needed.

After a comprehensive look at indirect and direct vocabulary instruction, with both showing value, the good news is developmental reading instructors do not have to choose one strategy over the other. It is our assertion, based on the research evidence presented throughout this article, the two instructional methods can and should be combined.

A Combination of Instructional Methods: Authentic Word Experiences

Given the multifaceted nature of vocabulary acquisition (Simpson & Randall, 2000; Zimmerman, 1997), it can be difficult to choose which instructional approach to implement. Although most studies indicated a preference for either indirect or direct instruction, many acknowledged vocabulary acquisition was actually a combination of multiple word experiences. What, then, is the most effective way to combine both types of instruction?

One promising idea for combining indirect and direct instruction is the use of literature discussion groups, defined as a time when students meet with peers to discuss what they have previously read (Daniels, 1994). Discussion groups provide opportunities for authentic word experiences as well as help promote word consciousness as students co-construct meanings and comment on words they know and words they do not yet fully understand (Blachowicz & Fisher, 2006). Students should engage in active word discussions (Francis & Simpson, 2003; McKeown, 1993). Dixon-Krauss (2001) called this the "mediational model design" (p. 310) for vocabulary teaching and learning. Mediational models seem especially beneficial for adult learners (Willingham & Price, 2006).

LITERATURE DISCUSSION GROUPS. When using literature discussion groups, students first read a book, poem, or short story. Then, as one part of the preparation for group discussion, students make a note of unfamiliar words in the reading. Next, they write their own definition from reading the word in context and then provide a dictionary definition. When the group meets, each participant's words are discussed in addition to the other components of literature discussion groups (Daniels, 1994; Willingham & Price, 2006). This integrated method is beneficial for several reasons. Primarily, students self-select salient words, or words they deem important. As discussed in an earlier section, word saliency promotes vocabulary acquisition (Blachowicz, Fisher, Ogle, & Watts-Taffe, 2006; Dixon-Krauss, 2001). Another reason discussion groups are effective is because students are engaged on numerous levels; they are reading, writing, speaking, and listening to new words along with directly learning the definitions which aids in long-term word acquisition (Zimmerman, 1997).

In their study of vocabulary strategies for college students, Simpson et al. (1987) spelled out specific suggestions for vocabulary advancement. They pointed out four necessary components of a successful program: (a) the use of mixed methods, (b) the necessity of learning words in context, (c) the importance of student interest, and (d) the need for learners to take an active role in their personal vocabulary growth. Students then must participate in realistic writing and verbal interactions using the newly learned words. Although Simpson et al. (1987) did not directly suggest using literature discussion groups by name, the methodology for effective teaching described above encompasses this strategy and serves as a foundational support for the use of literature discussion groups in community college developmental education reading classes for vocabulary growth and enhancement.

Simpson and Randall (2000) summed up the research best when they concluded,

> We must rely on some seminal research studies and our own practical teaching experiences with college students to describe some effective vocabulary practices. These seven characteristics, which are not mutually exclusive, include:
>
> > (a) an emphasis on definitional and contextual knowledge, (b) students' active and elaborative processing, (c) vocabulary in context,

(d) students' interest, (e) intense instruction, (f) a language-rich environment, and (g) wide reading. (p. 61)

Vocabulary instruction involves numerous levels and components, and each requires time, which might explain why so few community college reading professionals are interested in adding vocabulary instruction to their classes. With so much to cover and so little time, vocabulary instruction remains dispensable in the minds of many developmental educators. Unless the instructor has actually studied the research in detail, he or she does not realize the long term importance of this significant literacy component (Nist & Olejnik, 1995).

Once college reading professionals gain a better awareness of the need for dynamic vocabulary instruction, they will be passionate about their students' vocabulary development (Bromley, 2007). Instructor attitudes are contagious. In the past, if vocabulary instruction happened at all, it was typically routine and rote. Vocabulary was introduced, taught through assigned and graded dictionary work and then tested (Willingham, 2009). Fun and stimulating vocabulary instruction will awaken the excitement for learning inherent in all students. The study of adult vocabulary acquisition and instruction in the developmental education classroom should not be conducted to determine a superior teaching strategy (Simpson & Randall, 2000) since research shows there is no one magic answer; research should focus, instead, on the use of a wide variety of strategies with an emphasis on authentic word experiences—possibly in the form of literature discussion groups.

References

Blachowicz, C. L. Z., & Fisher, P. J. L. (2006). *Teaching vocabulary in all classrooms.* Upper Saddle River, NJ: Pearson.

Blachowicz, C. L. Z., & Fisher, P. J. L., Ogle, D., & Watts-Taffe, S. (2006). Vocabulary: Questions from the classroom. *Reading Research Quarterly, 41*(4), 524–539.

Bromley, K. (2007). Nine things every teacher should know about words and vocabulary instruction. *Journal of Adolescent & Adult Literacy, 50*(7), 528–535.

Burchers, S., Burchers M., & Burchers, S. (1997). *Vocabutoons, vocabulary cartoons: SAT word power.* Punta Gorda, FL: New Monic.

Daniels, H. (1994). *Literature circles: voice and choice in the student-centered classroom.* York, ME: Stenhouse.

DeRidder, I. (2002). Visible or invisible links: Does the highlighting or hyperlink affect incidental vocabulary learning, text comprehension, and the reading process? *Language, Learning, & Technology, 6,* 123–149.

Duin, A. H., & Graves, M. F. (1987). Intensive vocabulary instruction as a prewriting technique. *Reading Research Quarterly, 22*(3), 331–330.

Dixon-Krauss, L. (2001). Using literature as a context for teaching vocabulary. *Journal of Adolescent & Adult Literacy, 45*(4), 310–318.

Eeds, M., & Cockrum, W. A. (1985). Teaching word meanings by expanding schemata vs. dictionary work vs. reading in context. *Journal of Reading,* 492–497.

Fraser, C. A. (1999). Lexical processing strategy use and vocabulary learning through reading. *Studies in Second Language Acquisition, 21*, 225–241.

Francis, M. A., & Simpson, M. L. (2003). Using theory, our intuitions, and a research study to enhance students' vocabulary knowledge. *Journal of Adolescent & Adult Literacy, 47*(1), 66–78.

Freebody, P., & Anderson, R. C. (1983a). Effects of vocabulary difficulty, text cohesion, and schema availability on reading comprehension. *Reading Research Quarterly, 18*(3), 277–294.

Freebody, P., & Anderson, R. C. (1983b). Effects on text comprehension of differing proportions and locations of difficult vocabulary. *Journal of Reading Behavior, 15*(3), 19–39.

Gipe, J. (1979). Investigating techniques for teaching word meanings. *Reading Research Quarterly, 14*(4), 624–643.

Graves, M. F. (1986). Vocabulary learning and instruction. *Review of Research in Education, 13*, 49–89.

Graves, M. F., & Duin, A. H. (1985) Building students' expressive vocabularies. *Educational Perspectives, 23*(1), 4–10.

Herman, P. A., Anderson, R. C., Pearson, P. D., & Nagy, W. E. (1987). Incidental acquisition of word meaning from expositions with varied text features. *Reading Research Quarterly, 22*(3), 263–284.

Herman, P. A., & Dole, J. (1988). Theory and practice in vocabulary learning and instruction. *The Elementary School Journal, 89*(1), 42–54.

Jenkins, J. R., & Dixon, R. (1983). Vocabulary learning. *Contemporary Educational Psychology, 8*, 237–260.

Jenkins, J. R., Matlock, B., & Slocum, T. A. (1989). Two approaches to vocabulary instruction: The teaching of individual word meanings and practice in deriving word meanings from context. *Reading Research Quarterly, 24*(2), 215–235.

Juel, C., & Deffes, R. (2004). Making words stick. *Educational Leadership, 61*(6), 30–34.

Krashen, S. (1989). We acquire vocabulary and spelling by reading: Additional evidence for the input hypothesis. *The Modern Language Journal, 73*(4), 440–464.

Laufer, B. (2003). Vocabulary acquisition in a second language: Do learners really acquire most vocabulary by reading? Some empirical evidence. *The Canadian Modern Language Review, 59*(4), 567–587.

Marzano, R. J. (2004). *Building background knowledge for academic achievement.* Alexandria, VA: Association for Supervision and Curriculum Development.

McCarville, K. B. (1993). Keyword mnemonic and vocabulary acquisition for developmental college students. *Journal of Developmental Education, 16*(3), 2–6.

McKeown, M. G. (1993). Creating effective definitions for young word learners. *Reading Research Quarterly, 28*(1), 16–31.

Nagy, W. E., & Anderson, R. C. (1984). How many words are there in printed school English? *Reading Research Quarterly, 19*(3), 304–330.

Nagy, W. E., Anderson, R. C., & Herman, P. A. (1987). Learning word meanings from context during normal reading. *American Research Journal, 24*(2), 237–270.

Nagy, W., Anderson, R. C., Schommer, M., Scott, J. A., & Stallman, A. C. (1989). Morphological families in the internal lexicon. *Reading Research Quarterly, 24*(3), 262–282.

Nagy, W. E., Herman, P. A., & Anderson, R. C. (1985). Learning words from context. *Reading Research Quarterly, 20*(2), 232–253.

Nagy, W. E., & Scott, J. A. (1990). Word schemas: Expectations about the form and meaning of new words. *Cognition & Instruction, 7*(2), 105–127.

National Reading Panel (2000). *Teaching children to read: An evidence-based assessment of the scientific research literature in reading and its implications for reading instruction.* Washington, DC: National Institute of Child Health & Human Development.

Nilsen, A. P., & Nilsen, D. L. F. (2002). The lessons in the teaching of vocabulary from September 11 and Harry Potter. *Journal of Adolescent & Adult Literacy, 46*(3), 254–260.

Nist, S. L., & Olejnik, S. (1995). The role of context and dictionary definitions on varying levels of word knowledge. *Reading Research Quarterly, 30*(2), 172–193.

Pearson, P. D., Hiebert, E. H., & Kamil, M. L. (2007). Vocabulary assessment: What we know and what we need to learn. *Reading Research Quarterly, 42*(2), 282–296.

Pulido, D. (2003). Modeling the role of second language proficiency and the topic familiarity in second language incidental vocabulary acquisition through reading. *Language Learning, 53*(2), 233–284.

Rott, S., Williams, J., & Cameron, R. (2002). The effect of multiple-choice L1 glosses and input-output cycles on lexical acquisition and retention. *Language Teaching Research, 6*(3), 183–222.

Schatz, E. K., & Baldwin, R. S. (1986). Context clues are unreliable predictors of word meanings. *Reading Research Quarterly, 21*(4), 439–453.

Scott, J. A., & Nagy, W. E. (1997). Understanding the definitions of unfamiliar verbs. *Reading Research Quarterly, 32*(2), 184–200.

Simpson, M. L., Nist, S. L., & Kirby, K. (1987). Ideas in practice, vocabulary strategies designed for college students. *Journal of Developmental Education, 11*(2), 20–24.

Simpson, M. L., & Randall, S. N. (2000). Vocabulary development at the college level. In R.F. Flippo & D.C. Caverly (Eds.), *Handbook of college reading and study strategy research* (pp. 43–73). Mahwah, NJ: Lawrence Erlbaum.

Stahl, S. A., Jacobson, M. G., Davis, C. E., & Davis, R. L. (1989). Prior knowledge and difficult vocabulary in the comprehension of unfamiliar text. *Reading Research Quarterly, 24*(1), 27–43.

Stahl, S. A., & Nagy, W. E. (2006). *Teaching word meanings.* Mahwah, NJ: Lawrence Erlbaum.

Stahl, S. A., & Shiel, T. G. (1992). Teaching meaning vocabulary: Productive approaches for poor readers. *Reading and Writing Quarterly: Overcoming Language Difficulties, 8,* 223–241.

Stahl, S. A., Simpson, M. L., & Hayes, C. G. (1992). Ten recommendations from research for teaching high-risk college students. *Journal of Developmental Education, 16*(1). Retrieved October 17, 2006, from http://www.ncde.appstate.edu/reserve_reading/10_Recommendations_Article.htm

Stanovich, K. E. (1986). Matthew effects in reading: Some consequences of individual differences in the acquisition of literacy. Reading Research Quarterly, 21(4), 360–407.

Tekmen, E. A., & Daloglu, A. (2006). An investigation of incidental vocabulary acquisition and relation to learner proficiency level and word frequency. *Foreign Language Annals, 39,* 220–243.

Vygotsky, L. S. (1978). *Mind in society: The development of higher psychological processes.* Cambridge, MA: Harvard United Press.

Wallace, C. (2007). The key to teaching English language learners to read. *Reading Improvement, 44*(4), 189–193.

White, T. G., Power, M. A., & White, S. (1989). Morphological analysis: Implications for teaching and understanding vocabulary growth. *Reading Research Quarterly, 24*(3), 283–304.

Willingham, D., & Price, D. P. (2006). Literature discussion groups in the developmental classroom: Opportunities for students to reflect upon, interpret, and apply literacy learning. *The Journal of Teaching and Learning, 8*(1), 27–33.

Willingham, D., & Price, D. P. (2008). *Effective vocabulary instruction in the community college developmental education reading class.* Paper presented at the National Reading Conference in Orlando, FL.

Willingham, D. (2009). *Enhancing community college students' vocabulary acquisition: Literature discussion groups in developmental classes.* Unpublished Doctoral Dissertation, Sam Houston State University: Huntsville, TX.

Zimmerman, C. B. (1997). Do reading and interactive vocabulary instruction make a difference? An empirical study. *TESOL Quarterly, 31*(1), 121–140.

Literary Letters: Developmental Readers' Responses to Popular Fiction

Marty Frailey, Greta Buck-Rodriguez, and Patricia L. Anders

Marty Frailey, Greta Buck-Rodriguez, and Patricia L. Anders extend the work of Nancy Atwell, whose groundbreaking research demonstrated the academic promise of "literary letters" for building elaboration competencies with youngsters in the middle grades. Here, the authors extend that work with literary letters as written by college developmental readers. These students participated in a literature-oriented instructional unit designed to promote reading comprehension and positive attitudes for reading. As part of the curriculum the students received instruction with "elaborative thought patterns" so as to improve their response to narrative text. Participants demonstrated improvement not only in elaboration skills, comprehension, and attitude but also writing, discussion competency, and self-efficacy.

R esearch suggests that reading deficiencies are the greatest obstacle that underprepared students face in college (Wirt, et al., 2002). The problem is so acute that only 51% of the high school graduates tested by ACT are prepared for freshman courses (ACT, 2006). In part, this might be attributed to a lack of practice reading books for pleasure. According to Atwell (2007), "the major predictor of academic success is the amount of time that a student spends reading. In fact, the top 5 percent of U.S. students reads up to 144 times more than the kids at the bottom 5 percent" (p. 107). It follows that readers who enjoy books and become actively engaged in the reading process are more likely to read extensively and to experience success academically.

The study instructor, a 22-year veteran of community college instruction, has observed that most developmental reading students are disengaged, passive readers. In her experience, use of a skills-based approach (Crismore & Busch, 1984) has yielded low retention rates and limited advancement in reading ability. To promote self-efficacy and enjoyment of reading, she has added a literature-based component to her reading courses. This component features self-selected popular literature with multiple opportunities for writing and discussion.

This article describes pedagogy employed in a developmental reading class and presents findings from action research using class assignments and activities as formative data (Reinking & Bradley, 2008). The assignment we focus on is the literary letter (Atwell, 1984), an informal mode of teacher-learner correspondence: Students respond to books through letters and receive a personal reply from the instructor. In addition to writing a personal reply, for this study the instructor also "coded," or labeled thought patterns in, each letter. The instructor theorized that by using the literature component and coding system students might report improved comprehension, richer responses in writing and discussion, greater engagement and self-efficacy, and improved attitudes about reading. Three questions guided the inquiry:

1. How would the depth and breadth of students' literary letters change when we taught them different ways of elaborating in their written response to reading?

2. Would students report that learning elaborative thought patterns helped them to better comprehend, write about, and discuss their novels? If so, in what specific ways did it help them?

3. Would students report changes in their perceptions of themselves as readers, their attitudes about reading, and their engagement with books? If so, what sorts of changes would they report?

After exploring the literature that informs our study, we briefly describe the pedagogy used and then provide a description of the formative data collected and analyzed.

Interactive Pedagogy in English and Reading: Research and Applications

Theoretical Foundations

The intervention of focus in this study is informed by several theories related to literacy education. The strategy provides instructional engagements that elicit and affirm aesthetic responses to literature (Short & Burke, 2001). As personal engagement with the text is affirmed, students become invested in understanding both the text and the reading process itself (Tashlik, 1987).

If indeed "everything about learning and developing is social" (Vygotsky as cited in Wink & Putney, 2002, p. 62), then college literacy is not only an instructed process but also a "cultural learning process" (Gee, 2004, p. 11). A cultural learning process engages the learner through mentoring relationships and a set of expectations situated in an informal cultural context. Students can benefit from this added dimension of the literature-based component, as authentic interactions occur during literature circles, group presentations, and through written correspondence with the instructor. It is essential to provide developmental reading students with such opportunities for interaction (Sinagra, Battle, & Nicholson, 1998).

Although college literacy development can be influenced externally through the cultural learning process, there is also an internal transactional process (Rosenblatt, 1994), whereby the reader and the text create meaning synergistically. Rosenblatt's transactional theory describes a continuum representing readers' approaches to texts: At one end of the continuum is the efferent stance, in which readers focus on drawing information from the text; at the other end is the aesthetic stance, in which readers focus on the experience of reading itself. "Readers may respond to express their emotional reactions, to explore difficulties in understanding, to corroborate or verify their opinions with others, to build social relationships through sharing responses or to clarify their attitudes" (Beach, 1993, p. 6). To satisfy this great variety of purposes, teachers need to create a wide range of response strategies. "When there is active participation in literature—the reader living through, reflecting on, and criticizing his own responses to the text—there will be many kinds of benefits" (Rosenblatt, 1994, p. 276).

Some aesthetic responses to text have also been described as "elaboration" (Stein, 1989). Elaboration is comprised of "the processes by which relationships are formed between the reader-writer's background knowledge and a particular written text through inferencing, analogies, and connection making" (Schlumberger, 1991, p. 44). These processes are often required in college work and bear some attention in developmental education (Holschuh & Aultman, 2008). The term "elaborative thought patterns," devised for this study, refers to the various types of elaboration that emerge when readers respond to text.

Pedagogical Tools

The literature review also revealed examples of relevant, interactive pedagogical tools. The first pedagogical tool was self-selected literature. When using self-selected popular literature, students had the freedom to choose materials they found compelling, an essential ingredient in successful learning (Gee, 2004). In a study by Morris (1995), community college students who read self-selected literature in a workshop format made gains in reading skills that were equivalent to those made in a traditional reading course. In addition, they demonstrated improved attitudes about reading. Self-selected popular literature also afforded a prime opportunity for developmental reading students to gain the experience of "reading flow" (Flurkey, 2008). As students become completely absorbed in books, they experience the transcendent emotional state described by Csikszentmihalyi (1990) which is similar to Maslow's "peak experience" (as cited in Kramer, 1984) or Atwell's (2007) "reading zone." In a study by Nakamura (1988), high achievers experienced flow 40% of the time they studied as compared with 17% for low achievers. By offering self-selected literature, we hoped that students would enter a state of flow while reading and be motivated to repeat the experience.

A second tool is the literary letter. Similar assignments have been variously named "written dialogues," "teacher-learner correspondence," "literary gossip," "first draft chat" (Atwell, 1987); "dialectical notebooks" (Berthoff, 1987); and "booktalking" (Sinagra, Battle, & Nicholson, 1998). The common denominator in these assignments is that genuine communication is written to an authentic audience with the expectation of personal response rather than critical appraisal (Atwell, 1998). Through such correspondence, an instructor can not only affirm students' opinions about books but also model effective reading strategies (Stephens, Corey, & Chapman, 2003) and challenge students to think more deeply about what they read (Paris & Ayers, 1994).

Of the various assignments available, literary letters seemed to provide the best means for written dialogue between the instructor and her students. Our introduction to literary letters came from Atwell (1984), who described the letters she exchanged with middle-school students. These letters were first-draft, opinionated reflections to which the instructor responded. We hoped to expand on the successes of other community college instructors, specifically Henry's (1992, 1995) work with developmental reading students who wrote letters to her about self-selected literature.

Using a third tool, the coding system, the instructor provided feedback to students and evaluated the effectiveness of the literary letter. Kletzien and Hushion (1992) labeled student journal entries with "graphic thinking symbols" to represent the thought patterns that emerged. "Use of the symbols was probably the most powerful means of getting students to vary their responses and to stretch their thinking" (p. 449).

This study is based on assumptions drawn from the theories and research herein described. The teaching and research methods chosen reflect our belief that the reading process is both social and transactional and that reluctant readers can become motivated when offered appealing choices and a variety of response strategies. We also believe that, as students engage in a variety of literature-based activities, they can increase their sophistication in evaluating, revising, and reflecting on their understanding of both the text and their own reading process.

Methodology

Setting and Participants

This research took place in a developmental reading course at an urban community college in the southwestern part of the United States during the Spring 2003 semester. The class began with 23 students and ended with 19, an exceptionally high retention rate for reading courses at the college. Of the 19 students who completed the course, attendance was exemplary, with only five who had more than three absences in the 31 sessions. There were 10 female and 9 male students of diverse backgrounds and ages. They included three Native Americans, six Hispanics, two African Americans, two Africans, and six Caucasians. Of these students, six spoke English as their second language and nine spoke more than one language. There was some diversity in age, as eight students were 17–20 years of age; seven were 21–25; two were 26–30; and two were over 35. Students were placed in the course because of their reading level as measured by the *Compass Reading Test* (ACT, 2008), the college's placement test for newly enrolled students. Students' raw scores on this test ranged from 68 to 79 out of a possible 99 points. Fifteen of the students were enrolled in developmental writing courses, and four were enrolled in freshman composition courses.

Of the four students who withdrew from the course, three did so within the first 2 weeks of the semester without explanation. The fourth student who dropped did so after completing about three-fourths of the course, but he was not keeping up with assignments nor was he attending regularly. Two of these students were males, one Caucasian, and the other African American. The two female students were both Hispanic. The teacher researchers who participated in the study included the course instructor, a university reading professor, and a graduate student.

Instructional Design

The four-credit course was taught with a literature-based component similar to Atwell's (1987) reading workshop. This component comprised approximately 40% of the class time; the other 60% of class time was spent learning and applying reading and study strategies to academic texts and periodicals. Only the literature-based component was part of the study. Course materials included a minimum of four paperback books, a subscription to *Newsweek* magazine, and a 56-page packet of teacher-designed materials. The packet included handouts on a variety of reading and study strategies, directions for various assignments, rubrics for grading, self-evaluation forms, and record-keeping materials.

The literature-based component of the course was multifaceted. Students chose from a variety of books, wrote personal responses, and participated in discussions with others reading the same book. The students wrote literary letters and participated in discussions called literature circles. The instructor provided each student with two late passes that allowed them to turn in two assignments up to 1 week late without penalty. All students began the semester reading the same book, but as they became familiar with literature and the routines of the classroom, a wider degree of choice was introduced. A description of the procedures used for each book follows.

BOOK I. During the 1st month of the semester, the students read a teacher-selected book, *The Pilot's Wife*, by Anita Shreve (1998). They received directions for writing literary letters as well as a sample letter and a blank grading rubric. Students wrote three letters (Letters 1–3) about Book 1. They also studied related vocabulary and reading strategies, met in literature circles twice, and completed individual reader response projects such as creating collages, writing letters to authors, and designing original book jackets.

BOOK II. During the 2nd month of the course, approximately 30 books were introduced by the instructor, and students were encouraged to explore others. Students browsed books for 15 minutes in the classroom library. After narrowing book choices down to five novels, students selected from these titles, and literature circles were formed with each group consisting of three to six participants reading the same book. For this second book, students followed the same procedure of writing weekly literary letters (Letters 4–6), meeting in literature circles twice, and completing individual reader-response projects after finishing the books.

BOOK III. The procedure for Book II was followed for Book III. Students chose books, met in their respective literature circles, wrote literary letters (Letters 7–9).

BOOK IV. During the last month of the semester, students read individually chosen books, and each presented a 5-minute Book Talk to the class. They continued to write weekly literary letters (Letters 10–12), but the letters were excluded from the study because students were no longer reading group books, meeting in literature circles, and preparing group presentations.

Data and Analysis

Multiple data sources were collected and analyzed to better understand how students evolved as readers over the semester. The data sources included nine literary letters per student, a questionnaire with a corresponding focus-group activity, and a final self-evaluation. This methodology is common among teacher researchers (Short & Burke, 2001).

LITERARY LETTERS. The first data source was the nine literary letters which students wrote as they responded to Books I, II, and III. Letters were returned weekly with the instructor's response, including the coding of elaborative thought patterns. Letters 3, 6, and 9 were selected for in-depth analysis because the final letter written about each book was most likely to show students' most sophisticated thinking. The 17 descriptive codes (see Appendix A and B or http://dtc.pima.edu/~mfrailey/ DevReadingResources/Index.html) were based on our definition of elaborative thought patterns. The codes corresponded to four broad categories: (a) retelling/summarizing; (b) evaluation of self, author, and text; (c) personal response/reaction; and (d) going beyond the text. To analyze the letters, researchers coded phrases, sentences, or paragraphs according to the elaborative thought patterns that were manifested, referring to each one as a coded response (see Appendix B). They tallied the total number of coded responses.

In addition to categorizing and quantifying elaborative thought patterns, investigators rated the amount of support students provided for each coded response. They classified individual responses into three levels according to the degree of support provided. Claims with little or no support received one point; claims with limited support, such as justification, background knowledge, and/ or examples, received 3 points; claims with extensive support received 5 points. Examples of the three levels follow:

Little or no support: When the co-pilot pulled out that briefcase, I think it was a bomb, but I'm not sure (1 point)

Limited support: I wonder if he fell in love with someone else and he couldn't decide what to do so he killed himself and all those people. Then it was intentional. I really don't think it was pilot error. (3 points)

Extensive support: I am looking forward to the end to see if maybe Kathryn and Mattie and maybe Robert will go down and investigate the scene off the coast of Ireland. Maybe they will find something like Jack is still alive and he is off somewhere drinking martinis on the beach. Maybe he got money out of the deal and he is rich with his mother and living like a king. That would make this real interesting. (5 points)

For both types of subjective analysis—the coding of elaborative thought patterns and judgments about the degree of support provided—researchers followed specific procedures to establish inter-rater reliability. First they discussed, reviewed, and agreed upon definitions and common understandings of the criteria for coding letters and judging support. Next, the instructor and the graduate student independently analyzed each student's letter. Third, the university professor examined each analysis for agreement. There was almost complete agreement between the instructor and the graduate student (550/571, or 96%, for quantity of responses; 556/571, or 97%, for quality of responses). In the few cases of disagreement, the university professor did her own analysis and then led a discussion with the other researchers to decide on a code and/or a level of support that all three researchers agreed upon.

During Weeks 3–6 of the course, the instructor provided her class with minilessons on the various elaborative thought patterns and their respective codes. To understand the coding of thought patterns better, students engaged in colaborative activities during which they coded sample excerpts from former students' letters.

After coding and evaluating the responses, researchers next recorded the length of each letter (Letters 1–9) and noted variations across the semester. Their supposition was that length might indicate the extent of elaboration. The in-depth analysis began with Letter 3, the final letter on Book I, because it was the first one written after the instructor had begun minilessons on elaborative thought patterns. Letters 6 and 9 were comparable to Letter 3, as each was the final letter written on a book. Researchers graphed the data and analyzed changes in students' writing as they moved through the semester.

WRITTEN QUESTIONNAIRES AND FOCUS GROUPS. Another data source was the tape recordings of focus-group discussions about the value of the literature-based component in general and literary letters in particular. To prepare for the focus groups, each student first filled out a questionnaire with the following questions:

1. How did the literary letters help you prepare for the literature discussion groups?

2. Do you think the writing of literary letters had an impact on your comprehension of your books?

3. We taught you codes. How did the knowledge of codes help you with your writing?

4. What kinds of changes did you see in your letters as we moved through the semester?

5. In what ways did the reading of paperback books and the writing of literary letters impact your interest in reading and/or your attitude toward books?

6. What do you think of the letter writing activity as a way to talk about books? What did you think about the literature discussions?

During class, the 19 students and three researchers were divided into groups, each composed of six or seven students and one researcher. These groups discussed the same questions they had answered on the questionnaire. Using this dual procedure meant that input from students who were less fluent in one of the two forms of discourse would not be excluded. The discussions were tape recorded, and the responses were documented and analyzed using qualitative content analysis (Merriam, 1998). That is, researchers transcribed the tapes of the three group discussions and summarized the student comments, noting the number of students who made similar claims.

STUDENT SELF-EVALUATION. The third data source was a student self-evaluation. Students responded to a Likert-type set of questions, reporting their perceptions of themselves as readers (very poor, poor, average, good, or excellent) and their attitudes and interests in reading (strongly dislike, moderately dislike, neutral, moderately like, or strongly like) at the beginning and end of the semester. Investigators calculated the mean score for the class and then looked at changes made by individuals. In addition, each student reported the number of books read during the semester, the total number of pages read, and the types of books read.

Findings and Discussion

This section provides results of the data analysis, including literary letters, questionnaires, focus-group discussions, and self-evaluations. As these results are presented, we offer our interpretations and reflections.

Changes in Depth and Breadth of Literary Letters

First, researchers analyzed the types of elaborative thinking and the amount of support given for opinions. Then they looked at how these elements changed over the course of the semester.

TYPE AND QUANTITY OF RESPONSES. The total number of coded thought patterns in the literary letters changed little during the semester. For the entire class, the total number of coded responses for Letter 3 was

198, the total for Letter 6 was 184, and for Letter 9 it was 190. The total number of responses remained consistent in each of four broad categories: Retelling; Evaluating Self, Author, and Text; Personal Response; and Going Beyond the Text.

Within the four broad categories there were 17 specific codes, the analysis of which demonstrated considerable variability. For example, as students wrote Letter 3, Letter 6, and Letter 9, they used fewer predictions (16, 7, 1); they used fewer inferences (29, 25, 18); and they varied their use of judgments (57, 39, 52). However, in all three letters, judgments and inferences dominated student responses.

Although responses in some categories decreased over the semester, in other categories they increased. For example, students strengthened their focus on evaluating authors (3, 11, 8), connecting with other books and media (1, 3, 5), and discussing themes (0, 5, 4). Changes in the focus of student writing might have occurred for a variety of reasons. By midsemester, students had gotten more exposure and practice with the elaborative thought patterns and were becoming more aware of the variety of ways they could respond to their novels. Also, after students had completed a few novels, they had experienced different genres and authors and could therefore more easily compare books. In some cases, individual students changed their thought patterns to correspond with changes in the genre of novels they were reading. In addition, some books seemed to encourage deeper thinking than others, presenting lessons about life or profound ethical dilemmas that led to meaningful reflection.

Retelling was much more of a focus in Letters 1–2 than in later letters. Initially, an average of 36% of each letter was devoted to retelling. Analysis of these brief retellings revealed that the average percentage of the letter that was retelling actually declined to 22%. These data suggest that by the 6th and 9th letters 14 students used a range of elaborative thought patterns to respond to literature. Having quantified this range of thinking, the study focus turned to the quality of the responses.

QUALITY OF RESPONSES. The quality of the elaboration was scored with a 1, 3, or 5, depending on researchers' assessment of the level of support offered for each response. There was a pronounced change in the quality of responses over the semester, particularly in Letter 6, the final letter for Book II. In Letters 3, 6, and 9 respectively, the scores jumped from 155 points to 238 points and back down to 182 points (see Table 1). The marked improvement in Letter 6 was probably due to the fact that students were receiving in-depth instruction and practice identifying the elaborative thought patterns at this time in the semester. As students began reading Book III (Letters 6–9), coding of letters continued but in-class instruction on the topic was no longer provided. At that point the focus was to encourage spontaneous thinking and writing. Between Letter 3 (when instruction in the coding of thought patterns began) and Letter 6 (after coding instruction was completed), the quality of the responses improved in almost all 17 categories. Students were not only able to use a variety of thought patterns but were now able to support their ideas with more examples, descriptions, and reasons.

NUMBER AND LENGTH OF LETTERS. Of the 171 letters assigned during the study (9 per student), 159, or 93%, were submitted. The letters ranged in length from 126 to 964 words, with a median of 320 words. Letter 1 tended to be the shortest, probably because students were unfamiliar with the assignment. During the reading of the first book, students' letters ranged from an average of 266 words for Letter 1 to 357 words for Letter 3. By the reading of the third book, the average letter ranged from 309 words for Letter 7 to 361 words for Letter 9. In general, the length of the letters increased as students moved to the second and third letter of each book. Perhaps they had more to write about as they progressed through their books and discussed them in literature circles.

Student Perceptions

Late in the semester, students responded both in writing and in focus groups to six questions. Students reflected on the experience of learning and applying elaborative thought patterns through the writing of literary letters. They reported the impact they perceived these experiences had on their understanding of their books and their ability to write and talk about them. Student comments are reported according to categories that emerged from the qualitative content analysis (Merriam, 1998). These categories included impact on (a) reading comprehension improvement; (b) writing skill improvement; (c) self-efficacy enhancement; and (d) attitudes about reading, self-selection, and writing.

READING COMPREHENSION IMPROVEMENT. The 19 students discussed how the writing of literary letters impacted their comprehension. They provided a variety of responses that were over-whelmingly positive, such as the following: "the writing provided me with the opportunity to critically analyze my books," "it helped me organize ideas," "it stimulated my thought process," "it helped me go deeper into the book and read between the lines," and "it helped me question things more." One student stated, "the literary letters were the necessary pit stop I had to take while reading my book to help make sense of all the information I was taking in." Another student claimed, "I used to read a book and I didn't even know what was going on, they just looked like words to me and now I'm starting to understand the plot and stuff." Another student remarked, "literary letters helped me understand and keep track

Table 1. Quality Points Assigned to Coded Thought Patterns in Letters 3, 6, and 9

Thought Pattern	Code	Quality Points Assigned		
		Letter 3	Letter 6	Letter 9
Retelling/Summarizing	R	14	24	23
Evaluating Self and Author				
Metacognition	M	7	0	5
Evaluate Author	Ev@	3	14	8
Evaluate Book	EvB	10	27	16
Personal Response/Reaction				
Discover New Ideas	!!!	0	0	5
Connect with Books/Media	C	3	5	7
Respond Emotionally	☺☹	10	15	6
Predict/Set Expectations	P/Ex	12	7	8
Personally Identify with Text	ID	17	23	18
Visualize	Vis	2	1	5
Going Beyond the Text				
Make Judgments	J	43	44	34
Draw Inferences	I	18	31	16
Make Analogies	↓↓	2	3	2
Question Events/Characters	??	11	16	10
Rhetorical Structures	RH	3	5	7
Identify Themes	TH	0	17	8
Reflect on Personal Impact Per Im		0	6	4

more because once I wrote it down on paper, it's like a flashback remembering more about the book." Even students who were avid readers spoke of changes they noticed in their reading. One student stated,

> I have always read books just for pleasure but what I have learned this semester is that every book has some kind of lesson that you learn from. I have read books in the past but I never stopped to think about what I've learned and now that is what I look for.

WRITING SKILL IMPROVEMENT. Students also reflected on how the knowledge and use of different thought patterns helped them with their writing. The most common response they gave was that the letters got them to stop retelling and/or summarizing the book. It helped them generate ideas about what they read. They became more aware of different ways they could think about their reading. One student remarked, "the codes were a good guideline to show me how I was conveying my ideas." Students had a new way to define what they were doing as they wrote.

Two students stated that they were now able to identify elaborative thought patterns during the writing process. Students became aware of their own thinking processes when they read books and wrote about them. "It was interesting to read where you have your assumptions and then you go and turn the page and something else happens that makes you sad, angry or just excited about each character. I did something in this class that I haven't accomplished since the 5th grade which is finish a book."

Two students saw the labeling of thought patterns as merely a system of evaluation; they felt the coding let them know if they were "getting things right" or "doing what was expected." Two students remarked that they liked the concrete, specific information that coded letters provided. One student claimed that knowing her letter would be coded motivated her to pay attention and think before she wrote. Two students acknowledged that the letter writing provided the discipline they needed to keep up in the book, stay focused on the story, and "not get side-tracked." They kept reading regularly because letters were due each week. Only 4 students felt that the writing and coding of literary letters didn't really cause changes in their writing. Two of these students had the insight that any change in their letters was based primarily on the amount of time they dedicated to the assignment. One student ascribed the change in her letter writing to how much she liked the specific book. The fourth student said, "more sophisticated novels got me to do more in-depth thinking."

SELF-EFFICACY ENHANCEMENT. Students also exhibited greater self-efficacy. They spoke repeatedly about new awareness of themselves as competent, capable readers. Further, they became aware of the process of metacognition. They described themselves as "making predictions," "confirming inferences," and "drawing conclusions." Also, students were surprised by how much they read. The discipline involved in keeping up with their groups and the large amount of assigned reading forced them to read much more than they would have read on their own. One student, who was completing his 2nd semester in a course with a literature-based component, stated, "I wish I had taken a class like this in high school. I might have finished high school. I've gone through 12 novels since I had this instructor and I find reading enjoyable. I used to hate to read." Another said, "Usually I would fall asleep after a few pages and struggle to read the rest of the book. But now I have completed 6 books, which is a huge accomplishment for a person like me that used to hate books."

Students also had new confidence in their abilities as readers. One student commented, "I used to have to read a few pages and then go back. I don't have to reread what I read. I read it once. It used to take me forever to read a book before." Another stated, "I do feel that I have become a stronger reader and a quicker reader. I am able to read at a much faster pace and still understand completely what I read and get through more books!"

ATTITUDE ABOUT READING. Researchers queried the students about how the reading of paperback books and the writing of literary letters influenced their interest in reading and/or their attitudes toward books. In general, students reported a notable shift in attitude about reading. They demonstrated this change through the number of books they read and the compelling comments made during focus-group sessions. In both written and oral comments, students described the powerful engagement they had with books. The vast majority (14 out of 19, or 73%) of students felt that the experience had a significant or powerful impact on their interest in reading. Students made the following claims: "I now have a clearer idea of what I like to read," "I learned my favorite genres," "I discovered a new hobby," "I discovered that books could be fun," and "reading used to put me to sleep, now the right book can hold my attention."

Three students stated that they were able to complete a book for the first time, and they found a profound sense of achievement in doing so. Students mentioned that they began to look for books when they were in stores, and they tried to talk to people outside of class about what they were reading. Three students were surprised to find that they were motivated to try new books after they had already read the number required for the course. One student commented, "I didn't own no books before and now I do. I have, like, three at home and I want to read them after this one. It's a change in the way I think about things," Another claimed, "before I would never just stop and buy a book. Now everywhere I go, I buy books." One student stated, "I've actually started to pick up books more, believe it or not. I've started to read more magazines. I read the newspaper more since I've been in this class. I've read more than I have in my whole life, actually."

ATTITUDE ABOUT SELF-SELECTION. Students reported appreciating being able to select their own books, as it helped them discover what they liked. The experience of exploring a variety of books opened their minds to diverse reading materials. The self-selection allowed students the opportunity to read books with which they could identify. They read about issues that were meaningful to them personally. One student commented on his selection process:

> You know the good thing was we got to pick what we wanted to read so after reading the back of books and learning about them and reading and liking it, it changed my view on reading. It's not boring. I thought it was interesting. Now if I go to a store and see a book, I actually pick it up and

read the back and see what it's about. Before it was just a book and I didn't even pick it up.

After choosing an action-packed book (*Run*; Winter, 2000), another student made the following statement:

This is definitely my favorite book. I liked it so much that I read 150 pages in one sitting. I thought that I would never be able to read that much because I always had a hard time with reading books for a long period of time. I used to be able to read only like 20 pages, and that was the most. It was mostly because the books were just not interesting. Now I know there are books that I can enjoy reading and this is sure one of them.

ATTITUDE ABOUT WRITING. Two students commented that they liked literary letters because they could develop a friendly, casual dialogue with the instructor. They enjoyed relating to their instructor as a friend through letters rather than reporting back to a teacher in the traditional book report format. There was more fun associated with the informal letter approach as opposed to a formal paper.

Two students reported that letter writing helped them apply some of the principles they were learning in their writing classes. Three mentioned that the extra practice with writing was good for them as they were developing college-level writing skills. More than half of the students felt more confident and at ease with writing by the end of the semester. The only negative comment came from a student who deemed letter writing to be useless. He was uncomfortable communicating on paper and would have preferred talking in person about his book. He did admit, though, that the letters helped him rethink his book, analyze the facts, and remember what happened.

Student Self-Evaluation

As a final course activity, students completed a self-evaluation by responding to a Likert-type scale assessing their self-perception and attitude toward reading and reporting on the number of books read. Students compared their perceptions of themselves as readers at the beginning and end of the semester. At the beginning of the semester, students perceived themselves to be "average readers," with a mean score of 2.89 on a 5-point Likert scale. At the end of the semester they believed themselves to be "good readers," with a mean score of 3.94. Almost all students showed a positive shift.

Students also reported changes in their attitudes toward reading. At the beginning of the semester, their average score was 2.78, or a little below neutral. At the end of the semester, the average score was 4.52, about halfway between "moderately liking" and "strongly liking" reading. Individual changes in scores were as follow: three students reported no changes, nine students shifted up by 1 point, five students up 2 points, one student up 3 points, and one student up 4 points.

Students reported reading an average of 4.28 books (R = 3.5–9.0); the average number of pages they reported reading was 1,308 (R = 859–3,325). This evidence suggests that students will complete extensive amounts of reading when given the opportunity and motivation. Several students commented on exceeding their expectations about how much reading they could do in a semester. Perhaps this realization will help them feel less threatened by the world of academics.

The changes students reported in self-efficacy and attitude, as well as the substantial amount of reading reported, highlighted the importance of providing opportunities for free reading of independently chosen books. As Atwell (2007) stated, "it's reading that makes readers . . . frequent, voluminous, happy experiences with books" (p. 18).

Implications for Practice and Future Research

The shifts in quality and quantity of literary letters along with the changes in self-perception and attitude suggest profound implications for both practice and research. The literature-based component represented only 40% of the reading course. Therefore, we do not claim that a literature component of a college reading course can be used to replace instruction and practice applying reading and study strategies to academic texts. However, we do argue that, within the context of a developmental reading course, it is essential to provide time for "frequent, sustained, pleasurable experiences with books" (Atwell, 2007, p. 18) that self-selected authentic material can offer. In other content areas, such as history, reticent readers might be better engaged in their readings and exhibit improved comprehension if more current readings, including historic novels, are used along with course texts.

A current issue facing the field of higher education is the retention and success of male students (Manno, n.d.; Mortenson, 2007). Although not part of our original study, we found male students completed this course at an unexpectedly high rate, with 9 out of 11 finishing the course, including 5 of the 6 minority males. In general, the male students responded enthusiastically to self-selected reading materials and literary letters. In fact, many of the comments quoted in this paper regarding the value of books were provided by male students. For the last 12 years the instructor has included a literature-based component, and she has noticed consistent improvement in the retention of males, particularly minority males.

The apparent positive impact of a personalized student-teacher relationship and weekly interaction between students through groups could be applied to other courses and learning environments. Specifically, it could be integrated into programs designed for at-risk students, including minority males, who need to improve their reading prior to enrollment in college courses. Further study might shed light on the impact of a literature-based component on male developmental readers, particularly minority males.

The teaching methodology described in this paper could be applied to alternate systems: For example, instead of corresponding with an instructor, students could correspond with peers. Individual students could be responsible for coding the letters they receive before responding to them. This adaptation would reduce the amount of coding the reading instructors face and, thereby, make the approach less formidable. In addition, it would provide more opportunities for students to develop and apply their understanding of the various thought patterns. This added dimension of peer-to-peer correspondence could work effectively not only in brick-and-mortar classes but also to create opportunities for meaningful interaction in hybrid and online classes. The impact of the student coding experience and/or the dynamics of online peer correspondence through literary letters might also be explored in future research.

This study focused on changes in students' written responses (literary letters) and their self-reported changes in reading and writing. A next step would be a controlled experimental study investigating students' changes when compared with classes using other instructional designs.

Conclusion

This study provided persuasive evidence of the value of a literature-based component in a developmental reading course, instruction in elaborative thought patterns, and the use of a coding system with literary letters. Both data and anecdotal feedback from this study reflected an improvement in students' processing of text and an increase in their quantity of reading. Further, students claimed to enjoy reading more. All these outcomes in the literature-based component of the course demonstrated improvement in reading abilities for underprepared students.

This instructional design illustrates an approach that can provide students with the tools they need to become not only confident, competent readers but also "skilled, passionate, critical, habitual" readers (Atwell, 2007, p. 12). Given the pervasiveness of deficiencies in reading for college-bound students (Wirt et al., 2002) and the impact that extensive reading has on academic success (Atwell, 2007), such an approach should be more widely implemented. This instructional design could be utilized with developmental readers in community college, university, and even in middle school and high school. In any case, students' experiences in this course provided them with a much-desired taste of success in the academic realm; replicating this instructional design might provide the same successful experience to other underprepared, resistant readers.

References

ACT. (2008). *Compass* Iowa City, IA: Author, Retrieved from ACT website: http://www.act.org/compass/tests/index.html

ACT. (2006). *What the ACT reveals about college readiness in reading.* Iowa City, IA: Author.

Atwell, N. (1984). Writing and reading literature from the inside out. *Language Arts, 61*, 240–252.

Atwell, N. (1987). Building a dining room table: Dialogue journals about reading. In T. Fulwiler (Ed.), *The journal book* (pp. 157–170). Portsmouth, NH: Boynton/Cook.

Atwell, N. (1998). *In the middle: New understandings about writing, reading, and learning* (2nd ed.). Portsmouth, NH: Boynton/Cook.

Atwell, N. (2007). *The reading zone: How to help kids become skilled, passionate, habitual, critical readers.* New York: Scholastic.

Beach, R. (1993). *A teacher's introduction to reader-response theories.* Urbana, IL. National Council of Teachers of English.

Berthoff, A. E. (1987). Dialectical notebooks and the audit of meaning. In T. Fulwiler (Ed.), *The journal book* (pp. 11–18). Portsmouth, NH: Boynton/Cook.

Crismore, A., & Busch, K. M. (1984). *Landscapes: A state-of-the-art assessment of reading comprehension research 1974–1984: Final report.* Bloomington, IN: Language Education Dept., Indiana University.

Csikszentmihalyi, M. (1990). Literacy and intrinsic motivation. *Daedalus, 2*, 115–140.

Flurkey, A. D. (2008). Reading flow. In A. D. Flurkey, E. J. Paulson, & K. S. Goodman (Eds.), *Scientific realism in studies of reading* (pp. 267–304), New York: Erlbaum.

Gee, J. (2004). *Situated language and learning: A critique of traditional schooling.* New York: Routledge.

Henry, J. (1992). Belles lettres: A qualitative study of student-teacher exchange in literary letters. (Doctoral dissertation, University of Cincinnati, 1992). *Dissertation Abstracts International, 54*, A0875.

Henry, J. (1995). *If not now: Developmental readers in the college classroom.* Portsmouth, NH: Heinemann.

Holschuh, J. P., & Aultman, L. P. (2008). Comprehension development. In R. F. Flippo & D. C. Caverly (Eds.), *Handbook of college reading and study strategy research* (2nd ed.; pp. 121–144). New York: Routledge.

Kletzien, S., & Hushion, B. (1992). Reading workshop: Reading, writing, thinking. *Journal of Reading, 35*(6), 444–451.

Kramer, B. B. (1984). Bequest of wings: Three readers and special books, *Language Arts, 61*(3), 253–260.

Manno, A. J. (n.d.). *Male retention at the community college.* Retrieved from http://www.raritanval.edu/departments/English/full-time/Manno/Male%20Retention%20at%20the%20Community%20College%20.doc

Merriam, S. B. (1998). *Qualitative research and case study applications in education* (2nd ed.). San Francisco: Jossey-Bass.

Morris, L. A. A. (1995). The effects of a modified workshop approach on reading achievement and attitude toward reading of community college developmental students (Doctoral Dissertation, University of Houston). *Dissertation Abstracts International, 56*, A4711.

Mortenson, T. G. (2007). Enrollment rates and educational attainment by age and gender: Bachelor's degree attainment by gender for 25 to 29 year olds, 1950 to 2006. *Postsecondary Education Opportunity, 181.* Retrieved from http://www.postsecondary.org/archives/Reports/181_707pg1_16.pdf

Paris, S. G., & Ayers, L. R. (1994). *Becoming reflective students and teachers with portfolios and authentic assessment.* Washington, DC: American Psychological Association.

Reinking, D., & Bradley, B. A. (2008). *On formative and design experiments.* New York: Teachers College Press.

Rosenblatt, L. M. (1994). *The reader, the text, the poem: The transactional theory of the literary work.* Carbondale, IL: Southern Illinois University Press.

Schlumberger, A. (1991). *The effects of elaboration on community college students' execution of a reading-writing task.* Unpublished doctoral dissertation. University of Arizona, Tucson.

Short, K. G., & Burke, C. (2001). Curriculum as inquiry. In S. Boran & B. Comber (Eds.), *Critiquing whole language and classroom inquiry* (WLU Series; pp. 18–41). Urbana, IL; National Council of Teachers of English.

Shreve, A. (1998). *The pilot's wife.* Boston: Little, Brown and Co.

Sinagra, M. D., Battle, J., & Nicholson, S. A. (1998). E-mail "Booktalking": Engaging developmental readers with authors and others in the academic community. *Journal of College Reading and Learning, 29*(1), 30–39.

Stein, V. (1989). *Elaboration: Using what you know* (Reading-to-Write Report No. 6; Technical Report No. 25). Berkeley, CA: Center for the Study of Writing. (ED306596)

Stephens, J., Corey, J., & Chapman, I. (2003). Between the lines: Reading and misreading student writers. *Journal of College Reading and Learning, 33*(2), 197–213.

Tashlik, P. (1987). I hear voices: The text, the journal, and me. In T. Fulwiler (Ed.). *The journal book* (pp. 157–170). Portsmouth, NH: Boynton/Cook.

Wink, J., & Putney, L. G. (2002). *A vision of Vygotsky.* Boston: Allyn and Bacon.

Winter, D. (2000). *Run.* New York: Penguin Putnam Books.

Wirt, J., Choy, S., Gerald, D., Provasnik, S., Rooney, P., Watanabe, S., & Tobin, R. (2002). *The condition of education* (DHHS Publication No. NCES 2002-025). Washington, DC: U.S. Government Printing Office.

Appendix A

Abbreviated List of Elaborative Thought Patterns & Examples

Evaluating Self & Author

M — Metacognition	I have some questions about the book but I'll keep reading. I must say that this book has lots of words in it that I do not know but I have a dictionary to look things up.

Personal Response/Reaction

!!! — Discover New Ideas	This book shows how bad war is, what struggles kids faced fighting and killing people they didn't even know. They fought in a war no one supported. The book let you learn about stuff we never faced first hand. *The Things They Carried*
C — Connect with books/media	I expected this book to be a sweet romance like a Danielle Steel novel. I wanted the guy to get the girl back in the end. The Reader was a very different kind of book and the ending was perhaps more realistic than a typical romance novel but it was not as pleasant. *The Reader*
Vis — Visualize	Even when they talk about the food they are preparing, not only can I picture it but I can almost smell it and my mouth starts to water wanting A taste of the savory food that Tita makes. *Like Water for Chocolate*

Going Beyond the Text

RH — Rhetorical Structures	I always felt that way about the south. That beneath the smiles and southern hospitality and politeness was a lot of guns, liquor and secrets. A lot of secrets would end up floating down the Nansemond river. *Midnight in the Garden of Good and Evil*
TH — Identify Themes	After finding out that love was a burden and since that ring was a symbol of that love, throwing it in the ocean was a cleansing act. The end of the book showed us how you say goodbye to a relationship that isn't there anymore. *The Pilot's Wife*
Per Im — Reflect on Personal Impact	This particular quote has made me realize how important a true relationship with God is. Just the thought of being left behind scares me. I feel that now is the time to make myself right with God. *Left Behind*

Appendix B

Sample of Coded Letter (The Pilot's Wife, *Letter 3*)

Dear_____,

    I am currently on page 252 of "The Pilot's Wife." At this point [R]
in the story Kathryn is still coping with the loss of her husband.
In the midst of dealing with the loss, she is faced with many
questions about her late husband. As I suspected the rabbit's hole [↓↓]
got deeper. I don't think I was prepared for how deep it went. I [☺☺]
was surprised when Kathryn decided to go to London. I was even [J]
more surprised when Robert said he would go. I think Kathryn
was a very brave person to make this choice. Not only did she get
on an airplane but went to London to confront her biggest fears.
Robert seems to be the only one supporting Kathryn in her decisions. When Kathryn went to Murie Boland's house and saw her
holding the baby, I felt horrible for her. Never once did I think [☺☺]
Jack would go to such lengths to have a secret life. The author of [Ev@]
the book does an excellent job of putting characters [sic] feelings [EvB]
in perspective, however the book overall is quite depressing. I am [?]
currently wondering how Kathryn will tell Mattie about Jack's
secret life. I also wonder how Mattie will take the news about her
deceptive father. Even more than I thought before, Jack is a complete jerk. I can't believe he would do that to Kathryn, let alone
Mattie. [J]
    Murie strikes me as an extremely coldhearted person. Never [J]
once did she consider calling Kathryn to inform her of Jack's de-
ception. This says a lot about what type of person Murie was. This
character reminds me of my ex-girlfriend. Both my ex-girlfriend [JD]
and Murie show no concern for another person's feeling. While
reading this part of the book, I started to get very angry. I couldn't [☺☺]
believe what I was reading. At one point, I had to put the book
down and smoke a cigarette. I felt like Kathryn's stress and anger
were being transmitted to me like a radio station. With all of this [↓↓]
going on, the cause of the plane crash still eats at me. I can't wait
to find out what actually happened in the cockpit. Now that Jack's
secret life's been exposed, I find it hard to believe that Jack would [I]
commit suicide knowing he was leaving three children behind. If
he did however, it only shows he was extremely selfish. I'm still [J, P/Ex]
hoping that Robert and Kathryn will hook up. Also what will the [?]
impact be when Kathryn finds out what really happened on the
plane? Well, I can't wait to find out what happens.
    Sincerely

Facilitating Student Learning through Contextualization: A Review of Evidence

Dolores Perin

In this selection, Dolores Perin discusses two forms of contextualization (contextualized and integrated instruction) and reviews the extant research. Although this seems to be a relatively new conversation within the field, the need for such work has been long-established. At an early meeting of the American Reading Forum, literacy pioneer George Spache stated that college reading and study strategies should be taught to students as they progress through the academic literacy demands of their college classes. Yet this recommended best practice for promoting transfer and benefiting learning has been for the most part lost to a field awash in a sequential skills-oriented curricular model where college reading classes have been divorced from general education or occupational courses. In recent years Perin's influential work has advocated that "contextualization" will lead at-risk students to learn more effectively and proceed through college-level course work.

Proficiency in reading, writing, and mathematics is key to academic learning, but courses in these foundational skills[1] are conventionally taught separately from the disciplines to which the skills must be applied. For example, students may be taught writing skills in a developmental English class and then be expected to apply them in a college-level history class. Several problems arise with this structure. First, for reasons still to be determined, learners, even the most proficient, often do not readily transfer newly learned skills to novel settings (Barnett & Ceci, 2002). Second, students may not be motivated to learn the skills taught in developmental education courses because they do not perceive them to be directly connected to their personal educational goals (Cavazos, Johnson, & Sparrow, 2010). Third, weaknesses in academic skills may not be addressed by the disciplinary instructor whose objective is to teach the subject matter, not basic skills (Fisher & Ivy, 2005).

This situation has serious implications for the academic trajectory of the many students who enter community colleges without the ability to read, write, or solve mathematics problems at the college level. However, bringing basic skills and content area instruction closer together may increase proficiency in reading, writing, and mathematics skills as well as the capacity of students to apply those skills in meaningful ways to academic tasks (Baker, Hope, & Karandjeff, 2009; Heller & Greenleaf, 2007; Lee & Spratley, 2010). In particular, developmental educators have suggested that basic skills instruction should use "authentic materials like the textbooks used in college courses such as psychology or biology" (Simpson, Hynd, Nist, & Burrell, 1997, p. 41). Simpson et al. (1997) contrasted such "embedded" instruction with the predominant "generic" approach (p. 42), in which technical aspects of literacy or mathematics are taught apart from content. Embedding developmental education instruction in disciplinary content may be helpful because basic-skill demands differ considerably across disciplines (Goldman & Bisanz, 2002; Stahl & Shanahan, 2004). Furthermore, generic instruction has been criticized as uninteresting and ineffective (Grubb et al., 1999). In contrast, "people learn when they have a need that is meaningful and real" (Goode, 2000, p. 270). For many students, what is real is their career goals, which are furthered by the completion of a specific degree or certificate program. Thus, using authentic materials may result in more active, generalizable learning (Simpson & Nist, 2002). The purpose of this article is to examine evidence for the embedding of basic skills instruction through *contextualization*.

Contextualization has been defined as "a diverse family of instructional strategies designed to more seamlessly link the learning of foundational skills and academic or occupational content by focusing teaching and learning squarely on concrete applications in a specific context that is of interest to the student" (Mazzeo, Rab, & Alssid, 2003, pp. 3–4). As passing the disciplinary courses needed to earn a desired college credential is assumed to be of considerable interest to students, the specific content of these courses can create a context for the learning of reading, writing, and mathematics skills that are authentic and personally meaningful to them (Kalchik & Oertle, 2010). The alignment and integration of developmental and disciplinary courses has been associated with positive student outcomes (Levin, Cox, Cerven, & Haberler, 2010; Weiss, Visher, & Wathington, 2010) and connections between basic skills and disciplinary learning are highlighted in the national literacy standards for career and college readiness (National Governors' Association and Council of Chief State School Officers, 2010).

Identification of Studies

Literature was sought that focused on contextualization as a form of instruction in reading, writing, or mathematics. A keyword search for sources (journal articles, books, and technical reports) dated 1990 to 2010 was conducted using the ERIC, JSTOR, and Education Full Text databases, augmented by searches of the Web of Science Social Science Citation Index, Google Scholar, and bibliographies in identified references as well as by a hand search of the journals relevant to the purpose of the study, including *Community College Review, Community College Journal of Research and Practice, and Journal of Developmental Education*. Works were selected if they reported instructional procedures for the contextualization of basic academic skills or measured student outcomes associated with the approach. The contextualization of English as a second language (e.g., Song, 2006) and content area instruction (e.g., Reisman & Wineburg, 2008) was beyond the scope of this review. The initial intention was to confine the search to work in community colleges, but because a shortage of research on contextualization in this setting was immediately apparent, the search also screened in reports on contextualization in adult literacy and K–12 education. The search identified 61 sources, of which 34 were descriptive and 27 were quantitative reports. Later in this article, selected studies with quantitative evidence are discussed. A full bibliography, listing both the descriptive and quantitative work, is available from the author.

Terminology

Numerous terms are used in the literature for contextualization, both of basic skills and other areas, including *contextual teaching and learning* (Baker et al., 2009; Johnson, 2002), *contextualized instruction* (Parr, Edwards, & Leising, 2008; Wisely, 2009), *content area literacy* (McKenna & Robinson, 2009), *embedded instruction* (Simpson et al., 1997), *writing-to-learn* (Klein, 1999; McDermott, 2010), *integrative curriculum* (Dowden, 2007), *situated cognition* (Hattie, Biggs, & Purdie, 1996; Stone, Alfeld, Pearson, Lewis, & Jensen, 2006), *problem-based learning* (Gijbels, Dochy, Van den Bossche, & Segers, 2005), *theme-based instruction* (Dirkx & Prenger, 1997), *anchored instruction* (Bottge, Rueda, Serlin, Hung, & Jung, 2007), *curriculum integration* (Badway & Grubb, 1997), *academic-occupation integration* (Bragg, Reger, & Thomas, 1997; Grubb & Kraskouskas, 1992; Perin, 2001; Prentice, 2001), *work-based learning* (Raelin, 2008), and *functional context education* (Sticht, 2005). Furthermore, contextualization is an important component of learning communities involving developmental education and college English courses (Fallon, Lahar, & Susman, 2009; Tai & Rochford, 2007; Weiss et al., 2010) as well as workplace literacy (Mikulecky & Lloyd, 1997). Regardless of the term used, all of these applications center on the practice of systematically connecting basic skills instruction to a specific content that is meaningful and useful to students.

Extent of Use of Contextualization in Basic Skills Instruction

Estimating the extent of contextualization of basic skills instruction in community colleges is difficult, but the use of contextualization seems rare. A study in one state found the practice to be infrequent and confined mostly to mathematics instruction (Wisely, 2009). A search for contextualization in the form of academic integration at community colleges in several states also found low usage (Perin, 2001). Although learning communities connecting developmental and college-level content courses have been described (Weiss et al., 2010), it is not known whether these efforts last only when external funding is available or whether they are becoming regular practice. If contextualization is rare, it may be because it is expensive; Jenkins, Zeidenberg, and Kienzl (2009) reported that a program integrating adult basic education and college-credit occupational courses in the state of Washington received 75% more funds per student than did traditional basic skills and vocational courses. Other reasons for the low use of contextualization may be a lack of awareness of its existence and benefits, the effort required to modify curriculum, and general resistance to moving toward an interdisciplinary focus. If the research indicates positive outcomes and colleges wish to implement contextualization, these barriers will need to be overcome.

Two Forms of Contextualization of Basic Skills Instruction

An examination of the literature indicates that contextualization is implemented in two distinct forms, *contextualized* and *integrated* instruction. This distinction has not been made explicit in previous literature, but it is an important contrast for instructional design because each form of contextualization involves different teaching staff and instructional emphases. Contextualized instruction is employed by instructors of reading, writing, and mathematics, whereas integrated instruction is the province of discipline-area instructors.[2] To maintain consistency with previous literature, the umbrella term *contextualization* is used here to refer collectively to the two forms of instruction.

Contextualized basic skills instruction involves the teaching of reading, writing, or mathematics skills against a backdrop of specific subject matter such as philosophy (Snyder, 2002), statistical process control (Baker et al., 2009), allied health (Shore, Shore, & Boggs, 2004), business (Weiss et al., 2010), history (De La Paz, 2005), and science. The primary objective is to teach the academic skills rather than the subject matter, although there may be some implicit learning of the content as students are exposed systematically to material in the same discipline as they practice the basic skills over time. Although many developmental reading instructors routinely use passages from content area textbooks, what is different about contextualized instruction is the systematic use of text from a single college-credit subject area.

Whereas the venue for contextualized basic skills instruction is the basic skills classroom, *integrated basic skills instruction* occurs in content area classrooms. Examples have been reported for college courses in business and allied health (Artis, 2008; Badway & Grubb, 1997; Cox, Bobrowski, & Spector, 2004; Perin, 2001) and in K–12 science, social studies, and career and technical education (Barton, Heidema, & Jordan, 2002; Bulgren, Marquis, Lenz, Schumaker, & Deshler, 2009;

De La Paz & Felton, 2010; Krajcik & Sutherland, 2010; Massey & Heafner, 2004; McDermott, 2010; Nokes, 2008; Parr et al., 2008; Stone et al., 2006; Tilson, Castek, & Goss, 2010). Integrated instruction may be needed when a content instructor observes that many students are having difficulty with the basic skills needed to learn the material, such as, in one example, when teachers found it necessary to "sneak in" reading comprehension strategies in a college course on symbolic logic (Higbee, Lundell, & Arendale, 2005, p. 328).

While contextualized instruction aims to teach basic skills for the purpose of meaningful application, the goal of integrated instruction is to teach the disciplinary content, not basic skills; however, teaching basic skills is a necessary step toward critical thinking about the content (Pearson, 2010). As instruction must be customized for specific contexts, both approaches can require considerable effort on the part of instructors. However, given the serious difficulties with basic academic skills seen in both secondary and postsecondary classrooms in the United States (Bailey, Jeong, & Cho, 2009; Grigg, Donahue, & Dion, 2007; Salahu-Din, Persky, & Miller, 2008), it is important to find instructional methods that can promote improved outcomes. Theories of the transfer of learning as well as theories of learner motivation suggest that contextualization may serve this purpose.

Theoretical Framework: Underlying Mechanisms

The goal of contextualization is to create conditions for more effective learning, expressed, for example, in better skills, higher grades and rates of retention in courses, and progression to more advanced course work. Whether instruction is contextualized or integrated, the connection of basic skills instruction to applications and life goals is consistent with constructivism, which places students' interests and needs at the center of education (Dewey, 1916/1966; Dowden, 2007).

From a cognitive perspective, contextualization is thought to promote transfer of learning and the retention of information (Boroch et al., 2007; Dirkx & Prenger, 1997; Karweit, 1998; Stone et al., 2006; Weinbaum & Rogers, 1995). Stone et al. (2006) hypothesized that "the creation of explicit connections between situations is critical if students are to transfer their knowledge and skills outside the classroom, whether it is to another context or to an abstract testing situation" (p. 11). However, knowing when and where one should apply a previously learned skill requires metacognitive and self-regulation abilities that low-skilled students may lack (Bailer, 2006; Fox, 2009; Mayer & Wittrock, 1996; Nash-Ditzel, 2010). Linking basic skills instruction directly to authentic content area applications that students will encounter in a disciplinary course may increase the likelihood that skills will be transferred to that particular setting.[3]

Barnett and Ceci (2002) proposed that the extent to which the transfer of skills occurs will vary according to the type of skill being targeted, how transfer is measured, the demands placed on memory of the skill to be transferred, and the distance between learning and transfer. According to this framework, the distance between original learning and eventual transfer can be measured in terms of the similarity of the two domains; the physical, temporal, functional, and social contexts also come into play, as does the modality for expressing transfer. In the present context, modality is the application of a skill, such as verbalizing how a mathematics problem is solved in an accounting class or writing a summary in a history class.

In addition to the cognitive mechanism of transfer of learning, possible benefits of contextualization may be explained by the affective mechanism of intrinsic motivation, where a learner is drawn to engage in a task because it is perceived as interesting, enjoyable, or useful (Baker & Wigfield, 1999; Becker, McElvany, & Kortenbruck, 2010; Ryan & Deci, 2000). Academically underprepared college students may not be drawn to learn basic skills that they should have learned much earlier in their academic history (Cavazos et al., 2010; Dean & Dagostino, 2007; Gardenshire-Crooks, Collado, Martin, & Castro, 2010). Having graduated from high school, they may not realize that their academic skills are not at college standard, and they may resist the need yet again to sit in classrooms that teach basic skills. Levin and Calcagno (2008) summarized students' low motivation to learn from generic basic skills instruction:

> [Skill and drill] pedagogy has many drawbacks, including the fact that many remedial students face serious attitudinal obstacles that prevent them from learning in this way. Often it is the same style that the students were exposed to in high school and that may have contributed to their difficulties in the first place. Beyond that, its abstract and isolated nature may prevent students from seeing the usefulness of what is being taught in real-world situations and from applying the skills that are learned to later academic and vocational coursework. (Levin & Calcagno, 2008, p. 185)

Furthermore, underprepared students may not be motivated to attend class regularly and apply themselves to learning because they dislike appearing incompetent (Dean & Dagostino, 2007) or because of competing job and family responsibilities (Caverly, Nicholson, & Radcliffe, 2004; Kozeracki, 2005). Extrapolating from research on motivation, it is possible that students may be more inclined to try to overcome such obstacles if explicit connections are made in class between basic skills and personally meaningful content applications (Berns & Erickson, 2001; Bond, 2004; Boroch et al., 2007; Guthrie, Anderson, Alao, & Rinehart, 1999; Johnson, 2002; National Council for Workforce

Education & Jobs for the Future, 2010; Shore et al., 2004; Sticht, 2005).[4] Similarly, workplace literacy students, who may not generally see the appeal of basic skills instruction, may be more motivated to learn the skills when instruction is connected to job-specific applications (Jenkins et al., 2009; Sticht, Armstrong, Hickey, & Caylor, 1987; Washington State Board for Community and Technical Colleges, 2005).

Evidence on Contextualization

Twenty-seven studies provided evidence on contextualization. Sixteen of the studies were on contextualized instruction, 10 were on integrated instruction, and a further study, by Wisely (2009), reported on both contextualized and integrated instruction. Quantitative studies of contextualized instruction were conducted with college academic programs (six studies), adult basic education (six studies), and K–12 academic education (four studies of each), but no studies involving career and technical education (CTE) students were found for this form of contextualization. Five of the six studies on contextualized instruction in college involved developmental education (Caverly et al., 2004; Perin & Hare, 2010; Shore et al., 2004; Snyder, 2002; Wisely, 2009), and one (Martino, Norris, & Hoffman, 2001) focused on low-achieving students in a college-level content course. Among the six studies involving adult basic education students, five were conducted with workplace literacy programs (Ekkens & Winke, 2009; Lazar, Bean, & Van Horn, 1998; Mikulecky & Lloyd, 1997; Perin, 1997; Sticht, 1995) and one was conducted with a prison sample (Dirkx & Crawford, 1993). Three of four studies of K–12 contextualized instruction focused solely on mathematics (Bottge, 1999; Bottge & Hasselbring, 1993; Brenner et al., 1997), and one dealt with writing instruction (De La Paz, 2005).

Four of the 10 studies on integrated instruction were conducted with CTE programs, two in college (Cox et al., 2004; Jenkins et al., 2009) and two in secondary education (Parr et al., 2008; Stone et al., 2006). The other six studies were in academic programs in elementary (Guthrie et al., 1999; Tilson et al., 2010) and secondary education (Bulgren et al., 2009; De La Paz & Felton, 2010; Greenleaf et al., 2010; Vaughn et al., 2009). No studies of integrated instruction at the college level were identified.

Many of the studies had methodological weaknesses that limited conclusions that could be drawn about the effectiveness of contextualization. A table summarizing the studies and their limitations is available from the author. Twelve studies (six on contextualized and six on integrated instruction) that offer the best evidence for the impact of contextualization on basic skills are summarized in the next section.[5]

Contextualized Instruction

COLLEGE SETTINGS. Perin and Hare (2010) created a curricular supplement to provide developmental education students with weekly practice in selected reading and writing skills to complement their work in the classroom. The practice focused on written summarization, question generation, vocabulary, and persuasive writing skills. Students in 12 developmental reading and English classrooms in two community colleges were randomly assigned to two conditions. Both conditions practiced the same skills but used different text. In one condition called "science," the skills practice was contextualized in passages from biology textbooks. In the other condition called "generic," the students engaged in the same practice but instead of using science text, read passages on a wide assortment of topics taken from developmental education textbooks. A third group was a purposive sample of four classrooms that served as a business-as-usual comparison group. Both the science and generic groups showed statistically significant higher gain on three variables on a researcher-developed written summarization measure (the proportion of main ideas from source text, accuracy of information, and word count) than the comparison group, and the science group showed greater gain than the generic group on two summarization variables (proportion of main ideas and accuracy), with effect sizes of 0.33 to 0.62 SD units. However, pre-post gain on a generic standardized test of reading was not associated with participation in the instruction. The findings for the summarization measure suggest that systematic practice contextualized in content-specific text helps students learn to summarize the type of material they need to read to learn in college-credit courses. At the same time, the study is limited by the fact that it involved independent practice rather than direct instruction, and students received only a small amount of feedback, raising the possibility that results were perhaps due at least in part to student-related variables. Also, because randomization occurred within classrooms, there may have been contamination between conditions.

Caverly et al. (2004) investigated the use of a contextualized reading comprehension strategy with first-semester students in developmental reading classrooms in a 4-year college. Instruction was anchored in chapters from textbooks used in core curriculum courses that the students would have to pass to complete their degree. A strategy was taught based on the mnemonic "PLAN" (Predict, Locate, Add, and Note). Students first predicted what would be in the textbook chapters and examined the title, introduction, subtitles, pictures, graphs, summaries, and the use of boldface and italics. From the predictions and examination of the text, the students created a concept map (visual display of the information) and ascertained how they would approach the reading task. Next, they checked items in the concept map that they already knew and marked unfamiliar information with a question mark. They then read the text and expanded the concept map using new information. In the last step of the strategy, students reflected on what they had learned and estimated how well they thought they could now satisfy the task demands they had identified before reading. The students applied the strategy to both well- and poorly written textbook passages. Also, to promote transfer of learning, they were asked to apply it in other classes and were required to summarize this in writing.

Statistically significant differences were found between students ($n = 56$) who took the contextualized reading course and students in a random sample ($n = 72$) who had the same pretest reading levels but did not take developmental education. Measures used in the analysis were scores on a statewide standardized reading test as well as grades in a subsequent college-level history course with high reading demands. This study suggests that the strategy of contextualized instruction promoted achievement in college-credit courses, but the conclusions are tentative because the comparison group did not take developmental education, leaving a question as to what, specifically, was responsible for the improved performance: the developmental education course in general, the instructional strategy, or a combination of the two. Also, students who choose to take developmental education may differ from those who do not on variables (e.g., motivation) that may explain the group difference.

Similar to Caverly et al. (2004), Shore et al. (2004) contextualized basic skills instruction in college course content. Community college developmental mathematics students who were preparing for degrees in various health professions were taught problems based on topics from allied health (respiratory therapy, radiology, occupational therapy, medical laboratory, and physical therapy) and nursing curricula. The problems were developed collaboratively by a group of health and developmental education instructors who observed each other's classes. For example, a problem was developed to teach students to interpret a graph illustrating the relationship between the percentage of normal glomerular filtration, as measured by creatine clearance, and blood urea nitrogen; this information is used to yield a function needed by nurses when analyzing a patient's kidney function. Data were collected for cohorts over a 3-year period.

Compared with a comparison group made up of sections of a traditional developmental mathematics course, students receiving the contextualized instruction in the first 2 years of the study earned better mathematics scores and were more likely to respond on a questionnaire that they found the instruction useful. The proportion of contextualized problems on the mathematics test increased each year over the 3-year project period, increasing to 70% in the third year. The contextualization group participating in the third year did not show an advantage over the comparison group, which was attributed by the researchers to a larger number of seriously underprepared students than in previous years and to the fact that the contextualized problems were harder than the traditional problems. The positive findings for contextualization in the first 2 years of the study are encouraging, but firm conclusions cannot be drawn because it was not stated how classrooms were assigned to conditions or whether the groups had equivalent mathematics scores at the pretest stage. Furthermore, the authors referred to pre- and posttests but neither the specific amount of gain nor the statistics were reported.

ADULT BASIC EDUCATION. Based on a program evaluation, Mikulecky and Lloyd (1997) reported outcomes of contextualized instruction for 180 incumbent workers in six companies who participated in work-related literacy classes. The instruction was provided in five of the companies for 20 to 60 hours and for 200 hours in another—equivalent, as the authors pointed out, to 6 or 7 weeks of high school. Participants' initial reading levels ranged from high elementary school grades to college level. The industries in which the instruction was contextualized included automobile and other manufacturers, a prison, an insurance company, and a hospital. For example, hospital workers and correctional officers were taught writing skills needed to improve the quality of written reports and memoranda, and gasket makers were taught reading skills using company newsletter articles, procedure manuals, and productivity graphs. Some of the participants were taught skills to prepare for promotion tests.

Literacy gains were measured using pre and post self-reports on literacy practices, beliefs, and plans as well as self-reports on strategies used to read a workplace newsletter and on performance on a work-related reading scenario. The researchers created scores from the self-reports, compared the pre and post scores using t tests, and, finally, expressed the amount of gain on a 3-point scale (positive, neutral, and negative gain). Statistically significant gain was found on the reading scenario, reading strategies, literacy beliefs, and plans, and the gains in one company were higher than those for a waiting-list comparison group from the same company. Overall, increases in skill were found for students in classrooms in which more than 70% of instructional time was spent on reading and writing activities and in which students discussed and received feedback on reading and writing processes. Although encouraging, this is tentative because it is based on self-reports, which can be subjective.

SECONDARY EDUCATION. De La Paz (2005) contextualized writing instruction in social studies content in eighth-grade English language arts classrooms. This instruction took place after students had learned an approach to historical reasoning in the social studies class. In the language arts class, the students were taught self-regulation strategies to set and monitor progress toward reading and writing goals and to write persuasive essays on controversies related to westward expansion. The essay-writing instruction was contextualized in textbook passages, primary documents, and secondary sources from the social studies class based on two mnemonics, STOP (Suspend judgment; Take a side, Organize ideas; Plan as you write) and DARE (Develop a topic sentence; Add supporting ideas; Reject an argument for the other side; End with a conclusion). Students engaged in essay-writing practice using the self-regulation and mnemonic strategies until they were able to plan and compose an essay of at least five paragraphs within one class period after reading a set of social studies documents. Compared with a group receiving traditional instruction (no historical reasoning or contextualized writing instruction), the contextualized strategy group showed greater gain on measures of essay length, persuasive quality, the number of arguments included in the essay, and historical accuracy (effect sizes $d = 0.57$ to $d = 1.23$), providing some support for contextualization. Furthermore, the effects were seen for learners over a range of ability levels, from students with learning disabilities to average-and high-achieving learners. However, a post-only design was used, and although group pretest achievement scores did not differ, the comparison group was made up of English language learners, raising the possibility that there may have been unmeasured pretest differences between groups. Furthermore, the experimental condition consisted of both contextualization and strategy instruction, clouding attribution of results.

Brenner et al. (1997) conducted a contextualized mathematics intervention using an everyday life scenario. Seventh and eighth graders in a pre-algebra class were taught problem-solving skills including the manipulation of symbols in equations. Specifically, students learned to produce and represent functions such as $y = mx + b$. The problems were cast in a hypothetical scenario involving the selection of a pizza company as a vendor for the school cafeteria. Lessons included taste tests with data collection on student preferences, a computer malfunction scenario in which students searched for errors in the pizza maker's order forms and invoices, a pizza delivery game in which students had to determine the correct destination, formulas related to advertising the pizza, and tables about profit and loss in the pizza business. Students frequently worked in cooperative groups to discuss and solve the problems. Three teachers taught two sections each, one contextualized and one traditional; the classes were randomly assigned among teachers to treatment and control conditions, and the classrooms for each teacher were randomly assigned to conditions. Several curriculum-based and transfer measures were administered to test students' ability to represent and solve word problems. Participants in the intervention showed greater gain than the control group in the representation of problems, such as depicting the word problems in the form of tables and graphs. Both fluent speakers and English language learners showed this benefit.

The design of the study did not permit a clear attribution of the findings to contextualization. The intervention and control conditions differed not only in the use of contextualized materials but also in whether cooperative learning was used. Furthermore, because the materials were contextualized, the treatment focused more on problem representation than the symbol manipulation that, according to the researchers, is characteristic of traditional mathematics instruction at this level. In fact, the performance of the control group was better on symbol manipulation.

Integrated Instruction

CTE (COLLEGE). Jenkins et al. (2009) studied student outcomes in the Integrated Basic Education and Skills Training (I-BEST) program, a special initiative that combines CTE and adult basic education in community colleges throughout the state of Washington.[6] Students in this program are enrolled in noncredit adult basic education and simultaneously take a college-credit occupational course that integrates instruction in occupationally related reading, writing, and mathematics. Instruction lasts one college quarter, in accordance with the statewide community college calendar. Although the content and number of hours of instruction varies across sites, there is a stipulation that both an occupational and a basic skills instructor must be present in the classroom for at least half of the total instructional time. (It is not reported how this time is distributed across class sessions.)

Two-year outcomes were compared between a cohort of 900 I-BEST students and two other samples of adult basic education students: one group that did and another group that did not enroll in a traditional, college-level CTE course at the same time as the I-BEST students. The comparisons controlled for age, gender, intent (vocational or academic), enrollment status (full- or part-time) when first enrolled, and educational history. Net of controls, I-BEST students were more likely than the traditional group to take subsequent credit-bearing courses, earn credits toward a certificate or degree, persist to the next college year, and show gain in basic skills. I-BEST students' basic skills improvement was 18% higher than adult basic education students who did not enroll in a traditional occupational course and 9% higher than adult basic education students who took an occupational course. Thus, the major advantage of I-BEST was seen when the comparison group took only adult basic education but not an occupational course. These results provide encouraging evidence for integrated instruction, but conclusions remain tentative as the sample was self-selected, raising the possibility that results could be attributed at least partially to student motivation. As the authors noted, I-BEST correlated with, but did not necessarily cause, the positive outcomes.

CTE (SECONDARY EDUCATION). Stone et al. (2006) investigated the effects of integrating mathematics instruction into five CTE areas (agriculture, auto technology, business and marketing, health, and information technology) using a "Math-in-CTE" model. The purpose of the instruction was to broaden students' knowledge of mathematics concepts they learned in CTE and have students "recognize how to solve practical problems by using mathematics in their occupational area; recognize math occurring in other contexts; and do so without diminishing the acquisition of technical knowledge in the course" (p. 5). However, it was not explained why technical knowledge might diminish by a broadened approach to mathematics instruction, which assumed prior knowledge of algebra. Initially, highly contextualized mathematics problems were taught, along with more abstract examples. For instance, when students used a T-square during instruction in agricultural mechanics, the teacher presented the Pythagorean theorem by showing the formula $a^2 + b^2 = c^2$. However, ultimately, the goal was that "students would see the math as an essential component of the CTE content, a tool—like a saw, wrench, or thermometer—needed to successfully solve workplace problems" (p. 6).

Teachers in 12 states were recruited on a volunteer basis and randomly assigned to conditions (57 experimental and 74 control). The CTE teachers in the experimental condition collaborated with mathematics teachers to identify mathematics problems embedded in the existing CTE curricula and to create lessons highlighting mathematical operations. The math-enhanced CTE lessons constituted 10% of instructional time over one academic year. The mathematics lessons contained seven elements: introduce the CTE lesson; assess mathematics skills relating to the CTE lesson; work through a mathematics problem embedded in the CTE lesson; work through related, contextualized examples; work through traditional mathematics examples; have students demonstrate their understanding; and mathematics questions in formal assessment at the end of the CTE unit or course (Stone et al., 2006, p. 12).

Pre- and posttests on two standardized mathematics tests, the TerraNova and Accuplacer, showed significantly greater gain for the experimental group (effect sizes 0.42 and 0.55). When occupational tests used in each participating classroom were administered at posttest, no significant differences were found between the experimental and control groups. The authors interpreted this to mean that the mathematics instruction was not detrimental to a growth of knowledge in the CTE field, but because the mathematics enhancement was presumably in the interest of an increase in occupational knowledge, the findings can also be interpreted to mean that the mathematics enhancement did not advance CTE performance.

ACADEMIC PROGRAMS (K-12). Building on De La Paz's (2005) eighth-grade study of contextualized instruction described earlier, De La Paz and Felton (2010) investigated the effects of instruction that focused on both historical reasoning and persuasive writing in an 11th-grade 20th-century history course. Whereas in the earlier study, the writing skills were taught by language arts teachers, in the De La Paz and Felton study, history teachers provided this instruction.

Participants were students (n = 79) in experimental classrooms and students (n = 81) in business-as-usual comparison classrooms in two schools. In the experimental (integrated instruction) condition, the history teachers introduced and modeled steps in the writing of persuasive essays on historical topics and then taught the content using the historical reasoning strategy. Then, the students were given guided practice in the writing of two persuasive essays on the history topics using the STOP and DARE mnemonics from De La Paz's 2005 study. Instruction and guided practice focused on writing a topic sentence stating a position on a historical controversy, providing reasons, using evidence to support claims, presenting a counterargument (with evidence), and refuting the opposing point of view, presenting new evidence.

Pre- and posttest persuasive essays were analyzed for length, persuasive quality, and historical accuracy. At posttest, the essays written by the experimental group were longer (d = 0.66), approximately one third more likely to include elaborated claims, and three times more likely to include elaborated rebuttals than the essays written by the comparison group (controlling for essay length); in addition, the experimental group's essays cited historical documents in support of claims more often (effect size 1.42 SD units). These results support the practice of integrated instruction, although, as with the De La Paz (2005) study, it is not possible to determine whether the positive outcome was attributable to contextualization or the instructional strategies.

A study of integrated instruction was conducted by Vaughn et al. (2009) with low-income seventh-grade social studies students, approximately one third of whom spoke Spanish as a native language and were not proficient speakers of English. Assignment to condition was unusually rigorous; first, students were randomly assigned to classrooms and then classrooms were randomly assigned to an intervention or business-as-usual control condition. The social studies material was identical in both conditions. The intervention involved explicit reading comprehension and vocabulary instruction; the control group did not receive any literacy instruction but only focused on the social studies content. The integrated instruction was delivered for 50 minutes per day, 5 days per week for 9 to 12 weeks. Four new vocabulary words were taught per day. All vocabulary was drawn directly from the social studies text.

To teach vocabulary after giving an overview of a "big idea" relating to the historical topic, the teacher pronounced each vocabulary word, identified a Spanish cognate or translated the word into Spanish, provided a definition in everyday language, showed a visual representation of the word, and put each word into two sentences, one in historical context from the class reading and the other relating to students' everyday life experience. The students then discussed each word in pairs. A 2-to-4-minute video clip on the topic was then shown and discussed. Then a graphic organizer was used to support silent and oral reading comprehension, and students worked in pairs to read the text and answer questions. In the paired reading, one student read while the other followed along, with the first student interrupting to correct the reader as needed. The teacher then led a whole-class discussion of the answers to the questions and, as a writing activity, worked with students to summarize information on the topic using the graphic organizer.

On researcher-developed measures of vocabulary matching and reading comprehension, the experimental group showed greater gain than the control group, with effect sizes of $g = 1.12$ for reading comprehension and $g = 0.53$ for vocabulary. Importantly, the integrated instruction was equally effective with proficient and less proficient speakers of English.

Bulgren et al. (2009) used a short-term "content-enhancement routine" (CER, p. 274) with typically developing and learning disabled (LD) students ($n = 36$) in grades 9 to 12. Students were randomly assigned to CER and control groups, using stratification to ensure equal representation of LD and non-LD students. The CER group learned a strategy for taking notes and learning vocabulary based on a 30-minute film on ozone depletion as the basis of any essay on climate change. The note-taking process was taught using a "question exploration guide," an organizational structure for recording important information in the film. Sections of the guide listed several questions that students had to answer, including "What is the critical question?" "What are they key terms and explanations?" "What are the supporting questions and answers?" and "What is the main idea answer?" Other questions related to experiments that could be conducted as well as to how knowledge about ozone depletion could be applied to individual lives. The control group viewed the film twice and was asked to take notes with no further instruction.

Outcome measures were writing quality and content knowledge exhibited in post-test essays on a topic related to ozone depletion. Writing quality referred to the ideas expressed in the essay as well as organization, voice, word choice, sentence construction, and the use of written English conventions. The content score measured identification of the problem, cause, effect, solution, and the writer's conclusion on the issue. At posttest, the essay quality of the experimental group was 25% better than that of the control group ($d = 1.32$). Superior gains for the treatment group were seen for every writing quality variable except writing conventions. The CER group also showed greater gain than the control group on content knowledge ($d = 0.74$). However, when the scores for the LD and typically developing students were disaggregated, only the typically developing students showed greater gain than the control group ($d = 2.0$). The results of this integrated instruction approach are encouraging, but conclusions are limited by the fact that the activity in the control condition seems considerably less compelling. Other methodological limitations are that instruction was delivered by researchers rather than classroom teachers and the intervention was very short, lasting only two sessions.

Similar to Bulgren et al. (2009), Tilson et al. (2010) taught an experimental science unit that integrated literacy instruction. Whereas the study conducted by Bulgren et al. was a small-scale experiment in secondary education, participants in the study conducted by Tilson et al. were fourth graders in 94 classrooms in 48 elementary schools. Students were randomly assigned to experimental classrooms ($n = 217$ students) or control classrooms ($n = 241$ students). The science unit taught concepts on physical science (light and energy), with 40% of instructional time spent on science, 40% on literacy (reading, writing, speaking, and listening), and 20% on formative assessment.

Several types of science-related writing were embedded in the science instruction, including the recording of data, written responses to informational text, and reports on what students learned in group discussions. Instruction was provided on constructing topic sentences, including supporting evidence, and using scientific vocabulary in precise ways. The teacher modeled the entire writing process at the beginning of the unit. Moreover, the students were taught to use graphic organizers and worked in pairs to plan writing tasks. As an example of the integrated instruction, one of the lessons involved testing various materials to investigate the phenomenon of reflection. Students created a data table and read a text on the topic, after which they wrote explanations on the nature of reflection.

In the control condition, students used the same text and experiential activities but, instead of explicit strategy instruction, they only engaged in reading and writing practice. All students were tested pre and post on writing skills using an experimenter-designed instrument. The quality of students' writing was scored on the accuracy of the science content, the use of evidence, the quality of the introduction and conclusion, the clarity of expression, vocabulary usage, and vocabulary count (defined as how many of 32 science terms targeted during instruction were included in the writing sample). The treatment group showed greater gain from pre to post than the control group on all of the writing measures except vocabulary usage and quality of conclusion ($d = 0.69$ on a composite score of all of the writing dimensions). As with De La Paz (2005) and De La Paz and Felton (2010), a clear attribution cannot be made to contextualization in itself because the treatment was confounded with strategy instruction.

Trends in the Research

The studies identified in this review suggest that contextualization of basic skills instruction, especially when coupled with explicit strategy instruction, is a promising approach for academically underprepared community college students. Conclusions are tentative, however, because of the shortage of rigorous studies with college populations. Research with K–12 samples was included in the review because there was relatively little information on the use of contextualization with students in college or adult education settings, but there does not seem to be any reason why findings from elementary and secondary education cannot be extrapolated to older adolescent and adult learners.

Outcome measures for almost all of the studies focused exclusively on and found gains for specific basic skills outcomes, such as reading, writing, or mathematics scores. All of the outcomes of contextualization for basic skills achievement were positive, although there was minor variation in outcomes for subskills and different measures. It is also of note that most of the studies compared contextualization with a business-as-usual comparison group, indicating that contextualization is more effective than standard, noncontextualized practice. This is a good start in examining the potential of contextualization, but more definitive conclusions can only be made when contextualization is compared with other instruction in addition to conventional approaches so that effects of attention and novelty can be ruled out.

An assumption underlying integrated instruction is that when basic skills instruction is incorporated in disciplinary instruction, ability in both academic skills and content knowledge should increase. However, in five studies of integrated instruction that measured outcomes on knowledge development in a content area (Bulgren et al., 2009; De La Paz & Felton, 2010; Parr et al., 2008; Stone et al., 2006; Tilson et al., 2010), two found no improvement in content knowledge (Parr et al., 2008; Stone et al., 2006). Both of these studies embedded mathematics in occupational courses in high school CTE. As strong claims are made for the advantages of combining literacy with subject-area instruction, these mixed findings are disappointing and warrant further research.

Only two studies, Wisely (2009) and Jenkins et al. (2009), provided data on college advancement. Wisely found that participation in contextualization was associated with completion of developmental education courses and the speed of entry into, as well as the performance and completion of, college-level courses. However, these positive effects were limited to non-White students; no effect of contextualization was found for White students. Jenkins et al. found that adult education students who attended occupational classes that integrated basic skills and content area instruction were more likely than adult education students who either did or did not enroll in a traditional occupational course to take subsequent credit-bearing courses, earn credits toward a college credential, persist to the next college year, and show greater gain in basic skills. Given practitioners' enthusiasm about the value of contextualization (see program descriptions in Baker et al., 2009; Boroch et al., 2007; California Community Colleges, 2008), it is unfortunate that more evidence is not available.

Practical Implications

The presence of large numbers of low-skilled students in colleges, especially community colleges, along with low rates of retention and progress in course work (Bailey et al., 2009) and recent findings that traditionally low graduation rates are not increasing (Radford, Berkner, Wheeless, & Shepherd, 2010) suggest that instruction of academically underprepared college students needs to be reformed. Among the many different innovations underway that attempt to promote the learning of low-skilled college students (Perin & Charron, 2006), contextualization seems to have the strongest theoretical base and perhaps the strongest empirical support. (There is a striking lack of evidence for most instructional approaches used to teach foundational skills in community colleges; see Levin & Calcagno, 2008.) Both forms of contextualization (i.e., contextualized and integrated instruction) are supported by quantitative studies that include control or comparison groups. There are more studies on contextualized than integrated instruction, but both forms of contextualization appear potentially valuable.

Moving toward contextualization in general, and contextualized or integrated instruction in particular, will depend on practical conditions internal to the colleges. Most important among these conditions are instructors' willingness to modify their instruction and colleges' ability to provide incentives and support for this change. Many developmental education instructors are not highly aware of the day-to-day reading and writing requirements that students find so difficult in college-credit disciplinary courses. Furthermore, instructors tend to be strongly committed to the generic, decontextualized instruction in reading, writing, and mathematics that predominates in developmental education (Grubb et al., 1999). However, disciplinary instructors may be equally unwilling to consider contextualization because they feel that basic skills instruction is beyond their range of responsibility or competence. Strong college leaders will need to provide ongoing direction and support for either version of contextualization.

The following recommendations are offered to support the implementation of contextualization in community colleges to promote improved student outcomes.

1. Carefully select the context for basic skills instruction. Indeed, the selection of this context is perhaps the greatest challenge to contextualization. Instructors understandably do not wish to teach academic skills too narrowly. It may be most effective to segment basic skills instruction according to students' career goals so that different developmental education courses are contextualized in content from course work needed for a given degree or certificate. Selection of college-credit courses with high enrollments but low

success rates may be a useful direction. Block scheduling of developmental education students to provide appropriate contextualization will be needed. These reforms will initially take much effort but may be more effective than current developmental education practice.

2. Create conditions for interdisciplinary collaboration so that basic skills and content area instructors can familiarize each other with their curricula, assessment approaches, standards, and teaching techniques (Baker et al., 2009; Greenleaf et al., 2010; Kalchik & Oertle, 2010; Perin, 2005; Shore et al., 2004; Stone et al., 2006). It is important that instructors visit each other's classrooms, discuss their educational philosophy and instructional techniques, jointly analyze the literacy and mathematics demands of content instruction, look for intersects between their instructional topics, and collaborate to align curricula so that students can be taught reading, writing, or mathematics skills that are directly applicable to the subject areas they are learning. Substantial time is required for this effort. Although salary and time constraints are a major challenge, part-time instructors should be integral to this effort because they form a large proportion of the developmental education faculty.

3. Provide ongoing professional development led by experienced trainers, coaches and mentors to initiate and support contextualization. Professional development leaders should be experts from within the institution rather than outsiders (Kozeracki, 2005). Formal professional development should be conducted with interdisciplinary groups of instructors and should be designed to meet tangible targets for implementing contextualized or integrated courses. Evidence-based professional development methods should be used, such as interdisciplinary inquiry-based approaches that involve coaching and intensive institutes (Greenleaf et al., 2010). Furthermore, professional development should be guided by common cross-discipline agreement on desired learning outcomes for contextualization and the means of achieving them (Baker et al., 2009). Follow-up activities and supportive monitoring should be provided after the conclusion of formal training sessions to maintain instructors' interest and ability to contextualize or integrate basic skills instruction. Greenleaf et al. (2010) noted that "a long history of research in reading has demonstrated that reading comprehension strategies are not often taught in subject-area classes, even when teachers are trained to use these strategies during subject-area teaching" (p. 15). To avoid this situation, follow-up support by respected instructional leaders will be needed.

4. Develop assessment procedures that incorporate both basic skills and content area knowledge to evaluate the effects of

contextualization. For example, in the study conducted by Shore et al. (2004), developmental mathematics and allied health instructors collaborated to create allied health mathematics problems. Both De La Paz and Felton (2010) and Perin and Hare (2010) included measures of content accuracy in instruments to measure contextualized writing, and Guthrie et al. (1999) developed fine-grained assessment methods that simultaneously measured reading comprehension strategies and science knowledge. It appears that such measures will need to be locally developed because disciplinary curricula tend to change, and conventional standardized tests do not capture students' progress in contextualized basic skills (Greenleaf et al., 2010), although customized subject-specific basic skills tests can be developed and normed (Lazar et al., 1998).

5. As the basis of contextualization of basic skills instruction in community colleges, select discipline-area courses that are needed for graduation by large numbers of students but have high failure rates. As contextualization is a labor-intensive initiative, it will be necessary to select courses for implementation. Initial attempts should focus on courses that have the highest need, represented by failure rates. Anecdotal evidence suggests that introductory science courses such as anatomy and physiology, required for graduation in popular majors such as allied health, may be a useful place to start because these courses display high failure rates, and studies are available on the contextualization of basic skills in science (Bulgren et al., 2009; Guthrie et al., 1999; McDermott, 2010; Shore et al., 2004).

6. When contextualized courses are established, collect outcome data for examination by instructors and administrators. Instructors who implement contextualization and administrators who support this effort should be made aware of both short- and longer-term outcomes such as the rate of passing basic skills and disciplinary courses, grade point average, semester-to-semester retention, and degree or certificate attainment. Evaluating contextualization in this way will indicate whether the effort is worthwhile and may point to the need for modification of teaching techniques.

Future Research Directions

Many approaches to the instruction of academically underprepared students have been tried, but their level of effectiveness is often unknown (Perin & Charron, 2006). Furthermore, it is not clear that improving instruction is itself high on the community college educational reform agenda. For example, a study of a well-funded reform effort, "Achieving the Dream," reported that only 27% of a set of student achievement–oriented reform strategies implemented by 26 community colleges focused on changes in classroom instruction (Rutschow et al., 2011, Figure 5.2, p. 76). Colleges might be more likely to reform instruction if there were more evidence on which to base such efforts.

The lack of rigorous research suggests that it is currently premature to invest substantial funds in contextualization. However, practitioners have been enthusiastic about it for many years, trends in the available research are positive, and the approach is consistent with theories of learning and motivation. For these reasons, it would be worthwhile to mount a rigorous research and development effort to gather information about the potential efficacy of this approach, specifically with low-skilled adult learners, whether in community college degree and certificate programs or adult basic education programs.

A premise underlying the practice of contextualization of basic skills is that students are more likely to transfer the skills to subject-area learning when the instruction is connected to these subject areas rather than taught abstractly. A topic that has not been addressed in studying the effects of contextualization on transfer of learning is possible interactions between student ability, student motivation, type of skill to be learned, and amount of contextualization. Thus, in either research and development studies or basic research investigations, moderators of the possible effects of contextualization should be identified. Experiments investigating contextualization should include a comparison of performance on alternate approaches as well as business-as-usual comparison groups to ensure that effects of contextualization are not attributable simply to novelty or increased attention.

Anecdotal evidence from practitioners (e.g., Baker et al., 2009; Boroch et al., 2007; Johnson, 2002) suggests that lower skilled students benefit from contextualization, not because it helps them become flexible learners but only because it increases their mastery of basic skills as well as the likelihood of transfer of basic skills to content courses that is not occurring in traditional, decontextualized learning environments. There is very little research on the relationship between contextualization of basic skills instruction and subsequent course work, and based on the small number of available studies, it is not possible to attribute the gains exclusively to contextualization. Future research paradigms should control for variables such as the nature of the course, teacher expertise, and cognitive and affective characteristics of learners.

The issue of dosage of contextualization should also be studied in light of claims that instruction can be overcontextualized and as such can be counterproductive (e.g., see Bransford, Brown, & Cocking, 2000). Another area that needs attention is the nature of the dependent variable used in studies of contextualization. The studies in this review varied on whether they measured both basic skills and subject-area gain or just the former. Dependent variables in future research on contextualization of basic skills should include both basic skills and content knowledge because the intent is to bring the two areas closer together and increase learning in both.

Conclusion

The contextualization of basic skills in disciplinary content is used in elementary, secondary, adult and postsecondary education as a way to engage students, deepen content learning, and promote transfer of skill. The approach is well grounded in psychological theories of transfer and motivation. There is support in the literature for two forms of contextualization identified in this review: contextualized instruction, which is taught by developmental education instructors and English language arts teachers, and integrated instruction, which is provided by discipline-area instructors.

There is more descriptive than evaluative literature, but the 27 quantitative studies found in this review, taken together, suggest that contextualization has the potential to promote short-term academic achievement and longer term college advancement of low-skilled students. However, the studies suggest that considerable effort is needed to implement contextualization because instructors need to learn from each other and collaborate across disciplines, a practice that is not common in college settings. Furthermore, there is very little information on cost or what would be needed to scale up contextualization. However, the available evidence, taken in combination with practitioners' considerable enthusiasm for contextualization, suggests that this approach is a useful step toward improving the outcomes of academically underprepared college students.

Notes

1. The terms *foundational skills*, *basic skills*, and *developmental education* are used interchangeably in this article to refer to preparation in reading, writing, and mathematics that aims to bring underprepared student's skills to the college level. A further point is to recognize that all of these terms imply assumptions about the nature of learning. It is possible to interpret the word *skill* as implying a behaviorist framework, which is at odds with a view of learning as essentially sociocultural. The term *skill* is used here as shorthand for ability to engage in the reading, writing, and mathematics activities that undergird and are necessary for learning from the postsecondary curriculum. Also, the current intent is to be neutral with regard to explanations for the term *low skills;* no negative connotation should be inferred.

2. In rare cases, contextualization of reading, writing, or mathematics has been used in learning communities that link upper-division college courses, such as advanced composition and abnormal psychology (Cargill & Kalikoff, 2007).

3. Cognitive theory on transfer has a long history of unresolved debates (Anderson, Reder, & Simon, 1996; Barnett & Ceci, 2002; Billing, 2007; Bransford et al., 2000; Detterman & Stemberg, 1993; Greeno, 2009; Mikulecky, 1994; Perkins & Salomon, 1989; Smagorinsky & Smith, 1992; Son & Goldstone, 2009). One problem is the lack of a commonly agreed-on definition of transfer (Barnett & Ceci, 2002), but a more pressing question is that of "dosage," that is, how much contextualization is required to facilitate the transfer of learning. More specifically, the debate has focused on creating flexible learners who will apply knowledge and skill to diverse situations. It has been theorized that overcontextualization limits learner's flexibility in applying new knowledge and skill (Bransford et al., 2000). The debate has a slightly different focus from that in the current review, which is narrower in its concern with the learning and application of basic literacy and mathematics skills by low-achieving students. From a pragmatic point of view, although too much contextualization may inhibit flexibility in the application of skills, the simple application of basic skills to a subject area would be an improvement over the current situation in which many low-skilled students do not apply basic skills they have learned in remedial settings once in the content classroom. Furthermore, it appears that transfer is difficult to discern even when explicit instruction in transfer is provided (Hendricks, 2001).

4. The hypothesis here is that level of intrinsic motivation predicts level of future engagement in course work. However, it is noted that intrinsic motivation to read has not been found to be a statistically significant predictor of future reading ability. Rather, level of intrinsic motivation to read loses its independent predictiveness once prior reading ability is accounted for (Becker et al., 2010). The same may be true for intrinsic motivation as a predictor of students' engagement in learning, with the result that motivation may be confounded with prior academic achievement in predicting future course engagement.

5. Most of the studies of contextualization in college settings have serious limitations. However, all of the studies of contextualization in college identified in the search for this review are included in the following section because we are most concerned with this particular sector.

6. In the state of Washington, adult basic education serves students based on tested skill levels and, consequently, overlaps with developmental education courses.

References

Anderson, J. R., Reder, L. M., & Simon, H. A. (1996). Situated learning and education. *Educational Researcher, 25*(4), 5–11.

Artis, A. B. (2008). Improving marketing students' reading comprehension with the SQ3R method. *Journal of Marketing Education, 30*, 130–137.

Badway, N., & Grubb, W. N. (1997). *A sourcebook for reshaping the community college: Curriculum integration and the multiple domains of career preparation* (MDS-782, Vols. I–II). Berkeley, CA: National Center for Research in Vocational Education.

Bailer, D. L. (2006). *A multivariate analysis of the relationship between age, self-regulated learning, and academic performance among community college developmental education students* (Unpublished doctoral dissertation). Touro University International, Cypress, CA.

Bailey, T. R., Jeong, D. W., & Cho, S. W. (2009). Referral, enrollment, and completion in developmental education sequences in community colleges. *Economics of Education Review, 29,* 255–270.

Baker, E. D., Hope, L., & Karandjeff, K. (2009). *Contextualized teaching and learning: A faculty primer.* Retrieved from http://www.careerladdersproject .org/docs/CTL.pdf

Baker, L., & Wigfield, A. (1999). Dimensions of children's motivation for reading and their relations to reading activity and reading achievement. *Reading Research Quarterly, 34,* 452–477.

Barnett, S. M., & Ceci, S. J. (2002). When and where do we apply what we learn? A taxonomy for far transfer. *Psychological Bulletin, 128,* 612–637.

Barton, M. L., Heidema, C., & Jordan, D. (2002). Teaching reading in mathematics and science. *Educational Leadership, 60*(3), 24–29.

Becker, M., McElvany, N., & Kortenbruck, M. (2010). Intrinsic and extrinsic reading motivation as predictors of reading literacy: A longitudinal study. *Journal of Educational Psychology, 102,* 773–785.

Berns, R. G., & Erickson, P. M. (2001). Contextual teaching and learning: Preparing students for the new economy. *The highlight zone.* Research @ Work (No. 5). (ERIC Document Reproduction Service No. ED452376)

Billing, D. (2007). Teaching for transfer of core/key skills in higher education: Cognitive skills. *Higher Education, 53,* 483–516.

Bond, L. P. (2004, January). *Using contextual instruction to make abstract learning concrete.* Alexandria, VA: Association for Career and Technical Information. Retrieved from http://www.acteonline.org/content.aspx?id=5822 &terms=Using+Contextual+Instruction+to+Make+Abstract#contextual

Boroch, D., Fillpot, J., Hope, L., Johnstone, R., Mery, P., Serban, A., & Gabriner, R. S. (2007). *Basic skills as a foundation for student success in California community colleges.* Sacramento: Center for Student Success, Research and Planning Group, Chancellor's Office, California Community Colleges. Retrieved from http://css.rpgroup.org

Bottge, B. A. (1999). Effects of contextualized math instruction on problem solving of average and below-average achieving students. *Journal of Special Education, 33,* 81–92.

Bottge, B. A., & Hasselbring, T. S. (1993). A comparison of two approaches for teaching complex, authentic mathematics problems to adolescents in remedial math classes. *Exceptional Children, 59,* 556.

Bottge, B. A., Rueda, E., Serlin, R. C., Hung, Y.-H., & Jung, M. K. (2007). Shrinking achievement differences with anchored math problems: Challenges and possibilities. *Journal of Special Education, 41,* 31–49.

Bragg, D. D., Reger, W. I. V., & Thomas, H. S. (1997). *Integration of academic and occupational education in the Illinois Community College System.* Springfield: Illinois Community College Board. (ERIC Document Reproduction Service No, ED418757)

Bransford, J. D., Brown, A. L., & Cocking, R. R. (2000). *How people learn: Brain, mind, experience, and school.* Washington, DC: National Academy Press. Retrieved from http://www.nap.edu/

Brenner, M. E., Mayer, R. E., Moseley, B., Brar, T., Durán, R., Reed, B. S., & Webb, D. (1997). Learning by understanding: The role of multiple representations in learning algebra. *American Educational Research Journal, 34*, 663–689.

Bulgren, J., Marquis, J., Lenz, B. K., Schumaker, J. B., & Deshler, D. D. (2009). Effectiveness of question exploration to enhance students' written expression of content knowledge and comprehension. *Reading & Writing Quarterly, 25*, 271–289.

California Community Colleges. (2008). Teaming up for green technology. *Getting It Done with WPLRC, 6*(5), 1–2. Retrieved from http://www.wplrc.org/app/doc/WPLRC%20Getting%20It%20Done%20Vol6-5.pdf

Cargill, K., & Kalikoff, B. (2007). Linked psychology and writing courses across the curriculum. *Journal of General Education, 56*, 83–92.

Cavazos, J. J., Johnson, M. B., & Sparrow, G. S. (2010). Overcoming personal and academic challenges: Perspectives from Latina/o college students. *Journal of Hispanic Higher Education, 9*, 304–316.

Caverly, D. C., Nicholson, S. A., & Radcliffe, R. (2004). The effectiveness of strategic reading instruction for college developmental readers. *Journal of College Reading and Learning, 35*, 25–49.

Cox, P. L., Bobrowski, P. E., & Spector, M. (2004). Gateway to business: An innovative approach to integrating writing into the first-year business curriculum. *Journal of Management Education, 28*, 62–87.

De La Paz, S. (2005). Effects of historical reasoning instruction and writing strategy mastery in culturally and academically diverse middle school classrooms. *Journal of Educational Psychology, 97*, 139–156.

De La Paz, S., & Felton, M. K. (2010). Reading and writing from multiple source documents in history: Effects of strategy instruction with low to average high school writers. *Contemporary Educational Psychology, 35*, 174–192.

Dean, R. J., & Dagostino, L. (2007). Motivational factors affecting advanced literacy learning of community college students. *Community College Journal of Research and Practice, 31*, 149–161.

Detterman, D. K., & Sternberg, R. J. (Eds.). (1993). *Transfer on trial: Intelligence, cognition, and instruction.* Norwood, NJ: Ablex.

Dewey, J. (1966). *Democracy and education.* New York, NY: Free Press. (Original work published 1916)

Dirkx, J. M., & Crawford, M. (1993). Teaching reading through teaching science: Development and evaluation of an experimental curriculum for correctional ABE programs. *Journal of Correctional Education, 44*, 172–176.

Dirkx, J. M., & Prenger, S. M. (1997). *A guide for planning and implementing instruction for adults: A theme-based approach.* San Francisco, CA: Jossey-Bass.

Dowden, T. (2007). Relevant, challenging, integrative and exploratory curriculum design: Perspectives from theory and practice for middle level schooling in Australia. *Australian Educational Researcher, 34*, 51–71.

Ekkens, K., & Winke, P. (2009). Evaluating workplace English language programs. *Language Assessment Quarterly, 6*, 265–287.

Fallon, D., Lahar, C. J., & Susman, D. (2009). Taking the high road to transfer: Building bridges between English and psychology. *Teaching English in the Two-Year College, 37*(1), 41–55.

Fisher, D., & Ivy, G. (2005). Literacy and language as learning in content-area classes: A departure from "Every Teacher a Teacher of Reading." *Action in Teacher Education, 27*(2), 3–11.

Fox, E. (2009). The role of reader characteristics in processing and learning from informational text. *Review of Educational Research, 79,* 197–261.

Gardenshire-Crooks, A., Collado, H., Martin, K., & Castro, A. (2010). *Terms of engagement: Men of color discuss their experiences in community college.* New York, NY: Manpower Demonstration Research Corporation. (ERIC Document Reproduction Service No. ED508982)

Gijbels, D., Dochy, F., Van den Bossche, P., & Segers, M. (2005). Effects of problem-based learning: A meta-analysis from the angle of assessment. *Review of Educational Research, 75,* 27–61.

Goldman, S. R., & Bisanz, G. L. (2002). Toward a functional analysis of scientific genres: Implications for understanding and learning processes. In J. Otero, J. A. Leon, & A. C. Graesser (Eds.), *The psychology of science text comprehension* (pp. 19–50). Mahwah, NJ: Erlbaum.

Goode, D. (2000). Creating a context for developmental English. *Teaching English in the Two-Year College, 27,* 270–277.

Greenleaf, C. L., Litman, C., Hanson, T. L., Rosen, R., Boscardin, C. K, Herman, J., & Jones, B. (2010). Integrating literacy and science in biology: Teaching and learning impacts of reading apprenticeship professional development. *American Educational Research Journal, 48,* 1–71.

Greeno, J. G. (2009). A theory bite on contextualizing, framing, and positioning: A companion to Son and Goldstone. *Cognition and Instruction, 27,* 269–275.

Grigg, W., Donahue, P., & Dion, G. (2007). *The nation's report card: 12th grade reading and mathematics* (NCES 2007–468). Washington, DC: National Center for Education Statistics.

Grubb, W. N., & Kraskouskas, E. (1992). *A time to every purpose: Integrating academic and occupational education in community colleges and technical institutes* (MDS-251). Berkeley: University of California at Berkeley, National Center for Research in Vocational Education.

Grubb, W. N., Worthen, H., Byrd, B., Webb, E., Badway, N., Case, C., & Villeneuve, J. C. (1999). *Honored but invisible: An inside look at teaching in community colleges.* New York, NY: Routledge.

Guthrie, J. T., Anderson, E., Alao, S., & Rinehart, J. (1999). Influences of concept-oriented reading instruction on strategy use and conceptual learning from text. *Elementary School Journal, 99,* 343–366.

Hattie, J., Biggs, J., & Purdie, N. (1996). Effects of learning skills interventions on student learning: A meta-analysis. *Review of Educational Research, 66,* 99–136.

Heller, R., & Greenleaf, C. L. (2007). *Literacy instruction in the content areas: Getting to the core of middle and high school improvement.* Washington, DC: Alliance for Excellent Education.

Hendricks, C. C. (2001). Teaching causal reasoning through cognitive apprenticeship: What are results from situated learning? *Journal of Educational Research, 94,* 302–311.

Higbee, J. L., Lundell, D., & Arendale, D. R. (Eds.). (2005). *The general college vision: Integrating intellectual growth, multicultural perspectives, and student development.* Minneapolis: General College and the Center for Research on Developmental Education and Urban Literacy, University of Minnesota-Twin Cities.

Jenkins, D., Zeidenberg, M., & Kienzl, G. (2009). *Educational outcomes of I-BEST, Washington State Community and Technical College System's*

Integrated Basic Education and Skills Training Program: Findings from a multivariate analysis (CCRC Working Paper No. 16). New York, NY: Teachers College, Columbia University, Community College Research Center. Retrieved from http://ccrc.tc.columbia.edu/ContentByType.asp?t=1

Johnson, E. B. (2002). *Contextual teaching and learning: What it is and why it's here to stay.* Thousand Oaks, CA: Corwin.

Kalchik, S., & Oertle, K. M. (2010, September). *The theory and application of contextualized teaching and learning in relation to programs of study and career pathways. Transition highlights* (Issue 2). Retrieved from http://occrl.illinois.edu/files/Highlights/Highlight_09_2010.pdf

Karweit, N. (1998). Contextual learning: Review & synthesis. In A. M. Milne (Ed.), *Educational reform and vocational education* (pp. 53–84). Washington, DC: National Institute on Postsecondary Education, Libraries, and Lifelong Learning. (ERIC Document Reproduction Service No. ED421659)

Klein, P. D. (1999). Reopening inquiry into cognitive processes in writing-to-learn. *Educational Psychology Review, 11*, 203–270.

Kozeracki, C. (2005). Preparing faculty to meet the needs of developmental students. In C. A. Kozeracki (Ed.), *Responding to the challenges of developmental education* (New Directions for Community Colleges, No. 129, pp. 39–49). San Francisco, CA: Jossey-Bass.

Krajcik, J. S., & Sutherland, L. M. (2010). Supporting students in developing literacy in science. *Science, 328*, 456–459.

Lazar, M. K., Bean, R. M., & Van Horn, B. V. (1998). Linking the success of a basic skills program to workplace practices and productivity. *Journal of Adolescent & Adult Literacy, 41*, 352–362.

Lee, C. D., & Spratley, A. (2010). *Reading in the disciplines: The challenges of adolescent literacy.* New York: Carnegie Corporation of New York.

Levin, H. M., & Calcagno, J. C. (2008). Remediation in the community college: An evaluator's perspective. *Community College Review, 35*, 181–207.

Levin, J. S., Cox, E. M., Cerven, C., & Haberler, Z. (2010). The recipe for promising practices in community colleges. *Community College Review, 38*, 31–58.

Martino, N. L., Norris, J., & Hoffman, P. (2001). Reading comprehension instruction: Effects of two types. *Journal of Developmental Education, 25*, 2–10.

Massey, D. D., & Heafner, T. L. (2004). Promoting reading comprehension in the social studies. *Journal of Adolescent and Adult Literacy, 48*, 26–40.

Mayer, R. E., & Wittrock, M. C. (1996). Problem-solving transfer. In D. C. Berliner & R. C. Calfee (Eds.), *Handbook of educational psychology* (pp. 47–62). New York, NY: Macmillan.

Mazzeo, C., Rab, S. Y., & Alssid, J. L. (2003). *Building bridges to college and careers: Contextualized basic skills programs at community colleges.* Brooklyn, NY: Workforce Strategy Center. Retrieved from http://www.workforcestrategy.org/images/pdfs/publications/Contextualized_basic_ed_report.pdf

McDermott, M. (2010). Using multimodal writing tasks in the science classroom. *The Science Teacher, 77*, 32–36.

McKenna, M. C., & Robinson, R. D. (2009). *Teaching through text: Reading and writing in the content areas* (5th ed.). Boston, MA: Pearson Education.

Mikulecky, L. (1994). *Literacy transfer: A review of the literature.* Philadelphia: National Center on Adult Literacy, University of Pennsylvania. Retrieved from http://citeseerx.ist.psu.edu/viewdoc/download?doi=10.1.1.20.6494&rep=rep1&type=pdf

Mikulecky, L., & Lloyd, P. (1997). Evaluation of workplace literacy programs: A profile of effective instructional practices. *Journal of Literacy Research, 29,* 555–585.

Nash-Ditzel, S. (2010). Metacognitive reading strategies can improve self-regulation. *Journal of College Reading and Learning, 40,* 45–63.

National Council for Workforce Education & Jobs for the Future. (2010). *Breaking through: Contextualization toolkit.* Big Rapids, MI: Author. Retrieved from http://www.jff.org/sites/default/files/BT_toolkit_June7.pdf

National Governors' Association and Council of Chief State School Officers. (2010). *Common core state standards: English language arts and literacy in history/social studies, science, and technical subjects.* Retrieved from http://www.corestandards.org/assets/CCSSI_ELA%20Standards.pdf

Nokes, J. D. (2008). Aligning literacy practices in secondary history classes with research on learning. *Middle Grades Research Journal, 3*(3), 29–55.

Parr, B. A., Edwards, M. C., & Leising, J. G. (2008). Does a curriculum integration intervention to improve the mathematics achievement of students diminish their acquisition of technical competence? An experimental study in agricultural mechanics. *Journal of Agricultural Education, 49,* 61–71.

Pearson, P. D. (2010). Literacy and science: Each in the service of the other. *Science, 328,* 459–463.

Perin, D. (1997). Workplace literacy assessment. *Dyslexia, 3,* 190–200.

Perin, D. (2001). Academic-occupational integration as a reform strategy for the community college: Classroom perspectives. *Teachers College Record, 103,* 303–335.

Perin, D. (2005). Institutional decision making for increasing academic preparedness in community colleges. In C. A. Kozeracki (Ed.), *Responding to the challenges of developmental education* (New Directions for Community Colleges, No. 129, pp. 27–38). San Francisco, CA: Jossey-Bass.

Perin, D., & Charron, K. (2006). "Lights just click on every day": Academic preparedness and remediation in community colleges. In T. R. Bailey & V. S. Morest (Eds.), *Defending the community college equity agenda* (pp. 155–194). Baltimore, MD: Johns Hopkins Press.

Perin, D., & Hare, R. (2010). *A contextualized reading-writing intervention for community college students* (CCRC Brief No.44). New York, NY: Community College Research Center, Teachers College, Columbia University. Retrieved from http://ccrc.tc.columbia.edu/Publication.asp?UID=788

Perkins, D. H., & Salomon, G. (1989). Are cognitive skills context-bound? *Educational Researcher, 18,* 16–25.

Prentice, C. M. (2001). ERIC review: Integrating academic and occupational instruction. *Community College Review, 29*(2), 80–93.

Radford, A. W., Berkner, L., Wheeless, S., & Shepherd, B. (2010). *Persistence and attainment of 2003–04 beginning postsecondary students: After six years.* Washington, DC: National Center for Educational Statistics. Retrieved from http://nces.ed.gov/pubsearch/pubsinfo.asp?pubid=2011151

Raelin, J. A. (2008). *Work-based learning: Bridging knowledge and action in the workplace.* San Francisco, CA: Jossey-Bass.

Reisman, A., & Wineburg, S. (2008). Teaching the skill of contextualizing in history. *Social Studies, 99,* 202–207.

Rutschow, E. Z., Richburg-Hayes, L., Brock, T., Orr, G., Cerna, O., Cullinan, D., & Martin, K. (2011). *Turning the tide: Five years of achieving the dream in community colleges.* New York, NY: Manpower Demonstration Research Corporation. Retrieved from http://www.mdrc.org/publications/578/full.pdf

Ryan, R. M., & Deci, E. L. (2000). Intrinsic and extrinsic motivation: Classic definitions and new directions. *Contemporary Educational Psychology, 25,* 54–67.

Salahu-Din, D., Persky, H., & Miller, J. (2008). *The nation's report card: Writing 2007* (NCES 2008-468). Washington, DC: National Center for Education Statistics, Institute of Education Sciences, U.S. Department of Education.

Shore, M., Shore, J., & Boggs, S. (2004). Allied health applications integrated into developmental mathematics using problem based learning. *Mathematics and Computer Education, 38,* 183–189.

Simpson, M. L., Hynd, C. R., Nist, S. L., & Burrell, K. I. (1997). College academic assistance programs and practices. *Educational Psychology Review, 9,* 39–87.

Simpson, M. L., & Nist, S. L. (2002). Encouraging active reading at the college level. In C. C. Block & M. Pressley (Eds.), *Comprehension instruction: Research-based practices* (pp. 365–381). New York, NY: Guilford.

Smagorinsky, P., & Smith, M. W. (1992). The nature of knowledge in composition and literary understanding: The question of specificity. *Review of Educational Research, 62,* 279–305.

Snyder, V. (2002). The effect of course-based reading strategy training on the reading comprehension skills of developmental college students. *Research and Teaching in Developmental Education, 18*(2), 37–41.

Son, J. Y., & Goldstone, R. L. (2009). Contextualization in perspective. *Cognition & Instruction, 27,* 51–89.

Song, B. (2006). Content-based ESL instruction: Long-term effects and outcomes. *English for Specific Purposes, 25,* 420–437.

Stahl, S. A., & Shanahan, C. (2004). Learning to think like a historian: Disciplinary knowledge through critical analysis of multiple documents. In T. L. Jetton & J. A. Dole (Eds.), *Adolescent literacy research and practice* (pp. 94–115). New York, NY: Guilford.

Sticht, T. G. (1995). *The military experience and workplace literacy: A review and synthesis for policy and practice.* Philadelphia, PA: National Center on Adult Literacy. (ERIC Document Reproduction Service No. ED380570)

Sticht, T. G. (2005). *Functional context education: Making learning relevant in the 21st century—Workshop participant's notebook.* Retrieved from http://www.nald.ca/library/research/fce/FCE.pdf

Sticht, T. G., Armstrong, W. A., Hickey, D. T., & Caylor, J. S. (1987). *Cast-off youth: Policy and training methods from the military experience.* New York, NY: Praeger.

Stone, J. R., III, Alfeld, C., Pearson, D., Lewis, M. V., & Jensen, S. (2006). *Building academic skills in context: Testing the value of enhanced math learning in CTE* (Final study). St. Paul, MN: National Research Center for Career and Technical Education. Retrieved from http://136.165.122.102/UserFiles/File/Math-in-CTE/MathLearningFinalStudy.pdf

Tai, E., & Rochford, R. A. (2007). Getting down to basics in western civilization: It's about time. *Community College Journal of Research and Practice, 31,* 103–116.

Tilson, J. L., Castek, J., & Goss, M. (2010). Exploring the influence of science writing instruction on fourth graders' writing development. In R. T. Jimenez,

V. J. Risko, M. K. Hundley, & D. W. Rowe (Eds.), *59th yearbook of the National Reading Conference* (pp. 117–134). Oak Creek, CA: National Reading Conference.

Vaughn, S., Martinez, L. R., Linan-Thompson, S., Reutebuch, C. K., Carlson, C. D., & Francis, D. J. (2009). Enhancing social studies vocabulary and comprehension for seventh-grade English language learners: Findings from two experimental studies. *Journal of Research on Educational Effectiveness, 2*, 297–324.

Washington State Board for Community and Technical Colleges. (2005). *I-BEST: A program integrating adult basic education and workforce training* (Research Report No. 05-2). Olympia, WA: Author.

Weinbaum, A., & Rogers, A. M. (1995). *Contextual learning: A critical aspect of school-to-work transition programs*. Washington, DC: Academy for Educational Development. (ERIC Document Reproduction Service No. 381666)

Weiss, A. J., Visher, M. G., & Wathington, H. (2010). *Learning communities for students in developmental reading: An impact study at Hillsborough Community College*. New York, NY: Columbia University, Teachers College, the National Center for Postsecondary Research.

Wisely, W. C. (2009). *Effectiveness of contextual approaches to developmental math in California community colleges* (Unpublished doctoral dissertation). University of the Pacific, Stockton, CA.

Self-Selected Reading for Enjoyment as a College Developmental Reading Approach

Eric J. Paulson

Eric J. Paulson proposes that college reading programs should prepare students for a lifetime of reading and that the common developmental studies skills-based, direct-instruction methods found in so many college reading programs fall short of meeting the goal of preparing lifelong readers. In this article, Paulson argues that there is great value in delivering a program of self-selected reading for enjoyment with authentic texts. He covers theory and research from across the grade levels and with diverse populations.

The field of college developmental reading does not have a unified, agreed upon approach to creating effective and efficient readers at the college level, as Reynolds and Werner (2003) have pointed out. For example, Keefe and Meyer (1991) assert the appropriateness of a holistic, whole-langugage approach for adult readers, while Bohr (2003) maintained that a constructivist approach can confuse college readers. Despite college developmental educators calling for learner-centered approaches like reader response (e.g., Chamblee, 2003), a direct instruction, skills-based approach has a solid foothold in college developmental reading programs. The influence of the latter is evident in even the most cursory glance at many college reading textbooks, which show a focus on word-level skill building, with exercises that emphasize analyzing the roots of words and defining and memorizing vocabulary stems. When the text excerpts longer than a paragraph are provided in these textbooks, they are often followed by discrete point questions about factual, objective aspects of the text. If we accept that to an extent, textbooks reflect the type of teaching going on in the classroom (Wood, 2003), then college developmental reading practice is often typified by a focus on word-attack strategies and discrete-skill building. In addition, college developmental reading is often seen as consisting of content-area textbook reading and study assistance — a way to "get students through" their other college courses. In some contexts, a focus on skill building can be beneficial for many aspects of students' academic lives given an appropriate metacognitive, strategy-construction approach. However, I proposed that if we identify an important goal of college developmental reading programs as providing a foundation for life-long reading, a study-skills approach to college developmental reading falls short. Instead, we must focus on encouraging and instilling in developmental reading students the belief that reading has intrinsic value. It is through this approach that solid academic progress can be obtained as well.

The purpose of this article is to propose that encouraging *self-selected reading for enjoyment* by college developmental students is the key to generating both academic success and a love of reading. *Free voluntary reading* is a term coined by Krashen (2004) to describe "reading because you want to: no book reports, no questions at the end of the chapter" (p. 1). The term parallels others, such as *self-selected reading* (Cunningham, Hall, & Gambrell, 2002), *extensive reading* (Susser & Robb, 1990), *sustained silent reading* (McCraken, 1971), and more general descriptors like *pleasure reading* or *free reading*. *Self-selected reading for enjoyment*, shortened to SSRE for reasons of economy, will be the default term used here. A working definition of SSRE is reading for the sake of reading—fiction works independently chosen by college developmental readers to read for enjoyment or other intrinsically motivated reasons.

Concerns of reading educators about approaches that focus on and encourage holistic reading for the sake of reading understandably center around whether that approach can provide students with the vocabulary development and reading skills they need to succeed in college. The next section addresses how such an approach can be considered a viable part of a college developmental reading program.

Support for Self-Selected Reading for Enjoyment

Empirical Research on Self-Selected Reading

A curious, but fairly widespread, approach to developmental reading at many levels of education is that readers who are underperforming are given less opportunity to read authentic texts and instead given more drills and out-of-context instruction that involve little if any connected reading. In other words, poor readers get less reading and more worksheets, which only serves to increase the gap between good readers and poor readers (Allington, 1980; Krashen 2004). This trend toward giving troubled readers *less* authentic reading than their more proficient classmates is replicated in college developmental reading classes if the class is built around word analysis instead of being built around reading real texts. In fact, this bias toward explicit skill-and-drill instruction may be bolstered simply because of the lack of a tradition of SSRE approaches in college developmental reading programs. However, evidence that a SSRE approach provides significant academic progress abounds from other populations of students, as the following two sections illustrate.

SELF-SELECTED READING AND K-12 CONTEXTS. Krashen (2004) pointed out that K–12 students who were taught with free voluntary reading scored at least as well, if not better, on comprehension tests than students who were given traditional skills-based instruction: "in-school free reading programs are consistently effective. In 51 out of 54 comparisons (94 percent) readers do as well as or better than students who were engaged in traditional programs" (p. 2). There is a significant relationship between the amount of pleasure reading a student does and that student's spelling performance (Stanovich & West, 1989), and the amount of recreational reading a student does is the best predictor of vocabulary, comprehension, and reading speed (Krashen, 2004). Krashen (2004) summed up the relationship between reading and academic progress:

> Studies showing that reading enhances literacy development lead to what should be an uncontroversial conclusion: Reading is good for you. The research, however, supports a stronger conclusion: Reading is the only way we become good readers, develop a good writing style, an adequate vocabulary, advanced grammatical competence, and the only way we become good spellers. (p. 37)

In short, studies of approaches that share SSRE principles at the K–12 level show self-selected reading for enjoyment to be crucial to academic success.

SELF-SELECTED READING AND SECOND-LANGUAGE CONTEXTS. In the second-language acquisition field, the approach to reading termed "extensive reading" entails students reading large amounts of fiction throughout the course of a semester and responding to it holistically, as opposed to "intensive reading" where students read shorter passages and answer comprehension and vocabulary questions (Aebersold & Field, 1997). Extensive reading approaches have been found to increase reading speed and comprehension (Bell, 2001), increase scores on standardized assessments (Hitosugi & Day, 2004), have a demonstrable positive effect on students' writing (Hafiz & Tudor, 1989), build confidence in reading (Kembo, 1993), increase vocabulary (Day, Omura and Hiramatsu, 1991), and increase motivation to read (Constantino, 1994). Like the K–12 studies reviewed above, these studies of reading in a second or foreign language have shown the dramatic effects of utilizing SSRE-type approaches.

Findings from K–12 and second-language reading populations should be applicable to college developmental readers as well, as the following section describes.

SELF-SELECTED READING AT THE COLLEGE LEVEL. Unfortunately, there is little empirical research on SSRE programs at the college level and any corresponding academic gains. The few studies that have explored the efficacy of a holistic, self-selected reading curriculum, however, show dynamic improvement in standardized reading assessment (Henry, 1995) and in interest and joy in reading (Valeri-Gold, 1995). For example, Henry (1995) had her students read their choice of fiction throughout the semester and write literary letters to each other and to the instructor about the books they were reading. In addition to students demonstrating and articulating an increased desire to read in general, they made a leap of 3.6 grade levels in the 15 weeks of the course, as measured by the Nelson-Denny reading assessment (from 8.6 pre-test to 12.2 post-test averages). A similar result occurred in a version of Henry's class piloted at the University of Cincinnati. Similar to Henry's course, students in the UC course read books of their choice supplied by the instructor, bought from bookstores and borrowed from public libraries, and wrote literary letters to each other and the instructor about their books and reading processes. These students also showed great improvement on a standardized test, in this case the Degrees of Reading Power (DRP). Their pre-test average on the DRP was 26.13 and their post-test average was 45.81 (out of a possible score of 70), a gain similar to that found in Henry's (1995) study, albeit on a different nationally used standardized assessment.

Though there have not as yet been large, replicated studies focused on self-selected reading at the college level, there is evidence to suggest that even by the most quantitative standardized assessment measures, a SSRE approach shows important reading ability gains by students. More research in this area is encouraged.

Evidence from programs in K–12 and second-language learning contexts show SSRE-type approaches to be a powerful intervention in terms of both increases in reading proficiency and intrinsic interest in reading in general. In addition, though there are few empirical studies focused on self-selected reading programs at the college level, the research that does exist shows similar benefits. This convergence of evidence suggests that incorporating a SSRE approach into a college developmental reading program can have powerful instructional implications for students' attitudes toward reading, reading proficiency, and overall academic progress.

Problem: Access to Books

With evidence like that presented above, most would agree that a project designed to encourage college developmental students to read self-selected fiction for enjoyment on a regular basis is worthy, and that success in raising students' academic reading skills and general reading ability and confidence is likely. While step-by-step suggestions for a SSRE curriculum do not yet exist, Henry's (1995) book *If Not Now: Developmental Readers in the College Classroom* provides an engaging primer to such an approach. A key element in such a project, however, is access to books, as there is a positive correlation between access to books and reading ability (Krashen, 1995, 2004). Access in this sense means ability and tendency for students to easily obtain books—a public library a bus ride away seems accessible on paper, but in practical terms is not used as often as a source of books immediately accessible in, for example, the same building in which students attend classes. This is one reason that Elley's (1996) "book flood" programs, where the researcher provided numerous high interest books directly to students' classrooms, were so successful in generating patterns of extensive reading. In addition, in a multiple regression analysis that utilized data from 41 states in the U.S., Krashen (1995) found that significant predictors of National Assessment of Educational Progress (NAEP) reading comprehension test scores were the number of books per student in school libraries. These data point to a key element of extensive reading programs being the immediate accessibility of a variety of books for students to choose from.

The focus of this article concerns the importance of incorporating a SSRE approach in college developmental reading courses, and one important aspect of such an approach is encouraging reading above and beyond the class time frame. Because there is evidence that the longer a free voluntary reading program is run, the more effective it is (Krashen, 2004, p. 3), the more a college reading program can encourage and convince readers that reading for the sake of reading is intrinsically interesting and valuable, the more success those students will experience. To that end, a grant has recently been received at the University of Cincinnati to begin an on-site fiction lending library at the Center for Access and Transition, an open-access unit of the university that focuses on developmental education and underprepared readers. The make-up of the lending library will consist of high-interest fiction (novels, novellas, short stories, poetry, etc., from a wide variety of genre) which will alleviate the problem some of the university's students experience of limited access to books. One challenge will be to incorporate the lending library into curricula so that reading self-selected books for enjoyment eventually becomes part of the culture of the course of study at the Center.

Conclusion

Traditional college developmental reading approaches of word-attack strategies and textbook study assistance have their place in assisting students with their immediate study needs, if this instruction takes place within a constructivist curriculum. But an element conspicuous in its absence from many college developmental reading programs is a focus on long-term development of these students as readers. As Henry (1995) pointed out, students in college developmental reading classes generally do not consider themselves readers and do not enjoy reading in most contexts. While traditional college developmental reading approaches help students improve some aspects of their study habits, there may be little or no change in their view of reading in general, and no change in their reading habits overall. Without changing students' views of themselves as readers and their reading habits, college developmental reading instructors may be contributing to students' views of reading as something unenjoyable that is done out of necessity from time to time, like changing the oil in a car. Without "reading for reading's sake," students are missing a vital element in their development as college students—students who read only what is necessary for class, and do not read for choice, usually do not improve as effective and efficient readers. Stanovich (1986) refers to this as the "Matthew Effect," a rich-get-richer perspective on reading development: the more you read, the better a reader you become. This effect is, of course, part of a larger cycle: the more you read, the better a reader you become, the more you like reading, so the more you read, and so on. It is this cycle that a focus on discrete, word-level skill-building ignores, and it is this cycle that college developmental reading classes must strive to generate. Self-selected reading for enjoyment, with all its implementation challenges, is key to the goal of creating life-long readers at the college level.

References

Aebersold, J. A. & Field, M. L. (1997). *From reader to reading teacher: Issues and strategies for second language classrooms.* Cambridge: Cambridge University Press.

Allington, R. (1980). Poor readers don't get to read much in reading groups. *Language Arts, 57,* 872–876.

Bell, T. (2001). Extensive reading: Speed and comprehension. *The Reading Matrix, 1*(1). Retrieved September 14, 2005, from http://www.readingmatrix.com/articles/bell/index.html

Constantino, R. (1994). Pleasure reading helps, even if readers don't believe it. *Journal of Reading, 37*(6), 504–505.

Cunningham, P. M., Hall, D. P., & Gambrell, L. B. (2002). *Self-selected reading the four-blocks way.* Greensboro, NC: Carson-Dellosa Publishers.

Day, R., Omura, C., & Hiramatsu, M. (1991). Incidental EFL vocabulary learning and reading. *Reading in a Foreign Language, 7*(2), 541–551.

Elley, W. (1996). Using book floods to raise literacy levels in developing countries. In V. Greaney (Ed.), *Promoting reading in developing countries: Views on making reading materials accessible to increase literacy levels* (pp. 148–163). Newark, DE: International Reading Association.

Hafiz, F. M., & Tudor, I. (1989). Extensive reading and the development of language skills. *English Language Teaching Journal, 43,* 4–13.

Henry, J. (1995). *If not now: Developmental readers in the college classroom.* Portsmouth, NH: Heinemann.

Hitosugi, C. I. & Day, R. R. (2004). Extensive reading in Japanese. *Reading in a Foreign Language, 16*(1). Retrieved September 14, 2005, from http://nflrc.hawaii.edu/rfl/April2004/hitosugi/hitosugi.html.

Kembo, J. (1993). Reading: Encouraging and maintaining individual extensive reading. *English Teaching Forum, 31*(2), 36–38.

Krashen, S. D. (1995). School libraries, public libraries, and the NAEP reading scores. *School Library Media Quarterly, 22*(4), 235–237.

Krashen, S. D. (2004). *The power of reading: Insights from the research* (2nd ed.). Westport, CT: Libraries, Unlimited, Portsmouth, NH: Heinemann.

McCracken, R.A. (1971). Initiating sustained silent reading. *Journal of Reading, 14*(8), 521–524, 582–583.

Stanovich, K. E. (1986). Matthew effects in reading: Some consequences of individual differences in the acquisition of literacy. *Reading Research Quarterly, 21,* 360–406.

Stanovich, K. E. & West, R. (1989). Exposure to print and orthographic processing. *Reading Research Quarterly, 24,* 402–433.

Susser, B. & Robb, T. N. (1990). EFL extensive reading instruction: Research and procedure. *JALT Journal, 12*(2). Retrieved September 10, 2005, from http://www.kyoto-su.ac.jp/~trobb/sussrobb.html

Valeri-Gold, M. (1995). Uninterrupted sustained silent reading is an effective authentic method for college developmental learners. *Journal of Reading, 38*(5), 385–386.

Placement and Assessment

Introduction

The word *assessment* can be considered a buzzword, a bad word, or even a fighting word. It is, nonetheless, of major importance in the current educational culture, particularly as it relates to developmental reading.

Cross and Paris (1987) proposed a conception of "assessment" that encompasses the purposes of sorting, diagnosing, and evaluating— all of which are essential components of assessing developmental reading.

We begin with a historically significant work that, though published in 1992, continues to drive conversations about how and why to do assessment for college reading programs, one that carries forward Cross and Paris's triad of assessment purposes. Indeed, Michele Simpson and Sherrie Nist's *Journal of Reading* article is especially timely today given recent studies and reports that have questioned the efficacy of developmental programming (e.g., Alliance for Excellent Education, 2006; Bettinger & Long, 2004; 2005; Calcagno & Long, 2008; Complete College America, 2011; 2012; Jenkins, Jaggars, & Roksa, 2009; Martorell & McFarlin, 2007; Vandal, 2010; Wirt, Choy, Rooney, Provasnik, Sen, & Tobin, 2004) because it has become increasingly important for program administrators (and individual instructors) to provide an evidence base to support curricular decisions and to justify funding allocations. In many cases, this is a new expectation that requires professionals to learn about program evaluation protocols on their own.

We next move to a selection that explores a major purpose for assessment in developmental reading: "sorting." In the context of college reading, sorting essentially means placement, and Edward Behrman and Chris Street report on an investigation of an alternative approach to placement. Their approach incorporates a content-specific reading test rather than a general reading comprehension assessment.

The final selection examines effective assessments, an addition to the Cross and Paris triad of purpose that has recently become regarded as one of the most essential, yet traditionally overlooked aspects of a complete, student-centered assessment model. Kouider Mokhtari and Carla Reichard describe the Metacognitive Awareness of Reading Strategies Inventory (MARSI), an instrument designed to assess readers' metacognitve awareness and use of reading strategies.

Works Cited

Alliance for Excellent Education. (2006). *Paying double: Inadequate high schools and community college remediation.* Retrieved from http://www.all4ed.org/files/archive/publications/remediation.pdf

Bettinger, E., & Long, B. T. (2004). *Shape up or ship out: The effects of remediation on students at four-year colleges* (NBER Working Paper No. 10369). Cambridge, MA: National Bureau of Economic Research.

Bettinger, E., & Long, B. T. (2005). *Addressing the needs of under-prepared students in higher education: Does college remediation work?* (NBER Working Paper No. W11325). Retrieved from http://ssrn.com/abstract=720411

Boylan, H. R., & Bonham, B. S. (n.d.). Criteria for program evaluation. Retrieved from http://ncde.appstate.edu/sites/ncde.appstate.edu/files/evaluation.pdf

Calcagno, J. C., & Long, B. T. (2008). *The impact of postsecondary remediation using a regressions discontinuity approach: Addressing endogenous sorting and noncompliance.* (NBER Working Paper No. 14194). Cambridge, MA: National Bureau of Economic Research.

Complete College America. (2011). *Remediation: Higher education's bridge to nowhere.* Washington, DC: Complete College America.

Complete College America (2011). *Time is the enemy.* Washington, DC: Complete College America.

Cross, D. R., & Paris, S. G. (1987). Assessment of reading comprehension: Matching test purposes and test properties. *Educational Psychologist, 22*(3&4), 313–332.

Jenkins, D., Jaggars, S. S., & Roksa, J. (2009). *Promoting gatekeeper course success among community college students needing remediation.* Retrieved from http://ccrc.tc.columbia.edu/Publication.asp?UID=714

Martorell, P., & McFarlin, I. (2007). *Help or hindrance? The effects of college remediation on academic and labor market outcomes.* Unpublished manuscript.

Paulson, E. J., & Mason-Egan. P. (2007). Retrospective miscue analysis for struggling postsecondary readers. *Journal of Developmental Education, 31*(2), pp. 2–4, 6, 8, 10, 12–13.

Vandal, B. (2010). *Getting past go: Rebuilding the remedial education bridge to college success.* Retrieved from http://www.gettingpastgo.org/docs/GPGpaper.pdf

Wirt, J., Choy, S., Rooney, P., Provasnik, S., Sen, A., & Tobin, R. (2004). *The condition of education 2004* (NCES 2004–077). U.S. Department of Education, National Center for Education Statistics. Washington, DC: U.S. Government Printing Office.

Additional Readings

Belfield, C., & Crosta, P. (2012). *Predicting success in college: The importance of placement tests and high school transcripts* (CCRC Working Paper No. 42). New York, NY: Columbia University, Teacher's College, Community College Research Center.

Fields, R., & Parsad, B. (2012). *Tests and cutscores used for student placement in postsecondary education: Fall 2011.* Washington, DC: National Assessment Governing Board.

Flippo, R. F., & Schumm, J. S. (2009). Reading tests. In R. F. Flippo & D. C. Caverly (Eds.), *Handbook of College Reading and Study Strategies* (2nd ed., pp. 408–464). New York, NY: Routledge.

Flowers, L. A., Bridges, B. K., & Moore, J. L. (2012). Concurrent validity of the Learning and Study Strategies Inventory (LASSI): A study of African American precollege students. *Journal of Black Studies, 43*(2), 146–160.

Grubb, W. N. (2001). *From Black Box to Pandora's Box: Evaluating Remedial/Developmental Education.* New York, NY: Community College Research Center.

Hadden, C. (2000). The ironies of mandatory placement. *Community College Journal of Research and Practice, 24*, 823–838.

Hodara, M., Jaggars, S. S., & Karp, M. M. (2012). *Improving developmental education assessment and placement: Lessons from community colleges across the country* (CCRC Working Paper No. 51). New York, NY: Columbia University, Teachers College, Community College Research Center.

Hughes, K. L., & Scott-Clayton, J. (2011). *Assessing developmental education assessment in community colleges* (CCRC Working Paper No. 19, Assessment of Evidence Series). New York, NY: Columbia University, Teachers College, Community College Research Center.

James, C. L. (2006). *ACCUPLACER OnLine:* Accurate placement tool for developmental pograms? *Journal of Developmental Education, 30*(2), pp. 1–4, 6–8.

Johnston, P., & Costello, P. (2005). Principles for literacy assessment. *Reading Research Quarterly, 40*(20), 256–267.

Levine-Brown, P., Bonham, B. S., Saxon, D. P., & Boylan, H.R. (2008). Affective assessment for developmental students, part 2. *Research in Developmental Education, 22*(2), 1–4.

Meter, J. V., & Herrmann, B. A. (1986–1987). Use and misuse of the Nelson-Denny Reading Test. *Community College Review, 14*(3), 25–30.

Paulson, E. J., & Henry, J. (2002). Does the Degrees of Reading Power assessment reflect the reading process? An eye-movement examination. *Journal of Adolescent and Adult Literacy, 46*(3), 234–244.

Saxon, D. P., Levine-Brown, P., & Boylan, H. (2008). Affective assessment for developmental students, part 1. *Research in Developmental Education, 22*(1), 1–4.

Scott-Clayton, J. (2012). *Do high-stakes placement exams predict college success?* (CCRC Working Paper No. 41). New York, NY: Columbia University, Teachers College, Community College Research Center.

Simpson, M. L. (2002). Program evaluation studies: Strategic learning delivery model suggestions. *Journal of Developmental Education, 26,* 2–10.

Theurer, J. L. (2011). Does accuracy make a difference? Examining the miscues of proficient and less than proficient adult readers. *Literacy Research and Instruction, 50*(3), 173–182

Historically Significant Work

Toward Defining a Comprehensive Assessment Model for College Reading

Michele L. Simpson and Sherrie L. Nist

Michele L. Simpson and Sherrie L. Nist draw on David Cross and Scott Paris's work to define "assessment." Using the Cross and Paris triad of assessment purposes—sorting, diagnosing, and evaluating—the authors present their argument in favor of comprehensive assessment models for developmental reading programs. Simpson and Nist present the seven key characteristics of such a model, and describe an exemplar program.

Although literacy assessment is currently under scrutiny and reconceptualization in U.S. public schools, college reading programs have been slow or reluctant to examine traditional assessment methods. Many developmental programs rely exclusively on one standardized reading test not only to place and diagnose incoming students but also to evaluate program effectiveness (Wood, 1989).

In fact, assessment at the postsecondary level is often viewed only as an accountability issue—a means to an end—with the end being an improved score on a standardized reading test. Whether it is a percentile rank, a Degrees of Reading Power unit, or a cut-off score on a state mandated test, these scores all too often determine how many students will be in the program, in what materials they will be placed, and how long they will remain. Scores also can indicate the success or failure of college reading programs and thus affect funding.

To remedy the situation, some reading professionals search for a "better" standardized test, but unfortunately the solution is not that simple. Rather than simply changing tests or viewing assessment merely as an accountability issue, college reading programs need to conceptualize a comprehensive model of assessment that reflects current reading research and theory, is appropriate to the philosophy and goals of their program, and is unique to the characteristics of their students. Obviously, this task is not easy.

The purpose of this article, then, is to share our perspectives on college reading assessment through an examination of characteristics of a comprehensive assessment model and then to discuss how we have designed an assessment program unique to our university and students.

An Operational Definition

First, however, it is important to operationalize what we mean by the term assessment. Cross and Paris (1987) discuss three major purposes for reading assessment: sorting, diagnosing, and evaluating.

1. Reading tests that sort students do so by arranging them on a continuum from highest to lowest scores. Such tests are usually formal. Sorting is used to predict academic success or to indicate mastery of an instructional program and is usually part of a large-scale educational assessment. An example of sorting at the postsecondary level would be using a combination of Scholastic Achievement Test (SAT) or American College Test (ACT) scores and high level grade point averages to determine which students should be screened for a college reading program.

2. The second purpose of assessment, diagnosing individuals' reading problems, calls for gathering information about a particular student's strategies and processes. The diagnostic findings should be used to make informed decisions about individuals, not decisions about group changes. These diagnostic tests generally focus on a narrow range of reading skills or strategies, and they may be informal. Self-report measures, such as the Learning and Study Strategies Inventory (LASSI), are common, as are tests like the Self Concept of Academic Ability that target affective characteristics.

3. The final purpose of assessment, evaluating, calls for determining whether a particular experimental treatment or instructional program has had an effect on dependent variables such as persistence in college or improved reading performance. Program evaluations typically use standardized or formal tests that are specifically designed to measure the effects of institutional intervention on groups of students. Student improvement is often determined by formal tests such as the Nelson-Denny, the Degrees of Reading Power, or the Descriptive Test of Language Skills and by institutionally designed tests, any of which might be given at the beginning of the term and again at the end. Programmatic, instructional, or textbook changes are often made as a result of evaluations.

A comprehensive model of assessment, then, includes a variety of formal and informal instruments that sort, diagnose, and evaluate.

Characteristics of a Comprehensive Model of Assessment

It is obvious that assessment is multidimensional. The information gleaned should be viewed as an integral part of the instructional process that informs and empowers students and instructors.

Campione and Brown (1985) refer to this type of assessment as dynamic, and others label it interactive. As instructors interact with students and texts and model strategic reading processes, they look for patterns in how students construct meaning. This procedure, in turn, informs and shapes decisions about materials, tasks, pacing, and feedback for future lessons.

Such a recursive model of instruction and assessment can also empower students so that they become informed about and responsible for their own learning. When all pieces of the assessment puzzle are in place and operating effectively, students learn how to capitalize on their strengths and improve their weaknesses, instructors are well informed about students' progress, and institutions can make informed decisions about programmatic issues.

More specifically, we believe from our own experiences and a review of the literature that a comprehensive model of assessment has the following characteristics:

1. A match exists between the philosophical base, the short- and long-term goals of the reading program, and the assessment instruments used. Without this match, program validity is seriously compromised.

2. Sorting, diagnosing, and evaluating occur across tasks and texts since mastery of a strategy is a relative condition. Texts, especially those used for diagnosis, are lengthy, varied (theoretical versus factual, low prior knowledge versus high prior knowledge), and representative of the college texts students encounter (considerate as well as inconsiderate).

3. Multiple cutting scores and multiple variables are used for sorting and diagnosis, rather than a singular test or score (Morante, 1989).

4. Assessment instruments measure various types of processing. Wixson and Peters (1987) suggest assessing students' processing at the intersentence, text, and beyond-text levels. At the college level, assessing students' processing across texts is also important—knowing if students can modify their processing strategies according to content area and task is critical.

5. Diagnosis and evaluation are ongoing and inextricably involved with the recursive instructional phase. The information gained from

diagnosis and evaluation informs instructors about strengths and needs as students move toward strategy mastery.

6. Students are involved in their own diagnosis as well as in the evaluation of whether they accomplished short- and long-term programmatic goals.

7. Testing for testing's sake is avoided. Assessment measures provide pertinent and practical information that is used to improve instruction and inform students.

It is difficult, perhaps impossible, for one reading program to possess all of these characteristics. However, the difficulty of achieving perfection should not deter college reading professionals from incorporating as many of these characteristics as possible into their assessment program.

What follows is a description of our still evolving assessment model. As you will note, it is neither perfect nor complete. It does, however, incorporate many of the characteristics mentioned above.

Toward a Comprehensive Assessment Model

The assessment program described here sorts all university freshmen and diagnoses and evaluates those identified as at risk, using a variety of formal and informal measures. These measures were selected to reflect the short- and long-term goals of the program, not to dictate them. Because this assessment model is goal-driven, it is important first to discuss the nature of our college reading course.

The course could best be described as process-based in that we assume that reading is a constructive process and that meaning emerges from interactions among text, task, and students (Jenkins, 1979). As instructors, our short-term goal is to help students become strategic readers and active independent learners. The long-term goal is to help students succeed in college.

Rather than isolating discrete reading skills or objectives to be mastered, we describe the characteristics of strategic readers and directly teach strategies that lead to the development of these characteristics. We generally use longer pieces of text (e.g., an entire text chapter) and teach strategies that focus on cognitive and metacognitive processes such as encoding, organizing, monitoring, planning, and evaluating. Hence, our assessment procedures not only measure these processes, but also determine whether or not students have mastered them. To make this determination, we sort, diagnose, and evaluate students using a variety of measures.

SORTING. When students apply to our university, their SAT scores and high school grade point averages identify whether they need a college reading class. These two pieces of information together are used in a regression equation that predicts grade point averages for the end of their first year. Those identified as not needing a reading course enroll in regular courses; those needing intervention are further sorted to determine which level of reading course is most appropriate.

To make this determination we first administer a state-mandated test similar to traditional reading tests. Students read a series of short passages and answer multiple choice questions over vocabulary, main ideas, details, tone, and mood. Because this particular test supplies little information about process, except at the sentence and intersentence levels, and because we believe in the importance of using multiple measures, students are further sorted with two informal measures developed specifically for our purposes and population.

Second, students take a more informal sorting measure, an extended reading taken from a college level psychology textbook, to simulate a task that they will encounter frequently during their first 2 years of college. They read and study the 2,500-word excerpt in preparation for an objective test. Following reading and studying, they hand in the excerpt and any study materials (e.g., notes) and answer 15 text explicit and implicit multiple choice questions.

Scores on the extended reading yield information about students' abilities to process college level material. With additions beyond our format, instructors can gather even more information about individuals. For example, students could answer essay questions as well as objective items. These essays could be scored holistically or by using a template with assigned points.

Because of time constraints and the number of students involved at this stage of our sorting process (over 400), we have eliminated the essay portion. However, smaller programs might seriously consider including essay writing as it provides considerable insights into students' constructive processes that objective tests cannot.

Thus, in order to place students as accurately as possible, we use the multiple pieces of data that we have gathered. Using SAT scores, state-mandated test scores, and raw scores on the extended psychology excerpt, we sort the new students into three groups. Those who score above a predetermined cutting score on all three measures are exempted from taking any reading course. Those who score at or above the cutting scores on two of the three measures are placed in the upper level reading course. Those scoring below the cutting scores on two of the three measures are placed in the lower level course.

All students have been sorted prior to the first day of class. As they progress through the term, they enter the second phase of assessment, diagnosis.

DIAGNOSING. As mentioned earlier, many college reading programs use formal, standardized measures for student diagnosis. But some of these tests have not been designed for diagnostic purposes, so they provide only a static and limited sample of student outcomes (Wood, 1989). Diagnosis should be an ongoing process directly related to instruction. Moreover, we believe that diagnosis should evolve into a responsibility between students and instructor.

Over time we have depended on a wide variety of informal diagnostic measures, all of which are tied to the goals of the reading courses. Some of these measures rely on student self-report. Although self-report has some limitations (i.e., Alexander & Judy, 1988; Baker, 1982; Garner & Alexander, 1982), we find the information gained extremely useful.

One measure used at the beginning of the course is the Learning and Study Strategies Inventory (LASSI). The LASSI provides both students and instructors with valuable information about perceived strengths and weaknesses in both affective and cognitive domains and in skills such as time management, information processing, and self-testing.

Once students have completed the LASSI profile they write a brief journal entry answering the following questions:

1. According to the LASSI, what are your areas of strength? Do the results make sense with what you know about yourself? Explain. Any surprises? Explain.

2. According to the LASSI, on what areas do you need to focus this quarter (the low scores)? Do the results make sense with what you know about yourself? Explain. Any surprises? Explain.

3. Using the information from the LASSI and what you know about yourself as a reader and learner, what are your goals for this quarter?

Students hand in the LASSI profile and journal entry, which are saved for discussion in later conferences. In addition to providing meaningful discussion points for student conferences, these profiles and entries serve several other vital instructional purposes.

First, we compile a list of students who score low on test anxiety (indicating high anxiety) and refer them for special assistance. Second, we use the profiles as each strategy is introduced during the term. For example, when textbook marking is introduced, we ask students who scored low on the information processing scale to pay particular attention to and practice this strategy since it will improve their ability to read and process text information elaboratively.

Finally, at the end of the term, we return these journal entries to students so they can write their final self-evaluation journal entry, an evaluation measure we will describe later.

Perhaps the greatest amount of diagnostic information gathered about students, however, comes from their practice endeavors. After we introduce a strategy and provide modeling and examples, students practice the strategy on a full length content area chapter. For example, as students learn to mark text by noting key points in the margin, they complete a part of the chapter and receive extensive feedback before finishing the remainder of their chapter annotations.

This feedback takes two forms. First, we mark any key information missed and reword any misstatements of ideas. Second, we provide more global feedback in the form of a checklist. (For a detailed explanation of both the annotation procedure and the checklist see Simpson & Nist, 1990.)

From the checklist students learn what they did correctly and what needs revising before they prepare for the exam over the chapter. More importantly, the checklist informs instructors about the problems students are having as they construct meaning from the text and represent that meaning in their annotations. The checklist reveals which students are attempting to memorize the text as opposed to paraphrasing, or which students are focusing on details to the exclusion of superordinate ideas.

Using diagnostic information such as this, we design the next day's lessons. This cycle is repeated for each strategy taught and for each text chapter read and studied.

Gradually, we encourage students to take the responsibility of diagnosis on themselves. During class they meet with partners or in small groups to examine one another's strategies. In addition, they learn to diagnose errors on chapter exams using PLAE, a test evaluation strategy (Nist & Simpson, 1989).

As part of the PLAE diagnosis, students answer the following questions:

1. Was the test what I expected? Why or why not?

2. Did I follow my plan for studying? If not, what events or situations interfered with carrying out the plan. Explain.

3. How many hours did I study? Were those hours distributed or massed?

4. Did I miss questions because I didn't know or recognize information? If so, where did the information come from? Lectures? Textbooks?

5. Was there a pattern to my errors? What was the pattern?

6. Did I select the most appropriate study strategies for this test? If not, which ones would be more appropriate next time? List.

By the end of the term, many students become proficient in determining the strategies that work best for them in a particular learning situation. Those who struggle with self-diagnosis may find conferences helpful for examining the strategies they have created and going over the test in detail. Not only is the conference useful in helping students diagnose their efforts objectively, but it also provides instructors with additional diagnostic information to help those still having difficulty.

The process of ongoing diagnosis, consisting almost totally of informal measures, is perhaps the most important aspect of our assessment model. Because we continuously monitor student change and adaptation to strategies, we can modify instruction to meet student needs. But our model is still incomplete. The final step is to determine how well the diagnosing worked by once again examining the group as a whole to see how successful they have been in applying the strategies in actual college learning situations.

EVALUATING. Data are collected in the evaluating stage to examine both short- and long-term program goals. Every student enrolled in our program must retake the state-mandated reading test again at the end of the term. We administer this test merely to comply with the rules since it does not provide us with much evaluative information about whether students have become strategic learners. Consequently, we have developed several evaluation measures that are more reflective of our programmatic goals.

Perhaps the most useful short-term evaluative information comes from students' performance on the final exam given in the reading course. In some ways the kind of processing required to do well on the final exam is similar to but more complex than that which is needed to do well on the extended text excerpt used in the sorting stage.

For example, the final exam in the upper level course focuses on information about the U.S. in the 1960s. Students read a history chapter that covers Kennedy's and Johnson's presidential administrations as well as a *Newsweek* article about Vietnam. In addition, they listen to a lecture on the Vietnam War and see a film about civil rights. Hence, students have to process across a variety of texts, a more demanding task than the extended reading that covers only one piece of text.

Over time we have developed a final exam that we believe is a fair representation of tasks students will face once they enroll in regular classes. Students scoring a C or above appear to be strategic learners ready for those challenges in core college courses such as psychology, history, and sociology.

Students themselves are involved in the evaluation process in two different ways. At the end of the course, they are required to complete a final self-evaluation journal entry. They answer eight questions

Figure 1. Questions for the Final Self-Evaluation Journal Entry

1. What areas on the LASSI do you feel you have improved upon? Why do you feel this way? What strategies or ideas have helped you see this improvement?

2. What areas on the LASSI do you feel remained the same? Why? What could you do to improve them?

3. What have you learned since September about college level tasks?

4. How have your textbook reading and exam preparation methods changed since September? Compare your high school experiences to these past 10 weeks.

5. How have your reading fluency, flexibility, and rate changed since September? (Check your text for the meanings of these words if you have forgotten them.)

6. How has your reading, writing, listening, and speaking vocabulary changed since September?

7. How have your time management skills improved since September? If no change has occurred, why?

8. Imagine that a younger brother/sister or friend has asked you about college. What would you tell them that you have learned in these past 10 weeks that you wished you had learned in high school?

Note: The Learning and Study Skills Inventory (LASSI) is a self-report measure revealing perceived strengths and weaknesses in both affective and cognitive domains and in skills such as time management, information processing, and self-testing.

focusing on strategies and processes taught in the course (see Figure 1 for the questions). They refer to their LASSI profiles from the beginning of the term and to their practice endeavors to determine possible personal changes.

Marty's answers to four of the eight questions can be seen in Figure 2. His initial scores indicated that he needed work on almost all of the LASSI subscales, but, in particular, he needed to concentrate on Attitude, Motivation, Test Anxiety, and Self-Testing. Note that he evaluated himself as improving in most areas except for test anxiety.

The second way students become involved in the evaluation process is through responding to a questionnaire. After students have completed two quarters of the university's regular core courses, we often send them a questionnaire asking them to describe the strategies they are using, the difficulties they are having, and the strategies from the reading course that they find most and least useful. The return rate is never very high, but we still receive some insightful data.

To evaluate our long-term goal of improving student performance at the university, we examine how students perform in regular college

Figure 2. Marty's Answers to Four Questions from Final Self-Evaluation Journal Entry

1. What areas on the LASSI do you feel you have improved upon? Why do you feel this way? What strategies or ideas have helped you see this improvement?

   Marty's reply: The last 10 weeks have just seemed to speed by. I just reviewed my first journal entry and it seemed like I wrote it a couple weeks ago. I think I have improved in many areas that were covered by the LASSI. My attitude, motivation, and time management have all improved. I believe that I now select main ideas better thanks to the repeated annotation of chapters. And my use of support techniques and test strategies have improved due to annotations and the recitation strategies that we learned.

2. What areas on the LASSI do you feel remained the same? Why? What could you do to improve them?

   Marty's reply: I think my test anxiety has remained the same. It will improve with better preparation for examinations. It remained the same because I did not think it as a big problem and did not pay too much attention to it. I guess that it is good, in a way, not thinking about test anxiety.

3. What have you learned since September about college level tasks?

   *Marty's reply:*The college level assignments, lectures, and exams are a great deal larger than anything that I have had previously in high school. Specifically, the lectures and reading assignments are filled with much more material in greater detail than those in high school courses. In the last 10 weeks I have spent a greater percentage of my time studying than I ever had in high school.

8. Imagine that a younger brother/sister or friend has asked you about college. What would you tell them that you have learned in these past 10 weeks that you wished you had learned in high school?

   Finally, my advice to my younger sister. In the last 10 weeks I have learned many study skills and habits that make my study time more efficient. This is a big help because lately there just has not been a lot of my time in which I had absolutely nothing to work on. And if you fall behind it is not as easy to catch up in college as it was in high school. I just wish I knew some of these study methods in high school — I could have done so much better.

courses. Their grades are collected for 1 year following matriculation into the regular curriculum. Not only do we learn their grades for each course, but we also collect data concerning how they compare with students who were not enrolled in our courses.

This information is especially useful in determining how well we are preparing students for tasks required in a variety of content areas. If our students are experiencing problems in specific courses with specific task demands, we alter the curriculum to meet these needs. For example, 2 years ago we modified our curriculum to include more practice in writing essay examinations when we discovered that students were performing poorly in introductory history classes that used essay examinations.

Overall, our students are quite competitive with regularly admitted students. Approximately 70% of those who satisfactorily complete reading courses make a C or better in introductory courses such as psychology, history, sociology, and political science. About 85% of regularly admitted students' averages are also within the C range, but it is important to keep in mind that our students were predicted to make Ds in these courses without intervention.

While we cannot draw any causal links between reading course performance and performance in introductory content courses, we believe that continued collection of data such as these assists us in program evaluation.

Additional Considerations

Our assessment program is evolving, is in no way perfect, and continues to change. We are still developing and refining ways in which we sort, diagnose, and evaluate in an attempt to make our assessment procedures valid, reliable, and useful to instruction and students. Some other assessment measures that deserve consideration include the following:

1. The Sentence Verification Task (SVT) (Royer, Greene, & Sinatra, 1987; Royer, Marchant, Sinatra, & Lovejoy, 1990)—This instrument appears to have potential for both sorting and diagnosing. We are currently piloting this test as part of the initial sorting package, but the early data indicate that the SVT may be equally valuable as a diagnostic tool.

2. Student interviews—Although we feel that interviewing students would be a valuable way to gather important information for evaluation, we also realize that it is time consuming. One type of interview that we find particularly intriguing, however, is one that would focus on task specific and domain specific strategies. Finding out what particular strategies students find useful in specific courses for specific tasks would provide information that would help determine the reading curriculum.

3. Posttesting on instruments given during sorting—Although most programs give some sort of pre and post standardized test to measure cognitive growth, few give any kind of measures that look at affective growth. Instruments such as the LASSI, while expensive to use as both a pre- and posttest, would provide evidence in knowledge of study strategies, for example. In addition, programs might consider more informal measures, such as beginning and ending journal entries, as a

means of affective evaluation. We feel strongly that more evaluation procedures like these should be piloted.

College reading professionals who are grappling with assessment issues might start by asking the questions we did when we began examining our assessment model: What is it that we want to accomplish? Do we want more from our program than student improvement on a standardized reading text? If so, what do we want students to learn on a short- and long-term basis?

Once the questions of program goals and philosophy have been defined, the issue of outlining a comprehensive model of assessment designed for a unique and specific program can be addressed.

References

Alexander, P. A., & Judy, J. E. (1988). The interaction of domain-specific and strategic knowledge in academic performance. *Review of Educational Research, 58*, 375–404.

Baker, L. (1982). An evaluation of the role of metacognitive deficits in learning disabilities. *Topic in Learning and Learning Disabilities, 2*, 27–35.

Campione, J. C., & Brown, A. L. (1985). *Dynamic assessment: One approach and some initial data.* (Technical Report No. 361). Urbana, IL: Center for the Study of Reading.

Cross, D. R., & Paris, S. G. (1987). Assessment of reading comprehension: Matching test purposes and test properties. *Educational Psychologist, 22*, 313–322.

Garner, R., & Alexander, P. A., (1982). Strategic processing of text: An investigation of the effect of adults' question/answering performance. *Journal of Educational Research, 75*, 144–148.

Jenkins, J. J. (1979). Four points to remember: A tetrahedral model and memory experiments. In L. S. Cermack & F. I. M. Craik (Eds.), *Levels and processing in human memory* (pp. 429–445). Hillsdale, NJ: Erlbaum.

Morante, E. A. (1989). Selecting tests and placing students. *Journal of Developmental Education, 13*, 2–6.

Nist, S. L., & Simpson, M. L. (1989). PLAE, a validated study strategy. *Journal of Reading, 33*, 182–186.

Royer, J. M., Greene, B. A., & Sinatra, G. M. (1987). The Sentence Verification Technique: A practical procedure teachers can use to develop their own reading and listening comprehension tests. *Journal of Reading, 30*, 414–423.

Royer, J. M., Marchant, H. G. III, Sinatra, G. M., & Lovejoy, D. A. (1990). The prediction of college course performance from reading comprehension performance: Evidence for general and specific prediction factors. *American Educational Research Journal, 27*, 158–169.

Simpson, M. L., & Nist, S. L. (1990). Textbook annotation: An effective and efficient study strategy for college students. *Journal of Reading, 34*, 122–131.

Wixson, K. K., & Peters, C. W. (1987). Comprehension assessment: Implementing an interactive view of reading. *Educational Psychologist, 22*, 332–356.

Wood, N. V. (1989). Reading tests and reading assessment. *Journal of Developmental Education, 13*, 14–18.

The Validity of Using a Content-Specific Reading Comprehension Test for College Placement

Edward H. Behrman and Chris Street

Edward H. Behrman and Chris Street describe a study of the validity of a content-specific reading test used to place students in college-level coursework or developmental reading. The assessment instrument they describe provides readers with passages exclusively from the subject area for which the placement decision is intended. The authors' research concludes that the content-specific test is a significant predictor of course grades. Because most current college reading placement instruments do not account for the variability in reading across domains, Behrman and Street's article is both timely and relevant considering current conversations about disciplinary literacy instruction (see Chapter 5 in this text for additional discussion on this topic).

The scope and importance of reading placement testing at American colleges cannot be underestimated. Reading placement tests often determine whether incoming students will be allowed to pursue degree-level coursework immediately or be required first to enroll in developmental (remedial) courses. Each year a large proportion of entering college students are thus assigned to non-credit-level developmental reading courses. Of the 2.4 million freshmen attending 2-year and 4-year colleges in the United States in 2000, 11 percent or about 260,000 students were required to take a developmental reading course (Parsad & Lewis, 2003).

Unfortunately, despite the common wisdom that general reading ability should be related to academic achievement, reading placement tests have shown a negligible to modest relationship to grades in credit-level college courses (American College Testing Program, 1990; Armstrong, 1994; Brown, Fishco, & Hanna, 1993, citing Guidan; College of the Canyons, 1994; Feldt, 1989; Kessler, 1987). Reading tests in common use, such as ACCUPLACER, APS, ASSET, and Nelson-Denny, are grounded in a domain-generic model of comprehension that assumes "a good reader is a good reader," no matter the content. These content-general reading tests present passages from a variety of subject areas and yield a global comprehension score. However, research suggests that learning is based on both domain-specific and domain-generic factors, with emerging evidence that domain-specific factors may have primacy (for reviews, see Alexander & Judy, 1988; Byrnes, 1995). Further, both schema theory (Anderson, 1984; Anderson & Pearson, 1984; Mason & staff, 1984; Rumelhart, 1981; Wilson & Anderson, 1986) and the construction-integration model of reading (Kintsch, 1986, 1988; Kintsch & vanDijk, 1978; Mannes & Kintsch, 1987; Moravcsik &

Kintsch, 1993; vanDijk & Kintsch, 1983) support the domain-related nature of understanding and learning from text.

As an alternative to using content-general reading tests that mask the influence of domain-specific knowledge and domain-specific reading strategies on comprehension, it has been recommended that content-specific reading placement tests might be more valid predictors of course success (Behrman, 2000). A content-specific reading test would measure the reader's ability to comprehend text in a particular subject area, such as history, psychology, literature, or biology. Such a test would present passages exclusively from the academic discipline for which the placement decision would be made, and the comprehension score would indicate the examinee's ability to understand text in that subject area. The purpose of the present study is to explore the validity of using content-specific reading tests for college placement decisions by examining the relationship among scores on a content-general reading test, a content-specific reading test, a test of prior domain knowledge, and grades in an introductory human anatomy class.

Theoretical Framework

Establishing Validity of Placement Decisions

Because the intent of placement testing is to predict whether or not a student will be successful in credit-level coursework, the proper external measure of a placement test's validity is the relationship between placement test scores and grades in the target credit-level course rather than the developmental course (Sawyer, 1989, 1996). In the ideal placement situation we would be able to accurately predict which students are academically prepared for the demands of college study. Using Guilford's (1956) classification, each placement decision therefore falls into one of four quadrants: successful predictors, successful non-predictors, unsuccessful predictors, and unsuccessful non-predictors. A good placement test would minimize the proportion of successful non-predictors and unsuccessful predictors. Put another way, the majority of students placed directly in the credit-level course would be successful without the need for developmental coursework; and the majority of those placed into the developmental course would not have been successful if placed directly into the credit-level course.

However, the strength of the placement test-criterion relationship is not by itself sufficient for validity claims. AERA/APA/NCME standards emphasize that internal evidence, such as a conceptual framework underlying the test's development, may also be required to establish validity (Joint Committee, 1999). Although dissatisfied with current notions of reliability and validity, Schoenfeld (1999) echoes this same point: "If you are going to test for students' understanding of something, then (a) you have to have an adequate characterization of what it is you're assessing, and (b) you need to have a good idea of how performance on the assessment corresponds to being able to do whatever it is that's supposedly being assessed" (p. 11). Content-general reading tests may serve poorly as placement instruments because they score low in both areas: (a) they are founded on an assumption that reading comprehension is not mediated by the nature of the reading content; and (b) they attempt to predict performance in a particular course by presenting examinees with passages from different subjects altogether. An "adequate characterization" of reading comprehension would require attention to four areas of psychological and educational inquiry that build a theoretical basis for the role of content-specific factors in comprehension, and by extension, to the need for a domain-specific approach to placement testing: domain-knowledge research, schema theory, the construction-integration model, and expert-novice studies.

Domain-Knowledge Research

Although there has been a long-standing debate in cognitive psychology as to whether learning new concepts is more a function of domain-specific knowledge or general reasoning ability (Lawson et al., 1991), two extensive literature reviews (Alexander & Judy, 1988; Byrnes, 1995) provide evidence for the dominance of domain-specific knowledge. Byrnes (1995) found that declarative knowledge ("knowing what") is domain-specific, and that procedural knowledge ("knowing how"), which may be domain-specific or domain-general, always starts out as domain-specific. Byrnes concluded that domain-general ability was less important than domain-specific ability as a determinant of learning. According to Byrnes, any apparent ability to learn across content areas may be a function of processing speed, cross-disciplinary strategy use, or metacognitive skills, not general capacity.

Alexander and Judy (1988) found that although domain-specific declarative knowledge by itself will not lead to successful task performance unless the learner can use strategic knowledge, accurate and complete domain-specific declarative knowledge is a necessary precondition for efficient use of both domain-specific and domain-general strategic knowledge. In addition, they reported that incorrect or incomplete domain-specific declarative knowledge may hinder task performance and that lack of domain-specific declarative knowledge leads to use of inefficient strategies. They concluded that the relative importance of domain-specific declarative knowledge may depend upon the nature of the domain or the requirements of the task.

Taken together, these two reviews suggest that the ability to read with understanding would not be constant across disciplines, since learning depends upon domain-based declarative knowledge and domain-related strategies, in addition to more generalized strategies. To the extent that "general reading ability" exists, it may therefore be limited to the ability to process text fluently and automatically, recognize the opportunity to use generalized strategies when applicable, and monitor reading progress. Further, because application of reading strategies is enhanced by domain-specific declarative knowledge, a reader who possesses "general reading ability" but lacks domain-specific knowledge may still be unable to derive meaning from text.

Schema Theory

According to schema theory (Anderson, 1984; Anderson & Pearson, 1984; Mason & staff, 1984; Rumelhart, 1981; Wilson & Anderson, 1986), a reader's schema, or abstracted mental structure, for a topic is activated while reading about that topic. Schema theory has strongly influenced reading educators to conclude that meaning resides not in the text alone but also in the mind of the reader (e.g., National Institute of Child Health and Human Development, 2000). Efficient readers have the ability to quickly call up the appropriate schema and correctly use the schema to fill in information not provided in the text (Rumelhart, 1981). Readers also utilize schemata to generate tentative hypotheses about text to be confirmed or rejected as reading continues (Mason & staff, 1984). Anderson and Pearson (1984) concluded that prior experience or exposure improves comprehension, since a fully developed schema helps the reader make inferences, direct attention to important rather than trivial information, and plan for recall.

It follows that the reader may comprehend more from a passage dealing with familiar content than with unfamiliar content. But content-general reading assessments are insensitive to a reader's varied content, textual, and linguistic schemata. By amalgamating the examinee's responses across the range of passages from different subject areas, the composite reading-comprehension score purports to represent a trait (generic reading ability) that is difficult to interpret in light of schema theory, which posits that comprehension is highly content-dependent and thus differential across content areas. Proponents of content-general testing may claim that the effects of prior knowledge are "washed out" by the variety of content areas presented, but such a claim is unfounded. In fact, composite scores from content-general tests are biased, not controlled, by prior knowledge (Johnston, 1984). Examinees are placed at a great advantage (or disadvantage) depending on which subject areas and topics are presented on the content-general test.

Construction-Integration Model

The construction-integration model of reading (Kintsch, 1986, 1988; Kintsch & vanDijk, 1978; Mannes & Kintsch, 1987; Moravcsik & Kintsch, 1993; vanDijk & Kintsch, 1983) asserts that the reader engages text at three levels of representation. Surface-level representations are "processes concerned with the parsing of text" (Kintsch, 1986, p. 89) when words, phrases, and their linguistic relations are encoded into working memory. Textbase representation establishes meaning of text as the reader builds propositions and works toward coherence by finding the relationships among propositions. Situational representation occurs as the reader connects the overall situation described by the text to his or her knowledge system. Situational representation may involve adding to an existing situation model or developing a new one. In general, the textbase model allows the reader to recall or summarize the text and the situational model allows the reader to draw inferences, elaborate, and solve problems.

According to the construction-integration model, the representations needed by an examinee during a reading comprehension test would depend upon the nature of the test items. Comprehension-test items that require the examinee to reproduce or recall stated information may require only a sufficient textbase representation. On the other hand, items that require the examinee to expand, interpret, apply, or elaborate upon stated information may require a sufficient situational representation. Thus, reading tests that include items measuring inference or application would tend to favor readers who have enough knowledge to develop an adequate situational representation.

Expert-Novice Studies

Overall, empirical studies that compare high-knowledge subjects (domain experts) to low-knowledge subjects (domain novices) in relation to comprehension and other factors related to reading support the theoretical position that prior knowledge is strongly related to college students' understanding of text, although not all studies agree on the performance outcomes of prior knowledge. For example, Stahl, Hare, Sinatra, and Gregory (1991) found no differences in factual recall between high-knowledge and low-knowledge subjects, but high-knowledge subjects were better able to infer an organization of the facts. Shimoda (1993) found that topic familiarity improved speed and improved short-term accuracy for recognition questions. Royer, Carlo, Dufresne, and Mestre (1996) found that without domain expertise, a reader may be able to understand the gist of non-technical text, but is unable to draw inferences. Domain expertise of college students has been shown to be related to reading comprehension in history (Hall & Edmundson, 1992; McNamara & Kintsch, 1996; Shapiro, 2004; Voss & Silfies, 1996), literature (Zeitz, 1994), psychology (Royer et al., 1996; Shapiro, 2004), and physics (Alexander & Kulikowich, 1994; Royer et al., 1996).

Two studies emphasizing the important role of domain expertise among college students are of particular interest. In the first study, college students were pre-tested for history knowledge and then presented either expanded (well-developed causal structure) or unexpanded (poorly developed causal structure) versions of fictitious history accounts (Voss & Silfies, 1996). Prior knowledge was not significantly correlated with literal comprehension after reading expanded text but was significantly related with comprehension after reading unexpanded text. In other words, prior knowledge had a positive effect on literal comprehension when texts were sparse in content and readers had to rely more on schemata. It should be noted that since researchers used fictitious text, subjects could not use prior knowledge of the text topic, but rather background knowledge of more general history concepts as well as content-related reading skills.

In the second study, college students were asked to read a physics or psychology text to investigate how domain expertise was affected by complexity of cognitive task (Royer et al., 1996). Experts were advanced undergraduate majors and novices were students in an introductory class. Subjects were post-tested at three increasing levels of cognitive skill development: (1) surface-level understanding; (2) near inference (combining information from two different sections of text) and far inference (combining text information with outside knowledge); and (3) the representational stage of problem solving in which subjects decided whether or not an example problem conformed to the underlying concept or principle in a previously stated problem. Experts outperformed novices on all tests, even after controlling for verbal and math SAT scores. Overall, the differential in performance between experts and novices increased as the level of cognitive skill increased: in psychology, difference increased at each level, while in physics differences on inference and problem-solving tests were about the same, but greater than on surface-level understanding. Thus, after students read technical academic text in either content area, expertise was significantly related to test performance, with expertise becoming more advantageous as tasks became more complex. Such a finding makes the proposal for content-specific reading assessment even more compelling, as success in credit-level college courses may be more related to inferential thinking and problem-solving skills than upon lower-level cognitive tasks.

In the present study, college freshmen enrolled in an introductory human anatomy class were administered a content-general reading test, a content-specific reading test, and a test of prior domain knowledge on the first day of class in order to contrast the ability of each test to predict course grades. Three research questions are addressed in the study:

1. How well does a content-specific reading comprehension test predict grades in a credit-level college course?

2. Does the content-specific reading comprehension test predict course grades better than a content-general reading comprehension test?

3. Would the prediction of course grades be improved by using a combination of content-general reading comprehension, content-specific reading comprehension, and domain knowledge tests?

Method

Setting

The study was conducted in an introductory human anatomy class at a large community college in southern California. The anatomy course was required for students entering biology, nursing, or health-related majors. Although it was recommended that students entering the anatomy class be eligible to enroll in English 1 A (reading and composition), there was no formal reading prerequisite for the anatomy class. The course included a two-hour lecture and six-hour lab session each week over the 16-week semester. In addition to weekly class meetings, students were expected to devote a considerable amount of time reading and studying outside of the classroom.

Historically, the anatomy course had proven difficult for many students and tended to derail some students interested in health sciences, with failure or withdrawal rates as high as 50 percent. Many students who were unable to attain a grade of C in the course (even after several attempts) dropped out of their health-related major. Informal conversation with several department chairs from area community colleges indicated that the high attrition rate at this college was typical for this course across institutions.

Participants

Forty-nine community college students in an introductory human anatomy course participated in the study. At the first class meeting the instructor requested that the students voluntarily participate and all agreed. There was no compensation for participation. There were 28 women and 21 men in the class. The class comprised 16 Hispanic American, 14 European American, 10 African American, and 9 Asian American students. Fourteen of the students reported they were non-native English speakers.

Instruments and Procedure

A content-general reading comprehension test, a content-specific reading comprehension test, and a test of prior knowledge were used as predictors of course success. The content-general reading comprehension test was Form C1 of ASSET (*Assessment of Skills for Successful Entry and Transfer*). ASSET is described by its publisher as "an educational advising, course placement, and retention planning tool . . . to serve students entering two-year academic institutions" (American College Testing Program, 1990, p. 1). The reading section of ASSET/C1 contained three passages on topics from prose fiction, business, and social studies presumed to be "representative of the level and kinds of writing commonly encountered in college freshman curricula" (p.4): a Cajun festival, electronic mail service, and Hellenic ideas. Each passage was followed by eight multiple choice questions that measured literal comprehension, inferential comprehension, or vocabulary in context.

Researcher-developed tests served as measures of content-specific reading comprehension and prior domain knowledge. The content-specific reading test included three passages taken from the course textbook (Marieb & Mallatt, 2003). Topics were embryonic development of the brain, special parts of the skull, and epithelia and glands. Each passage included both the words and accompanying diagrams from the textbook. In order to eliminate testing format as a confounding variable in this study, the content-specific reading test was designed with a multiple-choice item format to mirror that of the commercially developed content-general reading test. The first two passages were followed by six items and the third passage was followed by eight items that measured literal or inferential comprehension.

The test of prior domain knowledge contained 20 multiple-choice items. A multiple-choice test is considered a valid and objective method for measuring prior domain knowledge (Dochy, Segers, & Buehl, 1999). Each item asked the student about a term related to human anatomy, in ascending order of difficulty. For example, an easy item was, "The *patella* is a bone in the (a) pelvis, (b) knee, (c) thigh, or (d) ankle." A more difficult item was, "Which of the following is not a type of white blood cell? (a) neutrophils, (b) eosinophils, (c) lymphocytes, or (d) thrombocytes."

All three predictor measures were administered in the same sequence (domain knowledge, content-specific reading, and content-general reading) to all subjects on the first day of class. Students were provided 15 minutes to complete the domain knowledge test and 25 minutes to complete each reading test. The criterion measure of course success was the final grade earned (A, B, C, D, F, or W) at the end of the semester. Although many factors influence final grade, and final grade is not always a true indicator of student learning, because college placement is specifically concerned with ensuring that students are not placed into courses that they will fail, final grade is the most appropriate measure of course success when validating placement decisions.

Results

A forward-solution multiple regression was computed using SPSS, with domain knowledge, content-specific reading comprehension, and content-general reading comprehension as predictor variables and course grade as the criterion variable. The three predictor variables were entered as

Table 1. Means, Standard Deviations, and Intercorrelations Among Course Grade, Domain Knowledge, Content-Specific Reading, and Content-General Reading (N = 49)

Variable	M	SD	GR	DK	CS	CG
Grade (GR)	1.53	1.65	—	.311*	.398**	.219
Domain Knowledge (DK)	11.29	3.60		—	.543**	.297*
CS Reading (CS)	11.48	3.22			—	.725**
CG Reading (CG)	17.33	5.00				—

*Significance level (two-tailed) < .05
**Significance level (two-tailed) < .01

scale values based on number of questions answered correctly on each test (maximum score was 24 for content-general reading comprehension, 20 for content-specific reading comprehension, and 20 for domain knowledge). Course grades were also entered as scale values with A = 4, B = 3, C = 2, D = 1, and F or W = 0. Although it may be argued that A, B, C grades are not technically scale values, the SPSS program treats scale and ordinal values identically (George & Mallery, 2003).

Means and standard deviations for all variables are shown in Table 1. The grade-point average for the class was 1.53 on a four-point scale. Consistent with the historical difficulty of the human anatomy course, only 25 of the 49 students passed with a grade of D or higher. All of the failing students were encouraged by the instructor to withdraw (W) rather than receive an F.

Zero-order correlations between all variables are also presented in Table 1. Prior domain knowledge was a significant predictor of course grade at the .05 level (r = .311, two-tailed p = .029). Content-specific reading comprehension was a significant predictor of course grade at the .01 level (r = .398, p = .005). Content-general reading comprehension was not a significant predictor of course grade (r = .219, p = .131). In addition, both prior domain knowledge (r = .543, p = .000) and content-general reading comprehension (r = .725, p = .000) were highly correlated with content-specific reading comprehension.

The forward-solution multiple regression analysis is shown in Table 2. In a forward-solution procedure, the predictor variable with the highest zero-order correlation with the criterion is entered first. The next variable entered is the one that produces the greatest increment in variance (R-squared), after partialing out the variable already in the equation (Kerlinger & Pedhazur, 1973). Because it had the highest zero-order correlation, content-specific reading comprehension was the first variable entered. The amount of variance accounted for by

Table 2. Forward-Solution Multiple Regression of Course Grade on Domain Knowledge, Content-Specific Reading, and Content-General Reading (N = 49)

Variable	R	R^2	ΔR^2	F	df	p
CS Reading	.398	.158	.158	8.824	1,47	.005
Domain Knowledge	.414	.171	.013	.722	2,46	NS
CG Reading	.422	.178	.007	.389	.3,45	NS

Variable entered: CS Reading
Variables excluded: Domain Knowledge, CG Reading
Entry criterion: Probability of F to enter < = .05

content-specific reading comprehension (R-squared) was .158 ($F = 8.824$, $p = .005$). However, neither prior domain knowledge nor content-general reading comprehension produced a significant increase in variance (R-squared) after partialing out the effects of content-specific reading comprehension, and both were excluded from the regression equation using a criterion of .05 for the significance of the change in F ratio. Post-hoc analysis showed that the incremental variance attributed to prior domain knowledge was only .013 ($F = .722$, NS) and to content-general reading comprehension was only .007 ($F = .389$, NS).

Table 3 displays the distribution of course grades by content-specific reading comprehension scores. Since a grade of C or higher is required for students in the anatomy course to continue in their health-related majors, course success is defined here as a grade of C or above. For students scoring 16 or above on the content-specific reading test, the success rate was 100 percent (6 of 6). For students scoring between

Table 3. Distribution of Course Grades by Content-Specific Reading Scores (N = 49)

	GRADE				
CS Reading Score	F/W	D	C	B	A
16 or above	0	0	0	3	3
12–15	9	1	2	1	5
10–11	5	0	3	2	1
9 or below	10	0	2	2	0

12 and 15 on the content-specific reading comprehension test, the success rate was 44 percent (8 of 18). For students scoring 10 or 11 on the content-specific reading comprehension test, the success rate was 55 percent (6 of 11). For students scoring 9 or below on the content-specific reading comprehension test, the success rate was only 29 percent (4 of 14).

Discussion

The first research question addressed the test-criterion relationship between a content-specific reading comprehension test and grades in a credit-level college course. In this study, a researcher-developed test of comprehension of text taken from a human anatomy textbook was a significant predictor (at the .01 level) of course grades in a community college introductory human anatomy class. The second research question addressed whether the content-specific reading comprehension test would predict course grades better than a commercially developed content-general reading comprehension test. Results indicate that the content-specific reading comprehension test was a significant predictor of course grades, while the content-general reading comprehension test was not. The third research question addressed whether the prediction of course grades would be improved by using a combination of content-general reading comprehension, content-specific reading comprehension, and domain knowledge tests. It was found that the tests of domain knowledge and content-general reading comprehension did not add significantly to the prediction of course grades after using the test of content-specific reading comprehension as a single predictor.

The present study therefore offers support for the validity of using content-specific rather than content-general reading comprehension tests for placement into credit-level college courses. Further, the present study does not support the validity of including a test of prior knowledge or a content-general reading test if a content-specific reading test is being used for course placement.

Conclusions

Content-general reading placement tests that measure comprehension across a variety of subject areas may have limited utility in academic placement decisions. As an alternative to using content-general reading placement tests, it is suggested that reading placement tests be specific to the courses for which placement decisions will be made. A content-specific reading comprehension test would draw passages from a defined subject area and yield a comprehension score intended to indicate reading comprehension ability in that subject rather than generic reading ability. The present study offers preliminary empirical evidence that a placement system using content-specific reading comprehension tests could enhance the validity of placement decisions over a placement system using content-general reading tests. Results of this study also suggest that there may be limited value in administering a content-general reading test if content-specific reading tests are being used to make placement decisions.

Although results underscore the important relationship between content-specific reading ability and academic performance, there may be limits to the ability of any single measure to predict course success. In this study about 16 percent of the variance in course grades was explained by scores on the content-specific reading comprehension test. The tests of domain knowledge and content-general reading comprehension did not improve the prediction, since both of these tests were highly correlated with content-specific reading comprehension. Nonetheless, it is likely that stronger prediction of course grades will require a multiple-factor model. However, many of the personal, social, economic, as well as academic factors that influence course success may be difficult to measure through a placement instrument. In addition, there may be statistical limits to the maximization of test-criterion coefficients, since either low reliability (Sawyer, 1989) or restricted range[1] of either the predictor or criterion variable can depress the magnitude of the observed correlation.

Ultimately, the validity of any placement testing system must be determined within the context of its use. Each college using a reading test to place students into credit-level courses has the responsibility for determining the extent to which the placement test really serves its intended purpose for each of the courses that require placement. The college should study which courses are most dependent upon content-specific reading ability and which other academic factors contribute to success in each course. In addition, the college may wish to consider whether the testing prompts and response formats are consistent with the kinds of tasks students will encounter in the target course.

There will never be a placement test with perfect predictability, so the goal of placement testing should be to reduce the proportion of successful non-predictors and unsuccessful predictors. Until researchers are able to identify reading placement tests that will improve the validity of placement decisions, large proportions of college students may continue to be misplaced based on the results of reading test scores. Any reduction in the number of students who are misplaced would be a move in the right direction.

Footnote

1. In the formula for a bivariate coefficient of correlation, both the numerator and denominator are based on calculations involving deviations of X and Y scores from the mean (Capon, 1988). The arithmetic effect of one of the variables having restricted range, or less deviation from the mean, is always a lower correlation.

References

Alexander, P. A., & Judy, J. E. (1988). The interaction of domain-specific and strategic knowledge in academic performance. *Review of Educational Research, 58,* 375–404.

Alexander, P. A., & Kulikowich, J. M. (1994). Learning from physics text: A synthesis of recent research. *Journal of Research in Science Teaching, 31,* 895–911.

American College Testing Program. (1990). *ASSET technical manual for use with Forms B and C.* Iowa City, IO: Author.

Anderson, R. C. (1984). Role of the reader's schema in comprehension, learning, and memory. In R. C. Anderson, J. Osborn, & R. J. Tierney (Eds.), *Learning to read in American schools: Basal readers and content texts* (pp. 243–257). Hillsdale, NJ: Erlbaum.

Anderson, R. C., & Pearson, P. D. (1984). A schema-theoretic view of reading comprehension. In P. D. Pearson (Ed.), *Handbook of reading research* (pp. 255–291). New York: Longman.

Armstrong, W. B. (1994). *English placement testing, multiple measures, and disproportionate impact: An analysis of the criterion-and content-related validity evidence for the reading & writing placement tests in the San Diego Community College District.* San Diego, CA: San Diego Community College District, Research and Planning. (ERIC Document Reproduction Service No. 398965)

Behrman, E. H. (2000). Developmental placement decisions: Content-specific reading assessment. *Journal of Developmental Education, 23*(3), 12–14, 16, 18.

Brown, J. I., Fishco, V. V., & Hanna, G. (1993). *Nelson-Denny Reading Test: Manual for scoring and interpretation, Forms G & H.* Chicago: Riverside.

Byrnes, J. P. (1995). Domain specificity and the logic of using general ability as an independent variable or covariate. *Merrill-Palmer Quarterly, 41,* 1–24.

Capon, J. A. (1988). *Elementary statistics for the social sciences.* Belmont, CA: Wadsworth.

College of the Canyons. (1994). *Predictive validity study of the APS Reading Test.* Santa Clarita, CA: Author. (ERIC Document Reproduction Service No. ED 374853)

Dochy, F., Segers, M., & Buehl, M. M. (1999). The relation between assessment practices and outcomes of studies: The case of research on prior knowledge. *Review of Educational Research, 69,* 145–186.

Feldt, R. C. (1989). Reading comprehension and critical thinking as predictors of course performance. *Perceptual and Motor Skills, 68,* 642.

George, D., & Mallery, P. (2003). *SPSS for Windows step by step. 11.0 update* (4th ed.). Boston: Allyn & Bacon/Pearson.

Guilford, J. P. (1956). *Fundamental statistics in psychology and education* (3rd ed.). New York: McGraw-Hill.

Hall, V. C., & Edmondson, B. (1992). Relative importance of aptitude and prior domain knowledge on immediate and delayed posttests. *Journal of Educational Psychology, 84,* 219–223.

Johnston, P. (1984). Prior knowledge and reading comprehension test bias. *Reading Research Quarterly, 19,* 219–239.

Joint Committee on Standards for Educational and Psychological Testing of the American Educational Research Association, the American

Psychological Association, and the National Council on Measurement in Education. (1999). *Standards for educational and psychological testing*. Washington, DC: American Educational Research Association.

Kerlinger, F. N., & Pedhazur, E. J. (1973). *Multiple regression in behavioral research*. New York: Holt, Rinehart and Winston.

Kessler, R. P. (1987). *Can reading placement scores predict classroom performance? A discriminant analysis*. Santa Ana, CA: Rancho Santiago Community College District. (ERIC Document Reproduction Service No. ED 291440)

Kintsch, W. (1986). Learning from text. *Cognition and Instruction, 3*, 87–108.

Kintsch, W. (1988). The role of knowledge in discourse comprehension: A construction-integration model. *Psychological Review, 95*, 163–182.

Kintsch, W. & vanDijk, T. A. (1978). Towards a model of discourse comprehension and production. *Psychological Review, 85*, 363–394.

Lawson, A. E., McElrath, C. B., Burton, M. S., James, B. D., Doyle, R. P., Woodward, S. L., et al. (1991). Hypothetico-deductive reasoning skill and concept acquisition: Testing a constructivist hypothesis. *Journal of Research in Science Teaching, 28*, 953–970.

Mannes, S., & Kintsch, W. (1987). Knowledge organization and text organization. *Cognition and Instruction, 4*, 91–115.

Marieb, E. N., & Mallat, J. (2003). *Human anatomy* (3rd ed. update). San Francisco: Benjamin Cummings.

Mason, J. M., & the staff of the Center for the Study of Reading, University of Illinois. (1984). A schema-theoretic view of the reading process as a basis for comprehension instruction. In G. G. Duffy, L. R. Roehler, & J. Mason (Eds.), *Comprehension instruction: Perspectives and suggestions* (pp. 26–38). New York: Longman.

McNamara, D. S., & Kintsch, W. (1996). Learning from texts: Effects of prior knowledge and text coherence. *Discourse Processes, 22*, 247–288.

Moravcsik, J. E., & Kintsch, W. (1993). Writing quality, reading skills, and domain knowledge as factors in text comprehension. *Canadian Journal of Experimental Psychology, 47*, 360–374.

National Institute of Child Health and Human Development. (2000). *Report of the National Reading Panel. Teaching children to read: An evidence-based assessment of the scientific research literature on reading and its implications for reading instruction*. (NIH Publication No. 00–4769). Washington, DC: U. S. Government Printing Office.

Parsad, B., & Lewis, L. (2003). *Remedial education at degree-granting postsecondary institutions in Fall 2000. Statistical analysis report*. (NCES Publication No. 2040-010). Washington, DC: U. S. Government Printing Office.

Royer, J. M., Carlo, M. S., Dufresne, R., & Mestre, J. (1996). The assessment of levels of domain expertise while reading. *Cognition and Instruction, 14*, 373–408.

Rumelhart, D. E. (1981). Schemata: The building blocks of learning. In J. T. Guthrie (Ed.), *Comprehension and teaching: Research reviews* (pp. 3–26). Newark, DE: International Reading Association.

Sawyer, R. (1989). *Validating the use of ACT Assessment scores and high school grades for remedial course placement in college*. (Research Report No. 89–4). Iowa City, IO: American College Testing.

Sawyer, R. (1996). Decision theory models for validating course placement tests. *Journal of Educational Measurement, 33*, 271–290.

Schoenfeld, A. H. (1999). Looking toward the 21st century: Challenge of educational theory and practice. *Educational Researcher, 28*(7), 4–14.

Shapiro, A. M. (2004). How including prior knowledge as a subject variable may change outcomes of learning research. *American Educational Research Journal, 41*, 159–189.

Shimoda, T. A. (1993). The effects of interesting examples and topic familiarity on text comprehension, attention, and reading speed. *Journal of Experimental Psychology, 61*, 93–103.

Stahl, S. A., Hare, V. C., Sinatra, R., & Gregory, J. F. (1991). Defining the role of prior knowledge and vocabulary in reading comprehension: The retiring of Number 41. *Journal of Reading Behavior, 23*, 487–508.

Van Dijk, T. A., & Kintsch, W. (1983). *Strategies of discourse comprehension.* New York: Academic.

Voss, J. F., & Silfies, L. N. (1996). Learning from history text: The interaction of knowledge and comprehension skill with text structure. *Cognition and Instruction, 14*, 45–68.

Wilson, P. T., & Anderson, R. C. (1986). What they don't know will hurt them: The role of prior knowledge in comprehension. In J. Orasanu (Ed.), *Reading comprehension: From research to practice* (pp. 31–48). Hillsdale, NJ: Erlbaum.

Zeitz, C. M. (1994). Expert-novice differences in memory, abstraction, and reasoning in the domain of literature. *Cognition and Instruction, 12*, 277–312.

Assessing Students' Metacognitive Awareness of Reading Strategies

Kouider Mokhtari and Carla A. Reichard

Kouider Mokhtari and Carla A. Reichard present an overview of the development and validation of the Metacognitive Awareness of Reading Strategies Inventory (MARSI), an instrument designed to assess readers' metacognitive awareness and perceived use of three types of strategies: global reading strategies, problem-solving strategies, and support reading strategies. The MARSI is presented in its entirety, complete with a discussion of the administration, scoring, interpretation, and potential uses of the instrument.

Recent trends within the domain of reading comprehension have led to an increasing emphasis on the role of metacognitive awareness of one's cognitive and motivational processes while reading (Alexander & Jetton, 2000; Guthrie & Wigfield, 1999; Pressley, 2000; Pressley & Afflerbach, 1995). Indeed, researchers agree that awareness *and* monitoring of one's comprehension processes are critically important aspects of skilled reading. Such awareness and monitoring processes are often referred to in the literature as *metacognition*, which can be thought of as the knowledge of the readers' cognition about reading and the self-control mechanisms they exercise when monitoring and regulating text comprehension.

The construct of metacognition has been richly built through the efforts of several prominent researchers representing diverse research traditions using various data sources. Although it is a challenge to account for all the characterizations of metacognition, we attempt, in our brief review, to reflect the richness of inquiry behind the construct, which provides a foundation for developing a valid and reliable instrument aimed at measuring readers' metacognitive awareness and control of the strategic processes invoked while reading. Researchers generally agree that *metacognition* refers to the "knowledge about cognitive states and abilities that can be shared among individuals while at the same time expanding the construct to include affective and motivational characteristics of thinking" (Paris & Winograd, 1990, p. 15). In his classic article "Metacognition and Cognitive Monitoring," Flavell (1979) described the process of cognitive monitoring as occurring through the actions and interactions of four classes or interrelated phenomena: Metacognitive knowledge, metacognitive experiences, goals (or tasks), and actions (or strategies). Other researchers (e.g., Wade, Trathen, & Schraw, 1990) have used examples of students' reflections about their thinking while reading to illustrate what they do when they read. Readers' reflections show how they plan, monitor, evaluate, and use information available to them as they make sense of what they read. Such reflections unveil judgments about the readers' thinking processes that serve as conventional descriptions of metacognition. Recent conceptions of reading comprehension depict efficient readers as strategic or "constructively responsive" readers who carefully orchestrate cognitive resources when reading (Pressley & Afflerbach, 1995).

Researchers investigating reading comprehension monitoring among skilled and unskilled readers have long recognized the importance of metacognitive awareness in reading comprehension because it distinguishes between skilled and unskilled readers. Paris and Jacobs (1984) provided an illustration of the differences between these two types of readers:

> Skilled readers often engage in deliberate activities that require planful thinking, flexible strategies, and periodic self-monitoring. They think about the topic, look forward and backward in the passage, and check their own understanding as they read. Beginning readers or poor readers do not recruit and use these skills. Indeed, novice readers often seem oblivious to these strategies and the need to use them. (p. 2083)

Skilled readers, according to Snow, Burns, and Griffin (1998), are good comprehenders. They differ from unskilled readers in "their use of general world knowledge to comprehend text literally as well as to draw valid inferences from texts, in their comprehension of words, and in their use of comprehension monitoring and repair strategies" (p. 62). Pressley and Afflerbach (1995) pointed out that skilled readers approach the reading task with some general tendencies. For example, they tend to be aware of what they are reading; they seem to know why they are reading; and they have a set of tentative plans or strategies for handling potential problems and for monitoring their comprehension of textual information.

Unskilled readers (typically young developing readers and some inexperienced adolescents and adults), on the other hand, are quite limited in their metacognitive knowledge about reading (Paris & Winograd, 1990). They do relatively little monitoring of their own memory, comprehension, and other cognitive tasks (Flavell, 1979; Markman, 1979) and tend to focus on reading as a decoding process rather than as a meaning-getting process (Baker & Brown, 1984). In addition, they are less likely than skilled readers to detect contradictions or resolve inconsistencies in understanding text (Snow et al., 1998). Finally, they seem not to realize that they do not understand (Garner & Reis, 1981) and as a result fail to exercise control of their reading processes (Wagner & Sternberg, 1987).

The central role of metacognition and comprehension monitoring in the current descriptions of the reading process is reflected in the steady growth of interest in reading comprehension monitoring research. The value placed by teachers and researchers on this important aspect of reading is supported in the literature that documents the link between comprehension monitoring and academic learning. Paris and Winograd (1990) maintained that metacognition can promote academic learning and motivation. The idea is that students can enhance their learning by becoming aware of their own thinking as they read, write, and solve problems at school. Teachers can promote this awareness by simply informing students about effective problem-solving strategies and discussing cognitive and motivational characteristics of thinking. Paris and Winograd (1990) argued that such "consciousness-raising" has twin benefits: "(a) it transfers responsibility for monitoring learning from teachers to students themselves, and (b) it promotes positive self-perceptions, affect, and motivation among students. In this manner, metacognition provides personal insights into one's own thinking and fosters independent learning" (p. 15).

Researchers have shown that students' awareness of their own reading comprehension processes can be enhanced through systematic, direct instruction (Paris & Winograd, 1990). They concurred with other researchers that strategic reading can be taught to students who need it through carefully devised instructional techniques (e.g., Brown, Armbruster, & Baker, 1986). However, they cautioned that "metacognition should not be regarded as a final objective for learning or instruction." Instead, it should be regarded as an opportunity to "provide students with knowledge and confidence that *enables* them to manage their own learning and *empowers* them to be inquisitive and zealous in their pursuits" (Paris & Winograd, 1990, p. 22).

According to Garner (1987), reading strategies, which she operationally defined as "generally deliberate, planful activities undertaken by active learners, many times to remedy perceived cognitive failure" (p. 50), facilitate reading comprehension and may be teachable. Garner (1994) concurred with Paris, Lipson, and Wixon (1994) that reading strategies can and should be learned to the point of automaticity, after which they become skills, and that learners must know not only what strategies to use but also when, where, and how to use them.

The research on metacognition and reading comprehension is extensive (for recent reviews of the multidimensional nature of text comprehension, see especially Alexander & Jetton, 2000; and Pressley, 2000). This work has been very important in prompting reading researchers to examine readers' own awareness of their cognitive and motivational processes while reading and the actions they use to monitor comprehension. In addition, such research has provided teacher educators and practicing teachers with practical suggestions for helping struggling readers increase their awareness and use of reading strategies while reading. However, there are relatively few instruments to measure students' awareness and perceived use of reading strategies while reading for academic purposes.

Efforts to develop metacognitive awareness inventories have been well intentioned but generally not satisfactory from a measurement perspective. The few instruments available have been quite useful in helping to determine metacognitive awareness and use of reading strategies among elementary school students. However, most have shortcomings that limit their use for middle- or upper-level students. Criticisms of existing measures of metacognitive awareness in reading pertain mainly to the use of scales with a small number of items, limited psychometric properties, evidence of reliability and validity, or an uncertain characterization of the construct of metacognition in particular and reading in general. For example, Jacobs and Paris (1987) developed the Index of Reading Awareness to measure metacognitive awareness of third-through fifth-grade students with grade-equivalent reading abilities ranging from second to seventh grade. The scale consists of 22 multiple-choice items measuring four aspects of metacognition in reading: evaluation, planning, regulation, and conditional knowledge. Its value as a measure of metacognitive awareness of reading strategies was assessed by McLain, Gridley, and McIntosh (1991), who obtained preliminary reliability and validity data and found the scale only marginally acceptable. McLain et al. (1991) found the reliability index (.61) to be "minimal" and stated that the Index of Reading Awareness "should be used cautiously as a measure of metacognition in reading" (p. 81).

Pereira-Laird and Deane (1997) developed a self-report measure called Reading Strategy Use (RSU) to assess the perceptions of adolescent students' use of cognitive and metacognitive strategies when reading narrative and expository texts. Pereira-Laird and Deane reported preliminary support for the reliability (.97) and validity of the RSU measure in assessing cognitive and metacognitive reading strategy use for adolescents. However, on close examination, we identified some critical shortcomings that lessen the validity of this scale. Several items from the scale do not appear to be reading strategies, which are deliberate actions taken by readers before, during, and after reading (e.g., "I find it hard to pay attention when reading," and "After I have been reading for a short time, the words stop making sense"). All items were forced into predetermined factors (Metacognitive and Cognitive) on the basis of judges' ratings, and then a confirmatory factor analysis was conducted. Because they skipped an exploratory factor analysis, Pereira-Laird and Deane retained some items that we feel are out of place, and therefore this scale, although valuable, can still be improved. Finally, it is unclear to what extent the RSU scale can be used reliably with students other than those used in the study (the majority being Caucasians) and different types of reading materials (text types used were narrative and expository).

Schmitt (1990) developed a 12-item multiple-choice questionnaire to measure elementary students' awareness of strategic reading processes. Although its reliability is good, it has limitations for use with research. Students are forced to choose among several alternatives (rather than choosing all that apply), and although the directions stress that there is no "right" answer, many of the choices do not make much sense, which would seem to lead students to the "correct" metacognitive answer. The instrument is strictly aimed at metacognition, excluding measurement of other types of reading strategies that might be helpful to readers.

Miholic (1994) developed a 10-item multiple-choice inventory aimed at stimulating students' metacognitive awareness of reading strategies. The inventory is intended for use with students from junior high through college. No reliability or validity data are presented. There is no scoring rubric. This instrument, like that of Schmitt, seems to have limitations for use in research. It is aimed at increasing student and teacher awareness of metacognition in reading rather than measurement of metacognitive or other reading strategies.

The present article describes a new self-report measure, the Metacognitive Awareness of Reading Strategies Inventory (MARSI), which is designed to assess 6th- through 12th-grade students' awareness and perceived use of reading strategies while reading academic or school-related materials. The major purposes were to devise an instrument that would permit one to assess the degree to which a student is or is not aware of the various processes involved in reading and to make it possible to learn about the goals and intentions he or she holds when coping with academic reading tasks. Such information can increase students' awareness of their own comprehension processes. As well, it can help teachers better understand the needs of their students.

In designing a measure sensitive to these purposes, we were guided by the premise that constructing meaning from text is an intentional, deliberate, and purposeful act. According to Pressley and Afflerbach (1995), skilled readers approach the reading task with some general tendencies. These tendencies are shaped into specific responses depending on the goals of reading and the nature of the text being read. Guthrie and Wigfield (1999) concurred that "constructing meaning during reading is a motivational act." In addition, they state the following:

> A person is unlikely to comprehend a text by accident. If the person is not aware of the text, not attending to it, not choosing to make meaning from it, or not giving cognitive effort to knowledge construction, little comprehension occurs. (p. 199)

Current reading research, which stresses the interactive, constructive nature of reading, suggests the need for all students (especially struggling ones) to become "constructively responsive" readers (Pressley & Afflerbach, 1995, p. 83), and "thoughtfully literate" individuals (Allington, 2000, p. 94) who are engaged, motivated readers in control of their own learning (Alvermann & Guthrie, 1993). This type of constructively responsive, thoughtful, and engaged reading clearly involves much more than simply having good decoding skills, an adequate reading vocabulary, and an ability to recall what the text said. Learning from text, like all learning, demands readers who are *strategically engaged in the construction of meaning*" (Alexander & Jetton, 2000, p. 295).

MARSI Scale Development and Validation

The development of the MARSI was guided by several efforts, including (a) a review of recent research literature on metacognition and reading comprehension (e.g., Alexander & Jetton, 2000; Baker & Brown, 1984; Garner, 1987; Paris & Winograd, 1990; Pressley, 2000; Pressley and Afflerbach, 1995), (b) the use of expert judgment with respect to assignment and categorization of items within the inventory, (c) insights gained from existing reading strategies instruments regarding format and content (e.g., Jacobs & Paris, 1987; Miholic, 1994; Pereira-Laird and Deane, 1997; Schmitt, 1990), and (d) the use of factor analyses to examine the structure of the scale.

Following standard measurement criteria for developing valid, reliable, and sensitive measures (e.g., Churchill, 1979; Crocker & Algina,

1986; Sax, 1997), we subjected the items used in the MARSI to successive cycles of development, field-testing, validation, and revision. After a thorough review of the research literature pertaining to text comprehension, we examined four published reading strategy instruments for ideas regarding general format and content. We also searched several reading methods textbooks for ideas that could be used in statements about global reading strategies.

We used an extensive body of work on metacognition and reading comprehension by several researchers (e.g., Alexander & Jetton, 2000; Baker & Brown, 1984; Garner, 1987; Paris & Winograd, 1990; Pressley & Afflerbach, 1995, to name only a few) who had provided much of what is currently known about this important topic. We drew on Pressley and Afflerbach's (1995) notion of constructively responsive reading, which appears to be quite consistent with recognized theories of reading such as Rosenblatt's (1978) reader response theory, in which the transaction between readers and texts is emphasized. The concept of constructively responsive reading also embraces key principles of the top-down processing model of reading reflected in schema theory (Anderson & Pearson, 1984), bottom-up text-processing strategies emphasized by van Dijk and Kintsch (1983), and the comprehension monitoring processes advocated by several notable researchers in this line of inquiry (e.g., Baker & Brown, 1984; Garner, 1987; Paris & Winograd, 1990). In their book, *Verbal Protocols of Reading: The Nature of Constructively Responsive Reading,* Pressley and Afflerbach (1995) offer a very helpful thumbnail sketch of various strategies skilled readers use before, during, and after reading. Appendix A provides a summary of some of these strategies.

Initially, we generated a pool of nearly 100 items from which the final set of items was constructed. Each of the 15 skilled reader strategies listed on Pressley and Afflerbach's (1995) thumbnail outline was accounted for in the original strategy pool. This summary of some of the strategies skilled readers use when responding to text constructively was quite important in our efforts to develop our own instrument because we believe they represent a research-based conceptualization of what constitutes a metacognitive reading strategy, informed by a richness of inquiry into the construct of metacognition. We concur with Pressley and Afflerbach that skilled readers approach the reading task with some general tendencies (such as the ones described in Appendix A). These tendencies, which constitute constructively responsive reading, are shaped into specific responses or reading strategies depending on the goals of reading and the nature of the text being read. The initial collection of 100 reader strategies was designed to contain some redundancy. As a result, we anticipated refining or deleting some of the items to produce a shorter version of the scale. We took special care to write the items in a positive and easy-to-read manner using a response format that would seem appealing to students.

When selecting and categorizing the strategy statements within the instrument, we were assisted by a group of three expert judges (two professional research colleagues and a research assistant) who were knowledgeable about and experienced in the teaching and assessment of reading strategies. These judges were instructed to review the initial pool of items for clarity, redundancy, and readability. The initial review resulted in the elimination of 40 items due mainly to redundancy among the items used. Throughout the review process, whenever disagreements occurred, a discussion ensued until consensus was reached. Sixty items were retained for initial testing, in addition to a short biographical section asking participants for their age, gender, ethnicity, and self-evaluation of reading ability and interest in reading.

Finally, we field-tested the inventory with a large sample of students ($N = 825$) in Grades 6–12 drawn from 10 urban, suburban, and rural school districts in five midwestern states. School records from each of the districts, indicating that the participants shared similar linguistic, cultural, and socioeconomic backgrounds, documented similarity of student populations. None of the participants were identified as having any specific learning problems or handicapping conditions. Of the respondents, 47.2% were boys, and 52.8% were girls. Of the total number of participants, 52.2% were Caucasian, 19.1% were Native American, 4.4% were Asian; 6.4% were African American; 7.2% were Hispanic; and 10.8% described themselves as "Other." The ethnic makeup of our sample was typical for the areas from which the majority was obtained.

In addition to completing the inventory, students were asked to mark the items that were unclear or confusing to them. They were also asked to provide written feedback, if any, about any aspect of the instrument, including the clarity of instructions, wording of items, time devoted to completing the inventory, response format, and content. The feedback obtained throughout these phases resulted in additional enhancements to the final version of the instrument. We used the results of this field testing to determine the psychometric attributes of the inventory.

Exploratory factor analysis using a common factor model was used to identify potential factors or subscales for the 60-item instrument and to help identify any items that might need to be refined or deleted. The scree plot from the first factor analysis suggested that three factors should be retained. There were 13 eigenvalues greater than 1 (eigenvalues for Factors 4 through 13 ranged from 1.68 down to 1.00.). Gorsuch (1983) recommended evaluating the scree plot, the eigenvalues, and the interpretability of factors in tandem to decide the number of factors to retain. On the basis of this combination of criteria, three factors were retained. A two-factor solution was also attempted; however, it appeared that in this solution, items from the first two factors (of the three-factor solution) grouped together, whereas items from the third factor (of the three-factor solution) made up the second factor. Because there was evidence of interpretability for the three-factor solution, it was preferable.

A second principal-axis factor analysis was performed using three factors and an oblique Harris–Kaiser rotation. Cronbach's alpha was calculated for each subscale and for each grade level. Coefficients ranged from .89 to .93, and reliability for the total sample was .93, indicating a reasonably reliable measure of metacognitive awareness of reading strategies.

Next, the items were examined to see whether the analyses suggested they should be modified or deleted. Crocker and Algina (1986) suggested looking at (a) whether each item contributed or detracted from the reliability of the subscales; (b) whether items exhibited simple structure (loaded primarily on only one factor); (c) whether items had high factor loadings; and (d) for items that failed any of the above criteria, whether they appeared ambiguous or out of place in comparison with other items. For the analysis of reliabilities, items were included in a factor if their factor loadings were at least .20 or above, so there was some overlap of items. In addition, we examined each statement for redundancy, in hopes of shortening the scale without greatly reducing its reliability. All items were examined for ambiguity and lack of fit with other questions in the scale. Some were deleted if they did not exhibit simple structure or had rotated factor loadings below .30 for all three factors. In some cases, certain items were deleted when they reduced subscale reliabilities and did not seem to provide useful information. A number of other items were reworded or considered for deletion owing to a combination of (a) low factor loadings, (b) loading on more than one subscale, (c) reduced reliabilities, or (d) duplication with other questions. The resulting instrument contained 30 items that were reviewed for readability, response format, and completeness.

These remaining 30 items were reviewed by three raters (the same raters used to cull the initial sample of 100 items down to 60). Each statement was scrutinized for appropriateness and clarity, and disagreements were discussed until consensus among the raters was reached. After some revisions in wording, the inventory was administered to a small pilot group of students similar to the one used in the initial study. The students were asked to provide feedback on the clarity and ease of understanding of each of the items. The feedback was used to produce the final draft of the inventory (Version 1.0), which is displayed in Appendix B.

This revised instrument was administered again to a similar sample of 443 students in Grades 6–12. As in the analysis of the 60-item instrument, the analysis of the 30-item revised instrument yielded three factors or subscales. A second principal-axis factor analysis was performed using three factors and an oblique Harris–Kaiser rotation. The rotated factor patterns are shown in Table 1. The three factors

Table 1. Rotated Factor Pattern (Standard Coefficients)

Inventory item	FACTOR 1	2	3
1. I have a purpose in mind when I read.	.639		
2. I take notes while reading to help me understand what I'm reading.			.728
3. I think about what I know to help me understand what I'm reading.	.418	.404	
4. I preview the text to see what it's about before reading it.	.470		
5. When text becomes difficult, I read aloud to help me understand what I'm reading.		.375	.375
6. I write summaries to reflect on key ideas in the text.			.773
7. I think about whether the content of the text fits my purpose.	.597		
8. I read slowly but carefully to be sure I understand what I'm reading.		.454	
9. I discuss my reading with others to check my understanding.			.573
10. I skim the text first by noting characteristics like length and organization.	.640		
11. I try to get back on track when I lose concentration.		.679	
12. I underline or circle information in the text to help me remember it.			.616
13. I adjust my reading speed according to what I'm reading.		.512	
14. I decide what to read closely and what to ignore.	.582		
15. I use reference materials such as dictionaries to help me understand what I'm reading.			.493
16. When text becomes difficult, I begin to pay closer attention to what I'm reading.		.553	
17. I use tables, figures, and pictures in text to increase my understanding.	.385		
18. I stop from time to time to think about what I'm reading.		.605	
19. I use context clues to help me better understand what I'm reading.	.407		
20. I paraphrase (restate ideas in my own words) to better understand what I'm reading.			.526
21. I try to picture or visualize information to help me remember what I'm reading.		.632	
22. I use typographical aids like boldface type and italics to identify key information.	.425		
23. I critically analyze and evaluate the information presented in the text.	.308		.354
24. I go back and forth in the text to find relationships among ideas in it.			.511
25. I check my understanding when I come across conflicting information.	.352	.325	
26. I try to guess what the text is about when reading.	.373	.303	
27. When text becomes difficult, I reread to increase my understanding.		.634	
28. I ask myself questions I like to have answered in the text.			.510
29. I check to see if my guesses about the text are right or wrong.	.389		
30. I try to guess the meaning of unknown words or phrases.		.533	

Note. Items were categorized using the highest factor loading, with the exception of Item 23, which appeared to fit best as a Global Reading Strategy. Factor 1 = Global Reading Strategies; Factor 2 = Problem-Solving Strategies; Factor 3 = Support Reading Strategies.

Table 2. Factor Correlations

Factor	1	2	3
1	.92	—	
2	.20	.79	—
3	.73	.09	.87

Note. Cronbach's alphas are presented on diagonal. Factor 1 = Global Reading Strategies; Factor 2 = Problem-Solving Strategies; Factor 3 = Support Reading Strategies.

explained 29.7% of the total variance. The correlations between factors and Cronbach's alpha reliabilities for each factor or subscale are shown in Table 2. Cronbach's alpha was calculated for each subscale (see Table 2) and for each grade level (see Table 3). Reliability for the total sample was .89.

The first factor (Global Reading Strategies) contained 13 items and represented a set of reading strategies oriented toward a global analysis of text (see Appendix C). Examples include "I decide what to read closely and what to ignore;" "I think about what I know to help me understand what I read;" and "I have a purpose in mind when I read." These strategies can be thought of as generalized, intentional reading strategies aimed at setting the stage for the reading act (e.g., setting purpose for reading, making predictions).

The second factor (Problem-Solving Strategies) contained 8 items that appeared to be oriented around strategies for solving problems when text becomes difficult to read. Examples of these strategies include "When the text becomes difficult, I reread to increase my understanding;" and "I adjust my reading speed according to what I read." These strategies provide readers with action plans that allow them to navigate through text skillfully. Such strategies are localized, focused problem-solving or repair strategies used when problems develop in understanding textual information (e.g., checking one's understanding on encountering conflicting information or rereading for better understanding).

The third factor (Support Reading Strategies) contained 9 items and primarily involved use of outside reference materials, taking notes, and other practical strategies that might be described as functional or support strategies. Examples include "I take notes while reading"; "I underline or circle information in the text to help me remember it"; and "I summarize what I read to reflect on important information in the text." Strategies such as these serve a useful function for some of the students who seem to invoke them as needed. These strategies provide the support mechanisms aimed at sustaining responses to reading

Table 3. Cronbach's Alpha Reliabilities by Grade Level

Grade	n	Cronbach's α
6	31	.91
7	76	.87
8	74	.86
9	76	.87
10	70	.91
11	71	.91
12	45	.93

(e.g., use of reference materials such as dictionaries and other support systems). These three types of strategies (i.e., Global, Problem-Solving, and Support Strategies) interact with each other and have an important influence on text comprehension. The information gleaned from the inventory serves as a catalogue of strategies students report using while reading academic or school-related materials such as textbooks, library materials, and magazine articles.

Looking at the relationship between self-reported reading ability and strategy usage provides preliminary evidence of construct validity. In keeping with prior research on the relationship between reading strategy awareness, usage, and reading ability (see, e.g., Alexander & Jetton, 2000; Pressley, 2000), we suspected that skilled readers would use strategies more frequently; in particular, we predicted highly skilled readers to use Global and Problem-Solving Strategies more frequently than less skilled readers. As Table 4 shows, we found significant differences in the use of Global and Problem-Solving Strategies by self-reported reading ability but no significant differences in the use of Support Strategies by self-reported reading ability. Post hoc comparisons of Global Reading Strategies scores using the Ryan–Einot–Gabriel–Welch multiple-range test with α equals 0.05 yields a critical range of 0.136, which is smaller than the differences between any two of the means shown in Table 4. This means that readers who rate their reading ability as excellent have a significantly higher use of Global Reading Strategies than readers who rate their reading ability as average or not so good, and readers who rate their reading ability as average have a significantly higher use of Global Reading Strategies than readers who rate their reading ability as not so good. Similarly, post hoc comparisons of Problem-Solving Strategies scores using the Ryan–Einot–Gabriel–Welch multiple-range test with α equals 0.05 yields a critical range of 0.165, which is smaller than the differences between

Table 4. One-Way Analysis of Variance of Perceived Strategy Use by Reading Ability

Strategy use	WHOLE GROUP		EXCELLENT		AVERAGE		NOT SO GOOD		MSE	F(2, 440)	p>
	M	SD	M	SD	M	SD	M	SD			
MARSI	2.83	0.63	2.96	0.68	2.80	0.60	2.70	0.62	.39	7.05	.0009
GLOB	2.77	0.65	2.94	0.70	2.74	0.62	2.57	0.60	.41	12.53	.0001
PROB	3.19	0.78	3.40	0.81	3.13	0.75	3.01	0.84	.60	11.34	.0001
SUP	2.59	0.79	2.60	0.68	2.59	0.77	2.61	0.75	.63	0.02	.9829

Note. MARSI = Metacognitive Awareness of Reading Strategies Inventory; GLOB = Global Reading Strategies; PROB = Problem-Solving Strategies; SUP = Support Reading Strategies.

excellent and the other ability levels shown in Table 4. This means that readers who rate their reading ability as excellent have a significantly higher use of Problem-Solving Strategies than readers who rate their reading ability as average or not so good.

Overall, the psychometric data demonstrate that the instrument is a reliable and valid measure for assessing students' metacognitive awareness and perceived use of reading strategies while reading for academic purposes. We have also shown promising evidence of construct validity through higher use of Global and Problem-Solving Strategies by those who rate themselves as good readers. Further research using external measures of reading ability can help solidify this finding. We can meaningfully isolate three measurable strategy components or categories, as reflected in the three-factor solution obtained. The instrument is ready to be used as a tool for assessing students' metacognitive awareness of reading strategies while reading.

Administration, Scoring, and Interpretation

Administration

The MARSI can be administered individually as well as to groups of adolescent and adult students with grade level equivalents ranging from fifth grade through college. Although there is no time limit set for the instrument, the average administration time is between 10 and 12 min., depending on the students' grade level and overall reading ability. After explaining the purpose of the inventory, teachers should direct students to read each statement and rate how often they report using the strategy described in that statement using a 5-point Likert-type scale ranging from 1 (*I never do this*) to 5 (*I always do this*). It is important at this point to remind students that their responses are to refer only to the strategies they use when reading school-related materials. They should also be encouraged to respond honestly to each statement in the inventory and to ask questions about any aspect of the inventory they do not understand. The following outline delineates the steps to be taken when administering MARSI.

1. Distribute copies of the inventory to each student.

2. Ask students to provide identifying information (e.g., grade level) in the spaces provided.

3. Read the directions aloud and work through the example provided with the students.

4. Discuss the response options and make sure the students understand the rating scale.

5. Ask if anyone has questions about any aspect of the inventory.

6. Instruct the students to read each statement carefully and circle the appropriate responses.

7. Encourage students to work at their own pace.

Scoring

Scoring the inventory is quite easy and can be done by the students themselves. Students simply transfer the scores obtained for each strategy to the scoring sheet, which accompanies the inventory. After the individual scores are recorded, they should be added up in each column to obtain a total score, then divided by the number of items to get an average response for the entire inventory as well as for each strategy subscale (i.e., Global, Problem-Solving, and Support strategies). These scores can then be interpreted using the interpretation guidelines provided.

Interpretation

The interpretation of the information derived from the instrument was inspired by interpretation schemes used in published instruments (e.g., Henk & Melnick, 1995; Oxford, 1990). In examining the reading strategy usage of individual and groups of students on the MARSI, which ranges from 1 to 5, three levels of usage were identified, as suggested by Oxford for language learning strategy usage: high (mean of 3.5 or higher), medium (mean of 2.5 to 3.4), and low (2.4 or lower). These usage levels provide a helpful standard that can be used for interpreting the score averages obtained by individual or groups of students. The scores obtained should be interpreted using the high, moderate, and low usage designations shown on the scoring rubric that accompanies the scale. These usage designations are based on the average performance of the students who were used to validate the MARSI (the norm group).

As a general rule, the overall score averages indicate how often students use all the strategies in the inventory when reading academic materials. The averages for each subscale in the inventory show which group of strategies (i.e., Global, Problem-Solving, and Support Strategies) students use most or least when reading. This information enables them to tell if they score very high or very low in any of these strategy groups. A low score on any of the subscales or parts of the inventory indicates that there may be some strategies in these parts that they might want to learn about and consider using when reading. Note, however, that the best possible use of these strategies will ultimately depend, to a great extent, on the students' age, their reading ability, text difficulty, type of material read, and other related factors.

Potential Uses of the MARSI

The MARSI is not intended to be used as a comprehensive measure of students' comprehension monitoring capabilities. Rather, it is designed as a tool for helping students increase metacognitive awareness and strategy use while reading. The results obtained can be used for enhancing assessment, planning instruction, or conducting classroom or clinical research.

First, it enables students to increase awareness of their own reading strategies. This information will allow them to evaluate themselves in relation to other readers and also to amend the conceptions they hold about reading and learning from text. Becoming aware of one's cognitive processes while reading is a first important step toward achieving the type of constructively responsive and thoughtful reading that is emphasized by current models of reading. According to Paris and Winograd (1990), such "consciousness-raising" has twin benefits: "(a) it transfers responsibility for monitoring learning from teachers to students themselves, and (b) it promotes positive self-perceptions, affect, and motivation among students. In this manner, metacognition provides personal insights into one's own thinking and fosters independent learning" (p. 15).

Second, the information derived from the MARSI can provide teachers with a useful means of assessing, monitoring, and documenting the type and number of the reading strategies used by students. For example, teachers can examine the overall responses to get a general sense of the students' awareness and use of the individual reading strategies invoked using the guidelines provided. Over- or underreliance on a particular strategy may provide a hint about how the students approach the reading task. Students' internalized conceptions of the reading process are often related to the textual information they attend to. A student who reports overusing support strategies such as "using the dictionary" to look up every word in text may have a restricted view of reading. Support for this observation comes from Garner and Alexander (1989), who found that "children, particularly younger and poorer readers, often rely on a single criterion for textual understanding: understanding of individual words" (p. 145). On the other hand, underusing problem-solving strategies such as "rereading to increase understanding" may indicate lack of awareness of reading strategies and inadequate control of one's comprehension processes. Research tells us that certain strategies, particularly text reinspection and summarization are often difficult to learn and easy to abandon. Garner and Alexander noted that students often avoid reinspecting text to answer questions because it takes time and effort and evade summarization because it is difficult.

Third, MARSI can serve as a useful tool for teachers and researchers in investigating the impact of teaching strategic reading on students' reading comprehension under a variety of conditions, including reading for different purposes (e.g., reading to answer questions on a test vs. reading to research a particular topic); reading texts varying in length, difficulty, structure, and topic familiarity (e.g., reading a chapter book vs. reading a computer manual); and reading assigned versus self-selected readings. Teachers and researchers can use the data obtained from the instrument as a means of monitoring students' progress in becoming constructively responsive readers. They can administer it as a pretest and posttest in studies aimed at evaluating the impact of instruction on students' awareness and use of strategies while reading. They can use the individual and group average scores to derive a profile designating students along the three subscales of the inventory. Depending on the students' individual profiles, teachers might consider devising specific instructional strategies for addressing the specific weaknesses and needs. Some educators recommend maintaining performance data in portfolios, which can be used to demonstrate changes in the metacognitive awareness and use of strategies over time. Differences in performance can be documented along with other measures of reading in portfolios for individual students (see, e.g., Henk & Melnick, 1995).

A Cautionary Note

Classroom teachers and researchers will find the MARSI to be a useful tool for assessing and promoting learner awareness of the underlying processes involved in reading. However, they should keep in mind some cautions when using it for making decisions about students' overall ability to read and to monitor their understanding while reading academic materials. First, like other measures of reading, it should be used to supplement rather than to supplant existing assessment measures of students' reading comprehension. Teachers should consider it as only one source of information about students' reading abilities that must be analyzed in conjunction with other measures of reading ability.

Second, although there is psychometric support for the adequacy of MARSI as a measure of metacognitive awareness of reading strategies, it remains a self-report measure, and as such, it should be interpreted with vigilance. For instance, one cannot tell from the instrument alone whether students actually engage in the strategies they report using. In other words, invoking certain strategies through an inventory such as MARSI may indicate that the students know about or are aware of those strategies. However, awareness of strategies does not guarantee that students actually use them. According to Baker and Brown (1984), it is not enough to simply know appropriate reading strategies. Students must also be able to regulate or monitor the use of such strategies to ensure success in reading comprehension. Teacher judgment and common sense are clearly required to validate the discrepancy between students' beliefs about using the strategies and actual practice. Teachers should carefully scrutinize the responses to the reading strategies students report using while reading and interpret them in light of their own experiences observing and working with their students before they can make instructional decisions.

Third, although there is widespread agreement that constructively responsive reading is amenable to assessment and instruction, teachers who have helped students learn to become strategic readers often say that this process is work intensive and time-consuming on the part of teachers and students alike. Some estimate that it takes several months, perhaps as long as 1 year or more, for students to become strategic readers (Pressley, Beard El-Dinary, & Brown, 1992). Others caution that metacognition should not be regarded as a final objective for curriculum or instruction. Instead, it should be regarded as an opportunity to "provide students with knowledge and confidence that *enables* them to manage their own learning and *empowers* them to be inquisitive and zealous in their pursuits" (Paris & Winograd, 1990, p. 22). In other words, as teachers, we should strive first to better understand the thinking processes that support students' attempts to learn from texts; we should also help all readers, particularly struggling readers, learn to become actively engaged in reading. Increasing students' awareness of their comprehension processes while reading is an important first step toward their becoming constructively responsive, strategic, and thoughtful readers.

References

Alexander, P. A., & Jetton, T. L. (2000). Learning from text: A multidimensional and developmental perspective. In M. Kamil, P. Mosenthal, P. D. Pearson, & R. Barr (Eds.), *Handbook of reading research* (Vol. 3, pp. 285–310). Mahwah, NJ: Erlbaum.

Allington, R. (2000). *What really matters for struggling readers: Designing research-based programs.* New York: Longman.

Alvermann, D. E., & Guthrie, J. T. (1993). *Themes and directions of the National Reading Research Center: Perspectives in reading research, No. 1.* Athens, GA: University of Georgia and University of Maryland at College Park.

Anderson, R. C., & Pearson, P. D. (1984). A schema-theoretic view of basic processes in reading. In R. Barr, M. L. Kamil, P. Mosenthal, & P. D. Pearson (Eds.), *Handbook of reading research* (Vol. 2, pp. 255–292). White Plains, NY: Longman.

Baker, L., & Brown, A. L. (1984). Metacognitive skills and reading. In R. Barr, M. L. Kamil, P. Mosenthal, & P. D. Pearson (Eds.), *Handbook of reading research* (Vol. 2, pp. 353–394). White Plains, NY: Longman.

Brown, A. L., Armbruster, B., & Baker, L. (1986). The role of metacognition in reading and studying. In J. Orasanu (Ed.), *Reading comprehension: From research to practice* (pp. 49–75). Hillsdale, NJ: Erlbaum.

Churchill, G. A. (1979). A paradigm for developing better measures of marketing constructs. *Journal of Marketing Research, 16,* 64–73.

Crocker, L., & Algina, J. (1986). *Introduction to classical and modern test theory.* New York: Harcourt.

Flavell, J. H. (1979). Metacognition and cognitive monitoring: A new area of cognitive-developmental inquiry. *American Psychologist, 34,* 906–911.

Garner, R. (1987). *Metacognition and reading comprehension.* Norwood, NJ: Ablex.

Garner, R. (1994). Metacognition and executive control. In R. B. Ruddell, M. R. Ruddell, & H. Singer (Eds.), *Theoretical models and processes of reading* (4th ed.). Newark, DE: International Reading Association.

Garner, R., & Alexander, P. A. (1989). Metacognition: Answered and unanswered questions. *Educational Psychologist, 24,* 143–158.

Garner, R., & Reis, R. (1981). Monitoring and resolving comprehension obstacles: An investigation of spontaneous lookbacks among upper-grade good and poor comprehenders. *Reading Research Quarterly, 16,* 569–582.

Gorsuch, R. (1983). *Factor analysis.* Newark, NJ: Erlbaum.

Guthrie, J., & Wigfield, A. (1999). How motivation fits into a science of reading. *Scientific Studies of Reading, 3,* 199–205.

Henk, W. A., & Melnick, S. A. (1995). The Reader Self-Perception Scale (RSPS): A new tool for measuring how children feel about themselves as readers. *The Reading Teacher, 48,* 470–482.

Jacobs, J. E., & Paris, S. G. (1987). Children's metacognition about reading: Issues in definition, measurement, and instruction. *Educational Psychologist, 22,* 255–278.

Markman, E. M. (1979). Realizing that you don't understand: Elementary school children's awareness of inconsistencies. *Child Development, 50,* 634–655.

McLain, K. V. M., Gridley, B. E., & McIntosh, D. (1991). Value of a scale used to measure metacognitive reading processes. *Journal of Educational Research, 85,* 81–87.

Miholic, V. (1994). An inventory to pique students' metacognitive awareness of reading strategies. *Journal of Reading, 38,* 84–86.

Oxford, R. (1990). *Language learning strategies: What every teacher should know.* Boston: Heinle & Heinle.

Paris, S. G., & Jacobs, J. E. (1984). The benefits of informed instruction for children's reading awareness and comprehension skills. *Child Development, 55,* 2083–2093.

Paris, S. G., Lipson, M. Y., & Wixon, K. K. (1994). Becoming a strategic reader. In R. B. Ruddell, M. R. Ruddell, & H. Singer (Eds.), *Theoretical models and processes of reading* (4th ed.). Newark, DE: International Reading Association.

Paris, S. G., & Winograd, P. (1990). How metacognition can promote academic learning and instruction. In B. F. Jones & L. Idol (Eds.), *Dimensions of thinking and cognitive instruction* (pp. 15–51). Hillsdale, NJ: Erlbaum.

Pereira-Laird, J. A., & Deane, F. P. (1997). Development and validation of a self-report measure of reading strategy use. *Reading Psychology: An International Journal, 18,* 185–235.

Pressley, M. (2000). What should comprehension instruction be the instruction of? In M. Kamil, P. Mosenthal, P. Pearson, & R. Barr (Eds.), *Handbook of reading research* (Vol. 3, pp. 545–561). Mahwah, NJ: Erlbaum.

Pressley, M., & Afflerbach, P. (1995). *Verbal protocols of reading: The nature of constructively responsive reading.* Hillsdale, NJ: Erlbaum.

Pressley, M., Beard El-Dinary, P., & Brown, R. (1992). Skilled and not-so-skilled reading: Good information processing of not-so-good processing. In M. Pressley, K. Harris, & J. Guthrie (Eds.), *Promoting academic competence and literacy in school* (pp. 91–127). San Diego, CA: Academic Press.

Rosenblatt, L. M. (1978). *The reader: The text: The poem.* Carbondale, IL: Southern Illinois University.

Sax, G. (1997). *Principles of educational and psychological measurement and evaluation.* Belmont, CA: Wadsworth.

Schmitt, M. C. (1990). A questionnaire to measure children's awareness of strategic reading processes. *The Reading Teacher, 43,* 454–461.

Snow, C. E., Burns, M. S., & Griffin, P. (1998). *Preventing reading difficulties in young children.* Washington, DC: National Academy Press.

van Dijk, T. A., & Kintsch, W. (1983). *Strategies of discourse comprehension.* Orlando, FL: Academic Press.

Wade, W., Trathen, W., & Schraw, G. (1990). An analysis of spontaneous study strategies. *Reading Research Quarterly, 25,* 147–166.

Wagner, R. K., & Sternberg, R. J. (1987). Executive control in reading comprehension. In B. K. Britton & S. M. Glyn (Eds.), *Executive control processes in reading* (pp. 1–21). Hillsdale, NJ: Erlbaum.

Appendix A

A Thumbnail Sketch of Conscious Constructive Responses to Text

- Overviewing before reading (determining what is there and deciding which parts to process).

- Looking for important information in text and paying greater attention to it than to other information (e.g., adjusting reading speed and concentration depending on the perceived importance of text to reading goals).

- Attempting to relate important points in text to one another in order to understand the text as a whole.

- Activating and using prior knowledge to interpret text (generating hypotheses about text, predicting text content).

- Relating text content to prior knowledge, especially as part of constructing interpretations of text.

- Reconsidering and/or revising hypotheses about the meaning of text based on text content.

- Reconsidering and/or revising prior knowledge based on text content.

- Attempting to infer information not explicitly stated in text when the information is critical to comprehension of the text.

- Attempting to determine the meaning of words not understood or recognized, especially when a word seems critical to meaning construction.

- Using strategies to remember text (underlining, repetition, making notes, visualizing, summarizing, paraphrasing, self-questioning, etc.).

- Changing reading strategies when comprehension is perceived not to be proceeding smoothly.

- Evaluating the qualities of text, with these evaluations in part affecting whether text has impact on reader's knowledge, attitudes, behavior, and so on.

- Reflecting on and processing text additionally after a part of text has been read or after a reading is completed (reviewing, questioning, summarizing, attempting to interpret, evaluating, considering alternative interpretations and possibly deciding between them, considering how to process the text). Additionally if there is a feeling it has not been understood as much as it needs to be understood, accepting one's understanding of the text, rejecting one's understanding of a text.

- Carrying on responsive conversation with the author.

- Anticipating or planning for the use of knowledge gained from the reading.

Note. From *Verbal Protocols of Reading: The Nature of Constructively Responsive Reading* (p. 105), by M. Pressley and P. Afflerbach, 1995, Hillsdale, NJ: Erlbaum. Copyright 1995 by Lawrence Erlbaum Associates. Reprinted with permission.

Appendix B

Metacognitive Awareness of Reading Strategies Inventory (Version 1.0)

Directions: Listed below are statements about what people do when they read *academic or school-related materials* such as textbooks or library books. Five numbers follow each statement (1, 2, 3, 4, 5), and each number means the following:

- **1** means "I **never or almost never** do this."

- **2** means "I do this **only occasionally**."

- **3** means "I **sometimes** do this" (about **50%** of the time).

- **4** means "I **usually** do this."

- **5** means "I **always or almost always** do this."

After reading each statement, **circle the number** (1, 2, 3, 4, or 5) that applies to you using the scale provided. Please note that there are **no right or wrong answers** to the statements in this inventory.

Type	Strategy	Scale				
GLOB	1. I have a purpose in mind when I read.	1	2	3	4	5
SUP	2. I take notes while reading to help me understand what I read.	1	2	3	4	5
GLOB	3. I think about what I know to help me understand what I read.	1	2	3	4	5
GLOB	4. I preview the text to see what it's about before reading it.	1	2	3	4	5
SUP	5. When text becomes difficult, I read aloud to help me understand what I read.	1	2	3	4	5
SUP	6. I summarize what I read to reflect on important information in the text.	1	2	3	4	5
GLOB	7. I think about whether the content of the text fits my reading purpose.	1	2	3	4	5
PROB	8. I read slowly but carefully to be sure I understand what I'm reading.	1	2	3	4	5
SUP	9. I discuss what I read with others to check my understanding.	1	2	3	4	5
GLOB	10. I skim the text first by noting characteristics like length and organization.	1	2	3	4	5
PROB	11. I try to get back on track when I lose concentration.	1	2	3	4	5
SUP	12. I underline or circle information in the text to help me remember it.	1	2	3	4	5
PROB	13. I adjust my reading speed according to what I'm reading.	1	2	3	4	5
GLOB	14. I decide what to read closely and what to ignore.	1	2	3	4	5
SUP	15. I use reference materials such as dictionaries to help me understand what I read.	1	2	3	4	5
PROB	16. When text becomes difficult, I pay closer attention to what I'm reading.	1	2	3	4	5
GLOB	17. I use tables, figures, and pictures in text to increase my understanding.	1	2	3	4	5
PROB	18. I stop from time to time and think about what I'm reading.	1	2	3	4	5
GLOB	19. I use context clues to help me better understand what I'm reading.	1	2	3	4	5

(continued)

Type	Strategy	Scale				
SUP	20. I paraphrase (restate ideas in my own words) to better understand what I read.	1	2	3	4	5
PROB	21. I try to picture or visualize information to help remember what I read.	1	2	3	4	5
GLOB	22. I use typographical aids like boldface and italics to identify key information.	1	2	3	4	5
GLOB	23. I critically analyze and evaluate the information presented in the text.	1	2	3	4	5
SUP	24. I go back and forth in the text to find relationships among ideas in it.	1	2	3	4	5
GLOB	25. I check my understanding when I come across conflicting information.	1	2	3	4	5
GLOB	26. I try to guess what the material is about when I read.	1	2	3	4	5
PROB	27. When text becomes difficult, I reread to increase my understanding.	1	2	3	4	5
SUP	28. I ask myself questions I like to have answered in the text.	1	2	3	4	5
GLOB	29. I check to see if my guesses about the text are right or wrong.	1	2	3	4	5
PROB	30. I try to guess the meaning of unknown words or phrases.	1	2	3	4	5

Reading Strategies Inventory

Scoring Rubric

Student name: _____ Age: _____ Date: _____

Grade in school: □ 6th □ 7th □ 8th □ 9th □ 10th
  □ 11th □ 12th □ College □ Other

1. Write your response to each statement (i.e., 1, 2, 3, 4, or 5) in each of the blanks.
2. Add up the scores under each column. Place the result on the line under each column.
3. Divide the subscale score by the number of statements in each column to get the average for each subscale.
4. Calculate the average for the whole inventory by adding up the subscale scores and dividing by 30.
5. Compare your results to those shown below.
6. Discuss your results with your teacher or tutor.

Global Reading Strategies (GLOB subscale)	Problem-Solving Strategies (PROB subscale)	Support Reading Strategies (SUP subscale)	Overall Reading Strategies
1. _____	8. _____	2. _____	GLOB _____
3. _____	11. _____	5. _____	PROB _____
4. _____	13. _____	6. _____	SUP _____
7. _____	16. _____	9. _____	
10. _____	18. _____	12. _____	
14. _____	21. _____	15. _____	
17. _____	27. _____	20. _____	
19. _____	30. _____	24. _____	
22. _____		28. _____	
23. _____			
25. _____			
26. _____			
29. _____			

_____ GLOB score   _____ PROB score   _____ SUP score   _____ Overall score

_____ GLOB mean   _____ PROB mean   _____ SUP mean   _____ Overall mean

Key to averages: 3.5 or higher = high   2.5–3.4 = medium   2.4 or lower = low

Interpreting your scores: The overall average indicates how often you use reading strategies when reading academic materials. The average for each subscale of the inventory shows which group of strategies (i.e., global, problem solving, and support strategies) you use most when reading. With this information, you can tell if you score very high or very low in any of these strategy groups. Note, however, that the best possible use of these strategies depends on your reading ability in English, the type of material read, and your purpose for reading it. A low score on any of the subscales or parts of the inventory indicates that there may be some strategies in these parts that you might want to learn about and consider using when reading.

Appendix C

Categories of Reading Strategies Measured by the Metacognitive Awareness of Reading Strategies Inventory

Global Reading Strategies

Examples include setting purpose for reading, activating prior knowledge, checking whether text content fits purpose, predicting what text is about, confirming predictions, previewing text for content, skimming to note text characteristics, making decisions in relation to what to read closely, using context clues, using text structure, and using other textual features to enhance reading comprehension. (Items 1, 3, 4, 7, 10, 14, 17, 19, 22, 23, 25, 26, 29)

Problem-Solving Strategies

Examples include reading slowly and carefully, adjusting reading rate, paying close attention to reading, pausing to reflect on reading, rereading, visualizing information read, reading text out loud, and guessing meaning of unknown words. (Items 8, 11, 13, 16, 18, 21, 27, 30)

Support Reading Strategies

Examples include taking notes while reading, paraphrasing text information, revisiting previously read information, asking self questions, using reference materials as aids, underlining text information, discussing reading with others, and writing summaries of reading. (Items 2, 5, 6, 9, 12, 15, 20, 24, 28)

Professional Development, Training, and Credentialing

Introduction

In the preface, we announced this book's underlying argument and our call to action for all postsecondary developmental reading instructors to continue *becoming* professionals in the field. Here we take that call to action to the next level—one that is noticeably more critical of the shortcomings of our field, especially with regard to professional preparation. This is nothing new, of course, as scholars such as Kenneth Ahrendt and Martha Maxwell have lamented this lack of training since the 1960s and 1970s. Professional organizations such as the Southwest Reading Conference (now the Literacy Research Association), the College Reading Association (now the Association of Literacy Educators and Researchers), and the North Central Reading Association (now defunct) were formed during the 1950s and early 1960s to provide college reading and study skills specialists with opportunities for professional development and to share research. In 1966, the Western College Reading Association (now the College Reading and Learning Association) was founded with a similar mission. Scholarship and camaraderie were promoted at conferences, but there were still no formal training programs across the country.

The generation of college reading professionals who were to provide national leadership and scholarship during the last two decades of the twentieth century and the first decade of the twenty-first century underwent doctoral training that required them to learn about postsecondary literacy on top of the standard K–12 fare provided in all literacy doctoral programs. The individuals who provided instruction in the wildly popular community college developmental reading and study skills programs of the latter twentieth century were asked to adapt their knowledge and competencies mastered in K–12 reading specialist certification programs (programming which was evolving itself).

Formal training programs began to evolve during this period by a form of happenstance. The birth of the developmental studies movement and educational opportunity programs in research on institutions brought cadres of individuals who would undertake impactful research on the populations of students enrolled in developmental reading programs together under one roof, and in a number of cases, these individuals formed alliances with graduate reading programs so as to provide master's level and doctoral programming (both actual and de facto) focusing on college reading and learning. However, these opportunities were few and far between.

More recently, graduate programs allowing candidates to specialize in postsecondary reading that promise to be exemplary have been established. However, not many other credentialing and training opportunities exist that are specific to the field of postsecondary developmental reading. We continue to recruit individuals who have been trained to serve in the K–12 milieu to serve in our programs.

Literacy professionals serving in the K–12 arena must meet the extensive and measurable professional standards of knowledge, skills, and dispositions espoused by the International Reading Association (IRA) to be certified as highly qualified. Furthermore, they must maintain that certification through ongoing professional development experiences. Developmental reading professionals, however, have neither an established nor consistent set of professional standards dictating any form of certification, nor any explicit guidelines on continued professional development. Although the IRA once had a set of professional standards for those who worked with college students and adults, it has not maintained these guidelines for several decades.

In an era when current practice is being questioned by a variety of higher education stakeholders, it is clearly a time when professional standards must be developed for both full-time and part-time college reading professionals.

This chapter begins with a historically significant work by William G. Brozo and Norman A. Stahl that provides a College Reading Specialist Competency Checklist built upon extensive research. Although written a quarter century ago, the recommendations for the knowledge, skills, and dispositions needed for college reading professionals remain remarkably current.

Ironically, little was written in the professional literature on standards for postsecondary reading specialists across the next quarter century. Hence, we present the work of Eric J. Paulson and Sonya L. Armstrong, who argue that a lack of a fieldwide coherence is to blame for issues related to theory, terminology, and teacher preparation. They provide suggestions in each area en route to arguing for increased coherence.

The final article, by Patricia R. Eney and Evelyn Davidson, focuses on the increasing number of colleges and universities turning to part-time instructors to teach courses in developmental education. Program directors are called on to provide training, support, and evaluation of adjunct instructors. As there is limited literature on this topic, the authors have drawn on best practices and research in presenting a set of recommendations for supervising part-time instructors.

We conclude this chapter with a list of professional resources that provides a good representation of the range of organizations and publications available for all professionals in the field of postsecondary developmental reading.

Additional Readings

Ahrendt, K. M. (1975). *Community college reading programs*. Newark, DE: IRA.

Aspen Institute. (2013). *Creating a faculty culture of student success*. Washington DC: Aspen Institute.

Bain, K. (2004). *What the best college teachers do*. Cambridge, MA: Harvard University Press.

L'Allier, S. K., & Elish-Piper, L. (2007). Ten best practices for professional development in reading. *Illinois Reading Council Journal, 35*(1), 22–27.

Maxwell, M. J. (1966). Training college reading specialists. *Journal of reading, 10*(3), 147–155.

Maxwell, M. J. (1969, March). *What the college reading teacher needs to know about reading*. Paper presented at the Western College Reading Association Meeting (ERIC Document Reproduction Service No. Ed 046646).

May, M. M. (1971). Training assistants in developmental reading. In G. B. Schick & M. M. May (Eds.), *Reading: Process and pedagogy, the nineteenth yearbook of the National Reading Conference* (Vol. II, pp. 128–132). Milwaukee, WI: National Reading Conference.

Paulson, E. J., & Barry, W. J. (2012). Survey of college reading instructors: Professional preparation and classroom practice, part 1. *Research in Developmental Education, 24*(3).

Stahl, N. A. (1981). *The professional preparation of reading specialists for the community college, liberal arts college and university*. Pittsburgh, PA: University of Pittsburgh. (ERIC Document Reproduction Service No. 207-006).

Stahl, N. A., Brozo, W. G., & Gordon, B. (1984). The professional preparation of college reading and study-skills specialists. In G. McNinch (Ed.), *Reading teacher education: Yearbook of the 4th annual conference of the American Reading Forum*. Carrollton, GA: West Georgia College.

Focusing on Standards: A Checklist for Rating Competencies of College Reading Specialists

William G. Brozo and Norman A. Stahl

William G. Brozo and Norman A. Stahl present the College Reading Specialist Competency Checklist, an informal measure for evaluating the competencies and experiences of college reading professionals. The checklist is based on a comprehensive literature review on professional standards, and can be used for several evaluation scenarios, including hiring, supervision, graduate training, and professional development.

The past two decades witnessed considerable growth in the number of college level reading and study skills courses, learning assistance centers, writing labs, and peer tutoring programs. In 1980 Sullivan observed that there were nearly 2,000 college learning centers in the U.S. and Canada. Never before has there been a greater need for trained reading and study skills specialists.

In the early 1960s the subject of standards for specialists began to surface in the literature. Several leaders in the field have made observations and recommendations on professional standards for specialists, and several surveys can be found that detail ideal training programs. But despite the continuing need, professional educators have yet to agree upon a set of generally accepted qualifications, instructional experiences, and credentials for such specialists (Simpson, 1983; Stahl, 1981).

What Competencies Should Specialists Possess?

After a comprehensive review of the literature on professional standards for reading and study skills specialists (Stahl, 1981; Stahl, Brozo, and Gordon, in press), we discovered that these standards had yet to be presented so that they could be applied to practical settings. Using the recommendations from 19 sources, we synthesized skills, knowledge, and attitudes that we later organized around five broad categories. What evolved from this process is the College Reading Specialist Competency Checklist (CRSCC).

The CRSCC is designed to evaluate a specialist's competencies in at least four common situations.

1. A search committee might use the CRSCC to help focus an interview on a candidate's qualifications and then later for comparing candidates.

2. Professors who are supervising undergraduate and graduate practicums in college reading might use the CRSCC diagnostically to evaluate competencies of preservice specialists and to suggest subsequent instructional experiences.

3. Professors and administrators responsible for periodic reviews might use the CRSCC when discussing professional growth and work progress of specialists under their supervision.

4. Specialists might use the CRSCC to monitor their own growth as professionals in the field of college reading.

How to Use the CRSCC

The CRSCC is organized around five categories—Undergraduate Training, Instruction, Research and Measurement, Administrative and Counseling, and Personal Characteristics. Under the first four categories are specific sections detailing skills, competencies, and knowledge prerequisites. For example, under the category of Instruction, the first skill is the ability to individualize instruction. The numbers following this particular skill indicate that it was cited six times in the literature we surveyed, with each number corresponding to the numbered source in the reference section at the end of this article. The fifth broad category, Personal Characteristics, does not contain a list of skills and knowledge but rather a list of ideal attitudes for the specialist.

Notice that at the end of each section of the CRSCC the evaluator has the opportunity to include institution-specific competencies. When using the CRSCC, the evaluator ranks the specialist's competencies on a 3 point scale ranging from low to high.

Beyond its obvious logical validity, no technical data has been gathered on the CRSCC. Our intent was not to create a formalized, all inclusive rating scale which defined competencies that guarantee success; rather, the intent was to apply practically the numerous recommendations and survey findings drawn from the literature.

A final word. Relying soley on this checklist or any other informal measure for the purposes of candidate evaluation, practicum evaluation, personnel evaluation, or self-evaluation is imprudent. Nevertheless, in the decision making process, the CRSCC can serve as one valuable tool along with traditional methods (i.e., interviews, observations of performance, etc.) for assessing the competencies held by reading and study skills specialists.

References

[1] Ahrendt, Kenneth M. *Community College Reading Programs*. Newark, Del.: International Reading Association, 1975.

[2] Carter, Homer, and Dorothy J. McGinnis. "Preparation of Reading Therapists for the Junior College Level." In *Reading Process and Pedagogy*, edited by George B. Schick. Nineteenth Yearbook of the National Reading Conference. Milwaukee, Wis.: National Reading Conference, 1970.

[3] Cranney, A. Garr, Eleanor Schenck, and Ward Hellstrom. "Initiating a Program for Training Junior College Reading Teachers." In *Programs and Practices for College Reading*, edited by Phil L. Nacke. Twenty-second Yearbook of the National Reading Conference. Boone, N.C.: National Reading Conference, 1973.

[4] Eanet, Marilyn G. "Do Graduate Reading Programs Prepare College Reading Specialists?" *Forum for Reading*, vol. 14 (Spring 1982), pp. 30–33.

[5] Hiler, M. Jean. "Wanted, Well Qualified College Remedial Reading Teachers." *Epistle*, vol. 2 (October 1975), pp. 1–3.

[6] Kazmierski, Paul R. *Training Faculty for Junior College Reading Programs*. Topical Paper No. 24. Los Angeles, Calif.: ERIC Clearinghouse for Junior Colleges, University of California at Los Angeles, 1971.

[7] Kinne, Ernest W. "Training Inexperienced Graduate Students as Instructors in a Reading Program." In *College and Adult Reading*, edited by Alton J. Raygor. First Annual Yearbook of the North Central Reading Association, 1962.

[8] Livingston, Cathy L. *The Mad Hatter or Responsibilities of a Reading Instructor in a Community College*. ED 103 818. Arlington, Va.: ERIC Document Reproduction Service, 1974.

[9] Maxwell, Martha J. "Skill Requirements for College Reading and Study Specialists." In *Programs and Practices for College Reading*, edited by Phil L. Nacke. Twenty-second Yearbook of the National Reading Conference. Boone, N.C.: National Reading Conference, 1973.

[10] Maxwell, Martha J. "Training College Reading Specialists." *Journal of Reading*, vol. 10 (December 1966), pp. 147-52.

[11] Maxwell, Martha J. *What the College Reading Teacher Needs to Know about Reading*. ED 046 646. Arlington, Va.: ERIC Document Reproduction Service, 1969.

[12] Parker, Gerald, and Barbara Ross. "Doctoral Programs for College Reading and Study Skills Teachers." *Epistle*, vol. 2 (October 1975), pp. 4-8.

[13] Price, Umberto, and Kay Wolfe. "Teacher Preparation of the Junior College Reading Teacher." In *Junior College Reading Programs*, edited by Paul Berg. Newark, Del.: International Reading Association, 1968.

[14] Raygor, Alton L., and Anastasia Vavoulis. "Training Reading and Study Skills Specialists at the University of Minnesota." In *Programs and Practices for College Reading*, edited by Phil L. Nacke. Twenty-second Yearbook of the National Reading Conference. Boone, N.C.: National Reading Conference, 1973.

[15] Simpson, Michele L. "The Preparation of a College Reading Specialist: Some Philosophical Perspectives." *Reading World*, vol. 22 (March 1983), pp. 213-23.

[16] Stahl, Norman A. *The Professional Preparational of Reading Specialists for the Community College, Liberal Arts College, and University*. ED 216 600. Arlington, Va.: ERIC Document Reproduction Service, 1981.

Stahl, Norman A., William G. Brozo, and Belita Gordon. "The Professional Preparation of College Reading and Study Skills Specialists." In *Reading*

Teacher Education, edited by George H. McNinch. Fourth Yearbook of the American Reading Forum, in press.

[17] Staiger, Ralph C. "Initiating the College or Adult Reading Program." In *Research and Evaluation in College Reading*, edited by Oscar S. Causey and Emery P. Bliesmer. Ninth Yearbook of the National Reading Conference for College and Adults. Fort Worth, Tex.: Texas Christian University Press, 1960.

[18] Streicher, Rosalind, and Joseph Nemeth. "Competencies for College Developmental Reading Teachers." In *Reading: Theory and Practice*, edited by P. David Pearson. Twenty-sixth Yearbook of the National Reading Conference. Clemson, S.C.: National Reading Conference, 1977.

Sullivan, LeRoy L. "Growth and Influence of the Learning Center Movement." In *New Directions for College Learning Assistance*, edited by Kurt V. Lauridsen. San Francisco, Calif.: Jossey-Bass, 1980.

[19] Wortham, Mary Harper. *Reading: Emerging Issues in the Two-Year Colleges*. ED 027 343. Arlington, Va.: ERIC Document Reproduction Service, 1967.

The College Reading Specialist Competency Checklist

Directions: Indicate the degree to which the candidate possesses each competency. [Numbers in brackets correspond to numbered sources cited in the reference list at the end of this article.]

	COMPETENCE/ATTITUDE LEVEL		
Undergraduate Training	Low	Medium	High
Skills			
Reads well with a command of all basic skills to be taught to college readers [3, 13]	_____	_____	_____
Additional competencies:	_____	_____	_____
Knowledge			
Has a broad academic background [1, 13, 16]	_____	_____	_____
Knows the sciences [13]	_____	_____	_____
Knows the humanities [13]	_____	_____	_____
Knows the social sciences [2, 13]	_____	_____	_____
Knows reading methods [2]	_____	_____	_____
Additional competencies:	_____	_____	_____
Instruction			
Skills			
Individualizes instruction [2, 3, 6, 12, 13, 17]	_____	_____	_____
Groups for instruction [2, 3, 16]	_____	_____	_____

(continued)

Uses a variety of techniques for teaching college reading and study skills [5, 8, 12, 18]   ____ ____ ____

Specific components:

    comprehension [3, 7, 12, 18]   ____ ____ ____

    critical reading [18]   ____ ____ ____

    rate/flexibility [3, 7, 12, 18]   ____ ____ ____

    reference skills [12]   ____ ____ ____

    retention/memory skills [12]   ____ ____ ____

    spelling [10, 12]   ____ ____ ____

    study reading [3, 10, 12, 18]   ____ ____ ____

    test taking skills [7, 10, 12]   ____ ____ ____

    time management [12, 14]   ____ ____ ____

    vocabulary development [7, 10, 12, 18]   ____ ____ ____

Integrates the language arts into the instructional program [13, 14]   ____ ____ ____

Devises original materials [1, 8, 10, 14, 19]   ____ ____ ____

Matches materials to students' needs [6, 12, 13]   ____ ____ ____

Plans instructional activities directly supportive of the students' mastery of subject matter [16, 18]   ____ ____ ____

Evaluates commercial instructional material [14]   ____ ____ ____

Additional competencies: ____ ____ ____

Knowledge

Knows theories and models of learning and reading [2, 9, 10, 11, 12, 15, 18]   ____ ____ ____

Knows psychological and sociological literature concerning developmental and remedial college readers [12]   ____ ____ ____

Knows published instructional materials [10, 12, 13, 18]   ____ ____ ____

Knows college course content for planning instruction [16, 18]   ____ ____ ____

Additional competencies: ____ ____ ____

Research and Measurement

Skills

Uses informal diagnostic procedures [2, 8, 10, 12, 15, 17]   ____ ____ ____

Develops informal diagnostic procedures [5, 6, 12, 15]   ____ ____ ____

Administers, scores, and interprets formal standardized diagnostic tests properly [2, 8, 10, 12, 17] ____ ____ ____

Critically evaluates the quality of instruments [2, 8, 12, 14, 18] ____ ____ ____

Diagnoses learning problems and evaluates student progress using tests, interviews, and case studies [3, 10, 14] ____ ____ ____

Uses formal and informal achievement measures [1, 8, 12, 14, 15, 17, 18] ____ ____ ____

Applies research skills to the evaluation of instruction and curriculum [15, 18] ____ ____ ____

Conducts research and applies findings [4, 6, 9, 10, 18] ____ ____ ____

Additional competencies: ____ ____ ____

Knowledge

Knows the research literature and its practical applications [4, 10, 14, 18] ____ ____ ____

Knows the literature on effective teaching and learning in higher education [4] ____ ____ ____

Knows current studies in developmental, late adolescent, and adult psychology [3, 4, 6] ____ ____ ____

Knows statistics and research design [6, 13, 14] ____ ____ ____

Additional competencies: ____ ____ ____

Administrative and Counseling

Skills

Supervises professionals [1, 10] ____ ____ ____

Provides appropriate training for staff [1, 8, 10, 12, 18] ____ ____ ____

Serves as a college reading consultant on and off campus [8, 14, 18] ____ ____ ____

Interacts with and trains content area teachers [8, 10, 12, 18, 19] ____ ____ ____

Sets program goals and objectives [1, 12] ____ ____ ____

Develops learning programs [1, 18] ____ ____ ____

Budgets programs [1, 8, 12, 14] ____ ____ ____

Engages in public relations and conducts advertising for programs [9, 11] ____ ____ ____

Publishes in-house program evaluation data in the form of annual reports [11, 12] ____ ____ ____

(continued)

Develops and maintains relationships with academic departments [2, 9, 11, 18] _____ _____ _____

Serves on campus-wide committees [9] _____ _____ _____

Refers and directs students to appropriate campus agencies [9] _____ _____ _____

Additional competencies: _____ _____ _____

Knowledge

Knows institutional traditions and requirements [9] _____ _____ _____

Knows the organization of curricula and courses within academic units [6] _____ _____ _____

Knows the courses with high failure rates [12] _____ _____ _____

Knows the history and role of the college reading program on that campus [9] _____ _____ _____

Knows scheduling procedures, campus regulations, transfer and graduation requirements [8] _____ _____ _____

Additional competencies: _____ _____ _____

Personal Characteristics

Attitudes

Positive regard for students from varied socioeconomic and academic backgrounds [5, 9, 11, 12, 13, 18] _____ _____ _____

Desire to assist young adults to meet their career objectives [12] _____ _____ _____

Empathy towards the problems students encounter in their coursework [2, 5, 9, 18] _____ _____ _____

Flexibility and willingness to carry out program procedures and instruction to meet students' needs [5, 6, 13] _____ _____ _____

Creativity in developing student-centered learning programs [13] _____ _____ _____

Persevervance in the face of adversity [6] _____ _____ _____

Feelings of self-worth [16] _____ _____ _____

Commitment to the college reading program and profession [5, 17, 18] _____ _____ _____

Additional competencies: _____ _____ _____

Postsecondary Literacy: Coherence in Theory, Terminology, and Teacher Preparation

Eric J. Paulson and Sonya L. Armstrong

Eric J. Paulson and Sonya L. Armstrong discuss current issues across three key areas within which postsecondary literacy instruction is still developing: theory, terminology, and teacher preparation. The authors further provide specific recommendations for increasing coherence within each of these areas.

Like emergent literacy or adolescent literacy, postsecondary literacy carries with it a connotation of the level or age of students being served as well as a certain type of literacy instruction needed on the part of those students. Relative to emergent literacy or adolescent literacy, however, postsecondary literacy is still developing as a field in some important ways. That is not to say that there is not a dedicated cohort of professionals who teach at this level (including the two authors of this article, before getting into the teacher-preparation side of the business). Nor is there a lack of a rich history of instruction in the field: postsecondary literacy instruction has a 100-plus year foundation of being a part of many students' college experiences (Casazza, 1999; Stahl & King, 2009; Wyatt, 2003). Rather, where postsecondary literacy instruction will continue to develop as a unified field is from increased coherence in areas that include theory, terminology, and teacher preparation. The goal of this article is to begin—and in some cases, continue—an examination of current issues related to those three areas, with a view toward laying the groundwork for more comprehensive discussions about establishing coherence across these areas within the field of postsecondary literacy. At the end of each section we include a synopsis of the key points in a bulleted format for further discussion on these issues.

Our purpose for discussing three major aspects of literacy instruction within one article warrants mention. Although each of these aspects is deserving of separate, focused treatment, we have made a deliberate decision to include discussions of all three in a single article because of the interconnectedness of these aspects. We view these aspects as part of a holistic discussion that is best begun with an approach that, at least implicitly, is imbued with an understanding of the interrelatedness of the topics. That is, discussing theory without mention of language is unwise; discussing teacher preparation without discussing theory is counterproductive, and so on. So as much as our purpose is one of furthering coherence in each of these areas, our purpose also includes furthering discussions of the interdependence between each aspect within the field as a whole. We begin with some general information about postsecondary literacy instruction to set the stage for the three areas of discussion that follow.

The Prevalence and Variability of Transitional, or Developmental, Literacy Coursework

Courses typically referred to as developmental, including reading, writing, and study strategies, are prevalent in higher education, being offered in 99% of 2-year institutions and 75% of 4-year institutions (Boser & Burd, 2009). Similarly, there is an increasing prevalence of incoming and returning college students who have demonstrated difficulty with reading at a postsecondary level for purposes common to college courses. For example, the ACT college entrance test indicated that only about half of incoming college students were prepared for the reading requirements of a typical first-year college course (ACT, 2006; Associated Press, 2006).

This prevalence is important because "given the large numbers of students involved, many of whom are minority, low-income or disadvantaged" (Jenkins & Boswell, 2002, p. 1), the effectiveness of developmental programs in transitioning students to upper level classes is a crucial part of access to higher education. Unfortunately, historically, more than a quarter of the students who begin developmental coursework do not successfully complete it (Wirt, Choy, Rooney, Provasnik, Sen, & Tobin, 2004), a troubling statistic that suggests that continued critical reflection on instructional practice is needed.

Although professionals in the field of postsecondary literacy as a whole understand that there is a lack of instructional effectiveness if theoretically sound best practices are not put to use (Boylan & Saxon, 1999), there is a great deal of variability in the effectiveness of instructional approaches within the field (Jenkins & Boswell, 2002). One specific problem is that reading and writing courses in postsecondary contexts continue to be reduced to a skills-only or basic-grammar based approach which assumes a deficiency at the most basic "skills" level without acknowledging students' unfamiliarity with academic discourse practices (Bartholomae, 1985). In addition, postsecondary literacy instruction is characterized by a relative lack of formal teacher education (Carnegie Foundation, 2008; Stahl, Simpson, & Hayes, 1992). In short, critical inquiry into the state of postsecondary literacy instruction, including teacher preparation, is imperative. especially if the field is to continue to move toward coherence as a body of professionals. In the next section, we initiate this critical inquiry by examining the need for coherence in theory development within postsecondary literacy.

Theory

Several scholars have already identified solid reasons for the need for theory development in postsecondary contexts that may be useful here (e.g., Collins & Bruch, 2000). Casazza (2003), for example, has acknowledged that a crucial gap in the field is "a theoretical framework that can inform educators about the learners' different understandings of what knowledge is and also how they approach the task of learning" (p. 183). Similarly, Chung and Brothen (2001) provide a reminder of a fundamental principle of education when they report Hunter Boylan's comment: "Some research suggests that if a course is explicitly informed by a theory—*any theory* [emphasis in original] (p. 40)—then students tend to be more successful". Although few would advocate for "any theory," it certainly is likely that the focused reflection and dialogue surrounding most theoretical issues can serve to tie together aspects of practice in a way that an atheoretical discussion does not.

As educators and professionals in postsecondary literacy contexts continue to move toward presenting themselves as a unified field, theoretical coherence is essential and must be at the heart of practice. Although we do not attempt to lay out a theoretical foundation for an entire field in this single article, we do propose general directions the field might take toward furthering coherence in postsecondary literacy theory.

A comprehensive theory of postsecondary literacy must center on the students who are enrolled in these classes. No matter what the educational level, one common aspect of teaching is that educators have no control over students' out-of-class backgrounds and previous experiences. Higbee (2009) and many others have noted that postsecondary literacy courses include a diverse population of students. Such diversity creates a twofold responsibility for educators: one, to create an environment and structure that do not assume particular prior experiences in order to create successful learning outcomes for students, and two, to ensure that learners' cultural and social backgrounds are represented in the curriculum (Bohr, 2003). Perspectives that consider the social, cognitive, and affective aspects of learning are essential.

We would caution against any perspective that positions literacy as a set of decontextualized skills; such a perspective usually involves a broad epistemological assumption that the knowledge needed for students to negotiate the transition to academic modes of literacy is somehow "provided" to students in their first year of required college-level reading and writing classes (Tinberg, 1997) through the development of basic skills. The model of learning underlying such widely assumed outcomes is characteristic of a transmission view of knowledge and learning, a basic-skills approach, or more generally as what Street (1984) has described as an "autonomous model of literacy." One potentially hazardous implication of such autonomous or basic-skills models is that postsecondary literacy transitions are assumed to be standardized and linear, which much research has already disputed (e.g., Sternglass, 1997).

Instead, a theoretical framework that foregrounds sociocultural models of literacy is more appropriately adopted since "the literacy practices of academic disciplines can be viewed as varied social practices associated with different communities" (Lea & Street, 2006, p. 368). Sociocultural models view literacies as multiple, complex, dynamic social practices embedded in specific purposes, which Street (1993) has conceptualized as a continuum of contextualized processes and which Dressman, Wilder, and Connor (2005) have noted allows literacies to be defined as "a set of historically, economically, and environmentally responsive practices that vary in accordance with a reader's subjectivity as a gendered, ethnic, economic user of language" (p. 11). Additionally useful, and related to this perspective, is a situated cognition perspective in which knowledge is constructed in direct response to the context and culture of learning (Brown, Collins, & Duguid, 1989). Academic literacies, like all literacies, must be understood within the specific context in which they are embedded.

We would also stress the importance of including an understanding of identity in postsecondary literacy educational contexts. Students' academic goals are not met through a linear process of mastering basic skills; the multifaceted purposes for reading in different academic contexts, and when and how to use which standard writing conventions, vary depending on the given discourse-community context (McCarthy, 1987). Recognizing these contexts and being able to navigate them involves sophisticated matters of socialization and acculturation, as much an identity issue as a language issue. Gee (1996) has argued that what is important is "saying *(writing)-doing-being-valuing-believing combinations* [emphasis in original]" (p. 127), combinations he terms "Discourses (with a capital D)" (p. vii). Gee's point, of course, is that literacy-learning involves much more than memorization of specific, isolated skills, though language-related skills such as grammar are certainly embedded in this process.

Viewed through Gee's (2001) lens, a primary Discourse "is the ways with words, objects, and deeds that are associated with his primary sense of self formed in and through his (most certainly class-based) primary socialization within the family (or other culturally relevant primary socializing group)" (p. 723); school-based modes of communicating and knowing become a secondary Discourse. The difference between a student's primary Discourse and the secondary Discourse of the academy may cause conflict and obstacles to learning. What are often difficulties attributed to "cognitive deficits" on the part of the students may in fact be more accurately described as a mismatch between Discourses.

The concept of "mismatch" is one that should prove useful to attempts at theoretical constructions of postsecondary literacy contexts, especially in terms of the general mismatch between students' primary and secondary Discourses. Rogers (2004) has discussed the issue of students' Discourses either aligning with or conflicting with the institution's goals, and Lundell and Collins (2001) have pointed out that conflicts between students' primary and secondary Discourses can greatly affect their success. Dressman, Wilder, and Connor (2005) argue that literacy difficulties are a "result of alienation from and/or resistance to the literate discourses of school settings" (pp. 8–9). To be successful in higher education, students must learn to negotiate the literacy practices of various discourse communities. Such awareness lends itself to metacognitive, self-reflective thinking that is needed to navigate academic literacies, and, as Bartholomae (1985) has argued, students are forced to "invent the university." Given this understanding of what successfully navigating a postsecondary academic literacy context entails, Lundell and Collins' (2001) conclusion that "the new Discourse of higher education must be organized and made available to latecomers in ways that will not promote conflict with their primary and other extant Discourses" (p. 15) is important and appropriate.

Toward Coherence in Theory: A Synopsis

What follows is a synopsis of the key points from this section in a bulleted format that we view as focal points for further discussion:

- Theory must proceed from an understanding of the participants in, and the context of, literacy instruction at the postsecondary level.

- An understanding of identity, and the potential difficulties caused by a mismatch of primary and secondary Discourses (Gee, 2001), is an important aspect of theory at this level.

- Any theoretical perspective that positions literacy as merely and exclusively a set of decontextualized skills should be understood as ultimately being theoretically unsupported and pedagogically ineffective.

- Our recommendation for theoretical bases of postsecondary literacy instruction include sociocultural and situated cognitive perspectives that view literacies as complex, dynamic social practices embedded in specific purposes in response to the specific contexts and culture of learning.

Terminology

Peirce (1932) speaks to the reasons behind the need for precise language: "Those reasons would embrace, in the first place, the consideration that the woof and warp of all thought and all research is symbols; so that it is wrong to say that good language is *important* [emphasis in original] to good thought, merely; for it is of the essence of it" (p. 129). Issues of terminology may be at the heart of any inquiry into a field, but the inconsistent use of terminology in postsecondary literacy deserves special attention. In a field such as postsecondary literacy—one that is rightly focused on language—educators must be more attentive to the terms they use and the conceptualizations those terms represent or suggest. Despite periodic attempts to include the vocabulary of issues germane to postsecondary literacy in glossaries, in explicit vocabulary sections of other publications, and on professional listservs, there still exist widespread discrepancies in how literacy and literacy-learners are described within the field and—especially—from outside the field. In this section, we aim to build upon existing discussions by acknowledging some of the discrepancies that persist and then making specific usage recommendations.

Since at least the late 1960s, a wide variety of terminology has shown up in works focused on postsecondary literacy. For example, Wortham (1967) uses *remedial, developmental, basic,* and others before condensing them all into *remedial;* Ahrendt (1975) uses *marginal, high-risk, remedial, developmental,* and *inadequately prepared;* and Cross (1976) discusses her term *new students* while drawing on distinctions between *remedial* and *developmental* described by Roueche and Wheeler (1973). Several researchers have also explicitly discussed the fact that there is such a wide variety of terms; for example, in an article in this journal, Sherrie Nist (1984) directly addressed the confusion of the terms *developmental* and *remedial,* and John Roueche's work (Roueche & Kirk, 1973; Roueche & Roueche, 1999) has been particularly useful in this area. Even today, these issues continue to confront postsecondary literacy professionals. And because our interest is in how these terms are used presently in the field, we will focus most of our attention on current usage and draw primarily from works within the last several years.

The limitations of short, formalized definitions of culturally loaded terms—regardless of the field—can be problematic. In addition, some of the differences between major terms in a particular glossary may be so subtle to those outside the immediate discipline that the risk is that the distinction between the terms is lost altogether. For example, in the useful article titled "A Glossary of Developmental Education and Learning Assistance Terms" (Arendale, 2007), the first definitions of the terms *underprepared* and *developmental* (p. 13 and p. 19) are exactly the same, and the second definitions of each term differ in the addition of only one word. Whereas the second definition of *underprepared* is "a student who, while meeting college admissions requirements, is not yet fully prepared to succeed in one or more college-level courses" (p. 13), the second definition of developmental is "a student who, while meeting college admissions requirements, is not yet fully prepared to succeed in one or more *introductory* [emphasis added] college-level courses" (p. 19). Thus, the difference between *underprepared* and *developmental* in this glossary comes down to the absence or presence of a single word, and this distinction will most likely be lost on those not fully versed in the nuances of the field.

Rather than work from official glossaries, our preference is to focus on how terms are currently used, *in situ*, in the professional literature, whether provided as an explicit definition or implicitly through contrast with other terms or usage in general. A sampling of the definitions of the terms previously introduced follows.

Common Terms

REMEDIAL. Remedial education has traditionally suggested a focus on students' cognitive deficits as learners (Arendale, 2005); Casazza (1999) describes *remedial* as stemming from a medical model frame (as does Higbee, 2009):

> [Remedial] is the most common term across educational levels used to describe student weaknesses or deficiencies. It implies a "fixing" or "correction" of a deficit. For this reason, it is often associated with a medical model where a diagnosis is made, a prescription is given, and a subsequent evaluation is conducted to see if the "patient," or student, has been brought up to speed. (Casazza, 1999, para, 24)

Don'ts

Many educators would agree that "at best, the term *remedial student* is offensive; at worst, it is destructive and insulting" (Roueche & Roueche, 1999, p. 17). Interestingly, this is also the term that the U.S. Department of Education seems to prefer (e.g., official reports like *Remedial Education at Degree-Granting Postsecondary Institutions in Fall 2000* [National Center for Education Statistics, 2003]).

DEVELOPMENTAL. The term *developmental* has focused on a wide spectrum of student attributes and aspects; as Higbee (2009) states, "the term 'developmental education' was coined to reflect the influence of *better* student development theory and to consider the development of 'the whole student'" (p. 67). Similarly, the National Association for Developmental Education defines developmental education as promoting "the cognitive and affective growth of all postsecondary learners, at all levels of the learning continuum" (2008, para. 1). This is the term perhaps most often contrasted with *remedial* and most educators agree that it is comparatively a more useful description of postsecondary literacy contexts in general.

UNDERPREPARED. Whereas *remedial* is often construed to assign agency—or blame—to students for their lack of scholastic success, *underprepared* places that blame on the students' previous school or schooling experiences. The term is not used consistently, however, even within the same source. For example, Dzubak (2007) describes underprepared students as students "whose 'college readiness skills' do not adequately prepare them for the rigors of college study and learning"

inconsistently used

(para. 4), but in a subsequent section of the article the definition is re-stated to include a "deficit in reading" (para. 31), which links the term directly to a deficit model usually associated with the term *remedial*, not *underprepared*. Similarly, as an example of how the term is used outside of the field in a broad sense, Astin (1998) implicitly equates re-mediation with underpreparedness when he writes that "no problem strikes me as being more important than the education of the so-called underprepared or 'remedial' student" (para. 3). Nevertheless, terminol-ogy like *underprepared*, which takes the onus off the student for diffi-culties experienced in educational contexts, has been a positive step forward for the field.

MISPREPARED. This term may be thought of as a "tweaking" of the term *underprepared* in that it moves away from an over/under (or good/bad) dichotomy and instead acknowledges that successful high school students can still struggle in college due to the difference in goals of the two institutions. Johnson and Carpenter (2000) describe the issue: "Students today may be 'misprepared,' earning high grades in high school from courses that do not prepare them for college. Even if stu-dents take college preparatory courses, grade inflation and lack of rigor may lead them to think they are prepared when they are not" (p. 325).

AT-RISK. Notorious for some educators because of its predictive uses and misuses (e.g., assigning students to certain academic tracks at the outset of their academic career), *at-risk* is usually used to label students who fit certain criteria and/or score at a certain level on standardized tests as being in danger of not performing up to standards in college (or other educational levels, as this term's usage is widespread). Chamblee (1998) notes that this term has been used interchangeably with *under-prepared* (e.g., "Many of these students, often referred to as underpre-pared or at risk, have experienced limited success in high school" [p. 532]), but Johnson and Carpenter (2000) set the terms in opposition to each other: "Rather than underprepared, many students are now called at *risk* [emphasis in original], a broader, more descriptive term" (p. 325).

TRANSITIONAL. Use of this term is relatively new and focuses on the changes—both in terms of identity and ability to navigate new kinds of texts—that take place when the learner moves from one academic context (like high school) to another (like college). The emphasis is on what the student needs to know about the new academic environment and how to navigate that new environment, instead of focusing on the student's deficits or previous educational experiences (Sanchez & Paul-son, 2008). Transitions can involve changes in literacy conceptualiza-tions, awareness of the relationship of different types of literacies to the student's academic and other contexts, and increased proficiency in navigating and negotiating literacies for different purposes.

Usage Issues

Compounding the variety of ways these terms are defined and used is the relative frequency with which they are also made to appear synonymous in the professional literature, as in the previous example of how *underprepared* has been linked to *remedial*; this is also evident in U.S. Department of Education official publications that use both terms (U.S. Department of Education Institute of Education Sciences, n.d.). Similarly, Cohen and Brawer (2008) note that *remedial*, *developmental*, *compensatory*, and *basic skills* have been used interchangeably in some literature; thus, convolution of terms is widespread and not limited to one or two specific terms.

Perhaps more importantly, there seems to be an impression outside the field that terms other than *remedial* are simply euphemisms. To this end, Phipps (1998) draws attention to the problem that "what the general public refers to as remedial education is often defined as 'developmental education' by professionals and practitioners in the academic community" (p. 1). For example, the South Carolina Commission on Higher Education, (n.d.) equates *remedial* with *developmental* in an "AKA" fashion when discussing "requirements for remedial (also known as 'developmental') education programs in public higher education" (para. 1). Likewise, Calcagno and Long (2008) explicitly eschew differences in these terms in their recent report and use the terms *remediation*, *college prep*, and *developmental education* interchangeably.

The lack of coherence is obvious: within the field some draw large distinctions among terms, some draw subtle distinctions among terms, and some claim interchangeability among terms. Outside of the field, some terms are viewed as euphemisms for a single term that is perceived to have fallen out of favor. In many cases, terms are used either idiosyncratically or simply inconsistently. Our main purpose here is to raise these issues with an eye toward initiating further discussion, and, to this end, we offer two recommendations: a suggestion for a general term and a suggestion for usage.

GENERAL TERM. Professionals involved in postsecondary literacy instruction should choose to use a term that does not construe blame on students or their previous institutions for what are perceived by some as shortcomings. Since the reasons for challenges in navigating academic literacies are varied, using a term that assumes a cognitive shortcoming on the part of the student is simply unacceptable. Our preference for a term is one that can apply to the learner as well as to the learning situation and does not imbue either with a negative connotation. The advantages of avoiding a negative connotation are obvious. Wyatt (2003) has commented on the difference in enrollment based on Harvard's choice of course titles; registration for a reading course experienced a dramatic uptick once the course name was changed to omit the word *remedial. Transitional* works well in this regard, since students can transition *from* any educational context to any educational context (e.g., not just from precollege coursework to college-level coursework); moreover, the term gets at transitions of discursive awareness and use within educational environments.

USAGE. An unfortunate reality of the terminology of the field is that there seem to be many more ways to modify the *learner* than the type of learning situation; that is, it seems more common to use terms that position the learner, instead of the learning context, in certain ways. It is important to choose a usage structure that does not always result in renaming the learner but still allows for accurate identification of the type and level of literacy instruction. Here, we follow the guidelines of both the American Psychological Association (APA, 2009) and Arendale (2007) by putting the person first when using a descriptor. Thus, instead of "a developmental student," Arendale (2007) suggests using a structure like "a student with developmental issues in college algebra" (p. 19). Though this structure still attributes "issues" to the student, it is a step in the right direction as it moves away from imposing a generalized label on the "type" of student. Building on this general approach, we would propose that educators adopt a usage that would be even more specific to the context in which it is used. Continuing with the "developmental student" example, we would phrase this as "a student placed into a developmental reading course." This leaves the student unmodified, while being very specific about what the learning context is (placement into a specific course).

Toward Coherence in Terminology: A Synopsis

Just as with the "Theory" section, we end this section with a synopsis of main points from our discussion related to terminology:

- Although different terms may provide different denotative distinctions, the connotations of each term must be taken into account as well. For example, if *developmental* can be used in place of *remedial*, then it should; if *at-risk* connotes an assignment of blame on a student's identity, then it should not be used.

- Educators in the field must endeavor to help those outside the field understand that terminology has real and important meanings, and distinctions and terms used within the field are not simply euphemisms for *remedial*.

- Educators in the field must be careful to select terminology that indicates the precise meaning: *underprepared* versus *misprepared*, for example. For a general term for concepts in the postsecondary literacy field, we recommend the term *transitional* for its denotative accuracy and its connotative acceptability.

- We strongly suggest that usage of terms is "person-first"—(i.e., modifies not the person but the context of his or her learning environment): for example, "a student placed into a transitional reading and writing course."

Teacher Preparation

Just as there is a direct link between terminology and theory—words reflect and are shaped by beliefs—there is also a link between theory and practice. As commonly understood theoretical bases for postsecondary literacy issues are identified and developed, the field should experience more theory-driven pedagogy. However, the development of firmer theoretical foundations for pedagogy alone is not enough: Such foundations must be accessible to and applied by practitioners in college classrooms in order to result in improvements to postsecondary literacy instruction. A more unified, structured approach to teacher preparation would address this need and could also result in greater instructional effectiveness across the field. In this section, we discuss the need for coherence in teacher preparation in postsecondary literacy contexts.

Given the widespread attitude traditionally held by higher education (and society in general) toward developmental education as having merely a service function, and the low status afforded these courses in many institutions, it may come as no surprise that training requirements for instructors of these courses historically have not been of a high standard or widespread. The effect was, as Ahrendt (1975) noted, "a severe lack of trained, competent reading personnel available for the community college" (p. 24). This is not to say that training programs for postsecondary literacy instructors did not exist; for example, graduate courses were reported as early as the mid-1960s (Maxwell, 1966) and early 1970s (May, 1971). Nevertheless, a consensus in the field from this period (Maxwell, 1969) through the mid-1980s (e.g., Brozo & Stahl, 1985; Simpson, 1983) concluded that "considering the extensive body of literature relating to college reading in general, remarkably little has been written about the training of specialists for college reading programs" (Eanet, 1983, p. 30). The issue of a lack of teacher preparation in the field continues to the present day (e.g., Collins & Bruch, 2000; Stahl, Simpson, & Hayes, 1992; see also Lundell, 2000), with most institutions requiring minimal graduate-level work in literacy, teaching experience, or knowledge of the field's rich history (Stahl, 2000) in order to be qualified to teach reading or writing in a community college or university academic assistance program.

Although some progress has been made in this area, the parallel inexperience of both students and teachers in postsecondary literacy contexts continues to be identified as a serious issue: "Students are not the only ones underprepared for the challenges presented by this scenario. Campuses, too, are underprepared, and on several levels. Most faculty teaching developmental courses have no particular training for the role" (Calcagno & Long, 2008, p. 5). In general, the field is challenged by a situation in which the type, quality, and amount of training required of those who provide college literacy instruction does not adequately reflect the needs of students who are already in the midst of such a crucial transition. In fact, often the requirements for teaching postsecondary literacy courses in a community college consist of submitting transcripts that demonstrate a certain number of graduate credits in literacy, English, or a related area, with no requirements for specialized training with diverse groups of students and no expectation for experience working with nonstandard and non-native English speakers. Because students placed into postsecondary literacy courses bring with them widely diverse linguistic, conceptual, social, and cultural backgrounds (Boylan, 1999), as well as far-ranging literacy experiences, educators in postsecondary literacy courses need to be sufficiently prepared to meet the needs of these students. However, the currently accepted employment requirements do not reflect sufficient teacher preparation.

Broaching the subject of the need for an increase in teacher preparation has the potential to be mistaken for a call for top-down accountability of teachers. That is not our intention, nor do we think that a constructive goal. Instead, we are observing that where colleagues teaching in K–12 levels may be overmanaged, instructors teaching postsecondary literacy courses are at the opposite end of the spectrum. Some form of coherence for teacher preparation and certification is needed at the postsecondary level.

In the 1970s and 1980s there were several descriptions of the type of knowledge and skill base a postsecondary literacy instructor should have. The 1971 *Yearbook of the National Reading Conference* (Schick & May, 1971) alone had numerous articles explicitly delineating requirements for instructors, as did other books (e.g., Ahrendt, 1975) and journal articles (e.g., Simpson, 1983). Brozo and Stahl's (1985) article reviewed and summarized such work to date, culminating in a checklist of standards for instructors based on the authors' review of the literature. Of primary importance, teachers of first-year college students need to be experts in literacy and specialists in academic modes of literacy. Instructors should be well-versed in reading and writing theories, and they also need an understanding of the various literacies (types, purposes, conditions, etc.) that students must navigate in academia (Simpson, 2003; Simpson, Stahl, & Francis, 2004). Shanahan and Shanahan (2008) argue that "as students move through school, reading and writing instruction should become increasingly disciplinary, reinforcing and supporting student performance with the kinds of texts and interpretive standards that are needed in the various disciplines or subjects" (p. 57). Decades earlier, Carter and McGinnis (1971) made a similar, general point that postsecondary literacy instructor preparation should include undergraduate coursework in areas like psychology, sociology, and history so instructions would be versed in the discursive contexts of those disciplines.

In recent years there has been a renewed interest in graduate-level certificate and degree programs designed specifically for preparation of future college literacy instructors. Although programs that focus on developmental education in general have historically had a firm foundation in some institutions, an interest in postsecondary literacy has made itself known both in program and course titles and descriptions that specifically target literacy instruction preparation at the postsecondary level in other universities. These opportunities for specialization and professionalization are crucial, and we are hopeful that the benefits of such programs will be felt by students in the near future.

In order for postsecondary literacy to continue developing as a field of professionals, such focused emphases on postsecondary teaching as a profession are imperative. To achieve such a goal, we offer the following as the major recommendations: collectively, professionals must insist on working toward increasing the credential requirements for new and developing postsecondary literacy teachers. At first glance this may seem to be a charge directed toward administrators, but we believe that any meaningful change to the current teacher-training problems needs to be initiated from within the field by the scholars and professionals who know this problem to have a major impact on the success of both programs and students. For example, those working in teacher education must ensure that graduate courses on postsecondary literacy education continue to be offered and that they become more visible to current and prospective college teachers. In addition, the postsecondary educational community should strive to improve both the initial and ongoing training for those who serve in transitional classrooms. Here again, a possible model exists with K–12 educators, who are providing in-service teacher workshops and school-based invited seminars and lectures.

Toward Coherence in Teacher Preparation: A Synopsis

Below are the two major points from this section that we believe are key to any discussion of teacher preparation related to postsecondary literacy instruction:

- In addition to greater attention paid to the theoretical bases for pedagogical choices, improvements in the quality and quantity of teacher preparation for postsecondary literacy instructors are important.

- It is crucial that instructors understand the discipline-specific literacy expectations that their students must navigate at the college level. Pedagogical focus on navigation and negotiation of these literacies should be explicit.

Discussion

One purpose of this article has been to initiate—and on some levels, renew—a conversation, one which focuses on how to move forward as a more coherent field of professionals and scholars. It is incumbent upon researchers, teachers, and teacher-educators to respond to the realities and perspectives of postsecondary literacy contexts. As this article proposes, the development of a unifying, comprehensive theoretical grounding for the field would provide such a cohesive framework and would tie together important aspects of postsecondary literacy education.

Additionally, a commonly agreed-upon set of terminology for the field allows communication with greater specificity and clarity. Given the well-established relationship between thought and language, movement toward terminological clarity is necessary both for issues of theory development and for issues of communication within and outside of the field. Such clarity is especially crucial in core documents like departmental and institutional mission statements that guide departments in their planning and implementation of programs and also act as the public description of the department's perspective and focus for those outside the program or field.

Finally, we feel strongly that some form of commonly accepted methods for teacher preparation and certification—credentialing—is needed at the postsecondary level. Teaching postsecondary literacy is a challenging and rewarding profession, as most in the field will acknowledge. However, at present it is clear that more can and should be done to ensure the success of the field's new and developing teachers, and, therefore, the success of students in transitional literacy courses.

Simpson (1983) noted a "lack of philosophical and pedagogical cohesiveness" (p. 222) in postsecondary literacy instruction. And although theory-pedagogy pairings are a commonly accepted connection (though not always connected where needed), adding terminological precision to the mix is important as well because theoretically grounded pedagogy deserves accurate and responsible articulation at all levels: among colleagues, with students, and to those outside of the field. All three of these areas—theory, terminology, and teacher preparation—must move forward on some level for any one of the areas to advance in any real sense.

Limitations

Directly related to the decision to include discussion of three important areas in a single article are limitations imposed on the amount of breadth allocated to each area. That decision was a deliberate one, made to emphasize the interconnectedness of the three areas, but it also meant that space for fully discussing any one of the areas would be limited. Whereas a full literature review and discussion for each of these three areas would be preferable, considerations of space prohibited that approach and posed limitations on the amount of background material included in this article.

Conclusion

A major purpose of this article is to move toward increased coherence in the postsecondary literacy field, and some areas in need of immediate attention have been outlined: theory, terminology, and teacher preparation. These three aspects of postsecondary literacy should not be considered in isolation. Indeed, what we presented in this paper is a cyclical, recursive, and interconnected process that is found in most dynamic, established fields. Also, the focus on coherence is not intended as an exercise in bureaucratic standardization but as a much-needed movement toward further developing postsecondary literacy as a unified academic field: one with a solid theoretical foundation, a common language with which to articulate a core set of guiding principles, and an evidence-based pedagogy taught by comprehensively prepared literacy educators.

This is an exciting period in the history of postsecondary literacy, with much possibility for change on the horizon. It is hoped that this overview of current issues in postsecondary literacy instruction—and our recommendations for possible directions—will be useful for professionals in the field as change is considered.

References

ACT. (2006). *Reading between the lines: What the ACT reveals about college readiness in reading*. Retrieved from http://www.act.org/path/policy/reports/reading.html.

American Psychological Association. (2009). *Publication manual of the American Psychological Association* (6th ed.). Washington, DC: Author.

Ahrendt, K. M. (1975). *Community college reading programs*. Newark, DE: IRA.

Arendale, D. R. (2005). Terms of endearment: Words that define and guide developmental education. *Journal of College Reading and Learning, 35*(2), 66–82.

Arendale, D. R. (2007). A glossary of developmental education and learning assistance terms. *Journal of College Reading and Learning, 38*(1), 10–34.

Associated Press. (2006). *High school reading linked to college success*. Retrieved from http://www.msnbc.msn.com/id/11608629/from/RL..2/

Astin, A. W. (1998). *Remedial education and civic responsibility*. Retrieved from http://www.highereducation.org/crosstalk/ct0798/voices0798-astin.shtml

Bartholomae, D. (1985). Inventing the university. In M. Rose (Ed.), *When a writer can't write: Studies in writer's block and other composing-process problems* (pp. 11–28). New York, NY: Guilford Press.

Bohr, L. (2003). College and precollege reading instruction: What are the real differences? In N. A. Stahl & H. Boylan (Eds.), *Teaching developmental reading: Historical, theoretical, and practical background readings* (pp. 60–71). Boston, MA: Bedford/St. Martin's.

Boser, U., & Burd, S. (2009). *Bridging the gap: How to strengthen the PK–16 pipeline to improve college readiness*. Retrieved from http://www.newamerica .net/publications/policy/bridging.gap

Boylan, H. R. (1999). Demographics, outcomes, and activities. *Journal of Developmental Education*, 23(2), 2–6.

Boylan, H. R., & Saxon, D. P. (1999). *What works in remediation: Lessons from 30 years of research*. Retrieved from http://www.ncde.appstate.edu/reserve _reading/what_works.htm

Brown, J. S., Collins, A., & Duguid, P. (1989). Situated cognition and the culture of learning. *Educational Researcher*, 18(1), 32–42.

Brozo, W. G., & Stahl, N. A, (1985). Focusing on standards: A checklist for rating competencies of college reading specialists. *Journal of Reading*, 28(4), 310–314.

Calcagno, J. C., & Long, B. T. (2008). *The impact of postsecondary remediation using a regression discontinuity approach: Addressing endogenous sorting and noncompliance*. Retrieved from http://www.postsecondaryresearch.org /i/a/document/8161_CalcagnoLongRevised.pdf

Carnegie Foundation for the Advancement of Teaching. (2008). *Basic skills for complex lives: Designs for learning in the community college* (Report from Strengthening Pre-collegiate Education in Community Colleges [SPECC]). Stanford, CA: Author.

Carter, H. L. L., & McGinnis, D. J. (1971). Preparation of reading therapists for the junior college level. In G. B. Schick & M. M. May (Eds.), *Reading: Process and pedagogy, the nineteenth yearbook of the National Reading Conference, Volume II* (pp. 45–49). Milwaukee, WI: The National Reading Conference.

Casazza, M. E. (1999). Who are we and where did we come from? *Journal of Developmental Education*, 23(1), 2–6.

Casazza, M. E. (2003). Strengthening practice with theory. In N. A. Stahl & H. Boylan (Eds.) *Teaching developmental reading: Historical, theoretical, and practical background readings* (pp. 179–192). Boston, M.A: Bedford/St. Martin's.

Chamblee, C. M. (1998). Bringing life to reading and writing for at-risk college students. *Journal of Adolescent & Adult Literacy*, 41(7), 532–537.

Chung, C., & Brothen, T. (2001). Some final thoughts on theoretical perspectives—over lunch. In D. B. Lundell & J. L. Higbee (Eds.), *Proceedings of the second meeting on future directions in developmental education* (pp. 39–44). Minneapolis, MN: Center for Research on Developmental Education and Urban Literacy, General College, University of Minnesota.

Cohen, A. M., & Brawer, F. B. (2008). *The American community college* (5th ed.). San Francisco, CA: Jossey-Bass.

Collins, T., & Bruch, P. (2000). Theoretical frameworks that span the disciplines. In D. B. Lundell & J. L., Higbee (Eds.), *Proceedings of the first intentional meeting on future directions in developmental education* (pp. 19–22). Minneapolis, MN: Center for Research on Developmental Education and Urban Literacy, General College, University of Minnesota.

Cross, K. P. (1976). *Accent on learning: Improving instruction and reshaping the curriculum*. San Francisco, CA: Jossey-Bass.

Dressman, M., Wilder, P., & Connor, J. J. (2005). Theories of failure and the failure of theories: A cognitive/sociocultural/macrostructural study of eight struggling students. *Research in the Teaching of English*, 40(1), 8–61.

Dzubak, C. M. (2007). *What skills and whose standards: Why are students under-prepared?* Retrieved from http://www.myatp.org/Synergy_1/Syn_a1.htm

Eanet, M. G. (1983). Do graduate reading programs prepare college reading specialists? *Forum for Reading, 14,* 30–33.

Gee, J. P. (1996). *Social linguistics and literacies.* London: Taylor & Francis.

Gee, J. P. (2001). Reading as situated language: A sociocognitive perspective. *Journal of Adolescent & Adult Literacy, 44*(8), 714–725.

Higbee, J. L. (2009). Student diversity. In R. F. Flippo & D. C. Caverly (Eds.). *Handbook of college reading and study strategy research* (pp. 67–94). New York, NY: Routledge.

Jenkins, D., & Boswell, K. (2002). *State policies on community college remedial education.* Retrieved from http://www.communitycollegepolicy.org/pdf/FINAL%20REMEDIAL%20POLICY.pdf

Johnson, L. L., & Carpenter, K. (2000). College reading programs. In R. F. Flippo & D. C. Caverly (Eds.), *Handbook of college reading and study strategy research* (pp. 321–363). Mahwah. NJ: Lawrence Erlbaum Associates.

Lea, M. R., & Street, B. V. (2006). The "academic literacies" model: Theory and applications. *Theory into Practice, 45*(4), 368–377.

Lundell, D. B. (2000). Standards: Implications for training, professional development, and education. In D. B. Lundell & J. L. Higbee (Eds.), *Proceedings of the first international meeting on future directions in developmental education* (pp. 60–62). Minneapolis, MN: Center for Research on Developmental Education and Urban Literacy, General College, University of Minnesota.

Lundell, D. B., & Collins, T. C. (2001). Toward a theory of developmental education: The centrality of "discourse." In D. B. Lundell & J. L. Higbee (Eds.), *Theoretical perspectives in developmental education* (pp. 49–61). Minneapolis, MN: Center for Research on Developmental Education and Urban Literacy, General College, University of Minnesota.

Maxwell, M. J. (1966). Training college reading specialists. *Journal of Reading, 10*(3), 147–155.

Maxwell, M. J. (1969). *What the college reading teacher needs to know about reading.* Retrieved from ERIC database. (ED046646)

May, M. M. (1971). Training assistants in developmental reading. In G. B. Schick & M. M. May (Eds.), *Reading: Process and pedagogy, the nineteenth yearbook of the National Reading Conference, Volume II* (pp. 128–132). Milwaukee, WI: The National Reading Conference.

McCarthy. L. P. (1987). A stranger in strange lands: A college student writing across the curriculum. *Research in the Teaching of English, 21*(3), 233–265.

National Association for Developmental Education. *Definition.* Retrieved from: http://www.nade.net/aboutDevEd/definition.html

National Center for Education Statistics, (2003). *Remedial education at degree-granting post-secondary institutions in Fall 2000.* Retrieved from http://nces.ed.gov/surveys/peqis/publications/2004010/3.asp

Nist. S. (1984). Developmental versus remedial: Does a confusion of terms exist in reading programs? *Journal of Developmental Education, 8*(3), 8–10.

Peirce, C. S. (1932). The ethics of terminology. In C. Hartshorne & P. Weiss (Eds.), *Collected papers of Charles Sanders Peirce, Vol. II.* Cambridge, MA: Harvard University Press.

Phipps, R. A. (1998). *College remediation: What it is, what it costs, what's at stake*. Washington, DC: The Institute for Higher Education Policy. Retrieved from http://www.ihep.org/Publications/publications-detail.cfm?id=22.

Rogers, R. (2004). Storied selves: A critical discourse analysis of adult learners' literate lives. *Reading Research Quarterly, 39*(3). 272–305.

Roueche, J. E., & Kirk, R. W. (1973). *Catching up: Remedial education*. San Francisco, CA: Jossey-Bass.

Roueche, J. E., & Roueche, S. D. (1999). *High stakes, high performance: Making remedial education work*. Washington, DC: American Association of Community Colleges.

Roueche, J. E., & Wheeler, C. L. (1973). Instructional procedures for the disadvantaged. *Improving College and University Teaching, 21*, 222–225.

Sanchez, D., & Paulson, E. J. (2008). Critical language awareness and learners in college transitional English. *Teaching English in the Two-Year College, 36*(2), 164–176.

Schick, G. B., & May, M. M. (Eds.), (1971). *Reading: Process and pedagogy, the nineteenth yearbook of the National Reading Conference, Volume II*. Milwaukee. WI: The National Reading Conference.

Shanahan, T., & Shanahan, C. (2008). Teaching disciplinary literacy to adolescents: Rethinking content-area literacy. *Harvard Educational Review, 78*(1), 40–59.

Simpson, M. L. (1983). The preparation of a college reading specialist: Some philosophical perspectives. *Reading World, 22*, 213–223.

Simpson, M. L. (2003). Conducting reality checks to improve students strategic learning. In N. A. Stahl & H. Boylan (Eds.). *Teaching developmental reading: Historical, theoretical, and practical background readings* (pp. 290–301). Boston, MA: Bedford/St. Martin's.

Simpson, M. L., Stahl, N. A., & Francis, M. A. (2004). Reading and learning strategies: Recommendations for the 21st century. *Journal of Developmental Education, 28*(2), 2–15.

South Carolina Commission on Higher Education. (n.d.). *Policies on remedial education in South Carolina*. Retrieved from http://www.che.sc.gov /AcademicAffairs/Adm/a_7.htm

Stahl, N. (2000). Historical perspectives: With hindsight we gain foresight. In D. B. Lundell & J. L. Higbee (Eds.), *Proceedings from the first intentional meeting on future directions in developmental education* (pp. 13–16). Minneapolis, MN: Center for Research on Developmental Education and Urban Literacy, General College, University of Minnesota.

Stahl, N. A., & King, J. R. (2009). History. In R. F. Flippo & D. C. Caverly (Eds.), *Handbook of college reading and study strategy research* (pp. 3–25). New York, NY: Routledge.

Stahl, N. A., Simpson, M. L., & Hayes, C. G. (1992). Ten recommendations from research for teaching high-risk college students. *Journal of Developmental Education, 16*(1), 2–10.

Sternglass, M. (1997). *Time to know them: A longitudinal study of writing and learning at the college level*. Mahwah, NJ: Lawrence Erlbaum Associates.

Street, B. (1984). *Literacy in theory and practice*. Cambridge, MA: Cambridge University Press.

Street, B. (1993). Introduction: The new literacy studies. In B. Street (Ed.), *Cross-cultural approaches to literacy* (pp. 1–22). Cambridge, MA: Cambridge University Press.

Tinberg, H. B. (1997). *Border talk: Writing and knowing in the two-year college.* Urbana, IL: NCTE.

U.S. Department of Education Institute of Education Sciences. (n.d.). *Handbooks online: Remedial education.* Retrieved from http://nces.ed.gov/ssbr/pages/remedialed.asp?IndID=15

Wirt, J., Choy, S., Rooney, P., Provasnik, S., Sen, A., & Tobin, R. (2004). *The condition of education 2004* (NCES 2004-077). Washington, DC: U.S. Department of Education, National Center for Education Statistics.

Wortham, M. H. (1967). *Emerging issues in the two-year colleges.* Retrieved from ERIC database. (ED027343)

Wyatt, M. (2003). The past, present, and future need for college reading courses in the U.S. In N. A. Stahl & H. Boylan (Eds.), *Teaching developmental reading: Historical, theoretical, and practical background readings* (pp. 12–28). Boston, MA: Bedford/St. Martin's.

Improving Supervision of Part-Time Instructors

Patricia R. Eney and Evelyn Davidson

Patricia R. Eney and Evelyn Davidson draw on research and best practices to provide developmental educators with guidance in adopting procedures to train, support, and evaluate part-time faculty who serve students in college reading courses as well as basic writing and developmental mathematics. Given that the professional demographics for the nation's postsecondary faculty, regardless of a school's classification, demonstrate that the number of part-time faculty is continuing to grow each year, this is a topic of much discussion in higher education, and especially relevant for professionals in developmental reading.

D evelopmental educators face two significant trends in postsecondary education that heavily impact their work: the increase in the number of underprepared students entering colleges today and the growing reliance on part-time faculty, which includes contingent, adjunct, and full-time faculty teaching some developmental courses (Boylan, 1999; Boylan, Bonham, Jackson, & Saxon, 1994; McCabe, 2000, 2003). Because part-time faculty have a major role in the delivery of developmental courses and programs, it is critical to provide a supportive environment and professional development opportunities that allow part-time faculty to focus on quality teaching and learning while also giving them a stake in the institution's mission.

According to Boylan (1999), "Developmental courses are found in over 90% of the nation's community colleges and in about 70% of our universities." In a policy report, McCabe (2000) states that "[41] percent of entering community college students and 29 percent of all entering college students are underprepared in at least one of the basic skills (reading, writing, mathematics)" (p. 5). A follow-up study (McCabe,

2003) confirms the trend by pointing out that "each year one million students—one in four who enter higher education—are underprepared" (p. 14). Among the issues McCabe raises is the need to provide effective developmental programs that prepare these students to become knowledgeable and productive members of society. Colleges and universities have a daunting responsibility that requires not only adequate funding but also skilled and committed developmental educators, many of whom are part time.

This second trend, the use of part-time faculty, is addressed by Boylan, Bonham, Jackson, and Saxon (1994), who have found that the majority (72%) of those teaching developmental courses do so on a part-time basis, either as adjunct instructors or as full-time faculty in academic departments who also teach developmental education courses part time (p. 1). Further, remedial education programs often survive on marginal budgets and rely on "large numbers of inexpensive, part-time faculty" (McCabe, 2000, p. 39). This study also reports that many college faculty "often shun developmental education," preferring instead to work with "the best and the brightest" (p. 44). In such cases developmental education becomes a low priority. Despite budget constraints and heavy use of part-time instructors, the study finds that 43% of community college students in developmental courses successfully complete their program and perform well in subsequent college work (p. 31).

Part-time faculty members are defined in the *NADE Self-Evaluation Guides* as "teachers who occupy positions that require less than 50 percent of full-time service and whose appointment includes only limited or no fringe benefits" (Clark-Thayer, 1995, p. 171). Part-time faculty are hired in developmental education as in other disciplines because they cost less both in salary and fringe benefits, they do not require long-term commitments and, in fact, they can be hired or dismissed as determined by rising or falling enrollments. Most colleges and universities depend on part-time instructors as a source of low-cost labor but also recognize that they provide a valuable service because many of them have advanced degrees and/or life experiences that can enhance the institutions' offerings. However, although they are knowledgeable in their content areas, many part-time instructors have had little training in classroom instruction and curriculum development. Part-time faculty members are given a major responsibility in instructing underprepared students (Boylan, Bonham, & Bliss, 1994); consequently, they should be trained, mentored, and valued by their institutions and colleagues.

Roueche and Roueche (1993) promote quality selection and development for faculty, including part timers: "All faculty should be provided with the training and preparation they need to be excellent teachers" (p. 115). To support successful preparation of students for college-level work, the National Study of Community College Remedial Education (as reported in McCabe, 2000) recommends sound "techniques, models and structures" (p. 45). Among these are staff training and professional development for those who work with under-prepared students. In *What Works: Research-Based Best Practices in Developmental Education* (2002), Boylan includes adjunct faculty as valued resources for developmental education, finding them as effective in teaching as full-time faculty (p. 55). In addition, he states that they should be offered the same professional development opportunities as full-time faculty (p. 56). Among the recommended adjunct support mechanisms are manuals, orientation programs, participation in departmental meetings, ongoing professional development including workshops and conference attendance, and mentoring programs.

Research reported in the literature describes training, instructional models, and strategies for faculty teaching developmental students (Angelo & Cross, 1991; Boylan, 2002; Casazza & Silverman, 1996; Cross, 1976, 1992; Kozeracki, 2005; Maxwell, 1997; Roueche & Roueche, 1993). However, few resources focus specifically on the integration of part timers into the developmental education community. Nevertheless, when part-time instructors are mentioned, two themes consistently emerge: Part timers should be treated as valued resources in the delivery of developmental courses, and they should be provided with comprehensive training and faculty development opportunities. Wallin (2005) provides advice and guidance on hiring and supervising adjunct faculty across the disciplines; much of what she writes is applicable to part-time faculty in developmental education, and her examples and models of support underscore the importance of treating adjuncts as valued members of the institution.

In Fall 2004, the NADE Adjunct Faculty Committee conducted an Adjunct Supervisors' Survey in an effort to determine what was currently being provided for adjuncts in the following areas: training, orientation, manuals, professional development opportunities, salaries, and evaluations. The results of the survey were presented at the National Association for Developmental Education (NADE) conference. Those who responded to the survey and those who attended the conference sessions concurred that more attention should be given to professional development and training opportunities for adjuncts (Eney, Davidson, Dorlac, & Whittington, 2005).

Seven Recommendations for Supervisors of Part-Time Instructors

Considering the historical background of the use of part-time faculty in developmental education, it is essential to begin to make changes in the way colleges and universities select part-time instructors and how they treat them once they are hired. Although there has been considerable discussion of the plight of part-time instructors in higher education (Cox & Leatherman, 2000; Nelson, 1997; Skinner, 2005; Spinetta, 1990), little discussion has focused on improving the quality of part-time instructors and their work in developmental education classes. Therefore, the following recommendations are suggested for supervisors of part-time instructors teaching developmental courses.

1. Employ Individuals with Appropriate Credentials, Personalities, and Beliefs

According to a recent study done by the National Center for Developmental Education (Boylan & Saxon, 2005), "careful hiring practices" were found to be among the best practices of the five participating Texas community colleges in the study. The study confirmed the importance of hiring individuals with experience in teaching at-risk students and not depending heavily on the use of untrained part-time faculty. When Roueche and Roueche (1993) examined how faculty were selected for teaching developmental education courses, they found that instructors who showed a strong interest in teaching underprepared students also "were more likely to seek a higher degree of preparedness for the task, provided highly relevant instruction, used motivational strategies, and possessed a caring attitude toward their students" (p. 109).

Developmental education instructors need to be not only sensitive to the needs of at-risk students but also agreeable to assisting them in meeting their academic goals. McCabe (2000) states that "underprepared students require more personal attention. They often have personal, job, and family issues that must be addressed if there is to be academic progress" (p. 48). Underprepared students generally not only have deficiencies in basic skills but also are filled with self-doubt, low self-esteem, and/or anxiety about their ability to learn. Therefore, "successful remediation occurs in direct proportion to priority given to the program by the college. Most important is a caring staff who believe in the students and in the importance of their work" (p. 49).

Those who teach developmental students need not only appropriate education and training but also personalities and core sets of beliefs that will allow them to interact appropriately—and empathetically—with their students. Cross (1976) recommends that "staff working with remedial students should be selected for their interest and commitment as well as for their knowledge about learning problems" (p. 43). Supervisors should resist the urge to hire someone interested in teaching college students who has not embraced the concept of accepting at-risk students into college. Boylan (2002) recognizes that best practice developmental programs hire adjuncts "who [express] a desire to teach developmental courses" (p. 56). Among the characteristics of excellent teachers identified by Roueche and Roueche (1993) is empathy: "the ability to recognize, interpret, and act on the clues that others give" (p. 106). At the heart of this developmental philosophy, the "whole learner is placed at the center of practice; respect and empathy for learners is a central and unifying value" (Malnarich, Dusenberry, Sloan, Swinton, & van Slack, 2003, p. 25).

2. Provide Adequate Compensation

For more than 3 decades, the ranks of part-time instructors have been growing while those of full-time instructors have been decreasing. According to the National Center for Education Statistics (2004), between 1973 and 2003 the number of part-time faculty increased 375% while the full-time faculty increased only 67%. Between 1993 and 2001 part-time faculty increased 70% while the full-time faculty increased only 15% (p. 291). As full-time instructors reach retirement age, colleges and universities are likely to replace them with far less expensive part-time instructors who not only rarely receive any insurance or retirement benefits but also receive up to two thirds less pay than full-time instructors.

The Coalition on the Academic Workforce's (CAW) Collaborative Study of Undergraduate Faculty (American Historical Association, 2000) has revealed that, although many full-time non-tenure-track faculty receive more than $32,000 per year, most part-time faculty receive less than $3,000 per three-credit course. About one-third of them earn less than $2,000 per course. At this rate, "most could earn comparable salaries as fast food workers, baggage porters, or theater lobby attendants" (para. 19).

As early as 1976, the National Education Association advocated equal pay for equal work (termed pro rata pay) for part-time faculty. However, 30 years later part timers are still struggling with the same inequitable pay structure while having the same level of expectations concerning classroom responsibilities and the care of at-risk students as full-time faculty (Longmate & Cosco, 2002). Having inequitable pay sometimes even affects these instructors' professionalism. Rifkin (1998) conducted a survey of 1554 faculty at 127 randomly selected community colleges: 1197 (77%) were full time and 353 (23%) were part time. According to Rifkin, "even though both full- and part-time faculty are equally committed to the occupation, this study suggests that the professional commitment of part-time faculty does not go beyond their interest in students to include aspects that are integral to the profession such as curriculum, instruction, and other forms of scholarship" (pp. 18–19). This means that they are less likely to attend professional conferences, belong to professional organizations, or take courses in their employment field. Such behavior can greatly affect those teaching developmental students because often they have previous training in their subject area and not in developmental education in particular.

Pro rata pay is the fair and equitable approach to address this issue. However, actually achieving this goal is somewhat more difficult since part-time instructors often have no voice in defining salary rates.

Though college administrators, college faculty unions, and other full-time employees should lobby for equal pay for part-time instructors, recent success by adjunct unions in attaining equitable collective bargaining agreements (Carnevale, 2004: "Contract Reached," 2004) gives credence to part timers using unions as bargaining agents in much the same way as full-time faculty members have done for years.

All members of an institution's faculty deserve equal pay for equal work and should be treated fairly regardless of employment status. If higher education institutions are able to achieve pro rata pay, everyone wins. Part-time faculty will be paid according to an equitable salary scale, so their job satisfaction, professionalism, and loyalty to the institution should increase; the department will be able to increase the responsibilities that it requires of part timers and reap the benefits of their expertise; and the students should receive better instruction and service from their instructors.

3. Provide Part-Time Instructors with Necessary Services

The inability to provide space and services for part-time employees has long been a concern for college administrators. Oftentimes, especially during the fall term, the ranks of part-time instructors swell to two or three times the number of part timers during the rest of the year. Assuring they all have the services they need can stress even the most organized administrator. However, it is one of the most important areas to adjuncts. In Cohen's survey of 149 part-time faculty at a community college in suburban Washington, 48% responded that office space was very important to them (as cited in Freeland, 1998, p. 9).

Institutions make it difficult for part-time instructors to do their jobs when basic services or facilities are not available. The CAW report confirms that "many part-timers don't have access to e-mail, or even their own offices or telephones on the campus" (Cox & Leatherman, 2000, para, 14). The report also cites Karen Thompson, head of a university part-time faculty union: "The importance of the conditions of teaching personnel is of the utmost because those are also the learning conditions of the students" (para. 13).

All instructors should have a number of important services. 1. Office space: Part-time instructors need to have an actual office where they can have a file drawer and possibly share a desk with several other part timers who may not teach at the same time. Though locating that space in the developmental education department is important, some institutions have had to delegate a section of their library where instructors can have their own study carrels or set up a sizable office for all part-time instructors on campus. 2. File drawers: Some kind of secure storage area is also essential for part timers. As all instructors know, past tests, notes, handouts, and assignments need to be readily available in order to serve the students, not in the instructor's car or at home. 3. Regular mail and e-mail: The ability to send students messages and receive messages from them as well as receive information from professional organizations and publishers is essential for a college instructor. Therefore, instructors should be given their own e-mail address and instruction on how to activate it. It is also important that support staff make the college mailroom aware of all new hires at the beginning of each college term. All intraoffice and institutional memos, announcements, and advertisements for college events need to be sent to all instructors, not just full timers. 4. Meetings and get-togethers: Except for meetings that affect only full-time faculty, part timers need to be informed of all department meetings and get-togethers.

4. Involve Part-Time Instructors in Institutional Processes

The American Association of University Professors (AAUP) has shown concern that "contingent" teachers—nontenure track adjuncts and professors—are excluded from campus decision-making processes and faculty meetings even though they make up 44.5% of teachers in American colleges and universities (Skinner, 2005, p. 1). This exclusion often makes part-time faculty feel as though they have "no decision-making power within the institution and, therefore, little autonomy" (Rifkin, 1998, p. 15).

Spann (2000) believes that "policy development without the input and continuing involvement of those persons who actually implement the policy is both demoralizing and dehumanizing" (p. 4). He suggests involving all developmental educators in making policy decisions. If most instructors teaching developmental education classes work part time, it is only logical to include them in policy making. Once part-time faculty members are included in the process, they will "be more loyal, feel more responsibility, and will more actively support organizational goals than those who [do] not participate" (Roueche & Roueche, 1993, p. 73).

5. Establish Practical Professional Development Activities and Resources

Professional development should focus not only on policies and procedures of the institution but also on information about teaching, learning, professional publication, and the field of developmental education. Kozeracki (2005) recommends graduate programs, in-service training, and professional association activities to help prepare faculty for the pedagogical challenges of teaching developmental classes. However, not all part timers have these opportunities. She recommends college-sponsored faculty development that takes place through "formal collegewide programs, departmental meetings and roundtables, and informal discussions among colleagues" (p. 48). Unfortunately, she says, "opportunities for these types of conversations are substantially reduced for part-time faculty, especially those without offices, and for instructors whose offices or classrooms are not in close proximity to those of their colleagues" (p. 45).

Rifkin (1998) found in his survey of full- and part-time faculty that there was no significant difference between full- and part-time instructors in their commitment to their profession (p. 14). However, several other researchers found a big difference between full- and part-time faculty in teaching experience and training in instructing adult learners (Galbraith & Shedd, 1990), understanding of nontraditional students (Galbraith & Shedd; Roueche & Roueche, 1993), and teaching remedial courses (Shults, 2000). In addition, part-time faculty often either were not as actively involved in professional development or did not even have any opportunities for continuing professional development (Clery, 1998; Freeland, 1998; Longmate & Cosco, 2002; Rifkin, 1998).

With the need so greatly defined, researchers (Galbraith & Shedd, 1990; Greive, 1995; Roueche & Roueche, 1993; Spinetta, 1990) have called for all faculty to have equal educational opportunities. Galbraith and Shedd (1990) maintain that "with the increased number of part-time faculty, it seems paramount that they be included in professional development activities . . . not only for instructional development and improvement but also to build a sense of belonging and importance" (para. 8).

Instructors should be strongly encouraged if not required to engage in as many activities as possible. There are some institutions that use a merit pay system that rewards professional development and scholarly activities. Instructors may also be rewarded by being given an increased teaching load the next semester since they are more prepared to teach at-risk students.

Professional development can and should take on many forms within an institution. It should start with an orientation day for all developmental faculty prior to the start of the academic year and then include a training manual, a professional development library, and ongoing professional development days.

ORIENTATION Faculty orientation is essential for new faculty to receive basic information about the institution and for returning faculty to get critical information about new policies and procedures. According to Wallin (2004), one of the most important commitments that institutions can make to new adjunct faculty is a comprehensive orientation (p. 385).

The orientation should take place as much as 3 weeks prior to the start of the academic year. The coordinator of the developmental programs should organize and conduct it with segments given by academic deans, the discipline supervisors, and support staff. It is important to involve the administration of the institution, for it not only engages them in the developmental program but also shows the faculty that the administration cares about them and the program in general. At the orientation, the coordinator should distribute information about policies, procedures, employment practices, and college resources. The discipline supervisors should discuss course syllabi, grading policies, and instructional information about teaching methods and use of technology. Support staff should highlight procedures for duplicating materials, securing an e-mail address, and other housekeeping concerns. According to the NADE Adjunct Supervisors' Survey (2004), only 41% of 2-year colleges and 20% of 4-year colleges surveyed gave tours of their campuses to new adjunct faculty. New hires need to have guided tours of the campus not only to find their own way the first few weeks of the semester but also to direct new students.

Orientation serves as a time to welcome new adjunct instructors to the campus and provide a refresher for those who have taught before. Along with providing needed information for successful teaching and learning, the orientation is an opportunity "to communicate key cultural values and attitudes about faculty, students, and the college culture" (Gadberry & Burnstad, 2005, p. 88).

DEPARTMENTAL INSTRUCTORS' MANUAL. Many colleges and universities have developed instructors' manuals that include the policies and procedures of each individual institution. Though this is a good place to start, instructors need resources that provide good advice on such topics as characteristics of developmental students, working with adult learners, conducting a stimulating class session, and dealing with disruptive or absentee students. Such a resource manual should include:

> orientation information, the goals and objectives of developmental education, academic policies and procedures, sources of assistance for faculty, and sources of referral for students. It should also include a selection of articles relevant to teaching developmental students as well as a bibliography of useful references. (Boylan, 2002, p. 57)

An instructors' manual will allow instructors to develop their teaching ability and/or have their questions answered without always involving the full-time faculty. This manual can be general in nature with all departmental instructors receiving a copy or specific in nature focusing on one discipline. It can be set up as a work in progress with all instructors being encouraged to submit stellar lesson plans for inclusion. Not only does this help all departmental instructors, it also increases part-time instructors' sense of belonging.

DEPARTMENTAL PROFESSIONAL LIBRARY. Building a professional library that is housed within the department and accessible by all faculty is essential for instructors' professional development. Boylan (2005) recommends a professional development library for faculty, which "should include copies of professional journals in developmental education and learning assistance as well as a variety of books and reports on teaching developmental students" (p. 12). Whether instructors are searching for new ideas or are involved in a research project, having a collection of classic works in developmental education and teaching and learning is important. Though coordinators will have their own favorites to include in such a library, some classics with which to start are listed in Table 1.

ONGOING PROFESSIONAL DEVELOPMENT DAYS. Providing professional development opportunities for part-time employees has long been a frustration for developmental educators.

Sending them to conferences is often financially impossible, and organizing in-house professional development often can be time-consuming and expensive. However, professional development is essential for keeping the instructors informed of the newest trends in developmental education and in their particular fields of expertise.

In their study of part-time community college faculty in a midwestern state, Keim and Biletzky (1999) found that the part-time faculty tended to use instructional methods that were very traditional. Lecture was used by part-time instructors 83% of the time and class discussion 62% of the time. Active learning and technology-style teaching were rately or never used by 60 to 70% of the respondents. However, those who participated in professional development were "more likely to use small group discussions, demonstrations, and instructional methods to encourage critical thinking than those who had not" (p. 733).

Boylan (1999) believes that all developmental instructors need to meet regularly in order to "share the problems they encounter and discuss the solutions they have implemented" (p. 6). He recommends that training programs for adjunct faculty should involve readings and workshops (Boylan, 2005). In order to be successful, these workshops need to be activities that "both the college and the individual have deemed purposeful and valuable to improve teaching and learning" (Roueche & Roueche, 1993, p. 258). It is essential that the professional development workshops are well organized and scheduled when most of the part-time instructors can attend. Certainly, coordinators should make use of the college teaching and learning center, if available, as both a focal point for general professional development and a resource for specific instruction on developmental education issues.

Roueche and Roueche (1993) maintain that there are three types of professional development: (a) *instructional development*, which focuses on "teaching skills, such as planning, organizing, evaluating, motivating, using technology, and developing teaching strategies" (p. 117); (b) *personal development*, which helps faculty develop interpersonal skills, especially relating to students; and (c) *institutional or*

Table 1. Book Recommendations for Professional Developmental Education Library

General Information	Classroom Assessment Techniques: A Handbook for College Teachers (Angelo & Cross, 1993)	Learning Assistance and Developmental Education: A Guide for Effective Practice (Casazza & Silverman, 1996)	Improving Student Learning Skills (Maxwell, 1997)	No One to Waste: A Report to Public Decision-Makers and Community College Leaders (McCabe, 2000)
	What Works: Research-Based Best Practices in Developmental Education (Boylan, 2002)	Raising Academic Standards: A Guide to Learning Improvement (Keimeg, 1983)	Yes We Can!: A Community College Guide for Developing America's Underprepared (McCabe, 2003)	Between a Rock and a Hard Place: The At-Risk Student in the Open-Door College (Roueche & Roueche, 1993)
Writing	Engaging Ideas: A Professor's Guide to Integrating Writing, Critical Thinking, and Active Learning in the Classroom (Bean, 1996)	Literacy With an Attitude: Educating Working-Class Children in Their Own Self-Interest (Finn, 1999)	Errors and Expectations (Shaughnessy, 1979)	Time to Know Them: A Longitudinal Study of Writing and Learning at the College Level (Sternglass, 1997)
Reading and Study Skills	How to Read a Book (Adler & Van Doren, 1972)	How to Speak How to Listen (Adler, 1997)	Questioning the Author: An Approach for Enhancing Students' Engagement with Texts (Beck, McKeown, Hamilton, & Kucan, 1997)	College Rules! How to Study, Survive and Succeed in College (Nist & Holschuh, 2002)
Mathematics	Winning at Math: Your Guide to Learning Mathematics Through Successful Study Skills (Nolting, 2002)	Mastering Mathematics: How to Be a Great Math Student (Smith, 1999)	Overcoming Math Anxiety (Tobias, 1995)	

organizational development, which helps faculty and the institution learn to create "an effective teaching and learning climate" (p. 117) for their students. Coordinators and supervisors need to include all three types as they plan workshops for their instructors.

Professional development in all forms is essential for providing the best instruction for at-risk students. Coordinators of learning centers or developmental programs are charged with providing the best professional development they can offer. Boylan (1999) believes that "not anyone can teach developmental courses just because they have an advanced degree. It takes more than subject knowledge: it also takes knowledge of developmental students and how they learn" (p. 6).

6. Establish a Faculty-to-Faculty Mentoring Program for New Hires

Part-time faculty face a great challenge as they start out at a college or university. They are often coming from the ranks of high school teachers or are just on campus for a limited amount of time each day. As one part of faculty development, Boylan (1999) recommends faculty-to-faculty mentoring, which can help new hires find their identity in their new environment as well as enhance their teaching. This, in turn, benefits both the individual and the institution (p. 2).

A mentoring program should be available for all new instructors for at least their 1st semester and possibly the 1st year and should be completely voluntary on the part of both the mentor and the mentee. Wallin (2004) believes that "veteran full-time faculty who serve as mentors to adjunct faculty should be carefully selected as role models committed to teaching and to the college" (p. 386). In a program including only one or two full-time instructors, experienced part-time instructors can certainly be mentors. All mentors should be compensated for serving in this important role.

A successful mentoring program can aid both the 1st-year teacher and the mentor, giving each new ideas to try in the classroom. The new faculty member also gains knowledge of the institution, begins to understand at-risk adult learners, and hones his or her teaching techniques to address the institution's unique student population. Participating in a mentoring program will help new faculty "[select] from teaching styles and skills without spending valuable time finding out on their own what students and the teaching and learning culture are like" (St. Clair, 1994, p. 4).

7. Develop a Goal-Setting and Evaluation Plan

All part-time faculty members should have their own goal-setting and evaluation plan. Though professional development is essential for part-time instructors, without a good evaluation program, the instructors will lack direction in how to use the new knowledge. Researchers have for years called for a well-planned evaluation process for developmental educators (Boylan, 1999, 2002; Casazza & Silverman, 1996; Roueche & Roueche, 1993). Since part-time faculty members often teach the bulk of the developmental classes, it is of paramount importance for them to collaborate with administrators to develop an evaluative plan that consists of both goal setting and evaluation.

Goal setting at the beginning of each year is essential for all instructors. Roueche and Roueche (1993) believe that "excellent teachers have set goals for themselves, goals that they have achieved and can point to with pride" (p. 104). Goal setting is especially important for part-time instructors who often need direction in how their classroom performance will affect their students particularly and the program in general. Casazza and Silverman (1996) believe that supervisors need to clearly define expectations for performance and set standards for achievement (p. 75). This needs to be done with part-time faculty before the start of the academic year if possible and certainly in the first 2 weeks for any late hires. Supervisors need to take care to have instructors set their own goals with their guidance and not expect them to set more than one or two goals per academic year.

During the year, there are several activities that the supervisor can engage in to aid the instructors in attaining their goals. The supervisor needs to observe all new hires at least once and invite them to visit his or her classroom. Also, engaging in spontaneous discussions of teaching strategies and available materials and resources throughout the year will help the part-time instructors reach their goals (Boylan, 1999). In addition, informal reviews throughout the year can keep the instructor on track. If any instructors are having problems in the classroom, supervisors need to offer constructive feedback to them so that they can adjust their instructional techniques.

At least once a year, preferably near the end of the spring term, the supervisor should begin the evaluation process. According to Casazza and Silverman (1996), there are several characteristics of effective evaluation. First of all, it is essential to involve the staff member in the process by asking him or her to produce a self-evaluation to be shared with the supervisor. Then, the supervisor should give the instructor a written evaluation preceding the review. This will allow the instructor to reflect on the comments before the actual meeting. During the review, both the supervisor and the instructor should offer feedback, discussing impressions and reactions and the instructor's strengths and weaknesses. Then, the instructor should be encouraged to offer comments about the supervisor's management style and administrative effectiveness (p. 80). Finally, the instructor should be asked to set some goals for the next year. This will allow the instructor to act on these goals as he or she writes syllabi and course materials as well as time for support staff to write up the goals and put them in the instructor's file. At the beginning of the academic year, the supervisor should remind the instructor of these goals to complete the evaluative cycle.

Conclusions

To adequately teach the growing number of underprepared students entering our college and university campuses, it is critical that all stakeholders involved—faculty, staff, and administration—value part-time faculty, acknowledge their contributions to the institution, and provide the resources necessary to support them. Part-time faculty in developmental education should be hired, trained, and compensated fairly. They should be provided professional development opportunities and allowed to participate in institutional governance and decision-making processes. Improving the services and opportunities that developmental educators provide to their part-time faculty can only enhance the quality that the instructors will bring to their classrooms.

References

American Historical Association. (2000, November). *Summary of data from surveys by the coalition on the academic workforce*. Retrieved October 21, 2005, from http://www.historians.org/caw/cawreport.htm

Angelo, T. A., & Cross, K. P. (1991). *Classroom assessment techniques: A handbook for college teachers*. San Francisco, CA: Jossey-Bass.

Boylan, H. R. (1999). Harvard Symposium 2000: Developmental education: Demographics, outcomes, and activities. *Journal of Developmental Education, 23*(2), 2–6.

Boylan, H. R. (2002), *What works: Research-based best practices in developmental education*. Boone, NC: Continuous Quality Improvement Network with the National Center for Developmental Education.

Boylan, H. R. (2005). *Consulting report on the Title III and Smart Start Program at Kodiak College* (Report). Kodiak, AK: Title III Project, Kodiak College.

Boylan, H., Bonham, B., & Bliss, L. (1994, March). *National study of developmental education: Characteristics of faculty and staff*. Paper presented at the National Association for Developmental Education Conference, Washington, DC.

Boylan, H. R., Bonham, B. S., Jackson, J., & Saxon, D. P. (1994). Staffing patterns in developmental education programs: Full-time/part-time, credentials, and program placement. *Research in Developmental Education, 11*(5), 1–4.

Boylan, H., & Saxon, D. P. (2005, July). *Affirmation and discovery: Learning from successful community college developmental programs in Texas* (Research funded by Texas Association of Community Colleges; TACC). Paper presented at the Texas Association of Community Colleges Conference, Midland, TX.

Carnevale, D. (2004, May 21). NYU adjuncts would get better pay and benefits under proposed contract. *Chronicle of Higher Education*, p. A14. Retrieved October 7, 2005, from Academic Search Elite database.

Casazza, M., & Silverman, S. (1996). *Learning assistance and developmental education*. San Francisco, CA: Jossey-Bass.

Clark-Thayer, S. (Ed.). (1995). *NADE self-evaluation guides*. Clearwater, FL: H & H Publishing.

Clery, S. (1998, September). Faculty in academe. *Update, 4*(4), 1–6.

Contract reached at Emerson College. (2004, May/June). *Academe, 90*(3), 27. Retrieved October 7, 2005, from Academic Search Elite database.

Cox, A. M., & Leatherman, C. (2000, December 1). Study shows colleges' dependence on their part-time instructors. *Chronicle of Higher Education*, p. A12. Retrieved October 21, 2005, from Academic Search Elite database.

Cross, K. P. (1976). *Accent on learning*. San Francisco, CA: Jossey-Bass.

Cross, K. P. (1992). *Adults as learners*. San Francisco, CA: Jossey-Bass.

Eney, P., Davidson, E., Dorlac, A., & Whittington, R. (2005, March). *Building a program for adjuncts: Help them soar!* Paper presented at the National Association for Developmental Education Conference, Albuquerque, NM.

Freeland, R. S. (1998). *Adjunct faculty in the community college*. (ERIC Document Reproduction Service No. ED 424 899)

Gadberry, J. L., & Burnstad, H. (2005). One faculty: Hiring practices and orientation. In D. L. Wallin (Ed.), *Adjunct faculty in community colleges: An academic administrator's guide to recruiting, supporting, and retaining great teachers* (pp. 1,6). Bolton, MA: Anker Publishing Co., Inc.

Galbraith, M. W., & Shedd, P. E. (1990, Fall). Building skills and proficiencies of the community college instructor of adult learners. *Community College Review, 18*(2), 6–14. Retrieved May 18, 2005, from Academic Search Elite database.

Grieve, D. (1995). *A handbook for adjunct/part-time faculty and teachers of adults* (3rd ed.). Elyria, OH: Info-Tec.

Keim, M. C., & Biletzky, P. E. (1999). Teaching methods used by part-time community college faculty. *Community College Journal of Research and Practice, 23*, 727–737.

Kozeracki, C. A. (Spring, 2005). Preparing faculty to meet the needs of developmental students. *New directions for community colleges, Vol. 129: Responding to the challenges of developmental education*. San Francisco: Jossey-Bass.

Longmate, J., & Cosco, F. (2002, May 3). Part-time instructors deserve equal pay for equal work. *Chronicle of Higher Education*, p. B14.

Maxwell, M. (1997). *Improving student learning skills*. San Francisco, CA: Jossey-Bass.

McCabe, R. (2000). *No one to waste: A report to public decision makers and community college leaders*. Washington, DC: Community College Press.

McCabe, R. (2003). *Yes, we can! A community college guide for developing America's underprepared*. Phoenix, AZ: League for Innovation in the Community College and American Colleges.

Malnarich, G., Dusenberry, P., Sloan, B., Swinton, J. & van Slack, P. (2003). *The pedagogy of possibilities: Developmental education, college-level studies, and learning communities* (National Learning Communities Project Monograph Series). Olympia, WA: The Evergreen State College, Washington Center for Improving the Quality of Undergraduate Education, in cooperation with the American Association for Higher Education.

NADE Adjunct Faculty Committee. (2004). *Adjunct supervisors' survey*. Unpublished manuscript.

National Center for Education Statistics. (2004). *Digest of education statistics. Chapter 3. Postsecondary education*. Washington, DC: U.S. Department of Education. Retrieved December 15, 2005, from http://nces.ed.gov/programs /digest/

Nelson, C. (Ed.). (1997). *Will teach for food—Academic labour in crisis*. Minneapolis: University of Minnesota Press.

Rifkin, T. (1998, April). *Differences between the professional attitudes of full- and part-time faculty*. Paper presented at the American Association of Community Colleges Convention, Miami, FL. (ERIC Document Reproduction Service No. ED 417 783)

Roueche, J., & Roueche, S. (1993). *Between a rock and a hard place: The at-risk student in the open door college*. Washington, DC: Community College Press.

Shults, C. (2000). *Remedial education: Practices and policies in community colleges* (Research Brief). Washington, DC: Community College Press.

Skinner, D. (2005, June 8). Ever vulnerable adjuncts. *Inside Higher Ed. Views*. Retrieved June 8, 2005, from http://insidehighered.com/views/2005/06/07 /skinner

Spann, M. G. (2000). *Remediation: A must for the 21st century learning society* (Policy Paper), Denver, CO: Education Commission of the States. (ERIC Document Reproduction Service No. ED 439 771)

Spinetta, K. I. (1990). Part-time instructors in the California community colleges: A need to revise current policies. *Community College Review, 18*(1), 43–49. Retrieved May 18, 2005, from Academic Search Elite database.

St. Clair, K. L. (1994, Winter). Faculty-to-faculty mentoring in the community college: An instructional component of faculty development. *Community College Review, 22*(3), 23–35. Retrieved May 23, 2005, from Academic Search Elite database.

Wallin, D. L. (2004). Valuing professional colleagues: Adjunct faculty in community and technical colleges. *Community College Journal of Research and Practice, 28*, 373–391.

Wallin, D. L. (Ed.). (2005). *Adjunct faculty in community colleges: An academic administrator's guide to recruiting, supporting, and retaining great teachers*. Bolton, MA: Anker Publishing Co., Inc.

Professional Resources

Whether you are a seasoned member of the profession or a neophyte teaching a course or workshop for the first time, the field of postsecondary reading and learning has a rich source of professional journals that should be read regularly in undertaking a personal professional development plan. Furthermore, a wealth of professional organizations offer myriad services, supports, and opportunities for camaraderie, day-to-day practice, scholarship, and personal professional development.

What follows in alphabetical order is a description of the journals that cover scholarship and practice in college and adult reading as well as other educational levels, followed by a listing of journals focused on developmental education and learning assistance that regularly cover college reading scholarship and instructional practice. In addition, there are listings and descriptions of the professional organizations that support the work of individuals interested in college reading and learning instruction and scholarship.

Journals

The journals of interest to the postsecondary reading and learning strategies specialist can be classified into two categories. First there are those generalist journals that focus on the field of literacy in a broadly defined manner. Although articles on postsecondary literacy do appear in these journals, readers are as likely to find articles pertaining to research or practice on a broad range of populations across the life span. These are the journals that are most likely to be the venues for cutting-edge theory and research employing a multitude of methods. Furthermore, given that these journals often have "impact" ratings, it is likely that researchers, even those working with postsecondary populations, will strive to publish their research in such journals. Still, we point out that due to the "big tent" nature of these journals keeping current with all of them would be difficult. Reading these journals is akin to going to a flea market; there is much to find, but one will have to dig deep to find articles explicitly about postsecondary reading and learning and dig even deeper to find theories and research that can be translated from another area of research or practice to our field. It should be noted that these journals regularly interchange "college students" with "adult readers."

The second category of journal focuses directly on the various fields comprising developmental education and learning assistance, and these are published by professional organizations. Hence, the articles on research and practice disseminated in these journals have direct and immediate implications for postsecondary reading and learning programs, classes, workshops, or tutorial applications. Professionals in the field generally author the articles in these journals for an audience comprised of fellow professionals. It is through the field-oriented journals that one learns of the best or evolving practices and the most current research from across North America. The foundations of these articles may come from the more generalist literacy or kindred educational psychology journals, or they may arise directly from the field of postsecondary literacy itself.

Generalist Journals

The *Journal of Adolescent & Adult Literacy* (*JAAL*) is the only literacy journal published exclusively for teachers of older learners. *JAAL* serves a broad audience of reading professionals interested in improving literacy instruction for adolescents and adults, current theory, research, and practice. Every issue includes practical ideas for instruction; reviews of student and teacher resources, including young adult literature; tips on how to integrate technology, media, and popular culture in the classroom; and reflections on current literacy trends, issues, and research. The International Reading Association issues *JAAL* eight times a year.

Long the flagship of the many journals for the reading profession, *Reading Research Quarterly* (*RRQ*) is essential reading for those committed to scholarship on literacy among learners of all ages. As the leading research journal in the field, each issue of *RRQ* includes multidisciplinary research employing various modes of investigation and conveying diverse viewpoints on literacy practices, teaching, and learning. There are also reports on important research investigations. The journal is peer-reviewed and distributed internationally. The International Reading Association releases *RRQ* four times a year.

The *Journal of Literacy Research* (*JLR*) is an interdisciplinary peer-reviewed journal that publishes research related to literacy, language, and literacy and language education from preschool through adulthood. *JLR* publishes research and scholarly papers, including original research, critical reviews of research, conceptual analyses, and theoretical essays. The articles represent diverse research paradigms and theoretical orientations. *JLR* is released internationally on a quarterly basis by the Literacy Research Association (formerly the National Reading Conference).

Literacy Research and Instruction (formerly *Reading Research and Instruction*) publishes peer-reviewed articles dealing with research and instruction in reading education and allied literacy fields. The journal is especially focused on instructional practices and applied or basic research of special interest to reading and literacy educators. *LRI* is released internationally by the Association of Literacy Educators and Researchers (formerly the College Reading Association) on a quarterly basis.

Reading Psychology is a reference journal publishing original manuscripts in the fields of literacy, reading, and related psychology disciplines. Articles appear in the form of completed research; practitioner-based "experiential" methods or philosophical statements; teacher and counselor preparation services for guiding all levels of reading skill development, attitudes, and interests; programs or materials; and literary or humorous contributions. The readership comprises reading researchers, psychologists, cognitive scholars, special educators, and reading educators. The journal is published six times per year.

Scientific Studies of Reading (SSR) publishes original empirical investigations dealing with all aspects of reading and its related areas, and, occasionally, scholarly reviews of the literature; papers focused on theory development; and discussions of social policy issues. Papers range from very basic studies to those whose main thrust is educational practice. The peer-reviewed journal also includes work on "all aspects of reading and its related areas," which includes investigations of eye movements, comparisons of orthographies, studies of response to literature, and more. *SSR* is issued by the Society for the Scientific Study of Reading.

College Reading and Learning Assistance Journals

The *Journal of College Literacy and Learning (JCLL)* publishes material related to advancing the scholarship on reading, writing, and academic success at the postsecondary level. It provides a forum for the exchange of information regarding research, theory, and best practice. The College Literacy and Learning Special Interest Group of the International Reading Association publishes *JCLL*, which is available online.

The *Journal of College Reading and Learning (JCRL)* is a national, peer-reviewed forum for theory, research, and policy related to reading improvement and learning assistance at two- and four-year colleges. It publishes reports of original research and articles linking theory, research, or policy to practice. *JCRL* is published in the fall and spring of each year. It is the official journal of the College Reading and Learning Association.

The *Journal of Developmental Education (JDE)* is published as a forum for educators concerned with practice, theory, research, and news in the postsecondary developmental and remedial community. Its content focuses on basic skills education and includes topics such as developmental writing, developmental mathematics, reading, tutoring, assessment and placement, and program evaluation. Emphasis is placed on manuscripts that relate education theory to practical teaching and learning, expand current knowledge, or clearly demonstrate impact on the field. The *JDE* is published three times each academic year, in the fall, winter, and spring, by the National Center for Developmental Education. *JDE* is the official publication of the National Association for Developmental Education.

The *Learning Assistance Review (LAR)* seeks to foster communication among learning center professionals. Its audience includes learning center administrators, teaching staff, and tutors, as well as other faculty members and administrators who are interested in improving the learning skills of postsecondary students. The *LAR* publishes scholarly articles and reviews that address issues of interest to a broad range of academic professionals with primary consideration on program design and evaluation, classroom-based research, the application of theory and research to practice, innovative teaching strategies, student assessment, and other topics that bridge gaps within our diverse profession. *LAR,* an official publication of the National College Learning Center Association, is published twice a year, in the spring and fall.

The *NADE Digest* is another official publication of the National Association for Developmental Education. The *NADE Digest* publishes articles that emphasize innovative approaches, best practices, effects of meaningful research on teaching and learning, and techniques to enhance student performance. It is a valued source of information for developmental education professionals including developmental educators, learning assistance personnel, academic counselors, and tutors who are interested in the discussion of practical issues in postsecondary developmental education.

Research and Teaching in Developmental Education (*RTDE*) focuses on a variety of topics related to developmental education across the disciplines. Of particular interest are measurement and evaluation procedures; program design and implementation; research and pedagogy as they inform, or are informed by, current theory; and interdisciplinary approaches to major concerns in developmental education. The journal has a biannual publication schedule. *RTDE* is the journal of the New York State College Learning Skills Association.

Research in Developmental Education (*RiDE*) is a research-based, single-article publication designed to review and analyze current developmental education practices or to report on up-to-date research literature and studies. *RiDE* provides invaluable research and resource information for students, instructors, researchers, and administrators. It is published by the National Center for Developmental Education at Appalachian State University.

Organizations

Professionals interested in the field of college reading and learning instruction have a wealth of opportunities to participate in organizations focused on postsecondary reading instruction. In some cases the mission and the goals of an association will explicitly pertain to postsecondary reading and learning, at least to some degree. In other cases organizations will have a separate special interest group, network, or division for college reading instruction and scholarship. In still other cases the interest is demonstrated in a more implicit manner. We list, in alphabetical order, as many organizations as makes sense. From our perspective, one must become active in a professional organization in order to have a successful career in the developmental education field.

The **Association of Literacy Educators and Researchers** (formerly the College Reading Association) has the following goals: promote standards and competency within the profession, stimulate the self-development and professional growth of teachers and reading specialists at all educational levels, encourage the continuing improvement of college and university curricula and preparation programs for teachers and reading specialists, and foster the continuing improvement of administrative, clinical, diagnostic, and instructional practices related to the learning process. Although ALER is composed of four divisions, the College Reading Division focuses on literacy practices and methods for teaching postsecondary students at all achievement levels, including developmental-level reading, writing, study skills, and English Language Learners (ELL) instruction through critical twenty-first-century literacy education and research. ALER publishes both *Literacy Research and Instruction* and *ALER Yearbook*. For additional information visit http://aleronline.org.

The mission of the **Association for the Tutoring Profession** (ATP) is to foster the advancement of tutoring to enhance student academic success. Its goals are to provide a network through which current trends in practice can be identified and innovations disseminated; to enhance the status of professionals, paraprofessionals, and students working in the field; to stimulate research in the field by offering a forum through which information can be shared; and to work collaboratively with other national, regional, and state organizations and persons having purposes supportive of, or in harmony with, the concerns of the ATP. Visit their Web site for more information at http://www.myatp.org.

The **College Literacy and Learning Special Interest Group (CLL/SIG)** exchanges information relating to reading and study skills, proposes adoption of teacher qualifications, acts as a resource center, and sponsors national conferences. It also publishes, in both print and online versions, the *Journal of College Literacy and Learning*. Membership is open to all members of the International Reading Association. For more information, go to http://j-cll.com/ and click on the CLL/SIG link.

The **College Reading and Learning Association (CRLA)** provides college reading and learning professionals with an open forum to discover and exchange the leading tools and techniques that enhance student academic success. It provides professional development for college professionals active in reading, learning assistance, writing, ESOL, learning strategies, mathematics, college success programs, mentoring, and tutoring programs. This group sponsors both the International Tutor Program Certification and the International Mentor Program Certification. CRLA also publishes the *Journal of College Reading and Learning*. There is an active special interest group for those interested in college reading. Members may also participate in regional or state groups. A highly respected national conference is offered every year. For more information, visit their Web site at http://crla.net.

The **Council of Learning Assistance and Developmental Education Associations (CLADEA)** provides leadership and a unified voice to advance the profession of postsecondary learning assistance and developmental education. Through its member council it fosters mutual support among national and international organizations dedicated to postsecondary learning assistance or developmental education. Member organizations include the College Reading and Learning Association, the Association for the Tutoring Profession, the National Association for Developmental Education, the National College Learning Center Association, and the National Center for Developmental Education. Visit http://cladea.net for more information.

The **National Association for Developmental Education (NADE)** seeks to improve the theory and practice of developmental education, the professional capabilities of developmental educators, and the design of programs to prepare developmental educators at all levels of the educational spectrum. In addition, NADE focuses on the academic success of students by providing professional development, supporting student learning, disseminating exemplary models of practice, and coordinating efforts with other organizations involved in facilitating communication among developmental education professionals. The organization publishes the *NADE Digest*, provides program certification, hosts an annual conference, and sponsors regional/state chapters and special interest groups, including one for reading. Go to http://nade.net to learn more.

The **National Center for Developmental Education (NCDE)**, housed at Appalachian State University, provides instruction, training programs, research, and other services consistent with the purpose of developmental education. These services are provided to a national audience of professionals dedicated to serving underprepared and disadvantaged college students. The NCDE sponsors the summer Kellogg Institute for the Training and Certification of Developmental Educators and publishes both the *Journal of Developmental Education* and *Research in Developmental Education*. For more information, visit http://ncde.appstate.edu.

The **National College Learning Center Association's (NCLCA)** mission is to support learning center professionals as they develop and to maintain learning centers, programs, and services that enhance student learning at the postsecondary level. The organization sponsors both an annual conference and the NCLCA Institute. It also offers the Learning Center Leadership Certification and publishes the *Learning Assistance Review*. For more information, go to http://nclca.org.

The **National Tutoring Association (NTA)** was formed as an organization for tutoring professionals. In recent years, its purpose has expanded to promote education, specialization, and scientific research. The NTA is dedicated exclusively to tutoring, and represents the interests of thousands of tutors practicing in all phases of tutoring, program administration, and supplemental student services in the United States and thirteen other countries. Members represent colleges, universities, high schools, middle schools, elementary schools, school districts, literacy programs, community programs, grant-supported programs, and No Child Left Behind/Supplemental Educational Services providers. The NTA Code of Ethics provides members with opportunities to achieve and maintain high professional standards for tutors and administrators of tutoring programs and services. For additional information, visit their Web site at http://www.ntatutor.com.

The **Studying and Self-Regulated Learning (SSRL)** Special Interest Group (SIG), which is part of the American Educational Research Association (AERA), is dedicated to promoting the development of theory and research in academic studying and self-regulated learning across the life span. The SIG brings together researchers and practitioners to share expertise in all aspects of self-regulated learning, including motivation, metacognition, learning and studying strategies, and the ways in which learners manage their emotions and environments.

Training Programs

Training programs specific to the instruction and administration of developmental reading courses and programs continue to emerge across the country. What follows are listings of graduate-level certificate or degree programs that focus exclusively on developmental reading. These listings are current as of January 1, 2013.

Institution:	California State University, Fullerton
Department Name and Address:	University Extended Education in cooperation with the Reading Department PO Box 6868 Fullerton, CA 92834–6868
Program Name:	Postsecondary Reading and Learning Certificate
Program Administrator and Contact Information:	JoAnne Greenbaum 657.278.5930 jgreenbaum@fullerton.edu
Web site:	http://extension.fullerton.edu/Professional development/PRL

Program Description:

This twelve-unit online certificate provides a cutting-edge curriculum that meets the emerging needs for community college faculty in the area of postsecondary reading. The certificate satisfies the California mandate under AB 1725 requiring certification in adult reading instruction for community college teachers of English.

Program Delivery Mode:	Online
Number of Credit Hours:	12 semester hours
Number of Enrolled Students:	45

Institution:	University of Cincinnati
Department Name and Address:	Graduate Program in Literacy 2610 McMicken Circle 615-L Teachers College Cincinnati, OH 45221–0022
Program Name:	Graduate Certificate in Postsecondary Literacy Instruction
Program Administrator and Contact Information:	Connie Kendall Theado 513.556.1427 connie.kendall@uc.edu
Web site:	http://cech.uc.edu/programs.html?cid=18GC-PLI

Program Description:

This is a stand-alone certificate that can be earned without being accepted into a graduate degree program, and all courses are taught online. The purpose of the Certificate in Postsecondary Literacy Instruction is to prepare instructors with theoretically and pedagogically sound expertise in literacy instruction at the postsecondary level, including teaching developmental reading and basic writing in the community college, four-year college, and adult literacy program contexts. With foci that incorporate both theory and practice, coursework in the Certificate in Postsecondary Literacy Instruction addresses educational issues that arise in most community colleges and adult literacy programs.

Program Delivery Mode:	Online
Number of Credit Hours:	18 semester hours
Number of Enrolled Students:	55

Institution:	Northern Illinois University
Department Name and Address:	Department of Literacy Education 147 Gabel Hall DeKalb, IL 60115

Program Name:	Certificate of Graduate Study in Postsecondary Developmental Literacy and Language Instruction
Program Administrator and Contact Information:	Sonya L. Armstrong 815.753.8486 sarmstrong@niu.edu
Web site:	http://www.cedu.niu.edu/ltcy/programs/certification.shtml

Program Description:

The Certificate of Graduate Study in Postsecondary Developmental Literacy and Language Instruction is a 15-credit-hour program of study intended to prepare current and future college educators to serve a diverse group of students in a variety of postsecondary literacy contexts, including learning assistance programs and developmental/transitional programs in community colleges and universities. The certificate allows students to demonstrate mastery in five areas related to postsecondary literacy instruction: theory, practice, assessment, research, and professional development.

Program Delivery Mode:	Blended (part online and part face-to-face)
Number of Credit Hours:	15 semester hours
Number of Enrolled Students:	35

Institution:	Texas Tech University
Department Name and Address:	Department of Curriculum and Instruction 104 Education Building Box 41071 Lubbock, TX 79409–1071
Program Name:	Graduate Certificate in Developmental Literacy
Program Administrator and Contact Information:	Mellinee Lesley 806.742.1997, Ext. 240 mellinee.lesley@ttu.edu
Web site:	http://www.depts.ttu.edu/gradschool/programs/gradcert.php

Program Description:

The Developmental Literacy Certificate is designed for individuals who want to teach high school "remedial" reading, adult literacy, adult basic education, GED preparation, and developmental reading courses at a community college.

Program Delivery Mode:	Online
Number of Credit Hours:	15 semester hours
Number of Enrolled Students:	5

Institution:	Texas State University
Department Name and Address:	Department of Curriculum and Instruction ASBN 410 601 University Dr. San Marcos, TX 78666
Program Name:	Graduate Program in Developmental Education/Specialization in Developmental Literacy (PhD, Ed.D., and M.S.Ed.)

Program Administrator and Contact Information:	Eric Paulson (Doctoral Program) 512.245.2048 eric.paulson@txstate.edu
	Jodi Patrick Holschuh (Master's Program) 512.245.7906 jh215@txstate.edu
Web site:	http://www.education.txstate.edu/ci/dev-ed/

Program Description:

The graduate program in developmental education provides its student-scholars the tools with which they can critically examine the current state of developmental education, define its essential role in postsecondary education, engage in research-based reconceptualizations of the field, and create new theory and innovative practices. The program's vision transcends narrow, static views of teaching and learning as well as deficit-oriented views of students that have traditionally dominated the field. The program values social, cultural, and critical perspectives on learning and learners. Through providing its graduate students with rigorous research, scholarly, and professional experiences in an apprenticeship model, the program aims to effect change in multiple areas of developmental education.

Program Delivery Mode:	Face-to-Face
Number of Credit Hours:	66 semester hours (doctorate)
Number of Enrolled Students:	12 per annual cohort (doctorate)

Institution:	San Francisco State University
Department Name and Address:	Department of English College of Liberal and Creative Arts HUM 289 1600 Holloway Avenue San Francisco, CA 94132
Program Name:	Certificate Program Courses in Teaching of Post-Secondary Reading
Program Administrator and Contact Information:	Mark Roberge 415.338.7457 roberge@sfsu.edu
Web site:	http://english.sfsu.edu/content/certificate-teaching-post-secondary-reading

Program Description:

The Certificate in Teaching Post-Secondary Reading is designed to assist prospective and already practicing postsecondary teachers in meeting specific individual professional needs in the areas of basic literacy and reading instruction. The certificate can help prepare students for teaching position in the community colleges and community agencies where specialized background and techniques in reading instruction are desirable.

Program Delivery Mode:	Face-to-Face
Number of Credit Hours:	12 semester hours
Number of Enrolled Students:	60

About the Contributors

Patricia A. Alexander is the Jean Mullan Professor of Literacy and Distinguished Scholar-Teacher in the Department of Human Development, Learning, and Quantitative Methodology at the University of Maryland. She has served as president of Division 15 (Educational Psychology) of the American Psychological Association, vice president of Division C (Learning and Instruction) of the American Educational Research Association, and past president of the Southwest Educational Research Association. A former middle school teacher, Dr. Alexander received her reading specialist degree from James Madison University (1979) and her Ph.D. in reading from the University of Maryland (1981). Since receiving her Ph.D., Dr. Alexander has published over 270 articles, books, or chapters in the area of learning and instruction. She has also presented over 400 papers or invited addresses at national and international conferences. She currently serves as the senior editor of *Contemporary Educational Psychology,* was past editor of *Instructional Science* and associate editor of *American Educational Research Journal-Teaching, Learning, and Human Development,* and presently serves on more than ten editorial boards including those for *Learning and Instruction, Educational Psychologist*, and the *Journal of Educational Psychology*. Dr. Alexander is a Fellow of the American Psychological Association and the American Educational Research Association, and was a Spencer Fellow of the National Academy of Education. She was recently named the second most productive scholar in Educational Psychology. Her honors include the Oscar S. Causey Award for outstanding contributions to literacy research from the National Reading Conference (2001), the E. L. Thorndike Award for Career Achievement in Educational Psychology from APA Division 15 and the Sylvia Scribner Award from AREA Division C.

Patricia L. Anders is a distinguished professor of the Language, Reading and Culture program in the Teaching, Learning and Sociocultural Department in the College of Education at the University of Arizona. Dr. Anders is currently leading projects in community literacy and adolescent literacy. She is the coauthor of *Literacy Instruction in the Content Area* and coeditor of *Literacy Development of Students in Urban Schools: Research and Policy*. Her research has been published in the *American Education Research Association Journal*, the *Reading Research Quarterly*, and the *Journal of Adolescent and Adult Literacy* among others. She is the past president of the Literacy Research Association, past president of the National Conference on Research in Language and Literacy, and a former board member of the International Reading Association. She is current coeditor of the *Journal of Literacy Research.*

Elaine DeLott Baker is the acceleration specialist for the Colorado Energy and Training Consortia, a USDOL-funded grant that includes a redesign of developmental education, with a focus on acceleration and contextualization. Ms. Baker's professional career spans curriculum development, teaching at the community college and graduate levels, program design and implementation, and research in adult education, K–12, community colleges, and workforce education and training. She has authored/coauthored numerous research reports, articles, and book chapters on educational topics, including acceleration, contextualization, career pathways, and educational innovation. Her work has been published by the *TESOL Quarterly*, the Community College Research Center, the *Language Teacher*, University of Colorado at Denver (UCD) Publications, Heinemann Press, Johns Hopkins Press, University of Georgia Press, and the University of Illinois Press. In addition to her work with the Colorado Community College system, Ms. Baker consults with several national foundations and nonprofits, including the Bill and Melinda Gates Foundation, the William and Flora Hewlitt Foundation, and the Aspen Institute. Ms. Baker is an alumna of Radcliffe College, University of Massachusetts at Amherst, and the University of Colorado at Denver.

Joy Banks is an associate professor and director of the doctoral program at Bowie State University. Joy's research explores the lived experiences of individuals whose identities reflect those of multiple marginalized groups, such as African American college students and students with disabilities. Her articles appear in *Journal of Transformative Education, Journal of College Reading and Learning, Multiple Voices for Ethnically Diverse Exceptional Learner, Multicultural Perspectives,* and *Journal of Negro Education.*

Social justice, critical race theory and culturally responsive pedagogy undergird the theoretical framework of her qualitative and quantitative writings. Prior to entering higher education, Dr. Banks taught middle school and high school students identified with mild and moderate special needs in Clark County Public School District, Las Vegas, Nevada, and Fairfax County Public Schools, Virginia.

Laura Bauer has been teaching developmental reading and writing as an adjunct at Truman College. Her scholarly interests remain rooted in developmental studies and developing appropriate, meaningful curriculum. She coauthored *Access, Opportunity, and Success: Keeping the Promise of Higher Education (Praeger, 2006)*, with Martha Casazza.

Edward H. Behrman is currently a contributing faculty member at Walden University. He previously held positions at the University of Pennsylvania, the University of Delaware, Rowan University, and National University. His scholarly interests are placement testing, critical literacy, and development of academic literacy at secondary and postsecondary levels. Publications include articles in the *Journal of Adolescent and Adult Literacy*, the *Journal of Developmental Education*, and *Reading Research and Instruction*. He has served on the editorial review boards for *Issues in Teacher Education*, the *Journal of Adolescent and Adult Literacy*, and the *Journal of Literacy Research*. He also served on the Critical Perspectives in Literacy Committee for the International Reading Association and was chair of the Research Committee for the California Council on Teacher Education.

William G. Brozo is a professor of literacy in the Graduate School of Education at George Mason University in Fairfax, Virginia. He earned his bachelor's degree from the University of North Carolina and his master's and doctorate from the University of South Carolina. He has taught reading and language arts in the Carolinas. He is the author of numerous articles and books on literacy development for children and young adults, including *To Be a Boy, To Be a Reader*. His newest book is *RTI and the Adolescent Reader: Responsive Literacy Instruction in Secondary Schools* (Teachers College Press/IRA). He is currently completing *Graphic Novels in the Disciplines* (Teachers College Press). Dr. Brozo's research focuses on adolescent literacy, content area/disciplinary literacy, and the literate lives of boys.

Greta Buck-Rodriguez earned a BS in education from Lesley University. She then taught ESL, ESP, and adult biliteracy for several years before developing an interest in adult basic literacy. She received an MA in Education from the Department of Language, Reading, and Culture at the University of Arizona, as well as certification in developmental education from the Kellogg Institute. Since 2003, Greta has been a full-time faculty member at Pima Community College in Tucson, Arizona, where she has developed hybrid and fully online reading courses. In addition, she and Marty Frailey recently designed a new course called Critical Reading for the Health Professions.

Martha E. Casazza is a partner in the consulting firm of TRPP Associates. Prior to that, she was the vice president of academic affairs at the Adler School of Professional Psychology and the dean of the College of Arts and Sciences at National-Louis University. She has served as president of the National College Learning Center Association, president of the National Association for Developmental Education, and coeditor of the *Learning Assistance Review*. She was president of the Illinois Network of Women in Higher Education, an affiliate of ACE. She currently serves on the editorial boards of the *Journal of Developmental Education* and the *Journal of College Reading and Learning*. Dr. Casazza is on the board for Heartland Alliance for Human Rights, and chairs the board for the Instituto Justice and Leadership Academy, an alternative charter high school. Dr. Casazza was a Fulbright Senior Scholar to South Africa in 2000. She received the Hunter R. Boylan Outstanding Research/Publication Award in 2004, is a Founding Fellow of CLADEA, and was named a Certification Trailblazer by the National Association for Developmental Education in 2010. Dr. Casazza has coauthored two books with Dr. Sharon Silverman: *Learning Assistance and Developmental Education: A Guide for Effective Practice* (1996, Jossey-Bass), and *Learning and Development* (2000, Jossey-Bass). She also coauthored *Access, Opportunity and Success: Keeping the Promise of Higher Education* (2006, Praeger) with Laura Bauer. She is currently working on *Dreaming Forward*, an oral history of a Latino community in Chicago.

Evelyn Davidson retired from Kodiak College, UAA, in January 2013; however, she remains a member of the College Reading and Learning Association (CRLA) and National Association for Developmental Educators (NADE). She served for ten years as coordinator of developmental education and the Learning Center at Kodiak College; for three years as co-chair of the University of Alaska Student Success committee; and as a copre-senter at CRLA and NADE annual conferences since 2002. She was a teacher of basic writing and Introduction to College Writing for twelve years. She has received a "Chancel-lor's Award for Excellence for Outstanding Contributions to Students," an "Outstanding Article in Journal for Developmental Education," and a "Staff Make Students Count" award. She is also a graduate of the Kellogg Institute and Advanced Kellogg at Appala-chian State University, Boone, North Carolina.

Lisa Schade Eckert is assistant professor of English education at Northern Michi-gan University, where she teaches English methods and literature courses. Her research interests include exploring intersections between literary theory and literacy pedagogy, English education and rural schooling, and the role of graduate education in rural teacher professional and personal identity development. Her publications include a book, *How Does It Mean? Engaging Reluctant Readers through Literary Theory* (Heinemann, 2006), as well as articles in *English Education, Reading Research Quarterly*, and the *English Journal*. Currently, she is working on a book project highlighting rural English teacher narratives. She regularly presents her work at national and international conferences, in-cluding those conducted by the National Council of Teachers of English and the Interna-tional Federation of Teachers of English.

Patricia R. Eney is an English instructor at College of Lake County in Grayslake, Il-linois. Besides this current article, she is the author of "Pointing Toward Self-Efficacy: Work-ing with a Disabled Writer" found in B. M. Hodge and J. Preston-Sabin's *Accommodations—or Just Good Teaching?* She also coauthored "Instructor Manuals That Reach Beyond the Ba-sics," which can be found in the *NADE Digest*. One of her current scholarly interests is inte-grating reading and writing. Patti is also interested in adjunct issues and conducts workshops for adjunct instructors on developmental education at her institution. She has been chair of NADE's Adjunct Faculty Committee for about eleven years.

Ellen Urquhart Engstrom is the director of Teacher Training at Groves Academy. She is certified to offer training in the WRS Levels I and II, Fundations®, and Just Words®. Ellen was the director of the Lower/Middle School at Groves before leaving in 1999 to join the faculty of Landmark College, a school specifically for students with learning disabili-ties and attention disorders. She was an associate professor at the college and a lead edu-cation specialist in the Landmark Institute for Research and Training. Ellen has given many workshops and courses for educators on the Wilson Reading System®, reading com-prehension, writing, study skills, assistive technology, universal design for learning, and executive function challenges.

Rona F. Flippo has authored seventeen books, most recently *Assessing Readers* (2nd ed., in press, Routledge); *Reading Researchers in Search of Common Ground: The Ex-pert Study Revisited* (2nd ed., 2012, Routledge); *Handbook of College Reading and Study Strategy Research* (2nd ed., 2009, Routledge); and *Preparing Students for Testing and Doing Better in School* (2008, Corwin/Sage); other fairly recent titles with Heinemann in-clude *Personal Reading* (2005), *Texts and Tests* (2004), *Assessing Readers* (2003), and *What Do the Experts Say?* (1999). Flippo has published over 100 articles/chapters in publications including *Journal of Adolescent & Adult Literacy, the Reading Teacher, Reading Psychology, Journal of Reading, Reading & Writing Quarterly, Phi Delta Kappan, Educational Leader-ship,* and the *Journal of Teacher Education*. She's served on professional organization committees, editorial and director boards, most recently, the International Reading Asso-ciation's board of directors (2012–2015).

Marty Frailey is a reading specialist with experience in both elementary and post-secondary instruction. For the last twenty-five years, she has taught reading and study skills at Pima College. She holds a bachelor's degree in elementary education from the University of Dayton and a master's degree in reading from the University of Arizona. More recent graduate work (1990–2007) has focused on developmental reading using a reading workshop. In 2000 she earned a certification as a developmental education spe-cialist from the Kellogg Institute. Marty has been a presenter at national conferences in-cluding CRLA, NADE, and SWADE. Her focus has included use of novels, literary letters, literature circles, integrating information literacy with novels, and linking reading and writing courses. For the past four summers, she has taught English at Huazhong Univer-sity in Wuhan China (2009–2012).

Sugie Goen-Salter is director of the Writing Program and professor of English at San Francisco State University where she cofounded SFSU's Integrated Reading and Writing Program for first-year students. She has published in the *Journal of Basic*

Writing, BWe, the *CATESOL Journal,* and in the edited volume *Generation 1.5 in College Composition: Teaching Academic Writing to US-Educated Learners of ESL.* Dr. Goen-Salter serves as co-chair of the Council on Basic Writing and is president of the California State University English Council. Professor Goen-Salter received her PhD in language and literacy in 1997 from Stanford University.

William S. Gray (1885–1960) earned one of the field's first PhDs in reading in 1916 while at the University of Chicago. His years in the professoriate were spent at the University of Chicago where he served as the director of research in reading in the Graduate School of Education. A prolific writer, Gray's scholarly interests in literacy covered the life span, but he forever will be known for his work with the *Dick and Jane* readers, which taught generations of youngsters to read. In addition, Gray served as the first president of the International Reading Association.

Major Josh W. Helms is a former assistant professor of Mathematics at the United States Military Academy at West Point and is currently an Army force structure analyst with the Center for Army Analysis at Fort Belvoir, Virginia. In his position as assistant professor, he taught principles of mathematical modeling to first-year cadets and probability and statistics, for which he was also course director, to second-year cadets. His research interests include the interdisciplinary application of mathematics and optimizing military operational processes.

Kimberly Turner Helms works under the auspices of the U.S. Army's Comprehensive Soldier and Family Fitness program, directing the Educational Delivery and Learning Enhancement branch within the Directorate of Curriculum. Her research interests include learner transitions and success and educational issues for armed services personnel and veterans. Currently, she is focusing on the subject of teaching appropriate study strategies to service members who have been diagnosed with traumatic brain injury and are now pursuing learning-related goals.

Katie Hern is an English instructor at Chabot College and has conducted extensive research into her department's long-standing accelerated academic literacy course. Hern is director of the California Acceleration Project, working with math colleague Myra Snell to support faculty from the state's 112 community colleges to redesign their reading, writing, and math curricula to increase student completion (http://cap.3csn.org). Hern and Snell's work has been featured by the *New York Times*, KQED public radio, and *Inside Higher Education*, along with national organizations Complete College America, Getting Past Go, the Developmental Education Initiative, and the American Association of Colleges and Universities. Hern speaks nationally on integrated reading and writing and accelerated models of remediation. Her article "Acceleration across California" appeared in *Change* magazine (May/June 2012).

Jodi Patrick Holschuh is an associate professor in the Graduate Program in Developmental Education at Texas State University. Dr. Holschuh is coauthor of several textbooks including *Effective College Learning, College Success Strategies,* and *Active Learning.* She has also coauthored a popular trade book on learning entitled *College Rules! How to Study, Survive and Succeed in College.* Her research has been published in the *Journal of Literacy Research,* and the *Journal of College Reading and Learning,* among others. She has presented numerous papers at national and international conferences on the topics of college reading and learning strategies. Her research interests include students' beliefs about learning, self-regulated learning, disciplinary literacy, making the transition from high school to college, strategies for academic success, and motivation.

Laura Hope earned a BA in English in 1987 and an MA in rhetoric and composition in 1988 from California State University at San Bernardino. She has been a professor of English at Chaffey College since 1990. During her tenure in the department, she has taught a wide variety of classes including developmental and transfer composition, advanced composition, honors courses, American literature, poetry, and literature and film. In 2000, she was elected Faculty Lecturer of the Year. Laura Hope was also a leader in the development of the Success Center network and a cofounder of the college's associate's degree program for inmates at the California Institution for Women. In 2008, she became the dean of instructional support at Chaffey College. As the dean of instructional support, Laura supervises a number of collegewide initiatives designed to enhance, improve, and diversify access to learning, such as distance education, the Success Centers including the Faculty Success Center, the honors program, professional development, student learning outcomes, supplemental instruction, Title V Grant activities, and the library.

Betty P. Hubbard is the chair of the Division of Education and Psychology at Concordia College Alabama. She is also the coordinator of assessment for academic affairs.

Holly Hungerford-Kresser is an assistant professor of English education in the College of Education and Health Professions at the University of Texas, Arlington. She teaches undergraduate courses in language arts methods and content area reading and writing, along with graduate courses in literacy research and advanced writing methods. Her research and publications have focused primarily on issues related to urban schools, college readiness, and identity. Recent publications include "Urban-schooled Latina/os, Academic Literacies, and Identities: (Re)Conceptualizing College Readiness," "Positioning and the Discourses of Urban Education: A Latino Student's University Experience," and "Addressing College Readiness Standards in the ELA Methods Course through Teacher Reflection." Prior to teaching at UTA, she taught courses at Texas State University and the University of Texas at Austin. Before beginning her career as a professor, she was a high school and middle school language arts teacher in Asunciòn, Paraguay, and Austin, Texas. She remains committed to public school education, with a particular focus on college readiness and urban education.

Kelley Karandjeff serves as a senior researcher with the Research and Planning Group for California Community Colleges. For fifteen years, Ms. Karandjeff has worked directly with community colleges and secondary schools as a program director focused on workforce development and career technical education. She now works as a researcher with a particular interest in dissemination designed to support practitioner action. She currently leads a large-scale evaluation of CTE bridge program and pathway development in San Francisco Bay Area community colleges and oversees communications for a multiyear study of student support. Ms. Karandjeff has coauthored numerous reports and publications, including a recent article in the *Journal of Applied Research in the Community College* titled "Improving Transfer Pathways in CTE Programs." Ms. Karandjeff holds an EdM from Harvard University and is an alumnus of the Coro Fellows Program in Public Affairs.

Gene Kerstiens was one of the founding members and later president of the College Reading and Learning Association. Gene's scholarly work included the *Study Behavior Inventory*, *Junior-Community College Reading/Study Skills: An Annotated Bibliography*, and numerous articles in journals and yearbooks of the profession. In 2000 he was named a Founding Fellow of the ACDEA. Dr. Kersteins passed away in 2009.

James R. King is a professor of literacy studies in the College of Education at the University of South Florida in Tampa. His research interests include multimedia literacies, early intervention in literacy, methods of text analyses, and interpretive inquiry in literacy. In addition, his inquiry addresses queer theory, feminist theory, and critical approaches to educational practice. Before USF, Dr. King taught at Texas Woman's University, University of Pittsburgh, and West Virginia University, where he earned a doctorate. He also taught first through sixth grades in Michigan and West Virginia. Dr. King is a trained Reading Recovery Teacher Leader. He has been actively publishing in education for over thirty years and is the author of *Uncommon Caring: Learning from Men Who Teach Young Children* (Teachers College Press).

Kouider Mokhtari serves as the Anderson-Vukelja-Wright Endowed Professor of Education within the School of Education at the University of Texas at Tyler, where he engages in research, teaching, and service initiatives aimed at enhancing teacher practice and increasing student literacy achievement outcomes. His research focuses on the acquisition of language and literacy by first and second language learners, with particular emphasis on children, adolescents, and adults who can read but have difficulties understanding what they read. His research has been published in books (e.g., *Reading Strategies of First and Second Language Learners: See How They Read*, Christopher-Gordon Publishers, with Ravi Sheory, 2008; and *Preparing Every Teacher to Reach English Learners*, Harvard Education Press, with Joyce Nutta and Carine Strebel, 2012), as well as journals such as the *Reading Teacher*, *Journal of Adolescent & Adult Literacy*, *Journal of Educational Psychology*, the *Canadian Modern Language Review*, *Journal of Research in Reading*, and *System: An International Journal of Educational Technology and Applied Linguistics*. His coauthored book *Preparing Every Teacher to Reach English Learners* has been selected for the 2013 AACTE Outstanding Book Award. He currently serves as co-chair of the Literacy and English Learners Committee of the International Reading Association, whose work is focused on enhancing the education of English learners. He also serves as coeditor of *Tapestry: An International Cross-Disciplinary Journal*, which is dedicated to the advancement of research and instruction for English language learners.

David W. Moore is an emeritus professor of education in the Mary Lou Fulton Teachers College at Arizona State University where he specialized in adolescent literacy and coordinated the doctoral program in Educational Leadership and Innovation. His vita shows a continuous publication record that balances research reports, professional articles, book chapters, books, and instructional programs. His publications have appeared in the *Elementary School Journal, Journal of Literacy Research*, and *Reading Research Quarterly*. Noteworthy coauthored publications include the *Handbook of Reading Research* chapter on secondary school reading and the first International Reading Association position statement on adolescent literacy. His most recent book is *Developing Readers and Writers in the Content Areas* (6th ed.). He served as president of the International Reading Association's History of Reading Special Interest Group and co-chaired its Commission on Adolescent Literacy.

Mary C. Newman has recently retired from the College of DuPage in Glen Ellyn, Illinois after teaching developmental reading and English composition courses for sixteen years. During that time, she gathered research data and now finds time for academic research and writing. Her research interests include intertextuality and discipline-specific reading strategies

Sherrie L. Nist is a professor emerita from the University of Georgia. She has published in professional journals and served on editorial boards of *Reading Research Quarterly, the Journal of Literacy Research,* and the *Journal of Contemporary Educational Psychology*. Her research interests include how college students study in different disciplines, how they learn from text, and how they transition from learning in high school to learning in college.

Eric J. Paulson is a professor in the Graduate Program in Developmental Education at Texas State University. His research interests center on postsecondary literacy in developmental education domains. He has taught in a variety of institutions in several different states and countries, including developmental reading in community colleges. He has published three books—*College Reading Research & Practice, Insight from the Eyes: The Science of Effective Reading Instruction,* and *Scientific Realism in Studies of Reading*—and numerous articles in journals that include *Reading Research Quarterly, Journal of Developmental Education, Journal of Adolescent and Adult Literacy, Research in the Teaching of English, Teaching English in the Two-Year College,* the *International Journal of Qualitative Methods,* and others. He is currently the editor of the *Journal of College Reading & Learning.*

Dolores Perin is a professor of psychology and education in the Health and Behavior Studies Department, and senior research associate at the Community College Research Center at Teachers College, Columbia University. Her research interests are in the reading and writing skills of underprepared postsecondary and adult education students. She has studied the contextualization of basic academic skills, academic-occupational integration, instructional approaches in developmental education and adult literacy programs, preparation of secondary science and social studies teachers for adolescent literacy, school-to-work transition of moderately handicapped adults, workplace literacy, and adult learning disabilities. She has published in journals including *Journal of College Reading and Learning, Community College Review, Journal of Developmental Education,* and the *Community College Journal of Research and Practice*. She is a licensed psychologist specializing in learning difficulties.

Debra Price is a professor in the Language, Literacy and Special Populations Department and director of the doctoral program in reading at Sam Houston State University in Huntsville, Texas. She is a member of and serves as a reviewer for the Literacy Research Association. She is a member, reviewer, and division chair elect with the Association of Literacy Educators and Researchers. Debra recently published an article titled "Digital literacies in multiuser virtual environments among college-level developmental readers," with colleagues, in the *Journal of College Reading and Learning*. Other recent research endeavors focus on helping classroom teachers bridge the gap between home and school digital literacies.

John E. Readence is an emeritus professor in the College of Education and former dean of the University College at the University of Nevada, Las Vegas. His professional interests include research and practice in content area literacy and teacher education.

Carla A. Reichard works in the Office of Sponsored Research at the University of Texas at Tyler. Her research interests include metacognition, measurement, and student retention.

Robert J. Rickelman is a former middle and high school teacher, who is currently a professor of literacy education at the University of North Carolina, Charlotte. He is past editor of *Reading Research and Instruction* and former president of the Association of Literacy Educators and Researchers. His research interests focus on reading across the content areas, the reading needs of adolescent learners, and alternate assessments for students with intellectual disabilities. He has been a consultant to a dozen state departments of education. His work has recently been published in *Reading Writing Quarterly*, the *Journal of Special Education*, and *Reading Psychology*. He is the author of three books, twenty book chapters, and over three dozen journal articles.

Emily Schneider is a doctoral student in learning science and technology design. Her research focuses on learning analytics for open online courses, with a particular emphasis on the design and evaluation of socio-technical systems to support community building and collective intelligence. Emily is on the pedagogy team at Stanford University's Office of the Vice Provost for Online Learning and coordinates the Lytics Lab, and interdisciplinary group of researchers working to understand and optimize online learning. As Lytics Lab coordinator, she enables ongoing conversations among researchers, designers, and technologists, and works to translate the collective knowledge of the group into frameworks and principles for the design of interfaces and instruction. Before coming to Stanford, she worked at MDRC conducting research on community college programs for academically underprepared students. Emily received a BA in English literature from Swarthmore College in 2007.

Cynthia Shanahan is a professor emerita of literacy, language and culture, and former director of the Council on Teacher Education, and associate dean of academic affairs at the University of Illinois at Chicago (UIC). She studies how students' knowledge of the discourses and practices of a subject matter (e.g., history or science) influences their ability to comprehend and critically think about text. Her extensive publications include *Learning from Text Across Conceptual Domains* (Lawrence Erlbaum Associates) and *Adolescent Literacy in the Academic Disciplines* (Guilford). Though a Carnegie project, she has investigated the differences in the disciplines in the ways experts approach reading and writing. Currently, she is working on Project READi, an IES-funded Reading for Understanding grant studying argumentation in science, history, and literature in grades 6–12.

Timothy Shanahan was Distinguished Professor of Urban Education at the University of Illinois at Chicago, where he was also director of the UIC Center for Literacy prior to his recent retirement. He has served as director of reading for the Chicago Public Schools, and has published more than 200 articles, chapters, and books. His research explores the connections between learning to read and learning to write, literacy in the disciplines, and improvement of reading achievement. He is past president of the International Reading Association (IRA). He received his PhD at the University of Delaware in 1980. He was inducted to the Reading Hall of Fame in 2007. For more information, visit his blog at www .shanahanonliteracy.com.

Michele L. Simpson has taught a variety of reading and learning strategy courses to undergraduates, served as a major professor for graduate students in reading education, and coordinated faculty development programs that focused on effective teaching techniques across many academic disciplines. During her tenure at the University of Georgia she coauthored three books, coedited one book, published over sixty articles and twenty chapters, and served on eight different editorial boards. One of the books she coauthored, *Readers, Teachers, Learners*, is in its fifth edition. For her research endeavors she received the International Reading Association's prestigious Elva Knight Research Award, several outstanding article awards from professional organizations (e.g., NADE), and was inducted as a Fellow into the American Council of Developmental Education Association. In addition to her teaching awards at the University of Georgia, she is most proud of a chapter on college studying that appeared in the widely respected *Handbook of Reading Research* edited by Barr, Kamil, Mosenthal, and Pearson.

Steven A. Stahl was a professor of curriculum and instruction at the University of Illinois at Urbana-Champaign at the time of his passing in 2004. Steven was the recipient of the Oscar Causey Award from the Literacy Research Association and the Gray Citation of Merit from the International Reading Association. He published extensively on topics of vocabulary instruction, reading fluency, reading comprehension, phonological awareness, and general reading instruction.

Chris Street is a professor of secondary education at California State University, Fullerton. He received his PhD from the University of Texas at Austin. He earned his MA from California State University, San Diego, and his BA from the University of California, Santa Barbara. A former English teacher, he now specializes in the development of academic literacy at secondary and postsecondary levels, reading and writing instruction, and teaching and learning at a distance. Additionally, he serves on the editorial board for the *Journal of Content Area Reading*. He also directs the Masters of Science in Education program at CSU Fullerton. His work has appeared in more than twenty journals and books.

Jed Teres is a research associate at MDRC, a nonprofit, nonpartisan education and social policy research organization, whose research areas include learning communities and developmental education.

Frances Oralind Triggs described herself as first a psychologist with special training in the field of reading, but in a larger sense she was first an educator. Such a philosophy drove both her day-to-day work and her scholarship at the University of Minnesota, the University of Illinois, the University of Maryland, and with the Committee on Diagnostic Reading Tests, Inc. She was particularly known for her texts *Remedial Reading: The Diagnosis and Correction of Reading Difficulties at the College Level*, *Improve Your Reading: A Manual of Remedial Reading Exercises*, *Reading: Its Creative Teaching and Testing Kindergarten Through College*, and articles in many of the impactful journals of the 1940s and 1950s.

Mary G. Visher is a senior associate in MDRC's K–12 and Young Adults and Postsecondary Education Policy areas. She has worked in public policy research for nearly three decades, specializing in research on community colleges and developmental education in the last decade. She was the project director for the Learning Communities Demonstration, funded by the National Center on Postsecondary Research (NCPR), which was a six-site experimental evaluation of the impacts of learning communities on student outcomes. She directs other major studies of reforms in developmental education. MDRC has published many reports authored by Dr. Visher (www.mdrc.org), and her work is published in several journals, including the *Journal of Research on Education Effectiveness* and the *Educational Evaluation and Policy Analysis*.

Heather Wathington is an assistant professor of education at the Curry School of Education at the University of Virginia. Her scholarship focuses on the academic achievement of low-income students and students of color in higher education, with a specific focus on understanding the educational contexts, levers, and practices that promote greater academic success for these students. Wathington's research examines college access, matriculation and persistence into higher education as well as postgraduate study and research training. Prior to her appointment at the University of Virginia, Wathington served as senior research officer at Lumina Foundation for Education. Before joining the Lumina Foundation, she served as director of programs in the Office of Diversity, Equity and Global Initiatives at the Association of American Colleges and Universities (AAC&U) in Washington, DC. Wathington is an honors graduate of Wellesley College in Wellesley, Massachusetts, and earned a master's degree in higher education management from the University of Pennsylvania. She has her doctorate from the University of Michigan in higher and postsecondary education.

Michael J. Weiss is a senior research associate at MDRC, a nonprofit, nonpartisan, education and social policy research organization. Weiss's research focuses on understanding the effectiveness of programs that aim to improve community college students' chances of academic success. In collaboration with his MDRC colleagues, Weiss has evaluated the effectiveness of learning community programs, enhanced counseling services, student success courses, and the City University of New York's (CUNY) Accelerated Study in Associates Program (ASAP). In addition to his focus on community colleges, Weiss also conducts methodological research to improve program evaluations. Weiss's research has been published in the *Journal of Research on Educational Effectiveness*, *Education Finance and Policy*, and *Education Week*.

Donna Willingham is a professor of developmental English and chair of developmental English, college success, ESOL, and languages at Lone Star College-Tomball. She is currently working on an integrated reading and writing text, *Kaleidoscopes: Focusing on College Reading & Writing*, which emphasizes authentic vocabulary development. In addition, Donna regularly presents student engagement seminars at national and local conferences as well as for other community colleges. Instructor training is a priority for Donna because she realizes that one of the most important contributors to student success is a highly trained, effective instructor.

About the Editors

Sonya L. Armstrong is an associate professor of literacy education at Northern Illinois University (NIU) and director of the College Learning Enhancement Program, the literacy component of NIU's developmental education program, CHANCE. She teaches developmental reading courses and graduate-level methods courses on postsecondary developmental literacy instruction. She has taught in developmental education programs and community colleges for over thirteen years. Currently, she serves as the associate editor for the *Journal of College Reading and Learning,* and leads the Research and Evaluation Special Interest Group of the College Reading and Learning Association. Her recent research examines program-level issues, including assessing the alignment of reading expectations in developmental reading and general/occupational education courses. With colleagues, she has published in the *Journal of Developmental Education, Literacy Research and Instruction,* the *Journal of Adolescent and Adult Literacy, Teaching English in the Two-Year College,* and *Research in the Teaching of English.*

Norman A. Stahl is a professor emeritus from the Department of Literacy Education at Northern Illinois University. Over the years his research has focused on postsecondary reading instruction with a particular interest in the field's history. Dr. Stahl's works include content analyses, quantitative research, instructional reviews, commentaries, organizational histories, and methodological pieces on documentary history and oral history. He has received honors from the National Association for Developmental Education, the College Reading and Learning Association, the College Literacy and Learning Special Interest Group of the International Reading Association, and the Association of Literacy Educators and Researchers for his scholarship pertaining to reading and learning. He has served as president of the College Reading and Learning Association, the Learning Research Association, the Association of Literacy Educators and Researchers, and the History of Literacy Special Interest Group of the International Reading Association, as well as serving as the Chair of the American Reading Forum. He is a national Fellow of the Council of Learning Assistance and Developmental Education Associations.

Hunter R. Boylan is the director of the National Center for Developmental Education and a professor of higher education at Appalachian State University in Boone, North Carolina. He is a member of the editorial boards of the *Journal of Developmental Education,* the *International Journal of Education and Development,* and the *Journal of Teaching and Learning* and serves on the advisory boards of the Carnegie Foundation Statway Project, the National Center for Postsecondary Research, the National Association for Developmental Education (NADE), and is a technical assistant for the Gates Foundation Developmental Education Initiative. He is the former chair of the Council of Learning Assistance and Developmental Education Associations, a past president of NADE, and the founding director of the nation's first doctoral program in developmental education at Grambling State University. He has received the NADE award for "Outstanding Leadership" and the association's "Outstanding Research" award is named after him, as are the research scholarships of the Association for the Tutoring Profession and the National College Learning Center Association. He is the author or coauthor of five books and more than a hundred research articles, book chapters, and monographs.

Acknowledgments *(continued from p. ii)*

Alexander, P. A. (2006). *The path to competence: A lifespan developmental perspective on reading.* Paper commissioned by the National Reading Conference. http://www.nrconline.org/publications/ThePathToCompetence.pdf

Armstrong, S. L., & Newman, M. (2011). Teaching textual conversations: Intertextuality in the college reading classroom. *Journal of College Reading and Learning, 41*(2). Reprinted by permission.

Banks, J. (2005). African american college students' perceptions of their high school literacy preparation. *Journal of College Reading and Learning, 32*(2). Reprinted by permission.

Behrman, E. H., & Street, C. (2005). The validity of using a content-specific reading comprehension test for college placement. *Journal of College Reading and Learning, 35*(2). Reprinted by permission.

Brozo, W. G., & Stahl, N. A. (1985). Focusing on standards: A checklist for rating competencies of college reading specialists. *Journal of Reading, 28*(4). Reprinted by permission of John Wiley & Sons, Inc.

Casazza, M. E., & Bauer, L. (2004). Oral history of postsecondary access: Martha Maxwell, a pioneer. *Journal of Developmental Education, 28*(1). Reprinted with permission from Appalachian State University, Boone, NC 28606.

DeLott Baker, E., Hope, L., & Karandjeff, K. (2009). *Contextualized teaching and learning: A faculty primer.* The Center for Student Success, California Community Colleges. RP Group. Reprinted by permission.

Eckert, L. S. (2008). Bridging the pedagogical gap: Intersections between literary and reading theories in secondary and postsecondary literacy instruction. *Journal of Adolescent & Adult Literacy, 52*(2). Reprinted by permission of John Wiley & Sons, Inc.

Eney, P. R., & Davidson, E. (2006). Improving supervision of part-time instructors. *Journal of Developmental Education, 30*(1). Reprinted with permission from Appalachian State University, Boone, NC 28606.

Engstrom, E. U. (2005). Reading, writing, and assistive technology: An integrated developmental curriculum for college students. *Journal of Adolescent & Adult Literacy, 49*(1). Reprinted by permission of John Wiley & Sons, Inc.

Flippo, R. F. (2011). Transcending the divide: Where college and secondary reading and study research coincide. *Journal of Adolescent & Adult Literacy, 54,*(6). Reprinted by permission of John Wiley & Sons, Inc.

Frailey, M., Buck-Rodriguez, G., & Anders P. L. (2009). Literary letters: Developmental readers' responses to popular fictions. *Journal of Developmental Education, 33*(1). Reprinted with permission from Appalachian State University, Boone, NC 28606.

Goen-Salter, S. (2008). Critiquing the need to eliminate remediation: Lessons from San Francisco state. *Journal of Basic Writing, 27*(2), 81–105. Reprinted by permission.

Gray, W. S. (1936). Reading difficulties in college: The nature and extent of reading deficiencies among college students. *Journal of Higher Education, 7*(7). Reprinted by permission.

Helms, J., & Helms, K. T. (2010). Note launchers: Promoting active reading of mathematics textbooks. *Journal of College Reading and Learning, 41*(1). Reprinted by permission.

Hern, K. (2012). Acceleration across California: Shorter pathways in developmental English and math. *Change: The Magazine of Higher Learning, 44*(3), 60–68. Reprinted by permission of the author.

Hungerford-Kresser, H. (2010). Navigating early college: Literacy experiences and identity negotiations of Latina/o students. *Journal of College Literacy & Learning, 36*. Reprinted by permission.

Hynd, C., Holschuh, J. P., & Hubbard, B. P. (2004). Thinking like a historian: College students' reading of multiple historical documents. *Journal of Literacy Research, 36*(2).

Kersteins, G. (1998). Studying in college, then & now: An interview with Walter Pauk. *Journal of Developmental Education, 21*(3). Reprinted with permission from Appalachian State University, Boone, NC 28606.

King, J. R., Stahl, N., & Brozo, W. G. (1984). Integrating study skills and orientation courses. *Forum for Reading, 16*(1), 6–13. Reprinted by permission.

Mokhtari, K., & Reichard, C. A. (2002). Assessing students' metacognitive awareness of reading strategies. *Journal of Educational Psychology, 94*(2), 249–259. Copyright © 2002 by the American Psychological Association. Reproduced with permission.

Moore, D. W., Readence, J. E., & Rickelman, R. T. (1983). An historical exploration of content area reading instruction. *Reading Research Quarterly, 18*(4). Reprinted by permission of John Wiley & Sons, Inc.

Paulson, E. J., & Armstrong, S. L. (2010). Postsecondary literacy: Coherence in theory, terminology, and teacher preparation. *Journal of Developmental Education, 33*(3). Reprinted with permission from Appalachian State University, Boone, NC 28606.

Paulson, E. J. (2006). Self-selected reading for enjoyment as a college developmental reading approach. *Journal of College Reading and Learning, 36*(2). Reprinted by permission.

Perin, D. (2011). Facilitating student learning through contextualization: A review of evidence. *Community College Review, 39*(3), 268–295. Reprinted by permission of SAGE Publications.

Shanahan, T., & Shanahan, C. (2012). What is disciplinary literacy and why does it matter? *Topics in Language Disorders, 32*(1), 7–18. Copyright © 2012 Lippincott Williams & Wilkins. Reprinted by permission.

Simpson, M. L., & Nist, S. L. (1992). Toward defining a comprehensive assessment model for college reading. *Journal of Reading, 35*(6). Reprinted by permission of John Wiley & Sons, Inc.

Stahl, N. A. (2013). Selected references of historical importance to the field of college reading and learning. Reprinted by permission of the author.

Stahl, N. A. (2006). Strategic reading and learning, theory to practice: An interview with Michele Simpson and Sherrie Nist. *Journal of Developmental Education, 29*(3). Reprinted with permission from Appalachian State University, Boone, NC 28606.

Stahl, S. A. (1985). To teach a word well: A framework for vocabulary instruction. *Reading World, 24*(3).

Triggs, F. O. (1948). The need for remedial reading in colleges. In *Remedial Reading: The Diagnosis and Correction of Reading Difficulties at the College Level*. Reprinted by permission of The New York Academy of Sciences, John Wiley & Sons.

Weiss, M. J., Visher, M.G., Washington, H., Teres, J., & Schneider, E. (2010). Learning communities for students in developmental reading: An impact study at Hillsborough Community College. *NCPR Brief*. Reprinted by permission of National Center for Postsecondary Research.

Willingham, D., & Price, D. (2009). Theory to practice: Vocabulary instruction in community college developmental education reading classes: What the research tells us. *Journal of College Reading and Learning, 40*(1). Reprinted by permission.

"Prior knowledge"